KONTAKTE

A Communicative Approach

Tracy D. Terrell
Late, University of California, San Diego

Erwin Tschirner
University of Iowa

Brigitte Nikolai
University of Iowa

Herbert Genzmer

CONSULTANTS:
Catherine C. Fraser
Indiana University
Dierk Hoffmann
Colgate University

The McGraw-Hill Companies, Inc.

New York ▪ St. Louis ▪ San Francisco ▪ Auckland ▪ Bogotá ▪ Caracas ▪ Lisbon ▪ London ▪ Madrid ▪ Mexico ▪ Milan ▪ Montreal ▪ New Delhi ▪ San Juan ▪ Singapore ▪ Sydney ▪ Tokyo ▪ Toronto

This is an EBI book.

McGraw-Hill

A Division of The ***McGraw-Hill*** *Companies*

Kontakte: A Communicative Approach

4 5 6 7 8 9 0 VNH VNH 9 0 9 8

ISBN 0-07-064643-0 (Student Edition)
ISBN 0-07-064644-9 (Instructor's Edition)

This book was set in Garamond by GTS Graphics, Inc.
The editors were Leslie Berriman, Gregory Trauth, Richard Lange, and Stacey Sawyer.
The production supervisor was Tanya Nigh.
Production and editorial assistance was provided by Edie Williams, Jeanine Briggs, and Susan Pezone.
Illustrations were by Sally Richardson.
The text and cover were designed by Vargas/Williams/Design.
Cover art: Paul Klee, *Hafen mit Segelschiffen* (Harbor with Sailboats), 1937. Oil on canvas (80 × 60.5 cm). Musée national d'art moderne, Paris.
The photo researcher was Stephen Forsling.
Von Hoffman Press was printer and binder.

Library of Congress Cataloging-in-Publication Data

Kontakte: a communicative approach / Tracy D. Terrell . . . [et al.].—
3rd. ed.
p. cm.
Includes index.
ISBN 0-07-064643-0 — ISBN 0-07-064644-9 (instructor's ed.)
1. German language—Grammar. 2. German language—Textbooks for foreign speakers—English. I. Terrell, Tracy D.
PF3112.K635 1996
838.2'421—dc20 95-43988
CIP

KAPITEL 1

Wer ich bin und was ich tue 48

KAPITEL 2

Besitz und Vergnügen 80

Talente, Pläne, Pflichten 110

Ereignisse und Erinnerungen 140

Geld und Arbeit 172

Wohnen 204

Unterwegs 238

Kindheit und Jugend 270

KAPITEL
9

Gesundheit und Krankheit 368

Partner 402

TO THE INSTRUCTOR

Welcome to the Third Edition of ***Kontakte***! To those of you who have used ***Kontakte*** in the past, we hope you'll find this new edition to be even more exciting and interesting to teach with than the last. To those of you who are teaching for the first time with ***Kontakte,*** we hope that you and your students will find teaching and learning German with ***Kontakte*** to be a rewarding experience. We are especially heartened by the enthusiasm of instructors who have written to say that ***Kontakte*** has increased not only their satisfaction in teaching German, but also their students' enjoyment in learning German, and that many of their students have chosen to continue beyond the first year.

In this Third Edition, we have placed the goal of cultural competence on equal footing with our longstanding commitment to communicative competence. The cultural base of the **Sprechsituationen** section has been greatly strengthened through completely new **Kultur . . . Landeskunde . . . Information** (**KLI**) boxes and new cultural features (see below). Needless to say, our communicative foundation has not changed. On the contrary, we believe that the synergy between the new interactive and content-based cultural sections and the communicative and task-based activities has made ***Kontakte*** even more versatile and, consequently, even more useful for our diverse North American German classes. ***Kontakte*** offers an exciting approach to language instruction that is a true alternative to the methodology of most German-language textbooks available today.

Changes in the Third Edition

Based on extensive input from instructors and students alike, we've undertaken a number of changes in the Third Edition without changing the basic concept of ***Kontakte.***

- In keeping with suggestions from the majority of users, who felt the text was too long for a standard first-year program, we have reduced the number of regular chapters from 14 to 12. Some of the material in **Kapitel 13** and **14** of the Second Edition has been integrated into other chapters of the Third Edition.
- To improve the flow of materials, we have resequenced the chapter dealing with illness and health; it is now **Kapitel 11.**
- While we have retained most of the activities in the **Sprechsituationen** section, we have made minor improvements to them. For example, dialogues, which now appear on a special audiotape to accompany the main text, have been turned into targeted listening comprehension activities.
- We have included several new narration series.
- Many pieces of line art have been modified to render them more culturally authentic. (For an example, see the vocabulary displays in **Kapitel 6.**)
- The cultural focus of the Third Edition has been greatly enhanced to help students develop the cultural literacy essential to understanding German life and language. We have redesigned the **KLI** boxes, making them interactive, and have added three new cultural features: **Kulturprojekt,** a task-based activity; **Porträt,** a presentation of famous German-speaking figures; and **Videoecke,** a video-based activities section. (See "Organization of Main Text," below, for a more detailed description of these new features.)
- We have trimmed back the **Wortschatz** by dropping the **Erinnern Sie sich** lists. Important review vocabulary has been retained in the regular lists and is indicated with "(**R**)."

- While we have retained the most popular reading texts from the Second Edition, almost two-thirds of the readings are new. Most of these texts are authentic or adapted from authentic texts. They include poetry, song lyrics, cartoons, short stories, and newspaper and magazine articles, to name a few.
- We have added more guidance in working with the reading texts in the marginal notes of the *Instructor's Edition*.
- In a number of chapters, activities and grammar explanations have been resequenced so that they better complement each other.
- Several grammar explanations have been rewritten to streamline the presentation. In some cases, previously separate sections were combined to provide a better overview.
- The simple past tense is now presented mainly for recognition.
- Marginal notes have been added to the grammar explanations to give students rules of thumb, hints, or a quick overview and orientation to the given grammar point.
- We have added several new ancillaries to build out the program, including a textbook audiotape, a video, a picture file, a separate *Instructor's Manual,* and a CD-ROM (see "Components," below, for a description of these ancillaries).

The *Kontakte* Program

The ***Kontakte*** program is a complete package of instructional materials for beginning German courses. Its primary goal is to help students achieve proficiency in oral and written communication skills and gain knowledge and understanding of the German-speaking world. The package provides oral and written activities that can be used as starting points for communication, and it introduces students to reading and writing strategies. The materials are designed to encourage you and your students to interact in German as naturally and as spontaneously as possible.

There are two student texts: the main text, ***Kontakte: A Communicative Approach,*** and the combined laboratory manual/workbook, ***Kontakte: Arbeitsbuch.*** The main text consists of two preliminary chapters, **Einführung A and B,** and twelve regular chapters. All chapters are organized by topics essential to communication at the beginning level and contain a wide variety of cultural materials that provide a context for language acquisition. Each regular chapter is divided into four parts:

- **Sprechsituationen**
- **Wortschatz**
- **Leseecke**
- **Strukturen und Übungen**

The **Sprechsituationen** are intended for oral and written communication practice in the classroom and are complemented by four culturally oriented features: the **Kultur . . . Landeskunde . . . Informationen (KLI)** boxes, the **Kulturprojekt,** the **Porträt,** and the **Videoecke** (see "Organization of Main Text," below, for further details). The **Sprechsituationen** are rounded out by ACTFL OPI-type **Rollenspiele,** and by creative-writing activities, **Zum Schreiben.**

The **Wortschatz** is a thematically organized reference list of all new vocabulary introduced in the **Sprechsituationen.**

The **Leseecke** contains two or three readings, many of which are authentic. Poems, short stories, newspaper and magazine articles, advertisements, polls, and interviews are among the many literary and nonliterary genres represented in ***Kontakte.*** Prereading and postreading activities help students not only to learn to read in German, but also to appreciate the literary, sociocultural, and historical value of the texts.

The **Strukturen und Übungen** provide concise explanations of grammar and usage followed by practice exercises.

Characters

A cast of characters helps provide a context for the presentation of vocabulary, culture, and grammar. The people who appear in the drawings, activities, readings, and grammar exercises of ***Kontakte*** belong to two groups of characters:

- a group of American students who are learning German at the University of California, Berkeley

- various individuals and families from Germany, Austria, and Switzerland

The characters are described in detail in the To the Student section. Although there is no "story line" to follow, the characters develop personalities as the text progresses and also help to provide a sense of unity to the textbook.

Components

The instructional package of ***Kontakte,*** Third Edition, includes the following components, designed to complement your instruction and to enhance your students' learning experience. Please contact your local McGraw-Hill sales representative for information on the availability and costs of these materials.

Available to adopters *and* to students:

- *Student Edition.* (See "Organization of the Main Text" below.)
- ***Arbeitsbuch.*** This combined laboratory manual and workbook contains listening activities and pronunciation exercises, as well as written exercises that practice the vocabulary and grammar of the chapter and cultural activities. (See "Organization of the ***Arbeitsbuch,***" below, for more details.)
- *Audiocassette Program.* A 7-hour taped program containing pronunciation practice and listening comprehension texts, including the dialogues and narration series from the main text.
- **New!** *Textbook Audiotape.* A 1-hour program containing the dialogues, selected texts from the **KLI** boxes, and poems from the **Leseecke** section.
- **New!** *CD-ROM.* A CD-ROM containing the vocabulary displays with pronunciation of vocabulary items, vocabulary exercises (including the narration series), as well as most of the exercises from the **Strukturen und Übungen** section.
- ***Kontakte*** *Electronic Language Tutor.* IBM™ or Macintosh™ diskettes containing single-response exercises from the **Strukturen und Übungen** section.
- *A Practical Guide to Language Learning: A Fifteen-Week Program of Strategies for Success,* by H. Douglas Brown (San Francisco State University). A brief introduction to language learning written for beginning students.

Available to adopters only:

- *Annotated Instructor's Edition.* The main text containing marginal notes with suggestions for using and expanding on the materials in the text, additional cultural information, teaching hints, and listening comprehension texts.
- **New!** *Instructor's Manual/Transparency Masters.* A handy two-section manual that provides a guided walk through **Einführungen A/B** and **Kapitel 1,** presents information on Natural Approach theory and practice, and offers hints and practical guidance to instructors. The *Transparency Masters* include all of the line art in the main text.
- *Tapescript.* Transcript containing all of the material recorded in the *Audiocassette Program.*
- *Test Bank* with *Testing Tape.* A collection of materials — many of them revised for the Third Edition — for testing listening comprehension, vocabulary, grammar, reading, culture, and writing. It also includes suggestions for testing oral proficiency.
- **New!** *Picture File.* 50 full-color, 9″ × 12″ photographs taken exclusively for ***Kontakte,*** Third Edition, in Germany, Austria, and Switzerland.
- **New!** ***Blickkontakte,*** a video to accompany ***Kontakte*** with a *User's Guide.* This 1-hour video, developed and produced by James P. Pusack and Erwin Tschirner (both at the University of Iowa), contains 27 video clips from recent ZDF broadcasts, including cartoons, short films, and excerpts from popular German TV series.
- **New!** *McGraw-Hill German Video* and *User's Guide.* A ½-hour video containing award-winning commercials.
- **New!** *From Input to Output: A Video Introduction.* A 1-hour instructional video containing demonstrations of the Natural Approach using ***Kontakte*** and filmed at the University of Iowa. Available for purchase from PICS.
- *Training/Orientation Manual,* by James F. Lee (University of Illinois, Urbana-Champaign). This

handy manual offers practical advice for beginning language instructors and coordinators.

Theoretical Basis for the Natural Approach

The materials in ***Kontakte*** are based on Tracy Terrell's "Natural Approach" to language instruction. This approach, in turn, draws on aspects of Stephen D. Krashen's theoretical model of second-language acquisition. His theory consists of five interrelated hypotheses, each of which is reflected in ***Kontakte.***

1. The *Acquisition-Learning Hypothesis* suggests that there are two kinds of linguistic knowledge that people use in communication: "Acquired knowledge" is normally used unconsciously and automatically to understand and produce language. "Learned knowledge," on the other hand, may be used consciously to produce carefully thought-out speech or to edit writing. ***Kontakte*** is designed to develop both acquired and learned knowledge.
2. The *Monitor Hypothesis* explains the functions of acquired and learned knowledge in normal conversation. Acquired knowledge, the basis of communication, is used primarily to understand and create utterances. Although learned knowledge is used primarily to edit what we write, some speakers are able to "monitor" their speech, using learned knowledge to make minor corrections before actually producing a sentence. Exercises in the **Strukturen und Übungen** sections ask students to pay close attention to the correct application of learned rules.
3. The *Input Hypothesis* suggests that the acquisition of language occurs when the acquirer comprehends natural speech. That is, acquisition takes place when acquirers are trying to understand and convey messages. For this reason, comprehension skills are given extra emphasis in ***Kontakte.*** Input in the target language is indispensable; no amount of explanation and practice can substitute for real communication experiences.
4. The *Natural Order Hypothesis* suggests that forms and syntax are acquired in a "natural order." For this reason, a topical-situation syllabus is followed in the **Sprechsituationen** and other acquisition-oriented sections; students learn the vocabulary and grammar they need to meet the communication demands of a given section. A grammatical syllabus, not unlike those in most beginning German textbooks, is the basis for the introduction of grammar in the **Strukturen und Übungen** sections, but activities to encourage the acquisition of forms and syntax are spread out over subsequent chapters.
5. The *Affective Filter Hypothesis* suggests that acquisition will take place only in "affectively" positive, nonthreatening situations. ***Kontakte*** promotes a positive classroom atmosphere by stressing student interest and involvement in activities that relate directly to their own experiences as well as in those that relate to the German-speaking countries and peoples; hence the title, ***Kontakte.***

Teaching with *Kontakte* and the Natural Approach

The following guidelines of ***Kontakte*** are based on the preceding five hypotheses and characterize a typical Natural Approach class.

1. *Comprehension precedes production.* Students' ability to use new vocabulary and grammar is directly related to the opportunities they have to listen to vocabulary and grammar in a natural context. Multiple opportunities to express their own meaning in communicative contexts must follow comprehension.
2. *Speech emerges in stages.* ***Kontakte*** allows for three stages of language development:
   Stage 1. Comprehension: **Einführung A**
   Stage 2. Early speech: **Einführung B**
   Stage 3. Speech emergence: **Kapitel 1**
   The activities in **Einführung A** are designed to give students an opportunity to develop good comprehension skills without being required to speak much German. The activities in **Einführung B** are designed to encourage the transition from comprehension to an ability to make natural responses with single words or short phrases. By the end of the **Einführung,** most students are making the transition from short answers to longer phrases and more complete sentences using the material of the **Einführung;** their ability to communicate

even at this early stage surpasses that of students learning by most other methods.

With the new material in each chapter, students will pass through the same three stages. The activities in the *Instructor's Edition,* the *Student Edition,* and the ***Arbeitsbuch*** are designed to provide comprehension experiences with new material before production.

3. *Speech emergence is characterized by grammatical errors.* It is to be expected that students will make many errors when they begin putting words together into sentences, because it is difficult to monitor spontaneous speech. These early errors do not become permanent, nor do they affect students' future language development. We recommend correcting errors by expanding and rephrasing students' responses into grammatically correct sentences.
4. *Group work encourages speech.* Most of the activities lend themselves to pair or small-group work, which allows for more opportunities to interact in German during a given class period and provides practice in a nonthreatening atmosphere.
5. *Students acquire language only in a low-anxiety environment.* Students will be most successful when they are interacting in communicative activities that they enjoy. The goal is for them to express themselves as best they can and to develop a positive attitude toward their second-language experience. The Natural Approach instructor will create an accepting and enjoyable environment in which to acquire and learn German.
6. *The goal of the Natural Approach is proficiency in communication skills.* Proficiency is defined as the ability to convey information and/or feelings in a particular situation for a particular purpose. Three components of proficiency are discourse competence (ability to interact with native speakers), sociolinguistic skills (ability to interact in different social situations), and linguistic skills (ability to choose correct forms and structures and express a specific meaning). Grammatical correctness is part of proficiency, but is neither the primary goal of a beginning foreign language course nor a prerequisite for developing communicative proficiency.

Organization of the Main Text

Each chapter opens with the **Sprechsituationen,** which provide oral and written activities for pair and small-group work intended to further the process of acquiring vocabulary and grammar. Subsections are organized by theme, and they include a variety of activities in which students practice listening, speaking, reading, and writing in communicative situations. These activities, sequenced according to relative difficulty, include:

vocabulary displays
interviews
autograph activities
information-gap activities
dialogues
interactions
narration series
role-plays
definitions
content-based activities
discussions
sequencing activities
matching activities
writing activities

Interspersed among the **Sprechsituationen** are **Kultur . . . Landeskunde . . . Informationen (KLI)** boxes. These interactive, cultural "mini-lessons" introduce significant cultural phenomena related to the chapter themes through visuals, texts, and tasks. First, students' examine their own cultural background, then they analyze the visual and/or texts, and, lastly, they compare and contrast their culture and cultural assumptions with those of the German-speaking world. The **Sprechsituationen** section closes with three additional culturally oriented features: the **Kulturprojekt,** the **Porträt,** and the **Videoecke.** The **Kulturprojekt** asks students to go beyond the classroom setting to gather additional cultural information by looking at German media, by browsing the library or "surfing the net," by interviewing native speakers of German who live in their community, and other similar tasks. One of the purposes of the **Kulturprojekt** is to make learning about culture a more active process for students and to allow them to explore areas of real interest to themselves. The **Porträt** introduces students to famous personalities from the German-speaking countries along with the cities they come from or are typically associated with. Hints for working with the **Porträt** and the **Kulturprojekt** can be found in both the *Instructor's Edition* notes as well as in the new *Instructor's Manual*. The **Sprechsituationen** section closes with the **Videoecke,** which features a still-frame picture from one of the video clips and presents questions to activate students' background knowledge and reveal their schemata of interpretation. The video can be viewed as an in-class activity or by students, independently, in the language laboratory. Activities for each video segment can be found in the *Video Guide* that accompanies the video.

The **Wortschatz** contains all new words that appear in the **Sprechsituationen.** These lists are organized by topic and divided into two further sections. In the first section, words are organized by parts of speech and presented with their English equivalents. Nouns are grouped by gender to help students see correspondences in word forms and plural formation. The second section, entitled **Ähnliche Wörter,** lists true cognates (e.g. **das Haus**) as well as compound words derived from previously active vocabulary (e.g. **der Spielplatz**). In essence, the **Ähnliche Wörter** lists are learning tools designed to help students realize that there are a large number of German words that are relatively easy to understand; these lists can also be used to help students develop strategies for making educated guesses about the meanings of the words.

Reading skills are developed primarily in the **Leseecke** section; however, texts are also found throughout the main text in the **KLI** boxes and in the **Porträt** section. In addition, a number of **Sprechsituationen** also offer practice in reading. Poetry, song lyrics, cartoons, advertisements, newspaper and magazine articles, graphs and charts, and narrative texts are among the many texts and genres represented. **Leseecke** readings are accompanied by the prereading **Vor dem Lesen** section that introduces, explains, and practices reading strategies, and by the postreading **Arbeit mit dem Text** section, which involves a more detailed analysis of the text, often followed by a creative or affective writing activity.

Grammar plays an important role in ***Kontakte.*** The **Strukturen und Übungen** section, appearing in the "purple pages" for quick reference, is closely linked to the rest of the chapter. Most of the thematic subsections in the **Sprechsituationen** open with a cross-reference to the pertinent grammar section(s) at the end of the chapter. The formal separation of grammar from the oral and written activities permits the instructor to adopt a deductive, an inductive, or a combined deductive-inductive approach, according to his or her preference. The grammar exercises are short and contextualized, and many are accompanied by visuals. While all grammar exercises can be assigned for homework, many can be done in class, and some even involve pair work. The answers for all single-response exercises can be found in Appendix F of the student text.

Organization of the *Arbeitsbuch*

The ***Arbeitsbuch,*** a combined laboratory manual and workbook, contains both activities for language acquisition as well as exercises for further language practice. The first part of each chapter contains laboratory material, the second part contains workbook material. An answer key is found at the end of the ***Arbeitsbuch.***

The laboratory component opens with the **Hörverständnis** section. Consisting of four parts, this section contains dialogues, narratives, radio ads, and other examples of oral texts recorded in the *Audiocassette Program*. (1) The **Dialoge aus dem Text** are recorded versions of the dialogues from the main text and the textbook audiotape that include brief follow-up activities. (2) **Weitere Hörtexte,** the core of the **Hörverständnis** section, contain listening passages that students encounter for the first time. Where appropriate, lists of unfamiliar words, called **Neue Wörter,** appear before the listening passages. Line drawings help orient students to the content of the passages, and listening tasks help students determine whether they have understood the main ideas and some of the supporting details of the passages. (3) The **Bildgeschichten** narration series, also found on the CD-ROM, includes the line drawings from the main text along with listening and reading activities, often followed by a short creative-writing task. (4) The **Rollenspiel** is an enactment of the same role-playing activity that appears in the main text and is designed to help prepare students to play the roles in class.

The laboratory component ends with the **Aussprache und Orthographie,** which provides explanations of the German sound system and orthographic rules along with guided practice in pronunciation and spelling.

The workbook component opens with the **Schriftliches** section, which contains additional writing activities for practice in vocabulary and grammatical structures. Within the limits of focused language practice, these activities have been designed to allow students to write German creatively. The **Schriftliches** section concludes with a guided writing task, **Schreiben Sie!,** designed to help students make the transition from writing simple sentences to composing paragraphs and texts.

The workbook component ends with the **Kulturecke,** which consists of two or three tasks designed to help students remember the cultural information and insights presented in class. In **Kapitels 6–12,** the **Kulturecke** includes short reading texts.

Acknowledgments

We would like to extend our heartfelt thanks to our two consulting editors, Catherine (Katy) C. Fraser (Indiana University) and Dierk Hoffmann (Colgate University), who were deeply involved in the revision of ***Kontakte*** from the very start to the very end. Their insights and advice, based on their extensive experience with the program, were indispensable. We would also like to acknowledge Katy for her work on the *Instructor's Edition* notes and the guided walk-through in the new *Instructor's Manual.*

We are also indebted to the many instructors who personally shared their experiences with us, especially James P. Pusack and the graduate student instructors of the University of Iowa. The following instructors invited us to present workshops at their colleges, presented workshops with us, presented ***Kontakte*** workshops of their own, wrote extensive reviews of ***Kontakte,*** tested some of the new materials out in their classrooms, and/or shared their thoughts with us in other important ways.

William Anthony, *Northwestern University*
Hamilton Beck, *Wabash College*
Claudia A. Becker, *University of Illinois, Chicago*
Philip D. Brandenburg, *Tarrant County Junior College*
Thomas Lovik, *Michigan State University*
Franziska Lys, *Northwestern University*
Kathleen Meyer, *Bemidji State University*
Linda Moehle-Vieregge, *The Pennsylvania State University*
Judith Moses, *Harold Washington College*
Stephen L. Newton, *University of California, Berkeley*
Elke Riebeling, *University of California, San Diego*
Ann W. Schmitt, *University of Michigan, Ann Arbor*
Gerhard Strasser, *The Pennsylvania State University*
Wiebke Strehl, *University of South Carolina*

In addition, we would like to express our gratitude to the many members of the language teaching profession whose valuable suggestions contributed to the preparation of this new edition. The appearance of their names does not necessarily constitute their endorsement of the text or its methodology.

Thomas P. Baldwin, *Western Kentucky University*
Johannes Balve, *Georgia Institute of Technology*
Carol Bander, *Saddleback College*
Marlena Bellaria, *Central Oregon Community College*
Françoise Bien, *Lincoln University*
Cheri A. Brown, *Moorhead State University*
Gabriele Buchenau, *New Mexico State University*
Steven R. Cerf, *Bowdoin College*
Russ Christensen, *Hamline University*
Petra Clayton, *Cuesta College*
Joe G. Delap, *Kansas Wesleyan University*
Ulrike Ebeling, *Douglas College*
James F. Ehrman, *University of Kentucky*
Lerke Foster, *Arizona State University*
Beverly Freeland, *Santa Monica College*
Erich A. Frey, *Occidental College*
Helen Frink, *Keene State College*
Marion Gehlker, *Columbia University*
Christian W. Hallstein, *Carnegie Mellon*
Ute Hartz, *Goucher College*
James L. Hodge, *Bowdoin College*
Adolf N. Hofmann, *Santa Rosa Junior College*
Jeanette Hudson, *University of Virginia*
Jeannette Iocca, *University of Missouri, Kansas City*
Bruce Kieffer, *Williams College*
John Kulas, *St. John's University, New Mexico*
Ruth L. Kuschmierz, *University of Pittsburgh at Greensburg*

Suzanne Lord, *California Polytechnic State University*
C. Ursula W. MacAffer, *Hudson Valley Community College*
Richard Meyer, *Arizona Western College*
Jennifer E. Michaels, *Grinnell College*
Stephanie Mignone, *College of Charleston*
Jorge R. Morgenstern, *Diablo Valley College*
Michael Myers, *Montana State University*
Carol Nolan, S.P., *Saint Mary of the Woods College*
Lisa Ohm, *Saint John's University*
Stephanie Pafenberg, *Queen's University, Kingston, Ontario*
Deborah Parker, *University of Missouri, Kansas City*
John Pizer, *Louisiana State University*
Teresa Reber, *Arizona State University*
W. Ann Rider, *Indiana State University*
Heidi M. Rockwood, *Georgia Institute of Technology*
Ingrid Rogers, *Manchester College*
Bianca Rosenthal, *California Polytechnic State University*
Elke Saylor, *University of Wisconsin, Milwaukee*
Patricia Schindler, *University of Colorado*
Katrin Schroeter, *University of New Mexico*
Lisa Shakoor, *Oxnard College*
Carola Hortmann Sprague, *Moorhead State University*
Gabriele Steiner, *Modesto Junior College*
Sigrid Suesse, *Georgetown College*
Welaria Wierenga, *Rochester Institute of Technology*
David V. Witkosky, *Auburn University at Montgomery*
Jerry T. Wood, *Baltimore City Community College*
Sue Wyman, *Santa Monica College*

These acknowledgments would not be complete without a word about the many people behind the scenes who, in one way or another, participated in the new edition. Special thanks is owed Lida Baldwin (Washington College), Angelika Blank and her family, Tracy Bartholomew, Dirk Haschenpusch, and Dierk Hoffmann (Colgate University) for their enthusiastic assistance to our gifted photographer Stuart Cohen. That Stuart was able to get some of the more unusual shots is largely due to their assistance. And, Stuart, thanks for your fine work! We would like to extend our gratitude to Heidi Madden, who, as the native reader, edited the language for style and authenticity; to Lihua Zhang and Sharla Volkersz, who painstakingly compiled the German-English and English-German end vocabularies; to Karin Vanderspek who compiled the index; to David Sweet, who secured reprint permissions for the realia and texts; and to Stephen Forsling, who researched many of the photos.

We would also like to acknowledge our Second Edition editors, Eileen LeVan and Jeanine Briggs, as well as Brian Lewis and Melanie Archangeli, whose work can still be found in the pages of this new edition.

The updated look of ***Kontakte*** is due to the artistry of Juan Vargas, who designed the cover and interior of the book, and to Edie Williams, who did the page layout. Special thanks goes to Sally Richardson, who worked closely with us to make the line drawings more culturally authentic and who was able to spare the cast of characters from the ravages of time!

We would also like to thank the GTS editing and production staff, especially Richard Lange and his colleagues, whose fine editorial and production work made our lives so much easier; the editing, production, and design teams at McGraw-Hill, especially Karen Judd and Sharla Volkersz, whose editorial expertise helped transform manuscript into book; Tanya Nigh, who saw the book through the complex manufacturing stages; Francis Owens, who oversaw the book and cover design and illustration programs; and Margaret Metz and the rest of the McGraw-Hill marketing and sales staff, who have so actively promoted ***Kontakte*** over the past years.

Finally, we would like to express our heartfelt gratitude to the McGraw-Hill foreign language editorial staff, especially Gregory Trauth, who expertly commented on all aspects of the manuscript and provided us with much needed assistance, and with whom we hope to have the pleasure of working again in the future; Leslie Berriman, whose constant support and encouragement are deeply appreciated; and Thalia Dorwick and Eirik Børve, whose vision made this book possible in the first place.

TO THE STUDENT

The course you are about to begin is based on a methodology called the "Natural Approach." It is designed to give you the opportunity to develop the ability to understand and speak "everyday German." You will also learn to read and write in German, and you will get to know the German-speaking world through readings, discussions, photos, video clips, and other visuals.

Researchers have distinguished two ways of developing ability in another language: *language acquisition,* which is the subconscious process of "picking up" a language, and *language learning,* which is the conscious process of learning the grammatical rules. Language acquisition gives us our fluency and much of our accuracy in speaking, and our ability to understand authentic language when we hear it. Language learning is limited; it helps us edit our speech and writing. The **Sprechsituationen** (*oral activities*) and the many readings of ***Kontakte*** will help you acquire German through listening to your instructor and through interaction with your instructor and your classmates. The **Strukturen und Übungen** (*grammar and exercises*) will help you to learn German and to apply the rules you have learned. Our goal in ***Kontakte*** is to help you *acquire,* not just learn, German. Language acquisition takes place when we understand the messages; that is, when we understand what we read or what we hear. The best ways for you to improve your German are to listen to it and to read it!*

Classes using ***Kontakte*** will provide you with a great deal of language you can understand. Your instructor will always speak German to you and will use gestures, photos, real objects, and sound effects to help you understand. To get the most out of a class session, you only need to think about *what* the instructor is saying. You do not have to think consciously about grammar or try to remember all the vocabulary that is being used.

Kontakte will also provide you with plenty of opportunities for reading. The more reading you do, the better your German will become. When you are reading, just pay attention to the message. You do not have to know every word or figure out every grammatical construction.

You will have many chances to speak German in the classroom, both with your instructor and with your classmates. Keep in mind that when you speak German, you will make mistakes. The best way to eliminate these errors is not to concentrate on grammar when you speak, but to continue to get more language input through listening, conversation, and reading. Don't worry; in time, your speaking will become more accurate.

*For a more in-depth discussion of acquisition and learning, you may want to read the preceding section, *To the Instructor*.

Getting Acquainted with the Materials

The Main Text

	WHAT IS IT?	HOW WILL IT HELP?
Sprechsituationen (*oral activities*)	Oral activities done in class with instructor and classmates.	Give you opportunities to listen to and interact with others in German.
Lektüre, KLI, Porträt (*reading, culture boxes, portrait*)	Short readings and visuals on interesting topics or cultural topics relevant to the German-speaking world. For class or homework.	Allow you to acquire German and help you to learn about the German-speaking world.
Kulturprojekt (*culture project*)	A task in which you investigate aspects of the culture of the German-speaking world.	Allows you to learn more about the German-speaking world by using sources such as encyclopedias, magazines, newspapers, and the Internet.
Wortschatz (*vocabulary list*)	A list of the new words that appear in the **Sprechsituationen.**	Use as a reference or to review vocabulary.
Strukturen und Übungen (*grammar and exercises*)	Explanations and examples of grammar rules followed by exercises; at the end of each chapter.	For self-study and for reference. Refer to grammar to edit your writing.
Appendix A–B	Part 2 of the **Informationsspiele** and **Rollenspiele.**	Use these appendices when you are working with a partner as you do these activities.
Appendix D	Grammar Summary Tables. Summaries of major grammatical points introduced.	Reference.
Appendix E	Verb charts of conjugation patterns of regular verbs and a list of strong and irregular weak verbs.	Reference.
Appendix F	Answers to single-response grammar exercises.	Use to check your answers.
Vokabeln (*end vocabularies*)	German-English/English-German end vocabularies containing all of the vocabulary used in ***Kontakte.***	Reference.

The *Arbeitsbuch* (*Laboratory Manual/Workbook*)

	WHAT IS IT?	**HOW WILL IT HELP?**
Hörverständnis (*listening comprehension*)	Authentic listening activities with short comprehension activities.	Provide you with more opportunities to listen to and acquire German outside of class.
Aussprache und Orthographie (*pronunciation and spelling*)	Taped pronunciation and spelling exercises.	Introduce you to the sound system and spelling conventions of German.
Schriftliches (*written work*)	Writing activities coordinated with the chapter theme, vocabulary, and grammar.	Allow you to practice vocabulary and grammatical structures and to express yourself creatively in writing.
Kulturecke (*cultural corner*)	Activities that review key cultural points found in the corresponding chapter of the main text.	Help you identify, review, and remember the important cultural information of the chapter.
Answer key	Answers to many of the taped **Hörverständnis** and **Aussprache und Orthographie** exercises as well as to some of the **Schriftliches** exercises.	Give you immediate feedback on comprehension, pronunciation and spelling, and written activities.

Getting Started with *Kontakte*

Sprechsituationen (*Oral Activities*)

The purpose of these acquisition activities is to provide you with the opportunity to hear and speak German. The idea is to focus on the content of *what* you are saying as opposed to *how* you are saying it. The acquisition activities should develop into natural and spontaneous conversations that center on you and your interests.

It is important to relax during an acquisition activity. Don't worry about not understanding every word your instructor says. Instead, concentrate on getting the main idea. And don't be afraid to ask your instructor to repeat or to clarify!

All beginners make mistakes when trying to speak a second language. Mistakes are natural and do not hinder the acquisition process. As your listening skills improve, you will make fewer mistakes, so make every effort to focus on getting the gist. Don't expect to be able to express yourself as well as you can in your native language. Do your best to express yourself in simple, direct sentences, using the vocabulary and structures you have acquired. Don't worry about your classmates' mistakes either. Some students will acquire German more rapidly than others, but everyone will be successful in the long run. Be attentive to your instructor's comments and feedback, especially as he or she rephrases, in a more complete and correct manner, what you or other students have said. The point of this technique is not to embarrass anyone, but rather to give the class a chance to hear more German.

Finally, speak *German* throughout the class and do your best to avoid using English. If you don't know a particular German word, think of another way to express yourself, such as with gestures. If you cannot think of a way to express an idea in German, ask your instructor: **Wie sagt man _____ auf deutsch?** (*How do you say _____ in German?*).

Wortschatz (*Vocabulary*)

Each chapter includes a vocabulary list organized by topics. This list, which contains all of the new words in the **Sprechsituationen,** is meant for reference and review. While you are not expected to *use* all of these words when you speak, you should *recognize* what they mean when you encounter them. Note that nouns are grouped together by gender. This arrangement is meant to help you see similarities in nouns of the same gender and to learn their plural forms.

Leseecke (*Readings*)

Reading is a valuable activity that will help you *acquire* German. There are many reasons for learning to read German. Perhaps you want to read signs, advertisements, and menus when you travel to a German-speaking country. Perhaps you want to be able to read German literature, or even research papers written in German.

The most important thing to remember when reading German is to focus on the meaning, that is, to "get into" the content of the story or reading selection. The reading skills and strategies that are practiced in ***Kontakte*** will help you do just that. Occasionally, you may need to check the meaning of a word in the list of glosses at the bottom of a reading or in the vocabulary list at the end of the book. If you find that you are doing this often and translating word-by-word into English, you are not reading. Learn to make educated guesses about what a word or sentence means based on the theme of the text and what you already understand about the text. The reading tasks, if followed closely, will help you get through the readings and to understand them.

Strukturen und Übungen (*Grammar and Exercises*)

The final section of each chapter is a study and reference manual. Here, you will study German grammar and verify your comprehension by doing the exercises. Since it is usually difficult to think of grammar rules and to apply them correctly when speaking, most of the verification exercises are meant to be written. This gives you time to check the forms you are unsure of.

We do not expect you to learn all of the rules in the grammar sections. To help you "get the hang" of German grammar, we have placed occasional grammar notes with "rules of thumb" in the margin. These notes, as well as the grammar explanations themselves and the grammar appendices, are your reference tools. Use them primarily when editing your writing.

Cross-references to the pertinent grammar points appear at the beginning of each subsection in the **Sprechsituationen.** Many students find it helpful to read the specific grammar section(s) when they start a new subsection in the **Sprechsituationen.**

Getting to Know the Characters

The people you will read and talk about in ***Kontakte*** reappear in activities and exercises throughout the text. Some are American students and others are people from Germany, Austria, and Switzerland.

First, there is a group of students learning German at the University of California at Berkeley. Although they all have different majors, they are all in Professor Karin Schulz's German class. You will meet eight students in the class: Steve (Stefan), Heidi, Al (Albert), Nora, Monique (Monika), Peter, Kathy (Katrin), and Thomas. Each uses the German version of his or her name.

Little by little, you will be introduced to people who live in various parts of the German-speaking world. For example, in Göttingen, Germany, you will meet Sylvia Mertens and her boyfriend, Jürgen Baumann. You will also get to know the Schmitz family. Rolf Schmitz, who is studying psychology at the University of California in Berkeley and who knows many of the students in Professor Schulz's German class, lives with his parents in Göttingen over the university holidays. He was born in Krefeld, a town near Düsseldorf, where his grandmother, Helene Schmitz, still lives. Rolf has twin sisters, Helga and Sigrid.

In Germany, you will also accompany an American student, Claire Martin, on her travels. Her best friends are Melanie Staiger and Josef Bergmann from Regensburg.

In Berlin, you will meet Renate Röder, who is single and who works for a computer company. Renate travels a lot and speaks several languages in addition to German. You will also meet Mehmet Segün. Mehmet, who came with his family to Berlin from Turkey when he was ten, works as a truck driver.

In Dresden, you will meet Sofie Pracht, a student at the Technische Universität. Sofie is studying biology and wants to become a biologist. Her best friend is Willi Schuster, who is also a student at the TU Dresden. Marta Szerwinski, a friend of Sofie's and Willi's, comes from Poland, but is currently working in Dresden.

In the Munich neighborhood of Schwabing, you will meet two families, the Wagners and the Rufs. In the Wagner family, you will meet Josie and Uli, their son Ernst, and their daughters, Andrea and Paula. Jens Krüger, their cousin, comes to visit quite often, so you will meet him as well. The Wagners' neighbors are the Ruf family: Jochen Ruf, a writer who works at home and takes care of the children and household, and Margret, a businesswoman who is president of Firma Seide, which manufactures toys. They have two children: Jutta, who is a student at the Goethe Gymnasium (*high school*) with Jens Krüger, and Hans, her younger brother.

There are others in the neighborhood as well, such as Herr Günther Thelen and Herr Alexander Siebert, Frau Sybille Gretter, Frau Judith Körner, Michael Pusch—who is very taken with himself—and his girlfriend, Maria Schneider.

In Austria, you will get to know Richard Augenthaler, who is 18 and has just graduated from high school.

In Switzerland, you will meet the Frisch family, Veronika and Bernd and their three children. Veronika and Bernd live and work in Zürich, but they like to travel, and we will follow them on different occasions.

Some Final Words

Keep the following hints in mind as you begin to learn German and throughout the rest of the course.

Understanding a New Language

Understanding a new language is not difficult once you realize that you don't need to understand every word. What is important in communication is getting the gist, that is, the message the speaker is trying to convey. Here are some techniques to help you develop good listening comprehension skills. First, learn to *guess* at meaning:

- Pay close attention to the context. For example, if someone greets you at 3:00 P.M. by saying **Guten Tag**, chances are it probably means *Good afternoon* and not *Good morning* or *Good evening*.
- In class, ask yourself what you *think* your instructor has said, even if you haven't understood all, or even any, of the words. What is he or she likely to have said in the given situation? Visual cues, such as gestures and body language, will help you along. Learn to make logical guesses.
- Pay close attention to key words. These are the words that carry the basic meaning of the sentence. For example, if your instructor points to a picture and says (in German) *Does the woman have brown hair?* you will know from the context and intonation that a question is being asked. By focusing on the key words, *brown* and *hair*, you will probably be able to answer the question correctly.

Second, realize that you do not need to know grammar to be able to understand much of what you hear. In the example sentence above, you would not need to understand *does*, *the*, or *have* in order to get the gist of the question. Nor do you need to have studied the rules of verb conjugation. You simply need to recognize and know the meaning of the two key words.

Vocabulary

The two preliminary chapters, **Einführung A** and **B,** will help you become familiar with many key words in

German. Each day your instructor will write new key words on the board. You should copy them into your notebook as they are introduced, for future reference and study. Copy them carefully, but don't worry now about the exact pronunciation or spelling rules.

Include the English equivalents if they help you remember the meaning. Review your vocabulary lists frequently: Look at the German word and try to visualize the person (for words like *man* or *child*), the thing (for words like *chair* or *pencil*), the person or thing with a particular characteristic (for words like *young* or *long*), or the activity or situation (for expressions like *stand up* or *is wearing*). You do not need to memorize these words, but you should concentrate on recognizing their meanings when you see them and when your instructor uses them in conversation with you in class.

Classroom Activities

In **Einführung A,** you will be doing three kinds of class activities: TPR, descriptions of classmates, and descriptions of pictures.

- In TPR ("Total Physical Response") activities, your instructor gives a command, which you then act out, a kind of "Simon says" game. While the TPR activities may seem childish at first, you will be surprised at how quickly and how much you can understand if you let your body and mind work together. What's more: In TPR activities, "cheating" is allowed! If you don't understand a command, sneak a look at your classmates to see what they are doing.
- On various occasions, your instructor will describe students in the class. You will have to remember the names of your classmates and identify who is being described. Through this kind of activity, you will begin to recognize the meaning of German words for colors and clothing and for descriptive words like *long, pretty, new,* and so forth.
- Your instructor will also bring many pictures to class and describe the people and things in them. Your goal is to identify the picture being described.

Finally, and just for fun, you will learn to say a few common phrases of greeting and leave-taking in German, such as *hello, good-bye, good afternoon,* and so on. You will practice these in short dialogues with your classmates, but don't memorize the dialogues; just have fun with them! Your pronunciation will not be perfect, of course, but it will improve as your listening skills improve.

Deutschland und Luxemburg
Einwohner
Deutschland (1995): 80,5 Mio
Luxemburg (1995): 400 000
Maßstab 2,0 cm = 100 km
DÄNEMARK
OSTSEE
NORDSEE
Flensburg
Hiddensee
Rügen
Stralsund
Kiel
Helgoland
SCHLESWIG-
HOLSTEIN
Rostock
Greifswald
MECKLENBURG-
VORPOMMERN
Güstrow
Ostfriesische Inseln
Cuxhaven
Lübeck
HAMBURG
Hamburg
Schwerin
Neubrandenburg
Bremerhaven
Emden
Leer
Oldenburg
BREMEN
Bremen
Lüneburg
Prenzlau
Elbe
BRANDENBURG
POLEN
NIEDERSACHSEN
LÜNEBURGER
HEIDE
Havel
Oder
BERLIN
Berlin
Potsdam
Ems
Weser
Osnabrück
Hannover
Wolfsburg
Brandenburg
Frankfurt
DIE NIEDERLANDE
Bielefeld
Braunschweig
Magdeburg
Eisenhüttenstadt
Hameln
Bad Harzburg
SACHSEN-
ANHALT
Münster
TEUTOBURGER WALD
Wernigerode
Dessau
Wittenberg
Cottbus
NORDRHEIN-WESTFALEN
Brocken
HARZ
Essen
Dortmund
Paderborn
Göttingen
Eisleben
Halle
Ruhr
Kassel
THÜRINGEN
Leipzig
SACHSEN
Dresden
Görlitz
Neiße
Krefeld
Düsseldorf
Fulda
Saale
Erfurt
Weimar
Meißen
Köln
Rhein
Eisenach
Jena
Aachen
Gera
Chemnitz
Bonn
Marburg
THÜRINGER WALD
Zwickau
Suhl
Gießen
Fulda
BELGIEN
Limburg
HESSEN
ERZGEBIRGE
Koblenz
RHÖN
Mosel
Wiesbaden
Frankfurt
Main
Bayreuth
EIFEL
RHEINLAND-
PFALZ
Mainz
TSCHECHIEN
HUNSRÜCK
LUXEMBURG
Luxemburg
Trier
Würzburg
Worms
Mannheim
Nürnberg
SAARLAND
Ludwigshafen
Saarbrücken
Kaiserslautern
Heidelberg
Rothenburg ob der Tauber
FRÄNKISCHE ALB
BAYERN
BÖHMER WALD
BADEN-
WÜRTTEMBERG
Regensburg
BAYERISCHER WALD
Karlsruhe
Straubing
Stuttgart
Passau
Donau
Isar
SCHWÄBISCHE ALB
VOGESEN
SCHWARZWALD
Neckar
Tübingen
FRANKREICH
Ulm
Augsburg
Inn
München
Rottweil
Chiemsee
Freiburg
BAYERISCHE ALPEN
Friedrichshafen
Garmisch-
Partenkirchen
Berchtesgaden
Konstanz
Lindau
ÖSTERREICH
Bodensee
DIE SCHWEIZ
Zugspitze

Österreich
Einwohner (1995): 7,9 Mio
Maßstab 1,5 cm = 50 km
TSCHECHIEN
DEUTSCHLAND
DIE SCHWEIZ
ITALIEN
SLOWENIEN
UNGARN
Gmünd
Horn
Krems
Donau
Linz
Sankt Pölten
WIEN
Wien
Melk
Amstetten
OBERÖSTERREICH
NIEDERÖSTERREICH
Baden
Gmunden
Eisenstadt
Wiener Neustadt
Neusiedler See
Salzburg
Bad Ischl
Salzkammergut
Mariazell
Bodensee
Bregenz
Kufstein
Wörgl
Sankt Johann in Tirol
Hallstatt
Liezen
Enns
Bruck an der Mur
BURGENLAND
Reutte
Bischofshofen
VORARLBERG
Innsbruck
Inn
Kitzbühel
Zell am See
Radstadt
STEIERMARK
Oberwart
Feldkirch
Arlberg
Bruck
Landeck
TIROL
SALZBURG
Mauterndorf
Sankt Georgen
Güssing
Graz
Mur
Osttirol
(zu Tirol)
Lienz
Spittal an der Drau
Feldkirchen
Vintschgau
Meran
SÜDTIROL
Drau
KÄRNTEN
Klagenfurt
Villach
Wörther See
Bozen
SCHAFFHAUSEN
Schaffhausen
DEUTSCHLAND
Kreuzlingen
BASEL
(STADT)
Rhein
THURGAU
Thur
Bodensee
Basel
Liestal
Winterthur
Frauenfeld
Baden
FRANKREICH
BASEL
(LAND)
ZÜRICH
St. Gallen
St. Margrethen
Delemont
AARGAU
Aarau
Zürich
Herisau
AUSSER-RHODEN
APPENZELL
JURA
SOLOTHURN
Reuss
Appenzell
Zürichsee
INNER-RHODEN
Solothurn
Aare
Zug
SANKT
GALLEN
Biel
LUZERN
ZUG
Einsiedeln
Vaduz
ÖSTERREICH
JURA
LIECHTENSTEIN
Luzern
SCHWYZ
Glarus
Neuchâtel
Vierwaldstätter See
GLARUS
NEUENBURG
Bern
Stans
Schwyz
BERNER
OBERLAND
Sarnen
NIDW.
Braunwald
Neuenburger See
UNTERWALDEN
Altdorf
Chur
Klosters
BERN
OBW.
Engelberg
Fribourg
Thun
Brienz
Davos
Brienzer See
Rhein
Thuner See
Interlaken
URI
Disentis
Inn
GRAUBÜNDEN
WAADT
Andermatt
FREIBURG
Jungfrau
Grindelwald
Lausanne
Jungfraujoch
St. Moritz
Montreux
Gstaad
Genfer See
Tessin
Rotten
TESSIN
Brig
Genf
Sion
Bellinzona
GENF
Rhône
WALLIS
Locarno
Zermatt
Lugano
Matterhorn
NIDW = NIDWALDEN
OBW = OBWALDEN
Langensee
ITALIEN
Die Schweiz
und Liechtenstein
Einwohner
Schweiz (1995): 6,9 Mio
Liechtenstein (1995): 29 600
Maßstab 2,0 cm = 50 km

Reykjavik
ISLAND
NORWEGEN
SCHWEDEN
FINNLAND
Helsinki
Oslo
Stockholm
Tallinn
ESTLAND
LETTLAND
Riga
LITAUEN
Wilna
Minsk
WEISSRUSSL
Schottland
Nordirland
NORDSEE
Kopenhagen
DÄNEMARK
OSTSEE
ATLANTISCHER OZEAN
IRLAND
Dublin
England
Wales
DIE NIEDERLANDE
GROSSBRITANNIEN
London
Amsterdam
Berlin
(ZU RUSSLAND)
Warschau
POLEN
Kiev
Brüssel
DEUTSCHLAND
Der Ärmelkanal
BELGIEN
Prag
Luxemburg
TSCHECHIEN
Paris
LUXEMBURG
DIE SLOWAKEI
MOLDAW
Kischin
Wien
LIECHTENSTEIN
Budapest
ÖSTERREICH
Bern
UNGARN
FRANKREICH
DIE SCHWEIZ
Ljubljana
RUMÄNIEN
SLOWENIEN
Zagreb
Bukarest
Belgrad
KROATIEN
JUGOSLAWIEN
BOSNIEN UND HERZEGOWINA
Sarajevo
BULGARIEN
ANDORRA
MONACO
VATIKANSTADT
Skopje
Sofia
Korsika
Rom
Tirana
PORTUGAL
Madrid
ITALIEN
ALBANIEN
MAZEDONIEN
Lissabon
Sardinien
SPANIEN
Mallorca
GRIECHENLAND
Athen
Straße von Gibraltar
Sizilien
Algier
Tunis
MALTA
Kreta
Rabat
TUNESIEN
MITTELMEER
MAROKKO
ALGERIEN
Tripolis
LIBYEN

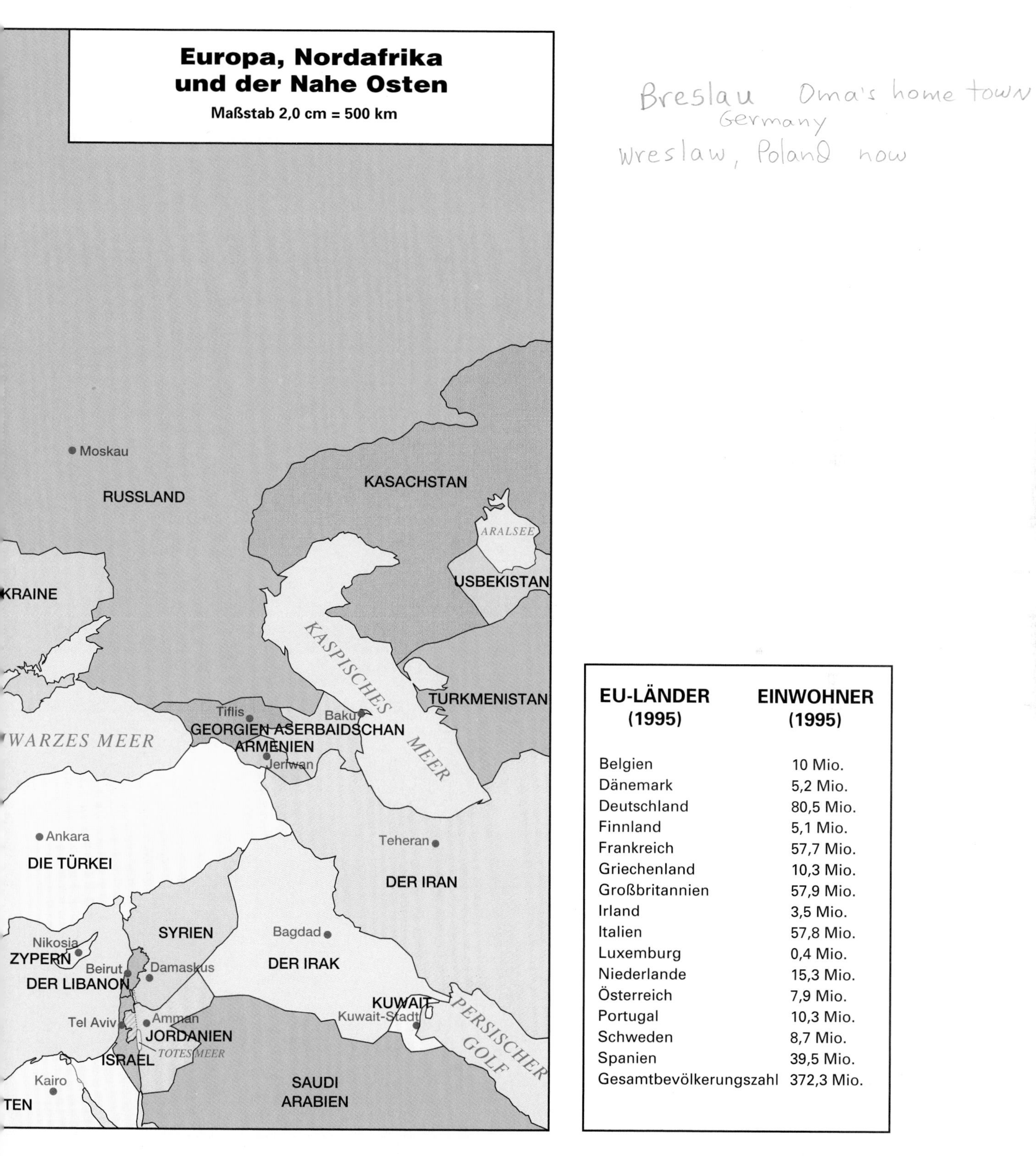

Breslau Oma's home town
Germany
Wreslaw, Poland now

EU-LÄNDER (1995)	EINWOHNER (1995)
Belgien	10 Mio.
Dänemark	5,2 Mio.
Deutschland	80,5 Mio.
Finnland	5,1 Mio.
Frankreich	57,7 Mio.
Griechenland	10,3 Mio.
Großbritannien	57,9 Mio.
Irland	3,5 Mio.
Italien	57,8 Mio.
Luxemburg	0,4 Mio.
Niederlande	15,3 Mio.
Österreich	7,9 Mio.
Portugal	10,3 Mio.
Schweden	8,7 Mio.
Spanien	39,5 Mio.
Gesamtbevölkerungszahl	372,3 Mio.

KONTAKTE

EINFÜHRUNG A

Grüß dich!

Your goals in **Einführung A** should be to relax, listen to as much German as possible, and get to know your classmates. The focus is primarily on listening skills; after you have heard German for several weeks, speaking it will come naturally to you.

THEMEN

Aufforderungen
Namen
Beschreibungen
Kleidung
Farben
Zahlen
Der Körper
Begrüßen und Verabschieden

KULTURELLES

Vornamen
Farben als Symbole
So zählt man . . . /So schreibt man . . .
Begrüßen und Verabschieden
Kulturprojekt: Deutschsprachige Zeitschriften und Zeitungen
Videoecke: Guten Tag und Auf Wiedersehen

STRUKTUREN

A.1 Giving instructions: polite commands
A.2 What is your name? The verb **heißen**
A.3 The German case system
A.4 Who are you? The verb **sein**
A.5 What do you have? The verb **haben**
A.6 Grammatical gender: nouns and pronouns
A.7 Addressing people: **Sie** versus **du** or **ihr**

SPRECHSITUATIONEN

Aufforderungen

Instructions

➤ **Grammatik A.1**

Grammar

Situation 1 Aufforderungen

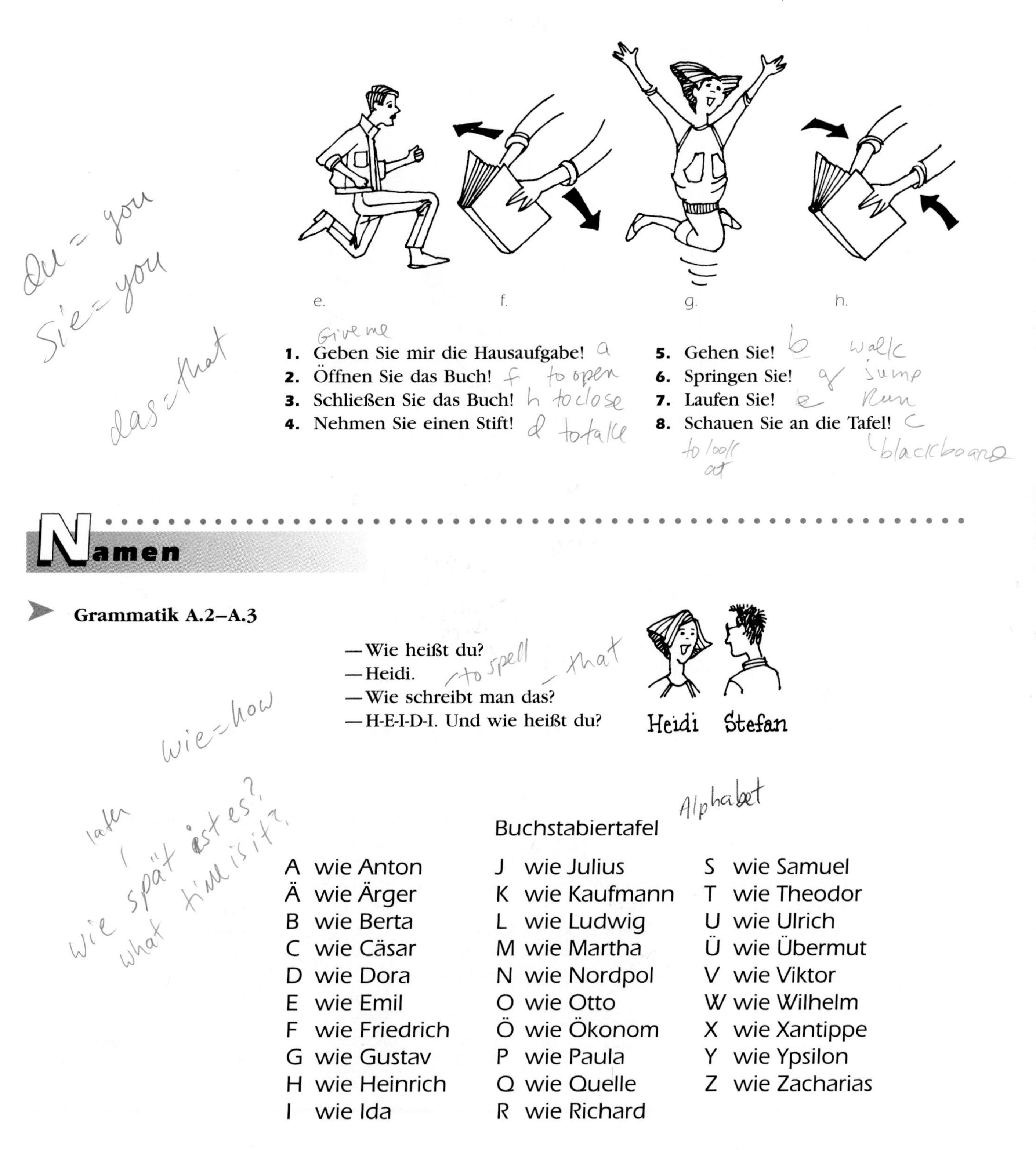

1. Geben Sie mir die Hausaufgabe!
2. Öffnen Sie das Buch!
3. Schließen Sie das Buch!
4. Nehmen Sie einen Stift!
5. Gehen Sie!
6. Springen Sie!
7. Laufen Sie!
8. Schauen Sie an die Tafel!

Namen

Grammatik A.2–A.3

—Wie heißt du?
—Heidi.
—Wie schreibt man das?
—H-E-I-D-I. Und wie heißt du?

Buchstabiertafel

A wie Anton
Ä wie Ärger
B wie Berta
C wie Cäsar
D wie Dora
E wie Emil
F wie Friedrich
G wie Gustav
H wie Heinrich
I wie Ida
J wie Julius
K wie Kaufmann
L wie Ludwig
M wie Martha
N wie Nordpol
O wie Otto
Ö wie Ökonom
P wie Paula
Q wie Quelle
R wie Richard
S wie Samuel
T wie Theodor
U wie Ulrich
Ü wie Übermut
V wie Viktor
W wie Wilhelm
X wie Xantippe
Y wie Ypsilon
Z wie Zacharias

Situation 2 Wie heißt . . . ?

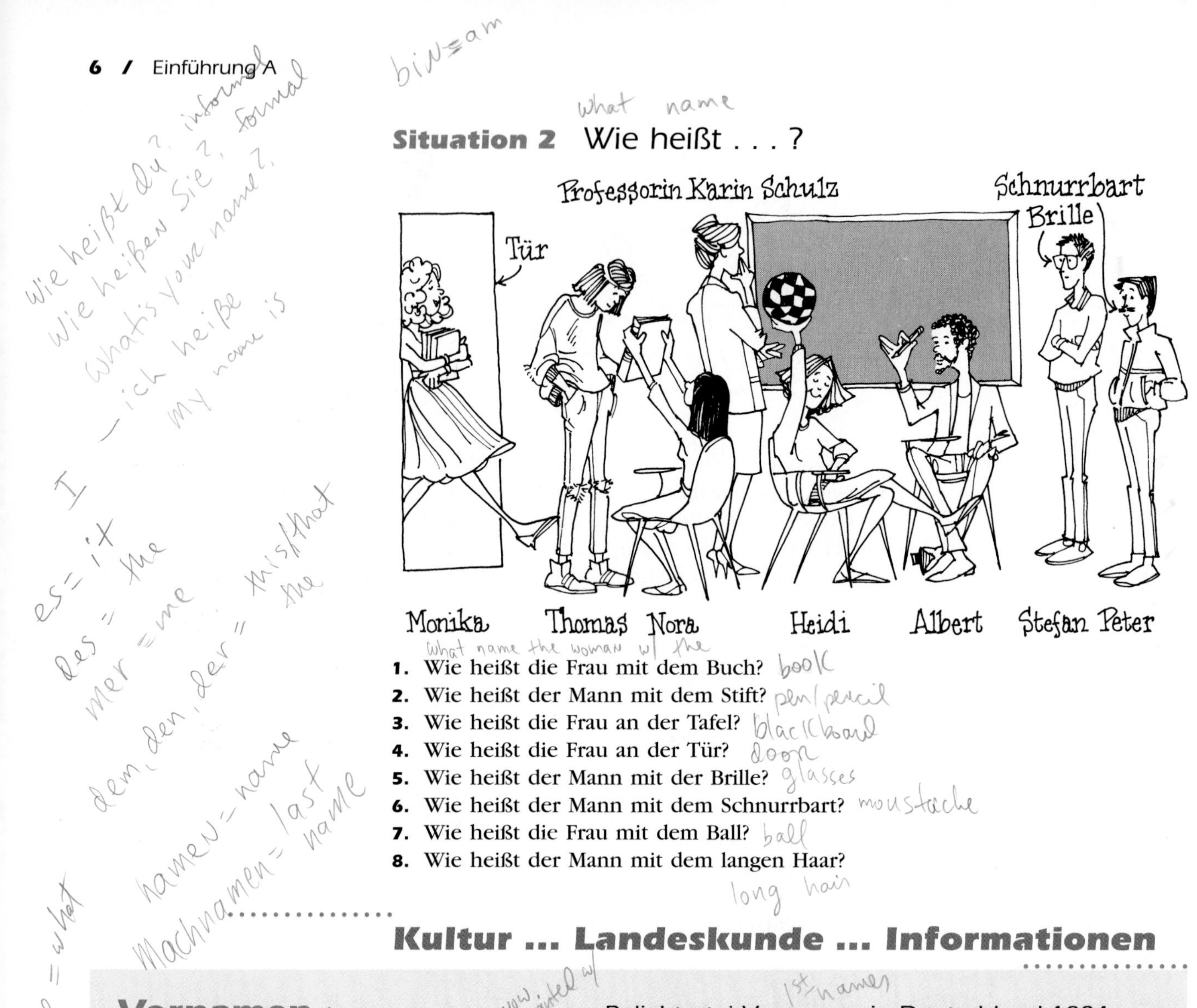

1. Wie heißt die Frau mit dem Buch?
2. Wie heißt der Mann mit dem Stift?
3. Wie heißt die Frau an der Tafel?
4. Wie heißt die Frau an der Tür?
5. Wie heißt der Mann mit der Brille?
6. Wie heißt der Mann mit dem Schnurrbart?
7. Wie heißt die Frau mit dem Ball?
8. Wie heißt der Mann mit dem langen Haar?

Kultur ... Landeskunde ... Informationen

Vornamen

- Wie heißen Sie mit Vornamen?
- Welche deutschen Vornamen kennen Sie?
- Welche deutschen Mädchennamen gibt es in Ihrem Deutschkurs?
- Welche deutschen Jungennamen gibt es in Ihrem Deutschkurs?
- Welche deutschen Familiennamen gibt es in Ihrem Deutschkurs?
- Welche Namen sind englische Namen?
- Welcher Name ist Ihr Lieblingsname?

[1]*most popular*

Beliebteste[1] Vornamen in Deutschland 1994

Mädchennamen		Jungennamen	
Ost	**West**	**Ost**	**West**
1. Lisa	Julia	1. Philipp	Alexander
2. Maria	Katharina	2. Maximilian	Daniel
3. Julia	Maria	3. Paul	Maximilian
4. Anna	Laura	4. Kevin	Christian
5. Sarah	Anna	5. Sebastian	Lukas
6. Franziska	Lisa	6. Florian	Tobias
7. Jessica	Sarah	7. Felix	Kevin
8. Sophie	Vanessa	8. Tobias	Marcel
9. Laura	Jessica	9. Max	Philipp
10. Jennifer	Franziska	10. Alexander	Sebastian

Quelle: Gesellschaft für Deutsche Sprache (Wiesbaden)

Beschreibungen

➤ **Grammatik A.4–A.5**

Situation 3 Im Deutschkurs

1. Wer ist _____ ?

- **a.** blond
- **b.** groß
- **c.** klein
- **d.** schlank
- **e.** jung
- **f.** alt

2. Wer hat _____ ?

- **a.** braunes Haar
- **b.** graues Haar
- **c.** kurzes Haar
- **d.** langes Haar
- **e.** einen Bart
- **f.** blaue Augen
- **g.** braune Augen

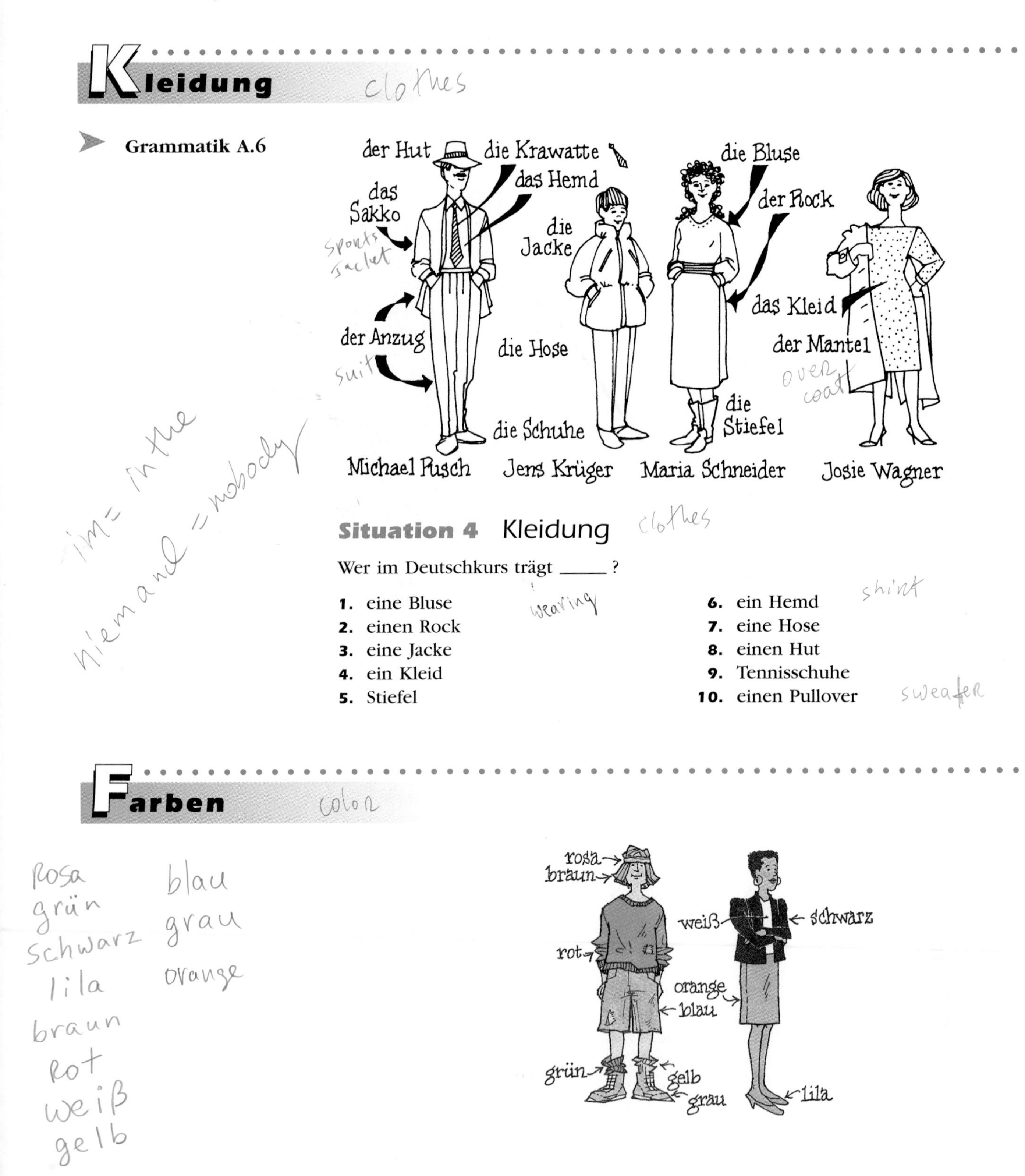

Kleidung

➤ **Grammatik A.6**

Situation 4 Kleidung

Wer im Deutschkurs trägt _____ ?

1. eine Bluse
2. einen Rock
3. eine Jacke
4. ein Kleid
5. Stiefel
6. ein Hemd
7. eine Hose
8. einen Hut
9. Tennisschuhe
10. einen Pullover

Farben

Situation 5 Meine Kommilitonen[1]

Schauen Sie Ihre Mitstudenten an. Was tragen sie?

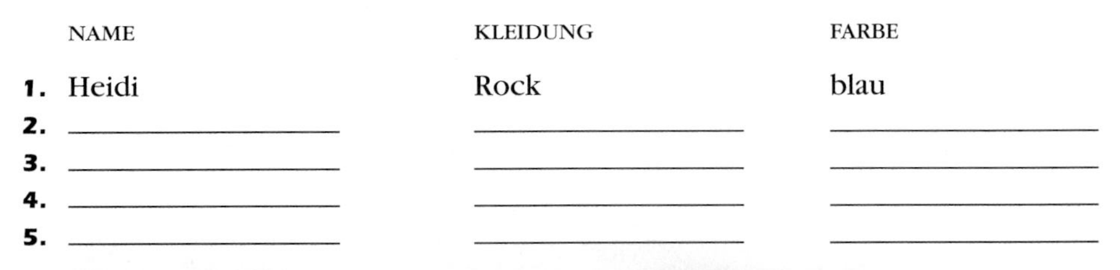

	NAME	KLEIDUNG	FARBE
1.	Heidi	Rock	blau
2.	______	______	______
3.	______	______	______
4.	______	______	______
5.	______	______	______

An einer Bushaltestelle in Basel

Kultur ... Landeskunde ... Informationen

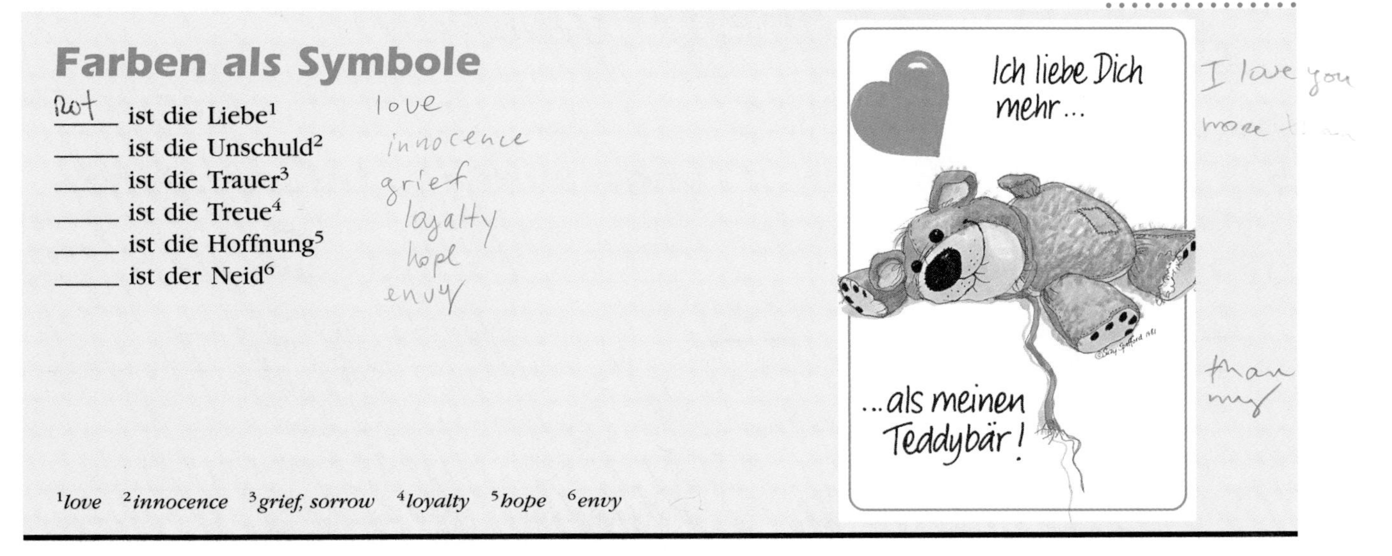

Farben als Symbole

_____ ist die Liebe[1]
_____ ist die Unschuld[2]
_____ ist die Trauer[3]
_____ ist die Treue[4]
_____ ist die Hoffnung[5]
_____ ist der Neid[6]

[1]*love* [2]*innocence* [3]*grief, sorrow* [4]*loyalty* [5]*hope* [6]*envy*

---

[1]*fellow students*

Zahlen

0	null	10	zehn	20	zwanzig	30	dreißig
1	eins	11	elf	21	einundzwanzig	40	vierzig
2	zwei	12	zwölf	22	zweiundzwanzig	50	fünfzig
3	drei	13	dreizehn	23	dreiundzwanzig	60	sechzig
4	vier	14	vierzehn	24	vierundzwanzig	70	siebzig
5	fünf	15	fünfzehn	25	fünfundzwanzig	80	achtzig
6	sechs	16	sechzehn	26	sechsundzwanzig	90	neunzig
7	sieben	17	siebzehn	27	siebenundzwanzig	100	hundert
8	acht	18	achtzehn	28	achtundzwanzig		
9	neun	19	neunzehn	29	neunundzwanzig		

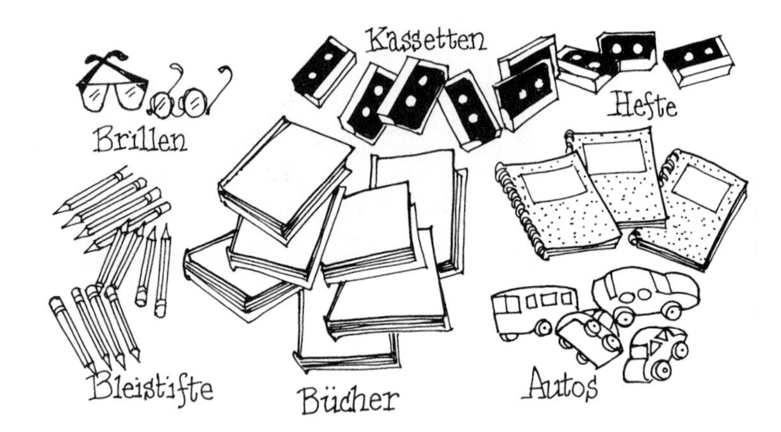

Kultur ... Landeskunde ... Informationen

So zählt man . . .

So schreibt man . . .

eine Eins. eine Sieben.

Situation 6 Wie viele?

Wie viele Studenten/Studentinnen im Kurs . . . ?

TRAGEN		HABEN	
eine Hose	_____	einen Bart	_____
eine Brille	_____	langes Haar	_____
eine Armbanduhr	_____	einen Schnurrbart	_____
eine Bluse	_____	braune Augen	_____
einen Rock	_____	blondes Haar	_____
Tennisschuhe	_____	grüne Augen	_____

Der Körper

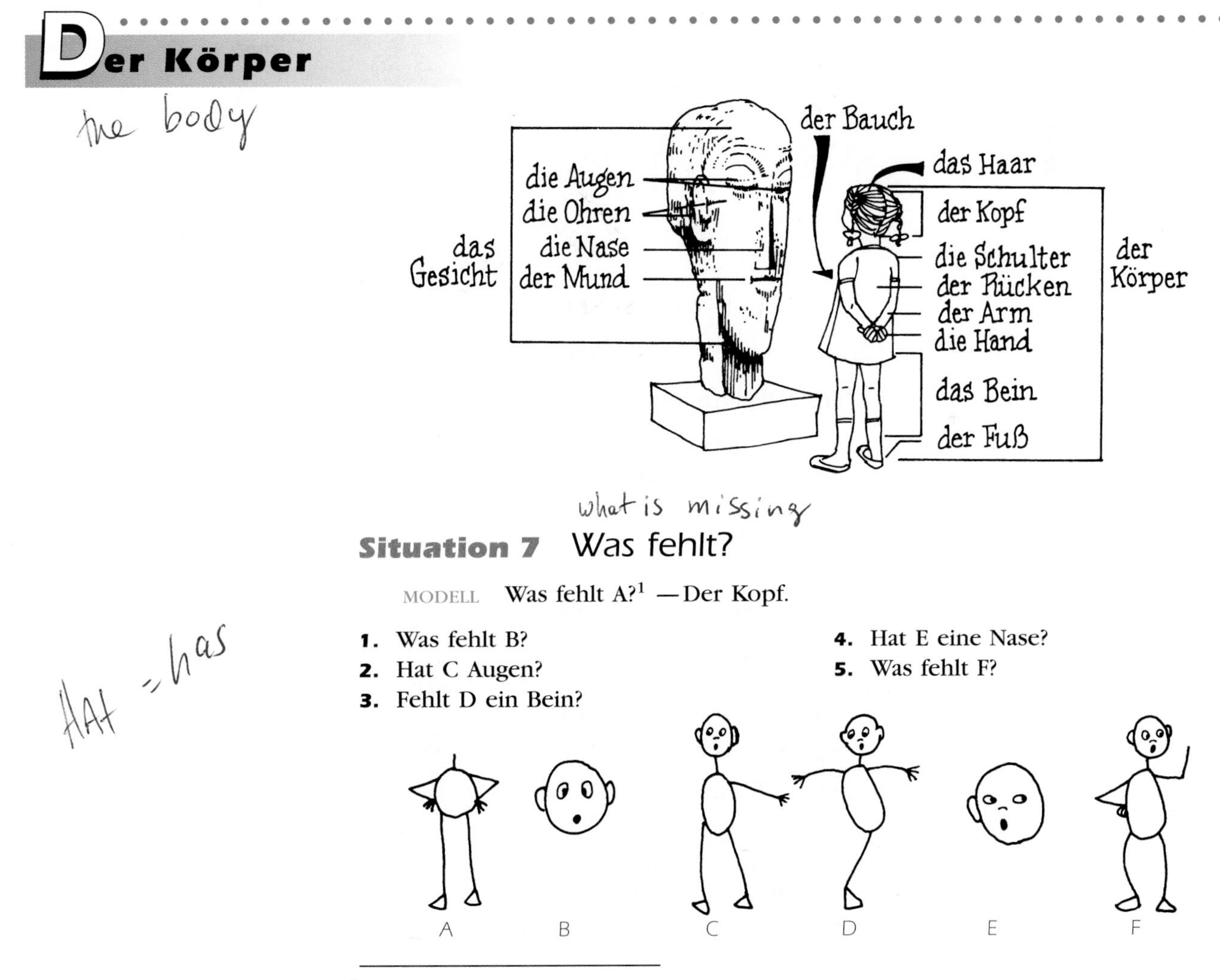

Situation 7 Was fehlt?

MODELL Was fehlt A?[1] —Der Kopf.

1. Was fehlt B?
2. Hat C Augen?
3. Fehlt D ein Bein?
4. Hat E eine Nase?
5. Was fehlt F?

[1] *What is A lacking?*

Begrüßen und Verabschieden

➤ **Grammatik A.7**

Guten Morgen!

Guten Tag!

Guten Abend!

Auf Wiedersehen!
Wiedersehen!

Tschüs!
Bis bald!

Situation 8 Dialoge

1. Jürgen Baumann spricht mit einer Studentin.

JÜRGEN: Hallo, bist du __ hier?
MELANIE: _. Du auch?
JÜRGEN: Ja. Sag mal, ________?
MELANIE: Melanie. Und _?
JÜRGEN: Jürgen.

2. Frau Frisch ruft Herrn Koch an.

HERR KOCH: ___.
FRAU FRISCH: Guten Tag. _____ Frau Frisch.
HERR KOCH: _______, Frau Frisch.
FRAU FRISCH: Herr Koch, unser Videorecorder funktioniert nicht.

3. Jutta trifft ihren Freund Jens.

JUTTA: Servus, Jens.
JENS: Ach, ____, Jutta.
JUTTA: Wo willst _ denn hin?
JENS: __ muß zum Fußballtraining.
JUTTA: Na, dann ______!
JENS: ____. Mach's gut, Jutta.

Kultur ... Landeskunde ... Informationen

Begrüßen[1] und Verabschieden[2]

Sie hören einen kurzen Text zum Begrüßen und Verabschieden. Was sagt man wann? Kreuzen Sie an.

WAS SAGT MAN ...	ZUR BEGRÜSSUNG?	ZUM ABSCHIED?
Auf Wiedersehen	☐	☐
Grüezi	☐	☐
Grüß Gott	☐	☐
Guten Abend	☐	☐
Guten Morgen	☐	☐
Guten Tag	☐	☐
Mach's gut	☐	☐
Servus	☐	☐
Tschüs	☐	☐

[1]*greeting* [2]*saying good-bye*

Ja, hallo! Wie geht's denn so?

Kulturprojekt Deutschsprachige Zeitschriften[1] und Zeitungen[2]

Gehen Sie in Ihre Bibliothek oder in einen Zeitungsladen und suchen Sie vier oder fünf deutschsprachige Zeitungen und Zeitschriften. Schreiben Sie auf:

- Wie heißen die Zeitungen/Zeitschriften?
- Wieviel kosten sie?
- Aus welcher Stadt kommen sie?
- Was sind die Hauptthemen: Freizeit, Kultur, Mode, Politik, Reisen,[3] Sport, Unterhaltung,[4] Wirtschaft[5]?

[1]*magazines* [2]*newspapers* [3]*travel* [4]*entertainment* [5]*economy*

Zeitungen aus aller Welt an einem Zeitungsstand in Innsbruck

Guten Tag. Quandt. Ich bin Paulines Mutter.

Guten Tag und Auf Wiedersehen

Sie sehen eine Reihe von Videoclips, in denen sich Leute begrüßen oder voneinander verabschieden. Sehen Sie sich die Clips an, und schreiben Sie zu jedem Clip auf:

- Wer sind diese Leute: Mann oder Frau, jung oder alt?
- Begrüßen sich die Leute oder verabschieden sie sich?
- Welche Tageszeit ist es: Morgen, Mittag, Nachmittag, Abend, Nacht?
- Sagen sie *Sie* oder *du*?

WORTSCHATZ

Aufforderungen — Instructions

Aufforderungen	Instructions
geben Sie mir	give me
gehen Sie	go, walk
hören Sie zu	listen
laufen Sie	go, run
lesen Sie	read
nehmen Sie	take
öffnen Sie	open
sagen Sie	say
schauen Sie	look
schließen Sie	close, shut
schreiben Sie	write; spell
setzen Sie sich	sit down
springen Sie	jump
stehen Sie auf	get up, stand up

Sonstige Verben — Other Verbs

Sonstige Verben	Other Verbs
funktionieren	to work
es funktioniert nicht	it's not working
haben	to have
heißen	to be called, be named
sein	to be
sprechen	to speak
er/sie spricht	he/she speaks
tragen	to wear; to carry
er/sie trägt	he/she is wearing
tun	to do
zählen	to count

Beschreibungen — Descriptions

Beschreibungen	Descriptions
er/sie ist . . .	he/she is . . .
dick	large, fat
groß	tall; big
klein	short; small
schlank	slender, slim

Ähnliche Wörter*

alt, blond, jung, lang, neu

er/sie hat . . .	he/she has . . .
einen **Bart**	a beard
einen **Schnurrbart**	a moustache
blondes Haar	blonde hair
braunes Haar	brown hair
graues Haar	grey hair
kurzes Haar	short hair
langes Haar	long hair
blaue Augen	blue eyes
braune Augen	brown eyes

Kleidung — Clothes

Kleidung	Clothes
er/sie trägt . . .	he/she is wearing . . .
eine **Armbanduhr**	a watch
eine **Brille**	glasses
eine **Hose**	pants
eine **Krawatte**	a tie

****Ähnliche Wörter** (*similar words; cognates*) lists contain words that are closely related to English words in sound, form, and meaning, and compound words that are composed of previously introduced vocabulary.

einen **Anzug**	a suit
einen **Mantel**	a coat; an overcoat
einen **Rock**	a skirt
ein **Hemd**	a shirt
ein **Kleid**	a dress
ein **Sakko**	a sports jacket
Stiefel	boots

Ähnliche Wörter

er/sie trägt . . . eine **Bluse**, eine **Jacke**, einen **Hut**, **Schuhe**, **Tennisschuhe**

Farben — Colors

gelb	yellow
lila	purple
rosa	pink
schwarz	black

Ähnliche Wörter

blau, braun, grau, grün, orange, rot, weiß

Zahlen — Numbers

1	**eins**	20	**zwanzig**
2	**zwei**	21	**einundzwanzig**
3	**drei**	22	**zweiundzwanzig**
4	**vier**	23	**dreiundzwanzig**
5	**fünf**	24	**vierundzwanzig**
6	**sechs**	25	**fünfundzwanzig**
7	**sieben**	26	**sechsundzwanzig**
8	**acht**	27	**siebenundzwanzig**
9	**neun**	28	**achtundzwanzig**
10	**zehn**	29	**neunundzwanzig**
11	**elf**	30	**dreißig**
12	**zwölf**	40	**vierzig**
13	**dreizehn**	50	**fünfzig**
14	**vierzehn**	60	**sechzig**
15	**fünfzehn**	70	**siebzig**
16	**sechzehn**	80	**achtzig**
17	**siebzehn**	90	**neunzig**
18	**achtzehn**	100	**hundert**
19	**neunzehn**		

Der Körper — The Body

der **Bauch**	belly, stomach
der **Kopf**	head
der **Mund**	mouth
der **Rücken**	back
das **Auge**	eye
die **Augen**	eyes
das **Bein**	leg
das **Gesicht**	face
das **Ohr**	ear
die **Ohren**	ears

Ähnliche Wörter

die **Hand**, die **Schulter** der **Arm**, der **Fuß** das **Haar**

Begrüßen und Verabschieden — Greeting and Leave-Taking

auf Wiedersehen!	good-bye
bis bald!	so long; see you soon
grüezi!	hi (*Switzerland*)
grüß Gott!	good afternoon; hello (*formal; southern Germany, Austria*)
guten Abend!	good evening
guten Morgen!	good morning
guten Tag!	good afternoon; hello (*formal*)
hallo!	hi (*informal*)
mach's gut!	take care (*informal*)
servus!	hello; good-bye (*informal; southern Germany, Austria*)
tschüs!	bye (*informal*)
viel Spaß!	have fun

Personen — People

die **Frau**	woman; Mrs.; Ms.
die **Lehrerin**	female teacher, instructor
der **Herr**	gentleman; Mr.
der **Lehrer**	male teacher, instructor
die **Mitstudenten**	fellow students

Ähnliche Wörter

die **Freundin**, die **Mutter**, die **Professorin**, die **Studentin** der **Freund**, der **Mann**, der **Professor**, der **Student**

Sonstige Substantive — Other Nouns

die **Tafel**	blackboard
die **Tür**	door
der **Stift**	pen
der **Bleistift**	pencil
Lieblings-	favorite
die **Lieblingsfarbe**	favorite color
der **Lieblingsname**	favorite name

Ähnliche Wörter

die **Kassette**, die **Schule** der **Ball**, der **Fußball**, der **Kurs**, der **Deutschkurs**, der **Name**, der **Familienname**, der **Vorname**, der **Videorecorder** das **Auto**, das **Buch**, das **Telefon**

Fragen	Questions
was fehlt?	what's missing?
welche Farbe hat . . . ?	what color is . . . ?
wer . . . ?	who . . . ?
wie heißen Sie?	what's your name? (*formal*)
wie heißt du?	what's your name? (*informal*)
ich heiße . . .	my name is . . .
wie schreibt man das?	how do you spell that?
wie viele . . . ?	how many . . . ?
wo willst du denn hin?	where are you going?

Wörter im Deutschkurs	Words in German Class
die **Antwort**	answer
die **Einführung**	introduction
die **Frage**	question
die **Grammatik**	grammar
die **Hausaufgabe**	homework
die **Sprechsituation**	conversational situation
die **Übung**	exercise
der **Wortschatz**	vocabulary
das **Kapitel**	chapter

Sonstige Wörter und Ausdrücke	Other Words and Expressions
aber	but
auch	also, too; as well
bitte	please
mein(e)	my
mit	with
nein	no
nicht	not
oder	or
sondern	but (rather/on the contrary)
viel	a lot, much
viele	many
von	of; from

Ähnliche Wörter

danke, dann, hier, und

STRUKTUREN UND ÜBUNGEN

A.1 Giving instructions: polite commands

command form = verb + **Sie**

The instructions your instructor gives you in class consist of a verb, which ends in **-en,** and the pronoun **Sie** (*you*).* Like the English *you,* German **Sie** can be used with one person (*you*) or with more than one (*you* [*all*]). In English instructions the pronoun *you* is normally understood, but not said. In German, **Sie** is a necessary part of the sentence.

Stehen Sie auf.	*Stand up.*
Nehmen Sie das Buch.	*Take the book.*

With certain instructions, you will also hear the word **sich** (*yourself*).†

Setzen Sie sich, bitte.	*Sit down, please.*

Übung 1 Im Klassenzimmer

Was sagt Frau Schulz zu den Studenten?

Nehmen Sie einen Stift!	Schreiben Sie „Tschüs"!
Sagen Sie „Guten Tag"!	Öffnen Sie das Buch!
Schauen Sie an die Tafel!	Hören Sie zu!
Schließen Sie das Buch!	Geben Sie mir die Hausaufgabe!

1. Peter **2.** Heidi **3.** Monika **4.** Nora

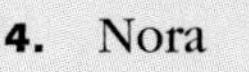

5. Albert **6.** Stefan **7.** Thomas **8.** Katrin

*The pronoun **Sie** (*you*) is capitalized to distinguish it from another pronoun, **sie** (*she; it; they*).
†**Sich** is a reflexive pronoun; its use will be explained in **Kapitel 11.**

A.2 What is your name? The verb *heißen*

heißen = *to be called*
Wie heißen Sie? (*formal*)
Wie heißt du? (*informal*)

Use a form of the verb **heißen** (*to be called*) to tell your name and to ask for the names of others.

Wie **heißen Sie?** / Wie **heißt du?***	*What is your name?*
Ich heiße . . .	*My name is . . .*

heißen (*singular forms*)		
ich	heiße	*my name is*
du	heißt	*your name is*
Sie	heißen	
er	heißt	*his name is*
sie	heißt	*her name is*

Übung 2 Minidialoge

Ergänzen Sie[1] das Verb **heißen:** heiße, heißt, heißen.

1. ERNST: Hallo, wie _____ᵃ du?
   JUTTA: Ich _____ᵇ Jutta. Und du?
   ERNST: Ich _____ᶜ Ernst.
2. HERR THELEN: Guten Tag, wie _____ᵃ Sie bitte?
   HERR SIEBERT: Ich _____ᵇ Siebert, Alexander Siebert.
3. CLAIRE: Hallo, ich _____ᵃ Claire und wie heißt ihr?
   MELANIE: Ich _____ᵇ Melanie und er _____ᶜ Josef.

A.3 The German case system

Case shows how nouns function in a sentence.

German speakers use a *case system* (nominative for the subject, accusative for the direct object, and so on) to indicate the function of a particular noun in a sentence. The article or adjective that precedes the noun shows its case. You will learn the correct endings in future lessons. For now, be aware that you will hear and read articles and adjectives with a variety of endings. These various forms will not prevent you from understanding German. Here are all the possibilities.

*The difference between **Sie** (*formal*) and **du** (*informal*) will be explained in Section A.7.
[1]**Ergänzen** . . . *Supply*

der, das, die, dem, den, des	*the*
ein, eine, einen, einem, einer, eines	*a, an*
blau, blaue, blauer, blaues, blauen, blauem	*blue*

In addition, definite articles may contract with some prepositions, just as *do* and *not* contract to *don't* in English. Here are some common contractions you will hear and read.

in	+ das	=	ins	*into the*
in	+ dem	=	im	*in the*
zu	+ der	=	zur	*to the*
zu	+ dem	=	zum	*to the*
an	+ das	=	ans	*to/on the*
an	+ dem	=	am	*to/at the*

A.4 Who are you? The verb *sein*

sein = *to be*

Use a form of the verb **sein** (*to be*) to identify or describe people and things.

—**Sind Heidi und Monika** blond?	*Are Heidi and Monika blonde?*
—Ja, **sie sind** blond.	*Yes, they are blonde.*
Peter ist groß.	*Peter is tall.*
Das Fenster ist klein.	*The window is small.*

sein

Singular			*Plural*		
ich	bin	*I am*	wir	sind	*we are*
du	bist	*you are*	ihr	seid	*you are*
Sie	sind	*you are*	Sie	sind	*you are*
er / sie / es	ist	*he / she / it is*	sie	sind	*they are*

Attention

Achtung!

NOT = **NICHT**

—Ist Jens dick? —Nein, er ist **nicht** dick, er ist schlank.

Übung 3 Minidialoge

Ergänzen Sie das Verb **sein:** bin, bist, ist, sind, seid.

1. MICHAEL: Ich bin Michael. Wer _____[a] du?
   JENS: Ich _____[b] Jens. Jutta und ich, wir _____[c] gute Freunde.
2. FRAU SCHULZ: Das ist Herr Thelen. Er _____[a] alt.
   STEFAN: Herr Thelen ist alt?
   FRAU SCHULZ: Ja, Stefan. Herr Thelen ist alt, aber Maria und Michael _____[b] jung.
3. HERR THELEN: Jutta und Hans, wie alt _____[a] ihr?
   JUTTA: Ich _____[b] 16, und Hans _____[c] 13.
4. MICHAEL: Wer bist du?
   HANS: Ich _____[a] Hans.
   MICHAEL: Wie alt bist du?
   HANS: Ich _____[b] 13.

A.5 What do you have? The verb *haben*

haben = *to have*

The verb **haben** (*to have*) is often used to show possession or to describe physical characteristics.

Ich habe eine Brille.	*I have glasses.*
Hast du das Buch?	*Do you have the book?*
Nora hat braune Augen.	*Nora has brown eyes.*

haben

Singular			*Plural*		
ich	habe	*I have*	wir	haben	*we have*
du Sie	hast haben	*you have*	ihr Sie	habt haben	*you have*
er sie es	hat	*he* *she* *it* *has*	sie	haben	*they have*

Übung 4 Minidialoge

Ergänzen Sie das Verb **haben:** habe, hast, hat, habt, haben.

1. FRAU SCHULZ: Nora, _____[a] Sie viele Freunde und Freundinnen?
   NORA: Ja, ich _____[b] viele Freunde und Freundinnen.
2. MONIKA: Stefan, _____ du einen Stift?
   STEFAN: Nein.
3. PETER: Hallo, Heidi und Katrin! _____[a] ihr das Deutschbuch?

HEIDI: Katrin ______[b] es, aber ich nicht.
PETER: Dann ______[c] wir zwei. Ich ______[d] es auch.

A.6 Grammatical gender: nouns and pronouns

In German, all nouns are classified grammatically as masculine, neuter, or feminine. When referring to people, grammatical gender usually matches biological sex.

MASCULINE	FEMININE
der Mann	**die** Frau
der Student	**die** Studentin

masculine = **der**
neuter = **das**
feminine = **die**
plurals (all genders) = **die**

When referring to things or concepts, however, grammatical gender obviously has nothing to do with biological sex.

MASCULINE	NEUTER	FEMININE
der Rock	**das** Hemd	**die** Hose
der Hut	**das** Buch	**die** Jacke

The definite article indicates the grammatical gender of a noun. German has three nominative singular definite articles: **der** (*masculine*), **das** (*neuter*), and **die** (*feminine*). The plural article is **die** for all genders. All mean *the.*

	Singular	*Plural*
Masculine	der	die
Neuter	das	die
Feminine	die	die

der → **er** = *he, it*
das → **es** = *it*
die → **sie** = *she, it*
die → **sie** = *they*

The personal pronouns **er, es, sie** (*he, it, she*) reflect the gender of the nouns they replace. For example, **er** (*he, it*) refers to **der Rock** because the grammatical gender is masculine; **es** (*it*) refers to **das Hemd** (*neuter*); **sie** (*she, it*) refers to **die Jacke** (*feminine*). The personal pronoun **sie** (*they*) refers to all plural nouns.

—Welche Farbe hat **der Rock**?	*What color is the skirt?*
—**Er** ist gelb.	*It is yellow.*
—Welche Farbe hat **das Hemd**?	*What color is the shirt?*
—**Es** ist weiß.	*It is white.*
—Welche Farbe hat **die Jacke**?	*What color is the jacket?*
—**Sie** ist braun.	*It is brown.*
—Welche Farbe haben **die Bleistifte**?	*What color are the pencils?*
—**Sie** sind gelb.	*They are yellow.*

Sometimes gender can be determined from the ending of the noun; for example, nouns that end in **-e,** such as **die Jacke** or **die Bluse,** are usually feminine. The ending **-in** indicates a female person: **die Studentin, die Professorin.**

In most cases, however, gender cannot be predicted from the form of the word. It is best, therefore, to learn the corresponding definite article along with each new noun.*

> **Achtung!**
>
> All German nouns are capitalized, whether they are common nouns (objects, concepts: **Jacke, Freund**) or proper nouns (names of people, countries, etc.: **Heidi, Deutschland**).

Übung 5 Welche Farbe?

Welche Farbe haben diese Kleidungsstücke?

MODELL S1: Welche Farbe hat **die Bluse**?
S2: **Sie** ist weiß.

Übung 6 Kleidung

Frau Schulz spricht über die Kleidung. Ergänzen Sie **er, es** oder **sie.**

Frau Schulz:

1. Hier ist die Jacke. _____ ist neu.
2. Und hier ist das Kleid. _____ ist modern.
3. Hier ist der Rock. _____ ist kurz.
4. Und hier ist die Bluse. _____ ist hübsch.
5. Hier ist das Hemd. _____ ist grün.
6. Und hier ist der Mantel. _____ ist schmutzig.
7. Hier ist der Hut. _____ ist schwarz.
8. Und hier ist die Hose. _____ ist weiß.
9. Hier ist die Krawatte. _____ ist rosa.
10. Und hier ist der Anzug. _____ ist alt.

A.7 Addressing people: *Sie* versus *du* or *ihr*

German speakers use two modes of addressing others: the formal **Sie** (*singular* and *plural*) and the informal **du** (*singular*) or **ihr** (*plural*). You usually use **Sie** with someone you don't know or when you want to show respect or social distance. Children are addressed as **du.** Students generally call one another **du.**

---

*Some students find the following suggestion helpful. When you hear or read new nouns you consider useful, write them down in a vocabulary notebook, using different colors for the three genders; for example, use blue for masculine, black for neuter, and red for feminine. Some students write nouns in three separate columns according to gender.

Use **du** and **ihr** with friends, family, and children. Use **Sie** with almost everyone else.

	Singular	*Plural*
Informal	du	ihr
Formal	Sie	Sie

Frau Ruf, **Sie** sind achtunddreißig, nicht wahr?	*Ms. Ruf, you are thirty-eight, aren't you?*
Jens und Jutta, **ihr** seid sechzehn, nicht wahr?	*Jens and Jutta, you are sixteen, aren't you?*
Hans, **du** bist dreizehn, nicht wahr?	*Hans, you are thirteen, aren't you?*

Übung 7 *Sie, du* oder *ihr*?

Was sagen diese Personen: **Sie, du** oder **ihr**?

1. Student → Student
2. Professor → Student
3. Freund → Freund
4. Studentin → zwei Studenten
5. Frau (40 Jahre alt) → Frau (50 Jahre alt)
6. Student → Sekretärin
7. Doktor → Patient
8. Frau → zwei Kinder

EINFÜHRUNG B

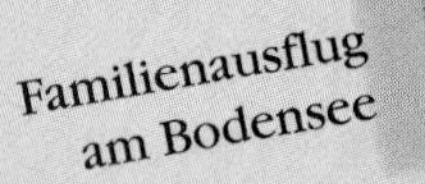

Familienausflug am Bodensee

In **Einführung B,** you will continue to develop your listening skills and will begin to speak German. You will learn to talk about your classroom, the weather, and people: their character traits, family relationships, and national origins.

THEMEN

Das Klassenzimmer
Eigenschaften
Die Familie
Wetter und Jahreszeiten
Herkunft und Nationalität

KULTURELLES

Das deutsche Klassenzimmer
Wie sind die jungen Deutschen?
Wetter und Klima
Die Lage Deutschlands in Europa
Kulturprojekt: Geographische Lage und Klima
Videoecke: Wie wird das Wetter?

STRUKTUREN

B.1 Definite and indefinite articles
B.2 Plural forms of nouns
B.3 Personal pronouns
B.4 Origins: **Woher kommen Sie?**
B.5 Possessive adjectives: **mein** and **dein/Ihr**

SPRECHSITUATIONEN

Das Klassenzimmer

➤ **Grammatik B.1–B.2**

Situation 1 Das Klassenzimmer

Wie viele _____ sind im Klassenzimmer?

1. Studenten
2. Tische
3. Fenster
4. Lampen
5. Uhren
6. Türen
7. Bücher
8. Tafeln
9. Professoren/Professorinnen

Situation 2 Gegenstände[1] im Klassenzimmer

MODELL S1: Was ist grün?
S2: Die Tafel und die Tür (sind grün).

1. weiß	**a.** der Boden
2. schmutzig	**b.** das Fenster
3. sauber	**c.** die Tafel
4. neu	**d.** die Uhr
5. alt	**e.** der Schwamm
6. klein	**f.** der Tisch
7. groß	**g.** das Buch
8. grün	**h.** die Tür
9. grau	**i.** die Decke
10. _____	**j.** _____

Kultur ... Landeskunde ... Informationen

Das deutsche Klassenzimmer

Was sehen Sie in diesem Klassenzimmer? Was haben Sie in Ihrem Klassenzimmer?

[1]*objects*

Eigenschaften

Ich bin tolerant.

Heidi ist sportlich.

Thomas ist intelligent.

Katrin ist optimistisch.

Albert und Stefan sind freundlich.

Mir geht's gut

Ach, wie traurig!

Situation 3 Interaktion: Wie bist du?

MODELL S1: Bist du glücklich?
S2: Ja, ich bin glücklich.
Nein, ich bin nicht glücklich.

	Ich	mein Partner	meine Partnerin
glücklich			
traurig			
konservativ			
schüchtern			
religiös			
ruhig			
freundlich			
verrückt			
sportlich			

Situation 4 Dialoge

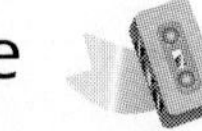

1. Gabi spricht mit Jutta auf einer Party.

JUTTA: Du, wer ist der Typ da drüben?
GABI: Der Typ mit dem ___?
JUTTA: Ja, genau.
GABI: Das ist ___ neuer Freund Sven.
JUTTA: Und wie ist ___ neuer Freund?
GABI: Er ist ein bißchen ______, aber sonst sehr ___.
JUTTA: Ich bin auch schüchtern. Macht das was?

2. Albert spricht mit Peter vor dem Unterricht.

ALBERT: Na, wie ist ___ neue Freundin, Peter?
PETER: Wirklich nett! Sie ist ___ und sehr ___.
ALBERT: Und wie ___ sie?
PETER: Karina.

Kultur ... Landeskunde ... Informationen

Wie sind die jungen Deutschen?

„Wie sind Sie?" Kreuzen Sie an. Was kreuzen 50 Prozent oder mehr junge Amerikaner (15–34 Jahre) wahrscheinlich[1] an?

	ICH	ANDERE JUNGE AMERIKANER
Ich bin glücklich.	☐	☐
Ich arbeite schwer.	☐	☐
Ich bin optimistisch.	☐	☐
Ich bin ernsthaft.	☐	☐
Ich habe Zukunftsangst.[2]	☐	☐
Ich interessiere mich für Politik.	☐	☐
Ich toleriere Seitensprünge.[3]	☐	☐
Ich bin religiös.	☐	☐

- Schauen Sie sich die Grafik an. Was sagen junge Amerikaner? Korrigieren Sie Ihre Antworten.
- Aus welchen Ländern kommen die jungen Menschen in der Studie?
- Wieviel Prozent der jungen Deutschen interessieren sich für Politik? Wieviel Prozent der jungen Amerikaner?
- Wieviel Prozent der jungen Deutschen tolerieren Homosexualität? Wieviel Prozent der jungen Amerikaner?
- Wieviel Prozent der jungen Deutschen finden Seitensprünge akzeptabel? Wieviel Prozent der jungen Amerikaner?

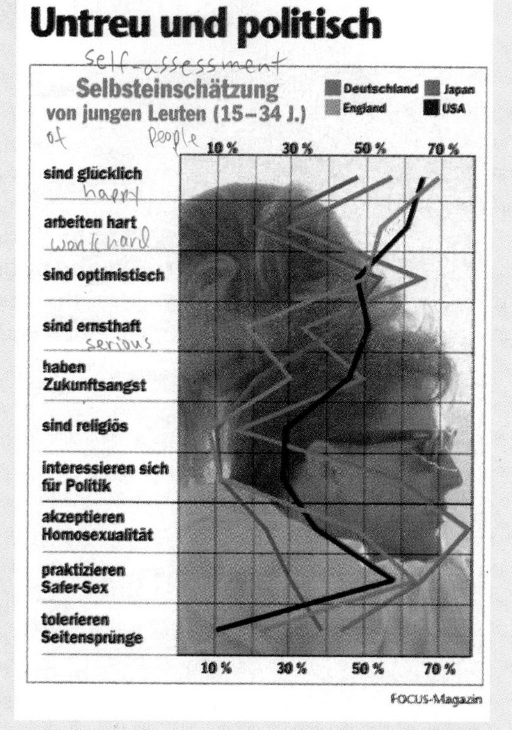

[1] *probably* [2] *fear about the future* [3] *extramarital affairs*

Die Familie

➤ **Grammatik B.3**

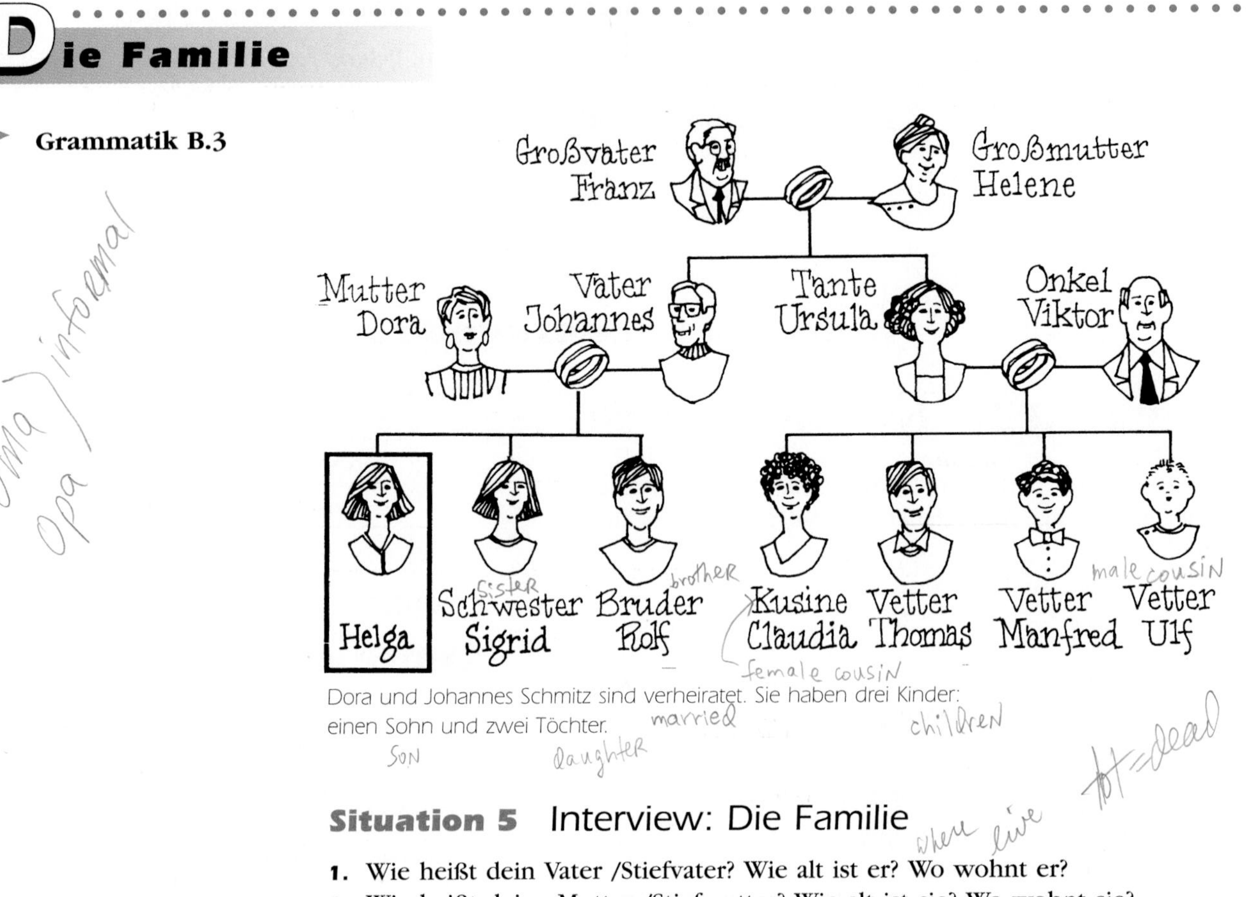

Dora und Johannes Schmitz sind verheiratet. Sie haben drei Kinder: einen Sohn und zwei Töchter.

Situation 5 Interview: Die Familie

1. Wie heißt dein Vater /Stiefvater? Wie alt ist er? Wo wohnt er?
2. Wie heißt deine Mutter /Stiefmutter? Wie alt ist sie? Wo wohnt sie?
3. Hast du Geschwister? Wie viele? Wie heißen sie? Wie alt sind sie? Wo wohnen sie?

Situation 6* Informationsspiel: Familie

MODELL S1: Wie heißt Claires Vater?
S2: Er heißt _____ .
S1: Wie schreibt man das?
S2: _____ .
S1: Wie alt ist Richards Mutter?
S2: Sie ist _____ Jahre alt.
S1: Wo wohnt Sofies Bruder?
S2: Er wohnt in _____ .

*This is the first of many information gap activities in ***Kontakte.*** Pair up with another student. One of you will work with the chart here, the other with the corresponding chart in Appendix A.

		Claire	Richard	Sofie	Mehmet
Vater	*Name*		Werner	Erwin	
	Alter	45		50	59
	Wohnort	Santa Fe	Innsbruck		Izmir
Mutter	*Name*	Sue		Elfriede	Sule
	Alter				
	Wohnort		Innsbruck	Dresden	
Bruder	*Name*	—	Alexander		Yakup
	Alter	—	15	27	34
	Wohnort	—			
Schwester	*Name*	Karen		—	
	Alter			—	
	Wohnort	Santa Fe	Innsbruck	—	Izmir

Wetter und Jahreszeiten

WIE IST DAS WETTER?

Es ist sonnig.

Es ist sehr schön.

Es ist sehr heiß.

Es ist kalt.

Es regnet.

Es ist kühl.

Es schneit.

Es ist windig.

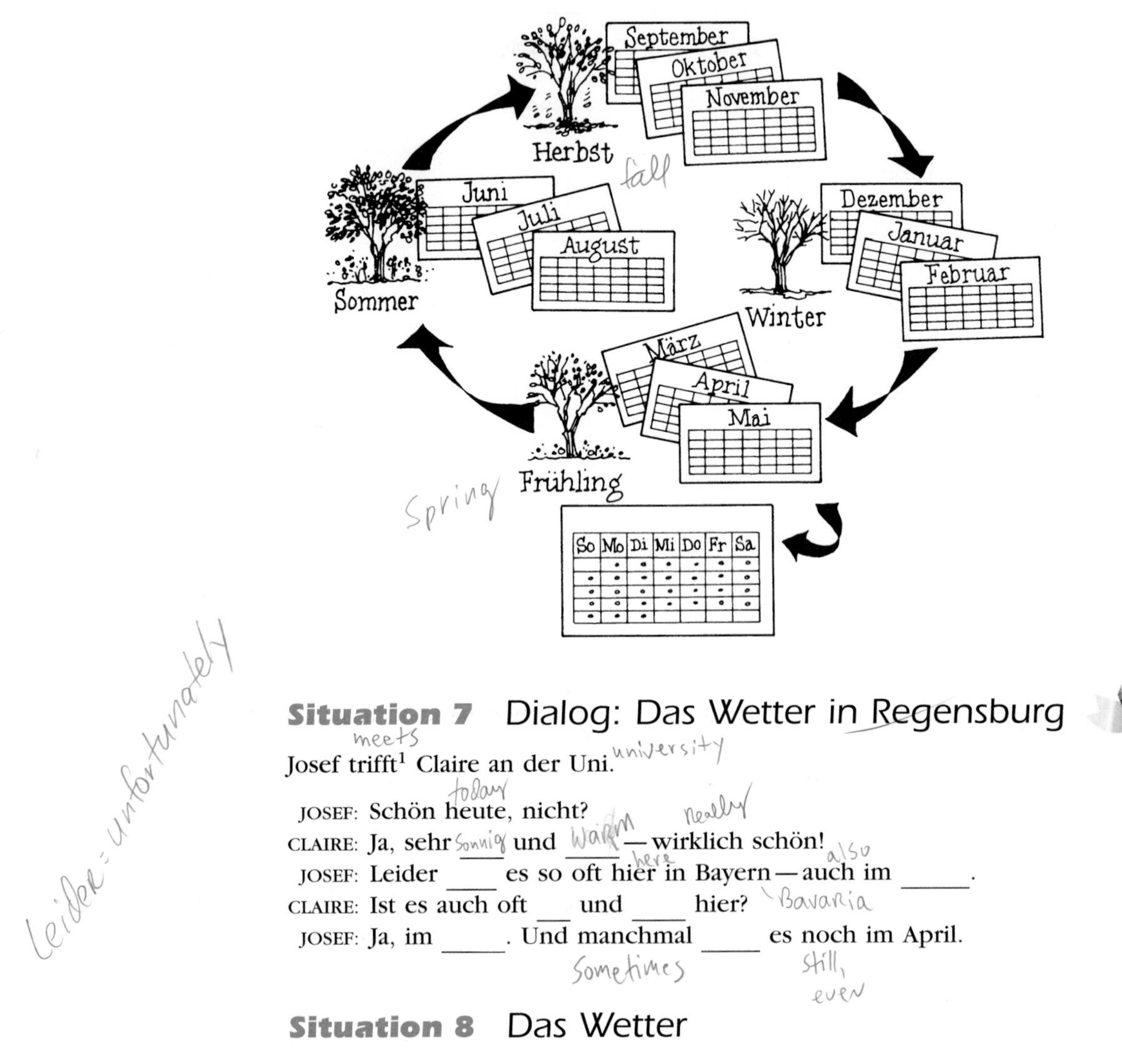

Situation 7 Dialog: Das Wetter in Regensburg

Josef trifft[1] Claire an der Uni.

JOSEF: Schön heute, nicht?
CLAIRE: Ja, sehr ____ und ____ —wirklich schön!
JOSEF: Leider ____ es so oft hier in Bayern—auch im _____.
CLAIRE: Ist es auch oft ___ und ____ hier?
JOSEF: Ja, im _____. Und manchmal _____ es noch im April.

Situation 8 Das Wetter

MODELL S1: Wie ist im Sommer das Wetter in Chicago?
S2: Es ist schön. Es ist warm und sonnig.

Frühling	Chicago	Es ist windig.
Sommer	Miami	Es ist kalt.
Herbst	Berlin	Es ist heiß.
Winter	Wien	Es regnet.
	Melbourne	Es ist sonnig.
	Moskau	Es schneit.
	Rom	Es ist warm.
		Es ist feucht.

[1]*meets*

Kultur ... Landeskunde ... Informationen

Wetter und Klima

Wie ist das Wetter in Ihrer Stadt? Kreuzen Sie an.

	IM WINTER	IM SOMMER
sonnig	☐	☐
warm	☐	☐
(sehr) heiß	☐	☐
(sehr) feucht	☐	☐
mild	☐	☐
(sehr) kalt	☐	☐
viel Niederschlag (Schnee/Regen)	☐	☐
windig	☐	☐
Temperaturschwankungen[1]	oft/selten[2]	oft/selten

An der Universität in Heidelberg. Es regnet wieder einmal.

Das Klima. Deutschland liegt in der Westwindzone zwischen dem Atlantischen Ozean und dem Kontinentalklima im Osten. Große Temperaturschwankungen sind selten. Niederschlag fällt in allen Jahreszeiten. Im Winter liegt die Temperatur zwischen 1,5 Grad Celsius im Tiefland[3] und minus 6 Grad im Gebirge.[4] Die Temperatur im Juli liegt zwischen 18 und 20 Grad Celsius.

Ausnahmen:[5] Am Rhein in Rheinland-Pfalz und Baden-Württemberg ist das Klima sehr mild. Oberbayern hat einen warmen alpinen Südwind, den Föhn. Im Harz sind die Sommer kühl, und im Winter gibt es viel Schnee.

Wie sind die Temperaturen in Deutschland? Benutzen Sie die Tabelle.

	Sommer	Winter Tiefland	Winter Gebirge
in C			
in F			

Welche Gebiete[6] bilden Ausnahmen?

wo			
Klima	sehr _____	warmer _____	Sommer: _____ Winter: _____

Temperaturen in Fahrenheit und Celsius

Fahrenheit → Celsius

32 subtrahieren und mit 5/9 multiplizieren

°F	°C
0	17.8
32	0
50	10
70	21.1
90	32.2
98.4	37
212	100

Celsius → Fahrenheit

Mit 9/5 multiplizieren und 32 addieren

°C	°F
-10	14
0	32
10	50
20	68
30	86
37	98.4
100	212

[1] *temperature variations* [2] *rare(ly)* [3] *lowlands* [4] *mountains* [5] *exceptions* [6] *areas*

Situation 9 Informationsspiel: Temperaturen

MODELL S1: Wieviel Grad Celsius sind 90 Grad Fahrenheit?
S2: _____ Grad Celsius.

F	90	65	32	0	−5	−39
C		18		−18		−39

Herkunft und Nationalität

➤ **Grammatik B.4–B.5**

Situation 10 Dialog: Woher kommst du?

Claire trifft Melanie auf einer Party.

CLAIRE: Wie heißt du?
MELANIE: Melanie. ____?
CLAIRE: Claire.
MELANIE: Bist du ________?
CLAIRE: Ja.
MELANIE: Und ____ kommst du?
CLAIRE: __ New York. Und du?
MELANIE: Aus Regensburg. Ich __ von hier.

Situation 11 Herkunft

MODELL
S1: Woher kommt Silvia Mertens?
S2: Sie kommt aus _____ .
S1: Wer kommt aus Dresden?
S2: _____ .
S1: Kommt Bernd Frisch aus Innsbruck?
S2: Nein, er kommt aus _____ .

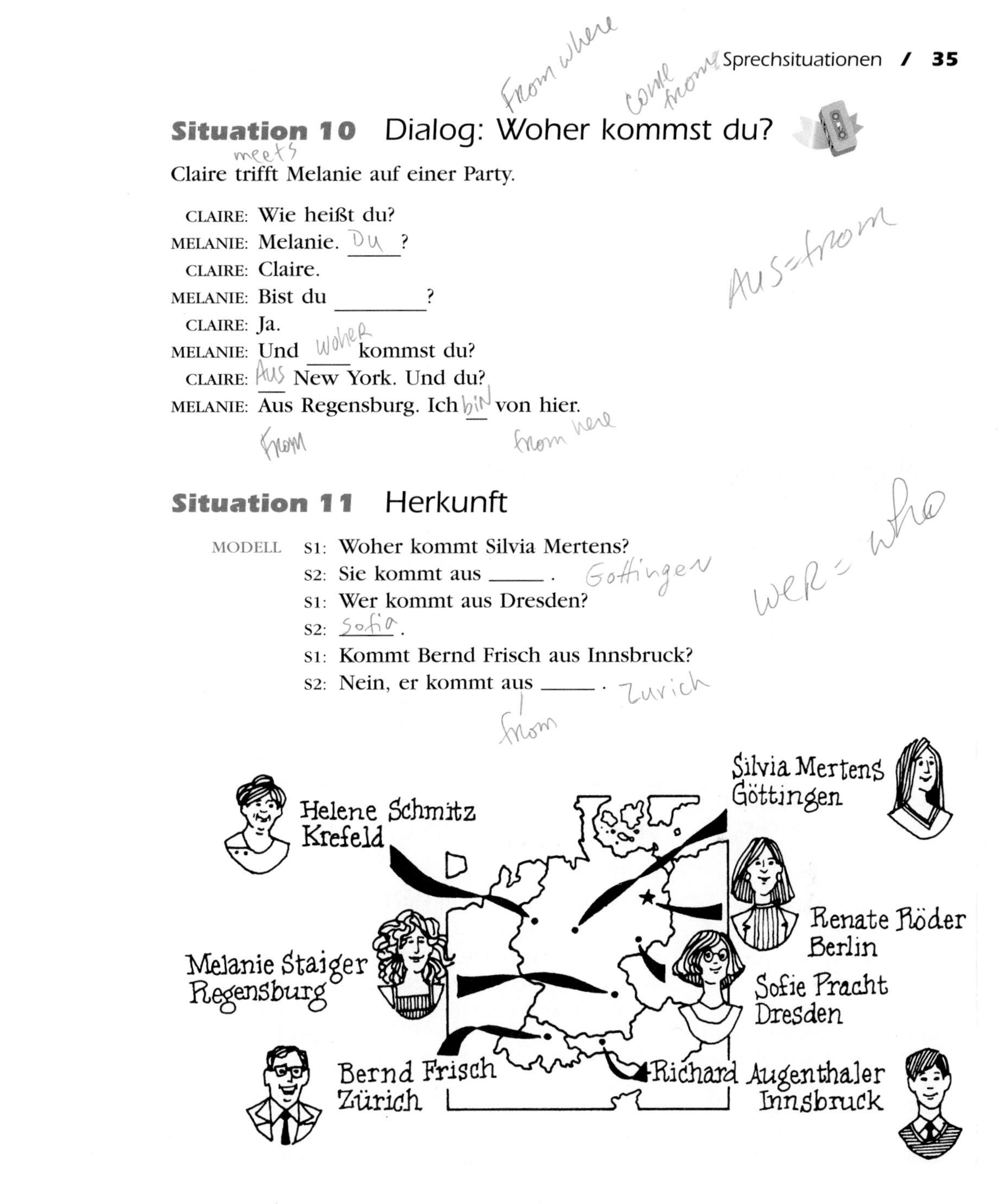

Situation 12 Nationalitäten

MODELL
S1: Woher kommt Mel Gibson?
S2: Aus _____ .
S1: Welche Sprache spricht er?
S2: _____ .

Mel Gibson	Schweden	Türkisch
Helmut Kohl	Südafrika	Spanisch
Sophia Loren	Deutschland	Englisch
Butros-Ghali	Australien	Arabisch
Tansu Çiller	Italien	Schwedisch
Nelson Mandela	Ägypten	Deutsch
Fidel Castro	der Türkei	Italienisch
Astrid Lindgren	Kuba	

Kultur ... Landeskunde ... Informationen

Die Lage Deutschlands in Europa

Deutschland liegt mitten in Europa. Es grenzt an Dänemark, ___, Tschechien, Österreich, die _____, Frankreich, Luxemburg, _____ und die Niederlande. Die Grenzen Deutschlands sind ___ Kilometer lang. Die längste Grenze ist die mit Österreich. Sie ist __ Kilometer lang. Die Grenze zu Dänemark ist nur _ Kilometer lang, die Grenze zu Polen __, zu Tschechien 356, zur Schweiz __, zu Frankreich 446, zu Luxemburg __, zu Belgien 155 und zu den Niederlanden __ Kilometer. Im Norden grenzt Deutschland an zwei Meere, die Nordsee und die _____. Deutschland gehört zur Europäischen Union. Welche Länder gehören noch zur Europäischen Union? Schauen Sie auf die Karte auf Seite 34.

Hints for working with the Kulturprojekt

You can find the approximate latitude of cities and towns in any world atlas. A reference work such as the *Information Please Almanac* usually lists the latitudes of major North American and world cities. (Look up *latitude* in the index.) A world atlas usually lists average monthly temperatures and average length of daylight for North American and world cities. The *Information Please Almanac,* e.g., provides weather data for 100 U.S. cities. If you have Internet access, you can also get information through the *World Wide Web.*

Situation 13 Interview

1. Woher kommst du?
2. Woher kommt dein Vater? Woher kommt deine Mutter? Woher kommen deine Großeltern?
3. Welche Sprachen sprichst du? Welche Sprachen sprechen deine Eltern?
4. Hast du Freunde / Freundinnen in Europa, Asien, Australien, Afrika oder Südamerika? Wie heißen sie? Woher kommen sie? Welche Sprachen sprechen sie?

Kulturprojekt Geographische Lage und Klima

Arbeiten Sie mit einem Weltatlas und lösen Sie die folgenden Aufgaben.

- Identifizieren Sie den Breitengrad[1] Ihrer Universitätsstadt, und suchen Sie große europäische oder nordafrikanische Städte, die ungefähr auf dem gleichen Breitengrad liegen.
- Identifizieren Sie die Breitengrade Hamburgs und Wiens, und suchen Sie nordamerikanische Städte, die ungefähr auf dem gleichen Breitengrad liegen.

[1] *latitude*

- Identifizieren Sie die durchschnittliche Sommertemperatur und die durchschnittliche Wintertemperatur Ihrer Universitätsstadt, und vergleichen Sie sie mit den durchschnittlichen Temperaturen Hamburgs und Wiens. Wo ist es wärmer im Sommer? kälter im Winter?
- Wie viele Stunden Tag und wie viele Stunden Nacht hat man bei Ihnen im Sommer? im Winter? Wie viele Stunden Tag und wie viele Stunden Nacht hat man in Hamburg (und in Wien) im Sommer? im Winter?

VIDEOECKE

Wie wird das Wetter?

Sie sehen eine Wettervorhersage.

- Ist es Winter oder Sommer?
- Scheint die Sonne?
- Schneit es oder regnet es?
- Wo ist das Wetter schön?

Am kältesten bleibt es auf den Bergen, aber auch sonst unter Null

WORTSCHATZ

Das Klassenzimmer / The Classroom

die **Decke, -n**	ceiling
die **Kreide**	(piece of) chalk
die **Tafel, -n** (R)*	blackboard
die **Uhr, -en**	clock
die **Wand, ¨-e**	wall
der **Boden, ¨**	floor
der **Schwamm, ¨-e**	eraser (*for blackboard*)
der **Stift, -e** (R)	pen
der **Bleistift, -e** (R)	pencil
der **Tisch, -e**	table
das **Fenster, -**	window
das **Heft, -e**	notebook

Ähnliche Wörter†

die **Lampe, -n**; die **Professorin, -nen** (R); die **Studentin, -nen** (R) der **Stuhl, ¨-e**; der **Professor, -en** (R); der **Student, -en** (R) das **Buch, ¨-er** (R); das **Papier, -e**

Eigenschaften / Characteristics

er/sie ist . . .	he/she is . . .
ernsthaft	serious
glücklich	happy
nett	nice
ruhig	quiet, calm
sauber	clean
schmutzig	dirty
schön	pretty, beautiful
schüchtern	shy
traurig	sad
verrückt	crazy

*(R) indicates words that were listed in a previous chapter and are presented again for review.

†**Ähnliche Wörter** (*similar words; cognates*) lists contain words that are closely related to English words in sound, form, and meaning, and compound words that are composed of previously introduced vocabulary.

Ähnliche Wörter

freundlich, intelligent, konservativ, nervös, optimistisch, progressiv, religiös, sportlich, tolerant

Die Familie	The Family
die **Frau, -en** (R)	woman; wife
die **Nichte, -n**	niece
die **Schwester, -n**	sister
die **Tante, -n**	aunt
der **Mann, ¨er** (R)	man; husband
der **Vetter, -n**	male cousin
das **Kind, -er**	child
die **Eltern**	parents
die **Großeltern**	grandparents
die **Geschwister**	siblings; brothers and sisters

Ähnliche Wörter

die **Kusine, -n;** die **Mutter, ¨;** die **Großmutter, ¨;** die **Tochter, ¨** der **Bruder, ¨;** der **Neffe, -n;** der **Onkel, -;** der **Sohn, ¨e;** der **Vater, ¨;** der **Großvater, ¨**

Das Wetter	The Weather
es ist . . .	it is . . .
feucht	humid
schön	nice
es . . .	it . . .
regnet	is raining; rains
schneit	is snowing; snows
18 Grad Celsius/ Fahrenheit	18 degrees Celsius/ Fahrenheit

Ähnliche Wörter

heiß, kalt, kühl, sonnig, warm, windig

Jahreszeiten	Seasons
der **Frühling**	spring
der **Herbst**	fall, autumn
im Frühling	in the spring

Ähnliche Wörter

der **Sommer**, der **Winter**

Monate	Months
der **Januar**	der **Juli**
der **Februar**	der **August**
der **März**	der **September**
der **April**	der **Oktober**
der **Mai**	der **November**
der **Juni**	der **Dezember**
im Januar	in January

Länder, Kontinente, Meere	Countries, Continents, Seas
Deutschland	Germany
Frankreich	France
Griechenland	Greece
Österreich	Austria
Rußland	Russia
Tschechien	Czech Republic
Ungarn	Hungary
Weißrußland	Belorussia
die **Ostsee**	Baltic Sea
die **Schweiz**	Switzerland
das **Mittelmeer**	Mediterranean Sea

Ähnliche Wörter

Afrika, Ägypten, Albanien, Algerien, Amerika, Asien, Australien, Belgien, Bosnien und Herzegowina, Bulgarien, Dänemark, England, Europa, Finnland, Großbritannien, Holland, Irland, Israel, Italien, Japan, Jugoslawien, Kanada, Kroatien, Kuba, Liechtenstein, Marokko, Mexiko, Moldawien, Neuseeland, Norwegen, Polen, Portugal, Rumänien, Schweden, Slowenien, Spanien, Südafrika, Südamerika, Tunesien
die **Nordsee**, die **Slowakei**, die **Türkei**, die **Ukraine**
die **Niederlande** (*pl.*), die **USA** (*pl.*)

Nationalitäten	Nationalities
die **Deutsche, -n**	female German
Ich bin Deutsche.	I am German.
die **Französin, -nen**	French woman
die **Österreicherin, -nen**	female Austrian
die **Schweizerin, -nen**	female Swiss
der **Deutsche, -n**	male German
Ich bin Deutscher.	I am German.

der **Franzose, -n**	French man
der **Österreicher, -**	male Austrian
der **Schweizer, -**	male Swiss

Ähnliche Wörter

die **Amerikanerin, -nen;** die **Australierin, -nen;** die **Engländerin, -nen;** die **Japanerin, -nen;** die **Kanadierin, -nen;** die **Mexikanerin, -nen**
der **Amerikaner, -**; der **Australier, -;** der **Engländer, -;** der **Japaner, -;** der **Kanadier, -;** der **Mexikaner, -**

Sprachen — Languages

Deutsch	German

Ähnliche Wörter

Arabisch, Englisch, Italienisch, Japanisch, Schwedisch, Spanisch, Türkisch

Sonstige Substantive — Other Nouns

die **Herkunft**	origin; nationality
die **Uni, -s** (*coll.*)	university
der **Typ, -en** (*coll.*)	character, person, guy
der **Unterricht**	class; instruction

Sonstige Verben — Other Verbs

wohnen (in)	to live (in)

Ähnliche Wörter

kommen (aus)

Fragewörter — Question Words

wer	who
wie	how
wie schreibt man das?	how do you spell that?
wo	where
woher	from where

Ähnliche Wörter

wann; was; welch-: welche Sprache(n), welcher Tag, welches Land

Sonstige Wörter und Ausdrücke — Other Words and Expressions

ein bißchen	a little (bit)
da drüben	over there
das ist . . .	this/that is . . .
das sind . . .	these/those are . . .
dein(e)	your (*informal*)
genau	exactly
heute	today
Ihr(e)	your (*formal*)
leider	unfortunately
macht das was?	does it matter?
manchmal	sometimes
nicht (R)	not
noch	even, still
sehr	very
sonst	otherwise
wirklich	really

Ähnliche Wörter

in, oft, so (oft)

STRUKTUREN UND ÜBUNGEN

B.1 Definite and indefinite articles

Recall that the definite article **der, das, die** (*the*) varies depending on gender, number, and case.* Similarly, the indefinite article **ein, eine** (*a, an*) has various forms.

Das ist **ein** Buch. Welche Farbe hat **das** Buch?	*This is a book. What color is the book?*
Das ist **eine** Tür. Welche Farbe hat **die** Tür?	*This is a door. What color is the door?*

Here are the definite and indefinite articles for all three genders in the singular and plural, nominative case. There is only one plural definite article for all three genders: **die.** The indefinite article (*a, an*) has no plural.

der → **ein**
das → **ein**
die → **eine**
die (*pl.*) → ∅

	Singular	*Plural*
Masculine	**der** Stift **ein** Stift	**die** Stifte Stifte
Neuter	**das** Buch **ein** Buch	**die** Bücher Bücher
Feminine	**die** Tür **eine** Tür	**die** Türen Türen

Übung 1 Im Klassenzimmer

Frau Schulz spricht über die Gegenstände im Klassenzimmer und ihre Farben. Ergänzen Sie den unbestimmten[1] Artikel, den bestimmten[2] Artikel und die Farbe.

MODELL FRAU SCHULZ: Das ist eine Lampe.
Welche Farbe hat die Lampe?
STUDENT(IN): Sie ist gelb.

*See Sections A.3 and A.6.
[1]*indefinite* [2]*definite*

1. Und das ist ______[a] Stift. Welche Farbe hat ______[b] Stift? Er ist ______[c].

2. Und das ist ______[a] Uhr. Welche Farbe hat ______[b] Uhr? Sie ist ______[c].

3. Und das ist ______[a] Stuhl. Welche Farbe hat ______[b] Stuhl? Er ist auch ______[c].

4. Und das ist ______[a] Buch. Welche Farbe hat ______[b] Buch? Es ist ______[c].

5. Und das ist ______[a] Tafel. Welche Farbe hat ______[b] Tafel? Sie ist ______[c].

6. Und das ist ______[a] Brille. Welche Farbe hat ______[b] Brille? Sie ist ______[c].

Übung 2 Was ist das?

Herr Frisch spricht mit seiner kleinen Tochter.

MODELL Ist das ein Heft? → Nein, das ist ein Bleistift.

1. Ist das eine Tür?
2. Ist das eine Uhr?
3. Ist das eine Lampe?
4. Ist das ein Tisch?
5. Ist das ein Stuhl?
6. Ist das eine Studentin?
7. Ist das ein Heft?
8. Ist das eine Tafel?
9. Ist das ein Fenster?

B.2 Plural forms of nouns

Just as with English nouns, there are different ways of forming the plurals of German nouns.

Albert hat ein Heft. Peter hat zwei Hefte.	*Albert has one notebook. Peter has two notebooks.*
Heidi hat eine Kusine. Katrin hat zwei Kusinen.	*Heidi has one cousin. Katrin has two cousins.*

Here are a few general guidelines to help you recognize and form the plural of German nouns.

1. Feminine nouns usually add **-n** or **-en.** They add **-n** when the singular ends in **-e;** otherwise, they add **-en.** Nouns that end in **-in** add **-nen: eine Studentin, zwei Studentinnen.**

eine Lampe	zwei Lampe**n**
eine Tür	zwei Tür**en**
eine Frau	zwei Frau**en**

2. Masculine and neuter nouns usually add **-e** or **-er.** Those plurals that end in **-er** have an umlaut when the stem vowel is **a, o, u,** or **au.** Many masculine plural nouns ending in **-e** have an umlaut as well. Neuter plural nouns ending in **-e** do not have an umlaut.

MASCULINE **(der)**		NEUTER **(das)**	
ein Rock	zwei R**ö**ck**e**	ein Heft	zwei Heft**e**
ein Mann	zwei M**ä**nn**er**	ein Buch	zwei B**ü**ch**er**

3. Masculine and neuter nouns that end in **-er** either add an umlaut or change nothing at all. Many nouns with a stem vowel of **a, o, u,** or **au** add an umlaut.

MASCULINE **(der)**		NEUTER **(das)**	
ein Bruder	zwei Br**ü**der	ein Fenster	zwei Fenster

4. Nouns that end in a vowel other than unstressed **-e** and many nouns of English or French origin add **-s.**

ein Auto	zwei Auto**s**
ein Hotel	zwei Hotel**s**

The following chart summarizes some common associations between gender and plural forms in German.

Singular	*Plural*	*Examples*
ein _____er	no change umlaut where possible	ein Lehrer, zwei Lehrer
ein _____	**-e** masculine words often add an umlaut, neuter words do not	ein Heft, zwei Heft**e** ein Rock, zwei R**ö**ck**e**
ein _____	**-er** umlaut where possible	ein Kind, zwei Kind**er** ein Mann, zwei M**ä**nn**er**

Singular	*Plural*	*Examples*
eine _____	**-n/-en/-nen** depending on final letter	eine Lampe, zwei Lampe**n** eine Tür, zwei Tür**en** eine Freundin, zwei Freun-dinn**en**
ein _____ (*foreign words*)	**-s**	ein Auto, zwei Auto**s** ein Hotel, zwei Hotel**s** ein Hobby, zwei Hobby**s**

Beginning with this chapter, the plural ending of nouns is indicated in the vocabulary lists as follows.

LISTING	PLURAL FORM
das **Fenster, -**	die **Fenster**
der **Bruder, ̈-**	die **Brüder**
das **Papier, -e**	die **Papiere**
der **Stuhl, ̈-e**	die **Stühle**
das **Kleid, -er**	die **Kleider**
der **Mann, ̈-er**	die **Männer**
die **Tante, -n**	die **Tanten**
die **Uhr, -en**	die **Uhren**
die **Studentin, -nen**	die **Studentinnen**
das **Auto, -s**	die **Autos**

Übung 3 Wer hat mehr?

Helga und Sigrid sind Zwillinge. Helga hat immer mehr als[1] Sigrid.

Sigrid hat . . .	Helga hat . . .
eine Hose	zwei _____
eine _____	zwei Lampen
eine _____	zwei Freundinnen
eine Uhr	zwei _____
ein Heft	zwei _____
ein Auto	zwei _____
ein Kleid	zwei _____
einen _____	zwei Stühle
einen Tisch	zwei _____
einen _____	zwei Röcke

[1]immer . . . *always more than*

Übung 4 Der Körper

1. Wie viele der folgenden Körperteile hat der Mensch[1]?

Arm	Fuß	Nase
Auge	Haar	Ohr
Bein	Hand	Schulter
Finger		

Der Mensch hat zwei _____ , . . .

2. Das Zimmer. Wie viele der folgenden Dinge sind in Ihrem[2] Zimmer? (ein[e], zwei, . . . , viele, nicht viele)

das Buch	der Stuhl	die Uhr
das Fenster	der Tisch	die Wand
die Lampe	die Tür	

In meinem Zimmer ist/sind _____ Buch/Bücher, . . .

B.3 Personal pronouns

Personal pronouns refer to the speaker (first person), to the person addressed (second person), or to the person(s) or object(s) talked about (third person).

	Singular	*Plural*
First person	ich *I*	wir *we*
Second-person informal *Second-person formal*	du *you* Sie *you*	ihr *you* Sie *you*
Third person	er *he, it* es *it* sie *she, it*	sie *they*

der → **er** = *it*
das → **es** = *it*
die → **sie** = *it*
die *(pl.)* → **sie** = *they*

As you know, third-person singular pronouns reflect the grammatical gender of the nouns they replace.

—Welche Farbe hat **der Hut?**	*What color is the hat?*
—**Er** ist braun.	*It is brown.*
—Welche Farbe hat **das Kleid?**	*What color is the dress?*
—**Es** ist grün.	*It is green.*
—Welche Farbe hat **die Bluse?**	*What color is the blouse?*
—**Sie** ist gelb.	*It is yellow.*

[1]*person* [2]*your*

The third-person plural pronoun is **sie** for all three genders.

—Welche Farbe haben **die Schuhe?** — *What color are the shoes?*
—**Sie** sind schwarz. — *They are black.*

> **Achtung!**
>
> Just as in English, an **s** added onto someone's name in German indicates possession. In German, however, there is no apostrophe before the **s.**
>
> Das ist Helga. Das ist Helgas Vater.
> *This is Helga. That is Helga's father.*

Übung 5 Welche Farbe?

Frau Schulz spricht über die Farbe der Kleidung. Antworten Sie!

1. Welche Farbe hat der Hut?
2. Welche Farbe hat das Hemd?
3. Welche Farbe hat die Hose?
4. Welche Farbe hat die Bluse?
5. Welche Farbe haben die Socken?
6. Welche Farbe hat das Kleid?
7. Welche Farbe hat der Rock?
8. Welche Farbe haben die Stiefel?
9. Welche Farbe hat die Jacke?
10. Welche Farbe hat der Mantel?

B.4 Origins: *Woher kommen Sie?*

kommen aus = *to come from (a place)*

To ask about someone's origin, use the question word **woher** (*from where*) followed by the verb **kommen** (*to come*). In the answer use the preposition **aus** (*from, out of*).

—Woher kommst du / kommen Sie? — *Where do you come from?*
—Ich komme aus Berlin. — *I'm from Berlin.*

kommen			
ich	komme	wir	kommen
du	kommst	ihr	kommt
Sie	kommen	Sie	kommen
er / sie / es	kommt	sie	kommen

Most verbs follow a conjugation pattern similar to that of **kommen.** The infinitive of German verbs, that is, the basic form of the verb, ends in **-n** or **-en.**

Kommen Sie heute abend? — *Are you coming tonight?*
Warten Sie! **Ich komme** mit! — *Wait! I'll come along.*

Übung 6 Minidialoge

Ergänzen Sie **kommen, woher** und **aus** und die Personalpronomen.

1. MEHMET: Woher _____[a] du, Renate?
   RENATE: Ich _____[b] aus Berlin.
2. FRAU SCHULZ: Woher _____[a] Lydia?
   KATRIN: Lydia kommt _____[b] Zürich.
   FRAU SCHULZ: _____[c] kommen Josef und Melanie?
   STEFAN: Sie _____[d] aus Regensburg.
   FRAU SCHULZ: Und woher komme _____[e]?
   ALBERT: Sie, Frau Schulz, Sie kommen _____[f] Kalifornien.
3. FRAU SCHULZ: Kommt Sofie aus Regensburg?
   HEIDI: Nein, _____[a] kommt aus Dresden.
   FRAU SCHULZ: Kommen Josef und Melanie aus Innsbruck?
   STEFAN: Nein, sie _____[b] aus Regensburg.
4. ANDREAS: Silvia und Jürgen, kommt _____[a] aus Göttingen?
   SILVIA: Ja, _____[b] kommen aus Göttingen.

der → mein, dein, Ihr
das → mein, dein, Ihr
die → meine, deine, Ihre
die *(pl.)* **→ meine, deine, Ihre**

B.5 Possessive adjectives: *mein* and *dein/Ihr*

The possessive adjectives **mein** (*my*), **dein** (*informal your*), and **Ihr** (*formal your*) have the same endings as the indefinite article **ein.** In the plural, the ending is always **-e.** Here are the forms of these possessive adjectives.

	Onkel (m.)	*Auto (n.)*	*Tante (f.)*	*Eltern (pl.)*
ich	mein	mein	meine	meine
du	dein	dein	deine	deine
Sie	Ihr	Ihr	Ihre	Ihre

Achtung!

Notice that the forms of **Ihr** are capitalized, just as **Sie** is, when they mean *your.*

—Woher kommen **deine** Eltern, Albert? — *Where are your parents from, Albert?*
—**Meine** Eltern kommen aus Mexiko. — *My parents are from Mexico.*

Wie heißt **Ihr** Vater, Frau Schulz? Und **Ihre** Mutter? — *What is your father's name, Ms. Schulz? And your mother's name?*

Übung 7 Minidialoge

Ergänzen Sie die Possessivpronomen und die Personalpronomen.

1. FRAU SCHULZ: Wo sind _____[a] Hausaufgaben?
   PETER: _____[b] liegen leider zu Hause.
2. ONKEL: Ist das _____[a] Hund?
   NICHTE: Nein, das ist nicht _____[b] Hund. Ich habe keinen Hund.
3. LYDIA: He, Rosemarie! Das ist _____[a] Kleid.
   ROSEMARIE: Nein, das ist _____[b] Kleid. _____[c] Kleid ist schmutzig.
4. KATRIN: Woher kommen _____[a] Eltern, Frau Schulz?
   FRAU SCHULZ: _____[b] Mutter kommt aus Schwabing, und _____[c] Vater kommt aus Germering.

Übung 8 Woher kommen sie?

Beantworten Sie die Fragen.

1. Woher kommen Sie?
2. Woher kommt Ihre Mutter?
3. Woher kommt Ihr Vater?
4. Woher kommen Ihre Großeltern?
5. Woher kommt Ihr Professor / Ihre Professorin?
6. Wie heißt ein Student aus Ihrem Deutschkurs, und woher kommt er?
7. Wie heißt eine Studentin aus Ihrem Deutschkurs, und woher kommt sie?

KAPITEL 1

Fahrradtour im Englischen Garten in München

In **Kapitel 1** you will learn to talk about how you spend your time: your studies, your recreational pursuits, and what you like and don't like to do.

Wer ich bin und was ich tue

THEMEN
Freizeit
Schule und Universität
Tagesablauf
Persönliche Daten

LEKTÜRE
Ein tabellarischer Lebenslauf
Guten Tag, ich heiße . . .

KULTURELLES
Freizeit
Schule und Universität in den USA und in Deutschland
Arbeitszeiten
Ausweise
Kulturprojekt: Tagesablauf
Porträt: Wilhelm von Humboldt und Berlin-Tegel
Videoecke: Was ist trendy?

STRUKTUREN
1.1 The present tense
1.2 Expressing likes and dislikes: **gern / nicht gern**
1.3 Telling time
1.4 Word order in statements
1.5 Separable-prefix verbs
1.6 Word order in questions

SPRECHSITUATIONEN

Freizeit

➤ **Grammatik 1.1–1.2**

Peter und Stefan wandern gern.

Ernst spielt gern Fußball.

Jutta und Gabi spielen gern Karten.

Melanie tanzt gern.

Veronika reitet gern.

Michael spielt gern Gitarre.

Thomas segelt gern.

Herr und Frau Ruf gehen gern spazieren.

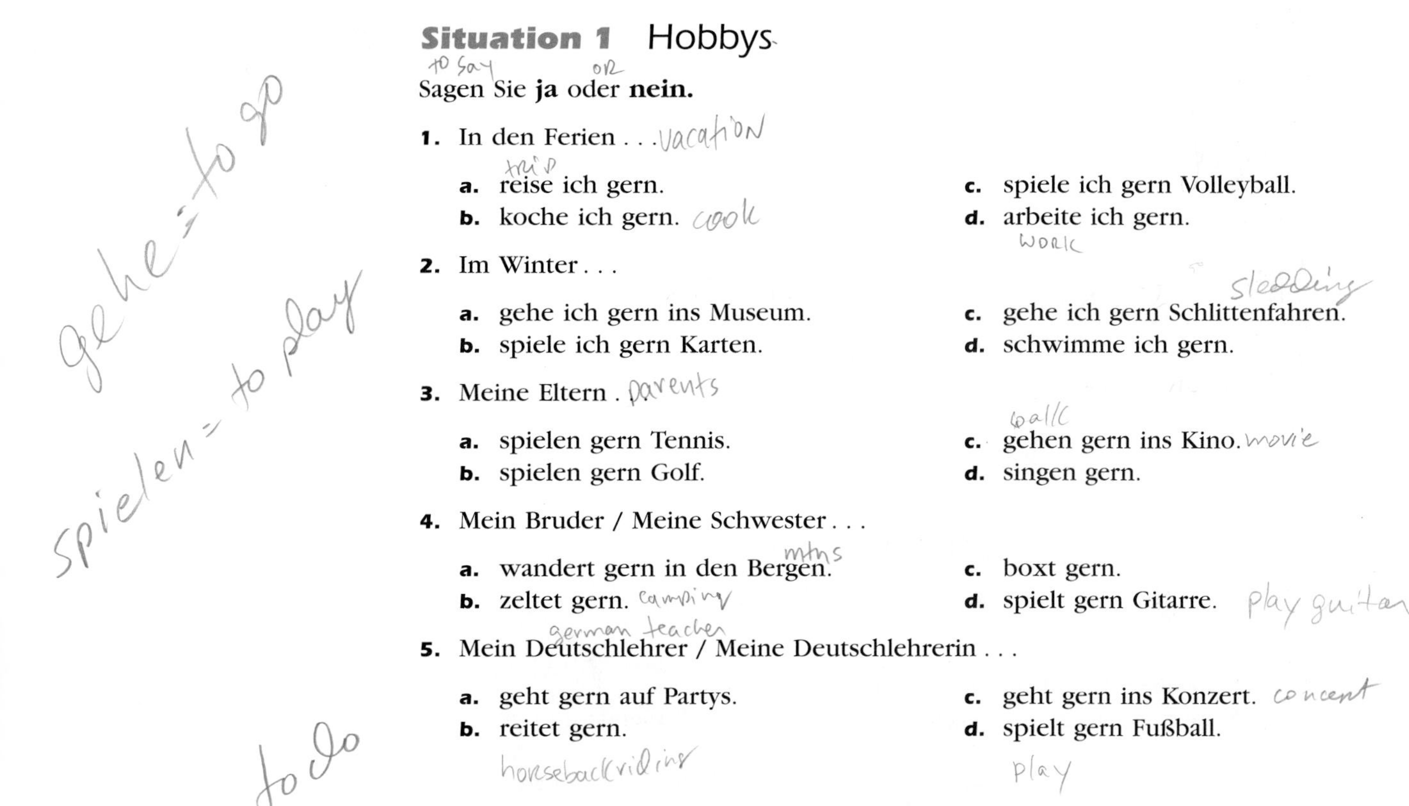

Situation 1 Hobbys

Sagen Sie **ja** oder **nein.**

1. In den Ferien . . .

a. reise ich gern.
b. koche ich gern.
c. spiele ich gern Volleyball.
d. arbeite ich gern.

2. Im Winter . . .

a. gehe ich gern ins Museum.
b. spiele ich gern Karten.
c. gehe ich gern Schlittenfahren.
d. schwimme ich gern.

3. Meine Eltern . . .

a. spielen gern Tennis.
b. spielen gern Golf.
c. gehen gern ins Kino.
d. singen gern.

4. Mein Bruder / Meine Schwester . . .

a. wandert gern in den Bergen.
b. zeltet gern.
c. boxt gern.
d. spielt gern Gitarre.

5. Mein Deutschlehrer / Meine Deutschlehrerin . . .

a. geht gern auf Partys.
b. reitet gern.
c. geht gern ins Konzert.
d. spielt gern Fußball.

Situation 2 Informationsspiel: Freizeit

MODELL

S1: Wie alt ist Rolf?
S2: ______ .
S1: Woher kommt Richard?
S2: Aus ______ .
S1: Was macht Richard gern?
S2: Er ______ .

S1: Wie alt bist du?
S2: ______ .
S1: Woher kommst du?
S2: ______ .
S1: Was machst du gern?
S2: ______ .

	Alter	Wohnort	Hobby
Richard	18		
Rolf		Berkeley	
Jürgen	21		geht gern tanzen
Sofie	22	Dresden	
Jutta			hört gern Musik
Melanie	21		besucht gern Freunde
mein Partner / meine Partnerin			

Situation 3 Interview: Was machst du gern?

MODELL S1: Ich spiele gern Karten. Du auch?
S2: Ja, ich spiele auch gern Karten.
Nein, ich spiele nicht gern Karten.

1. spiele Schach
2. wandere
3. gehe spazieren
4. reite
5. singe
6. spiele Volleyball
7. höre Musik
8. koche
9. tanze
10. lerne Deutsch

Kultur ... Landeskunde ... Informationen

Freizeit

- Was machen Amerikaner in ihrer Freizeit?
- Was machen Sie in Ihrer Freizeit? am Wochenende? abends? in den Ferien?
- Was machen Ihre Eltern in ihrer Freizeit? am Wochenende? abends? in den Ferien?
- Wie viele Stunden Freizeit haben Sie am Tag?
- Was machen Deutsche in ihrer Freizeit? Was ist anders als in Nordamerika? Was ist ähnlich?
- Wie viele Stunden Freizeit haben Deutsche am Tag? Raten[1] Sie!

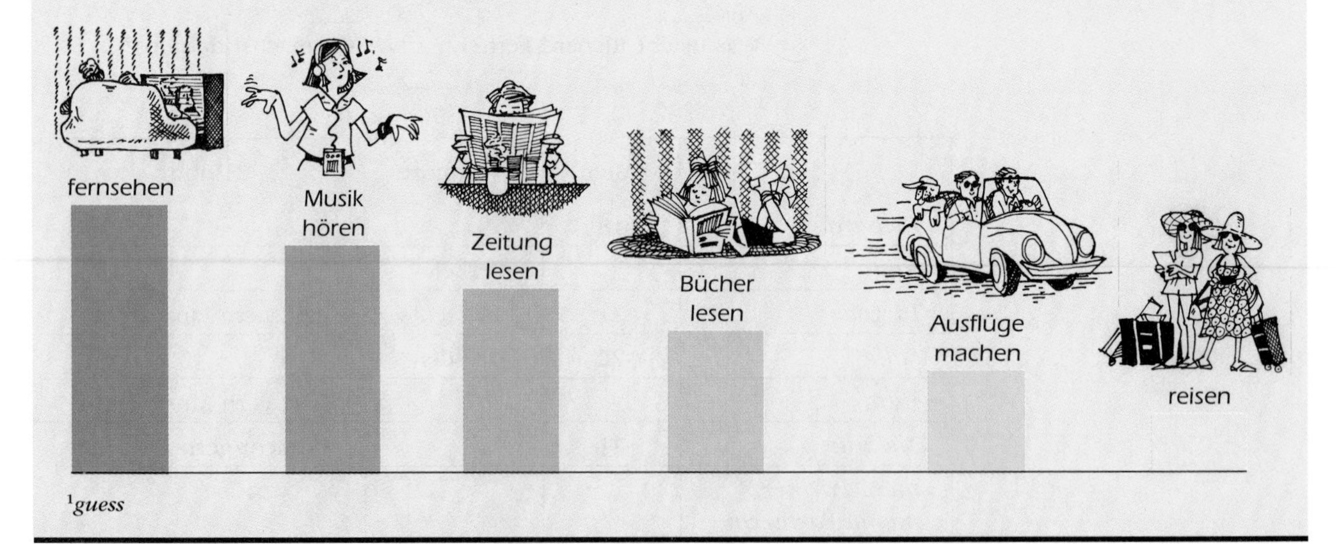

[1] *guess*

Situation 4 Umfrage

MODELL S1: Schwimmst du gern im Meer?
S2: Ja.
S1: Unterschreib bitte hier.

UNTERSCHRIFT

1. Schwimmst du gern im Schwimmbad?
2. Trinkst du gern Kaffee?
3. Spielst du gern Gitarre?
4. Hörst du gern Musik?
5. Gehst du gern zelten?
6. Arbeitest du gern?
7. Gehst du gern joggen?
8. Tanzt du gern?
9. Spielst du gern Golf?
10. Machst du gern Fotos?

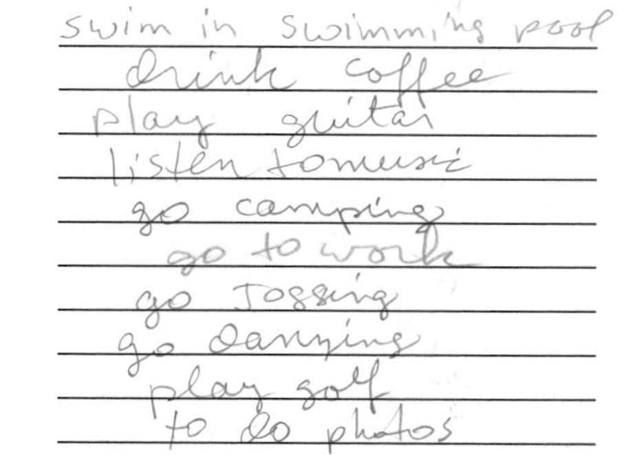

Schule und Universität

➤ **Grammatik 1.3**

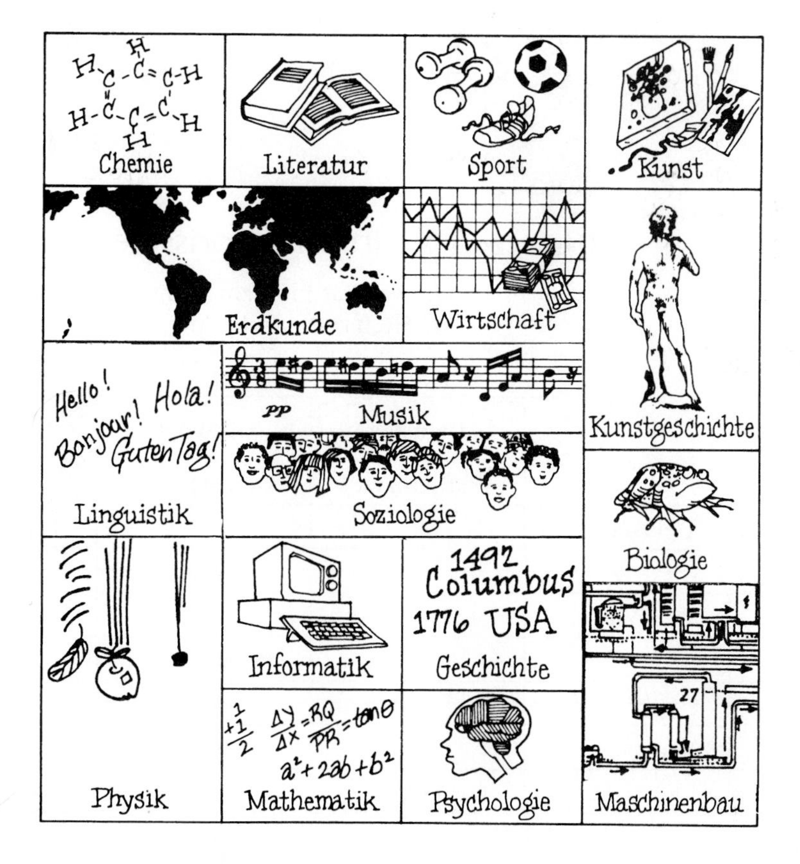

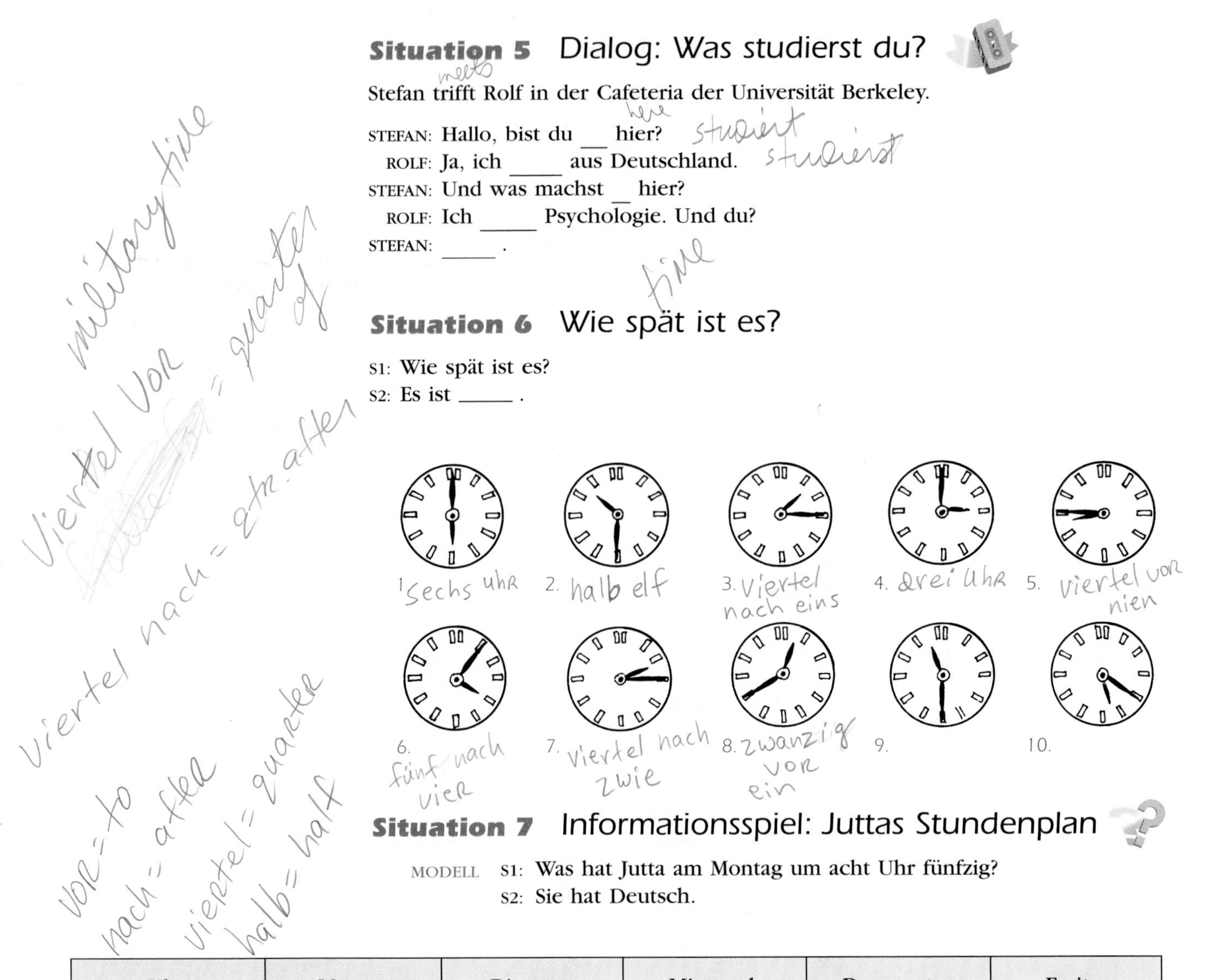

Situation 5 Dialog: Was studierst du?

Stefan trifft Rolf in der Cafeteria der Universität Berkeley.

STEFAN: Hallo, bist du __ hier?
ROLF: Ja, ich _____ aus Deutschland.
STEFAN: Und was machst __ hier?
ROLF: Ich _____ Psychologie. Und du?
STEFAN: _____ .

Situation 6 Wie spät ist es?

S1: Wie spät ist es?
S2: Es ist _____ .

1. 2. 3. 4. 5.
6. 7. 8. 9. 10.

Situation 7 Informationsspiel: Juttas Stundenplan

MODELL S1: Was hat Jutta am Montag um acht Uhr fünfzig?
S2: Sie hat Deutsch.

Uhr	Montag	Dienstag	Mittwoch	Donnerstag	Freitag
8.00 - 8.45		Mathematik	Deutsch		Französisch
8.50 - 9.35	Deutsch			Latein	
9.35 - 9.50	←		Pause		→
9.50 - 10.35	Biologie	Sozialkunde		Geschichte	
10.40 - 11.25			Physik		Deutsch
11.25 - 11.35	←		Pause		→
11.35 - 12.15	Sport		Erdkunde		Latein
12.20 - 13.00		Deutsch		Sozialkunde	

Situation 8 Interview

1. Welche Fächer studierst du in diesem Semester? Welche Fächer hast du gern? Welche Fächer hast du nicht gern?
2. Wann beginnt am Montag dein erster (1.) Kurs? Welcher Kurs ist das? Wann gehst du am Montag nach Hause?
3. Wann beginnt am Dienstag dein erster Kurs? Welcher Kurs ist das? Wann gehst du am Dienstag nach Hause?
4. Arbeitest du? An welchen Tagen arbeitest du? Wann beginnt deine Arbeit?
5. Wann gehst du in der Woche ins Bett? Und am Wochenende?

Kultur ... Landeskunde ... Informationen

Schule und Universität in den USA und in Deutschland

- Wann beginnt in den USA morgens die Schule?
- Wann gehen die Schüler nach Hause?
- Wann und wo machen sie Hausaufgaben?
- Wann haben sie Freizeit?
- Welche Fächer haben Schüler in den USA in der Schule?
- Welches sind Pflichtfächer[1]?
- An welchen Tagen gehen sie in die Schule?

Schauen Sie auf Juttas Stundenplan (Situation 7).

- Wann beginnt für Jutta die Schule?
- Wann geht sie nach Hause?
- Welche Fächer hat Jutta?
- Wie viele Fremdsprachen hat sie?
- An welchen Tagen geht sie in die Schule?

Spekulieren Sie:

- Wann und wo macht Jutta Hausaufgaben?
- Wann hat sie Freizeit?

Große Pause an einem Gymnasium in Berlin

[1] *required subjects*

Tagesablauf

➤ **Grammatik 1.4–1.5**

Herr Wagner steht auf.

Er duscht.

Er frühstückt.

Er geht zur Arbeit.

Er geht einkaufen.

Er räumt die Wohnung auf.

Er geht im Park spazieren.

Er geht ins Bett.

Situation 9 Bildgeschichte: Ein Tag in Sofies Leben

Situation 10 Informationsspiel: Diese Woche

MODELL S1: Was macht Renate am Montag?
S2: Sie frühstückt um acht Uhr.

	Silvia Mertens	Renate Röder	Mehmet Sengün
Montag		Sie frühstückt um 8 Uhr.	Er geht um 7 Uhr zur Arbeit.
Dienstag	Sie arbeitet am Abend in einer Kneipe.		Er lernt eine neue Kollegin kennen.
Mittwoch		Sie kauft eine Bluse.	
Donnerstag		Sie ruft ihre Eltern an.	Er geht einkaufen.
Freitag	Sie holt Jürgen von der Uni ab.		
Samstag	Sie geht mit Freunden ins Kino.		
Sonntag	Sie bleibt den ganzen Tag zu Hause.		Er repariert sein Motorrad.

Situation 11 Interview

1. Was machst du samstags?

a. Spielst du Fußball?
b. Stehst du spät auf?
c. Gehst du im Park spazieren?
d. Rufst du deine Eltern an?
e. Gehst du einkaufen?
f. Besuchst du Freunde?

2. Was machst du montags?

a. Stehst du früh auf?
b. Frühstückst du zu Hause?
c. Trinkst du Kaffee?
d. Kaufst du ein?
e. Arbeitest du in der Bibliothek?
f. Hast du Zeit für Sport? Was machst du?

3. Was machst du freitags?

a. Gehst du tanzen?
b. Bleibst du zu Hause?
c. Hörst du Musik?
d. Rufst du Freunde an?
e. Räumst du dein Zimmer auf?
f. Spielst du Tennis?

Situation 12 Freizeit und Arbeit

Was ist Freizeit? Was ist Arbeit? Machen Sie zwei Listen.

Freizeit	Arbeit
Karten spielen	Hausaufgaben machen

die Eltern anrufen
Musik hören
das Zimmer aufräumen
aufstehen
einkaufen gehen
eine Hose kaufen
kochen
Deutsch lernen
in der Sonne liegen
Hausaufgaben machen
eine Prüfung schreiben
einen Brief schreiben
singen
Karten spielen
Arbeit suchen
tanzen
wandern

Kultur ... Landeskunde ... Informationen

Arbeitszeiten

	Japan	USA	Schweiz	Schweden	Frankreich	Italien	Großbritannien	Niederlande	Belgien	Bundesrepublik
Jahresurlaub (Tage)	11	12	23	25	25	31	27	36	25	30
Feiertage[1]	14	10	8	9	9	9	8	5	11	10
Wochenarbeitszeit (Stunden)	42	40	41	40	39	40	39	40	38	37,9

- Wie viele Tage Urlaub im Jahr haben die Deutschen? Wer hat mehr?
- Wie viele Tage Urlaub haben die Amerikaner? Wer hat weniger?
- In welchem Land gibt es sehr viele Feiertage? In welchem Land gibt es sehr wenige?
- Wie viele Stunden in der Woche arbeiten die Italiener? Wer arbeitet auch so viel?

[1] *holidays*

Situation 13 Interview

1. Wann stehst du auf?
2. Wann duschst du?
3. Wann frühstückst du?
4. Wann gehst du zur Uni?
5. Wann kommst du nach Hause?
6. Wann machst du das Abendessen?
7. Wann gehst du ins Bett?

Persönliche Daten

➤ **Grammatik 1.6**

Antrag auf Ausstellung eines Personalausweises

Familienname: Ruf

geborene(r): Schuler

Vornamen: Margret

Geburtstag: 13. April 1957

Geburtsort: Augsburg

Staatsangehörigkeit: deutsch

Augenfarbe: blau, grau, (grün), braun   Größe 172 cm

München Sonnenstr. 11
Straße   Hausnummer

München, den 30.5.1996

Margret Ruf
Unterschrift des Antragstellers

Situation 14 Dialog: Auf dem Rathaus

Melanie ist auf dem Rathaus in Regensburg. Sie braucht einen neuen Personalausweis.

BEAMTER: Grüß Gott!
MELANIE: Grüß Gott. Ich brauche einen neuen ________.
BEAMTER: __ ist Ihr Name, bitte?
MELANIE: Staiger, Melanie Staiger.
BEAMTER: Und __ wohnen Sie?
MELANIE: In Regensburg.
BEAMTER: __ ist die genaue Adresse?
MELANIE: Gesandtenstraße 8.
BEAMTER: Haben Sie auch ____?
MELANIE: Ja, die Nummer ist 24352.
BEAMTER: ___ sind Sie geboren?
MELANIE: Am 3. ___ 1975.
BEAMTER: Was sind Sie _____?
MELANIE: Ich bin Studentin.
BEAMTER: Sind Sie verheiratet?
MELANIE: ___. Ich bin ledig.

Situation 15 Interview: Auf dem Rathaus

1. Wie heißen Sie?
2. Wie alt sind Sie?
3. Wo sind Sie geboren?
4. Wo wohnen Sie?
5. Was ist Ihre genaue Adresse?
6. Was ist Ihre Telefonnummer?
7. Was studieren Sie?
8. Sind Sie verheiratet?
9. Welche Augenfarbe haben Sie?
10. Welche Haarfarbe?

Kultur ... Landeskunde ... Informationen

Ausweise

- Haben Sie einen Ausweis? Was für einen?
- Welche persönlichen Daten stehen in Ihrem Ausweis?
- Wann brauchen Sie einen Ausweis? Kreuzen Sie an.
  - Wenn Sie Auto fahren ☐
  - Wenn Sie Fahrrad fahren ☐
  - Wenn Sie ins Ausland fahren ☐
  - Wenn Sie Bier kaufen ☐
  - Wenn Sie ins Kino gehen ☐
  - Wenn Sie spazierengehen ☐
- Wo bekommen Sie einen Ausweis? Kreuzen Sie an:
  - auf dem Rathaus ☐
  - im Supermarkt ☐
  - auf dem Postamt ☐
  - auf der Polizei ☐
  - an der Uni ☐

Gegenwärtige Anschrift/Address/Adresse
MÜNCHEN 71
AM LEHWINKEL 9
Größe/Height/Taille
172 cm
Augenfarbe/Colour of eyes/Couleur des yeux
BLAU
Ordens- oder Künstlername/Religious name or pseudonym/Nom de religion ou pseudonyme
Behörde/Authority/Autorité
LANDESHAUPTSTADT MÜNCHEN
KREISVERWALTUNGSREFERAT
Datum/Date/Date
17.07.92
WEBER<<MARION<<<<<<<<<<<<<<<<<<
Bundesdruckerei

BUNDESREPUBLIK DEUTSCHLAND FEDERAL REPUBLIC OF GERMANY REPUBLIQUE FEDERALE D'ALLEMAGNE
PERSONALAUSWEIS
IDENTITY CARD/CARTE D'IDENTITE 8011474816
Name/Surname/Nom
WEBER
Vornamen/Given names/Prénoms
MARION ILSABETH
Geburtstag und -ort/Date and place of birth/Date et lieu de naissance
20.09.68 AMBERG
Staatsangehörigkeit/Nationality/Nationalité Gültig bis/Date of expiry/Date d'expiration
DEUTSCH / 16.07.97
Unterschrift des Inhabers/Signature of bearer/Signature du titulaire
M. Weber
IDD<<WEBER<<MARION<<<<<<<<<<<<<<<<<
8011474816D<<6809205<9707162<<<<<<0

Das ist ein deutscher Personalausweis. In Deutschland brauchen[1] alle Leute, die älter als 16 Jahre sind, einen Ausweis. Sie müssen ihn immer dabeihaben[2]. Mit einem Computer kann die Polizei in drei Sekunden die Identität überprüfen[3]. Man bekommt[4] den Personalausweis auf dem Rathaus.

- Welche persönlichen Daten stehen in diesem Ausweis?

[1] *need* [2] *have it with them* [3] *check* [4] *gets*

Situation 16* Rollenspiel: Im Auslandsamt

S1: Sie sind Student/Studentin und möchten ein Jahr lang in Österreich studieren. Gehen Sie ins Auslandsamt und sagen Sie, daß Sie ein Stipendium möchten. Beantworten Sie die Fragen des Angestellten/der Angestellten. Sagen Sie am Ende des Interviews „Auf Wiedersehen“.

Situation 17 Zum Schreiben: Lebenslauf

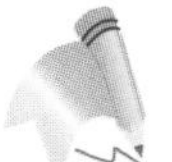

Schreiben Sie einen tabellarischen Lebenslauf mit Ihren persönlichen Daten.

Name: ....

Adresse: ....

Geburtstag: ....

Geburtsort: ....

Familienstand: ....

Schule:

19.... - 19.... ....

19.... - 19.... ....

Studium:

19.... - 19.... ....

19.... - 19.... ....

Hobbys: ....

....

Sprachen: ....

....

Hints for working with the **Kulturprojekt**

Ask your German instructor if he/she knows of a German club on campus or in town. The office for international students might also know if there are German, Austrian, or Swiss students who meet regularly and who would like to get to know American students. There also may be teaching assistants, instructors, or professors from a German-speaking country who would not mind being interviewed about their home country.

Kulturprojekt Tagesablauf

Fragen Sie Deutsche, Österreicher oder Schweizer oder fragen Sie Ihren Lehrer/Ihre Lehrerin nach den folgenden Informationen.

- Wann beginnen die meisten Menschen in Deutschland, Österreich oder der Schweiz mit ihrer Arbeit? Wie lange machen sie Mittagspause? Wann hören sie mit der Arbeit auf?
- Wann beginnt die Schule? Wann hört sie auf?
- Wann machen die Geschäfte auf? Wann machen sie zu? Wie ist es am Wochenende?
- Wann frühstücken viele Menschen? Wann essen sie zu Mittag? zu Abend?
- Was machen Studenten während der Woche am Abend? am Wochenende?
- Was machen 30- oder 40-jährige während der Woche am Abend? am Wochenende?

---

*This is the first of many role-playing activities in ***Kontakte.*** Pair up with another student. One of you takes the role of S1, the other of S2. The corresponding role for S2 appears in Appendix B.

Nach dem Abendessen. Arbeit und Vergnügen zu Hause.

Porträt

Wilhelm von Humboldt (1767 - 1835), Gelehrter[1] und Politiker, war unter anderem Philosoph, Sprachwissenschaftler und Bildungsreformer.[2] Er war mit berühmten Deutschen wie Goethe und Schiller befreundet[3] und konzipierte[4] die Berliner Humboldt-Universität. Sein Bruder Alexander war Naturforscher[5] und Geograph.

Tegel ist ein Stadtteil von Berlin. Dort steht das Humboldt-Schloß.[6] Der berühmte klassizistische Baumeister[7] Karl Friedrich von Schinkel hat es für Wilhelm und Alexander gebaut. Im Park des Schlosses ist auch das Grab[8] der Brüder von Humboldt.

[1] *scholar* [2] *educational reformer* [3] *friends* [4] *conceived* [5] *naturalist* [6] *palace* [7] *architect* [8] *tomb*

Schloß Tegel in Berlin

VIDEOECKE

Was ist trendy?

Was ist trendy?—Fußball, Handball, Skateboardfahren

Sie sehen einen Clip, der zeigt, was in Deutschland gerade „in" ist.

- Was ist gerade in Deutschland „in"?
- Welche Trends finden Sie gut?
- Welche Trends kommen aus den USA?
- Was ist bei Ihnen „in"?

WORTSCHATZ

Freizeit — Leisure Time

lesen	to read
er/sie liest	he/she reads
Zeitung lesen	to read the newspaper
liegen	to lie
in der Sonne liegen	to lie in the sun
reisen	to travel
segeln	to sail
spielen	to play
wandern	to hike
zelten	to camp

Ähnliche Wörter*

die **Karte, -n**; die **Musik**   der **Ball, ¨-e** (R); der **Fußball, ¨-e**; der **Volleyball, ¨-e**   das **Golf**; das **Hobby, -s**; das **Schach**; das **Squash**; das **Tennis**   **boxen; hören; kochen; reiten; schwimmen gehen; singen; tanzen; windsurfen gehen**

Orte — Places

die **Arbeit, -en**	work; job
zur Arbeit gehen	to go to work
der **Berg, -e**	mountain
in die Berge gehen	to go to the mountains
in den Bergen wandern	to hike in the mountains
das **Kino, -s**	movie theater, cinema
ins Kino gehen	to go to the movies
das **Meer, -e**	sea
im Meer schwimmen	to swim in the sea
das **Rathaus, ¨-er**	town hall
auf dem Rathaus	at the town hall
das **Schwimmbad, ¨-er**	swimming pool
ins Schwimmbad fahren	to go to the swimming pool

Ähnliche Wörter

die **Party, -s; auf eine Party gehen**; die **Uni, -s; zur Uni gehen; auf der Uni sein**   der **Park, -s; im Park spazierengehen**   das **Bett, -en; ins Bett gehen**; das **Haus, ¨-er; zu Hause sein; nach Hause gehen**; das **Konzert, -e; ins Konzert gehen**; das **Museum, Museen; ins Museum gehen**

---

*__Ähnliche Wörter__ (*similar words; cognates*) lists contain words that are closely related to English words in sound, form, and meaning, and compound words that are composed of previously introduced vocabulary.

Schul- und Studienfächer — Academic Subjects

die **Erdkunde**	earth science; geography
die **Geschichte**	history
die **Kunstgeschichte**	art history
die **Informatik**	computer science
die **Kunst**	art
die **Sozialkunde**	social studies
die **Wirtschaft**	economics
der **Maschinenbau**	mechanical engineering

Ähnliche Wörter

die **Biologie**, die **Chemie**, die **Linguistik**, die **Literatur**, die **Mathematik**, die **Musik**, die **Physik**, die **Religion**, die **Soziologie** der **Sport** das **Latein**

Schule und Universität — School and University

die **Hausaufgabe, -n** (R)	homework assignment
die **Lehrerin, -nen** (R)	female teacher, instructor
die **Prüfung, -en**	test
die **Schülerin, -nen**	female pupil
der **Lehrer, -** (R)	male teacher, instructor
der **Schüler, -**	male pupil
der **Stundenplan, ¨-e**	schedule
das **Auslandsamt, ¨-er**	center for study abroad
das **Fach, ¨-er**	academic subject
das **Stipendium, Stipendien**	scholarship
das **Studium**	university studies
die **Ferien** (*pl.*)	vacation

Ähnliche Wörter

die **Pause, -n** der **Kurs, -e** (R) das **Semester, -** **lernen; studieren**

Tage — Days

welcher Tag ist heute?	what day is today?
der **Montag**	Monday
der **Dienstag**	Tuesday
der **Mittwoch**	Wednesday
der **Donnerstag**	Thursday
der **Freitag**	Friday
der **Samstag**	Saturday
der **Sonntag**	Sunday

Persönliche Daten — Biographical Information

die **Farbe, -n**	color
die **Augenfarbe**	color of eyes
die **Haarfarbe**	color of hair
die **Größe, -n**	height
die **Staatsangehörigkeit, -en**	nationality, citizenship
die **Unterschrift, -en**	signature
der **Beruf, -e**	profession
was sind Sie von Beruf?	what's your profession?
der **Familienstand**	marital status
der **Geburtstag, -e**	birthday
der **Personalausweis, -e**	(personal) ID card
der **Wohnort, -e**	residence
das **Alter**	age
ledig	unmarried
verheiratet	married

Ähnliche Wörter

die **Adresse, -n**; die **Nummer, -n**; die **Hausnummer, -n**; die **Telefonnummer, -n**; die **Person, -en**; die **Präferenz, -en** der **Name, -n** (R); der **Familienname, -n**; der **Vorname, -n** **geboren; wann sind Sie geboren?**

Zeitausdrücke — Time Expressions

die **Freizeit**	leisure time
die **Woche, -n**	week
in der Woche	during the week
der **Abend, -e**	evening
der **Tag, -e**	day
der **ganze Tag**	all day long, the whole day
das **Wochenende, -n**	weekend
am Wochenende	over the weekend
früh	early
spät(er)	late(r)
wie spät ist es?	what time is it?
wieviel Uhr ist es?	what time is it?
um wieviel Uhr . . . ?	at what time . . . ?
wann?	when?
um halb drei	at two thirty
um sechs (Uhr)	at six o'clock
um sieben Uhr zwanzig	at seven twenty
um Viertel vor vier	at a quarter to four
um zwanzig nach fünf	at twenty after/past five

Ähnliche Wörter

die **Sekunde, -n** der **Moment, -e; im Moment**

Sonstige Substantive — Other Nouns

die **Tasche, -n**	bag; purse; pocket
die **Unterschrift, -en**	signature
die **Wohnung, -en**	apartment
der **Brief, -e**	letter
der **Wohnort, -e**	place of residence
das **Abendessen, -**	supper, evening meal
das **Motorrad, ⸚er**	motorcycle
Motorrad fahren	to ride a motorcycle

Ähnliche Wörter

die **Gitarre, -n** der **Kaffee** das **Foto, -s**

Verben mit trennbaren Präfixen — Verbs with Separable Prefixes

ab·holen	to pick (somebody) up (from a place)
an·kommen	to arrive
an·rufen	to call up
auf·hören (mit)	to stop (doing something)
auf·räumen	to clean (up)
auf·stehen	to get up
aus·füllen	to fill in
aus·gehen	to go out
ein·kaufen (gehen)	to (go) shop(ping)
ein·packen	to pack up
fern·sehen	to watch TV
er/sie sieht fern	he/she is watching TV
kennen·lernen	to get acquainted with
spazieren·gehen	to go for a walk

Sonstige Verben — Other Verbs

arbeiten	to work
besuchen	to visit
bleiben	to stay, remain
brauchen	to need; to use
duschen	to (take a) shower
fliegen	to fly
frühstücken	to eat breakfast
kaufen	to buy
suchen	to look for
unterschreiben	to sign

Ähnliche Wörter

beginnen, reparieren, trinken

Sonstige Wörter und Ausdrücke — Other Words and Expressions

gern	gladly, willingly, with pleasure
wir singen gern	we like to sing
ihr(e)	her
sein(e)	his

LESEECKE

LEKTÜRE 1

Vor dem Lesen

With the help of a few simple strategies, you will learn how to orient yourself to the content of a reading; that is, you will learn how to make use of clues to a reading's content even before you begin to read. Look closely at the document you see here and check the most likely answers to the following questions.

1. Was für[1] ein Text ist es?

- ☐ ein Brief[2]
- ☐ eine Einkaufsliste[3]
- ☐ ein Gedicht[4]
- ☐ eine Kurzgeschichte[5]
- ☐ ein Lebenslauf[6]
- ☐ eine Reklame[7]

2. Wann schreibt man so[8] einen Text?

- ☐ Wenn man Arbeit sucht.[9]
- ☐ Wenn man einkaufen geht.[10]
- ☐ Wenn man etwas kaufen möchte.[11]
- ☐ Wenn man etwas verkaufen[12] möchte.
- ☐ Wenn man heiraten[13] möchte.

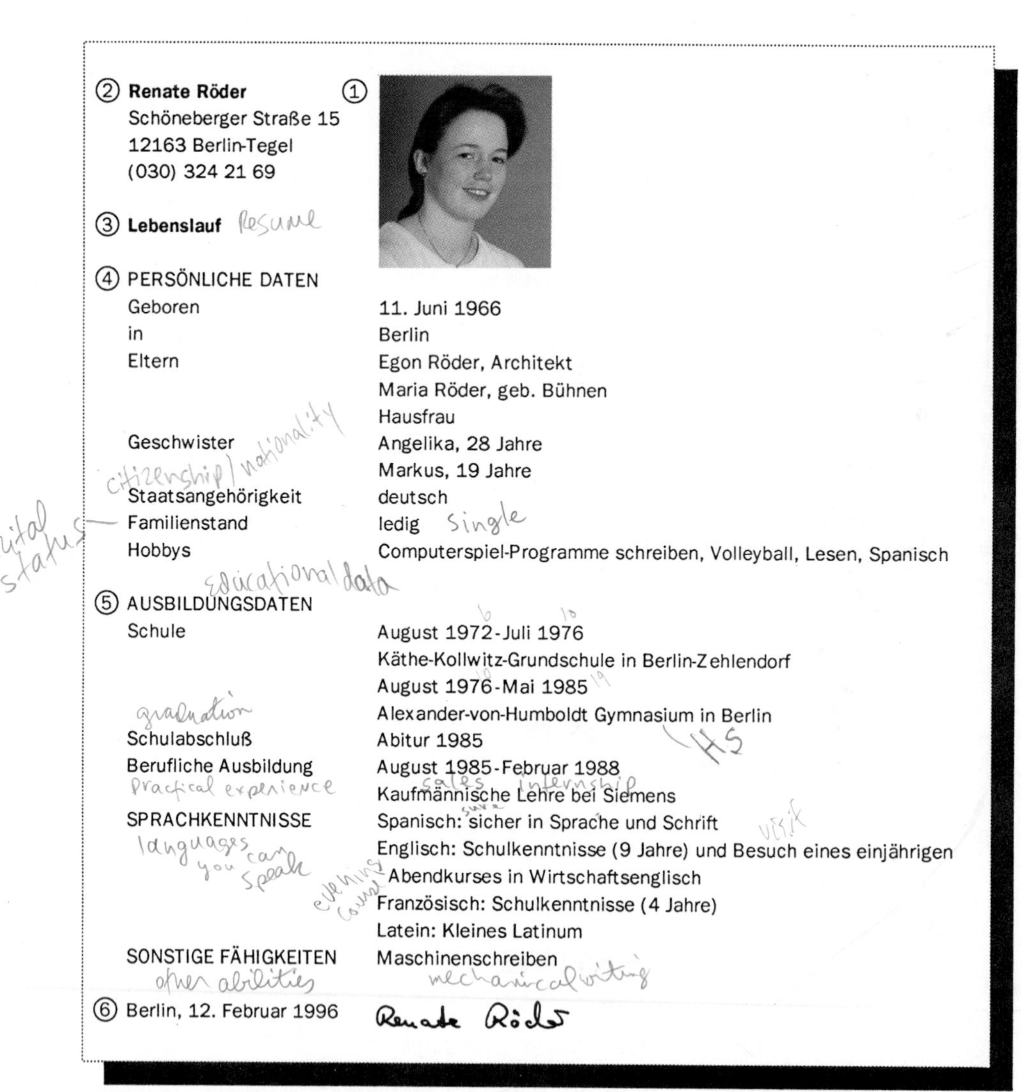

② **Renate Röder**
Schöneberger Straße 15
12163 Berlin-Tegel
(030) 324 21 69

①

③ **Lebenslauf**

④ PERSÖNLICHE DATEN

Geboren	11. Juni 1966
in	Berlin
Eltern	Egon Röder, Architekt Maria Röder, geb. Bühnen Hausfrau
Geschwister	Angelika, 28 Jahre Markus, 19 Jahre
Staatsangehörigkeit	deutsch
Familienstand	ledig
Hobbys	Computerspiel-Programme schreiben, Volleyball, Lesen, Spanisch

⑤ AUSBILDUNGSDATEN

Schule	August 1972-Juli 1976 Käthe-Kollwitz-Grundschule in Berlin-Zehlendorf August 1976-Mai 1985 Alexander-von-Humboldt Gymnasium in Berlin
Schulabschluß	Abitur 1985
Berufliche Ausbildung	August 1985-Februar 1988 Kaufmännische Lehre bei Siemens
SPRACHKENNTNISSE	Spanisch: sicher in Sprache und Schrift Englisch: Schulkenntnisse (9 Jahre) und Besuch eines einjährigen Abendkurses in Wirtschaftsenglisch Französisch: Schulkenntnisse (4 Jahre) Latein: Kleines Latinum
SONSTIGE FÄHIGKEITEN	Maschinenschreiben

⑥ Berlin, 12. Februar 1996 Renate Röder

---

[1]Was . . . *What kind of* [2]*letter* [3]*shopping list* [4]*poem* [5]*short story* [6]*résumé* [7]*advertisement* [8]*such* [9]Arbeit . . . *is looking for a job* [10]einkaufen . . . *is going shopping* [11]kaufen . . . *would like to buy* [12]*to sell* [13]*to get married*

Arbeit mit dem Text

A. Information suchen. The circled numbers refer to information that is essential to a German résumé. Write the appropriate number next to the keywords in the list.

NUMMER	STICHWORT
___	Titel, Überschrift
___	Name und Adresse
___	Datum und Unterschrift
___	Lichtbild (Foto)
___	Persönliche Daten
___	Schule und Ausbildung

B. Kulturelle Unterschiede. The kinds of information official documents typically contain and what is considered personal or private differ from country to country. Compare this German **Lebenslauf** with an American résumé. What are some of the differences? Was steht *nicht* in Ihrem Lebenslauf?

C. Ausbildungsdaten. Look at this section of the résumé closely. What different types of schools can you identify? For how many years did Renate attend her first school? For how many years did she attend the secondary school? When did she graduate (**Schulabschluß**)? Where did she get her professional training? Vervollständigen[1] Sie die Tabelle.

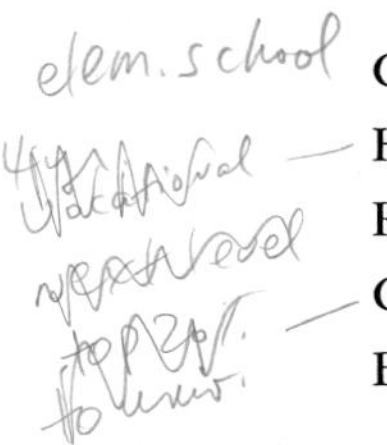

	JA?	JAHRE
Grundschule	☐	___
Hauptschule	☐	___
Realschule	☐	___
Gymnasium	☐	___
Berufsausbildung[2]	☐	___

D. Weitere Fragen

1. Wie heißt Renates Schulabschluß?
2. Wie alt ist Renate bei ihrem Schulabschluß?
3. Wo hat sie ihre Berufsausbildung gemacht?
4. Welche Sprachen spricht sie?

[1]*complete* [2]*occupational (career) training*

LEKTÜRE 2

Vor dem Lesen

Welche Informationen geben Sie, wenn Sie sich vorstellen[1]? Kreuzen Sie an.

Name	☐	Gewicht[2]	☐
Alter	☐	Hobbys	☐
Beruf/Studienfach	☐	Herkunft	☐
Familie	☐	Schulnoten[3]	☐
Freunde	☐	Interessen	☐
Geburtsdatum	☐	Adresse	☐

[1]sich . . . *introduce yourself* [2]*weight* [3]*grades*

Guten Tag, ich heiße . . .

Guten Tag, ich heiße Veronika Frisch. Ich bin verheiratet und habe drei Töchter. Sie heißen Natalie, Rosemarie und Lydia. Ich lebe mit meinem Mann Bernd und unseren Töchtern in der Schweiz. Wir wohnen in Zürich. Ich komme aus Zürich, und mein Mann kommt aus Luzern. Ich bin dreiunddreißig Jahre alt, und Bernd ist fünfzig. Bernd ist Geschäftsmann[1] hier in Zürich, und ich bin Lehrerin. Ich unterrichte[2] Französisch und Sozialkunde.[3] Meine Freizeit verbringe[4] ich am liebsten mit meiner Familie. Außerdem reise ich gern.

Guten Tag, ich heiße Sofie Pracht, bin 22 und komme aus Dresden. Ich studiere Biologie an der Technischen Universität Dresden. Ein paar Stunden in der Woche arbeite ich in einer großen Gärtnerei.[5] In meiner Freizeit gehe ich oft ins Kino, oder ich besuche Freunde. Ich spiele Gitarre und tanze sehr gern.

Mein Freund heißt Willi Schuster. Er studiert auch hier in Dresden an der Technischen Universität. Er kommt aus Radebeul. Das ist ein kleiner Ort[6] ganz in der Nähe von Dresden. Am Wochenende fahren wir manchmal mit dem Fahrrad[7] nach Radebeul und besuchen seine Familie.

Guten Tag, ich heiße Mehmet Sengün. Ich bin 29 und in Izmir, in der Türkei, geboren. Ich lebe jetzt seit[8] 19 Jahren hier in Berlin. Ich wohne in Kreuzberg, einem Stadtteil von Berlin, in einer kleinen Wohnung. In Kreuzberg leben sehr viele Türken — die Berliner nennen es Klein-Istanbul — und viele meiner türkischen Freunde wohnen ganz in der Nähe.

[1]*businessman* [2]*teach* [3]*social studies* [4]*spend (time)* [5]*nursery (gardening) business* [6]*town* [7]*bicycle* [8]*for*

Berlin-Kreuzberg, die türkische Hauptstadt Deutschlands

Meine Eltern sind seit sechs Jahren wieder in Izmir. Mein Vater hatte immer Heimweh[9] nach der Türkei. Die Deutschen waren ihm zu unfreundlich und kalt. Ich war auch ein halbes Jahr in Izmir, aber alle meine Freunde, Türken und Deutsche, leben hier in Berlin; und ich spreche inzwischen[10] auch fast[11] besser Deutsch als Türkisch. In Izmir war ich auch ein Fremder.[12] (25)

Im Moment arbeite ich für eine Speditionsfirma[13] hier in der Stadt. Ich fahre einen Lastwagen[14] und bin viel unterwegs.[15]

Ich weiß nicht, aber richtig zu Hause fühle ich mich in Berlin auch nicht, und für die Deutschen bin ich immer der Türke.

[9]hatte . . . *was homesick* [10]*meanwhile* [11]*almost* [12]*stranger, foreigner* [13]*trucking company* [14]*truck* [15]*on the road*

Arbeit mit dem Text

Was erfahren Sie über Veronika Frisch, Sofie Pracht und Mehmet Sengün? Vervollständigen Sie die Tabelle.

Name	Veronika Frisch	Sofie Pracht	Mehmet Sengün
Alter			
Geburtsort			
Familie/Freunde			
Wohnort			
Beruf			
Studienfach			
Freizeit			
Sonstiges[1]			

[1]*other information*

STRUKTUREN UND ÜBUNGEN

1.1 The present tense

One German present-tense form expresses three different ideas in English.

Ich spiele Gitarre. — *I play the guitar.* / *I'm playing the guitar.* / *I'm going to play the guitar.*

Most German verbs form the present tense just like **kommen** (**Einführung B**).

ich	**-e**
du	**-st**
er/sie/es	**-t**
wir	**-en**
ihr	**-t**
Sie, sie	**-en**

spielen			
ich	spiele	wir	spielen
du	spielst	ihr	spielt
Sie	spielen	Sie	spielen
er / sie / es	spielt	sie	spielen

Gabi und Jutta **spielen** gern Karten. — *Gabi and Jutta like to play cards.*

Verbs that end in an **s**-sound, such as **s, ß, z** (**ts**), or **x** (**ks**), do not add an additional **s** in the **du**-form: **du tanzt, du heißt, du reist.**

—Wie **heißt du?** — *What's your name?*
—**Ich heiße** Natalie. — *My name's Natalie.*

Verbs that end in **d** or **t** (and a few other verbs such as **regnen** [*to rain*] and **öffnen** [*to open*]) insert an **e** between the stem and the **-st** or **-t** endings. This happens in the **du-**, **ihr-**, and **er/sie/es**-forms.

Reitest du jeden Tag? — *Do you go horseback riding every day?*

reiten			
ich	reite	wir	reiten
du	reitest	ihr	reitet
Sie	reiten	Sie	reiten
er / sie / es	reitet	sie	reiten

Übung 1 Was machen sie?

Kombinieren Sie die Wörter. Achten Sie auf die Verbendungen.

MODELL Ich besuche Freunde.

1. ich	lernen	Freunde
2. ihr	besuche	ins Kino
3. Jutta und Jens	studiert	Spaghetti
4. du	hört	ein Buch
5. Melanie	reisen	gut Tennis
6. ich	kochen	nach Deutschland
7. wir	lese	in Regensburg
8. Richard	spielst	Spanisch
9. Jürgen und Silvia	geht	gern Musik

Übung 2 Minidialoge

Ergänzen Sie das Pronomen.

1. CLAIRE: Arbeitet Melanie?
   JOSEF: Nein, _____ arbeitet nicht.
2. MICHAEL: Schwimmen _____ gern im Meer?
   FRAU KÖRNER: Ja, sehr gern. Und Sie?
3. MEHMET: Was machst _____[a] im Sommer?
   RENATE: _____[b] fliege nach Spanien.
4. CLAIRE: Woher kommt _____[a]?
   HELGA UND SIGRID: _____[b] kommen aus Krefeld.
5. JÜRGEN: _____[a] studiere in Göttingen. Und _____[b]?
   KLAUS UND CHRISTINA: _____[c] studieren in Berlin.

Übung 3 Minidialoge

Ergänzen Sie die Verbendungen.

1. CLAIRE: Du tanz_____[a] gern, nicht?
   MELANIE: Ja, ich tanz_____[b] sehr gern, aber mein Freund tanz_____[c] nicht gern.
2. FRAU SCHULZ: Richard geh_____[a] im Sommer in den Bergen wandern.
   STEFAN: Und was mach_____[b] seine Eltern?
   FRAU SCHULZ: Seine Mutter reis_____[c] nach Frankreich, und sein Vater arbeit_____[d].
3. JÜRGEN: Wir koch_____[a] heute abend. Was mach_____[b] ihr?
   KLAUS: Wir besuch_____[c] Freunde.

1.2 Expressing likes and dislikes: *gern / nicht gern*

*verb + **gern** = to like to do something*
*verb + **nicht gern** = to dislike doing something*

To say that you like doing something, use the word **gern** after the verb. To say that you don't like to do something, use **nicht gern.**

Ernst spielt **gern** Fußball.	*Ernst likes to play soccer.*
Josef spielt **nicht gern** Fußball.	*Josef doesn't like to play soccer.*

I	II	III	IV
Sofie	spielt	gern	Schach.
Willi	spielt	auch gern	Schach.
Ich	spiele	nicht gern	Schach.
Monika	spielt	auch nicht gern	Schach.

The position of **auch/nicht/gern** (in that order) is between the verb and its complement.*

Übung 4 Was machen die Studenten gern?

Bilden Sie Sätze.

MODELL Heidi und Nora schwimmen gern.

Heidi / Nora

1. Monika / Albert
2. Heidi
3. Stefan
4. Nora (KINO)
5. Peter
6. Katrin
7. Monika
8. Albert (Tee)

Übung 5 Und diese Personen?

Sagen Sie, was die folgenden Personen gern machen.

---

*The complement provides additional information and thus "completes" the meaning of the verb: **ich spiele → ich spiele Tennis; ich höre → ich höre Musik.**

MODELL Jutta liegt gern in der Sonne. Frau Ruf liegt auch gern in der Sonne, aber Herr Ruf liegt nicht gern in der Sonne.

Frau Ruf Jutta Herr Ruf

1.

2.

Jens Jutta Andrea

3.

Michael Maria die Rufs die Wagners

4.

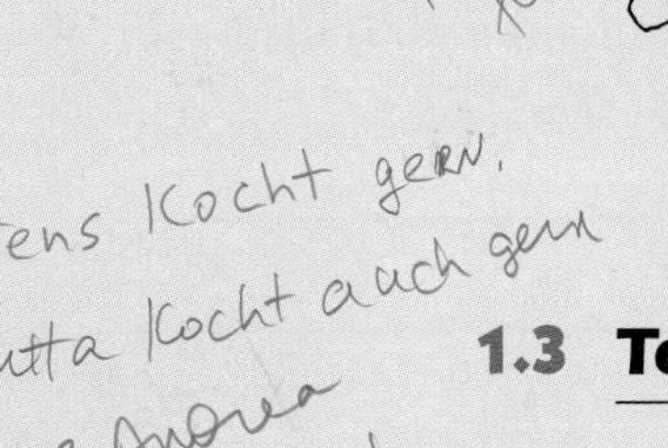

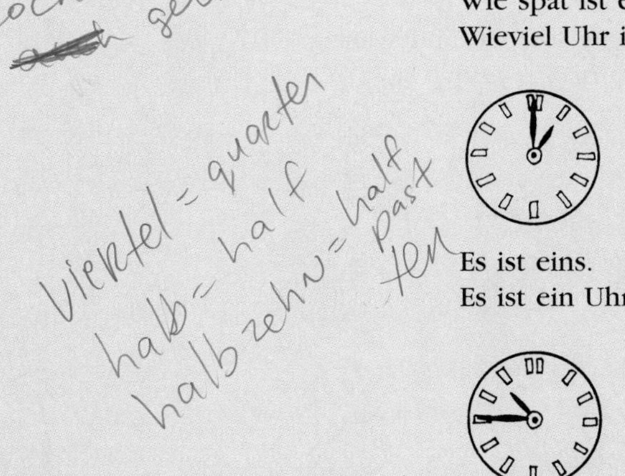

1.3 Telling time

Ask the time in German in one of two ways.

Wie spät ist es? Wieviel Uhr ist es?	*What time is it?*

Es ist eins.
Es ist ein Uhr.

Es ist drei.
Es ist drei Uhr.

Es ist Viertel vor elf.
Es ist zehn Uhr fünfundvierzig.

Es ist Viertel nach elf.
Es ist elf Uhr fünfzehn.

vor = *to*
nach = *after*

Es ist zehn (Minuten) vor acht.
Es ist sieben Uhr fünfzig.

Es ist zehn (Minuten) nach acht.
Es ist acht Uhr zehn.

The expressions **Viertel, nach, vor,** and **halb** are used in everyday speech. In German, the half hour is expressed as "half before" the following hour, not as "half after" the preceding hour, as in English.

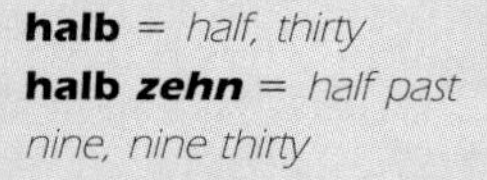

halb = *half, thirty*
halb zehn = *half past nine, nine thirty*

Es ist halb zehn. *It is nine thirty (halfway to ten).*

The 24-hour clock (0.00 to 24.00) is used when giving exact or official times as in time announcements, schedules, programs, and the like. With the 24-hour clock only the pattern (*number*) **Uhr** (*number of minutes*) is used.

Ankunft	km	Abfahrt	Anschlüsse	
14.22	**Potsdam Stadt**	**14.24**		
	↓	14.43	Wildpark 14.49 Werder (Havel) 14.56	(204)
	24	*E* 15.01	Wustermark 15.39 Nauen 15.57	(204.4)
			S-Bahnanschlüsse (Taktverkehr) bestehen in Richtung: Wannsee – Westkreuz – Charlottenburg – Zool Garten (S 3)	

Der Zug geht um vierzehn Uhr vierundzwanzig.
The train leaves at two twenty-four p.m.

Übung 6 Die Uhrzeit

Wie spät ist es?

MODELL Es ist acht Uhr.

1. 2. 3. 4.

5. 6. 7. 8.

1.4 Word order in statements

In English, the verb usually follows the subject of a sentence.

SUBJECT	VERB	COMPLEMENT
Peter	takes	a walk.

Even when another word or phrase begins the sentence, the word order does not change.

	SUBJECT	VERB	COMPLEMENT
Every day,	Peter	takes	a walk.

In statements, verb second.

In German statements, the verb is always in second position. If the sentence begins with an element other than the subject, the subject follows the verb.

I	II	III	IV
SUBJECT	VERB		COMPLEMENT
Wir	spielen	heute	Tennis.
	VERB	SUBJECT	COMPLEMENT
Heute	spielen	wir	Tennis.

Übung 7 Rolf

Unterstreichen[1] Sie das Subjekt des Satzes. Steht das konjugierte Verb vor[2] oder nach[3] dem Subjekt?

1. Rolf kommt aus Krefeld. ____________
2. Im Moment studiert er in Berkeley. ____________
3. Seine Großmutter wohnt noch in Krefeld. ____________
4. Samstags geht Rolf oft ins Kino. ____________
5. Am Wochenende wandert er oft in den Bergen. ____________
6. Außerdem treibt er gern Sport. ____________
7. Im Sommer geht er surfen. ____________
8. Er geht auch ins Schwimmbad der Uni. ____________

[1]*underline* [2]*before* [3]*after*

1.5 Separable-prefix verbs

Many German verbs have prefixes that change the verb's meaning. They combine with the infinitive to form a single word.

stehen	*to stand*	aufstehen	*to stand up*
gehen	*to go*	ausgehen	*to go out*
kommen	*to come*	ankommen	*to arrive*

In statements, verb second, prefix last.

When you use a present-tense form of these verbs, put the conjugated form in second position and put the prefix at the end of the sentence. The two parts of the verb form a frame or bracket, called a **Satzklammer,** that encloses the rest of the sentence.

Claire kommt an.

Claire kommt am Donnerstag an.

Claire kommt am Donnerstag in Frankfurt an.

Here are some common verbs with separable prefixes.

abholen	*to pick up, fetch*	ausfüllen	*to fill out*
ankommen	*to arrive*	ausgehen	*to go out*
anrufen	*to call up*	einkaufen	*to go shopping*
aufhören	*to stop, be over*	einpacken	*to pack up*
aufräumen	*to clean up, tidy up*	kennenlernen	*to meet*
aufstehen	*to get up*	spazierengehen	*to go for a walk*

Übung 8 Sie und Ihr Freund

Bilden Sie Sätze. Beginnen Sie die Sätze mit dem ersten Wort oder den ersten Wörtern in einer Zeile. Beachten[1] Sie die Satzstellung.[2]

MODELL Heute (ich/sein _____) → Heute bin ich fröhlich.

1. Ich (studieren _____)
2. Im Moment (ich / wohnen in _____)
3. Heute (ich / kochen _____)
4. Manchmal (ich / trinken _____)
5. Ich (spielen gern _____)
6. Mein Freund (heißen _____)
7. Jetzt (er / wohnen in _____)
8. Manchmal (wir / spielen _____)

Übung 9 Eine Reise in die Türkei

Mehmet fliegt morgen in die Türkei. Was macht er heute? Ergänzen Sie die folgenden Wörter: **ab, an, auf, auf, auf, aus, aus, ein, ein, spazieren.**

---

[1]*pay attention to* [2]*word order*

1. Er steht um 7 Uhr _____ .
2. Er räumt die Wohnung _____ .
3. Er packt seine Sachen[1] _____ .
4. Er ruft Renate _____ .
5. Er füllt ein Formular _____ .
6. Er holt seinen Reisepaß _____ .
7. Er kauft Essen[2] _____ .
8. Abends geht er _____ .
9. Er geht ins Kino. Der Film hört um 22 Uhr _____ .
10. Er geht noch ein bißchen _____ .

Übung 10 Was machen die Leute?

Verwenden Sie die folgenden Verben.

abholen
ankommen
anrufen
aufräumen
aufstehen
ausfüllen
ausgehen
einpacken
kennenlernen
spazierengehen

MODELL Frau Schulz geht spazieren.

[1]*things* [2]*food*

1.6 Word order in questions

When you begin a question with a question word **(wie, wo, wer, was, wann, woher),** the verb follows in second position. The subject of the sentence is in third position.

In **w**-questions, verb second.

I	II	III	IV	
Wann	beginnt	das Spiel?		*When does the game start?*
Was	machst	du	heute abend?	*What are you doing tonight?*
Wo	wohnst	du?		*Where do you live?*

Here are the question words you have encountered so far.

wann	*when*	wie	*how*
was	*what*	wie viele	*how many*
welcher*	*which*	wo	*where*
wer	*who*	woher	*from where*

Questions that can be answered by *yes* or *no* begin with the verb.

Tanzt du gern?	*Do you like to dance?*
Arbeitest du hier?	*Do you work here?*
Gehst du ins Kino?	*Are you going to the movies?*

Übung 11 Ein Interview mit Marta Szerwinski

Schreiben Sie die Fragen.

MODELL du + heißen + wie + ? → Wie heißt du?

1. du + sein + geboren + wann + ?
2. du + kommen + woher + ?
3. du + wohnen + wo + ?
4. du + haben + Augenfarbe + welch- + ?
5. du + sein + groß + wie + ?
6. du + studieren + ?
7. du + studieren + Fächer + welch- + ?
8. du + arbeiten + Stunden + wie viele + ?
9. du + machen + gern + was + ?

---

*The endings of **welcher** vary according to gender, number, and case of the following noun. They are the same endings as those of the definite article. Therefore, **welcher** is called a **der**-word.

(M)	(N)	(F)	(Pl)
welch**er** Name	welch**es** Alter	welch**e** Adresse	welch**e** Studienfächer

Übung 12 Noch ein Interview

Stellen Sie die Fragen.

1. —Ich heiße Sofie.
2. —Nein, ich komme nicht aus München.
3. —Ich komme aus Dresden.
4. —Ich studiere Biologie.
5. —Er heißt Willi.
6. —Er wohnt in Dresden.
7. —Nein, ich spiele nicht Tennis.
8. —Ja, ich tanze sehr gern.
9. —Nein, ich trinke kein Bier.
10. —Ja, Willi trinkt gern Bier.

KAPITEL 2

Flohmarkt!
Was wollen
Sie kaufen?

In **Kapitel 2** you will learn to talk more about things: your own possessions and things you give others. You will also learn how to describe what you have and don't have and to give your opinion on matters of taste or style.

Besitz und Vergnügen

THEMEN
Besitz
Geschenke
Geschmacksfragen
Vergnügen

LEKTÜRE
Höflichkeit am Telefon
Guten Tag, ich heiße . . .

KULTURELLES
Flohmarkt
Die Deutsche Bundespost
Vergnügen
Kulturprojekt: Deutsche Produkte
Porträt: Carl Friedrich Benz, Gottlieb Daimler und Karlsruhe
Videoecke: Mode ist, wie man sich fühlt

STRUKTUREN
2.1 The accusative case
2.2 The negative article **kein, keine**
2.3 What would you like? **Ich möchte . . .**
2.4 Possessive adjectives
2.5 The present tense of stem-vowel changing verbs
2.6 Asking people to do things: The **du**-imperative

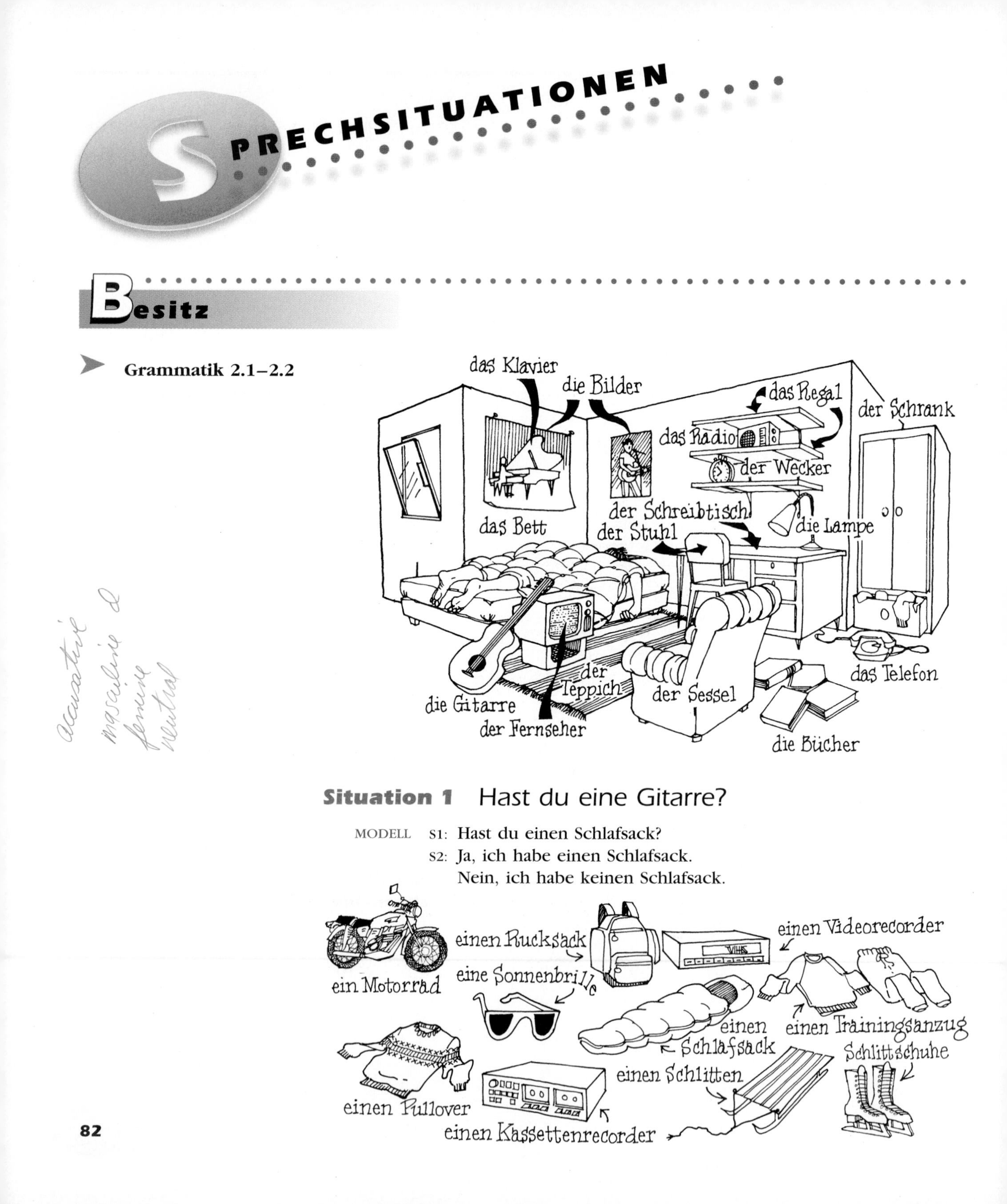

SPRECHSITUATIONEN

Besitz

➤ **Grammatik 2.1–2.2**

Situation 1 Hast du eine Gitarre?

MODELL S1: Hast du einen Schlafsack?
S2: Ja, ich habe einen Schlafsack.
Nein, ich habe keinen Schlafsack.

Situation 2 Dialog: Stefan zieht in sein neues Zimmer

Katrin trifft Stefan im Möbelgeschäft.

KATRIN: Hallo, Stefan. Was machst du denn hier?
STEFAN: Ach, ich brauche noch ein paar Sachen. Morgen ziehe ich in ________ _____.
KATRIN: Was brauchst du denn?
STEFAN: Ach, alles Mögliche.
KATRIN: Was hast du denn schon?
STEFAN: Ich habe einen _______, eine ____ und . . . und . . . und einen _____.
KATRIN: Das ist aber nicht viel. ________ hast du denn?
STEFAN: So 30 Dollar.
KATRIN: Ich glaube, du bist im falschen Geschäft. Der Flohmarkt ist viel besser _____.
STEFAN: Ja, vielleicht hast du recht.

Kultur ... Landeskunde ... Informationen

Flohmarkt

Sie sind für ein Jahr in Deutschland und brauchen ein paar Sachen. Leider haben Sie nur ungefähr DM 250,-. Alles ist auf dem Flohmarkt sehr billig. Suchen Sie etwas aus. Was nehmen Sie?

Plattenspieler[1] mit 2 Boxen,[2] 50 DM. ☎ 05326/85577.

Elektrische Schreibmaschine, älteres Modell, 30,– DM, ☎ 05321/26699.

2 Sessel, 1 Hocker,[3] Cord braun, 50 DM, Selig, Talstr. 17, Seesen.

Schreibtisch mit Stuhl u. Lampe 50 DM, ☎ 05323/723140 am Abend 5050.

Tramper-Rucksack, Alugestell, Preis 35 DM, ☎ 05321/84724.

3 Lautsprecher-Boxen, 40,– DM, ☎ 05321/80664.

Schreibtisch, ca. 120 x 50 cm, Limba, 50 DM. ☎ 05324/6194 oder 05321/40877.

Stereo-Kompakt-Anlage, Boxen leicht defekt, 50 DM. Ahrens, Nordwinkel 3, Goslar.

2 Matratzen,[4] eintlg., neuw., 50 DM, ☎ 05582/1796.

Gut erh. Schreibmaschine (Adler) 50 DM, ☎ 05321/24943 od. 43234.

Tennisschläger, Plus 30, neue Bespannung, 50 DM, ☎ 05321/1388 ab 18.30 Uhr.

Farbfernseher ohne Fernbedienung,[5] 42 cm Bild, 50 DM. ☎ 05322/1741.

Grünes Sofa zum Kippen[6] 50 DM, 1 Kippcouch zu verschenken.[7] ☎ 05321/20173.

Kleine Katze, 8 Wochen, stubenrein[8] zu verschenken, ☎ 05335/5562.

2 Paar schwarze Schuhe, Gr. 39, zum Servieren geeignet, 20 DM, ☎ 05321/61248.

Bett, 90x200 cm, gut erh., 50 DM. ☎ 05321/24241, 19-20 Uhr.

Yucca-Palme, 2,40 m, sehr schönes Exemplar, 50 DM. ☎ 05321/41179.

[1] *turntable, record player* [2] *loudspeakers* [3] *stool* [4] *mattresses* [5] *remote control* [6] zum . . . *reclinable* [7] *to give away* [8] *housebroken*

Situation 3 Informationsspiel: Was machen sie morgen?

MODELL S1: Schreibt Jürgen morgen einen Brief?
S2: Nein.
S1: Schreibst du morgen einen Brief?
S2: Ja. (Nein.)

	Jürgen	Silvia	mein(e) Partner(in)
einen Brief schreiben	–		
ein Buch kaufen	+		
einen Film anschauen			
eine Freundin anrufen	–	+	
die Hausaufgaben machen	+		
den Computer reparieren			
einen Freund besuchen	+	+	
das Zimmer aufräumen	–		

Geschenke

➤ **Grammatik 2.3**

Situation 4 Was möchten sie?

MODELL S1: Was möchte Herr Thelen?
S2: Er möchte ______ .

Situation 5 Was möchtest du zum Geburtstag?

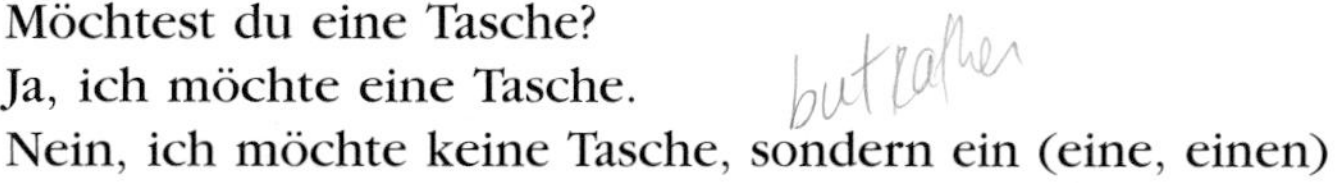

MODELL S1: Möchtest du eine Tasche?
S2: Ja, ich möchte eine Tasche.
Nein, ich möchte keine Tasche, sondern ein (eine, einen) ______ .

Auf der Suche nach dem coolsten Computerspiel

1. eine Armbanduhr
2. eine Sonnenbrille
3. einen Rucksack
4. einen Tennisschläger
5. einen Pulli
6. eine Schreibmaschine
7. einen Computer
8. einen Hund
9. einen Trainingsanzug
10. ______

Situation 6 Umfrage

MODELL S1: Möchtest du ein Auto?
S2: Ja.
S1: Unterschreib hier bitte.

	UNTERSCHRIFT		UNTERSCHRIFT
1. einen Fußball	______	6. einen Schlafsack	______
2. eine Gitarre	______	7. einen Tennisschläger	______
3. Schuhe	______	8. ein Wörterbuch	______
4. eine Uhr	______	9. ein Autotelefon	______
5. eine Katze	______	10. eine Sonnenbrille	______

Situation 7 Dialog: Ein Geschenk für Josef

Melanie trifft Claire in der Mensa.

MELANIE: Josef hat nächsten Donnerstag ______.
CLAIRE: Wirklich? Dann brauche ich ja noch ein ______ für ihn. Mensch, das ist schwierig. Hat er denn Hobbys?
MELANIE: Er ___ Gitarre und ___ gern Musik.
CLAIRE: Hast du schon ein Geschenk?
MELANIE: Ich _____ ein Songbuch kaufen. Aber es ist ziemlich ___. Kaufen wir es zusammen?
CLAIRE: Ja, klar. Welche Art Musik hat er denn ___?
MELANIE: Ich glaube, Soft Rock und Oldies. Simon und Garfunkel, Cat Stevens und so.

Kultur ... Landeskunde ... Informationen

Die Deutsche Bundespost

Was machen Sie, wenn Ihr Freund / Ihre Freundin Geburtstag hat? Kreuzen Sie an.

- Ich gratuliere persönlich. ☐
- Ich gratuliere am Telefon. ☐
- Ich schicke eine Geburtstagskarte. ☐
- Ich schicke ein Telegramm. ☐
- Ich schicke ein Fax. ☐

Sie hören eine Beschreibung der Deutschen Bundespost. Hören Sie gut zu und schreiben Sie die Sätze zu Ende.

1. Postautos, Briefkästen und Telefonzellen sind ___.
2. Für Briefe und Telefon hat die Post das _____.
3. Außerdem gibt es einen Paketdienst und eine _____.
4. Ein Brief kostet _____.
5. Zum Telefonieren in einer Telefonzelle braucht man oft eine ______.

Das Hauptpostamt in Bad Harzburg. Hier kann man Briefmarken kaufen und Briefe einwerfen.

Geschmacksfragen

➤ **Grammatik 2.4–2.5**

Situation 8 Interaktion: Wie findest du meine Tennisschuhe?

1. Kreuzen Sie an, was Sie heute tragen.
2. Fragen Sie, wie Ihr Partner / Ihre Partnerin es findet.

MODELL S1: Wie findest du meine Schuhe?
S2: Deine Schuhe? Nicht schlecht.

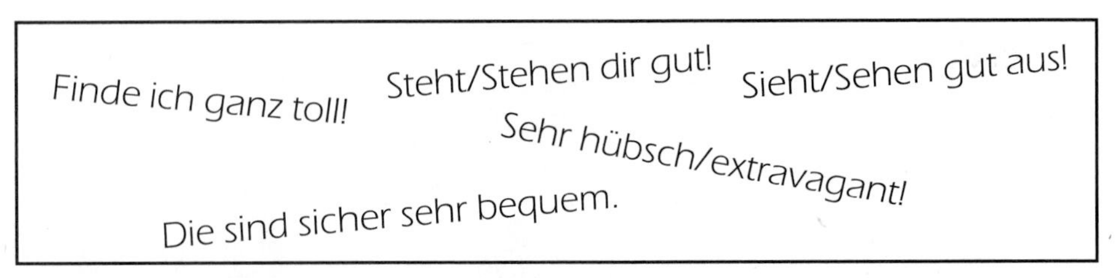

	Was Sie heute tragen	Wie Ihr(e) Partner(in) es findet
Schuhe		
einen Ring		
einen Gürtel		
Ohrringe		
eine Armbanduhr		
ein T-Shirt		

Situation 9 Frau Gretters neue Jacke

Bringen Sie die Sätze in die richtige Reihenfolge.

___ Von Karstadt. Sie ist wirklich sehr schön.
___ Ich finde sie einfach toll. Woher haben Sie Ihre Jacke?
___ Tag, Frau Körner.
___ Mein Mantel ist schon sehr alt. Ich brauche dringend etwas für den Winter.
___ Guten Tag, Frau Gretter. Wie geht's denn so?
___ Gehen Sie doch zu Karstadt! Sie können dort auch schicke Mäntel kaufen.
___ Danke, ganz gut. Wie finden Sie denn meine neue Jacke?

Situation 10 Interview: Besitz

1. Was hast du in deinem Zimmer? Was möchtest du haben?
2. Hast du wertvolle Sachen? Videorecorder, Auto, Computer? Was möchtest du haben?
3. Hast du Schmuck? Was möchtest du haben?
4. Hast du einen Hund oder eine Katze? Möchtest du einen Hund oder eine Katze haben?

Vergnügen

➤ **Grammatik 2.6**

Herr Wagner schläft gern.

Jens fährt gern Motorrad.

Sofie trägt gern Hosen.

Melanie lädt gern Freunde ein.

Mehmet läuft gern im Wald.

Ernst ißt gern Eis.

Hans liest gern Bücher.

Natalie sieht gern fern.

Situation 11 Interview: Was machst du lieber?

MODELL S1: Schwimmst du lieber im Meer oder lieber im Schwimmbad?
S2: Lieber im Meer.

1. Ißt du lieber zu Hause oder lieber im Restaurant?
2. Spielst du lieber Volleyball oder lieber Basketball?
3. Trägst du lieber ein Hemd (eine Bluse) oder lieber ein T-shirt?
4. Fährst du lieber Fahrrad oder lieber Motorrad?
5. Schreibst du lieber Postkarten oder lieber Briefe?
6. Liest du lieber Zeitungen oder lieber Bücher?
7. Lädst du lieber Freunde ein oder lieber Verwandte?
8. Läufst du lieber im Wald oder lieber in der Stadt?
9. Fährst du lieber ans Meer oder lieber in die Berge?
10. Schläfst du lieber im Hotel oder lieber im Zelt?

Situation 12 Dialoge: Was machst du heute abend?

1. Willi trifft Sofie vor der Bibliothek der Universität Dresden.

WILLI: Was machst du ________?
SOFIE: Ich weiß noch nicht. Was machst du denn?
WILLI: Ich weiß auch noch nicht.
SOFIE: Also . . . bei Rudi ist ein Fest. ________?
WILLI: Rudi? Ach nee, seine Feste sind immer ______.
SOFIE: Aber, Willi, wenn wir auf ein Fest ____, ist es nie langweilig!

2. Claire spricht mit Melanie am Telefon.

CLAIRE: Ihr geht ins Kino? __________?
MELANIE: „Schindlers Liste."
CLAIRE: Ja? Wo denn?
MELANIE: __ Gloria.
CLAIRE: Und wann?
MELANIE: _________.
CLAIRE: Da komme ich __.

Situation 13 Zum Schreiben: Eine Einladung

Schreiben Sie eine Einladung zu einer Party. Benutzen Sie das Modell unten und Ihre Phantasie!

CALIGVLA* PARTY

Wann: Mittwoch den 11. Juni – ab 20 Uhr.
Wo: Ludwig-Thomaheim – Neubau 5. Stock.
Wie: Im Kostüm der Epoche, mit eigenem Kissen, um darauf zu ruhen.

B.D.E.A. (Bring Deinen Eigenen Alkohol)
* Der wahnsinnige römische Kaiser

Situation 14 Rollenspiel: Am Telefon

S1: Sie rufen einen Freund/eine Freundin an. Sie machen am Samstag ein Fest. Laden Sie Ihren Freund/Ihre Freundin ein.

Situation 15 Informationsspiel: Was machen sie gern?

MODELL S1: Was sprechen Josef und Melanie gern?
S2: Englisch.
S1: Was sprichst du gern?
S2: ______

	Richard	Josef und Melanie	mein(e) Partner(in)
fahren	Motorrad		
tragen		Jeans	
essen	Wiener Schnitzel		
sehen	Fußball		
vergessen		ihr Alter	
waschen	sein Auto		
treffen	seine Freundin		
einladen	seinen Bruder		
sprechen		Englisch	

Situation 16 Bildgeschichte: Ein Tag in Silvias Leben

Kultur ... Landeskunde ... Informationen

Vergnügen

Was ist am Wochenende für Sie am wichtigsten[1]? Kreuzen Sie an:

Ausschlafen	☐
Fernsehen	☐
Sport	☐
Lesen	☐
Hobbys	☐
Freunde einladen	☐

Lesen Sie zuerst, was den Deutschen am Wochenende am wichtigsten ist. Beantworten Sie dann die Fragen.

- „Glotze" ist ein anderes Wort für ____ .
- In welchen vier Bereichen gibt es Unterschiede zwischen Männern und Frauen?
- Sind Hobbys wichtiger für Frauen oder für Männer?
- Wer liest lieber, Männer oder Frauen?
- Machen Sie dieselbe Umfrage in Ihrem Kurs. Wie ist das Resultat? Gibt es auch Unterschiede zwischen Männern und Frauen? Ist das Resultat typisch (repräsentativ) für Studenten?

FOCUS-FRAGE

„Was ist Ihnen am Wochenende am wichtigsten?"

GLOTZE TOTAL

von 1300 Befragten* antworteten

Fernsehen	**49%**
Familienleben	**45%**
Ausschlafen	**44%**
Ausflüge[2] machen	**37%**
Natur erleben[3]	**35%**
Hobbys	**34%**
Lesen	**32%**
Partnerschaft pflegen[4]	**27%**
Faulenzen[5]	**26%**
Ausgehen/Kneipen[6]	**23%**
In Ruhe einkaufen	**19%**
Sport	**18%**
Kultur/Kino/Konzerte	**17%**
Reparaturen erledigen[7]	**16%**

Deutliche[8] Unterschiede[9] zwischen Männern und Frauen gibt es in den Bereichen[10] „Familienleben" (38 % zu 51 %), „Hobbys" (43 % zu 26 %), „Lesen" (24 % zu 39 %) und „Reparaturen" (28 % zu 6 %). Die alten und neuen Bundes-länder unterscheiden sich am meisten bei „Familienleben" (43 % zu 52 %) und „Faulenzen" (29 % zu 17 %)

* Repräsentative Umfrage des Sample-Instituts für Focus im Mai. Mehrfachnennungen möglich

[1]am . . . *most important* [2]*excursions* [3]*to experience* [4]*to nurture* [5]*to take it easy, be lazy* [6]*bar, tavern* [7]*to take care of, handle* [8]*significant* [9]*differences* [10]*areas*

Kulturprojekt Deutsche Produkte

Hints for working with the Kulturprojekt

Use a reference work such as *The Universal Almanac* to look up the largest foreign companies doing business in North America. Some of the German firms listed may do business in your area.

Arbeiten Sie mit deutschen Zeitungen oder Zeitschriften. Suchen Sie Anzeigen[1] für vier bis fünf deutsche Produkte.

- Identifizieren Sie das Produkt. Was ist es?
- Wie heißt die Firma, die es produziert?
- Wie ist das Produkt? Welche besonderen Eigenschaften[2] hat es?
- Wo bekommt man mehr Informationen über das Produkt?
- Wieviel kostet das Produkt? Ist es ein teures oder nicht so teures Ding?
- Welche Anzeigen finden Sie besonders interessant oder originell?
- Gibt es deutsche Firmen in Ihrer Nähe? Wenn ja, welche?

[1]*advertisements* [2]*characteristics*

Porträt

Carl Benz

Gottlieb Daimler

Das Schloß in Karlsruhe. 1715 im barocken Stil erbaut.

Carl Friedrich Benz (1844–1929) aus Karlsruhe war Ingenieur. 1883 gründete[1] er eine Motorenfabrik in Mannheim, und 1886 konstruierte er ein Fahrzeug[2] mit drei Rädern[3] und einem Einzylinder-Viertakt-Benzinmotor.[4] Die erste Testfahrt endete leider an einer Mauer.[5] Gottlieb Daimler (1834–1900) aus Cannstadt arbeitete zur gleichen Zeit wie Benz an einem motorisierten Fahrzeug. 1901 produzierte er den ersten Mercedes. 1926 gründeten die Firmen Daimler und Benz die Daimler-Benz AG.[6]

Karlsruhe liegt zwischen dem Schwarzwald und dem Rhein. Die barocke Stadt „Carols Ruhe"[7] wurde im 18. Jahrhundert von Markgraf[8] Karl Wilhelm gegründet und diente ihm als[9] Residenz. Heute ist Karlsruhe das Zentrum des Bundesverfassungsgerichts[10] und des Bundesgerichtshofs[11] und eines wichtigen naturwissenschaftlich-technischen Forschungszentrums.[12]

[1]*founded* [2]*vehicle* [3]*wheels* [4]*one-cylinder four-stroke gas engine* [5]*wall* [6]*Inc. (stock company)* [7]*rest* [8]*margrave (an aristocratic title, similar to a count)* [9]diente . . . *served as his* [10]*Federal Constitutional Court* [11]*Federal Court of Justice* [12]*research center*

VIDEOECKE

Mode ist, wie man sich fühlt

Sie sehen einen Bericht über Jugendmode in Deutschland:

- Wie nennt man diese Mode?
- Ist es teuer, sich so zu kleiden?
- Was sind die Hauptbestandteile[1] dieser Mode?
- Wie finden Sie diese Mode?

[1]*main components* [2]*cool*

„In" ist, was grell[2] ist

Besitz — Possessions

die **Schreibmaschine, -n**	typewriter
der **Fernseher, -**	TV set
der **Koffer, -**	suitcase
der **Rucksack, ¨e**	backpack
der **Schlafsack, ¨e**	sleeping bag
der **Schlitten, -**	sled
der **Schlittschuh, -e**	ice skate
der **Schmuck**	jewelry
der **Schreibtisch, -e**	desk
der **Tennisschläger, -**	tennis racket
der **Wecker, -**	alarm clock
das **Bild, -er**	picture
das **Fahrrad, ¨er**	bicycle
das **Faxgerät, -e**	fax machine
das **Klavier, -e**	piano
das **Surfbrett, -er**	surfboard

Ähnliche Wörter

der **CD-Spieler, -**; der **Computer, -**; der **Kassettenrecorder, -**; der **Walkman, Walkmen** (*pl.*); der **Videorecorder, -** das **Buch, ¨er** (R); das **Kochbuch, ¨er;** das **Songbuch, ¨er;** das **Wörterbuch, ¨er;** das **Radio, -s;** das **Telefon, -e;** das **Autotelefon, -e**

Haus und Wohnung — Home and Apartment

der **Schrank, ¨e**	wardrobe
der **Sessel, -**	armchair
der **Stuhl, ¨e**	chair
der **Teppich, -e**	carpet
das **Regal, -e**	bookshelf, bookcase
das **Zimmer, -**	room

Ähnliche Wörter

die **Katze, -n** der **Hund, -e** das **Haus, ¨er**

Kleidung und Schmuck — Clothes and Jewelry

die **Kette, -n**	necklace
die **Sonnenbrille, -n**	sunglasses
der **Gürtel, -**	belt
das **Armband, ¨er**	bracelet
das **Halstuch, ¨er**	scarf
der **Trainingsanzug, ¨e**	sweats

Ähnliche Wörter

die **Jeans** (*pl.*); der **Pullover, -;** der **Pulli, -s;** der **Ring, -e;** der **Ohrring, -e** das **T-shirt, -s**

Sonstige Substantive — Other Nouns

die **Art, -en**	kind, type
die **Bibliothek, -en**	library
die **Einladung, -en**	invitation
die **Lust**	desire
hast du Lust?	do you feel like it?
die **Mensa, -s**	student cafeteria
die **Mitbewohnerin, -nen**	female roommate, housemate
die **Reihenfolge, -n**	order, sequence
die **Sache, -n**	thing
die **Stadt, ¨e**	city
die **Stunde, -n**	hour
die **Tasse, -n**	cup
die **Telefonzelle, -n**	telephone booth
die **Zeitung, -en**	newspaper
der **Gruselfilm, -e**	horror film
der **Haarschnitt**	hair cut
der **Mensch, -en** (*wk. masc.*)	person
Mensch!	Man! Oh boy! (*coll.*)
der **Mitbewohner, -**	male roommate, housemate
der **Wald, ¨er**	forest, woods
im Wald laufen	to run in the woods
das **Fest, -e**	party
das **Frühstück, -e**	breakfast
das **Geld**	money
das **Geschäft, -e**	store
das **Geschenk, -e**	present
das **Jahr, -e**	year
das **Studentenheim, -e**	dorm
das **Vergnügen**	pleasure
das **Zelt, -e**	tent
die **Verwandten** (*pl.*)	relatives

Ähnliche Wörter

die **Karte, -n;** die **Geburtstagskarte, -n;** die **Postkarte, -n;** die **Telefonkarte, -n;** die **Pizza, -s** der **Basketball, ¨e;** der **Bus, -se;** der **Film, -e;** der **Flohmarkt, ¨e;** der **Geburtstag, -e;** der **Kilometer, -** das **Bier, -e;** das **Ding, -e;** das **Eis;** das **Fax, -e;** das **Hotel, -s;** das **Restaurant, -s;** das **Telegramm, -e**

Verben / Verbs

an·schauen	to look at
aus·sehen, sieht . . . aus	to look
es sieht gut aus	it looks good
ein·laden, lädt . . . ein	to invite
essen, ißt	to eat
fahren, fährt	to drive, ride
glauben	to believe
klingeln	to ring
laufen, läuft (R)	to run
was läuft im Kino?	what's playing at the movies?
lieben	to love
schicken	to send
schlafen, schläft	to sleep
sport treiben	to do sports
stehen	to stand
das steht / die stehen dir gut!	that looks / they look good on you
treffen, trifft	to meet
treffen wir uns . . .	let's meet . . .
wissen, weiß	to know
ziehen	to move

Ähnliche Wörter

bringen; finden; gratulieren; mit·kommen; sehen, sieht; vergessen, vergißt; waschen, wäscht

Adjektive und Adverbien / Adjectives and Adverbs

bequem	comfortable
billig	cheap, inexpensive
dringend	urgent(ly)
echt	real(ly)
einfach	simple, simply
falsch	wrong
ganz	whole; *here:* quite
grell	gaudy, shrill; *here:* cool, neat
häßlich	ugly
hübsch	pretty
langweilig	boring
richtig	right, correct
schlecht	bad
schwierig	difficult
teuer	expensive
toll	neat, great
wertvoll	valuable, expensive
wichtig	important
ziemlich	rather
ziemlich groß	pretty big

Ähnliche Wörter

besser, extravagant, schick

Possessivpronomen / Possessive Adjectives

dein, deine, deinen	your (*informal sg.*)
euer, eure, euren	your (*informal pl.*)
ihr, ihre, ihren	her, its
Ihr, Ihre, Ihren	your (*formal*)
mein, meine, meinen	my
sein, seine, seinen	his, its
unser, unsere, unseren	our

Präpositionen / Prepositions

an	at; on; to
am Samstag	on Saturday
am Telefon	on the phone
ans Meer	to the sea
bei	with; at
bei Rudi	at Rudi's place
bei McDonald's	at McDonald's
bis	until
bis acht Uhr	until eight o'clock
für	for
zu	to; for (*an occasion*)
zur Uni	to the university
zum Geburtstag	for someone's birthday

Sonstige Wörter und Ausdrücke / Other Words and Expressions

alles	everything
alles Mögliche	everything possible
also	well, so, thus
da	there
dich	you (*accusative case*)
diese, diesen, dieser, dieses	this; these
ein paar	a few
etwas	something
heute abend	this evening
ihn	him; it (*accusative case*)
kein, keine, keinen	no; none
klar!	of course!
lieber	rather
ich gehe lieber . . .	I'd rather go . . .
mittags	at noon
morgen	tomorrow
natürlich	naturally
nie	never
niemand	no one, nobody
recht	right
du hast recht	you are right
schon	already
vielleicht	perhaps
wenn	if; when
zusammen	together

LESEECKE

LEKTÜRE 1

Vor dem Lesen

A. Skimming is reading a text quickly to look for clues about the content. Read the title and skim the text for words and phrases you recognize. What do you think it is about?

Was man beim Telefonieren tun und nicht tun sollte.[1] ☐
Wie man einen Telefonanschluß bestellt.[2] ☐
Wie man einen Anrufbeantworter[3] programmiert. ☐

B. Regeln[4] fürs Telefonieren in den USA.

1. Gibt es gute und schlechte Zeiten zum Telefonieren?
   gute Zeit:
   von _____ bis _____
   von _____ bis _____
   schlechte Zeit:
   von _____ bis _____
   von _____ bis _____
2. Wie melden Sie sich[5]?
3. Stellen Sie sich vor,[6] wenn Sie anrufen?
4. Begrüßen Sie die andere Person? Wie?

C. Scanning is looking for specific information in a text. Scan the text and underline words or phrases that answer the following questions.

1. Welche Uhrzeiten kommen vor[7]?
2. Wie meldet man[8] sich?
3. Wie stellt man sich vor?
4. Wie begrüßt man sich[9]?

---

[1] *should* [2] Telefonanschluß . . . *orders telephone service* [3] *answering machine* [4] *rules* [5] melden . . . *answer a call* [6] Stellen . . . *Do you introduce yourself* [7] *are mentioned* [8] *one, you, people* [9] begrüßt . . . sich *greet each other*

Höflichkeit am Telefon

Das Telefon ist sehr praktisch; es kann aber auch zu einem Quälgeist[1] werden, wenn gewisse Regeln nicht eingehalten werden.[2]

Zum Beispiel sollte man nicht zu unmöglichen[3] Zeiten anrufen. Es ist nicht sehr höflich, morgens vor 9 Uhr und abends nach 22 Uhr anzurufen. Auch die 5 üblichen[4] Essenszeiten und eine mögliche Mittagsruhe sollte man respektieren, ebenso[5] die Abendnachrichten[6] im Fernsehen, für die sich die andere Person interessieren könnte.

Unhöflich ist es auch, sich beim Telefonieren nur mit einem „Hallo!" oder mit dem anonymen „Ja, bitte?" zu melden.[7] Normalerweise meldet man sich kurz mit 10 seinem Nachnamen, wenn man angerufen wird, also „Schulze". Der Sohn oder die Tochter meldet sich mit dem Vornamen, also „Anna Schulze" oder „Thomas Schulze". Hausangestellte[8] oder Gäste sagen: „Hier bei Schulze". Der Anrufer sagt dann seinen Namen und grüßt, also zum Beispiel: „Meier, guten Morgen!" Möchte man, daß jemand[9] ans Telefon gerufen wird,[10] sollte man immer höflich sein, zum 15 Beispiel: „Guten Tag, Frau Schulze, ich würde gerne Ihren Mann sprechen!"

[1]*pain, nuisance* [2]eingehalten . . . *are observed* [3]*impossible* [4]*customary* [5]*as well as* [6]*evening news* [7]*answer* [8]*domestic help* [9]*someone* [10]ans . . . *is called to the telephone*

Arbeit mit dem Text

A. In a text about "how to do something" you can also expect information referring to the opposite: "The do's and don'ts of . . .". Negation markers are therefore very important. Scan the text again and underline **nicht.** Also look for and underline the prefix **un-,** which indicates something negative like **Unhöflichkeit** (versus **Höflichkeit**).

B. Füllen Sie die Tabelle aus. Was ist beim Telefonieren höflich? Was nicht? Wenn Sie im Text keine Informationen finden, machen Sie einen Strich.[1]

	Zeiten	sich melden	sich vorstellen/begrüßen
höflich			
unhöflich			

C. Kulturelle Unterschiede. Vergleichen Sie die Informationen aus dem Text mit Ihren Antworten in **Vor dem Lesen B.** Was ist in deutschsprachigen Ländern anders?

[1]machen . . . *draw a line*

LEKTÜRE 2

Vor dem Lesen

Schauen Sie sich die Zeichnungen[1] an. Welche Personen sind das? Was wissen Sie schon aus dem Vorwort[2] über diese Personen?

Name	Alter (ungefähr)[3]	verheiratet ledig	Kinder	Beruf

[1]*drawings* [2]*preface* [3]*approximately*

Guten Tag, ich heiße . . .

Guten Tag, ich heiße Michael Pusch. Ich möchte mich selbst und ein paar Freunde und Bekannte[1] vorstellen. Ich bin fünfundzwanzig, ledig und arbeite bei einer Werbeagentur.[2] Meine Hobbys: ich gehe gern gut essen—am liebsten Italienisch—und interessiere mich für Kunst, Theater, Filme und so weiter. Ich habe eine feste Freundin, sie heißt Maria Schneider, ist intelligent und sehr erfolgreich[3] in ihrem Beruf. Sie ist Grafikerin.[4] Wir sind schon seit zwei Jahren zusammen.

Ich wohne in München, Stadtteil Schwabing. Das ist ein sehr schöner (und teurer) Teil der Stadt, sehr zentral.

Ich möchte jetzt ein paar von meinen Schwabinger Nachbarn und Bekannten vorstellen. Zuerst die Familie Wagner, Josie und Uli Wagner. Sie wohnen direkt neben mir und haben drei Kinder, einen Jungen, Ernst, und zwei Mädchen, Andrea und Paula. Nette Kinder. Sie haben gerade ein neues Auto gekauft.

[1]*acquaintances* [2]*advertising agency* [3]*successful* [4]*graphic designer*

Gegenüber[5] wohnt Familie Ruf. Herr Ruf ist Schriftsteller.[6] Hält sich für was Besseres.[7] Spielt immer den Künstler. Aber sein Hobby ist Fußball, er sieht immer die Sportschau im Fernsehen, liegt auf dem Sofa und trinkt Bier. Na ja. Seine Frau Margret ist Geschäftsführerin[8] in einer Spielzeugfabrik.[9] Sie verdient[10] das Geld, der Herr Künstler paßt auf die Kinder auf und kocht, spielt Hausmann. Sie haben einen Jungen, Hans, und ein Mädchen, Jutta. Auch nette Kinder.

Dann sind da noch Herr Thelen, er ist der Hausmeister[11] von Nummer 14, wo die Rufs wohnen, und Herr Siebert, ein pensionierter[12] Lehrer. Junggeselle.[13] Er wohnt in der Wohnung über mir. Ja, und dann sind da noch zwei Nachbarinnen, Frau Gretter und Frau Körner. Beide sind ledig und wohnen im selben Haus wie die Wagners.

So, das wär's erstmal für heute. Also, Servus, bis später.

[5] *across the way* [6] *writer* [7] Hält... *considers himself to be better (than other people)* [8] *manager* [9] *toy factory* [10] *earns* [11] *maintenance man* [12] *retired* [13] *bachelor*

Arbeit mit dem Text

Was gehört zusammen?

1.	Familie Wagner	**a.**	ist der Hausmeister von Nr. 14.
2.	Herr Ruf schreibt Romane,	**b.**	wohnt direkt neben Michael Pusch.
3.	Michael und Maria	**c.**	sind die Kinder der Rufs.
4.	Herr Thelen	**d.**	ist pensionierter Lehrer.
5.	Hans und Jutta	**e.**	sind schon zwei Jahre zusammen.
6.	Frau Ruf verdient das Geld,	**f.**	aber sein Hobby ist Fußball.
7.	Herr Siebert	**g.**	wohnt im selben Haus wie die Wagners.
8.	Frau Gretter	**h.**	und ihr Mann paßt auf die Kinder auf.

STRUKTUREN UND ÜBUNGEN

2.1 The accusative case

nominative = subject
accusative = direct object

The nominative case designates the subject of a sentence; the accusative case commonly denotes the object of the action implied by the verb, such as what is being possessed, looked at, or acted on by the subject of the sentence.

Jutta hat einen Wecker. — *Jutta has an alarm clock.*
Jens kauft eine Lampe. — *Jens buys a lamp.*

Here are the nominative and accusative forms of the definite and indefinite articles.

	Tisch (m.)	*Bett (n.)*	*Lampe (f.)*	*Bücher (pl.)*
Nominative *Accusative*	der den	das	die	die
Nominative *Accusative*	ein einen	ein	eine	—

Note that only the masculine has a different form in the accusative case.

Der Teppich ist schön. Kaufst du **den** Teppich? — *The rug is beautiful. Are you going to buy the rug?*

Übung 1 Auf dem Flohmarkt

Was kaufen diese Leute? Was kaufen Sie?

MODELL Jens kauft den Wecker, das Regal und den Videorecorder.

	Jens	Ernst	Melanie	Jutta	Sie
der Pullover	–	–	–	+	
der Wecker	+	–	–	–	
die Tasche	–	+	+	–	
das Regal	+	–	+	–	
die Lampe	–	–	–	+	
die Stühle	–	+	–	–	
der Videorecorder	+	–	–	+	
der Schreibtisch	–	+	+	–	

Übung 2 Ihr Zimmer

Was haben Sie in Ihrem Zimmer?

MODELL Ich habe einen/eine/ein/— _____ , . . .

das Bett
das Bild / die Bilder
die Bücher
der Fernseher
die Gitarre
das Klavier
die Lampe / die Lampen
das Radio
das Regal / die Regale
der Schrank
der Schreibtisch
der Sessel
der Stuhl / die Stühle
das Telefon
der Teppich
der Wecker
_____

2.2 The negative article *kein, keine*

Kein and **keine** (*not a, not any, no*) are the negative forms of **ein** and **eine.**

Im Klassenzimmer sind **keine** Fenster. — *There aren't any / are no windows in the classroom.*

Stefan hat **keinen** Schreibtisch. — *Stefan doesn't have a desk.*

The negative article has the same endings as the indefinite article **ein.** It also has a plural form: **keine.**

	Teppich (m.)	*Regal (n.)*	*Uhr (f.)*	*Stühle (pl.)*
Nom./Acc.	ein/einen	ein	eine	—
Nom./Acc.	kein/keinen	kein	keine	keine

— Hat Katrin **einen** Schrank? — *Does Katrin have a wardrobe?*
— Nein, sie hat **keinen** Schrank. — *No, she doesn't have a wardrobe.*

— Hat Katrin **Bilder** an der Wand? — *Does Katrin have pictures on the wall?*
— Nein, sie hat **keine** Bilder an der Wand. — *No, she has no pictures on the wall.*

Übung 3 Vergleiche[1]

Wer hat was? Was haben Sie?

MODELL Albert hat keinen Computer. Er hat einen Fernseher und eine Gitarre, aber er hat kein Fahrrad. Er hat ein Telefon und Bilder, aber er hat keinen Teppich.

	Albert	Heidi	Peter	Monika	Sie
der Computer	–	+	+	–	
der Fernseher	+	–	–	–	
die Gitarre	+	+	–	–	
das Fahrrad	–	–	+	+	
das Telefon	+	+	+	+	
die Bilder	+	–	–	+	
der Teppich	–	+	+	+	

2.3 What would you like? *Ich möchte . . .*

Use **möchte** (*would like*) to express that you would like to have something. The thing you want is in the accusative case.

Ich möchte **eine Tasse Kaffee**, bitte. — *I'd like a cup of coffee, please.*
Hans möchte **einen Fernseher** zum Geburtstag. — *Hans would like a TV set for his birthday.*

Möchte is particularly common in polite exchanges, for example in shops or restaurants.

KELLNER: Was möchten Sie? — WAITER: *What would you like?*
GAST: Ich möchte ein Bier. — CUSTOMER: *I'd like a beer.*

[1]*comparisons*

möchte = *would like*

Following are the forms of **möchte.** Note that the **er/sie/es**-form does not follow the regular pattern; it does not end in **-t.**

möchte			
ich	möchte	wir	möchten
du	möchtest	ihr	möchtet
Sie	möchten	Sie	möchten
er / sie / es	möchte	sie	möchten

To say that someone would like to do something, use **möchte** with the infinitive of the verb that expresses the action. This infinitive appears at the end of the sentence. Think of the **Satzklammer** used with separable-prefix verbs, and pattern your **möchte** sentences after it. **Möchte** and similar verbs are explained in more detail in **Kapitel 3.**

Peter möchte einen Mantel kaufen.

Sofie möchte ein Eis essen.

Übung 4 Der Wunschzettel

Was, glauben Sie, möchten diese Personen? Die folgenden Sachen stehen zur Wahl.[1]

MODELL Meine beste Freundin möchte einen Ring.

das Auto	der Koffer	die Rollerblades
der Computer	das Motorrad	die Sonnenbrille
der Fernseher	die Ohrringe	die Tennisschuhe
die Hose	der Pullover	der Teppich
der Hund	das Radio	der Videorecorder
die Katze	der Ring	der Walkman

1. Ich _____
2. Mein bester Freund / Meine beste Freundin _____
3. Meine Eltern _____
4. Mein Mitbewohner / Meine Mitbewohnerin und ich _____
5. Mein Nachbar / Meine Nachbarin in der Klasse _____
6. Mein Professor / Meine Professorin _____
7. Mein Bruder / Meine Schwester _____

[1] stehen . . . *are options*

2.4 Possessive adjectives

Use the possessive adjectives **mein, dein,** and so forth to express ownership.

—Ist das **dein** Fernseher?	*Is this your TV?*
—Nein, das ist nicht **mein** Fernseher.	*No, this is not my TV.*
—Ist das Sofies Gitarre?	*Is this Sofie's guitar?*
—Ja, das ist **ihre** Gitarre.	*Yes, this is her guitar.*

Here are the nominative forms of the possessive adjectives.

Singular	*Plural*
mein Auto (*my car*)	**unser** Auto (*our car*)
dein Auto (*your car*) **Ihr*** Auto (*your car*)	**euer** Auto (*your car*) **Ihr*** Auto (*your car*)
sein Auto (*his car*) **ihr** Auto (*her car*)	**ihr** Auto (*their car*)

Note the three forms for English *your:* **dein** (*informal singular*), **euer** (*informal plural*), and **Ihr** (*formal singular* or *plural*).

Albert und Peter, wo sind **eure** Bücher?	*Albert and Peter, where are your books?*
Öffnen Sie **Ihre** Bücher auf Seite 133.	*Open your books to page 133.*

Possessive adjectives have the same endings as the indefinite article **ein.** They agree in case (*nominative* or *accusative*), gender (*masculine, neuter,* or *feminine*), and number (*singular* or *plural*) with the noun that they precede.

Mein Pulli ist warm. Möchtest du **meinen** Pulli tragen?	*My sweater is warm. Would you like to wear my sweater?*
Josef verkauft **seinen** Computer.	*Josef is selling his computer.*

Like **ein,** the forms of possessive adjectives are the same in the nominative and accusative cases—except for the masculine singular, which has an **-en** ending in the accusative.

Achtung!

Note that German **ihr** means both *her* and *their.*

Jutta füttert **ihre** Katze.	*Jutta feeds her cat.*
Herr und Frau Ruf füttern **ihren** Hund.	*Mr. and Mrs. Ruf feed their dog.*

*The formal possessive adjective **Ihr** is capitalized just like the personal pronoun **Sie** (*you*).

Possessive Adjectives Nominative and Accusative Cases				
	Ring (m.)	*Armband (n.)*	*Kette (f.)*	*Ohrringe (pl.)*
my	mein/meinen	mein	meine	meine
your	dein/deinen	dein	deine	deine
your	Ihr/Ihren	Ihr	Ihre	Ihre
his	sein/seinen	sein	seine	seine
her	ihr/ihren	ihr	ihre	ihre
our	unser/unseren	unser	unsere	unsere
your	euer/euren	euer	eure	eure
your	Ihr/Ihren	Ihr	Ihre	Ihre
their	ihr/ihren	ihr	ihre	ihre

Übung 5 Hans und Helga

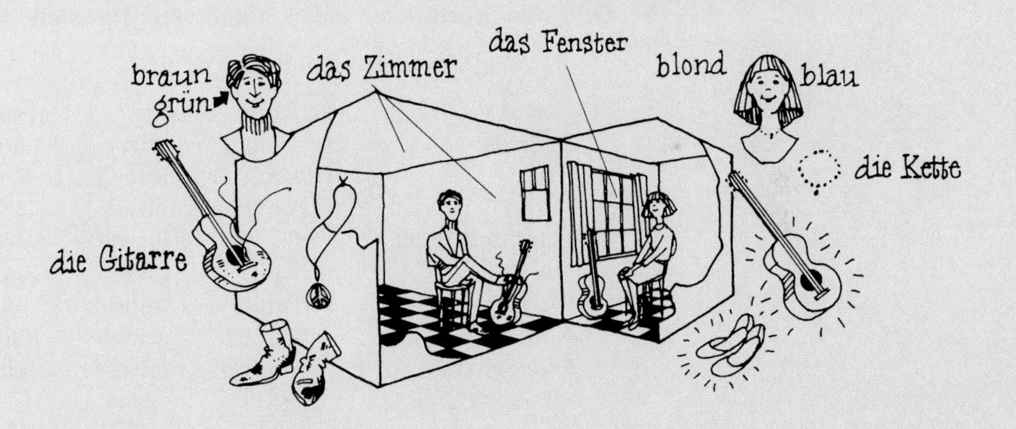

Beschreiben Sie Hans und Helga.

Seine Haare sind braun.	Ihre Haare sind blond.
_____ Augen sind grün.	_____ Augen sind blau.
_____ Kette ist lang.	_____ Kette ist . . .
_____ Schuhe sind schmutzig.	. . .
_____ Gitarre ist alt.	. . .
_____ Zimmer ist groß.	. . .
_____ Fenster ist klein.	. . .

Übung 6 Minidialoge

Ergänzen Sie **dein, euer** oder **Ihr.** Verwenden Sie die richtige Endung.

1. FRAU GRETTER: Wie finden Sie meinen Pullover?
   HERR WAGNER: Ich finde _____ Pullover sehr schön.
2. BERND: Weißt du, wo meine Brille ist, Veronika?
   VERONIKA: _____ Brille ist auf dem Tisch.
3. OMA SCHMITZ: Helga! Sigrid! Räumt _____ Schuhe auf!
   HELGA UND SIGRID: Ja, gleich, Oma.
4. HERR RUF: Jutta! Komm mal ans Telefon! _____ Freundin ist am Apparat.[1]
   JUTTA: Ich komme.
5. HERR SIEBERT: Beißt _____ Hund?
   FRAU KÖRNER: Was glauben Sie denn! Natürlich beißt mein Hund nicht.
6. NORA: Morgen möchte ich zu meinen Eltern fahren.
   PETER: Wo wohnen _____ Eltern?
   NORA: In Santa Cruz.
7. JÜRGEN: Silvia und ich, wir verkaufen unseren Computer.
   ANDREAS: _____ Computer! Der ist so alt, den kauft doch niemand!

Übung 7 Flohmarkt

Sie und die Studenten und Studentinnen in Frau Schulz' Deutschkurs brauchen Geld und organisieren einen Flohmarkt. Schreiben Sie Sätze. Wer verkauft was?

MODELL Monika verkauft ihre CDs.

(Monika)	verkaufe	ihr	Computer (der)
Thomas	verkaufen	(ihre)	Ohrring (der)
ich	verkaufen	ihre	Wörterbuch (das)
Katrin	verkaufen	ihren	Trainingsanzug (der)
Peter und Heidi	(verkauft)	ihren	(CDs) (*pl.*)
wir	verkauft	mein	Bücher (*pl.*)
Stefan	verkauft	seine	Gitarre (die)
Nora und Albert	verkauft	seinen	Bilder (*pl.*)
Frau Schulz	verkauft	unsere	Telefon (das)

2.5 The present tense of stem-vowel changing verbs

In some German verbs, the vowel changes in the **du**- and the **er/sie/es**-forms.

—**Schläfst** du gern?	*Do you like to sleep?*
—Ja, ich **schlafe** sehr gern.	*Yes, I like to sleep very much.*
Ich **lese** viel, aber Ernst **liest** mehr.	*I read a lot, but Ernst reads more.*

[1] *phone*

There are four types of stem vowel changes: **a → ä, au → äu, e → i, e → ie.**

learn these

These are the types of vowel changes you will encounter.

a → ä	fahren:	du fährst	er/sie/es fährt	*to drive*
	schlafen:	du schläfst	er/sie/es schläft	*to sleep*
	tragen:	du trägst	er/sie/es trägt	*to wear*
	waschen:	du wäschst	er/sie/es wäscht	*to wash*
	einladen:	du lädst . . . ein	er/sie/es lädt . . . ein*	*to invite*
au → äu†	laufen:	du läufst	er/sie/es läuft	*to run*
e → i	essen:	du ißt‡	er/sie/es ißt§	*to eat*
	sprechen:	du sprichst	er/sie/es spricht	*to speak*
	treffen:	du triffst	er/sie/es trifft	*to meet*
	vergessen:	du vergißt§	er/sie/es vergißt	*to forget*
e → ie#	lesen:	du liest‡	er/sie/es liest	*to read*
	sehen:	du siehst	er/sie/es sieht	*to see*
	fernsehen:	du siehst . . . fern	er/sie/es sieht . . . fern	*to watch TV*

Jürgen **läuft** jeden Tag 10 Kilometer. — *Jürgen runs 10 kilometers every day.*
Ernst **ißt** gern Pizza. — *Ernst likes to eat pizza.*
Michael **sieht** gern **fern.** — *Michael likes to watch TV.*

Achtung!

—Läufst du **gern** in der Stadt? — *Do you like to jog in the city?*
—Nein, ich laufe **lieber** im Wald. — *No, I prefer jogging in the forest.*

Übung 8 Minidialoge

Ergänzen Sie das Pronomen.

1. OMA SCHMITZ: Seht _____[a] gern fern?
   HELGA UND SIGRID: Ja, _____[b] sehen sehr gern fern.
2. FRAU GRETTER: Lesen _____[a] die Zeitung?
   MARIA: Im Moment nicht. _____[b] lese gerade ein Buch.
3. HERR SIEBERT: Ißt Ihre Tochter gern Eis?
   HERR RUF: Nein, _____[a] ißt lieber Joghurt. Aber da kommt mein Sohn, _____[b] ißt sehr gern Eis.

---

*Recall that verb stems ending in **d** or **t** insert an **-e-** before another consonant: **ich arbeite, du arbeitest.** Verb forms that contain a vowel change do not insert an **-e-**. Verb forms without this vowel change, however, do insert an **-e-: ihr lad*e*t ein.**
†Recall that **äu** is pronounced as in English *boy.*
‡Recall that verb stems that end in **s, ß, z,** or **x** do not add **st** in the **du**-form, but only **t.**
§When **-ss-** is followed by a consonant or when it is at the end of a word, it is spelled **-ß-: ich esse, wir essen;** but: **du ißt, er/sie/es ißt, ihr eßt.**
#Recall that **ie** is pronounced as in English *niece.*

4. SILVIA: Wohin[1] fährst _____[a] im Sommer?
ANDREAS: _____[b] fahre nach Spanien. Und wohin fahrt _____[c]?
SILVIA: _____[d] fahren nach England.

Übung 9 Jens und Jutta

Ergänzen Sie das Verb. Verwenden Sie die folgenden Wörter.

machen (2×)	sehen
fahren (2×)	lesen
essen (3×)	schlafen

MICHAEL: Was _____[a] Jutta und Jens gern?
ANDREA: Jutta _____[b] sehr gern Motorrad. Jens _____[c] lieber fern.
MICHAEL: Was essen sie gern? _____[d] Jens gern Chinesisch?
ERNST: Jens _____[e] gern Italienisch, aber nicht Chinesisch. Und Jutta _____[f] gern bei McDonald's.
MICHAEL: Und ihr, was _____[g] ihr gern?
ANDREA: Ich _____[h] gern Bücher und Ernst _____[i] gern. Und im Winter _____[j] wir gern Schlitten.

Übung 10 Was machen Sie gern?

Sagen Sie, was Sie gern machen, und bilden Sie Fragen.

MODELL ich/du: bei McDonald's essen →
Ich esse (nicht) gern bei McDonald's. Ißt du auch (nicht) gern bei McDonald's?

1. wir/ihr: Deutsch sprechen
2. ich/du: Freunde einladen
3. ich/du: im Wald laufen
4. ich/du: Pullis tragen
5. wir/ihr: fernsehen
6. ich/du: Fahrrad fahren
7. wir/ihr: die Hausaufgabe vergessen
8. ich/du: schlafen

2.6 Asking people to do things: The *du*-imperative

Use the **du**-imperative when addressing people you normally address with **du,** such as friends, relatives, other students, and the like. It is formed by dropping the **-(s)t** ending from the present-tense **du**-form of the verb. The pronoun **du** is not used.

Drop the **-(s)t** from the **du**-form to get the **du**-imperative.

(du) kommst →	Komm!	*Come!*
(du) tanzt →	Tanz!	*Dance!*
(du) arbeitest →	Arbeite!	*Work!*

[1] *Where*

(du) öffnest →	Öffne!	*Open!*
(du) ißt →	Iß!	*Eat!*
(du) siehst →	Sieh!	*See!*

Verbs whose stem vowel changes from **a(u)** to **ä(u)** drop the umlaut in the **du**-imperative.

(du) fährst →	Fahr!	*Drive!*
(du) läufst →	Lauf!	*Run!*

Imperative sentences always begin with the verb.

Trag mir bitte die Tasche.	*Please carry the bag for me.*
Öffne bitte das Fenster.	*Open the window, please.*
Reite nicht so schnell!	*Don't ride so fast!*
Sieh nicht so viel fern!	*Don't watch so much TV!*

Übung 11 Ach, diese Geschwister!

Ihr kleiner Bruder macht alles falsch. Sagen Sie ihm, was er machen soll.

MODELL Ihr kleiner Bruder ißt zu viel. → Iß nicht so viel!

1. Ihr kleiner Bruder schläft den ganzen Tag.
2. Er liegt den ganzen Tag in der Sonne.
3. Er vergißt seine Hausaufgaben.
4. Er liest seine Bücher nicht.
5. Er sieht den ganzen Tag fern.
6. Er trinkt zu viel Cola.
7. Er spricht mit vollem Mund.
8. Er trägt seine Brille nicht.
9. Er geht nie spazieren.
10. Er treibt keinen Sport.

Übung 12 Vorschläge[1]

Machen Sie Ihrem Freund / Ihrer Freundin Vorschläge.

MODELL deinen Eltern einen Brief / schreiben →
Schreib deinen Eltern einen Brief.

1. heute ein T-Shirt / tragen
2. keine laute Musik / spielen
3. den Wortschatz / lernen
4. deine Freunde / anrufen
5. nicht allein im Park / laufen
6. nicht zu lange in der Sonne / liegen
7. dein Zimmer / aufräumen
8. heute abend in einem Restaurant / essen
9. nicht zu spät ins Bett / gehen
10. früh / aufstehen

---

[1]*suggestions*

KAPITEL 3

Harfenspieler in der Fußgängerzone in Freiburg

In **Kapitel 3,** you will learn how to describe your talents and those of others. You will learn how to express your intentions and how to talk about obligation and necessity. You will also learn additional ways to describe how you or other people feel.

Talente, Pläne, Pflichten

THEMEN
Talente und Pläne
Pflichten
Ach, wie nett!
Körperliche und geistige Verfassung

LEKTÜRE
mal eben
Kleine Geschenke

KULTURELLES
Stadtprofil: Bad Harzburg
Schuljahr und Zeugnisse
Kulturprojekt: Deutschland, Österreich und die Schweiz
Porträt: Ingeborg Bachmann und Klagenfurt
Videoecke: Fünf Schulfächer

STRUKTUREN
3.1 The modal verbs **können, wollen, mögen**
3.2 The modal verbs **müssen, sollen, dürfen**
3.3 Accusative case: personal pronouns
3.4 Word order: dependent clauses
3.5 Dependent clauses and separable-prefix verbs

SPRECHSITUATIONEN

Talente und Pläne

➤ **Grammatik 3.1**

Peter kann ausgezeichnet kochen.

Rosemarie und Natalie können gut zeichnen.

Claire kann gut Deutsch.

Melanie und Josef wollen heute abend zu Hause bleiben und lesen.

Silvia will für Jürgen einen Pullover stricken.

Sofie und Willi wollen tanzen gehen.

Situation 1 Kochen

Bringen Sie die Sätze in die richtige Reihenfolge.

_____ Spaghetti esse ich besonders gern.
_____ Dann komm doch mal vorbei.
_____ Nicht so gut. Aber ich kann sehr gut Spaghetti machen.
_____ Kannst du chinesisch kochen?
__1__ Kochst du gern?
_____ Ja, ich koche sehr gern.
_____ Ja, gern! Vielleicht Samstag?
_____ Gut! Bis Samstag.

Situation 2 Informationsspiel: Kann Katrin kochen?

MODELL S1: Kann Katrin kochen?
S2: Ja, ganz gut.
S1: Kannst du kochen?
S2: Ja, aber nicht so gut.

[+]		[0]		[−]	
	ausgezeichnet fantastisch sehr gut gut		ganz gut		nicht so gut nur ein bißchen gar nicht kein bißchen

	Katrin	Peter	mein(e) Partner(in)
kochen	ganz gut		
zeichnen		kein bißchen	
tippen	nur ein bißchen		
Witze erzählen	ganz gut		
tanzen		sehr gut	
stricken		kein bißchen	
Skateboard fahren	ganz gut		
Geige spielen	ausgezeichnet		
schwimmen	gut		
ein Auto reparieren		nicht so gut	

Situation 3 Umfrage: Wünsche und Absichten

MODELL S1: Willst du heute abend ins Kino gehen?
S2: Ja.
S1: Unterschreib hier bitte.

UNTERSCHRIFT

1. Willst du heute abend ins Kino gehen? __________
2. Willst du mit mir tanzen gehen? __________
3. Willst du mit mir Hausaufgaben machen? __________
4. Möchtest du in der nächsten Prüfung ein A schreiben? __________
5. Willst du heute abend einen Roman lesen? __________
6. Willst du in diesem Semester 20 Stunden pro Woche arbeiten? __________
7. Möchtest du im Winter einen Pullover stricken? __________
8. Möchtest du am Wochenende mit mir Tennis spielen? __________
9. Willst du mit mir chinesisch kochen? __________
10. Möchtest du morgen mit mir Deutsch sprechen? __________

Kultur ... Landeskunde ... Informationen

Stadtprofil: Bad Harzburg

ungefähr[1] 23 000 Einwohner
Bade- und Kurort[2] im Harz
Attraktionen: Spielbank[3] und Pferderennbahn[4], viele Wanderwege, vier Parks, Tennisplätze, Golfplatz, drei Schwimmbäder, Stadtbücherei[5]
Schulen: 4 Grundschulen[6], 1 Hauptschule[7], 1 Realschule[8], 2 Gymnasien[9], 6 Kindergärten

- Was kann man in der Stadtbücherei von Bad Harzburg machen?
- Was kann man noch machen, wenn man Bad Harzburg besucht?
- Vergleichen Sie Ihre Heimatstadt oder Universitätsstadt mit Bad Harzburg.

MODELL Meine Heimatstadt hat 67 000 Einwohner und liegt am Mississippi. Attraktionen: Heimatmuseum, . . .

Bad Harzburg, Bade- und Kurort im Harz mit Pferderennbahn und Kasino

[1] *approximately* [2] Bade- . . . *spa and resort town* [3] *casino* [4] *horse racing track* [5] *public library* [6] *elementary schools* [7] *basic secondary school* [8] *intermediate secondary school* [9] *advanced secondary schools*

Situation 4 Bingo-Interview

MODELL Kannst du Gitarre spielen? Ja = 2 Punkte
Kann deine Mutter / dein Vater Gitarre spielen? Ja = 1 Punkt

1. Walzer tanzen
2. Schlittschuh laufen
3. Französisch
4. einen Salat machen
5. einen Fernseher reparieren
6. einen Pullover stricken
7. Haare schneiden
8. gute Fotos machen
9. Tischtennis spielen
10. ein deutsches Lied singen

Pflichten

➤ **Grammatik 3.2**

Jens ist faul, er muß mehr lernen.

Er darf nicht mit Jutta ins Kino gehen.

Frau Frisch muß den Tisch decken.

Darf ich die Kerzen anzünden?

Sag Vati, er soll den Fernseher ausmachen.

Vati sagt, du sollst sofort nach Hause kommen.

Situation 5 Ein schlechtes Zeugnis

Jens hat drei Fünfen im Zeugnis. Was muß er machen? Was darf er nicht machen?

1. Freitagabend in die Disko gehen
2. Latein lernen
3. den ganzen Tag in der Sonne liegen
4. seine Hausaufgaben machen
5. dreimal in der Woche Fußball spielen
6. am Wochenende ins Schwimmbad gehen
7. eine Woche nach Italien fahren
8. Nachhilfe nehmen
9. mit seinen Lehrern sprechen
10. _____

Kultur ... Landeskunde ... Informationen

Schuljahr und Zeugnisse

Sie hören einen Text über die deutschen Schulen. Hören Sie gut zu und beantworten Sie dann die Fragen.

- Von wann bis wann dauert das Schuljahr? Es dauert von ____ bis ___ oder ___.
- Wann gibt es Zeugnisse[1]? In der ___ und am ___ des Jahres.
- Schreiben Sie neben die Wörter die richtige Note[2] (Zahl) und was es in Nordamerika gibt.

	IN DEUTSCHLAND	IN NORDAMERIKA
„sehr gut"	______	______
„gut"	______	______
„befriedigend"[3]	______	______
„ausreichend"[4]	______	______
„mangelhaft"[5]	______	______
„ungenügend"[6]	______	______

- Wann bleibt man sitzen[7]?

Mini-Wörterbuch zum Hörtext

entscheiden to decide
die **Klasse, -n** grade, level
das **Resultat, -e** result
die **Versetzung** graduation into the next grade

[1]*report cards* [2]*grade* [3]*satisfactory* [4]*sufficient* [5]*poor* [6]*insufficient* [7]bleibt . . . sitzen *flunks, is held back a grade*

Zeugnis

für Jens Krüger

geboren am 22. August 1981 Klasse 9 b

Allgemeine Beurteilung: Jens ist ein schwacher Schüler. Er muß mehr lernen.

Deutsch	4	Mathematik	4
mündlich 3- schriftlich 4		Physik	5
Geschichte / Sozialkunde	3	Chemie	3
Geschichte 4 Sozialkd. 2		Biologie	3
Erdkunde	3	Musik	2
1. Fremdsprache: Englisch	5	Bildende Kunst / Werken	2
mündlich 5 schriftlich 5		Bildende Kunst 2 Werken 3	
2. Fremdsprache: Latein	5	Sport	1
mündlich 5 schriftlich 5			

Wahlpflichtfach

3. Fremdsprache: Italienisch	4		
mündlich 4 schriftlich 4			

Freiwillige Unterrichtsveranstaltungen

Versäumte Tage:	davon unentschuldigt:	Verspätungen:	Versäumte Einzelstunden:	davon unentschuldigt:
12	0	17	/	/

nicht versetzt in die Klasse 10

Bemerkungen: Jens ist bei seinen Mitschülern beliebt.

Berlin, 17. Juli 1996

Cramer — Schulleiter(in)   U. Möller — Klassenlehrer(in)

Gelesen: Arnd Krüger — Erziehungsberechtigte(r)

Beurteilung der Leistungen: 1 = sehr gut, 2 = gut, 3 = befriedigend, 4 = ausreichend, 5 = mangelhaft, 6 = ungenügend

Schul II 721 – Zeugnis des Gymnasiums, Klasse 7 bis 10 (ggf. 5 bis 10) (4.85)
Mat. 1822. Sätze à 2 Blatt. 098

Situation 6 Pflichten

Sagen Sie **ja** oder **nein.**

1. Ich darf nicht

a. jeden Tag bis Mittag schlafen.
b. Bier trinken.
c. einkaufen gehen.
d. _____ .

2. Ich muß mal wieder

a. das Haus putzen.
b. einen Roman lesen.
c. Hausaufgaben machen.
d. _____ .

3. In den Ferien muß mein Freund / meine Freundin

a. Sport treiben.
b. seine / ihre Eltern besuchen.
c. in die Universität gehen.
d. _____ .

4. Meine Eltern müssen mal wieder

a. miteinander essen gehen.
b. ein neues Auto kaufen.
c. miteinander sprechen.
d. _____ .

5. Meine Kinder dürfen nicht

a. Bungee-jumping gehen.
b. rauchen.
c. ihr ganzes Geld ausgeben.
d. _____ .

Situation 7 Dialog

Rolf trifft Katrin in der Cafeteria.

ROLF: Hallo Katrin, ist hier noch __?
KATRIN: Ja, klar.
ROLF: Ich hoffe, ich ___ dich nicht beim Lernen.
KATRIN: Nein, ich muß auch mal ____ machen.
ROLF: Was machst du denn?
KATRIN: Wir haben morgen eine _____, und ich ___ noch das Arbeitsbuch machen.
ROLF: ___ ihr viel für euren Kurs arbeiten?
KATRIN: Ja, ganz schön viel. Heute abend ___ ich bestimmt nicht fernsehen, ___ ich so viel lernen muß.
ROLF: Ich glaube, ich störe dich nicht länger. ______ für die Prüfung.
KATRIN: Danke, tschüs.

Situation 8 Stefans Zimmer

Stefans Mutter kommt zu Besuch.

Das ist Stefans Zimmer.

So soll es sein.

Was muß Stefan machen?

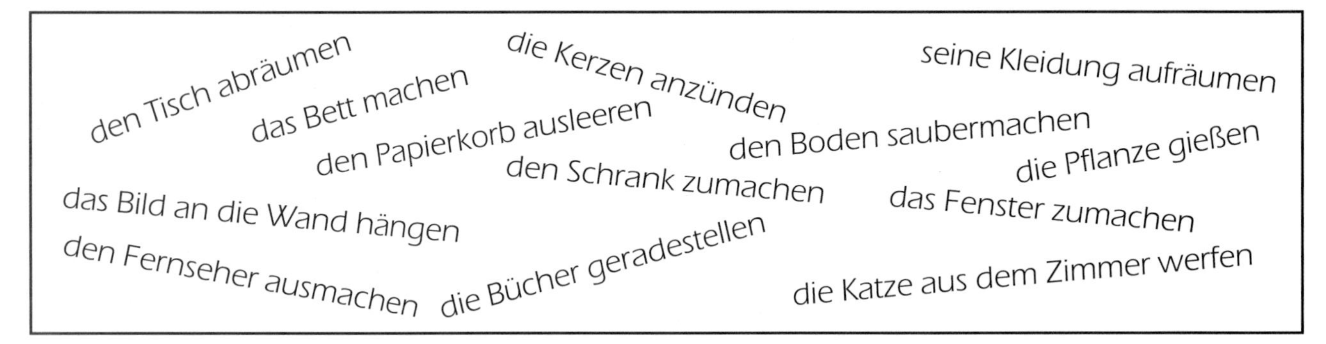

Ach, wie nett!

➤ **Grammatik 3.3**

—Der Fernseher läuft ja den ganzen Tag.
—Soll ich ihn ausmachen?

—Ich finde den Mantel einfach toll!
—Kaufen Sie ihn doch!

—Die Tasche ist so schwer.
—Komm, Oma, ich trage sie.

—Hier ist mein Taschentuch. Du darfst mich nie vergessen.
—Nein, Geliebte, ich vergesse dich nie!

Samstag machen wir ein Fest. Ich möchte euch gern einladen.

Hallo, wir wollen nach Regensburg. Nehmt ihr uns mit?

Situation 9 Minidialoge

Was paßt?

1. Es ist kalt und das Fenster ist offen!
2. Der Wein ist gut.
3. Du hast nächste Woche Geburtstag?
4. Der Koffer ist so schwer.
5. Die Suppe ist wirklich gut!

a. Komm, ich trage ihn.
b. Machen Sie es bitte zu.
c. Darf ich ihn probieren?
d. Ich mag sie aber nicht.
e. Ja, ich gebe eine Party, und ich lade euch ein.

6. Wie findest du Paul Simon?
7. Das Haus ist schmutzig.
8. Kannst du deinen CD-Spieler mitbringen?
9. Sprecht bitte ein bißchen lauter!
10. Mein Auto ist leider kaputt.

f. Warum? Verstehst du uns denn nicht?
g. Ich mag ihn ganz gern.
h. Steig ein, ich nehme dich mit.
i. Ich mache es morgen sauber.
j. Ja, gut, ich bringe ihn mit.

Situation 10 Dialog

Heidi sucht einen Platz in der Cafeteria.

HEIDI: Entschuldigung, __________?
STEFAN: Ja, sicher.
HEIDI: Danke.
STEFAN: __________?
HEIDI: Ja, ich glaube schon. Bist du nicht auch in dem Deutschkurs um neun?
STEFAN: Na, klar. Jetzt ___ ich's wieder. Du ___ Stefanie, nicht wahr?
HEIDI: Nein, ich heiße Heidi.
STEFAN: Ach ja, richtig . . . Heidi. Ich heiße Stefan.
HEIDI: ____ kommst du eigentlich, Stefan?
STEFAN: ___ Iowa City, und du?
HEIDI: Ich bin aus Berkeley.

STEFAN: Und was studierst du?
HEIDI: ____________. Vielleicht Sport, vielleicht Geschichte oder vielleicht Deutsch.
STEFAN: Ich studiere auch Deutsch, Deutsch und ______. Ich möchte in Deutschland bei einer amerikanischen Firma arbeiten.
HEIDI: Toll! Da verdienst du sicherlich viel Geld.
STEFAN: _______.

Situation 11 Umfrage

MODELL S1: Machst du gern das Arbeitsbuch für „Kontakte"?
S2: Ja, ich mache es gern. / Nein, ich mache es nicht gern.
S1: Unterschreib hier bitte. / Schade. Tschüs.

	UNTERSCHRIFT
1. Machst du gern das Arbeitsbuch für „Kontakte"?	________________
2. Kannst du das deutsche Alphabet?	________________
3. Kennst du den beliebtesten deutschen Vornamen für Jungen?	________________
4. Trinkst du gern deutschen Wein?	________________
5. Liest du gern die Grammatik?	________________
6. Lernst du gern den Wortschatz?	________________
7. Kennst du alle Studenten und Studentinnen im Kurs?	________________
8. Vergißt du oft die Hausaufgabe für den Deutschkurs?	________________
9. Magst du unseren Lehrer/unsere Lehrerin?	________________
10. Schreibst du gern deutsche Briefe?	________________

Situation 12 Rollenspiel: In der Mensa

S1: Sie sind Student/Studentin an der Uni in Regensburg. Sie gehen in die Mensa und setzen sich zu jemand an den Tisch. Fragen Sie, wie er/sie heißt, woher er/sie kommt und was er/sie studiert.

Die Mensa der Universität Regensburg. Haben Sie Hunger?

Körperliche und geistige Verfassung

➤ **Grammatik 3.4–3.5**

Er ist glücklich.

Sie sind traurig.

Er ist wütend.

Sie sind betrunken.

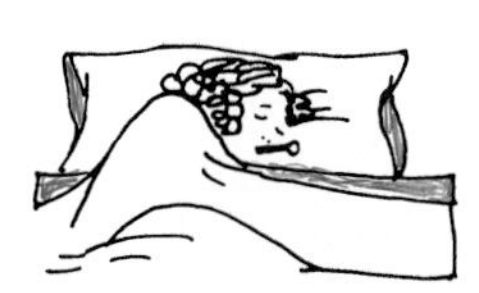
Sie ist krank.

Er ist besorgt.

Sie sind in Eile.

Sie ist müde.

Sie haben Hunger.

Er hat Langeweile.

Er hat Durst.

Er hat Angst.

Situation 13 Wohin gehst du, wenn . . . ?

MODELL S1: Wohin gehst du, wenn du Hunger hast?
S2: Wenn ich Hunger habe, gehe ich ins Restaurant.

1. Wenn ich Hunger habe,		**a.** in die Stadt.
2. Wenn ich Angst habe,		**b.** ins Kino.
3. Wenn ich Langeweile habe,		**c.** nach Hause.
4. Wenn ich Durst habe,		**d.** in eine Kneipe.
5. Wenn ich Heimweh habe,	gehe ich	**e.** ins Krankenhaus.
6. Wenn ich traurig bin,		**f.** ins Bett.
7. Wenn ich müde bin,		**g.** in den Wald.
8. Wenn ich krank bin,		**h.** in die Klasse.
9. Wenn ich frustriert bin,		**i.** ins Restaurant.
10. Wenn ich wütend bin,		**j.** ______ .

Situation 14 Informationsspiel: Was machen sie, wenn . . . ?

MODELL S1: Was macht Renate, wenn sie traurig ist?
S2: Sie weint.
S1: Was machst du, wenn du traurig bist?
S2: Ich gehe ins Bett.

	Renate	Mehmet	Ernst	mein(e) Partner(in)
traurig sein	ruft ihre Freundin an		weint	
müde sein		schläft		
in Eile sein	nimmt ein Taxi		ist nie in Eile	
wütend sein	wirft mit Tellern		schreit ganz laut	
krank sein		ißt Hühnersuppe		
glücklich sein	lädt Freunde ein		lacht ganz laut	
Hunger haben	ißt einen Apfel		schreit ganz laut „Hunger!“	
Langeweile haben		geht in eine Kneipe		

Situation 15 Interview: Wie fühlst du dich, wenn . . . ?

MODELL S1: Wie fühlst du dich, wenn du um fünf Uhr morgens aufstehst?
S2: Ausgezeichnet!

[+]	ausgezeichnet fantastisch sehr gut gut	[0]	ganz gut	[−]	nicht besonders gut ziemlich schlecht mies total mies

1. wenn du um fünf Uhr morgens aufstehst
2. wenn du die ganze Nacht nicht schlafen kannst
3. wenn du drei Filme hintereinander ansiehst
4. wenn deine Freunde dich auf eine Party einladen
5. wenn du von der Arbeit nach Hause kommst
6. wenn du ein Referat schreiben mußt
7. wenn dein bester Freund / deine beste Freundin dich anruft
8. wenn du einkaufen gehen willst, aber kein Geld hast
9. wenn dein Mitbewohner / deine Mitbewohnerin dich zur Uni mitnimmt
10. wenn du ein A in Deutsch bekommst

Situation 16 Warum fährt Frau Ruf mit dem Bus?

Kombinieren Sie!

MODELL S1: Warum fährt Frau Ruf mit dem Bus?
S2: Weil ihr Auto kaputt ist.

1. Warum fährt Frau Ruf mit dem Bus?
2. Warum hat Hans Angst?
3. Warum geht Jutta nicht ins Kino?
4. Warum geht Jens nicht in die Schule?
5. Warum kauft Andrea Hans eine CD?
6. Warum fährt Herr Wagner nach Leipzig?
7. Warum ist Ernst wütend?
8. Warum fährt Frau Gretter in die Berge?
9. Warum geht Herr Siebert um zehn Uhr ins Bett?
10. Warum ruft Maria ihre Freundin an?

a. Er hat Geburtstag.
b. Ihr Auto ist kaputt.
c. Er ist allein.
d. Sie hat eine Prüfung und muß lernen.
e. Er ist krank.
f. Er will seinen Bruder besuchen.
g. Sie geht wandern.
h. Er muß sein Zimmer aufräumen.
i. Sie will sie ins Kino einladen.
j. Er steht jeden Tag um sechs Uhr auf.

Situation 17 Zum Schreiben: Auch in Ihnen steckt ein Dichter!

Schreiben Sie ein Gedicht!

MODELL

Wasser	ein Nomen = Thema
kühl, naß	zwei Adjektive
schwimmen, segeln, tauchen	drei Verben
Sonne auf meiner Haut	vier Wörter, die ein Gefühl ausdrücken[1]
Sommer	ein Nomen = Zusammenfassung[2]

Mögliche Themen: Hund, Oma, Wochenende, Uni, Deutsch usw.

Hints for working with the Kulturprojekt

Use an atlas or a reference work such as the *Information Please Almanac.* Also, you will find answers to many of these questions in your textbook.

Kulturprojekt Deutschland, Österreich und die Schweiz

Suchen Sie in der Bibliothek oder in einer Enzyklopädie nach den folgenden Informationen zu Deutschland, Österreich und der Schweiz, und tragen Sie sie in die Tabelle ein.[3]

---

[1]*express* [2]*summary* [3]tragen . . . ein *write into*

1. Wie heißt die Hauptstadt?
2. Welche Währung[1] hat das Land?
3. Welche Farben hat die Flagge, und wie sieht sie aus? (Zeichnen Sie eine kleine Skizze.)
4. Welche Sprache(n) spricht man da?
5. Wie groß ist das Land in Quadratkilometern (km^2)?
6. Wie viele Einwohner[2] hat das Land?
7. Welches Nationalitätskennzeichen[3] hat das Land? (z.B. GB für Großbritannien, I für Italien)
8. Wie heißen die drei größten Städte?

Porträt

Der Lindwurmbrunnen in Klagenfurt

Ingeborg Bachmann (1926–1973) kam aus Klagenfurt und studierte Philosophie in Innsbruck, Graz und Wien. Sie schrieb Gedichte, Hörspiele[1] und Kurzgeschichten.[2] Bachmann zählt zu[3] den wichtigsten Autorinnen der deutschsprachigen Literatur der Gegenwart.[4] Zu ihren Werken gehören[5] der Roman *Malina* (1971) und die Erzählung[6] „Das dreißigste Jahr" (1961), die beide verfilmt wurden.[7] Sie erhielt[8] Preise für Literatur in Österreich und Deutschland, unter anderem den Preis der Gruppe 47 und den Georg-Büchner-Preis. Sie starb[9] 1973 unter mysteriösen Umständen[10] in Rom.

Klagenfurt ist die Hauptstadt von Kärnten, Österreichs südlichstem Bundesland, und liegt ganz in der Nähe des Wörther Sees. Auf dem Marktplatz steht der Lindwurmbrunnen.[11] Er erinnert an[12] den Drachen, der früher im Wörther See gelebt haben soll.

[1] *radio plays* [2] *short stories* [3] zählt . . . *is among* [4] *present time* [5] *belong* [6] *story* [7] verfilmt . . . *were made into a movie* [8] *received* [9] *died* [10] *circumstances* [11] *dragon fountain (a lindworm is a type of wingless dragon)* [12] erinnert . . . *reminds one of*

[1] *currency* [2] *inhabitants* [3] *national abbreviation*

Danke, Maxi. Du kanst dich setzen.

Fünf Schulfächer

Sie sehen verschiedene Klassenszenen aus einer deutschen Oberschule. Beantworten Sie für jede Szene die folgenden Fragen:

- Wie heißt das Unterrichtsfach?
- Was ist das Thema?
- Haben Sie das auch an Ihrer Oberschule gelernt?
- Wie finden Sie den Lehrer/die Lehrerin?
- Wie verhalten sich die Schüler/Schülerinnen? Arbeiten sie mit, stören sie usw.?

Talente und Pläne — Talents and Plans

der **Schlittschuh, -e** (R)	ice skate
Schlittschuh laufen, läuft	to go ice-skating
der **Witz, -e**	joke
Witze erzählen	to tell jokes
schneiden	to cut
Haare schneiden	to cut hair
stricken	to knit
tauchen	to dive
tippen	to type
zeichnen	to draw

Ähnliche Wörter

der **Ski, -er; Ski fahren;** der **Walzer, -** das **Bungee-jumping; Bungee-jumping gehen;** das **Skateboard, -s; Skateboard fahren, fährt;** das **Tischtennis**

Pflichten — Obligations

ab·räumen	to clear
den Tisch ab·räumen	to clear the table
decken	to set; to cover
den Tisch decken	to set the table
gerade·stellen	to straighten
die Bücher gerade·stellen	to straighten the books
gießen	to water
die Blumen/Pflanzen gießen	to water the flowers/plants
putzen	to clean
sauber·machen	to clean

Ähnliche Wörter

hängen; das Bild an die Wand hängen

Körperliche und geistige Verfassung — Physical and Mental States

die **Angst, ¨e**	fear
Angst haben	to be afraid
die **Eile**	hurry
in Eile sein	to be in a hurry
die **Langeweile**	boredom
Langeweile haben	to be bored
das **Glück**	luck; happiness
viel Glück!	lots of luck, good luck
das **Heimweh**	homesickness
Heimweh haben	to be homesick
ärgern	to annoy; to tease
schreien	to scream, yell
stören	to disturb
weinen	to cry

beschäftigt	busy
besorgt	worried
betrunken	drunk
eifersüchtig	jealous
faul	lazy
glücklich (R)	happy
krank	sick
müde	tired
traurig	sad
wütend	angry

Ähnliche Wörter

der **Durst; Durst haben;** der **Hunger; Hunger haben**
das **Gefühl, -e** **fühlen; wie fühlst du dich?; ich fühle mich . . . ; frustriert**

Essen und Trinken — Eating and Drinking

die **Kneipe, -n**	bar, tavern
das **Mittagessen**	midday meal, lunch
zu Mittag essen, ißt	to eat lunch
probieren	to try, taste

Ähnliche Wörter

die **Cola, -s;** die **Schokolade;** die **Spaghetti** (*pl.*); die **Suppe, -n** der **Apfel, ¨;** der **Hamburger, -;** der **Salat, -e** das **Brot, -e;** ein **Stück Brot**

Schule, Zeugnisse und Noten — School, Report Cards, and Grades

die **Nachhilfe**	tutoring
Nachhilfe geben	to tutor
Nachhilfe nehmen	to be tutored
die **Sprechstunde, -n**	office hour
der **Satz, ¨e**	sentence
der **Sommerkurs, -e**	summer school
das **Arbeitsbuch, ¨er**	workbook
das **Beispiel, -e**	example
zum Beispiel	for example
das **Referat, -e**	report
eine **Eins**	excellent, very good
eine **Zwei**	good
eine **Drei**	satisfactory
eine **Vier**	sufficient
eine **Fünf**	poor
eine **Sechs**	insufficient, failing
belegen	to take (a course)

Unterhaltung — Entertainment

die **Geige, -n**	violin
der **Besuch, -e**	visit
zu Besuch kommen	to visit
der **Roman, -e**	novel
das **Gedicht, -e**	poem
das **Lied, -er**	song

Ähnliche Wörter

die **CD, -s;** die **Disko, -s**

Sonstige Substantive — Other Nouns

die **Ärztin, -nen**	female physician
die **Blume, -n**	flower
die **Geliebte, -n**	beloved female friend, love
die **Hauptstadt, ¨e**	capital city
die **Haut**	skin
die **Kerze, -n**	candle
die **Oma, -s**	grandma
die **Pflicht, -en**	duty; requirement
der **Arzt, ¨e**	male physician
der **Papierkorb, ¨e**	wastebasket
der **Punkt, -e**	point
das **Krankenhaus, ¨er**	hospital
das **Taschentuch, ¨er**	handkerchief

Ähnliche Wörter

die **Firma, Firmen;** die **Pflanze, -n;** die **Nacht, ¨e;** die **Vase, -n** der **Mittag;** der **Plan, ¨e;** der **Platz, ¨e** das **Alphabet;** das **Aspirin;** das **Licht, -er;** das **Talent, -e;** das **Taxi, -s**

Modalverben — Modal Verbs

dürfen, darf	to be permitted (to), may
können, kann	to be able (to), can; may
mögen, mag	to like, care for
möchte	would like (to)
müssen, muß	to have to, must
sollen, soll	to be supposed to
wollen, will	to want; to intend, plan (to)

Sonstige Verben — Other Verbs

an·machen	to turn on, switch on
an·sehen, sieht . . . an	to look at; to watch

an·ziehen	to put on (clothes)
an·zünden	to light
auf·machen	to open
auf·passen	to pay attention; to watch out
aus·geben, gibt . . . aus	to spend
aus·machen	to turn off
aus·leeren	to empty
den **Papierkorb aus·leeren**	to empty the wastebasket
aus·ziehen	to take off (clothes)
bekommen	to get, receive
ein·steigen	to board
erzählen	to tell
kennen	to be acquainted with, know
mit·nehmen, nimmt . . . mit	to take along
nehmen, nimmt (R)	to take
rauchen	to smoke
stellen	to put, place (in an upright position)
verreisen	to go on a trip
vorbei·kommen	to come by, visit
werfen, wirft	to throw
zu·machen	to close

Ähnliche Wörter

baden, hoffen, kämmen, kombinieren, lachen, leben, mit·bringen

Adjektive und Adverbien / Adjectives and Adverbs

ausgezeichnet	excellent
beliebt	popular
besonders	particularly
bestimmt	definitely, certainly
eigentlich	actually
fertig	ready; finished
ganz	whole; quite; rather
die ganze Nacht	all night long
ihr ganzes Geld	all her money
ganz schön viel	quite a bit
kaputt	broken
naß	wet
schnell	quick, fast
schwer	heavy; hard, difficult
wahr	true

Ähnliche Wörter

amerikanisch; beste, bester, bestes; chinesisch; fantastisch; frei; ist hier noch frei?; laut; offen

Sonstige Wörter und Ausdrücke / Other Words and Expressions

bei (R)	with; at
bei dir	at your place
bis	until
dreimal	three times
einander	one another, each other
hintereinander	in a row
miteinander	with each other
ein bißchen (R)	a little
kein bißchen	not at all
Entschuldigung!	excuse me
gar nicht	not at all
immer	always
jede	each, every
jede Woche	every week
jemand	someone, somebody
jetzt	now
mit	with
mit mir	with me
na	well
nur	only
pro	per
pro Woche	per week
schade!	too bad
schon	already
ich glaube schon	I think so
schon wieder	once again
sicher	sure
sicherlich	certainly
sofort	immediately
von (R)	of; from
von der Arbeit	from work
warum	why
weil	because
wenn (R)	if; when(ever)
wieder	again
schon wieder	once again
wohin	where to
zu (R)	to; for
zu Fuß	on foot
zum Arzt	to the doctor
zum Mittagessen	for lunch

Ähnliche Wörter

allein, hoffentlich, lange, nicht länger, mehr, morgens, so

LESEECKE

LEKTÜRE 1

Vor dem Lesen

Lyrik. A short text like a poem usually requires intensive reading. Every single word is carefully chosen by the author to convey the meaning or feelings he or she wants to express. Look at the poem and listen as your instructor reads it.

- Was fühlen Sie, wenn Sie das Gedicht hören?

mal eben

von Ralf Kaiser

mal eben aufstehen
mal eben essen
mal eben schule
mal eben pause
mal eben schule (5)
mal eben essen
mal eben hausaufgaben
mal eben freizeit
mal eben fernsehen
mal eben pinte[1] (10)
mal eben schlafen

mal eben leben

[1]Bar, Kneipe

Arbeit mit dem Text

1. „Mal eben" bedeutet „schnell einmal".[1] Dann kommt in jeder Zeile[2] ein anderes Wort. Was stellen die Wörter von „aufstehen" bis „schlafen" dar?[3]
2. Wie finden Sie den „Tagesablauf" in dem Gedicht?

[1]*just* [2]*line* [3]stellen . . . dar *represent*

3. Die letzte Zeile steht allein. Was drückt sie aus? Schreiben Sie den Satz zu Ende:
   Das Leben ist _____ .
4. Schreiben Sie ein Gedicht, z.B. Ihren Tagesablauf, das Leben eines Freundes oder Verwandten. Benutzen Sie „mal eben" oder einen anderen Ausdruck, z.B. „hoffentlich", „nicht nur", „einfach", „nie wieder".

LEKTÜRE 2

Vor dem Lesen

Title, subtitle, and visuals such as illustrations, photos, and graphs as well as the general layout of a text all provide clues about its content. Look at the title and the layout of the following text. What kind of text is it? What is it about?

1. Der Mann (Er) oder die Frau (Sie)?
   _____ trägt einen Rollkragenpullover[1]
   _____ trägt eine Nickelbrille[2]
   _____ liest Zeitung
   _____ sitzt auf dem Sofa
   _____ lehnt sich auf[3] das Sofa
   _____ stützt den Kopf auf[4]
   _____ ist wütend
   _____ dreht sich[5] um
   _____ verschränkt die Arme
   _____ legt sich über das Sofa
2. Wie alt, glauben Sie, sind diese Leute?
3. Sind die Leute eher individualistisch, konformistisch oder traditionell?
4. Der Titel des Cartoons ist „Kleine Geschenke". Spekulieren Sie: Wer möchte ein Geschenk? Bekommt er/sie es?
5. Warum macht man Geschenke? Kreuzen Sie an.

	POSITIVER GRUND	NEGATIVER GRUND
um sich zu bedanken[6]	☐	☐
um eine Freude zu machen[7]	☐	☐
um auch ein Geschenk zu bekommen	☐	☐
um andere an uns zu binden	☐	☐
um Hilfe in der Zukunft[8] zu bekommen	☐	☐
aus Tradition	☐	☐
_____ ?	☐	☐

---

[1] *turtleneck sweater* [2] *chrome-rimmed glasses* [3] lehnt . . . auf *is leaning on* [4] stützt . . . auf *is resting one's head on* [5] dreht . . . *is turning around* [6] sich . . . *to thank someone for something* [7] eine . . . *to make someone happy* [8] *future*

KLEINE GESCHENKE

[1]Mir . . . *I don't care* [2]*still* [3]übt . . . *exerts power over him* [4]*acts of extortion* [5]sind . . . *don't matter to me* [6]nach . . . *are longing for oppression* [7]*fault* [8]Ich . . . *I don't need other people to boost my ego* [9]*garbage* [10]statt . . . *instead of doing something reasonable with it*

Arbeit mit dem Text

A. Zur Handlung[1]

1. Wer möchte ein Geschenk?

2. Der Mann ist gegen[2] Geschenke (Bild 2). Warum? Hier sind seine Argumente. In welchen Bildern sagt er das? Schreiben Sie die Nummer des Bildes neben das Argument.

_____ Man kauft jemanden mit Geschenken.
_____ Jemand, der ein Geschenk möchte, sehnt sich nach Unterdrückung.
_____ Geschenke sind etwas für Kinder.
_____ Man sollte nur vernünftige Sachen kaufen.
_____ Die Frau kauft sich selbst, was sie haben will.
_____ Geschenke sind Fremdbestätigung.

3. Wie reagiert die Frau auf die Argumente des Mannes?

Sie wird ärgerlich. ☐
Sie wird traurig. ☐
Sie ignoriert seine Argumente. ☐

Woher wissen Sie das? Was sagt sie?

4. Wer „gewinnt" die Debatte?

5. Was für ein Geschenk möchte die Frau?

B. Zur Sprache

Charakterisieren Sie die Sprache des Mannes und die Sprache der Frau. Wer spricht so: der Mann (Er) oder die Frau (Sie)?

_____ sagt immer das gleiche.
_____ spricht in langen Sätzen.
_____ spricht in kurzen Sätzen.
_____ verwendet viele lange Wörter.
_____ verwendet die Sprache der Psychologie.
_____ verwendet kurze Wörter.
_____ ist aggressiv.

Nach dem Lesen

Spielen Sie diese Szene nach.

---

[1] *plot* [2] *against*

STRUKTUREN UND ÜBUNGEN

3.1 The modal verbs *können, wollen, mögen*

Modal verbs, such as **können** (*can, to be able to, know how to*), **wollen** (*to want to*), and **mögen** (*to like to*) are auxiliary verbs that modify the meaning of the main verb. The main verb appears as an infinitive at the end of the clause.

The modal **können** usually indicates an ability or talent but may also be used to ask permission. The modal **wollen** expresses a desire or an intention to do something. The modal **mögen** expresses a liking; just as its English equivalent, *to like,* it is commonly used with an accusative object.

Kannst du kochen?	*Can you cook?*
Kann ich mitkommen?	*Can I come along?*
Sofie und Willi wollen tanzen gehen.	*Sofie and Willi want to go dancing.*
Ich mag aber nicht tanzen.	*I don't like to dance.*

Modals do not have endings in the **ich-** and **er/sie/es-**forms. Note also that these modal verbs have one stem vowel in all plural forms and in the polite **Sie**-form, and a different stem vowel in the **ich-, du-,** and **er/sie/es-**forms.

können = *can*
wollen = *to want to*
mögen = *to like (to)*

	können	wollen	mögen
ich	kann	will	mag
du	kannst	willst	magst
Sie	können	wollen	mögen
er / sie / es	kann	will	mag
wir	können	wollen	mögen
ihr	könnt	wollt	mögt
Sie	können	wollen	mögen
sie	können	wollen	mögen

Übung 1 Talente

A. Wer kann das?

MODELL Ich kann Deutsch. *oder* Wir können Deutsch.

1. Deutsch	mein Freund / meine Freundin
2. Golf spielen	meine Eltern
3. Ski fahren	ich/wir
4. Klavier spielen	mein Bruder / meine Schwester
5. gut kochen	der Professor / die Professorin

B. Kannst du das?

MODELL Gedichte schreiben → Kannst du Gedichte schreiben?
oder Könnt ihr Gedichte schreiben?

1. Gedichte schreiben	du
2. Auto fahren	ihr
3. tippen	
4. stricken	
5. zeichnen	

Übung 2 Pläne und Fähigkeiten

Was können oder wollen diese Personen (nicht) machen?

MODELL am Samstag / ich / wollen →
Am Samstag will ich Schlittschuh laufen.

fernsehen	kochen	viel Geld verdienen
Golf spielen	nach Europa fliegen	Witze erzählen
Haare schneiden	schlafen	zeichnen
ins Kino gehen	Ski fahren	_____ ?

1. heute abend / ich / wollen
2. morgen / ich / nicht können
3. mein Freund (meine Freundin) / gut können
4. am Samstag / mein Freund (meine Freundin) / wollen
5. mein Freund (meine Freundin) und ich / wollen
6. im Winter / meine Eltern (meine Freunde) / wollen
7. meine Eltern (meine Freunde) / gut können

3.2 The modal verbs *müssen, sollen, dürfen*

The modal **müssen** stresses the necessity to do something. The modal **sollen** is less emphatic than **müssen** and may imply an obligation or a strong suggestion made by another person. The modal **dürfen,** used primarily to indicate permission, can also be used in polite requests.

Jens muß mehr lernen.	*Jens has to study more.*
Vati sagt, du sollst sofort nach Hause kommen.	*Dad says you're supposed to come home immediately.*
Frau Schulz sagt, du sollst morgen zu ihr kommen.	*Ms. Schulz says you should come to see her tomorrow.*
Darf ich die Kerzen anzünden?	*May I light the candles?*

müssen = *must*
sollen = *to be supposed to*
dürfen = *may*

	müssen	sollen	dürfen
ich	muß	soll	darf
du Sie	mußt müssen	sollst sollen	darfst dürfen
er / sie / es	muß	soll	darf
wir	müssen	sollen	dürfen
ihr Sie	müßt müssen	sollt sollen	dürft dürfen
sie	müssen	sollen	dürfen

nicht müssen = *not to have to, not to need to*
nicht dürfen = *mustn't*

When negated, the English expressions *to have to* and *must* undergo a change in meaning. The expression *not have to* implies that there is no need to do something, while *must not* implies a strong warning. These two distinctions are expressed in German by **nicht müssen** and **nicht dürfen,** respectively.

Du mußt das nicht tun. — *You don't have to do that.*
or: *You don't need to do that.*

Du darfst das nicht tun. — *You mustn't do that.*

Achtung!

Remember the two characteristics of modal verbs:

1. no ending in the **ich-** and **er/sie/es-**forms;
2. one stem vowel in the **ich-, du-,** and **er/sie/es-**forms and a different one in the plural, the formal **Sie,** and the infinitive. (Note, however, that **sollen** has the same stem vowel in all forms.)

Übung 3 Jutta hat eine Fünf in Englisch.

Was muß sie machen? Was darf sie nicht machen?

1. mit Jens zusammen lernen
2. viel fernsehen
3. in der Klasse aufpassen und mitschreiben
4. jeden Tag tanzen gehen
5. jeden Tag ihren Wortschatz lernen
6. amerikanische Filme im Original sehen
7. ihren Englischlehrer zum Abendessen einladen
8. für eine Woche nach London fahren
9. fleißig[1] die englische Grammatik lernen

---

[1] *diligently*

Übung 4 Minidialoge

Ergänzen Sie **können, wollen, müssen, sollen, dürfen.**

1. ALBERT: Hallo, Nora. Peter und ich gehen ins Kino. _____[a] du nicht mitkommen?
   NORA: Ich _____[b] schon, aber leider _____[c] ich nicht mitkommen. Ich _____[d] arbeiten.
2. JENS: Vati, _____[a] ich mit Hans fischen gehen?
   HERR WAGNER: Nein! Du hast eine Fünf in Physik, eine Fünf in Latein und eine Fünf in Englisch. Du _____[b] zu Hause bleiben und deine Hausaufgaben machen.
   JENS: Aber, Vati! Meine Hausaufgaben _____[c] ich doch heute abend machen.
   HERR WAGNER: Nein, aber du _____[d] zu Hans gehen, und dann _____[e] ihr eure Hausaufgaben zusammen machen.
3. HEIDI: Hallo, Stefan. Frau Schulz sagt, du _____[a] morgen in ihre Sprechstunde kommen.
   STEFAN: Morgen _____[b] ich nicht, ich habe keine Zeit.
   HEIDI: Das _____[c] du Frau Schulz schon selbst sagen. Bis bald.

3.3 Accusative case: personal pronouns

As in English, certain German pronouns change depending on whether they are the subject or the object of a verb.

Ich bin heute abend zu Hause. Rufst du **mich** an?	*I will be home tonight. Will you call me?*
Er kommt aus Wien. Kennst du **ihn**?	*He is from Vienna. Do you know him?*

A. First- and second-person pronouns: nominative and accusative forms

Nominative	*Accusative*	
ich	mich	*me*
du Sie	dich Sie	*you* *you*
wir	uns	*us*
ihr Sie	euch Sie	*you* *you*

Wer bist **du**? Ich kenne **dich** nicht.	*Who are you? I don't know you.*
Wer seid **ihr**? Ich kenne **euch** nicht.	*Who are you (people)? I don't know you.*

B. Third-person pronouns: nominative and accusative forms

	Nominative	*Accusative*	
Masc.	er	ihn	*him, it*
Fem.	sie		*her, it*
Neuter	es		*it*
Plural	sie		*them*

der → er
den → ihn
das → es
die → sie

Recall that third-person pronouns reflect the grammatical gender of the noun they stand for: **der Film → er; die Gitarre → sie; das Foto → es.** This relationship also holds true for the accusative case: **den Film → ihn; die Gitarre → sie; das Foto → es.** Notice that only the masculine singular pronoun has a different form in the accusative case.

Wo ist der Spiegel? Ich sehe **ihn** nicht.	*Where is the mirror? I don't see it.*
Das ist meine Schwester Jasmin. Du kennst **sie** noch nicht.	*This is my sister Jasmin. You don't know her yet.*
—Wann kaufst du die Bücher?	*When will you buy the books?*
—Ich kaufe **sie** morgen.	*I'll buy them tomorrow.*

Übung 5 Minidialoge

Ergänzen Sie **mich, dich, uns, euch, Sie.**

1. KATRIN: Holst du mich heute abend ab, wenn wir ins Kino gehen?
   THOMAS: Natürlich hole ich _____ ab!
2. STEFAN: Hallooo! Hier bin ich, Albert! Siehst du _____[a] denn nicht?
   ALBERT: Ach, *da* bist du. Ja, jetzt sehe ich _____[b].
3. SABINE: Guten Tag, Frau Schulz. Sie kennen _____ noch nicht. Wir sind neu in Ihrer Klasse. Das ist Rick, und ich bin Sabine.
   FRAU SCHULZ: Guten Tag, Rick. Guten Tag, Sabine.
4. MONIKA: Hallo, Albert. Hallo, Thomas. Katrin und ich besuchen _____ heute.
   ALBERT UND THOMAS: Toll! Bringt Kuchen mit!
5. STEFAN: Heidi, ich mag _____[a]!
   HEIDI: Das ist schön, Stefan. Ich mag _____[b] auch.
6. FRAU SCHULZ: Spreche ich laut genug? Verstehen Sie _____[a]?
   KLASSE: Ja, wir verstehen _____[b] sehr gut, Frau Schulz.
7. STEFAN UND ALBERT: Auf Wiedersehen, Frau Schulz! Schöne Ferien! Und vergessen Sie uns nicht!
   FRAU SCHULZ: Natürlich nicht! Wie kann ich _____ denn je vergessen?

Übung 6 Was machen diese Personen?

MODELL Kauft Michael das Buch? →
Nein, er kauft es nicht, er liest es.

Verwenden Sie diese Verben.

anrufen, ruft an	essen, ißt	trinken
anziehen, zieht an	kaufen	verkaufen
anzünden, zündet an	schreiben	waschen, wäscht
ausmachen, macht aus		

1. Liest Maria den Brief?

2. Ißt Michael die Suppe?

3. Macht Maria den Fernseher an?

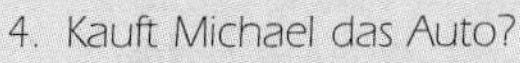

4. Kauft Michael das Auto?

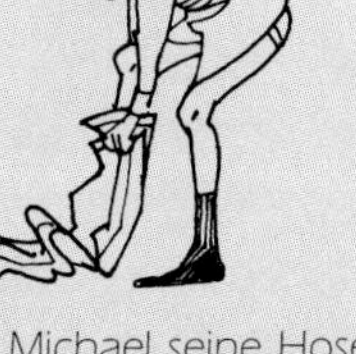

5. Zieht Michael seine Hose aus?

6. Trägt Maria den Rock?

7. Bestellt[1] Michael das Schnitzel?

8. Besucht Michael seinen Freund?

9. Kämmt Maria ihr Haar?

10. Bläst Michael die Kerzen aus[2]?

3.4 Word order: dependent clauses

Use a conjunction such as **wenn** (*when, if*) or **weil** (*because*) to add a modifying clause to a sentence.

Mehmet hört Musik, **wenn** er traurig ist.	*Mehmet listens to music whenever he is sad.*
Renate geht nach Hause, **weil** sie müde ist.	*Renate is going home because she is tired.*

---

[1]bestellen *to order (in a restaurant)* [2]Bläst . . . aus *is (he) blowing out*

In the preceding examples, the first clause is the main clause. The clause introduced by a conjunction is called a *dependent clause.* In German, the verb in a dependent clause occurs at the end of the clause.

MAIN CLAUSE	DEPENDENT CLAUSE
Ich bleibe im Bett,	wenn ich krank **bin.**
I stay in bed	*when I am sick.*

When **wenn** or **weil** begins a clause, the conjugated verb occurs at the end of the clause.

In sentences beginning with a dependent clause, the entire clause acts as the first element in the sentence. The verb of the main clause comes directly after the dependent clause, separated by a comma. As in all German statements, the verb is in second position. The subject of the main clause follows the verb.

I	II	III	
DEPENDENT CLAUSE	VERB	SUBJECT	
Wenn ich krank bin,	bleibe	ich	im Bett.
When I'm sick, I stay in bed.			
Weil sie müde ist,	geht	Renate	nach Hause.
Because she's tired, Renate is going home.			

Übung 7 Warum denn?

Beantworten Sie die Fragen.

MODELL Warum gehst du nicht in die Schule? → Weil ich krank bin.

1. Warum gehst du nicht in die Schule?
2. Warum liegt dein Bruder im Bett?
3. Warum eßt ihr denn schon wieder?
4. Warum kommt Nora nicht mit ins Kino?
5. Warum sieht Jutta schon wieder fern?
6. Warum sitzt du allein in deinem Zimmer?
7. Warum trinken sie Bier?
8. Warum machst du denn das Licht an?
9. Warum singt Jens den ganzen Tag?
10. Warum bleibst du zu Hause?

- **a.** Durst haben
- **b.** krank sein
- **c.** traurig sein
- **d.** Langeweile haben
- **e.** Angst haben
- **f.** glücklich sein
- **g.** lernen müssen
- **h.** müde sein
- **i.** Hunger haben
- **j.** keine Zeit haben

Übung 8 Ist das immer so?

Sagen Sie, wie das für andere Personen ist und wie das für Sie ist.

MODELL S1: Was macht Albert, wenn er müde ist?
S2: Wenn Albert müde ist, geht er nach Hause.
S1: Und du?
S2: Wenn ich müde bin, trinke ich einen Kaffee.

1. Albert ist müde.
2. Maria ist glücklich.
3. Herr Ruf hat Durst.
4. Frau Wagner ist in Eile.
5. Heidi hat Hunger.
6. Frau Schulz hat Ferien.
7. Hans hat Angst.
8. Stefan ist krank.

a. Sie trifft Michael.
b. Er geht nach Hause.
c. Sie fährt mit dem Taxi.
d. Sie kauft einen Hamburger.
e. Er trinkt eine Cola.
f. Er geht zum Arzt.
g. Er ruft: „Mama, Mama".
h. Sie fliegt nach Deutschland.

3.5 Dependent clauses and separable-prefix verbs

As you know, the prefix of a separable-prefix verb occurs at the end of an independent clause.

Rolf **steht** immer früh **auf.**	*Rolf always gets up early.*

In a dependent clause, the prefix is attached to the verb form, which is placed at the end of the clause.

Rolf ist immer müde, wenn er früh **aufsteht.**	*Rolf is always tired when he gets up early.*
Helga, bitte **mach** das Fenster nicht **auf!** Es wird kalt, wenn du es **aufmachst.**	*Helga, please don't open the window. It gets cold when you open it.*

When there are two verbs in a dependent clause, such as a modal verb and an infinitive, the modal verb comes last, following the infinitive.

INDEPENDENT CLAUSE	Rolf **muß** früh **aufstehen.**	*Rolf has to get up early.*
DEPENDENT CLAUSE	Er ist müde, wenn er früh **aufstehen muß.**	*He is tired when he has to get up early.*
INDEPENDENT CLAUSE	Helga hat kein Geld. Sie **kann** nichts **machen.**	*Helga doesn't have any money. She can't do anything.*
DEPENDENT CLAUSE	Sie hat Langeweile, weil sie nichts **machen kann.**	*She's bored because she can't do anything.*

Übung 9 Warum ist das so?

MODELL Jürgen ist wütend, weil er früh aufstehen muß.

1. Jürgen ist wütend.
2. Silvia ist froh.
3. Claire ist in Eile.
4. Josef ist traurig.
5. Thomas geht nicht zu Fuß.
6. Willi hat selten Langeweile.
7. Marta hat Angst vor Wasser.
8. Mehmet fährt in die Türkei.

a. Sie muß noch einkaufen.
b. Er steht immer so früh auf.
c. Seine Freundin nimmt ihn zur Uni mit.
d. Er sieht immer fern.
e. Sie kann nicht schwimmen.
f. Er will seine Eltern besuchen.
g. Melanie ruft ihn nicht an.
h. Sie muß heute nicht arbeiten.

KAPITEL 4

Blick über Freiburg, eine Stadt mit einer fast 900-jährigen Geschichte

In **Kapitel 4,** you will begin to talk about things that happened in the past: your own experiences and those of others. You will also talk about different kinds of memories.

Ereignisse und Erinnerungen

THEMEN
Tagesablauf
Erlebnisse anderer Personen
Geburtstage und Jahrestage
Ereignisse

LEKTÜRE
Invasion der Ahnenforscher
Thomas fliegt nach Deutschland

KULTURELLES
Universität und Studium
Ladenschluß in Deutschland
Feiertage und Brauchtum
Kulturprojekt: Deutsche Einwanderer
Porträt: Hannah Arendt und Hannover
Videoecke: Christkindl

STRUKTUREN
4.1 Talking about the past: the perfect tense
4.2 Strong and weak past participles
4.3 Dates and ordinal numbers
4.4 Prepositions of time: **um, am, im**
4.5 Past participles with and without **ge-**

SPRECHSITUATIONEN

Tagesablauf

➤ **Grammatik 4.1**

Ich habe geduscht.

Ich habe gefrühstückt.

Ich bin in die Uni gegangen.

Ich bin in einem Kurs gewesen.

Ich habe mit meinen Freunden Kaffee getrunken.

Ich bin nach Hause gekommen.

Ich habe zu Mittag gegessen.

Ich bin nachmittags zu Hause geblieben.

Ich habe abends gelernt.

Situation 1 Was haben Sie gemacht?

Bringen Sie diese Aktivitäten in eine chronologische Reihenfolge.

Gemüsemarkt in Freiburg. Waren Sie heute schon beim Einkaufen?

1. Heute morgen . . .
   _____ habe ich meine Bücher genommen.
   _____ habe ich gefrühstückt.
   _____ habe ich geduscht.
   _____ bin ich in die Uni gegangen.
2. Gestern nachmittag . . .
   _____ bin ich nach Hause gekommen.
   _____ habe ich Basketball gespielt.
   _____ habe ich Essen gemacht.
   _____ bin ich einkaufen gegangen.
3. Gestern abend . . .
   _____ habe ich einen Film gesehen.
   _____ habe ich zu Abend gegessen.
   _____ bin ich ins Bett gegangen.
   _____ habe ich das Geschirr gespült.
4. Letzten Samstag . . .
   _____ bin ich spät ins Bett gegangen.
   _____ habe ich viel getanzt.
   _____ habe ich mit einer Freundin gesprochen.
   _____ bin ich auf ein Fest gegangen.
5. Letzten Mittwoch . . .
   _____ bin ich ins Kino gegangen.
   _____ habe ich in der Bibliothek gearbeitet.
   _____ bin ich in die Uni gefahren.
   _____ habe ich gearbeitet.

Situation 2 Dialog: Das Fest

Silvia und Jürgen sitzen in der Mensa und essen zu Mittag.

SILVIA: Ich bin furchtbar ____.
JÜRGEN: Bist du wieder so spät ins Bett ______?
SILVIA: Ja. Ich bin heute früh erst um vier Uhr nach Hause _______.
JÜRGEN: Wo ____ du denn so lange?
SILVIA: Auf einem Fest.
JÜRGEN: _____________?
SILVIA: Ja, ich habe ein paar alte Freunde _____, und wir haben uns sehr gut _______.
JÜRGEN: Kein Wunder, ___________!

Situation 3 Das letzte Mal

MODELL Wann hast du mit deiner Mutter gesprochen?
Ich habe gestern mit meiner Mutter gesprochen.

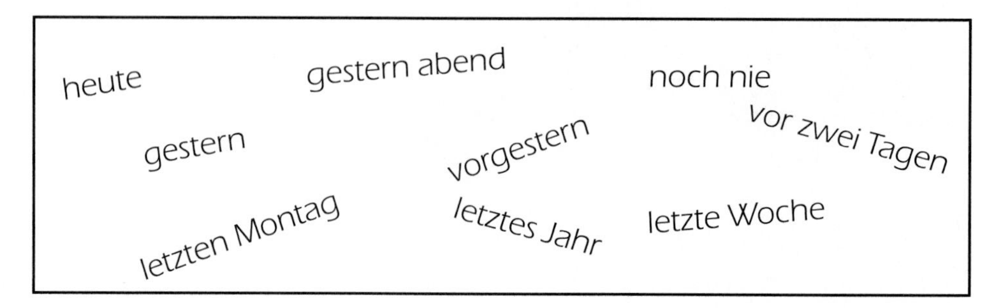

1. Wann hast du dein Auto gewaschen?
2. Wann hast du gebadet?
3. Wann bist du ins Theater gegangen?
4. Wann hast du deine beste Freundin / deinen besten Freund getroffen?
5. Wann hast du einen Film gesehen?
6. Wann bist du in die Disko gegangen?
7. Wann hast du gelernt?
8. Wann bist du einkaufen gegangen?
9. Wann hast du eine Zeitung gelesen?
10. Wann hast du das Geschirr gespült?
11. Wann bist du spät ins Bett gegangen?
12. Wann bist du den ganzen Abend zu Hause geblieben?

Kultur ... Landeskunde ... Informationen

Universität und Studium

- Wann haben Sie mit dem Studium am College oder an der Universität angefangen?
- Welche Voraussetzungen[1] (High-School-Abschluß, Prüfungen usw.) braucht man zum Studium?
- An welchen Universitäten haben Sie sich beworben[2]?
- Studieren Sie an einer privaten oder staatlichen Hochschule[3]?
- Müssen Sie Studiengebühren[4] bezahlen?
- Wie lange dauert Ihr Studium wahrscheinlich?
- Welchen Abschluß[5] haben Sie am Ende Ihres Studiums?
- Was für Kurse müssen Sie belegen?

Heinrich-Heine-Universität Düsseldorf

[1]*prerequisites* [2]sich . . . *applied* [3]*college, university* [4]*fees, tuition* [5]*degree; diploma*

Die Universitäten in Deutschland sind Institutionen der Bundesländer, also nicht privat. Studiengebühren gibt es nicht. Man braucht normalerweise das Abitur,[6] um an einer Universität zu studieren. Beim Abitur nach 13 Schuljahren sind die Studienanfänger ungefähr 20 Jahre alt.

Für viele Fächer, vor allem Medizin, Zahnmedizin,[7] Pharmazie und Psychologie gibt es einen „Numerus Clausus". Das bedeutet, nur wer sehr gute Noten hat, wird zum Studium zugelassen.[8] Manchmal gibt es außerdem noch einen Test.

Das Studium für die meisten Fächer dauert fünf bis sieben Jahre. Oft dauert es auch länger, wenn man promoviert, das heißt, einen Doktor[9] als Abschluß haben will. Andere Abschlüsse sind Magister,[10] Diplom[11] oder Staatsexamen.[12] Die Studierenden haben meistens viel Freiheit in der Wahl[13] ihrer Seminare und Vorlesungen. Wenn die Studierenden oder ihre Eltern den Lebensunterhalt[14] nicht selbst finanzieren können, gibt es finanzielle Hilfe vom Staat, das sogenannte BAföG.

- Vergleichen Sie das Studium in Deutschland und in den USA. Was ist anders? Was ist ähnlich?

[6] roughly: *high school diploma* [7] *dentistry* [8] *admitted* [9] *doctorate* [10] *master's degree* [11] *certificate (usually in the technical fields)* [12] *state certified exam* [13] *choice* [14] *living costs*

Erlebnisse anderer Personen

➤ **Grammatik 4.2**

Jutta ist ins Schwimmbad gefahren.

Sie hat in der Sonne gelegen.

Sie ist geschwommen.

Sie hat Musik gehört.

Jens und Robert haben Postkarten geschrieben.

Sie sind in den Bergen gewandert.

Sie haben Tennis gespielt.

Sie haben viel gelesen.

Situation 4 Richards Wochenende

Situation 5 Dialog: Hausaufgaben für Deutsch

Heute ist Montag. Auf dem Schulhof[1] des Albertus-Magnus-Gymnasiums sprechen Jens, Jutta und ihre Freundin Angelika übers Wochenende.

JENS: Na, habt ihr die Hausaufgaben für Deutsch ______?
JUTTA: Hausaufgaben? Haben wir für Deutsch Hausaufgaben auf?
JENS: Habt ihr das erste Kapitel von dem Roman nicht _____?
JUTTA: Hast du das _____, Angelika?
ANGELIKA: Ich habe keine Ahnung, wovon Jens spricht!
JENS: Also ihr habt es _______. Habt ihr denn wenigstens Mathe gemacht?
ANGELIKA: Wir haben es _____, aber die Aufgaben waren zu schwer. Da haben wir ______.
JENS: Was habt ihr denn übers Wochenende überhaupt ______?
ANGELIKA: Eigentlich eine ganze Menge. Ich habe Musik _____ und ______.
JENS: Das ist aber nicht viel.
ANGELIKA: Doch! Und am Samstagabend haben Jutta und ich über alles Mögliche ________ und ________.
JUTTA: Ich bin am Sonntag mit meinen Eltern und Hans _____________. Wir waren an der Isar[2] und haben ein Picknick ______.
JENS: Kein Wunder, daß ihr keine Zeit für Hausaufgaben hattet!

---

[1] *school yard* [2] *river that flows through Munich*

Situation 6 Zum Schreiben: Ein Tagebuch

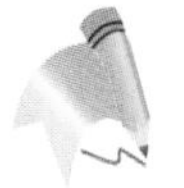

28. Juli 1996

Habe einen total coolen Jungen kennengelernt! Er heißt Billy, eigentlich Paul, aber er sieht aus wie Billy Idol. Er ist total süß!! Habe gleich einen Brief an Geli geschrieben und ihr von Billy erzählt. Warte jetzt auf Gelis Antwort... Außerdem haben wir Zeugnisse bekommen. Das war nicht so gut...

Juttas Tagebuch

Schreiben Sie auch ein Tagebuch. Vielleicht haben Sie das früher schon einmal auf englisch gemacht. Machen Sie sich zuerst ein paar Notizen. Was ist letzte Woche passiert? Was haben Sie gemacht? Was wollen Sie nicht vergessen?

MODELL Letzte Woche habe/bin ich . . .

Situation 7 Informationsspiel: Wochenende

MODELL S1: Was hat Frau Ruf am Samstag gemacht?
S2: Sie hat einen Brief geschrieben.
S1: Was hast du am Samstag gemacht?
S2: Ich ______ .

	am Freitag	am Samstag	am Sonntag
Frau Ruf		hat einen Brief geschrieben	hat mit einer Freundin gefrühstückt
Herr Ruf	hat das Haus geputzt		
Jutta	ist tanzen gegangen	ist ins Kino gegangen	
Hans	hat seine Hausaufgaben gemacht		
Michael		hat sein Auto gewaschen	hat Tennis gespielt
Maria			ist den ganzen Tag zu Hause geblieben
mein Partner / meine Partnerin			

Kultur ... Landeskunde ... Informationen

Ladenschluß in Deutschland

Wie ist das in Ihrem Land?

- Zu welchen Zeiten kann man einkaufen?
- Welche Geschäfte sind am Wochenende geöffnet? Welche Geschäfte sind am Wochenende geschlossen?
- Wann kann man Lebensmittel einkaufen?
- Gibt es Tage, an denen alles geschlossen ist?

Wie ist das in Deutschland? Lesen Sie den Artikel und beantworten Sie die Fragen.

- Zu welchen Zeiten kann man in Deutschland einkaufen?
- Kann man am Wochenende einkaufen? Wenn ja, wann?
- An welchen Samstagen ist bis 18 Uhr geöffnet?
- Wie lange ist am „langen Donnerstag" geöffnet?
- In welchen europäischen Ländern gibt es auch nur *einen* „langen" Verkaufstag pro Woche?

Öffnungszeiten des Postamts im österreichischen Bregenz

Deutschland ist geöffnet
von montags bis freitags von 7 bis 18.30 Uhr, samstags von 7 bis 14 Uhr, am ersten Samstag im Monat und an den vier Samstagen im Monat vor Heiligabend[5] bis 18 Uhr, zwischen April und September bis 16 Uhr. Das ergibt maximal 68,5 Stunden in der Woche. Wer die nicht komplett ausnutzt,[6] darf am langen Donnerstag bis 20.30 Uhr offen halten. Bäckereien dürfen täglich eine halbe Stunde früher öffnen. Hinzu kommen jeweils die Sonderbestimmungen[7] für Tankstellen,[8] Apotheken und Zeitungsläden, für Shops auf Bahn-, Flug- und Fährhäfen sowie in den Kur- und Erholungsorten.[9]

[1] *individual regulations* [2] *variable* [3] *communities* [4] *limit* [5] *Christmas Eve* [6] *takes advantage of* [7] *special regulations* [8] *gas stations* [9] *spa and resort towns*

Geburtstage und Jahrestage

➤ **Grammatik 4.3–4.4**

Marta hat am ersten Oktober Geburtstag.
Richard hat am zwölften Oktober Geburtstag.
Frau Schmitz hat am achten Juli Geburtstag.
Mehmet hat am einunddreißigsten Juli Geburtstag.
Josef hat am fünfzehnten April Geburtstag.
Veronika hat am siebenundzwanzigsten April Geburtstag.

Situation 8 Dialog: Welcher Tag ist heute? 

Marta und Sofie sitzen im Café.

SOFIE: Welcher Tag ist heute?
MARTA: _____.
SOFIE: Nein, welches Datum?
MARTA: Ach so, der ______.
SOFIE: Mensch, heute ist Willis Geburtstag! Er hat am _______ Geburtstag.
MARTA: Wirklich? Ich dachte, er hat ______ Geburtstag.
SOFIE: Nein, Christian hat im August Geburtstag, aber Willi ____.
MARTA: Hast du denn schon ________?
SOFIE: Das ist es ja! Ich muß gleich noch ein Geschenk kaufen.
MARTA: Na, dann ______!

Situation 9 Geburtstage

MODELL S1: Wann ist Willi geboren?
S2: Am dreißigsten Mai 1972.

1. Willi (30. Mai 1972)
2. Sofie (9. November 1971)
3. Claire (1. Dezember 1971)
4. Melanie (3. April 1975)
5. Nora (4. Juli 1979)
6. Thomas (17. Januar 1979)
7. Heidi (23. Juni 1976)
8. Ihr Partner / Ihre Partnerin (_____)
9. sein/ihr Vater (_____)
10. seine/ihre Mutter (_____)

Situation 10 Erfindungen und Entdeckungen

MODELL S1: Wer hat den Bleistift erfunden?
S2: _____
S1: Wann hat er ihn erfunden?
S2: _____

Cyril Demian 1829

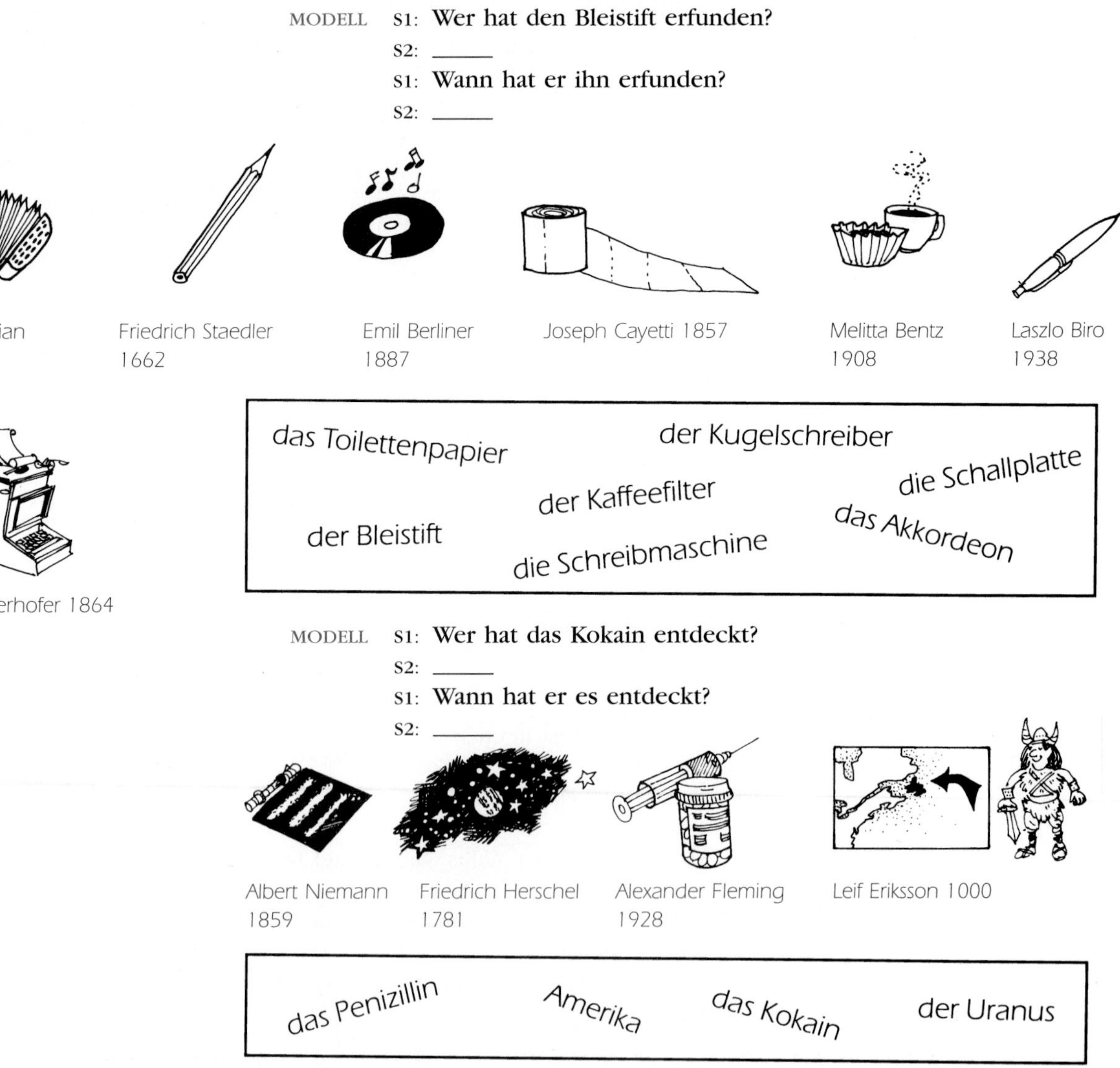

Friedrich Staedler 1662

Emil Berliner 1887

Joseph Cayetti 1857

Melitta Bentz 1908

Laszlo Biro 1938

Peter Mitterhofer 1864

das Toilettenpapier · der Kugelschreiber · der Kaffeefilter · die Schallplatte · der Bleistift · die Schreibmaschine · das Akkordeon

MODELL S1: Wer hat das Kokain entdeckt?
S2: _____
S1: Wann hat er es entdeckt?
S2: _____

Albert Niemann 1859

Friedrich Herschel 1781

Alexander Fleming 1928

Leif Eriksson 1000

das Penizillin · Amerika · das Kokain · der Uranus

Kultur ... Landeskunde ... Informationen

Feiertage und Brauchtum[1]

- Welches sind *die* Familienfeste in Ihrem Land?
- Was macht man an diesen Festen?
- Wer feiert[2] zusammen?
- Kennen Sie deutsche Feiertage und Bräuche[3]? Wenn ja, welche?

Auf dem Christkindlmarkt in München im Jahre 1897

Der Adventskalender: Ein deutscher Exportartikel in christlicher Tradition wird 85 Jahre alt. Amerika ist das Exportland Nummer 1.

- Weihnachten in Deutschland: An welchen Tagen feiert man? Der Adventskalender gibt Ihnen einen Tip.
- Welche deutschen Weihnachtstraditionen kennen Sie?
- Wie feiern die Deutschen am liebsten Weihnachten? Analysieren Sie die Umfrage.

TAG FÜR TAG: Adventskalender lassen die Erwartungen steigen

FOCUS-FRAGE

„Wo verbringen Sie Weihnachten?"

EIN FAMILIENFEST ZU HAUSE

von 1300 Befragten* antworteten

zu Hause	73 %
bei den Eltern/Kindern	21 %
bei Freunden	3 %
im Urlaub	3 %

83 Prozent der Deutschen verbringen Weihnachten im Kreis der Familie, 7 Prozent zusammen mit dem Partner, 6 Prozent mit Freunden, 4 Prozent feiern alleine.

* Repräsentative Umfrage des Sample-Instituts für FOCUS im Dezember

[1] *tradition* [2] *celebrates* [3] *customs*

Situation 11 Interview

1. Wann bist du geboren (Tag, Monat, Jahr)? Wann ist dein Freund / deine Freundin geboren (Tag, Monat, Jahr)? Wann ist dein Vater / deine Mutter geboren (Tag, Monat, Jahr)?
2. Wann bist du in die Schule gekommen (Monat, Jahr)? Wann hast du angefangen zu studieren (Monat, Jahr)?
3. Was war der wichtigste Tag in deinem Leben? Was ist da passiert? In welchem Monat war das? In welchem Jahr?
4. In welchem Monat warst du zum ersten Mal verliebt? hast du zum ersten Mal Geld verdient? hast du einen Unfall gehabt?
5. An welchen Tagen in der Woche arbeitest du? hast du frei? gehst du ins Kino? besuchst du deine Eltern? hast du Geld? gehst du ins Sprachlabor?
6. Um wieviel Uhr stehst du auf? ist dein erster Kurs? gehst du nach Hause? gehst du ins Bett?

Ereignisse

➤ **Grammatik 4.5**

1. Wann sind Sie aufgewacht?
2. Wann sind Sie aufgestanden?
3. Wann sind Sie von zu Hause weggegangen?
4. Wann hat Ihr Kurs angefangen?
5. Wann hat Ihr Kurs aufgehört?
6. Wann sind Sie nach Hause gekommen?
7. Wann haben Sie unsere Prüfungen korrigiert?

1. Wann hast du eingekauft?
2. Wann hast du das Geschirr gespült?
3. Wann hast du mit deiner Freundin telefoniert?
4. Wann hast du ferngesehen?
5. Wann hast du dein Fahrrad repariert?
6. Wann bist du abends ausgegangen?

Situation 12 Informationsspiel: Das Wochenende der Nachbarn

MODELL S1: Was hat Herr Siebert am Freitag gemacht?
S2: Er hat einen Fernseher repariert.

	am Freitag	am Samstag	am Sonntag
Herr Siebert	hat einen Fernseher repariert		hat seine Nichte besucht
Herr Thelen		ist verreist	
Frau Gretter		hat Ernst ein Märchen erzählt	
mein Partner / meine Partnerin			

Situation 13 Interview: Gestern

1. Wann bist du aufgestanden?
2. Was hast du gefrühstückt?
3. Wie bist du zur Uni gekommen?
4. Was war dein erster Kurs?

5. Was hast du zu Mittag gegessen?
6. Was hast du getrunken?
7. Wen hast du getroffen?
8. Was hast du nachmittags gemacht?
9. Wie war das Wetter?
10. Wo bist du um sechs Uhr abends gewesen?
11. Was hast du abends gemacht?
12. Wann bist du ins Bett gegangen?
13. Ist gestern etwas Interessantes passiert? Was?

Situation 14 Erinnerungen: Ein indiskretes Interview

1. Wann hast du deinen ersten Kuß bekommen? Von wem?
2. Wann bist du zum ersten Mal ausgegangen? Mit wem?
3. Wann hast du deinen Führerschein gemacht?
4. Wann hast du dein erstes Bier getrunken?
5. Wann hast du deine erste Zigarette geraucht?
6. Wann hast du zum ersten Mal ein F bekommen? In welchem Fach?
7. Wann bist du zum ersten Mal nachts nicht nach Hause gekommen?
8. Wann _____ ?

Situation 15 Rollenspiel: Das Studentenleben

S1: Sie sind Reporter/Reporterin von einer Unizeitung in Österreich und machen ein Interview zum Thema: Studentenleben in Nordamerika. Fragen Sie, was Ihr Partner / Ihre Partnerin gestern alles gemacht hat: am Vormittag, am Mittag, am Nachmittag und am Abend.

Hints for working with the Kulturprojekt

Use an historical atlas such as *The Times Atlas of World History.* Immigration data are also usually included in standard reference works such as the *Information Please Almanac* (look up "immigration" in the index).

Kulturprojekt Deutsche Einwanderer[1]

A. Suchen Sie in der Bibliothek oder in einem Nachschlagewerk[2] nach den folgenden Informationen. Ergänzen Sie die Tabelle.

- In welchen Jahrzehnten sind besonders viele Menschen in Ihr Land eingewandert?
- Wie viele von ihnen waren Deutsche?
- Wieviel Prozent aller Einwanderer in Ihr Land waren Deutsche?

---

[1]*immigrants* [2]*reference work*

Deutsche Einwanderer im 19. Jahrhundert

Jahrzehnt	Gesamteinwanderung[1]	Deutsche Einwanderung	Prozent der Deutschen an der Gesamteinwanderung

B. Suchen Sie folgende Informationen in einem Geschichtsbuch oder -atlas.

- Wie war die politische und gesellschaftliche[2] Situation in Deutschland oder Europa, als besonders viele Deutsche ausgewandert sind?
- Schreiben Sie die zehn wichtigsten Ereignisse[3] in Deutschland oder Europa seit 1830 mit Jahreszahlen auf.

C. Spuren[4] der Deutschen

- Gibt es in Ihrer Nähe Städte oder Orte mit deutschen Namen? Wie heißen sie?
- Gibt es in Ihrer Stadt ein Viertel[5] mit deutschen Geschäften und Restaurants?

---

[1] *total number of immigrants* [2] *social* [3] *events* [4] *traces* [5] *district, neighborhood*

Porträt

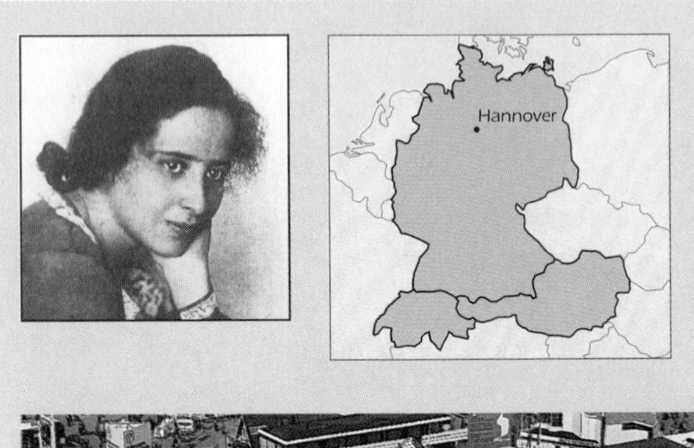

Die Soziologin und Politologin Hannah Arendt (1906–1975) wurde als Kind jüdischer[1] Eltern in Hannover geboren. Sie emigrierte 1933 nach Frankreich und 1940 in die USA. 1959 wurde sie Professorin in Princeton. Sie interessierte sich für totalitäre Regime im 20. Jahrhundert und wie sie das Volk kontrollieren: durch Terror, Konzentrationslager[2] und Verletzung[3] der Menschenrechte.[4] Von New York aus half sie vielen Juden, aus Europa zu fliehen.

Hannover ist bekannt als Messestadt.[5] Die Messe in Hannover ist die größte Industriemesse der Welt. Sie findet zweimal im Jahr statt.[6] Die Stadt Hannover wurde im 2. Weltkrieg fast völlig[7] zerstört[8] und sehr modern wiederaufgebaut.[9]

Die hannoversche Messe

[1] *Jewish* [2] *concentration camps* [3] *violation* [4] *human rights* [5] *trade fair city* [6] findet . . . statt *takes place* [7] *completely* [8] *destroyed* [9] *reconstructed*

Christkindl

Der Christkindlmarkt in Nürnberg wird jedes Jahr zur Weihnachtszeit vom Christkindl eröffnet. In diesem Clip lernen Sie das Christkindl kennen.

- Wer spielt die Rolle des Nürnberger Christkindls?
- Wie alt ist diese Person?
- Was für Fragen stellen ihr die Kinder?
- Was sind ihre Hobbys?

Was braucht das Nürnberger Christkindl am dringendsten? Jawohl, warme Schuhe und gute Nerven.

Unterwegs — On the Road

die **Fahrkarte, -n** — ticket

der **Bahnhof, ¨-e** — train station
der **Führerschein, -e** — driver's license
der **Schlafwagen, -** — sleeping car
der **Unfall, ¨-e** — accident

ab·fahren, fährt . . . ab, ist abgefahren* — to depart

Zeit und Reihenfolge — Time and Sequence

der **Abend, -e** (R) — evening
am Abend — in the evening
der **Nachmittag, -e** — afternoon
der **Vormittag, -e** — late morning

das **Datum, Daten** — date
welches Datum ist heute? — what is today's date?
das **Mal, -e** — time
das **letzte Mal** — the last time
zum ersten Mal — for the first time

abends — evenings, in the evening
gestern — yesterday
gestern abend — last night
letzt- — last
letzte Woche — last week
letzten Montag — last Monday
letzten Sommer — last summer
letztes Wochenende — last weekend
nachmittags — afternoons, in the afternoon
nachts — nights, at night
vorgestern — the day before yesterday

an — on; in
am Abend — in the evening
am ersten Oktober — on the first of October
an welchem Tag? — on what day?
bis (R) — until
bis um vier Uhr — until four o'clock
einmal — once
warst du schon einmal . . . ? — were you ever . . . ?
erst — not until
erst um vier Uhr — not until four o'clock
früh (R) — in the morning
bis um vier Uhr früh — until four in the morning
schon (R) — already
seit — since; for
seit zwei Jahren — for two years
über — over
übers Wochenende — over the weekend
vor — ago
vor zwei Tagen — two days ago

Schule und Universität — School and University

die **Aufgabe, -n** — assignment
die **Grundschule, -n** — elementary school
die **Vorlesung, -en** — lecture

der **Kugelschreiber, -** — ballpoint pen

das **Gymnasium, Gymnasien** — high school, college prep school

auf·haben — to be assigned
was haben wir auf? — what's our homework?
halten, hält, gehalten — to hold
ein **Referat halten** — to give a paper / oral report

Feste und Feiertage — Holidays

der **Feiertag, -e** — holiday
der **Nationalfeiertag, -e** — national holiday

das **Familienfest, -e** — family celebration

Weihnachten — Christmas

Ähnliche Wörter

die **Tradition, -en**; das **Picknick, -s**; der **Muttertag**; der **Valentinstag**

Ordinalzahlen — Ordinal Numbers

erst-
der erste Oktober
zweit-
dritt-

*Strong and irregular verbs are listed in the **Wortschatz** with the third-person singular, if there is a stem-vowel change, and with the past participle. All verbs that use **sein** as the auxiliary in the present perfect tense are listed with **ist.**

viert-	**zehnt-**
fünft-	**elft-**
sechst-	**zwölft-**
siebt-	**dreizehnt-**
acht-	**zwanzigst-**
neunt-	**hundertst-**

Sonstige Substantive — Other Nouns

die **Ahnung**	idea, suspicion
keine Ahnung	(I have) no idea
die **Erinnerung, -en**	memory, remembrance
die **Limonade, -n**	soft drink
die **Menge, -n**	amount
eine ganze Menge	a whole lot
die **Nachbarin, -nen**	female neighbor
die **Rechnung, -en**	bill; check (in restaurant)
die **Umfrage, -n**	survey
die **Unizeitung, -en**	university newspaper
der **Einwanderer, -**	immigrant
der **Keller, -**	basement, cellar
der **Kuß, Küsse**	kiss
der **Nachbar, -n** (*wk. masc.*)	male neighbor
der **Ort, -e**	place, town
der **Strand, ¨e**	beach
das **Erlebnis, -se**	experience
das **Geschirr**	dishes
Geschirr spülen	to wash the dishes
das **Jahrzehnt, -e**	decade
das **Märchen, -**	fairy tale
das **Sprachlabor, -s**	language laboratory
das **Tagebuch, ¨er**	diary

Ähnliche Wörter

die **Computerfirma, Computerfirmen;** die **Information, -en;** die **Reporterin, -nen;** die **Rolle, -n;** die **Wäsche;** die **Zigarette, -n** der **Garten, ¨;** der **Kaffeefilter, -;** der **Reporter, -;** der **Tee;** der **Uranus** das **Akkordeon, -s;** das **Café, -s;** das **Interview, -s;** das **Penizillin;** das **Prozent, -e;** das **Studentenleben;** das **Theater, -;** das **Thema, Themen;** das **Toilettenpapier;** das **Wunder; kein Wunder**

Sonstige Verben — Other Verbs

an·fangen, fängt . . . an, angefangen	to begin
antworten*	to answer
auf·wachen	to wake up
aus·wandern, ist ausgewandert	to emigrate
bezahlen	to pay (for)
dauern	to last
entdecken	to discover
erfinden, erfunden	to invent
ergänzen	to complete, fill in the blanks
passieren, ist passiert	to happen
spülen	to wash; to rinse
verdienen	to earn
verstehen	to understand
war, warst, waren	was, were

Ähnliche Wörter

diskutieren; essen, ißt, gegessen (R); **zu Abend essen; fotografieren; gewinnen, gewonnen; halten, gehalten; korrigieren; sitzen, gesessen; telefonieren; weg·gehen, ist weggegangen**

Adjektive und Adverbien — Adjectives and Adverbs

furchtbar	terrible
geschlossen	closed
links	left
mit dem linken Fuß auf·stehen, ist aufgestanden	to get up on the wrong side of the bed
süß	sweet
verliebt	in love

Ähnliche Wörter

politisch, total

Sonstige Wörter und Ausdrücke — Other Words and Expressions

diese, dieser, dieses (R)	this, that, these, those
doch!	yes (on the contrary)
etwas	something
etwas Interessantes/Neues	something interesting/new
genug	enough
gleich	right away
in (R)	in; at
im Garten	in the garden
im Café	at the cafe
ja	indeed
das ist es ja!	that's just it
stimmt!	that's right
überhaupt	anyway
wem	whom (*dative*)
wen	whom (*accusative*)
wenigstens	at least
zu	too
zu schwer	too heavy

*Regular weak verbs are listed only with their infinitive.

LESEECKE

LEKTÜRE 1

Vor dem Lesen

1. Machen Sie Ahnenforschung.[1] Aus welchem Land / welchen Ländern sind Ihre Vorfahren[2] gekommen? Zeichnen Sie einen Stammbaum.[3]
2. Welche deutschen Nachnamen kennen Sie? Wer in Ihrem Deutschkurs hat einen ursprünglich[4] deutschen Nachnamen?
3. Wie viele US-Bürger tragen einen deutschen Nachnamen? Raten Sie: Jeder dritte? jeder vierte? jeder fünfte? jeder zehnte?
4. Kennen Sie berühmte US-Amerikaner mit einem deutschen Nachnamen? Wen?
5. Lesen Sie den Titel, Untertitel und den ersten Absatz[5] des Textes. Was ist das Thema? Kreuzen Sie den richtigen Nebensatz[6] an.

Amerikaner/Amerikanerinnen mit deutschen Familiennamen sind nach Deutschland gekommen,

- □ weil sie in Goslar Station machen wollten.[7]
- □ weil sie den Großen Teich[8] sehen wollten.
- □ weil sie Leute mit dem gleichen Familiennamen kennenlernen wollten.
- □ weil sie alte Bekannte und Verwandte besuchen wollten.

---

[1]*genealogy* [2]*ancestors* [3]*family tree* [4]*originally* [5]*paragraph* [6]*clause* [7]Station . . . *wanted to stop* [8]den . . . *the Great Pond (Atlantic Ocean)*

Tausende von Amerikanern machten in Goslar Station

Invasion der Ahnenforscher[1]

Im Frühsommer des Jahres 1994 sind mehrere hundert amerikanische Familien über den Großen Teich gekommen, um ihre unbekannten Namensvettern und -cousinen zu besuchen. Vom 19. bis 22. Juni haben sie auch in Goslar und Umgebung Station gemacht. Eine Invasion der Ahnenforscher!

Der Hintergrund in imponierenden[2] Zahlen: Exakt 57,9 Millionen US-Bürger[3] tragen einen deutschen Namen, was bedeutet, daß etwa jeder 4. Amerikaner deutsche Vorfahren hat. So hat es das Amt[4] für Bevölkerungsstatistik in Washington in seinem Bericht[5] für das Jahr 1992 ausgewiesen.[6] Der Urahn[7] der Rockefellers war ein fränkischer[8] Bauer[9] namens Roggenfelder, die Automobilfirmen Studebaker und Chrysler sind auf die deutschen Auswandererfamilien Stutenbäcker und Kreisler zurückzuführen,[10] ebenfalls deutscher Abstammung[11] sind Stars der Filmgeschichte wie Clark Gable oder Doris Day.

[1]*genealogists* [2]*impressive* [3]*U.S. citizens* [4]*office* [5]*report* [6]*shown* [7]*forefather* [8]*Franconian* [9]*farmer, peasant* [10]sind . . . zurückzuführen *can be* [11]*descent*

Nicht zu vergessen das bekannteste Beispiel aus dieser Region: 1849 wanderte der Klaviertischler[12] Heinrich Engelhard Steinweg aus Wolfshagen in die Staaten aus, schon zehn Jahre später hatte er die größte Klavierfabrik der Welt, „Steinway & Sons", deren Flügel zur Legende wurden.

[12] *piano-maker*

Arbeit mit dem Text

1. Wie viele Amerikaner haben deutsche Vorfahren? Haben Sie richtig geraten?[9]
2. Schreiben Sie die deutschen Namen aus dem Text auf. Wie heißen die amerikanisierten Formen?
3. Wann ist der Klaviertischler ausgewandert?

LEKTÜRE 2

Vor dem Lesen

1. Sind Sie schon einmal in einem anderen Land oder einem anderen US-Bundesstaat gewesen? Wie sind Sie dahin gekommen? mit dem Auto oder dem Flugzeug? Was haben Sie da gemacht?
2. Orientierung im Text: Wer? Was? Wo? Überfliegen Sie den Text und schreiben Sie die Antworten in die Kreise.

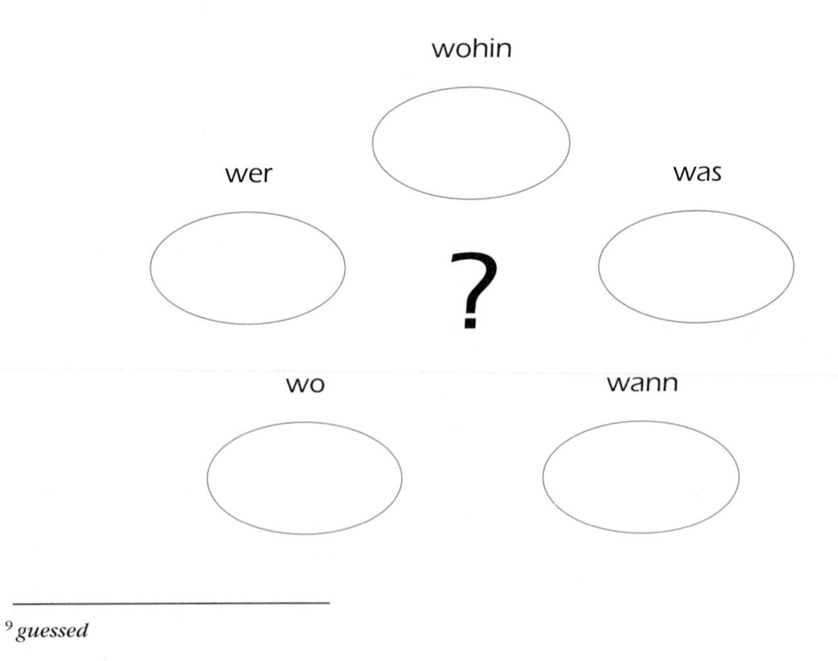

[9] *guessed*

Thomas fliegt nach Deutschland

Ein junger Mann mit dunklen Haaren, Stirnband und dunkelbraunen Augen geht an den Flugzeugschalter im Flughafen und sagt: „Hi, ich bin Thomas Jones. Ich fliege heute nach Deutschland, Frankfurt am Main natürlich, total cool, Mann. Hier ist mein Flugschein."

Der Angestellte schaut den jungen Mann von oben bis unten an, nimmt den Flugschein und sagt: „Alles in Ordnung. Gehen Sie bitte ins Flugzeug."

Thomas sagt: „Cool, danke schön." Er geht ins Flugzeug und setzt sich. Er sagt zu seinem Nachbarn: „Hi, ich bin der Thomas. Ich fliege zuerst nach Frankfurt, aber ich fahre nach München, sobald ich kann. Ich glaube, daß München die coolere Stadt ist. Fliegen Sie nach Deutschland, um zu studieren oder zu arbeiten oder um Urlaub zu machen?" Thomas wartet nicht auf eine Antwort, sondern sagt: „Früher habe ich geglaubt, daß München die coolste Stadt der Welt wäre, aber jetzt glaube ich natürlich etwas anderes. Berkeley, wo ich wohne, ist am coolsten. Es ist cool, Mann, toll, einfach ausgezeichnet, einfach grell! Heute fliege ich nach Deutschland, weil mein Bruder ein Konzert da gibt, echt wahr. Wenn ich seine Musik höre, denke ich: Wow, das ist echt cool, Mann! Ich habe ein paar Tonbänder mitgebracht, damit ich während des Fliegens zuhören kann. Möchten Sie auch zuhören? Ich habe zwei Walkmen mitgebracht."

Während Thomas spricht, starrt sein Nachbar ihn an. Er sagt: „Das klingt sehr attraktiv, aber leider muß ich nein sagen. Ich muß dieses Buch zu Ende lesen, bevor wir in Frankfurt ankommen."

Thomas antwortet: „Oh Mann, das ist wirklich schade. Ich hasse Bücher."

Arbeit mit dem Text

1. Was wissen Sie über die Hauptperson?

Name	Thomas Jones
Haare	
Augen	
Wohnort	
Wohin will er?	
Beruf des Bruders	
Wie spricht er?	
Lieblingsausdruck	

2. Wie finden Sie Thomas? Wie finden Sie seine Sprache?

STRUKTUREN UND ÜBUNGEN

4.1 Talking about the past: the perfect tense

In conversation, German speakers generally use the perfect tense to describe past events. The simple past tense, which you will study in **Kapitel 8,** is used more often in writing.

Ich **habe** gestern abend ein Glas Wein **getrunken.**	*I drank a glass of wine last night.*
Nora **hat** gestern Basketball **gespielt.**	*Nora played basketball yesterday.*

German forms the perfect tense with an auxiliary (**haben** or **sein**) and a past participle (**gewaschen**). Participles usually begin with the prefix **ge-.**

	AUXILIARY		PARTICIPLE
Ich	**habe**	mein Auto	**gewaschen.**

The auxiliary is in first position in yes/no questions and in second position in statements and word questions. The past participle is at the end of the clause.

Hat Heidi gestern einen Film **gesehen?**	*Did Heidi see a movie last night?*
Ich **habe** gestern zuviel Kaffee **getrunken.**	*I drank too much coffee yesterday.*
Wann **bist** du ins Bett **gegangen?**	*When did you go to bed?*

Verbs with **sein** = no direct object; change of location or condition.

Whereas most verbs form the present perfect tense with **haben,** several others use **sein.** To use **sein,** a verb must fulfill two conditions.

1. It cannot take a direct object.
2. It must indicate change of location or condition.

sein	**haben**
Ich **bin aufgestanden.** *I got out of bed.*	Ich **habe gefrühstückt.** *I ate breakfast.*
Stefan **ist** ins Kino **gegangen.** *Stefan went to the movies.*	Er **hat** einen neuen Film **gesehen.** *He saw a new film.*

Here is a list of common verbs that take **sein** as an auxiliary. For a more complete list, see the appendix.

ankommen	*to arrive*	ich bin angekommen
aufstehen	*to get up*	ich bin aufgestanden
einsteigen	*to board*	ich bin eingestiegen
fahren	*to go, drive*	ich bin gefahren
gehen	*to go, walk*	ich bin gegangen
kommen	*to come*	ich bin gekommen
schwimmen	*to swim*	ich bin geschwommen
wandern	*to hike*	ich bin gewandert

In addition to these verbs, **sein** itself and the verb **bleiben** (*to stay*) take **sein** as an auxiliary.

Bist du schon in China **gewesen?**	*Have you ever been to China?*
Gestern **bin** ich zu Hause **geblieben.**	*Yesterday I stayed home.*

Übung 1 Rosemaries erster Schultag

Ergänzen Sie **haben** oder **sein.**

Rosemarie _____[a] bis sieben Uhr geschlafen. Dann _____[b] sie aufgestanden und _____[c] mit ihren Eltern und ihren Schwestern gefrühstückt. Sie _____[d] ihre Tasche genommen und _____[e] mit ihrer Mutter zur Schule gegangen. Ihre Mutter und sie _____[f] ins Klassenzimmer gegangen, und ihre Mutter _____[g] noch ein bißchen dageblieben. Die Lehrerin, Frau Dehne, _____[h] alle begrüßt. Dann _____[i] Frau Dehne „Herzlich Willkommen" an die Tafel geschrieben.

Beantworten Sie die Fragen.

1. Wann ist Rosemarie aufgestanden?
2. Wohin sind Rosemarie und ihre Mutter gegangen?
3. Wer ist Frau Dehne?
4. Was hat Frau Dehne an die Tafel geschrieben?

Übung 2 Eine Reise nach Istanbul

Ergänzen Sie **haben** oder **sein.**

Josef und Melanie:

Wir _____[a] ein Taxi genommen. Mit dem Taxi _____[b] wir zum Bahnhof gefahren. Dort _____[c] wir uns Fahrkarten gekauft. Dann _____[d] wir in den Orientexpress eingestiegen. Um 5.30 _____[e] wir abgefahren. Wir _____[f] im Speisewagen[1] gefrühstückt. Den ganzen Tag _____[g] wir Karten gespielt. Nachts _____[h] wir in den Schlafwagen gegangen. Wir _____[i] schlecht geschlafen. Aber wir _____[j] gut in Istanbul angekommen.

---

[1] *dining car*

Beantworten Sie die Fragen.

1. Wohin sind Josef und Melanie mit dem Taxi gefahren?
2. Wann sind sie mit dem Zug abgefahren?
3. Wo haben sie gefrühstückt?
4. Was haben sie nachts gemacht?

Übung 3 Ein ganz normaler Tag

Ergänzen Sie das Partizip. Verwenden Sie die Liste.

aufgestanden	gefrühstückt	gehört
gearbeitet	gegangen	getroffen
geduscht	gegessen	getrunken

Heute bin ich um 7.00 Uhr _____[a]. Ich habe _____[b], _____[c] und bin an die Uni _____[d]. Ich habe einen Vortrag _____[e]. Um 10 Uhr habe ich ein paar Mitstudenten _____[f] und Kaffee _____[g]. Dann habe ich bis 12.30 Uhr in der Bibliothek _____[h] und habe in der Mensa zu Mittag _____[i].

4.2 Strong and weak past participles

weak verbs = **ge** + verb stem + **(e)t**

German verbs that form the past participle with **-(e)t** are called *weak verbs.*

arbeiten	gearbeitet	*work*	*worked*
spielen	gespielt	*play*	*played*

To form the regular past participle, take the present tense **er/sie/es**-form and precede it with **ge-**.

er	spielt	er	hat	gespielt
sie	arbeitet	sie	hat	gearbeitet
es	regnet	es	hat	geregnet

strong verbs = **ge** + verb stem + **en**; the verb stem may have vowel or consonant changes.

Verbs that form the past participle with **-en** are called *strong verbs.* Many verbs have the same stem vowel in the infinitive and the past participle.

kommen gek**o**mmen

Some verbs have a change in the stem vowel.

schwimmen geschw**o**mmen

Some also have a change in consonants.

gehen gega**ng**en

Here is a reference list of common irregular past participles.

Mit dem Fahrrad zum Einkaufen

PARTICIPLES WITH **haben**

essen, gegessen	*to eat*
lesen, gelesen	*to read*
liegen, gelegen	*to lie, be situated*
nehmen, genommen	*to take*
schlafen, geschlafen	*to sleep*
schreiben, geschrieben	*to write*
sehen, gesehen	*to see*
sprechen, gesprochen	*to speak*
tragen, getragen	*to wear, carry*
treffen, getroffen	*to meet*
trinken, getrunken	*to drink*
waschen, gewaschen	*to wash*

PARTICIPLES WITH **sein**

ankommen, angekommen	*to arrive*
aufstehen, aufgestanden	*to get up*
bleiben, geblieben	*to stay*
einsteigen, eingestiegen	*to board*
fahren, gefahren	*to go (using a vehicle), drive*
gehen, gegangen	*to go*
kommen, gekommen	*to come*
schwimmen, geschwommen	*to swim*
sein, gewesen	*to be*

Übung 4 Das ungezogene[1] Kind

Stellen Sie die Fragen!

MODELL SIE: Hast du schon geduscht?
DAS KIND: Heute will ich nicht duschen.

1. Heute will ich nicht frühstücken.
2. Heute will ich nicht schwimmen.
3. Heute will ich keine Geschichte lesen.
4. Heute will ich nicht Klavier spielen.
5. Heute will ich nicht schlafen.
6. Heute will ich nicht essen.
7. Heute will ich nicht Geschirr spülen.
8. Heute will ich den Brief nicht schreiben.
9. Heute will ich nicht ins Bett gehen.

---

[1] *ill-bred*

Übung 5 Katrins Tagesablauf

Was hat Katrin gestern gemacht? Schreiben Sie zu jedem Bild einen Satz. Verwenden Sie diese Ausdrücke.

arbeiten
abends zu Hause bleiben
ein Referat halten
nach Hause kommen
bis neun im Bett liegen
regnen
mit Frau Schulz sprechen
einen Rock tragen
Freunde treffen
ihre Wäsche waschen

4.3 Dates and ordinal numbers

Ordinals 1–19 add **-te** to the cardinal number (but note: **erste, dritte, siebte, achte**).

To form ordinal numbers, add **-te** to the cardinal numbers 1 through 19 and **-ste** to the numbers 20 and above. Exceptions to this pattern are **erste** (*first*), **dritte** (*third*), **siebte** (*seventh*), and **achte** (*eighth*).

	1–19 **-te**	
eins	**erste**	*first*
zwei	zweite	*second*
drei	**dritte**	*third*
vier	vierte	*fourth*
fünf	fünfte	*fifth*
sechs	sechste	*sixth*
sieben	**siebte**	*seventh*
acht	**achte**	*eighth*
neun	neunte	*ninth*
. . .		
neunzehn	neunzehnte	*nineteenth*

Ordinals 20 on add **-ste** to the cardinal number.

	20– **-ste**	
zwanzig	zwanzigste	*twentieth*
einundzwanzig	einundzwanzigste	*twenty-first*
zweiundzwanzig	zweiundzwanzigste	*twenty-second*
. . .		
dreißig	dreißigste	*thirtieth*
vierzig	vierzigste	*fortieth*
. . .		
hundert	hundertste	*hundredth*
. . .		

Ordinal numbers usually end in **-e** or **-en.** Use the construction **der** + **-e** to answer the question **Welches Datum . . . ?**

All dates are masculine:
***der* zweite Mai**
***am* zweit*en* Mai**

Welches Datum ist heute?	*What is today's date?*
Heute ist der achtzehnte Oktober.	*Today is October eighteenth.*

Use **am** + **-en** to answer the question **Wann . . . ?**

Wann sind Sie geboren?	*When were you born?*
Am achtzehn**ten** Juni 1969.	*On the eighteenth of June 1969.*

Ordinal numbers in German can be written as words or figures.

am zweiten Februar	*on the second of February*
am 2. Februar	*on the 2nd of February*

Übung 6 Wichtige Daten

Beantworten Sie die Fragen.

1. Welches Datum ist heute?
2. Welches Datum ist morgen?
3. Wann feiert man Weihnachten?
4. Wann feiert man den amerikanischen Nationalfeiertag?
5. Wann feiert man das neue Jahr?
6. Wann feiert man Valentinstag?
7. Wann ist dieses Jahr Muttertag?
8. Wann ist nächstes Jahr Martin-Luther-King-Tag?
9. Wann beginnt der Frühling?
10. Wann beginnt der Sommer?

4.4 Prepositions of time: *um, am, im*

Use the question word **wann** to ask for a specific time. The preposition in the answer will vary depending on whether it refers to clock time, days and parts of days, months, or seasons.

um

um CLOCK TIME

—Wann beginnt die Klasse?	*When does the class start?*
—**Um** neun Uhr.	*At nine o'clock.*

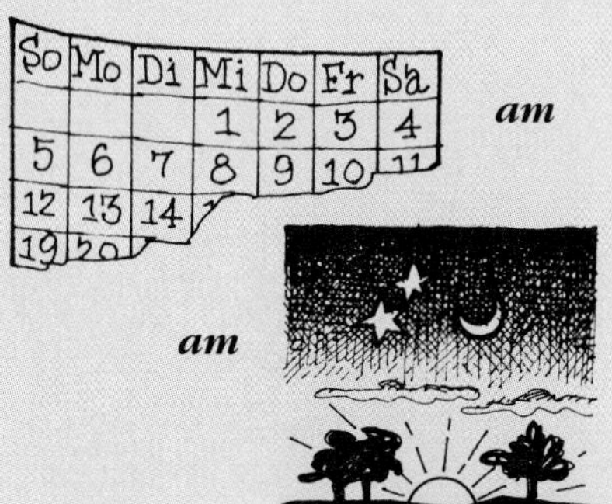

am DAYS AND PARTS OF DAYS*

—Wann ist das Konzert?	*When is the concert?*
—**Am** Montag.	*On Monday.*
—Wann arbeitest du?	*When do you work?*
—**Am** Abend.	*In the evening.*

im SEASONS AND MONTHS

—Wann ist das Wetter schön?	*When is the weather nice?*
—**Im** Sommer und besonders **im** August.	*In the summer and especially in August.*

No preposition is used when stating the year in which something takes place.

—Wann bist du geboren?	*When were you born?*
—Ich bin 1970 geboren.	*I was born in 1970.*

Übung 7 Melanies Geburtstag

Ergänzen Sie **um, am, im** oder —.

Melanie hat _____[a] Frühling Geburtstag, _____[b] April. Sie ist _____[c] 1974 geboren, _____[d] 4. April 1974. _____[e] Dienstag kommen Claire und Josef _____[f] halb vier zum Kaffee. Melanies Mutter kommt _____[g] 16 Uhr. _____[h] Abend gehen Melanie, Claire und Josef ins Kino.
Josef hat auch _____[i] April Geburtstag, aber erst _____[j] 15. April.

Übung 8 Interview

Beantworten Sie die Fragen.

1. Was machst du im Winter? im Sommer?
2. Wie ist das Wetter im Frühling? im Herbst?
3. Was machst du am Morgen? am Abend?
4. Was machst du am Freitag? am Samstag?
5. Was machst du heute um sechs Uhr abends? um zehn Uhr abends?
6. Was machst du am Sonntag um Mitternacht?

---

*Note the exceptions: **in der Nacht** (*at night*) and **um Mitternacht** (*at midnight*).

4.5 Past participles with and without *ge-*

A. Participles with **ge-**

Separable-prefix verbs form their past participles with **-ge-:**
weak verbs = prefix + **ge** + verb stem + **(e)t**
strong verbs = prefix + **ge** + verb stem + **en**
The verb stem may have vowel or consonant changes.

German past participles usually begin with **ge-.** The past participles of separable-prefix verbs begin with the prefix; the **ge-** goes between the prefix and the verb: **einladen → ein*ge*laden.**

Frau Schulz **hat** Heidi und Nora zum Essen **eingeladen.**	*Frau Schulz invited Heidi and Nora for dinner.*

Here are the infinitives and past participles of some common separable-prefix verbs.

PAST PARTICIPLES WITH **haben**

anfangen	angefangen	*to start*
anrufen	angerufen	*to call up*
aufräumen	aufgeräumt	*to tidy up*
auspacken	ausgepackt	*to unpack*
fernsehen	ferngesehen	*to watch TV*

PAST PARTICIPLES WITH **sein**

ankommen	angekommen	*to arrive*
aufstehen	aufgestanden	*to get up*
ausgehen	ausgegangen	*to go out*
weggehen	weggegangen	*to go away, leave*

B. Participles without **ge-**

Verbs ending in **-ieren** are weak: verb stem + **t.**

There are two types of verbs that do not add **ge-** to form the past participle: verbs that end in **-ieren** and verbs with inseparable prefixes.

1. Verbs ending in **-ieren** form the past participle with **-t: studieren → studiert.**

Paula **hat** zwei Semester Deutsch **studiert.**	*Paula studied German for two semesters.*
Thomas **hat** gestern sein Fahrrad **repariert.**	*Thomas repaired his bicycle yesterday.*

Here is a list of common verbs that end in **-ieren.**

buchstabieren	buchstabiert	*to spell*
diskutieren	diskutiert	*to discuss*
fotografieren	fotografiert	*to take pictures*
korrigieren	korrigiert	*to correct*
probieren	probiert	*to try, taste*
reparieren	repariert	*to repair, fix*
studieren	studiert	*to study*
telefonieren	telefoniert	*to telephone*

Verbs with inseparable prefixes may be weak or strong:
weak verbs =
verb stem + **(e)t**
strong verbs =
verb stem + **en**
The verb stem may have vowel or consonant changes.

SEPARABLE PREFIXES
an
auf
aus
mit
weg
wieder
zusammen
and others

INSEPARABLE PREFIXES
be-
ent-
er-
ge-
ver-
zer-

Separable prefixes can stand alone as whole words; inseparable prefixes are always unstressed syllables.

Almost all verbs ending in **-ieren** form the perfect tense with **haben.** The verb **passieren** (*to happen*) requires **sein** as an auxiliary: **Was ist passiert?** (*What happened?*)

2. The past participles of inseparable-prefix verbs do not include **ge: verstehen → verstanden.**

Stefan **hat** heute nicht viel **verstanden.**	*Stefan didn't understand much today.*

Whereas separable prefixes are words that can stand alone (**auf, aus, wieder,** and so forth), inseparable prefixes are simply syllables: **be-**, **ent-**, **er-**, **ge-**, **ver-**, and **zer-.** The past participles of most inseparable-prefix verbs require **haben** as an auxiliary. Here is a list of common inseparable-prefix verbs and their past participles.

bekommen	bekommen	*to get*
besuchen	besucht	*to visit*
bezahlen	bezahlt	*to pay*
entdecken	entdeckt	*to discover*
erfinden	erfunden	*to invent*
erzählen	erzählt	*to tell*
verdienen	verdient	*to earn*
vergessen	vergessen	*to forget*
verstehen	verstanden	*to understand*

Übung 9 Ein schlechter Tag

Herr Thelen ist gestern mit dem linken Fuß aufgestanden. Zuerst hat er seinen Wecker nicht gehört und hat verschlafen.[1] Dann ist er in die Küche gegangen und hat Kaffee gekocht. Nach dem Frühstück ist er mit seinem Auto in die Stadt zum Einkaufen gefahren. Er hat geparkt und ist erst nach zwei Stunden zurückgekommen. Herr Thelen hat einen Strafzettel[2] bekommen und DM 15,- bezahlt für falsches Parken. Er ist nach Hause gefahren, hat die Wäsche gewaschen und hat aufgeräumt. Beim Aufräumen ist eine teure Vase auf den Boden gefallen und zerbrochen.[3] Als die Wäsche fertig war, war ein Pullover eingelaufen.[4] Herr Thelen ist dann schnell ins Bett gegangen. Fünf Minuten vor Mitternacht ist das Haus abgebrannt.[5]

A. Richtig (R) oder falsch (F)?

1. _____ Herr Thelen hat gestern verschlafen.
2. _____ Vor dem Frühstück ist er in die Stadt gefahren.
3. _____ Herr Thelen hat falsch geparkt.
4. _____ Er hat seine Wohnung aufgeräumt.
5. _____ Herr Thelen braucht ein neues Haus.

[1]*overslept* [2]*ticket* [3]*broken* [4]*shrunk* [5]*burned down*

B. Suchen Sie die Partizipien heraus, bilden Sie die Infinitive und schreiben Sie sie auf.

PARTIZIPIEN MIT **ge-**	INFINITIV	PARTIZIPIEN OHNE **ge-**	INFINITIV
______	______	______	______
______	______	______	______

Übung 10 In der Türkei

Mehmet ist in der Türkei. Was hat er gestern gemacht? Verwenden Sie die Verben am Rand.[1]

Mehmet ist in der Türkei bei seinen Eltern. Gestern _____ er um 17 Uhr _____[a]. Er _____ seine Eltern und Geschwister _____[b] und einen Tee mit ihnen _____[c]. Dann _____ er in sein Zimmer _____[d] und _____ _____[e].

gehen
ankommen
trinken
schlafen
begrüßen

Nach einer Stunde _____ er zum Abendessen in die Küche _____[f]. Seine Eltern _____ ihn viel über sein Leben in Deutschland _____[g], und Mehmet _____ über seine Arbeit und seine Freunde _____[h]. Sie _____ noch einen Tee _____[i] und _____ um 23 Uhr ins Bett _____[j].

gehen
trinken
fragen
sprechen
gehen

Übung 11 Interview

Fragen Sie Ihren Partner / Ihre Partnerin. Schreiben Sie die Antworten auf.

MODELL mit deinen Eltern telefonieren (wie lange?) →
S1: Hast du gestern mit deinen Eltern telefoniert?
S2: Ja.
S1: Wie lange?
S2: Eine halbe Stunde.

1. früh aufstehen (wann?)
2. jemanden fotografieren (wen?)
3. jemanden besuchen (wen?)
4. ausgehen (wohin?)
5. etwas bezahlen (was?)
6. etwas reparieren (was?)
7. etwas Neues probieren (was?)
8. fernsehen (wie lange?)
9. etwas nicht verstehen (was?)
10. dein Zimmer aufräumen (wann?)

[1] *margin*

KAPITEL 5

Straßenarbeiter in Salzburg. Straßenbau wie in alten Zeiten.

In **Kapitel 5,** you will talk about shopping, jobs and the workplace, and daily life at home. You'll expand your ability to express your likes and dislikes and learn to describe your career plans.

Geld und Arbeit

THEMEN

Geschenke und Gefälligkeiten
Berufe
Arbeitsplätze
In der Küche

LEKTÜRE

Schwitzen fürs Image
Lebe wohl!

KULTURELLES

Weihnachtsbräuche
Ausbildung und Beruf
Studium oder Berufsausbildung?
Traumküche der Deutschen
Kulturprojekt: Arbeit und Geschäftswelt
Porträt: Werner von Siemens und Siemensstadt
Videoecke: Wie finanziert man das Studium?

STRUKTUREN

5.1 Dative case: articles and possessive adjectives
5.2 Question pronouns: **wer, wen, wem**
5.3 Expressing change: the verb **werden**
5.4 Location: **in, an, auf** + dative case
5.5 Dative case: personal pronouns

SPRECHSITUATIONEN

Geschenke und Gefälligkeiten

➤ **Grammatik 5.1–5.2**

Situation 1 Ist das normal?

Welches Bild gehört zu welchem Satz?

1. a. b.

_____ Jens gießt seiner Tante die Blumen.

_____ Jens gießt seine Tante.

2. a. b.

______ Jutta repariert ihren Bruder.
______ Jutta repariert ihrem Bruder das Radio.

3. a. b.

______ Silvia kauft das Kind.
______ Silvia kauft dem Kind die Schokolade.

4. a. b.

______ Herr Ruf kocht der Familie das Essen.
______ Herr Ruf kocht die Familie.

Situation 2 Sagen Sie *ja, nein* oder *vielleicht.*

1. Wem geben die Studenten ihre Hausaufgaben?

a. dem Professor
b. ihren Eltern
c. dem Hausmeister
d. dem Taxifahrer

2. Wem schreibt Rolf einen Brief?

a. seiner Katze
b. dem Präsidenten der USA
c. seinem Friseur
d. seinen Eltern

3. Wem kauft Andrea das Hundefutter?

a. ihrer Mutter
b. ihrem Freund Jens
c. ihrem Hund
d. ihren Geschwistern

4. Wem repariert Herr Ruf das Fahrrad?

a. seinem Hund
b. seiner Mutter
c. seinen Nachbarn
d. seinem Sohn

Situation 3 Bildgeschichte: Josef kauft Weihnachtsgeschenke.

Morgen ist Weihnachten, und Josef hat noch keine Geschenke.

Kultur ... Landeskunde ... Informationen

Weihnachtsbräuche[1]

- Feiern Sie Weihnachten?
- Wem kaufen Sie Weihnachtsgeschenke?
- Wer bringt Geschenke für die Kinder?
- Wann ist bei Ihnen Bescherung[2]? Wer ist alles dabei?

[1]*Christmas traditions* [2]*exchange of gifts*

Für die Zeit vor Weihnachten gibt es in Deutschland besonders viele Bräuche. Man nennt die vier Sonntage vor dem Heiligen Abend[3] den ersten, zweiten, dritten und vierten Advent. Viele Familien haben Adventsdekorationen mit vier Kerzen, und jeden Sonntag zündet man eine weitere Kerze an, bis am vierten Advent alle Kerzen brennen.[4] Am 6. Dezember ist Nikolaustag. An diesem Tag bekommen Kinder Süßigkeiten in ihre Schuhe gelegt, die vor der Tür oder vor dem Fenster stehen. Am 24. Dezember kommt die Familie zur Bescherung zusammen. In Süddeutschland warten die Kinder aufs Christkind[5] und im Norden auf den Weihnachtsmann. Wen sieht man auf dieser Weihnachtskarte?

[3] *Christmas Eve* [4] *burn* [5] *Baby Jesus* [6] *Happy New Year* (lit. *have a good slide* [*into the new year*])

Situation 4 Interaktion: Was schenkst du deiner Mutter?

Sie haben in der Lotterie 4 000 DM gewonnen. Für 1 000 DM wollen Sie Ihrer Familie und Ihren Freunden Geschenke kaufen. Was schenken Sie ihnen?

S1: Was schenkst du deiner Mutter?
S2: Einen/Ein/Eine ______ .
S2: Was schenkst du deinem Vater?
S1: Einen/Ein/Eine ______ .

	ich	mein(e) Partner(in)
Mutter		
Vater		
Schwester		
Bruder		
Großvater		
Großmutter		
Freund(in)		
Professor(in)		
Zimmerkamerad(in)		

Berufe

➤ **Grammatik 5.3**

Situation 5 Definitionen

Finden Sie den richtigen Beruf.

1. Dieser Mann unterrichtet in einer Schule. Er ist _____ .
2. Diese Frau untersucht Patienten im Krankenhaus. Sie ist _____ .
3. Dieser Mann lenkt ein Flugzeug. Er ist _____ .
4. Diese Person arbeitet im Restaurant. Sie ist _____ .
5. Diese Person zeichnet Pläne für Häuser. Sie ist _____ .
6. Diese Frau arbeitet auf dem Gericht. Sie ist _____ .

7. Diese Frau pflegt kranke Menschen. Sie ist _____ .
8. Dieser Mann schreibt Romane. Er ist _____ .
9. Diese Frau arbeitet in einem Supermarkt. Sie ist _____ .

Situation 6 Bildgeschichte: Was Michael Pusch schon alles gemacht hat

Situation 7 Berufe

Machen Sie Listen. Suchen Sie zu jeder Frage drei Berufe.

1. In welchen Berufen verdient man sehr viel Geld?
2. In welchen Berufen verdient man nur wenig Geld?
3. In welchen Berufen gibt es mehr Männer als Frauen?
4. In welchen Berufen gibt es mehr Frauen als Männer?
5. In welchen Berufen muß man gut in Mathematik sein?
6. In welchen Berufen muß man gut in Sprachen sein?
7. In welchen Berufen muß man viel reisen?
8. In welchen Berufen muß man viel Kraft[1] haben?
9. In welchen Berufen hat man sehr viel Verantwortung[2]?
10. In welchen Berufen braucht man einen Sinn für Schönheit[3]?

---

[1]*strength* [2]*responsibility* [3]Sinn . . . *sense of aesthetics*

Kultur ... Landeskunde ... Informationen

Ausbildung und Beruf

Jens hat keine Lust auf Schule und später Studium. Wenn er die zehnte Klasse erfolgreich[1] abschließt,[2] hat er den Realschulabschluß. Er möchte am liebsten eine praktische Ausbildung machen, z.B. als Gärtner, Automechaniker oder Koch. Ein Facharbeiter[3] verdient mehr als ein ungelernter Arbeiter. Die Grafik zeigt, wie die Ausbildung für Jens weitergeht.

- Wie lange dauert eine Ausbildung oder Lehre?
- Wo bekommt man die theoretische Ausbildung?
- Wo lernt man die praktische Seite des Berufs?
- Was bekommt man nach der Gesellenprüfung am Ende?
- Was ist man am Schluß[9]?

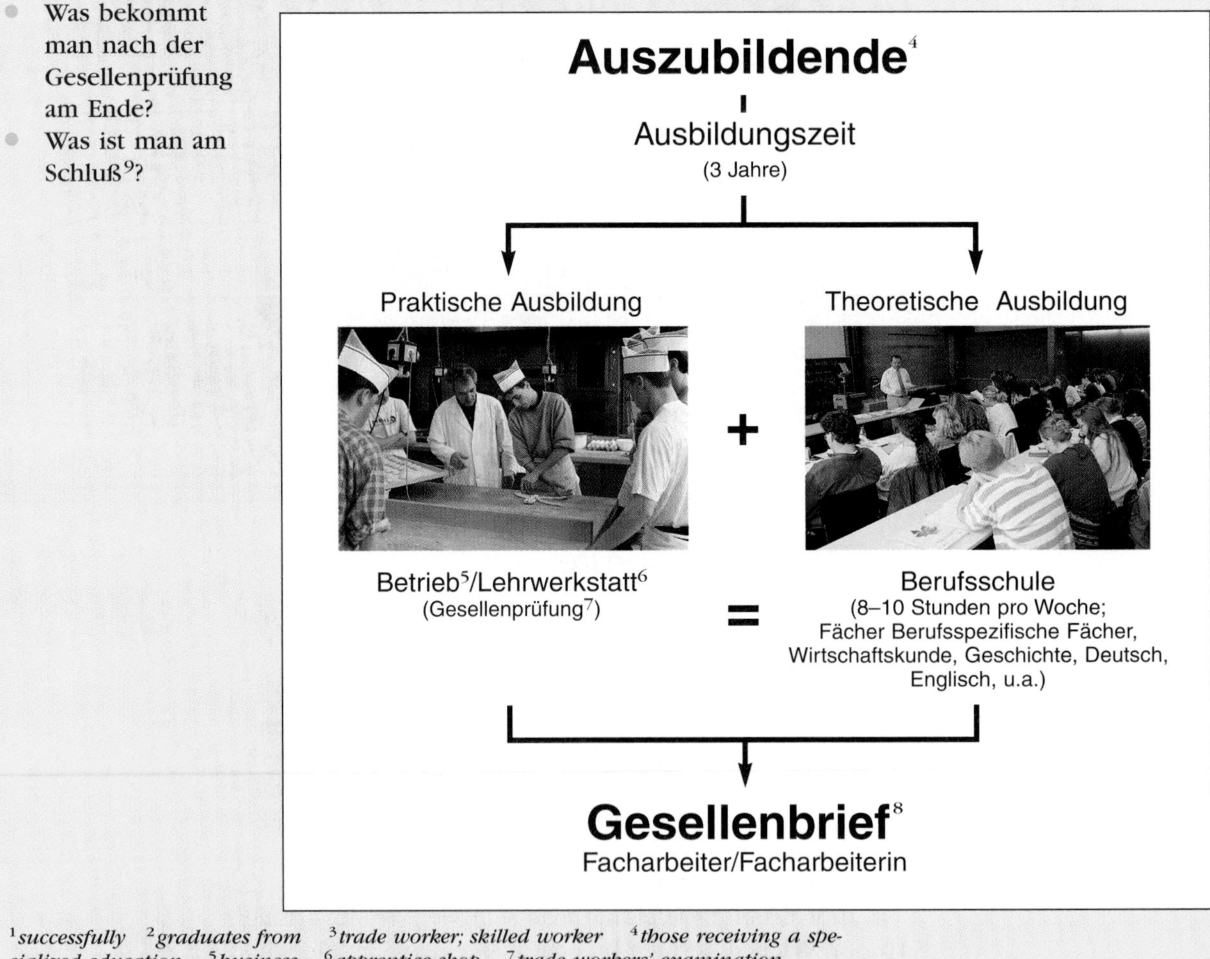

[1] *successfully* [2] *graduates from* [3] *trade worker; skilled worker* [4] *those receiving a specialized education* [5] *business* [6] *apprentice shop* [7] *trade workers' examination* [8] *certificate of completed apprenticeship* [9] am . . . *in the end*

Situation 8 Interview

1. a. Arbeitest du? Wo? Als was? Was machst du? An welchen Tagen arbeitest du? Wann beginnst du? Wann hörst du auf?
   b. Hast du gearbeitet? Wo? Als was? Was hast du gemacht? An welchen Tagen hast du gearbeitet? Wann hast du begonnen? Wann hast du aufgehört?
2. Was studierst du? Wie lange dauert das Studium? Was möchtest du werden? Verdient man da viel Geld? Ist das ein Beruf mit viel Prestige?
3. Was ist dein Vater von Beruf? Was hat er gelernt (studiert)? Was ist deine Mutter von Beruf? Was hat sie gelernt (studiert)?

Arbeitsplätze

➤ **Grammatik 5.4**

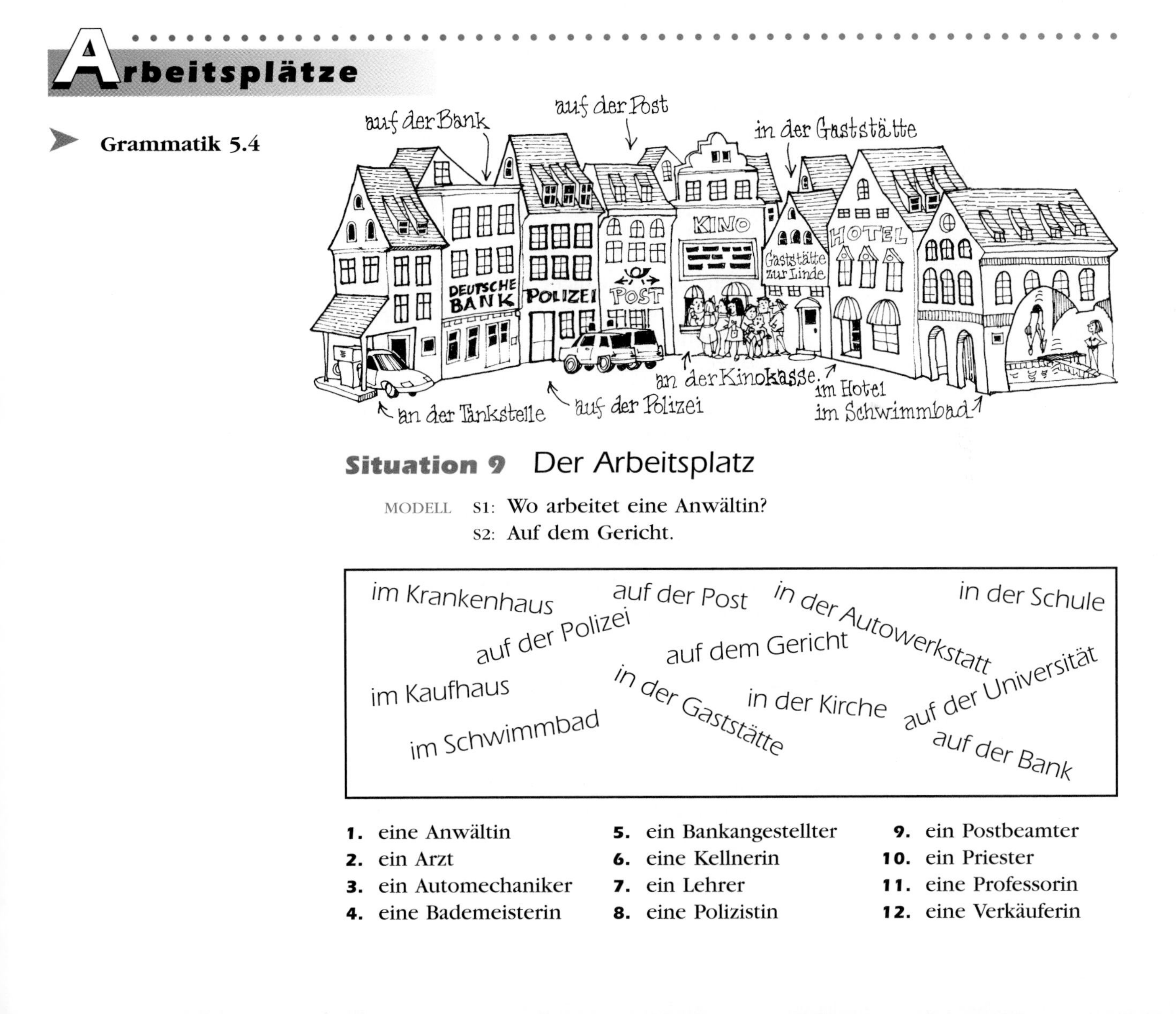

Situation 9 Der Arbeitsplatz

MODELL S1: Wo arbeitet eine Anwältin?
S2: Auf dem Gericht.

im Krankenhaus · auf der Post · in der Autowerkstatt · in der Schule · auf der Polizei · auf dem Gericht · im Kaufhaus · in der Gaststätte · in der Kirche · auf der Universität · im Schwimmbad · auf der Bank

1. eine Anwältin
2. ein Arzt
3. ein Automechaniker
4. eine Bademeisterin
5. ein Bankangestellter
6. eine Kellnerin
7. ein Lehrer
8. eine Polizistin
9. ein Postbeamter
10. ein Priester
11. eine Professorin
12. eine Verkäuferin

Situation 10 Minidialoge

Wo finden diese Dialoge statt?

auf der Post	im Hotel	in der Gaststätte
an der Kinokasse	im Schwimmbad	
in der Bäckerei	auf der Bank	auf dem Bahnhof
an der Tankstelle		

1. —Guten Tag, ich möchte ein Konto eröffnen.
   —Bitte. Füllen Sie bitte dieses Formular aus, und gehen Sie zum Schalter 3.
2. —Guten Tag, ich hätte gern eine Fahrkarte nach Bonn.
   —Hin und zurück oder einfach?
   —Hin und zurück, bitte.
3. —Guten Tag, ich brauche zwei Briefmarken für Postkarten in die USA, bitte.
   —Das sind zweimal drei Mark, sechs Mark zusammen.
   —Bitte sehr.
   —Danke.
4. —Guten Tag, einmal volltanken, bitte, und kontrollieren Sie auch das Öl.
   —Wird gemacht.
5. —Guten Tag, geben Sie mir bitte ein Bauernbrot.
   —Bitte sehr! Sonst noch etwas?
   —Nein, das ist alles, danke.
6. —Guten Tag, ich hätte gern ein Einzelzimmer für eine Nacht.
   —Mit oder ohne Dusche?
   —Mit Dusche bitte.
7. —Entschuldigen Sie bitte, können Sie mir sagen, wo die Umkleidekabinen sind?
   —Ja, die sind gleich hier um die Ecke.
8. —Guten Abend, zwei Eintrittskarten für *Schindlers Liste,* bitte.
   —Tut mir leid, der Film ist leider schon ausverkauft.
9. —Hallo! Zahlen, bitte!
   —Gerne. Zusammen oder getrennt?

Kultur ... Landeskunde ... Informationen

Studium oder Berufsausbildung?

- Was kann man in den USA machen, wenn man mit der Schule fertig ist?
- Welche Vorteile[1] hat ein Studium in den USA? Welche Nachteile[2]? Entscheiden[3] Sie Pro oder Kontra.

	PRO	KONTRA
Man hat nach dem Studium kein Geld.	☐	☐
Man verdient nicht gleich Geld.	☐	☐
Man verdient später mehr Geld.	☐	☐
Das Studium dauert oft sehr lange.	☐	☐
Das Studium ist teuer.	☐	☐
Man muß viele Prüfungen machen.	☐	☐
Das Studium ist anstrengend.[4]	☐	☐
Man bekommt nach dem Studium eine bessere Arbeitsstelle.	☐	☐
Man ist später arbeitslos.	☐	☐
Man muß mehr lernen.	☐	☐

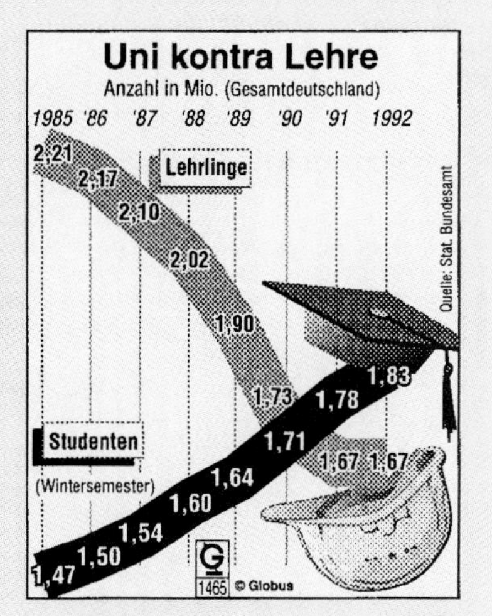

- In den USA gehen circa 60% der Jugendlichen nach der Schule aufs College. Wie ist es in Deutschland? Interpretieren Sie die Grafik.
- Warum, glauben Sie, wollen in Deutschland immer mehr Jugendliche studieren?

[1] *advantages* [2] *disadvantages* [3] *decide* [4] *strenuous*

Situation 11 Zum Schreiben: Vor der Berufsberatung

Morgen haben Sie einen Termin beim Berufsberater. Bereiten Sie sich auf das Gespräch vor. Machen Sie sich Notizen zu den Stichwörtern auf der Liste.

- Schulbildung
- familiärer[1] Hintergrund (Beruf der Eltern usw.)
- Interessen, Hobbys
- Lieblingsfächer, besondere Fähigkeiten
- Qualifikationen (Fremdsprachen, Computerkenntnisse usw.)
- Erwartungen[2] an den zukünftigen[3] Beruf (Geld, Arbeitszeiten, Urlaub usw.)

[1] *family* [2] *expectations* [3] *future*

Situation 12 Rollenspiel: Bei der Berufsberatung

S1: Sie arbeiten bei der Berufsberatung. Ein Student / Eine Studentin kommt in Ihre Sprechstunde. Stellen Sie ihm/ihr Fragen zu diesen Themen: Schulbildung, Interessen und Hobbys, besondere Kenntnisse, Lieblingsfächer.

In der Küche

➤ **Grammatik 5.4–5.5**

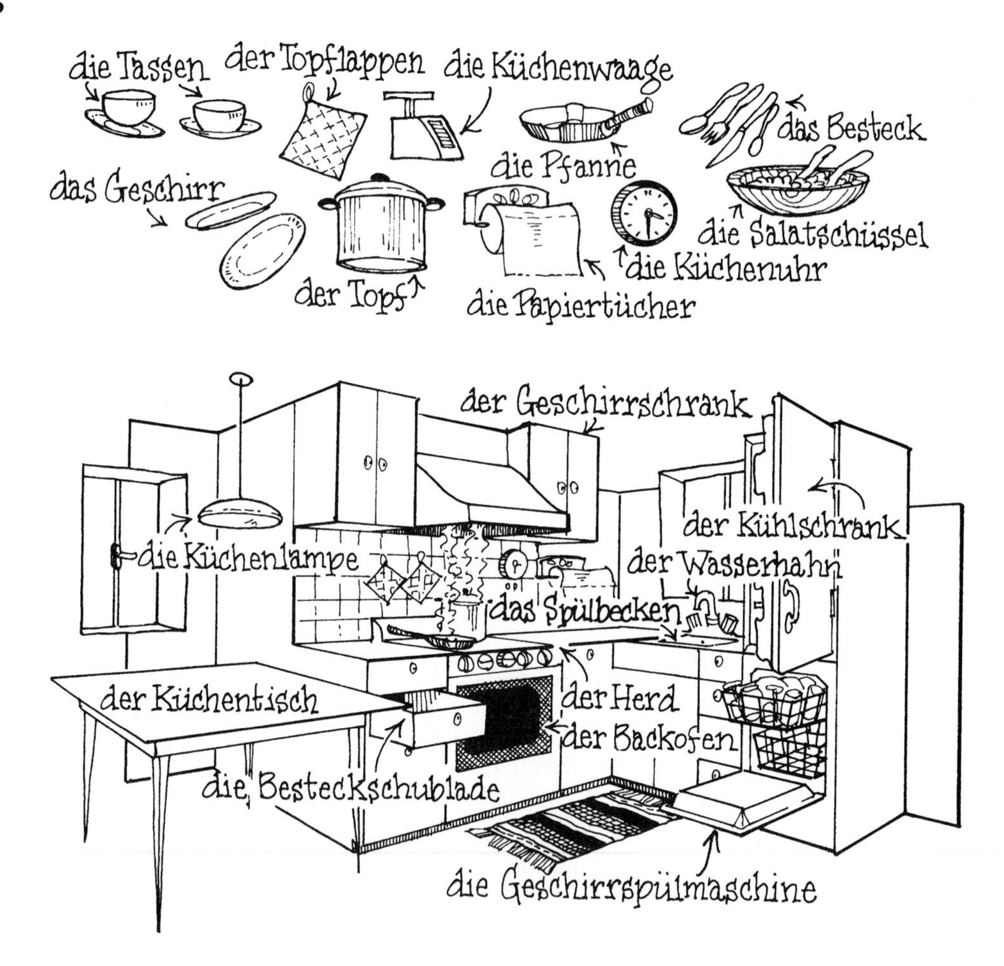

Situation 13 Wo ist . . . ?

MODELL S1: Wo ist der Küchentisch?
S2: Unter der Küchenlampe.

1. Wo ist die Geschirrspülmaschine?
2. Wo ist die Küchenuhr?
3. Wo ist der Backofen?
4. Wo ist das Spülbecken?
5. Wo sind die Papiertücher?
6. Wo ist die Pfanne?
7. Wo ist das Geschirr?
8. Wo ist der Topf?
9. Wo sind die Gläser?
10. Wo ist das Besteck?

Situation 14 Interaktion: Küchenarbeit

Wie oft spülst du das Geschirr?

mehrmals am Tag
jeden Tag
fast jeden Tag
zwei- bis dreimal in der Woche
einmal in der Woche
einmal im Monat
selten
nie

Wie oft . . . ?	ich	mein(e) Partner(in)
gehst du einkaufen		
kochst du		
deckst du den Tisch		
spülst du das Geschirr		
stellst du das Geschirr weg		
machst du den Herd sauber		
machst du den Tisch sauber		
machst du den Kühlschrank sauber		
fegst du den Boden		
bringst du die leeren Flaschen weg		

Kultur ... Landeskunde ... Informationen

Traumküche der Deutschen

Eine Traumküche? Bei dem Wettbewerb[1] „Wählen Sie Ihre Traumküche" hat diese moderne Küche den ersten Preis gewonnen. Wie finden Sie diese Küche? Was gibt es alles? Was fehlt? Was gibt es alles in Ihrer Traumküche?

[1] *contest*

Situation 15 Umfrage: Kochst du mir ein Abendessen?

MODELL S1: Kochst du mir morgen ein Abendessen?
S2: Ja.
S1: Unterschreib bitte hier.

	UNTERSCHRIFT
1. Kochst du mir morgen ein Abendessen?	____________
2. Backst du mir einen Kuchen zum Geburtstag?	____________
3. Kaufst du mir ein Eis?	____________
4. Verkaufst du mir deine Schuhe?	____________
5. Schenkst du mir deinen Kugelschreiber?	____________
6. Hilfst du mir heute bei der Hausaufgabe?	____________
7. Kannst du mir die Grammatik erklären?	____________
8. Schreibst du mir in den Ferien einen Brief?	____________
9. Kannst du mir ein Lied vorsingen?	____________
10. Kannst du mir hundert Dollar leihen?	____________

Hints for working with the Kulturprojekt

Current exchange rates may be found in major daily newspapers. Use a reference work such as *The Universal Almanac* to find the largest international companies and their place of origin. The *Britannica World Data,* a yearly supplement to the *Encyclopedia Britannica* found in most libraries, lists average household incomes. You can find information about average work and vacation schedules in your textbook.

Kulturprojekt Arbeit und Geschäftswelt

Suchen Sie nach folgenden Informationen. Benutzen Sie die Bibliothek, Zeitungen oder andere Nachschlagewerke.[1]

- Wie viele Stunden pro Woche muß man in Deutschland arbeiten? in Österreich? in der Schweiz?
- Wie viele Tage Urlaub pro Jahr hat man in Deutschland? in Österreich? in der Schweiz?
- Wie hoch ist der durchschnittliche Jahresverdienst[2]?
- Wieviel Deutsche Mark (österreichische Schillinge, Schweizer Franken) bekommen Sie zur Zeit für einen Dollar?
- Welche deutschen (österreichischen, Schweizer) Konzerne[3] kennen Sie? Was stellen sie her?
- Gibt es in Ihrer Umgebung Zweigstellen[4] deutscher (österreichischer, Schweizer) Firmen?
- Gibt es in Ihrer Stadt deutsche (österreichische, Schweizer) Produkte im Supermarkt oder in Geschäften?
- Kennen Sie jemanden, der in Deutschland (Österreich, der Schweiz) gearbeitet hat? Als was? Wann und wo?

[1]*reference works* [2]durchschnittliche . . . *average yearly income* [3]*large companies, concerns* [4]*branches*

Porträt

Werner von Siemens (1816–1892) ist der Begründer[1] der Elektrotechnik. Er entwickelte[2] die ersten elektrischen Telegraphen und baute die erste Telegraphenlinie von Berlin nach Frankfurt. Später erfand[3] Siemens unter anderem[4] eine Dynamomaschine, baute die erste brauchbare[5] elektrische Lokomotive, die erste elektrische Straßenbahn und den ersten Aufzug.[6] Seine Firma, die er 1847 zusammen mit dem Mechaniker J. G. Halske in Berlin gegründet[7] hatte, verlegte[8] das erste Tiefseekabel im Atlantik von Europa nach Amerika. Werner von

[1]*founder* [2]*developed* [3]*invented* [4]unter . . . *among other things* [5]*feasible* [6]*elevator* [7]*founded* [8]*laid*

Siemens arbeitete immer eng[9] mit seinen Brüdern Wilhelm und Carl zusammen, die in London und St. Petersburg Firmen leiteten.[10] Alle drei Brüder wurden für ihre Leistungen[11] geadelt,[12] Werner in Preußen,[13] Wilhelm in Großbritannien und Carl in Rußland.

Die Siemens AG ist heute das größte deutsche Unternehmen[14] der elektrotechnischen Industrie mit Hauptsitzen in Berlin und München. Schon am Anfang des 20. Jahrhunderts wurde das Unternehmen in Berlin-Spandau so groß, daß ein Teil der Stadt 1914 einen neuen Namen bekam: Siemensstadt. Neben den Werksanlagen[15] findet man in Siemensstadt Werkswohnungen für viele tausend Arbeiter und Angestellte der Firma Siemens.

Berlin-Siemensstadt. Wohnungen für Arbeiter und Angestellte der Firma Siemens.

[9] *closely* [10] *ran* [11] *achievements*
[12] *knighted* [13] *Prussia* [14] *company*
[15] *factory complex*

VIDEOECKE

Wie finanziert man das Studium?

Sie sehen zwei Clips, die zeigen, wie sich Studierende in Deutschland ihr Studium finanzieren können.

- Warum arbeitet Uwe Krüger im Altenheim?
- Wieviel verdient er dabei?
- Wieviel Geld braucht ein Student im Monat?
- Woher kommt das Geld?

Fast jedes Wochenende arbeitet Uwe Krüger, Student der Wirtschaftswissenschaften, in einem Saarbrücker Altenheim

Berufe — Professions

der **Anwalt, ¨e** / die **Anwältin, -nen**	lawyer
der **Arzt** (R), **¨e** / die **Ärztin, -nen**	physician
der **Bademeister, -** / die **Bademeisterin, -nen**	swimming-pool attendant
der/die **Bankangestellte, -n** (*wk. masc.*)	bank employee
der **Berufsberater, -** / die **Berufsberaterin, -nen**	career counselor
der **Dirigent, -en** (*wk. masc.*) / die **Dirigentin, -nen**	(orchestra) conductor
der **Friseur, -e** / die **Friseurin, -nen**	hairdresser
der **Hausmeister, -** / die **Hausmeisterin, -nen**	custodian
der **Kassierer, -** / die **Kassiererin, -nen**	cashier
der **Kellner, -** / die **Kellnerin, -nen**	waiter/waitress
der **Krankenpfleger, -** / die **Krankenpflegerin, -nen**	nurse
der **Postbeamte, -n** (*wk. masc.*) / die **Postbeamtin, -nen**	postal employee
der **Richter, -** / die **Richterin, -nen**	judge
der **Schriftsteller, -** / die **Schriftstellerin, -nen**	writer
der **Verkäufer, -** / die **Verkäuferin, -nen**	salesperson
der **Zahnarzt, ¨e** / die **Zahnärztin, -nen**	dentist

Ähnliche Wörter

der **Arbeiter, -** / die **Arbeiterin, -nen**; der **Architekt, -en** (*wk. masc.*) / die **Architektin, -nen**; der **Automechaniker, -** / die **Automechanikerin, -nen**; der **Bibliothekar, -e** / die **Bibliothekarin, -nen**; der **Fernsehreporter, -** / die **Fernsehreporterin, -nen**; der **Ingenieur, -e** / die **Ingenieurin, -nen**; der **Koch, ¨e** / die **Köchin, -nen**; der **Pilot, -en** (*wk. masc.*) / die **Pilotin, -nen**; der **Polizist, -en** (*wk. masc.*) / die **Polizistin, -nen**; der **Präsident, -en** (*wk. masc.*) / die **Präsidentin, -nen**; der **Priester, -** / die **Priesterin, -nen**; der **Sekretär, -e** / die **Sekretärin, -nen**; der **Steward, -s** / die **Stewardeß, Stewardessen**; der **Taxifahrer, -** / die **Taxifahrerin, -nen**

Orte — Places

die **Ecke, -n**	corner
um die Ecke	around the corner
die **Gaststätte, -n**	restaurant
in der Gaststätte	at the restaurant
die **Kinokasse, -n**	movie theater ticket booth
an der Kinokasse	at the movie theater ticket booth
die **Kirche, -n**	church
in der Kirche	at church
die **Polizei**	police station
auf der Polizei	at the police station
die **Post**	post office
auf der Post	at the post office
die **Tankstelle, -n**	gas station
an der Tankstelle	at the gas station
der **Bahnhof, ¨e**	train station
auf dem Bahnhof	at the train station
der **Schalter, -**	ticket booth
am Schalter	at the ticket booth
das **Büro, -s**	office
im Büro	at the office
das **Gericht, -e**	courthouse
auf dem Gericht	at the courthouse
das **Kaufhaus, ¨er**	department store
im Kaufhaus	at the department store
das **Krankenhaus, ¨er**	hospital
im Krankenhaus	in the hospital
das **Schwimmbad, ¨er** (R)	swimming pool
im Schwimmbad	at the swimming pool

Ähnliche Wörter

die **Bäckerei, -en; in der Bäckerei**; die **Bank, -en; auf der Bank**; die **Schule, -n; in der Schule**; die **Universität, -en; auf der Universität** der **Supermarkt, ¨e; im Supermarkt** das **Hotel, -s** (R); **im Hotel**

In der Küche — In the Kitchen

die **Fensterbank, ¨e**	window sill
die **Flasche, -n**	bottle
die **Geschirrspülmaschine, -n**	dishwasher

die **Küche, -n**	kitchen
die **Küchenwaage, -n**	kitchen scale
die **Salatschüssel, -n**	salad (mixing) bowl
die **Schublade, -n**	drawer
die **Tasse, -n** (R)	cup
der **Backofen, ¨**	oven
der **Herd, -e**	stove
der **Kühlschrank, ¨e**	refrigerator
der **Topf, ¨e**	pot, pan
der **Topflappen, -**	potholder
der **Wasserhahn, ¨e**	faucet
das **Besteck**	silverware, cutlery
das **Geschirr** (R)	dishes
das **Papiertuch, ¨er**	paper towel
das **Spülbecken, -**	sink

Ähnliche Wörter

die **Kaffeemaschine, -n;** die **Küchenarbeit, -en;** die **Küchenlampe, -n;** die **Küchenuhr, -en;** die **Pfanne, -n** der **Küchentisch, -e** das **Glas, ¨er** / das **Weinglas, ¨er**

Einkäufe und Geschenke — Purchases and Presents

die **Badehose, -n**	swim(ming) trunks
die **Briefmarke, -n**	stamp
die **Halskette, -n**	necklace
die **Münze, -n**	coin
die **Mütze, -n**	cap
die **Tasche, -n** (R)	purse, handbag; pocket
der **Badeanzug, ¨e**	bathing suit
der **Regenschirm, -e**	umbrella
der **Reiseführer, -**	travel guidebook
der **Roman, -e** (R)	novel
das **Handtuch, ¨er**	hand towel
das **Weihnachtsgeschenk, -e**	Christmas present
das **Zelt, -e**	tent

Ähnliche Wörter

die **Blumenvase, -n;** die **Kamera, -s;** die **Skibrille, -n** der **Bikini, -s;** der **Fahrradhelm, -e** das **Briefpapier;** das **Computerspiel, -e;** das **Parfüm, -e;** das **T-Shirt, -s** (R)

Schule und Beruf — School and Career

die **Ausbildung**	specialized training
praktische Ausbildung	practical (career) training
die **Bundeswehr**	German army
bei der Bundeswehr	in the German army
die **Schulbildung**	education, schooling
das **Abitur**	college-prep-school degree

Sonstige Substantive — Other Nouns

die **Dusche, -n**	shower
die **Eintrittskarte, -n**	admissions ticket
die **Kundin, -nen**	female customer
die **Lehre**	apprenticeship
die **Möglichkeit, -en**	possibility
die **Tätigkeit, -en**	activity
die **Umgebung, -en**	surrounding area, environs
die **Umkleidekabine, -n**	dressing room
die **Versicherung, -en**	insurance
die **Werkstatt, ¨en**	repair shop, garage
der **Kuchen, -**	cake
der **Kunde, -n** (*wk. masc.*)	male customer
der **Rasen**	lawn
der **Rat, Ratschläge**	advice
der **Termin, -e**	appointment
der **Urlaub**	vacation
der **Vorschlag, ¨e**	suggestion
das **Bauernbrot, -e**	(loaf of) farmer's bread
das **Einzelzimmer, -**	single room
das **Hundefutter**	dog food
das **Interesse, -n**	interest
Interesse haben an (+ *dat.*)	to be interested in
das **Konto, Konten**	bank account
ein Konto eröffnen	to open a bank account
das **Lieblingsfach, ¨er**	favorite subject
das **Öl**	oil
das Öl kontrollieren	to check the oil
die **Kenntnisse** (*pl.*)	skills; knowledge about a field

Ähnliche Wörter

die **Klasse, -n; erster Klasse;** die **Liste, -n;** die **Lotterie, -n; in der Lotterie gewinnen;** die **Patientin, -nen;** die **Politik;** die **Touristenklasse** der **Patient, -en** (*wk. masc.*) das **Pfund, -e;** das **Prestige**

Verben — Verbs

aus·tragen, trägt . . . aus, ausgetragen	to deliver
Zeitungen austragen	to deliver newspapers
einkaufen gehen, ist einkaufen gegangen	to go shopping
entschuldigen	to excuse
entschuldigen Sie!	excuse me
erklären	to explain
erzählen (R)	to tell (a story, joke)
fegen	to sweep
feiern	to celebrate
heiraten	to marry

interessieren	to interest
sich interessieren für	to be interested in
leihen, geliehen	to lend
lenken	to steer; to guide, direct
mähen	to mow
pflegen	to attend to; to nurse
raten, geraten (+ *dat.*)	to advise (a person)
sagen (R)	to say, tell
schenken	to give (as a present)
statt·finden, stattgefunden	to take place
stellen	to place, put
eine Frage stellen	to ask a question
unterrichten	to teach, instruct
untersuchen	to investigate; to examine
verkaufen	to sell
voll·tanken	to fill up (with gas)
vor·schlagen, schlägt . . . vor, vorgeschlagen	to suggest
weg·stellen	to put away
werden, wird, ist geworden	to become
zahlen	to pay
zeichnen	to draw

Ähnliche Wörter

backen, gebacken; heilen; vor·singen, vorgesungen; weg·bringen, weggebracht; wieder·kommen, ist wiedergekommen

Adjektive und Adverbien	Adjectives and Adverbs
ausverkauft	sold out
getrennt	separately; separate checks

Ähnliche Wörter

arbeitslos, flexibel, normal, praktisch, relativ

Sonstige Wörter und Ausdrücke	Other Words and Expressions
alles zusammen	all together; one check
als	as; when
als was?	as what?
als ich acht Jahre alt war	when I was eight years old
außerdem	besides
etwas	something, anything
sonst noch etwas?	anything else?
fast	almost
gern	gladly
ich hätte gern	I would like
hin und zurück	round-trip
irgendwelche, irgendwelcher, irgendwelches	any (+ *noun*)
jede, jeder, jedes	each
mehrmals	several times
nebenan	next door
von nebenan	from next door
tut mir leid!	sorry
und so weiter	and so forth
unter	under, underneath
unter dem Fenster	under the window
zweimal	twice

LESEECKE

LEKTÜRE 1

Vor dem Lesen

1. Haben Sie als Schüler/Schülerin gejobbt[1]? Was haben Sie gemacht? Wann haben Sie gejobbt? in den Ferien oder auch während des Schuljahres?
2. Was haben Sie mit Ihrem Lohn[2] gemacht?

[1] *worked a part-time job* [2] *pay*

3. Ab welchem Alter[3] darf man in Ihrem Bundesstaat arbeiten?
4. Was wissen Sie schon über Jens Krüger und Jutta Ruf? Lesen Sie im Vorwort[4] des Buches nach.
5. Lesen Sie den Titel, Untertitel und die Kurztexte zu den Fotos, und tragen Sie die Informationen in die Tabelle ein.

---

[3] Ab . . . *From what age* [4] *preface*

Name	Alter	Job	Stundenlohn	Geld für . . .
Marco				
Katrin				
Jens				
Jutta				

Marco, 16, jobbt als Hilfsarbeiter auf dem Bau. Verdienst: 12 Mark die Stunde. Wunschtraum: ein Honda-Moped

Kathrin, 14, Nachmittags Bürohilfskraft, abends Babysitting. 2-3mal die Woche. Ausgaben: CD's, USA-Urlaub

KINDERARBEIT

Schwitzen fürs Image

Mehr als 400 000 deutsche Schulkinder jobben, viele illegal. Ihr Antrieb[1] fast immer: Designerklamotten, Statussymbole, mit anderen mithalten

[1] *motivation*

Zum Beispiel Jens Krüger aus München: Pünktlich morgens um sieben ist Jens im Supermarkt. Er räumt Regale ein[2] und hilft hier und dort aus. Acht Stunden arbeitet er am Tag — für acht Mark pro Stunde. Samstags, während der Ferien und manchmal auch in der Woche.

5 Jens ist Gymnasiast[3] in München, geht in die neunte Klasse. Im Supermarkt jobbt er seit seinem zwölften Lebensjahr.

Jens ist einer von vielen. Die meisten seiner Klassenkameraden[4] und -kameradinnen jobben. Von seinem Lohn kauft sich Jens „Nike"-Turnschuhe, „Stüssy"-Jacken für 450 Mark oder die schwarzen „Levi's" für 180 Mark. „Es gefällt mir, 10 soviel Geld für Klamotten[5] auszugeben, und es sieht einfach cool aus", sagt er. Auch da ist er nicht der einzige. 90 Prozent aller „Kinderarbeiter" jobben, um sich ihren Lifestyle zu erhalten.[6] Denn das ist wichtig in der Clique. „Chevignon"-Rucksack, „Levi's"-Jeans oder „Scott"-Mountainbike sind genauso wichtig fürs Image wie das „Mercedes"-Cabrio für die Eltern.

15 Jens' Lehrer finden seine Freizeitaktivitäten nicht so toll, denn für Lernen und Hausaufgaben hat er natürlich wenig Zeit. Genauso wie Jutta. Sie jobbt als Babysitterin und in einer Boutique. „Wenn ich die Hausaufgaben nicht machen kann, schreibe ich eben ab[7]", sagt sie. Zweimal die Woche hütet[8] sie zwei Kleinkinder aus der Nachbarschaft. An zwei Nachmittagen und samstagvormittags jobbt sie 20 jeweils[9] drei Stunden in einer Boutique — für zehn Mark die Stunde. Außerdem bekommt sie die Kleidung in der Boutique billiger. Sie braucht das Geld für Kino, Disko und CDs.

Jens bekommt nur 30 Mark Taschengeld im Monat von seinen Eltern. Das reicht[10] natürlich vorn und hinten nicht. Sein Vater hat nichts dagegen, daß Jens 25 jobbt: „Solange er arbeitet, kommt er nicht auf dumme Gedanken", sagt er.

Jugendarbeitsschutzgesetz:[11] Kinderarbeit unter 14 Jahren ist nicht erlaubt.[12] Schüler und Schülerinnen bis 16 dürfen nur in bestimmten Jobs und nur zwei Stunden täglich arbeiten.

[2]räumt . . . ein *stocks* [3]*pupil at a Gymnasium* [4]*classmates* [5]*clothes (slang)* [6]*maintain* [7]schreibe . . . ab *copy (from another person)* [8]*looks after* [9]*in both cases* [10]*is enough* [11]*law governing working conditions for adolescents* [12]*permitted*

Arbeit mit dem Text

1. Tragen Sie in die Tabelle auf Seite 192 ein, wo Jens und Jutta jobben, wieviel sie verdienen und wofür sie das Geld ausgeben.
2. Woher kommen die meisten „Markenklamotten"[1]? Wie finden Sie die Preise?
3. Warum ist die Kleidung so wichtig für die Jugendlichen?
4. Wofür haben Jutta und Jens wenig Zeit?
5. Ist das legal, was Jutta und Jens machen? Warum (nicht)?
6. Wann hat Jens angefangen, im Supermarkt zu arbeiten? War das legal?

[1]*brand-name clothes*

LEKTÜRE 2

Lebe wohl!

	Stationen eines Lebens
Wenn du erst mal[1] laufen kannst	*erste Schritte*
wenn du erst mal versetzt bist[2]	
wenn du erst mal konfirmiert bist	
wenn du erst mal richtig arbeiten lernst	
wenn du erst mal selber Geld ins Haus bringst	
wenn du erst mal bei den Soldaten[3] gewesen bist	
wenn du erst mal die Prüfung in der Tasche hast	
wenn du erst mal die Frau fürs Leben gefunden hast	
wenn du erst mal eigene Kinder in die Welt gesetzt hast	
wenn du erst mal deine Raten[4] für die neuen Möbel bezahlt hast	
wenn du erst mal die Kinder aus dem Haus hast	
wenn du erst mal eine Lohngruppe[5] höher bist	
wenn du erst mal die Rente[6] durch hast	
wenn du erst mal im Jenseits[7] bist	*Tod*
dann hast du's	
geschafft.[8]	

[1]wenn . . . erst mal *once* [2]versetzt . . . *have gone into the next grade* [3]*soldiers* [4]*installments* [5]*income bracket* [6]*pension* [7]*afterlife* [8]dann . . . *then you have made it*

1. Stationen eines Lebens. Schreiben Sie die folgenden Stichworte[1] neben die entsprechenden[2] Zeilen[3] des Gedichts.

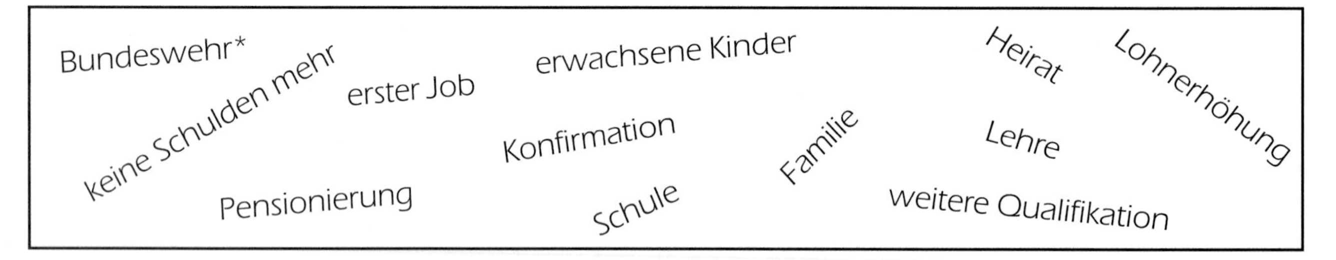

2. Wann haben Sie es geschafft? Schreiben Sie ein eigenes Gedicht. Was wollen Sie erreichen?

MODELL Wenn ich erst mal mit dem College fertig bin
wenn ich erst mal Geld verdiene
. . .

[1]*keywords* [2]*corresponding* [3]*lines*
*In Deutschland müssen alle jungen Männer unter 27 zum Militär- oder Zivildienst.

STRUKTUREN UND ÜBUNGEN

5.1 Dative case: articles and possessive adjectives

The dative case indicates the person to or for whom something is done.

A noun or pronoun in the dative case is used to designate the person to or for whom something is done.

Ernst schenkt **seiner Mutter** ein Buch.	*Ernst gives his mother a book.*
Sofie gibt **ihrem Freund** einen Kuß.	*Sofie gives her boyfriend a kiss.*

Notice that the dative case frequently appears in sentences with three nouns: a person who does something, a person who receives something, and the object that is passed from the doer to the receiver. The doer, the subject of the sentence, is in the nominative case; the recipient, or beneficiary, of the action is in the dative case; and the object is in the accusative case.

Doer		*Recipient*	*Object*
Nominative Case	*Verb*	*Dative Case*	*Accusative Case*
Maria	kauft	ihrem Freund	ein Hemd.

Maria is buying her boyfriend a shirt.

In German, the signal for the dative case is the ending **-m** in the masculine and neuter, **-r** in the feminine, and **-n** in the plural. Here are the dative forms of the definite, indefinite, and negative articles, and of the possessive adjectives.

	Masculine & Neuter	*Feminine*	*Plural*
Definite Article	dem	der	den
Indefinite Article	einem	einer	—
Negative Article	keinem	keiner	keinen
Possessive Adjective	meinem deinem seinem ihrem unserem eurem	meiner deiner seiner ihrer unserer eurer	meinen deinen seinen ihren unseren euren

Jutta schreibt **einem Freund** einen Brief. — *Jutta is writing a letter to a friend.*

Jens erzählt **seinen Eltern** einen Witz. — *Jens is telling his parents a joke.*

All plural nouns end in **n** in the dative unless they form their plural with **s.**

All plural nouns add an **-n** in the dative unless they already end in **n** or in **s.**

Claire erzählt **ihren Freunden** von ihrer Reise nach Deutschland. — *Claire is telling her friends about her trip to Germany.*

Here is a short list of verbs that often take an accusative object and a dative recipient.

erklären	*to explain something to someone*
erzählen	*to tell someone (a story)*
geben	*to give someone something*
leihen	*to lend someone something*
sagen	*to tell someone something*
schenken	*to give someone something as a gift*

Achtung!

Certain masculine nouns, in particular those denoting professions, add **-(e)n** in the dative and accusative singular as well as in the plural.

	Singular	*Plural*
Nominative	der Student	die Studenten
Accusative	den Studenten	die Studenten
Dative	dem Studenten	den Studenten

Übung 1 Was machen Sie für diese Leute?

Schreiben Sie mit jedem Verb einen Satz.

MODELL Ich schenke meiner Mutter eine Kamera.

backen	Bruder/Schwester	ein Abendessen
erklären	Freund/Freundin	meine Bilder
erzählen	Großvater/Großmutter	einen Brief
geben	Vetter/Kusine	ein Buch
kaufen	Vater/Mutter	eine CD
kochen	Onkel/Tante	mein Deutschbuch
leihen	Partner/Partnerin	50 Dollar
schenken	Professor/Professorin	eine Geschichte
schreiben	Mitbewohner/Mitbewohnerin	Kaffee
verkaufen		eine Krawatte
		einen Kuchen
		einen Kuß
		einen Tennisball
		einen Witz

Übung 2 Was machen diese Leute?

Bilden Sie Sätze.

MODELL Heidi schreibt ihren Eltern einen Brief.

Bikini (*m.*) = der Bikini
Grammatik (*f.*) = die Grammatik
Zelt (*n.*) = das Zelt

Heidi	erklären	Eltern	Bikini (*m.*)
Peter	erzählen	Freund	Grammatik (*f.*)
Thomas	geben	Freundin	Karte (*f.*)
Katrin	kaufen	Mann	Regenschirm (*m.*)
Stefan	kochen	Mutter	Armband (*n.*)
Albert	leihen	Professor	Rucksack (*m.*)
Monika	schenken	Schwester	Suppe (*f.*)
Frau Schulz	schreiben	Tante	Märchen (*n.*)
Nora	verkaufen	Vetter	Zelt (*n.*)

5.2 Question pronouns: *wer, wen, wem*

wer (Who is it?) = nominative
wen (Whom do you know?) = accusative
wem (Whom did you give it to?) = dative

Use the pronouns **wer, wen,** and **wem** to ask questions about people: **wer** indicates the subject, the person who performs the action; **wen** indicates the accusative object; **wem** indicates the dative object.

Wer arbeitet heute abend um acht?	*Who's working tonight at eight?*
Wen triffst du heute abend?	*Whom are you meeting tonight?*
Wem leihst du das Zelt?	*To whom are you lending the tent?*

Übung 3 Minidialoge

Ergänzen Sie **wer, wen** oder **wem.**

1. JÜRGEN: _____ hat meinen Regenschirm?
   SILVIA: Ich habe ihn.
2. MELANIE: _____ hast du in der Stadt gesehen?
   JOSEF: Claire.
3. SOFIE: _____ willst du die CD schenken?
   WILLI: Marta. Sie wünscht sie sich schon lange.
4. FRAU AUGENTHALER: Na, erzähl doch mal. _____ hast du letztes Wochenende kennengelernt?
   RICHARD: Also, sie heißt Uschi und . . .
5. MEHMET: _____ wollt ihr denn euren neuen Computer verkaufen?
   RENATE: Schülern und Studenten.
6. NATALIE: Weißt du, _____ heute abend zu uns kommt?
   LYDIA: Nein, du?
   NATALIE: Tante Christa, natürlich.

5.3 Expressing change: the verb *werden*

Use a form of **werden** to talk about changing conditions.

Ich werde alt.	*I am getting old.*
Es wird dunkel.	*It is getting dark.*

werden: e → i
du wirst; er/sie/es wird

werden			
ich	werde	wir	werden
du	wirst	ihr	werdet
Sie	werden	Sie	werden
er / sie / es	wird	sie	werden

In German, **werden** is also used to talk about what somebody wants to be.

Was willst du werden?	*What do you want to be (become)?*
Natalie will Ärztin werden.	*Natalie wants to be (become) a physician.*

Übung 4 Was passiert?

Bilden Sie Fragen, und suchen Sie dann eine logische Antwort darauf.

MODELL Was passiert im Winter? —Es wird kalt.

1. am Abend
2. wenn man Bücher schreibt
3. wenn man Fieber bekommt
4. im Frühling
5. im Herbst
6. wenn Kinder älter werden
7. wenn man in der Lotterie gewinnt
8. wenn man Medizin studiert
9. am Morgen
10. im Sommer

a. Man wird Arzt.
b. Man wird bekannt.[1]
c. Die Blätter werden bunt.[2]
d. Es wird dunkel.
e. Sie werden größer.
f. Es wird wärmer.
g. Es wird hell.[3]
h. Man wird krank.
i. Die Tage werden länger.
j. Man wird reich.

Übung 5 Was werden sie vielleicht?

Suchen Sie einen möglichen Beruf für jede Person.

[1]*well-known* [2]*colorful* [3]*bright*

MODELL Jens mag Autos und Motorräder. →
Vielleicht wird er Automechaniker.

1. Lydia kocht gern.
2. Sigrid interessiert sich für Medikamente.
3. Ernst fliegt gern.
4. Jürgen hat Interesse an Pädagogik.
5. Jutta zeichnet gern Pläne für Häuser.
6. Helga geht gern in die Bibliothek.
7. Hans heilt gern kranke Menschen.
8. Andrea hört gern klassische Musik.

Apotheker/Apothekerin
Architekt/Architektin
Bibliothekar/Bibliothekarin
Dirigent/Dirigentin
Koch/Köchin
Krankenpfleger/Krankenpflegerin
Lehrer/Lehrerin
Pilot/Pilotin

5.4 Location: *in, an, auf* + dative case

When indicating where something is located, **in, an,** and **auf** take the dative case.

To express the location of someone or something, use the following prepositions with the dative case.

in (*in, at*)
auf (*on, at*)
an (*on, at*)
+
dem/einem ____ (*m., n.*)
der/einer ____ (*f.*)
den ____ (*pl.*)

Katrin wohnt **in der Stadt.** — *Katrin lives in the city.*
Stefan und Albert sind **auf der Bank.** — *Stefan and Albert are at the bank.*

A. Forms and Contractions

Remember the signals for dative case.

	Masculine and Neuter	*Feminine*	*Plural*
Dative	dem einem	der einer	den

in + dem = im
an + dem = am

Note that the prepositions **in** and **an** + **dem** are contracted to **im** and **am.**

Masculine and Neuter	*Feminine*	*Plural*
im Kino **in einem** Kino	**in der** Stadt **in einer** Stadt	**in den** Wäldern **in** Wäldern
am See **an einem** See	**an der** Tankstelle **an einer** Tankstelle	**an den** Wänden **an** Wänden
auf dem Berg **auf einem** Berg	**auf der** Bank **auf einer** Bank	**auf den** Bäumen **auf** Bäumen

B. Uses

1. Use **in** when referring to enclosed spaces.

im Supermarkt	*in the supermarket* (enclosed)
in der Stadt	*in (within) the city*

2. **An,** in the sense of English *at,* denotes some kind of border or limiting area.

am Fenster	*at the window*
an der Tankstelle	*at the gas pumps*
am See	*at the lake*

3. Use **auf,** in the sense of English *on,* when referring to surfaces.

auf dem Tisch	*on the table*
auf dem Herd	*on the stove*

4. **Auf** is also used to express location in public buildings such as the bank, the post office, or the police station.

auf der Bank	*at the bank*
auf der Post	*at the post office*
auf der Polizei	*at the police station*

Übung 6 Was macht man dort?

Stellen Sie einem Partner / einer Partnerin Fragen. Er/Sie soll eine logische Antwort darauf geben.

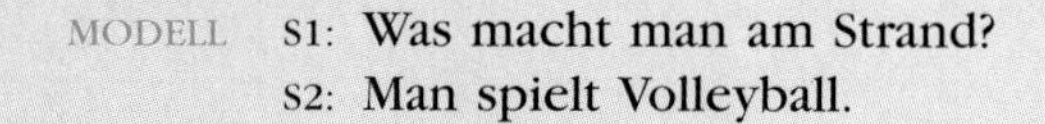
MODELL S1: Was macht man am Strand?
S2: Man spielt Volleyball.

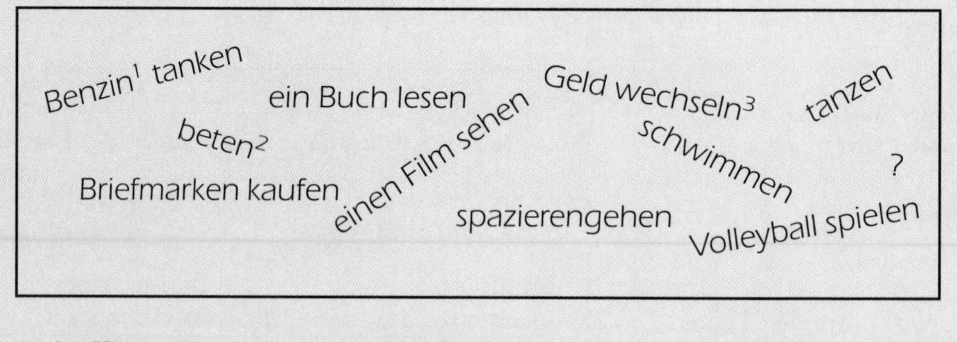

1. im Kino
2. auf der Post
3. an der Tankstelle
4. in der Disko
5. in der Kirche
6. auf der Bank
7. im Meer
8. in der Bibliothek
9. im Park

[1]*gasoline* [2]*to pray* [3]*to exchange*

Übung 7 Wo?

Wo sind die Leute? Wo sind das Poster, der Topf und der Wein?

MODELL Stefan ist am Strand.

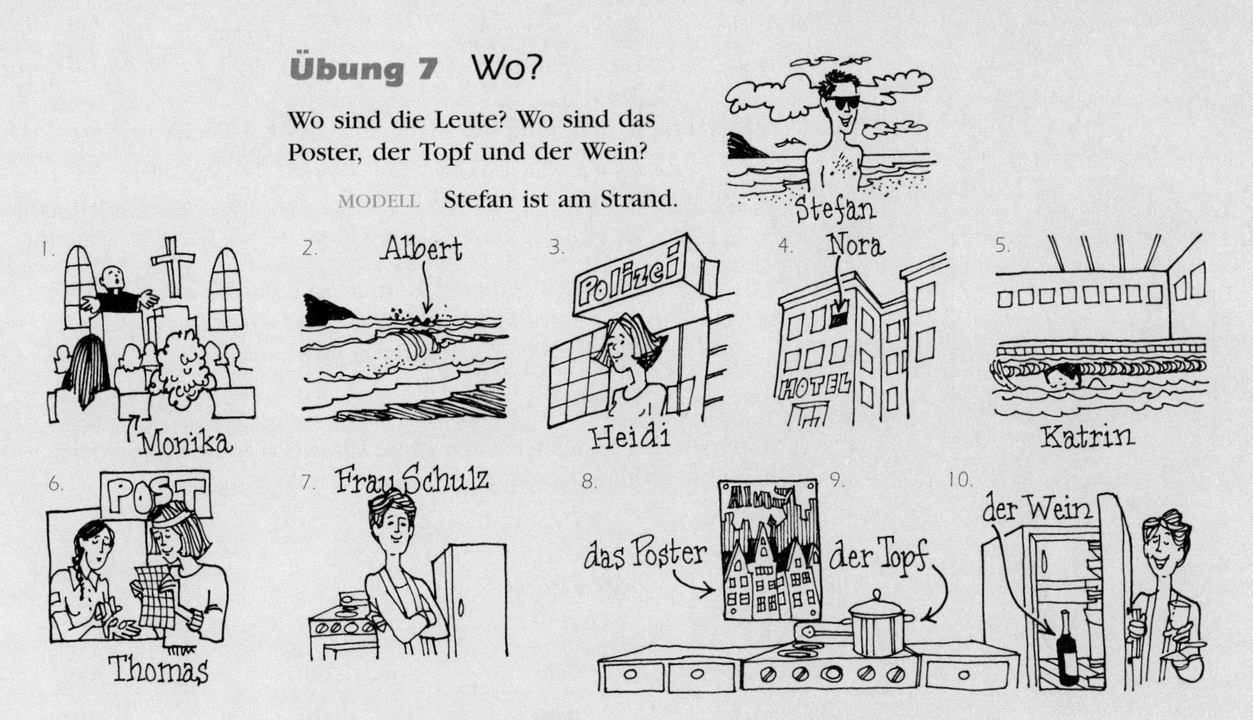

5.5 Dative case: personal pronouns

Personal pronouns in the dative case designate the person to or for whom something is done. (See also **Strukturen 5.1.**)

Kaufst du mir ein Buch?	*Are you buying me a book?*
Nein, ich schenke dir eine CD.	*No, I'm giving you a CD.*

A. First- and Second-person Pronouns

Here are the nominative and dative forms of the first- and second-person pronouns.

Singular		*Plural*	
Nominative	*Dative*	*Nominative*	*Dative*
ich	mir	wir	uns
du	dir	ihr	euch
Sie	Ihnen	Sie	Ihnen

Notice that German speakers use three different pronouns to express the recipient or beneficiary in the second person (English *you*): **dir, euch,** and **Ihnen.**

RICHARD: Leihst du mir dein Auto, Mutti? (*Will you lend me your car, Mom?*)
FRAU AUGENTHALER: Ja, ich leihe **dir** mein Auto. (*Yes, I'll lend you my car.*)

HERR THELEN: Viel Spaß in Wien! (*Have fun in Vienna!*)
HERR WAGNER: Danke! Wir schreiben **Ihnen** eine Postkarte. (*Thank you! We'll write you a postcard.*)

HANS: Ernst und Andrea! Kommt in mein Zimmer! Ich zeige **euch** meine Briefmarken. (*Ernst and Andrea! Come to my room! I'll show you my stamp collection.*)

B. Third-person Pronouns

The third-person pronouns have the same signals as the dative articles: **-m** in the masculine and neuter, **-r** in the feminine, and **-n** in the plural.

de**m** → ih**m**
de**r** → ih**r**
de**n** → ihn**en**

	Masculine and Neuter	*Feminine*	*Plural*
Article	dem	der	den
Pronoun	**ihm**	**ihr**	**ihnen**

Was kaufst du deinem Vater?	*What are you going to buy your dad?*
Ich kaufe **ihm** ein Buch.	*I'll buy him a book.*
Was schenkst du deiner Schwester?	*What are you going to give your sister?*
Ich schenke **ihr** eine Bluse.	*I'll give her a blouse.*
Was kochen Sie ihren Kindern heute?	*What are you going to cook for your kids today?*
Ich koche **ihnen** Spaghetti mit Ketchup.	*I'm making them spaghetti with catsup.*

Notice that the dative-case pronoun precedes the accusative-case noun.

Ich schreibe dir einen Brief. *I'll write you a letter.*

Übung 8 Minidialoge

Ergänzen Sie **mir, dir, uns, euch** oder **Ihnen.**

1. HANS: Mutti, kaufst du _____ Schokolade?
   FRAU RUF: Ja, aber du weißt, daß du vor dem Essen nichts Süßes essen sollst.
2. MARIA: Was hat denn Frau Körner gesagt?
   MICHAEL: Das erzähle ich _____ nicht.

3. ERNST: Mutti, kochst du Andrea und mir einen Pudding?
FRAU WAGNER: Natürlich koche ich _____ einen Pudding.

4. HERR SIEBERT: Sie schulden[1] mir noch zehn Mark, Herr Pusch.
HERR PUSCH: Was!? Wofür denn?
HERR SIEBERT: Ich habe _____ doch für 100 Mark mein altes Motorrad verkauft, und Sie hatten nur 90 Mark dabei.
HERR PUSCH: Ach, ja, richtig.

5. FRAU KÖRNER: Mein Mann und ich gehen heute abend aus. Können Sie _____ vielleicht ein gutes Restaurant empfehlen, Herr Pusch?
MICHAEL: Ja, gern . . .

Übung 9 Wer? Wem? Was?

Beantworten Sie die Fragen mit Hilfe der Tabelle.

MODELL Was hat Renate ihrem Freund geschenkt?
Sie hat ihm ein T-Shirt geschenkt.

	Renate	*Mehmet*
schenken	ein T-Shirt	einen Regenschirm
leihen	ihr Auto	1.000 Mark
erzählen	einen Witz	eine Geschichte
verkaufen	ihre Sonnenbrille	seinen Fernseher
zeigen	ihr Büro	seine Wohnung
kaufen	eine neue Brille	einen Kinderwagen

1. Was hat Mehmet seiner Mutter geschenkt?
2. Was hat Renate ihrem Vater geliehen?
3. Was hat Mehmet seinem Bruder geliehen?
4. Was hat Renate ihrer Friseurin erzählt?
5. Was hat Mehmet seinen Nichten erzählt?
6. Was hat Renate ihrer Freundin verkauft?
7. Was hat Mehmet seinen Eltern verkauft?
8. Was hat Renate ihrem Schwager gezeigt?
9. Was hat Mehmet seinem Freund gezeigt?
10. Was hat Renate ihrer Großmutter gekauft?
11. Was hat Mehmet seiner Schwägerin gekauft?

---

[1] *owe*

KAPITEL 6

Traumwohnung im österreichischen Kitzbühel

In **Kapitel 6**, you will learn vocabulary and expressions for describing where you live, for finding a place to live, and for talking about housework.

Wohnen

THEMEN
Haus und Wohnung
Das Stadtviertel
Auf Wohnungssuche
Hausarbeit

LEKTÜRE
Wohnungsanzeigen
Wohnträume

KULTURELLES
Carl Spitzweg: Der arme Poet
Wohnen in Nordamerika und in Deutschland
Regionale Stile
Das Hundertwasser-Haus
Auf Wohnungssuche
Kulturprojekt: Architektur und Baustile
Porträt: Walter Gropius und Weimar
Videoecke: Ein neues Studentenwohnheim

STRUKTUREN
6.1 Making comparisons with adjectives and adverbs
6.2 Location vs. destination: two-way prepositions with the dative or accusative case
6.3 Word order: time before place
6.4 Direction: **in/auf** vs. **zu/nach**
6.5 Separable-prefix verbs: the present and perfect tenses
6.6 The prepositions **mit** and **bei** + dative

Sprechsituationen

Haus und Wohnung

➤ **Grammatik 6.1–6.2**

Situation 1 Wo ist das?

MODELL S1: Wo ist die Badewanne?
S2: Im Bad.

die Badewanne	die Kopfkissen	im Bad
das Bett	der Kühlschrank	im Eßzimmer
die Dusche	der Nachttisch	in der Küche
die Geschirrspülmaschine	der Schrank	im Schlafzimmer
die Handtücher	das Sofa	im Wohnzimmer
der Herd	der Spiegel	
das Klavier	der Teppich	

Situation 2 Interview: Die Wohnung

1. Was ist größer, dein Schlafzimmer oder dein Wohnzimmer?
2. Was ist moderner, deine Küche oder dein Bad?
3. Was ist älter, deine Stereoanlage oder dein Fernseher?
4. Was ist neuer, dein Kühlschrank oder dein Computer?
5. Was ist kleiner, dein Bett oder dein Sofa?
6. Was ist schöner, dein Teppich oder deine Vorhänge?
7. Was ist teurer, eine Geschirrspülmaschine oder ein Mikrowellenherd?
8. Was ist billiger, ein Handtuch oder ein Schrank?

Kultur ... Landeskunde ... Informationen

Carl Spitzweg: Der arme Poet

- Beschreiben Sie das Zimmer so genau wie möglich: Ist das ein Wohnzimmer, ein Schlafzimmer oder eine Küche? Was gibt es alles in diesem Zimmer?
- Was macht der Mann? Warum ist er im Bett?
- Warum hängt der Regenschirm von der Decke?
- Was ist der Mann von Beruf? Geht er zur Arbeit?
- Ist der Mann verliebt, verlobt,[1] verheiratet oder ledig?
- Erfinden Sie einen Titel für das Bild.
- Ist das Ihre Traumwohnung? Wie sieht Ihre Traumwohnung aus? Bringen Sie ein Foto mit, oder malen[2] Sie ein Bild.

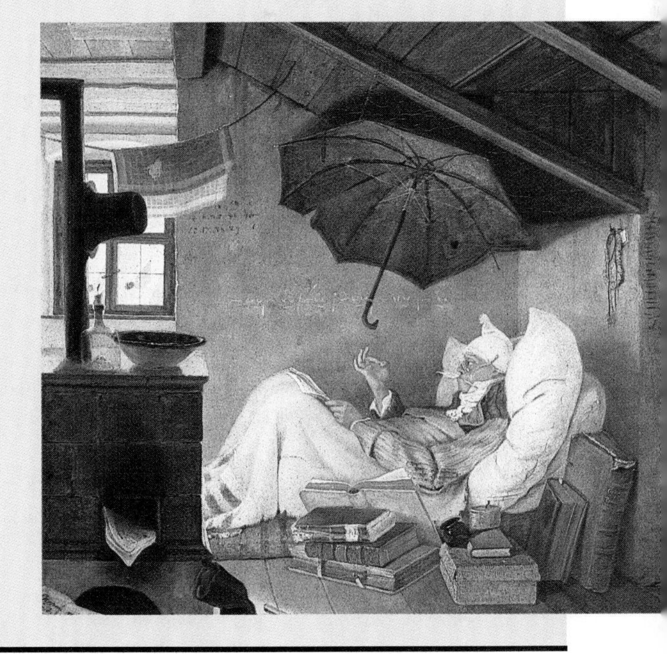

[1] *engaged (to be married)* [2] *paint*

Situation 3 Interview

1. Wo wohnst du? (in einer Wohnung, in einem Studentenheim, in einem Haus, auf dem Land, in der Stadt, _____)
2. Wohnst du allein? (in einer Wohngemeinschaft, bei deinen Eltern, bei einer Familie, mit einem Mitbewohner, mit einer Mitbewohnerin, _____)
3. Wie lange brauchst du zur Uni? (zehn Minuten zu Fuß, fünf Minuten mit dem Fahrrad, eine halbe Stunde mit dem Auto, eine Viertelstunde mit dem Bus, _____)
4. Was kostet dein Zimmer / deine Wohnung pro Monat?
5. Wie groß ist dein Zimmer / deine Wohnung? (20 Quadratmeter, _____)
6. Wie viele Zimmer sind in deiner Wohnung / deinem Haus?
7. Hat deine Wohnung / dein Haus einen Balkon oder eine Terrasse?
8. Was für Möbel hast du in deinem Zimmer / in der Wohnung? Was für Fotos oder Poster?
9. Wie gefällt dir deine Wohnung? (gut, ziemlich gut, nicht besonders gut, schlecht, ziemlich schlecht)
10. Möchtest du eine neue Wohnung? Wie soll sie sein? (größer, mehr Zimmer, billiger, näher an der Uni, schöner, _____)

Kultur ... Landeskunde ... Informationen

Wohnen in Nordamerika und in Deutschland

In Nordamerika:

- Haben moderne nordamerikanische Häuser einen Keller,[1] eine Terrasse, einen Balkon?
- Haben sie einen Garten vor oder hinter dem Haus?
- Aus welchem Material sind die Häuser normalerweise? (aus Stein, aus Holz,[2] aus Beton[3])
- Gibt es einen Zaun[4] um das ganze Grundstück[5] herum oder nur um den Garten hinter dem Haus?
- Wie viele Garagen sind üblich[6]? Wie groß sind die Garagen? (Platz für ein Auto, zwei Autos, drei Autos)
- Aus welchem Material ist das Dach? (aus Asphaltschindeln,[7] aus Holzschindeln,[8] aus Ziegeln[9])

Einfamilienhaus in München

[1]*basement* [2]*wood* [3]*concrete* [4]*fence* [5]*property* [6]*customary* [7]*asphalt shingles* [8]*wooden shingles* [9]*clay tiles*

Wohnblöcke in Ostberlin

Mehrfamilienhaus in Wernigerode

In Deutschland:

- Schauen Sie sich die Fotos an. Welche Unterschiede[10] gibt es zu Häusern in Nordamerika? Hören Sie sich den Text an, und beantworten Sie die folgenden Fragen.
- Wie viele Menschen leben in Deutschland?
- Wie groß ist Deutschland?
- In Deutschland leben ungefähr[11] 200 Menschen auf einem Quadratkilometer,[12] das sind 563 auf einer Quadratmeile. In Nordamerika sind es im Durchschnitt[13] 65. Wie viele sind es in Ihrem Bundesstaat?

[10] *differences* [11] *approximately* [12] *square kilometer* [13] im . . . *on average*

Situation 4 Das Zimmer

MODELL S1: Wo ist die Katze?
S2: Auf dem Sofa.

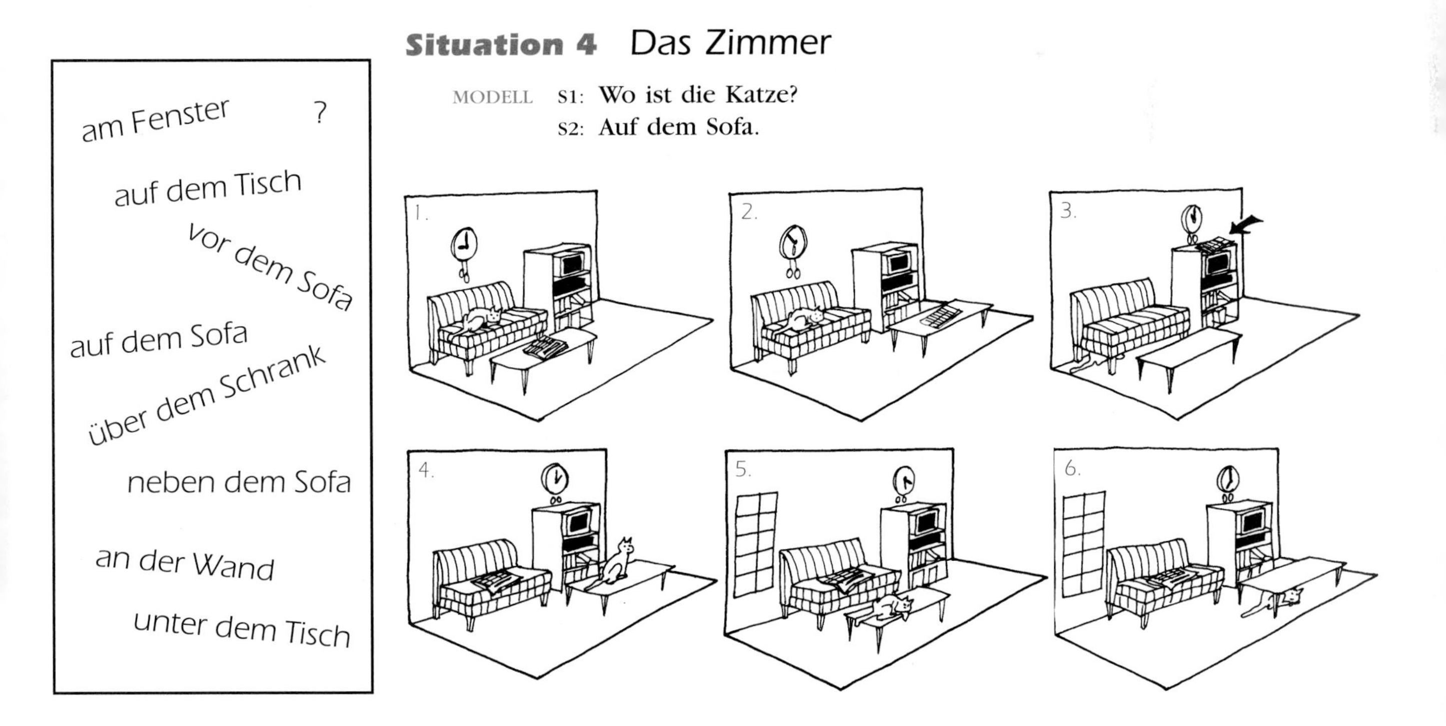

Das Stadtviertel

➤ **Grammatik 6.3–6.4**

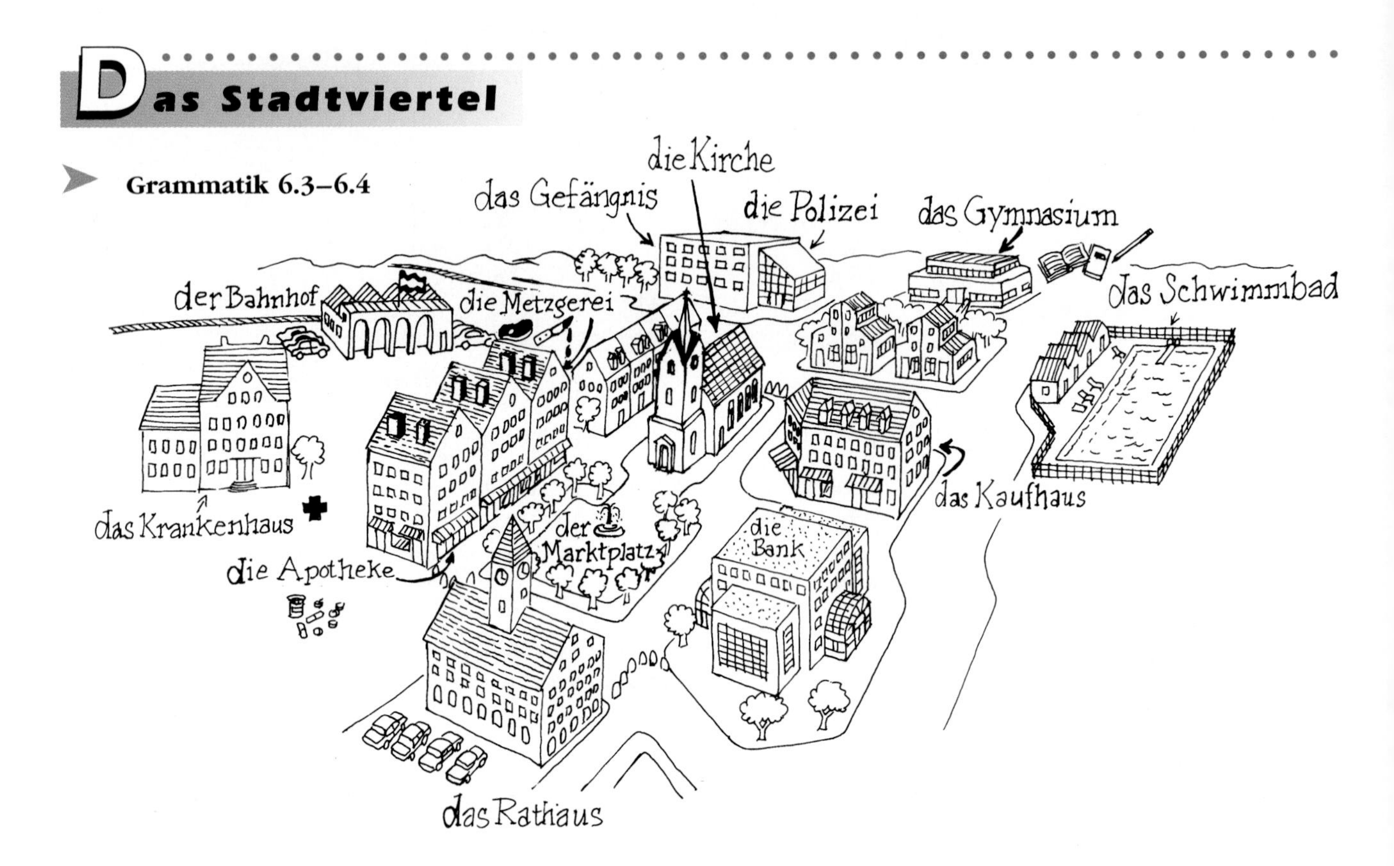

Situation 5 Gleich um die Ecke oder weiter weg?

MODELL S1: Wie weit weg sollte die Apotheke von deiner Wohnung sein?
S2: ______

1. die Apotheke
2. die Universität
3. die Polizei
4. der Flughafen
5. das Kino
6. das Krankenhaus
7. das Gefängnis
8. der Kindergarten
9. der Supermarkt
10. die Kirche
11. der Bahnhof
12. das Rathaus
13. die Bank
14. die Tankstelle
15. das Schwimmbad

gleich um die Ecke
gleich gegenüber
fünf Minuten zu Fuß
zwei Straßen weiter
eine halbe Stunde mit dem Auto
am anderen Ende der Stadt
fünf Minuten mit dem Auto
so weit weg wie möglich
zehn Minuten mit dem Fahrrad
im gleichen Gebäude
mir egal

Kultur ... Landeskunde ... Informationen

Regionale Stile

Welche Beschreibung paßt zu welcher Stadt?

______ ist eine typische Barockstadt. Diesen Baustil[1] gibt es in Deutschland seit ungefähr 1700. Man findet ihn vor allem im Süden von Deutschland und in Österreich. Kirchen, Klöster[2] und Residenzen[3] sind im barocken Baustil gebaut.

________ hat auch den Namen „Die bunte Stadt am Harz", weil die Holzbalken[4] der Häuser so bunt bemalt sind. Diesen Baustil nennt man Fachwerk.[5] Man findet ihn in ganz Deutschland, aber ganz besonders in Norddeutschland, zum Beispiel in Niedersachsen, in Sachsen-Anhalt und in Hessen. Die ältesten Häuser im Fachwerkstil stammen aus dem 14. Jahrhundert.

In _____ findet man viele Häuser aus roten Backsteinen;[6] diesen Baustil nennt man Backsteingotik. Kirchen, Rathäuser, Wohnhäuser und Stadttore wurden aus diesem Material gebaut. Es gibt ihn vor allem in den Hansestädten[7] entlang der Nord- und Ostseeküste.

Die Innenstadt von ______ wurde im 2. Weltkrieg fast völlig zerstört. Man hat diese Stadt als moderne Landeshauptstadt wieder aufgebaut. Trotz einiger alter Gebäude hat man das Gefühl eine neue und moderne Stadt zu besuchen. Viele Industrie- und Wirtschaftszentren in Deutschland, die im zweiten Weltkrieg stark zerstört wurden, sind in diesem modernen Stil geplant und aufgebaut.

Wernigerode

Lübeck

Die Würzburger Residenz

Kröpke-Uhr in Hannover

[1] *architectural style* [2] *monasteries* [3] *palaces* [4] *wooden beams* [5] *half-timber* [6] *bricks* [7] *Hanseatic cities*

Situation 6 Umfrage

MODELL S1: Wohnst du in der Nähe der Universität?
S2: Ja.
S1: Unterschreib bitte hier.

		UNTERSCHRIFT
1.	Wohnst du in der Nähe der Universität?	________
2.	Übernachtest du manchmal in Hotels?	________
3.	Gibt es in deiner Heimatstadt ein Schwimmbad?	________
4.	Warst du letzte Woche auf der Post?	________
5.	Arbeitet ein Freund / eine Freundin von dir bei einer Bank?	________
6.	Warst du gestern im Supermarkt?	________
7.	Gibt es in deiner Heimatstadt ein Rathaus?	________
8.	Warst du letzten Freitag in der Disko?	________
9.	Bist du oft in der Bibliothek?	________
10.	Warst du letzten Sonntag in der Kirche?	________

Situation 7 Wohin gehst du / fährst du, wenn . . . ?

MODELL S1: Wohin gehst du, wenn du ein Buch lesen willst?
S2: Wenn ich ein Buch lesen will? In die Bibliothek.

1.	du schwimmen gehen willst?	zum Bahnhof
2.	du Briefmarken kaufen willst?	ins Hotel
3.	du Geld brauchst?	in die Bäckerei
4.	du Benzin brauchst?	zum Flughafen
5.	du Brot brauchst?	zum Arzt
6.	du krank bist?	auf die Bank
7.	du verreisen willst?	zur Tankstelle
8.	du übernachten willst?	auf die Post
9.	du eine Zugfahrkarte kaufen willst?	ins Schwimmbad
10.	_____ ?	_____

Wohin fahren Sie, wenn Sie Benzin brauchen?

Situation 8 Gestern und heute

MODELL S1: Was war hier früher?
S2: Ein Restaurant.

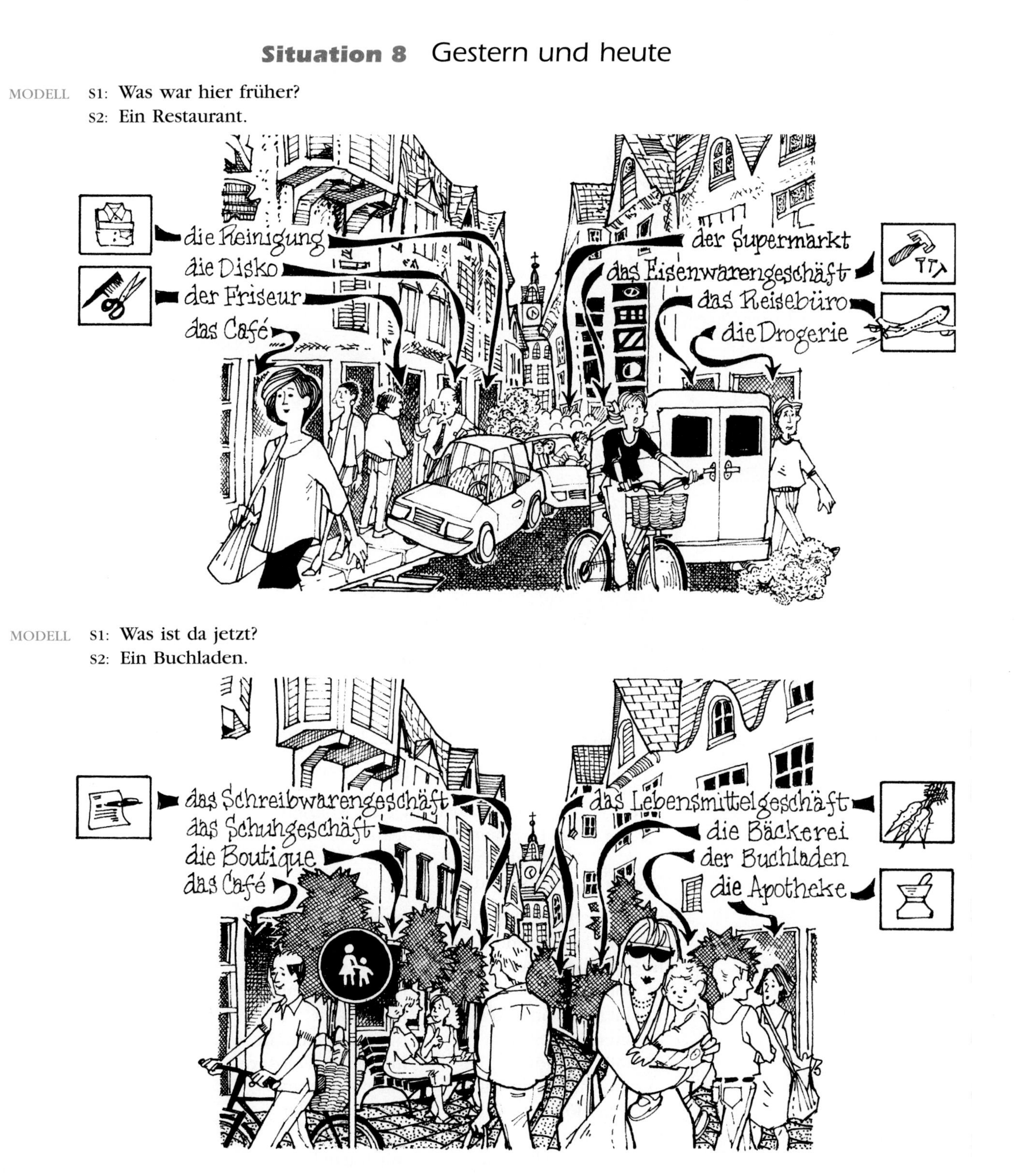

MODELL S1: Was ist da jetzt?
S2: Ein Buchladen.

Auf Wohnungssuche

Situation 9 Wo möchtest du gern wohnen?

Fragen Sie fünf Personen, und schreiben Sie die Antworten auf.

MODELL S1: Wo möchtest du gern wohnen?
S2: In einem Bauernhaus mit alten Möbeln.
S1: Und wo soll es stehen?
S2: Im Wald.

in einem Bauernhaus	mit Weinkeller	am Strand
in einer Raumstation	mit Terrasse	im Wald
in einem Baumhaus	mit Ausblick	in der Innenstadt
in einem Iglu	mit Schwimmbad	am Stadtrand
in einem Wohnwagen	mit Balkon	im Ausland
in einer Palmenhütte	mit alten Möbeln	auf dem Land
in einem Schloß	mit vielen Fenstern	in den Bergen
in einem Wolkenkratzer	mit einem Park	in der Nähe der Stadt
in einer Höhle	mit einem Garten	in einer Bucht
in einer Burg	mit Garage	unter Palmen
in einem Leuchtturm	mit Kachelofen	im Park

Kultur ... Landeskunde ... Informationen

Das Hundertwasser-Haus

Ein Haus von Friedensreich Hundertwasser. Es steht in Bad Soden in Hessen und ist ein Beispiel für kreatives und menschliches Wohnen. Hundertwasser findet, daß Menschen ein „Recht auf Fenster" haben. In seinen Häusern gibt es „Bäume[1] als Mieter[2]", zum Beispiel auf dem Balkon, damit das Wohnen natürlicher ist. Wie finden Sie dieses Haus? Vergleichen[3] Sie es mit den Häusern auf Seite 208 und 209.

Hundertwasser-Haus in Bad Soden im Taunus (Hessen)

[1] *trees* [2] *renters* [3] *compare*

Situation 10 Umfrage

MODELL S1: Möchtest du gern in der Innenstadt leben?
S2: Ja.
S1: Unterschreib bitte hier.

	UNTERSCHRIFT
1. Möchtest du gern in der Innenstadt leben?	____________
2. Möchtest du gern am Stadtrand leben?	____________
3. Kannst du dir ein Leben auf dem Land vorstellen?	____________
4. Möchtest du gern im Ausland wohnen?	____________
5. Möchtest du in einem Schloß wohnen?	____________
6. Möchtest du in einem Wohnwagen leben?	____________
7. Kannst du dir ein Leben auf einem Hausboot vorstellen?	____________
8. Möchtest du gern drei Monate in einer Raumstation wohnen?	____________
9. Möchtest du gern eine Woche unter Wasser wohnen?	____________

Kultur ... Landeskunde ... Informationen

Auf Wohnungssuche

Wie haben Sie Ihr Zimmer / Ihre Wohnung gefunden? Kreuzen Sie an.

durch eine Anzeige[1] in der Zeitung	□	durch eine Anzeige am Schwarzen Brett	□
mit Hilfe der Uni	□	durch die Gelben Seiten im Telefonbuch	□
durch Freunde oder Bekannte	□		

Schauen Sie sich das Foto und die Anzeigen an.

- Wer sucht ein Zimmer?
- Wo kann man eine Wohnung mieten?
- Wo kann man in eine Wohngemeinschaft einziehen?

ER IST WIEDER DA . . .
ALIEN XIV
—DER NACHMIETER[2]—

. . . Ein halbes Jahr war er in Schweden. Aber plötzlich[3] ist er wieder in Hamburg. Manche nennen[4] ihn EL SYMPATICO. Doch die meisten Karsten. Er will nur eines: DEINE WOHNUNG! (1–2 Zi bis 400,– incl.)

Wenn Du ihn anrufst, ruft er zurück . . .

Niemand hat es bis jetzt gewagt[5] . . .

04451 -83591 | 04451 -83591 | 04451 -83591 | 04451 -83591 | 04451 -83591 | 04451 -83591 | 04451 -83591 | 04451 -83591 | 04451 -83591

Vermiete[6] im September
2-Zimmer-Whg in St. Pauli (Hinterhof).
Miete 400,– + Heizung, Strom, Telefon.
wenn Katzenliebhaber/in[7] auch den Kater mitversorgt,[8] gibt es die Wohnung billiger.

2te Person für 3-Zimmer Wohnung in Ottensen (HH50) ab Juli gesucht.
Miete: DM 400,– + Kaution[9]
Tel. (040) 39 22 93

Studentin sucht Wohnung

[1]*ad* [2]*subletter* [3]*suddenly* [4]*call* [5]*dared* [6]*renting out* [7]*cat lover* [8]*helps take care of* [9]*security deposit*

Situation 11 Zum Schreiben: Wohnung gesucht!

Sie haben ein Stipendium an der Universität Basel bekommen. Jetzt suchen Sie eine Wohnung oder ein Zimmer in einer Wohngemeinschaft. Schreiben Sie eine Suchanzeige für das Schwarze Brett. Wohnungen sind sehr knapp—machen Sie Ihre Anzeige also möglichst attraktiv!

Situation 12 Dialog: Auf Wohnungssuche

Silvia ist auf Wohnungssuche.

FRAU SCHUSTER: _______!

SILVIA: Guten Tag. Hier Silvia Mertens. Ich rufe wegen des Zimmers an. Ist es noch __?

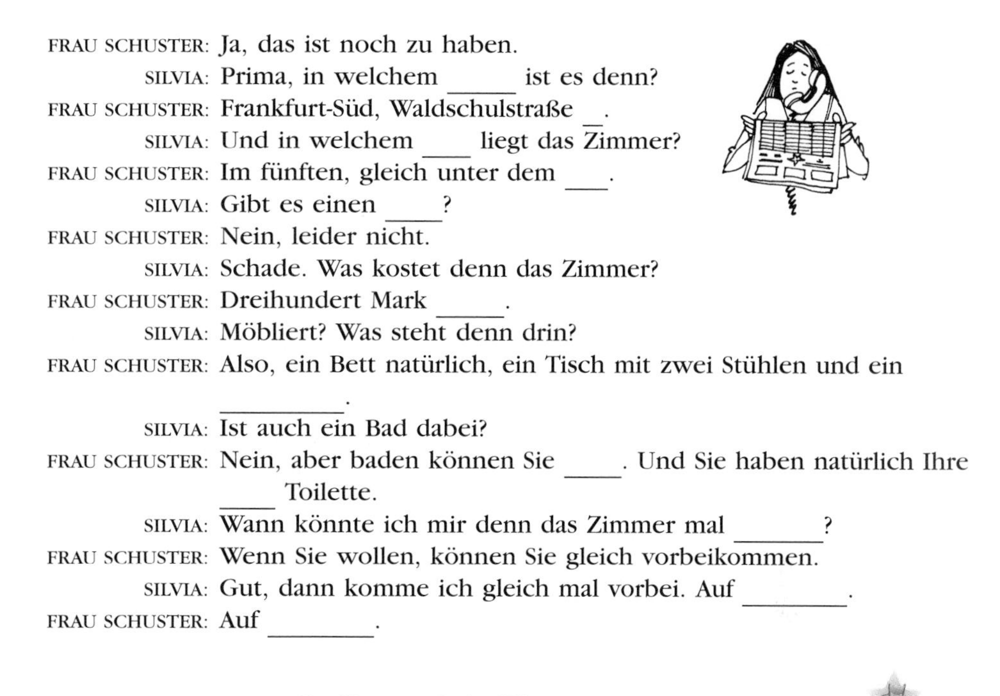

FRAU SCHUSTER: Ja, das ist noch zu haben.
SILVIA: Prima, in welchem _____ ist es denn?
FRAU SCHUSTER: Frankfurt-Süd, Waldschulstraße _.
SILVIA: Und in welchem ____ liegt das Zimmer?
FRAU SCHUSTER: Im fünften, gleich unter dem ___.
SILVIA: Gibt es einen ____?
FRAU SCHUSTER: Nein, leider nicht.
SILVIA: Schade. Was kostet denn das Zimmer?
FRAU SCHUSTER: Dreihundert Mark _____.
SILVIA: Möbliert? Was steht denn drin?
FRAU SCHUSTER: Also, ein Bett natürlich, ein Tisch mit zwei Stühlen und ein _________.
SILVIA: Ist auch ein Bad dabei?
FRAU SCHUSTER: Nein, aber baden können Sie ____. Und Sie haben natürlich Ihre ____ Toilette.
SILVIA: Wann könnte ich mir denn das Zimmer mal _______?
FRAU SCHUSTER: Wenn Sie wollen, können Sie gleich vorbeikommen.
SILVIA: Gut, dann komme ich gleich mal vorbei. Auf ________.
FRAU SCHUSTER: Auf ________.

Situation 13 Rollenspiel: Zimmer zu vermieten

S1: Sie sind Student/Studentin und suchen ein schönes, großes Zimmer. Das Zimmer soll hell und ruhig sein. Sie haben nicht viel Geld und können nur bis zu 500 DM Miete zahlen, inklusive Nebenkosten. Sie rauchen nicht und hören keine laute Musik. Fragen Sie den Vermieter / die Vermieterin, wie groß das Zimmer ist, was das Zimmer kostet, ob das Zimmer im Winter warm ist, ob Sie kochen dürfen, ob Ihre Freunde Sie besuchen dürfen. Sagen Sie dann, ob Sie das Zimmer mieten möchten.

Hausarbeit

➤ **Grammatik 6.5–6.6**

Andrea putzt ihre Schuhe.

Paula wischt den Tisch ab.

Ernst mäht den Rasen.

Jens fegt den Boden.

Josie saugt Staub.

Uli bügelt sein Hemd.

Jochen macht die Toilette sauber.

Jutta wäscht die Wäsche.

Margret putzt den Boden.

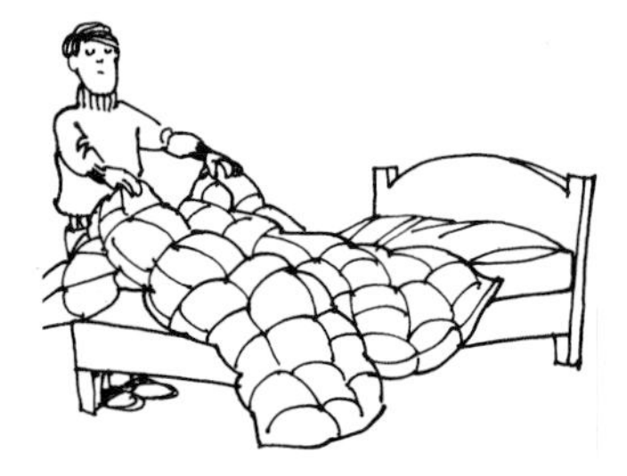

Hans macht sein Bett.

Situation 14 Was macht man mit einem Staubsauger?

MODELL S1: Was macht man mit einem Staubsauger?
S2: Mit einem Staubsauger saugt man Staub.

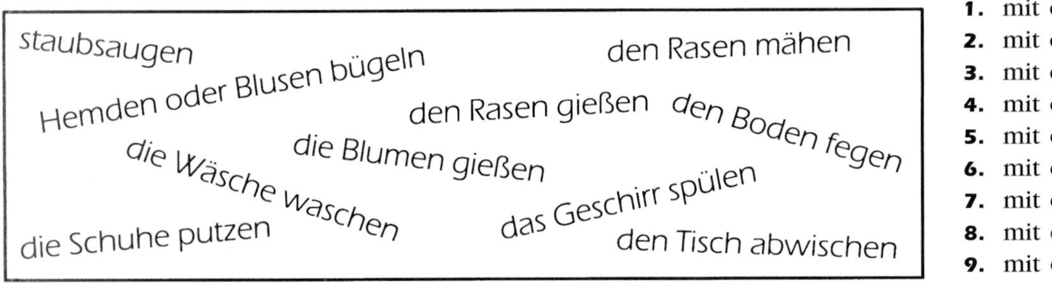

1. mit einem Staubsauger
2. mit einer Geschirrspülmaschine
3. mit einer Waschmaschine
4. mit einem Besen
5. mit einem Rasenmäher
6. mit einer Gießkanne
7. mit einem Bügeleisen
8. mit einem Putzlappen
9. mit einem Gartenschlauch

Situation 15 Bildgeschichte: Frühjahrsputz

Situation 16 Informationsspiel: Haus- und Gartenarbeit

MODELL
S1: Was macht Nora am liebsten?
S2: Sie _____ am liebsten _____ .
S1: Was hat Thomas letztes Wochenende gemacht?
S2: Er hat _____ .

S2: Was muß Nora diese Woche noch machen?
S1: Sie muß _____ .
S2: Was machst du am liebsten?
S1: Ich _____ am liebsten _____ .

	Thomas	Nora	mein(e) Partner(in)
am liebsten	den Rasen mähen		
am wenigsten gern		die Fenster putzen	
jeden Tag		den Tisch abwischen	
einmal in der Woche	sein Bett machen		
letztes Wochenende		ihre Bluse bügeln	
gestern		ihr Zimmer aufräumen	
diese Woche	seine Wäsche waschen		
bald mal wieder	die Flaschen wegbringen		

Hints for working with the Kulturprojekt

The *Encyclopedia Britannica* provides an excellent overview of the history of Western architecture (look under "architecture"). Additional information on famous architects can be found in its articles on the various German-speaking countries (e.g., look up "Austria" and then read the section on "Cultural Life").

Kulturprojekt Architektur und Baustile

Suchen Sie Bücher zur deutschen Architektur und Kunstgeschichte oder einen Reiseführer und beantworten Sie die folgenden Fragen.

- Welche berühmten deutschsprachigen Architekten gibt es? Was haben sie z.B. gebaut? Gibt es in den USA Gebäude von deutschen, österreichischen oder schweizerischen Architekten?
- Welche Baustile gibt es in Deutschland (Österreich, der Schweiz), z.B. in Berlin, Dresden, Rostock, München, Wien, Zürich?
- Welchen Baustil finden Sie typisch deutsch (österreichisch, schweizerisch)? Geben Sie ein Beispiel (Name, Foto oder Zeichnung).
- Gibt es in Ihrer Stadt oder Gegend Häuser im deutschen (österreichischen, schweizerischen) Stil? Wie sehen sie aus?

Porträt

Das Goethe-Schiller-Denkmal vor dem Hoftheater in Weimar

Der Architekt Walter Gropius (1883–1969) gründete[1] 1919 in Weimar das Bauhaus. So berühmte Künstler[2] wie Lyonel Feininger, Gerhard Mercks, Paul Klee und Wassily Kandinsky arbeiteten im Bauhaus, zuerst in Weimar und ab 1925 in Dessau. Ein moderner, funktionaler Stil in der Architektur und strenges,[3] pragmatisches Design waren die Ausdrucksformen dieser neuen Kunstrichtung.[4] Ein Beispiel für Architektur im Bauhausstil ist Siemensstadt in Berlin (vgl.[5] S. 188). 1933 vertrieben[6] die Nazis Gropius aus Deutschland. 1937 emigrierte er in die USA und wurde Professor für Architektur an der Harvard Universität.

Weimar ist nicht nur wegen des Bauhauses berühmt. In dieser kleinen Stadt in Thüringen lebten und arbeiteten auch die berühmtesten deutschen Dichter[7] der Klassik, Johann Wolfgang von Goethe und Friedrich Schiller. Der Komponist Johann Sebastian Bach war Organist in der Stadtpfarrkirche,[8] und Johann Gottlieb Herder war dort Prediger.[9] 1919 tagte[10] in Weimar die Nationalversammlung[11] und verabschiedete[12] die neue Verfassung[13] für die Weimarer Republik (1919–1933). Auf dem Ettersberg bei Weimar war das berüchtigte[14] Konzentrationslager[15] Buchenwald.

[1]*founded* [2]*artists* [3]*disciplined* [4]*artistic form* [5](= vergleiche) *compare* [6]*expelled* [7]*poets* [8]*main parish church* [9]*preacher* [10]*convened* [11]*national congress* [12]*passed* [13]*constitution* [14]*notorious* [15]*concentration camp*

Videoecke

Ein neues Studentenwohnheim

Zu Beginn des Semesters überall an den Universitäten das gleiche Bild.

In Universitätsstädten gibt es kaum freie Zimmer oder Wohnungen. Nur wenige Glückliche kommen im Studentenheim unter.[1] Der Clip zeigt, wie schön es diese kleine Gruppe hat.

- In welcher Stadt steht das neue Studentenwohnheim?
- Wie viele Studenten können in diesem Heim wohnen?
- Wieviel kostet ein Zimmer?
- Wieviel Prozent der Studenten bekommt einen Platz im Wohnheim?

[1]kommen . . . unter *get accommodations*

WORTSCHATZ

In der Stadt — In the City

die **Apotheke, -n** — pharmacy
die **Bushaltestelle, -n** — busstop
die **Drogerie, -n** — drugstore
die **Fabrik, -en** — factory
die **Metzgerei, -en** — butcher shop
die **Reinigung, -en** — dry cleaner's
die **Stadt, ¨e** — town, city
  die **Heimatstadt, ¨e** — hometown
  die **Innenstadt, ¨e** — downtown
die **Straße, -n** — street, road

der **Buchladen, ¨** — bookstore
der **Flughafen, ¨** — airport
der **Stadtrand, ¨er** — city limits
der **Stadtteil, -e** — district, neighborhood
der **Wolkenkratzer, -** — skyscraper

das **Bürohaus, ¨er** — office building
das **Eisenwarengeschäft, -e** — hardware store
das **Gebäude, -** — building
das **Gefängnis, -se** — prison, jail
das **Lebensmittelgeschäft, -e** — grocery store
das **Rathaus, ¨er** — town hall
das **Schreibwarengeschäft, -e** — stationery store
das **Stadtviertel, -** — district, neighborhood

Ähnliche Wörter

die **Boutique, -n**   der **Kindergarten, ¨**; der **Marktplatz, ¨e**; der **Parkplatz, ¨e**   das **Reisebüro, -s**; das **Schuhgeschäft, -e**

Haus und Wohnung — House and Apartment

die **Badewanne, -n** — bathtub
die **Diele, -n** — front entryway
die **Eßecke, -n** — dining area
die **Treppe, -n** — stairway
die **Waschküche, -n** — laundry room
die **Zentralheizung** — central heating

der **Aufzug, ¨e** — elevator
der **Ausblick, -e** — view
der **Flur, -e** — hallway
der **Kachelofen, ¨** — tile stove, hearth
der **Quadratmeter (qm)** — square meter (m^2)
der **Stock, Stockwerke** — floor, story
  im ersten Stock* — on the second floor

das **Dach, ¨er** — roof
das **Waschbecken, -** — (wash) basin

Ähnliche Wörter

die **Garage, -n**; die **Terrasse, -n**; die **Toilette, -n**   der **Balkon, -e**; der **Keller, -**; der **Weinkeller, -**   das **Bad, ¨er**; das **Eßzimmer, -**; das **Schlafzimmer, -**; das **Wohnzimmer, -**

Haus und Garten — House and Garden

die **Bürste, -n** — brush
die **Gießkanne, -n** — watering can
die **Kommode, -n** — dresser
die **Seife, -n** — soap

der **Besen, -** — broom
der **Frühjahrsputz** — spring cleaning
der **Gartenschlauch, ¨e** — garden hose
der **Putzlappen, -** — cloth, rag (for cleaning)
der **Rasenmäher, -** — lawn mower
der **Schrank, ¨e** — closet; cupboard
  der **Kleiderschrank, ¨e** — clothes closet, wardrobe
der **Sekretär, -e** — fold-out desk
der **Sessel, -** (R) — armchair
der **Spiegel, -** — mirror
der **Staubsauger, -** — vacuum cleaner
der **Vorhang, ¨e** — drapery

das **Bügeleisen, -** — iron
das **Kopfkissen, -** — pillow

die **Möbel** (*pl.*) — furniture

Ähnliche Wörter

die **Palme, -n**; die **Pflanze, -n**; die **Zimmerpflanze, -n**; die **Stereoanlage, -n**; die **Waschmaschine, -n**   der **Nachttisch, -e**; der **Wohnzimmertisch, -e**   **das Bett machen**; das **Handtuch, ¨er**; das **Poster, -**; das **Sofa, -s**

---

*The first floor is called **das Erdgeschoß.** All levels above the first floor are referred to as **Stockwerke.** Thus, **der erste Stock** refers to the second floor, and so on.

Wohnmöglichkeiten — Living Arrangements

die **Burg, -en** — fortress
die **Höhle, -n** — cave
die **Palmenhütte, -n** — hut made of palms
die **Raumstation, -en** — space station
die **Wohngemeinschaft, -en** — shared housing

der **Leuchtturm, ¨-e** — lighthouse

der **Haus, ¨-er** — house
  das **Bauernhaus, ¨-er** — farmhouse
  das **Baumhaus, ¨-er** — tree house
das **Schloß, Schlösser** — palace

Ähnliche Wörter

das **Hausboot, -e;** das **Iglu, -s**

Auf Wohnungssuche — Looking for a Room or Apartment

die **Anzeige, -n** — ad
die **Kaution, -en** — security deposit
die **Miete, -n** — rent
die **Mieterin, -nen** — female renter
die **Suchanzeige, -n** — housing-wanted ad
die **Vermieterin, -nen** — landlady

der **Mieter, -** — male renter
der **Vermieter, -** — landlord

die **Nebenkosten** (*pl.*) — extra costs (e.g., utilities)

Sonstige Substantive — Other Nouns

die **Bucht, -en** — bay
die **Nähe** — vicinity
  in der Nähe — in the vicinity
die **Seite, -n** — side; page
die **Viertelstunde, -n** — quarter hour
die **Zugfahrkarte, -n** — train ticket

das **Ausland** — foreign countries
  im Ausland — abroad
das **Benzin** — gasoline
das **Land, ¨-er** — country (*rural*)
  auf dem Land — in the country
das **Mitglied, -er** — member

Verben — Verbs

ab·trocknen — to dry (dishes)
ab·wischen — to wipe clean
bügeln — to iron
geben, gibt, gegeben — to give
  es gibt . . . — there is/are . . .
  gibt es . . . ? — is/are there . . . ?
mieten — to rent
putzen — to clean; to mop
rad·fahren, fährt . . . Rad, ist radgefahren — to bicycle
staub·saugen — to vacuum
stehen, gestanden — to stand
tippen — to type
übernachten — to stay overnight
vermieten — to rent out
vor·stellen — to introduce, present
  sich etwas vorstellen — to imagine something

Ähnliche Wörter

kosten; wieder·hören; auf Wiederhören!; zurück·kommen, ist zurückgekommen

Adjektive und Adverbien — Adjectives and Adverbs

dunkel — dark
eigen — own
hell — light
hoch — high
möbliert — furnished
nah — close
warm — heated, heat included
weit — far
  wie weit weg? — how far away?

Ähnliche Wörter

attraktiv, dumm, leicht, liberal, modern

Sonstige Wörter und Ausdrücke — Other Words and Expressions

bei — at; with
  bei deinen Eltern — with/at your parents'
  bei einer Bank — at a bank
  ist ein/eine . . . dabei? — does it come with a . . . ?
drin/darin — in it
egal — equal, same
  das ist mir egal — it doesn't matter to me
gegenüber — opposite; across
  gleich gegenüber — right across the way
gleich — right, directly
  gleich um die Ecke — right around the corner
inklusive — included (utilities)
knapp — just, barely
möglichst (+ *adverb*) — as . . . as possible
ob — if, whether
prima! — great!
unter — below, beneath; among
wegen — on account of; about

LESEECKE

LEKTÜRE 1

Vor dem Lesen

Wenn Sie eine Wohnung suchen, können Sie in der Zeitung eine Anzeige aufgeben[1] oder einfach die Wohnungsanzeigen lesen. Meistens gibt es zwei Kategorien: Vermietungen und Mietgesuche.[2]

1. Lesen Sie die Anzeigen flüchtig[3] und ordnen Sie sie ein. Wer will eine Wohnung vermieten? Wer sucht eine Wohnung?
2. In welchem Land hat man diese Anzeigen aufgegeben? Suchen Sie Hinweise[4] im Text. Welche Städte oder Bundesländer kommen vor?

---

[1]*post* [2]*apartment-wanted ads* [3]Lesen . . . flüchtig *Skim* [4]*clues*

a. Kleinwohnung, (bzw. Einzelzimmer), Hötting, Zentralheizung, Duschbenützung, für ordentlichen[1] Tiroler oder Vorarlberger Studenten (männlich) frei. Zuschriften[2] an TT[3] unter Nr. b824829-9

b. **Sie oder Er,** Nichtraucher im Beruf, guter Leumund,[4] sauber, hilfsbereit,[5] bietet sich schöne, komplett möblierte Wohngelegenheit[6] (längerfristig). Zuschriften an TT unter Nr. w824654-9

c. **Garçonniere**[7] in Innsbruck, auch teilmöbliert, baldmöglichst gesucht. Telefon 05 12/29 56 46 (ab 18 Uhr). 822633-8

d. **Freundlicher Student** sucht ruhige Wohnung, Zimmer oder ähnliches. Helfe auch bei kleineren Arbeiten im Haus, Garten, gehe mit dem Hund. Telefon 02 22/310 82 68 oder Zuschriften an TT unter Nr. w822091-8

e. Vermiete an Student/Studentin ab sofort in der Reichenau[8] Zimmer um 2000.-. Nur Wochenendheimfahrer. Zuschriften an TT unter Nr. t825228-9

f. Tyrolean-Airways-Pilot sucht günstige Großgarçonniere oder 2-Zimmer-Wohnung im Raum Innsbruck-Stadt bis Telfs.[9] Zuschriften an TT unter Nr. w825571-8

[1]*neat* [2]*application in writing* [3](TT = *"Tiroler Tageblatt"*) *regional newspaper of Tyrol* [4]*reputation* [5]*helpful* [6]*housing opportunity* [7]Einzimmerwohnung [8]*region in Austria* [9]*town near Innsbruck*

Arbeit mit dem Text

A. Sie arbeiten bei der Wohnungsvermittlung. Welche Wohnung (oder welcher Mieter) kommt für die folgenden Personen in Frage?

1. Julia Maierhofer studiert in Innsbruck und fährt jedes Wochenende nach Hause. Sie kann ungefähr 2000 Schilling für ein Zimmer ausgeben. An welche Nummer kann sie schreiben?

2. Paul Obermeier, Polizist, ledig, sehr seriös, arbeitet jetzt in Innsbruck und sucht eine möblierte Wohnung. An welche Nummer kann er schreiben?
3. Sebastian Buchner aus Arlberg studiert Betriebswirtschaft. Er sucht ein Zimmer oder eine kleine Wohnung. An welche Nummer kann er schreiben?
4. Frau Hohler hat eine sehr preisgünstige Wohnung zu vermieten. Sie möchte jemanden, der ihr den Rasen mäht und ihren Hund betreut, wenn sie nicht da ist. Welche Nummer ruft sie an?
5. Familie Augenthaler hat in ihrem Haus ab sofort eine Garçonniere frei; bei Bedarf auch teilmöbliert. Unter welcher Telefonnummer sucht jemand so eine Wohnung?
6. Herr Kliegl hat in seinem Appartementhaus zwei große Einzimmerwohnungen frei. Er vermietet nur an Leute mit sicherem Arbeitsplatz und Einkommen. Wem bietet er eine Wohnung an?

B. Auf dem Wohnungsmarkt gibt es bestimmte Fachbegriffe.[1] Kombinieren Sie die Begriffe mit den Definitionen.

1. Es gibt eine Gas-, Öl- oder Warmluftheizung für das ganze Haus.
2. Die Dusche muß man sich mit anderen Mietern teilen.
3. Der Vermieter möchte nur an Leute mit gutem Ruf[2] vermieten.
4. Eine Wohnung, die nur aus einem Zimmer mit Bad (oder Dusche) und Kochgelegenheit[3] besteht.
5. Der Vermieter möchte, daß der Mieter längere Zeit bei ihm wohnt.
6. Der Mieter möchte so schnell wie möglich eine Wohnung finden.

a. längerfristig
b. guter Leumund
c. Garçonniere
d. baldmöglichst
e. Zentralheizung
f. Duschbenutzung

[1]*specialized terminology* [2]*reputation* [3]*kitchen facilities*

LEKTÜRE 2

Wohnträume

So möchten vier junge Leute aus Deutschland, Österreich und der Schweiz wohnen.

SUSANNE, 17 JAHRE

Ich wünsch' mir ein altes Schloß in Österreich, in das ich mit meiner Freundin einziehe. Das Schloß soll groß sein und viele Zimmer mit vielen alten Möbeln haben. Dazu gehört auch ein riesiger Park mit Reitpferden, Hunden und vielen anderen Tieren.

CLAUDIA, 16 JAHRE

Ein total rundes Haus, wie eine Kugel, ganz modern, mit vielen Stockwerken—das wäre toll. Viele Fenster müssen auch drin sein. Die Möbel darin dürfen allerdings nicht zu modern sein. Stehen sollte das Kugelhaus an der Côte d'Azur in Frankreich, mit Blick aufs Meer. Da möchte ich mit meinem Freund und meiner besten Freundin und ihrem Freund wohnen.

PETER, 20 JAHRE

Ich möchte mit meiner Freundin auf einer kleinen Insel in der Nordsee wohnen, einer Hallig vor der Küste von Schleswig-Holstein. Auf einem renovierten alten Bauernhof mit kleinen Zimmern, vielen Fenstern und alten Bauernmöbeln. Außer uns wohnt niemand auf der Insel.

MARTIN, 18 JAHRE

Meine Traumwohnung ist mitten in Zürich, in einem großen Altbau. Es ist eine große Wohnung mit hohen Zimmern, die alle miteinander verbunden sind. Im Bad möchte ich eine große alte Badewanne. Es sind nicht viele Möbel in meiner Traumwohnung, in einem Raum steht nur ein riesiges Bett. Die Wände müssen gut isoliert sein, damit ich den ganzen Tag laut Musik hören kann.

Arbeit mit dem Text

A. Ergänzen Sie das Raster.

	Susanne	Claudia	Peter	Martin
In welchem Land?				
Auf dem Land oder in der Stadt?				
Wohnung oder Haus?				
Möbel?				
Mit wem?				

B. Antworten Sie bitte.

1. Wer träumt von einem alten Haus (einer alten Wohnung)?
2. Wie viele Leute möchten Tiere haben?
3. Wer träumt von alten Möbeln?
4. Wer will ein unkonventionelles Haus?

STRUKTUREN UND ÜBUNGEN

6.1 Making comparisons with adjectives and adverbs

A. Comparisons of Equality: so . . . wie

so . . . wie = *as . . . as*

To say that two or more persons or things are alike or equal in some way, use the phrase **so . . . wie** (*as . . . as*) with an adjective or adverb.

Die Küche ist **so groß wie** das Wohnzimmer. — *The kitchen is as big as the living room.*

Ein guter Staubsauger kostet **so viel wie** ein Mikrowellenherd. — *A good vacuum cleaner costs as much as a microwave oven.*

Inequality can also be expressed with this formula and the addition of **nicht.**

Eine Waschmaschine ist **nicht so schwer wie** ein Kühlschrank. — *A washing machine is not as heavy as a refrigerator.*

B. Comparisons of Superiority and Inferiority

All comparatives in German are formed with **-er.**

To compare two unequal persons or things, add **-er** to the adjective or adverb. Note that the comparative form of German adjectives and adverbs always ends in **-er,** whereas English sometimes uses the adjective with the word *more.*

Ein Radio ist **billiger als** ein Fernseher. — *A radio is cheaper than a TV.*

Lydia ist **intelligenter als** ihre Schwester. — *Lydia is more intelligent than her sister.*

Jens läuft **schneller als** Ernst. — *Jens runs faster than Ernst.*

Adjectives that end in **-el** and **-er** drop the **e** in the comparative form.

teuer → teu~~e~~rer
dunkel → dunk~~e~~ler

Eine Wohnung in Regensburg ist teuer, aber eine Wohnung in München ist noch **teurer.** — *An apartment in Regensburg is expensive, but an apartment in Munich is even more expensive.*

Gestern war es dunkel, aber heute ist es **dunkler.** — *Yesterday it was dark, but today it is darker.*

C. Umlaut in the Comparative

Certain one-syllable adjectives and adverbs whose stem vowel is **a, o,** or **u** add an umlaut in the comparative.

alt → älter	groß → größer	dumm → dümmer
kalt → kälter	oft → öfter	jung → jünger
lang → länger		kurz → kürzer
stark → stärker		
warm → wärmer		

Richard ist **jung,** aber Ernst ist **jünger.**	*Richard is young, but Ernst is younger.*
Ich bin **älter** als mein Bruder.	*I am older than my brother.*
Mein Bad ist **größer** als meine Küche.	*My bathroom is bigger than my kitchen.*

D. Irregular Comparative Forms

As in English, there are some German adjectives and adverbs that have an irregular comparative form.

gut	besser	viel	mehr
gern	lieber	hoch	höher

Ich spreche **besser** Deutsch als Französisch.	*I speak German better than French.*
Monika schläft **lieber** auf dem Sofa als im Bett.	*Monika likes sleeping on the sofa better than in the bed.*
Ernst ißt **mehr** als seine Schwestern.	*Ernst eats more than his sisters.*
Der Kühlschrank ist **höher** als die Tür.	*The refrigerator is taller than the door.*

Übung 1 Vergleiche

Vergleichen Sie.

MODELL Wien / Göttingen / klein → Göttingen ist kleiner als Wien.

1. Berlin / Zürich / groß
2. San Francisco / München / alt
3. Hamburg / Athen / warm
4. das Matterhorn / Mount Everest / hoch
5. der Mississippi / der Rhein / lang
6. die Schweiz / Liechtenstein / klein
7. Leipzig / Kairo / kalt
8. ein Fernseher / eine Waschmaschine / billig
9. Schnaps / Bier / stark
10. ein Haus in der Stadt / ein Haus auf dem Land / schön

11. zehn Mark / zehn Dollar / viel
12. eine Wohnung in einem Studentenheim / ein Appartement / teuer
13. ein Fahrrad / ein Motorrad / schnell
14. ein Sofa / ein Stuhl / schwer
15. Milch / Bier / gut

Übung 2 Jeder Mensch ist anders[1]

Vergleichen Sie die Personen.

	Herr Wagner	Frau Gretter	Frau Ruf	Herr Thelen
Alter	45	34	34	53
Größe	1,79	1,70	1,68	1,70
Gewicht	72 kg	60 kg	58 kg	80 kg
IQ	110	110	125	90
wählt	CSU	SPD	FDP	SPD

INFORMATION ZU DEN PARTEIEN

CSU = Christlich-Soziale Union: konservativ
FDP = Freie Demokratische Partei: liberal
SPD = Sozialdemokratische Partei Deutschlands: progressiv

MODELL Frau Ruf / Frau Gretter / alt →
Frau Ruf ist so alt wie Frau Gretter.
Frau Gretter / Herr Wagner / alt →
Herr Wagner ist älter als Frau Gretter.

1. Herr Wagner / Herr Thelen / alt
2. Frau Gretter / Herr Thelen / groß
3. Frau Gretter / Frau Ruf / groß
4. Frau Ruf / Herr Thelen / klein
5. Frau Gretter / Herr Thelen / leicht
6. Herr Wagner / Frau Ruf / schwer
7. Herr Wagner / Frau Ruf / intelligent
8. Frau Gretter / Herr Wagner / intelligent
9. Frau Ruf / Herr Wagner / progressiv
10. Herr Thelen / Frau Gretter / progressiv
11. Herr Wagner / Herr Thelen / konservativ

---

[1] *different*

6.2 Location vs. destination: two-way prepositions with the dative or accusative case

Wo asks about location. Questions about location are answered with a preposition + dative.

The prepositions **in** (*in*), **an** (*on, at*), **auf** (*on top of*), **vor** (*before*), **hinter** (*behind*), **über** (*above*), **unter** (*underneath*), **neben** (*next to*), and **zwischen** (*between*) are used with both the dative and accusative cases. When they refer to a fixed location, the dative case is required. In these instances, the prepositional phrase answers the question **wo** (*where* [*at*]).

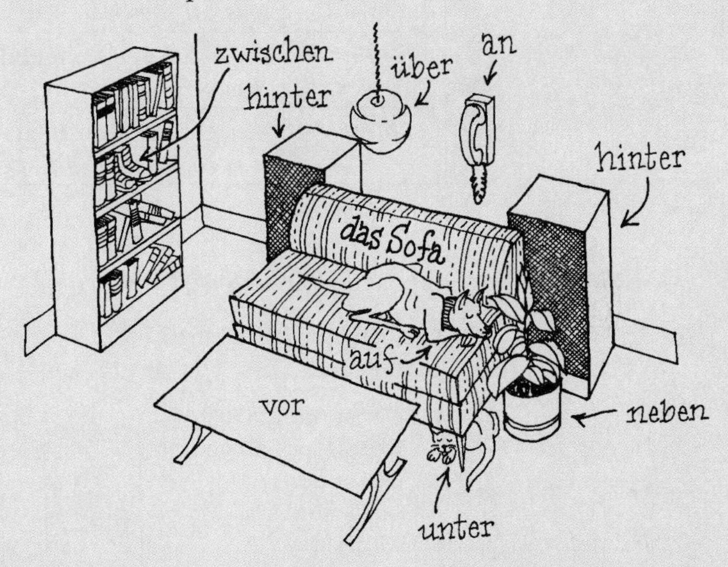

Im Wohnzimmer steht ein Sofa.
Hinter dem Sofa stehen zwei große Boxen.
An der Wand hängt ein Telefon.
Auf dem Sofa liegt ein Hund.
Unter dem Sofa liegt eine Katze.
Vor dem Sofa steht ein Tisch.
Über dem Sofa hängt eine Lampe.
Neben dem Sofa steht eine große Pflanze.
Zwischen den Büchern stehen Tennisschuhe.

Wohin asks about placement or destination. Questions about placement or destination are answered with a preposition + accusative.

When these prepositions describe movement toward a place or a destination, they are used with the accusative case. In these instances, the prepositional phrase answers the question **wohin** (*where* [*to*]).

Peter hat das Sofa **ins Wohnzimmer** gestellt.
Die Boxen hat er **hinter das Sofa** gestellt.
Das Telefon hat er **an die Wand** gehängt.
Der Hund hat sich gleich **auf das Sofa** gelegt.
Die Katze hat sich **unter das Sofa** gelegt.
Peter hat den Tisch **vor das Sofa** gestellt.
Die Lampe hat er **über das Sofa** gehängt.
Die große Pflanze hat er **neben das Sofa** gestellt.
Und seine Tennisschuhe hat er **zwischen die Bücher** gestellt.

	Wo?	*Wohin?*
	Location *Dative*	*Placement / Destination* *Accusative*
Masculine	Es ist auf **dem** Stuhl. *It is on the table.*	Leg es auf **den** Stuhl. *Put it on the table.*
Neuter	Es ist auf **dem** Bett. *It is on the bed.*	Leg es auf **das** Bett. *Put it on the bed.*
Feminine	Es ist auf **der** Kommode. *It is on the bureau.*	Leg es auf **die** Kommode. *Put it on the bureau.*
Plural	Es steht vor **den** Boxen. *It is in front of the speakers.*	Stell es vor **die** Boxen. *Put it in front of the speakers.*

Achtung!

in + dem = im
an + dem = am

in + das = ins
an + das = ans

Übung 3 Alberts Zimmer

Schauen Sie sich Alberts Zimmer an.

1. Wo ist die Katze?
2. Wo ist der Spiegel?
3. Wo ist der Kühlschrank?
4. Wo ist das Deutschbuch?
5. Wo ist die Lampe?
6. Wo ist der Computer?
7. Wo sind die Schuhe?
8. Wo ist die Hose?
9. Wo ist das Poster von Berlin?
10. Wo ist Albert?

Übung 4 Mein Zimmer

Beschreiben Sie Ihr Zimmer. Schreiben Sie acht Sätze mit verschiedenen Präpositionen.

MODELL Ich wohne in einem Studentenheim. In meinem Zimmer sind ein Bett, ein Schreibtisch, ein Bücherregal und ein Kleiderschrank. Das Bett ist unter dem Fenster. Neben dem Bett steht ein Nachttisch . . .

6.3 Word order: time before place

Time before place

In a German sentence, a time expression usually precedes a place expression. Notice that this sequence is often reversed in English sentences.

Ich gehe heute abend in die Bibliothek.

I'm going to the library tonight.

Übung 5 Wo sind Sie wann?

Bilden Sie Sätze aus den Satzteilen.

MODELL heute abend → Ich bin heute abend im Kino.

1. heute abend	in der Klasse
2. am Nachmittag	bei meinen Eltern
3. um 16 Uhr	im Bett
4. in der Nacht	auf einer Party
5. am frühen Morgen	im Urlaub
6. am Montag	am Frühstückstisch
7. am ersten August	in der Mensa
8. an Weihnachten	in der Bibliothek
9. im Winter	?
10. am Wochenende	

6.4 Direction: *in/auf* vs. *zu/nach*

Direction: **in/auf** + accusative; **zu/nach** + dative

To refer to the place where you are going, either use **in** or **auf** + accusative or use **nach** or **zu** + dative.

Albert geht **in die** Kirche.	*Albert goes to church.*
Katrin geht **auf die** Bank.	*Katrin goes to the bank.*
Heidi fährt **zum** Flughafen.	*Heidi drives to the airport.*
Rolf fliegt **nach** Deutschland.	*Rolf is flying to Germany.*

A. in + accusative

in for most buildings and enclosed spaces

In general, use **in** when you plan to enter a building or an enclosed space.

Heute nachmittag gehe ich **in die Bibliothek.**	*This afternoon I'll go to (into) the library.*
Abends gehe ich **ins Kino.**	*In the evening I go to (into) the movies.*
Morgen fahre ich **in die Stadt.**	*Tomorrow I'll drive to the city.*

in for countries with a definite article

Also use **in** with the names of countries that have a definite article, such as **die Schweiz, die Türkei,** and **die USA.**

Herr Frisch fliegt oft **in die** USA.	*Mr. Frisch often flies to the USA.*
Claire fährt **in die** Schweiz.	*Claire is going to Switzerland.*

B. auf + accusative

auf for public buildings and open spaces

Use **auf** instead of **in** when the destination is a public building such as the post office, the bank, or the police station.

Ich brauche Briefmarken. Ich gehe **auf die** Post.	*I need stamps. I'm going to the post office.*
Ich brauche Geld. Ich gehe **auf die** Bank.	*I need money. I'm going to the bank.*

Also use **auf** when the destination is an open space: **aufs Land** (*to the country*) and **auf den Markt** (*to the market*).

C. zu + dative

Use **zu** to refer to destinations that are specific names of buildings, places, or open spaces such as a playing field, or people.

Ernst geht **zu** McDonald's.	*Ernst goes to McDonald's.*
Hans geht **zum** Sportplatz.	*Hans goes to the playing field.*
Andrea geht **zum** Friseur.	*Andrea goes to the hairdresser's.*

zu Hause = *at home*

Note that **zu Hause** (*at home*) does not indicate destination but rather location.

D. nach

Use **nach** with names of countries and cities that have no article. Note that this applies to the vast majority of countries and cities.

Renate fliegt **nach Paris.**	*Renate is flying to Paris.*
Melanie fährt **nach Österreich.**	*Melanie is driving to Austria.*

nach Hause = *(going/coming) home*

Also use **nach** in the idiomatic construction **nach Hause** (*going/coming home*).

Achtung!

in + das = ins
auf + das = aufs
zu + dem = zum
zu + der = zur

Übung 6 Situationen

Heute ist Montag. Wohin gehen oder fahren die folgenden Personen?

MODELL Katrin sucht ein Buch. → Sie geht in die Bibliothek.

der Arzt	die Post
der Flughafen	der Supermarkt
der Freund	die Tankstelle
der Fußballplatz	das Theater
das Hotel	der Wald

1. Albert ist krank.
2. Hans möchte Fußball spielen.
3. Frau Schulz ist auf Reisen in einer fremden[1] Stadt. Sie braucht einen Platz zum Schlafen.
4. Herr Ruf braucht Benzin.
5. Herr Thelen braucht Lebensmittel.
6. Herr Wagner muß Briefmarken kaufen.
7. Jürgen und Silvia gehen Pilze[2] suchen.
8. Jutta möchte mit ihrem Freund sprechen.
9. Mehmet möchte in die Türkei fliegen.
10. Renate möchte *Das Phantom der Oper* sehen.

6.5 Separable-prefix verbs: the present and perfect tenses

The infinitive of a separable-prefix verb consists of a prefix such as **auf, mit,** or **zu** followed by the base verb.

aufstehen	*to get up*
mitkommen	*to come along*
zuschauen	*to watch*

Many prefixes are derived from prepositions. Others may derive from adverbs (**fern**), nouns (**Rad**), or even other verbs (**spazieren**).

fernsehen	*to watch TV*
radfahren	*to ride a bike*
spazierengehen	*to go for a walk*

A. The Present Tense

Separable prefixes are placed at the end of the independent clause.

1. Independent clauses: In an independent clause in the present tense, the conjugated form of the base verb is in second position and the prefix is in last position.

Ich **stehe** jeden Morgen um sieben Uhr **auf.**	*I get up at seven every morning.*

Separable prefixes are "reconnected" to the base verb in dependent clauses.

2. Dependent clauses: In a dependent clause, the prefix and the base verb form a single verb. It appears at the end of the clause and is conjugated.

Rolf sagt, daß er jeden Morgen um sechs Uhr **aufsteht.**	*Rolf says that he gets up at six every morning.*
Hast du nicht gesagt, daß du heute **abwäschst?**	*Didn't you say that you would do the dishes today?*

---

[1]*foreign* [2]*mushrooms*

Separable prefixes stay attached to the infinitive.

3. Modal verb constructions: In an independent clause with a modal verb (**wollen, müssen,** etc.), the infinitive of the separable-prefix verb is in last position. In a dependent clause with a modal verb, the separable-prefix verb is in the second-to-last position, and the modal verb is in the last position.

Jutta möchte nach dem Essen **spazierengehen.** — *Jutta wants to go for a walk after the meal.*

Ernst hat schlechte Laune, wenn er nicht **fernsehen** darf. — *Ernst is in a bad mood when he's not allowed to watch TV.*

B. The Perfect Tense

Separable prefixes precede the **-ge-** marker in past participles

The past participle of a separable-prefix verb is a single word, consisting of the past participle of the base verb + the prefix.

Infinitive	*Past Participle*
aufstehen	aufgestanden
kennenlernen	kennengelernt
wegbringen	weggebracht

Note that the prefix does not influence the formation of the past participle of the base verb; it is simply attached to it.

Herr Wagner **hat** gestern die Garage **aufgeräumt.** — *Mr. Wagner cleaned up his garage yesterday.*

Ich **habe** vor einer Stunde **angerufen.** — *I called an hour ago.*

Übung 7 Minidialoge

Ergänzen Sie die Sätze.

ankommen	aufstehen	fernsehen	mitnehmen
anrufen	ausmachen	mitkommen	umziehen
aufräumen	einladen		

1. HERR WAGNER: Ernst, aufwachen! Hast du nicht gestern gesagt, daß du heute um 7 Uhr _____ ?

ERNST: Ich bin aber doch noch so müde!

2. FRAU WAGNER: Andrea, jetzt aber Schluß[1]! Ich _____[a] den Fernseher jetzt _____[b]. Du wirst noch dumm, wenn du den ganzen Tag nur _____[c].

ANDREA: Aber, Mami, nur noch das Ende. Der Film ist doch gleich vorbei!

3. SILVIA: Entschuldigen Sie bitte! Wann _____[a] der Zug aus Hamburg _____[b]?

BAHNBEAMTER: Um 14 Uhr 56.

[1] jetzt . . . *finish up now*

4. ANDREAS: Hallo, Jürgen. Ich habe gehört, daß ihr bald eine neue Wohnung habt. Wann _____[a] ihr denn _____[b]?
   JÜRGEN: Nächstes Wochenende.
5. MARTA: Hallo, Sofie. Ich habe morgen Geburtstag, und ich möchte dich gern zu einer kleinen Feier _____ .
   SOFIE: Das ist aber nett von dir. Ich komme gern.
6. CLAIRE: Hallo, Melanie. Wo ist Josef?
   MELANIE: Er ist zu Hause. Er _____[a] heute sein Zimmer _____[b], und das dauert bei ihm immer etwas länger.
7. JÜRGEN: Hallo, Silvia. Ich fahre heute mit dem Auto zur Uni. Willst du _____[a]?
   SILVIA: Ja, gern. Schön, daß du mich _____[b].
8. KATRIN: Hier ist meine Telefonnummer. Warum _____[a] du mich nicht mal _____[b]!
   HEIDI: Gut, das mach' ich mal.

Übung 8 Am Sonntag

Gestern war Sonntag. Was haben die folgenden Personen gestern gemacht?

Nützliche Wörter: abtrocknen, anrufen, anziehen, aufwachen, ausgehen, ausziehen, fernsehen, radfahren, spazierengehen, zurückkommen

6.6 The prepositions *mit* and *bei* + dative

The prepositions **mit** (*with, by*) and **bei** (*near, with*) are followed by the dative case.

Masculine	*Neuter*	*Feminine*	*Plural*
mit dem Staubsauger	mit dem Bügeleisen	mit der Bürste	mit den Eltern
beim Onkel	beim Fenster	bei der Tür	bei den Eltern

Mit corresponds to the preposition *with* in English and is used in similar ways.

Herr Wagner fegt die Terrasse **mit** seinem neuen Besen. — *Mr. Wagner sweeps the terrace with his new broom.*
Ich gehe **mit** meinen Freunden ins Kino. — *I'm going to the movies with my friends.*
Ich möchte ein Haus **mit** einem offenen Kamin. — *I want a house with a fireplace.*

Use **mit** with means of transportation.

The preposition **mit** also indicates the means of transportation; in this instance it corresponds to the English preposition *by.* Note the use of the definite article in German.

Rolf fährt **mit** dem Bus zur Uni. — *Rolf goes to the university by bus.*
Renate fährt **mit** dem Auto zur Arbeit. — *Renate drives to work (goes to work by car).*

The preposition **bei** may refer to a place in the vicinity of another place; in this instance it corresponds to the English preposition *near.*

Bad Harzburg liegt **bei** Goslar. — *Bad Harzburg is near Goslar.*

The preposition **bei** also indicates placement with a person, a company, or an institution; in these instances it corresponds to the English prepositions *with, at,* or *for.*

Ich wohne **bei** meinen Eltern. — *I'm living (staying) with my parents/at my parents'.*
Hans arbeitet **bei** McDonald's. — *Hans works at (for) McDonald's.*

	German	*English*
Instrument	mit dem Hammer	*with the hammer*
Togetherness	mit Freunden	*with friends*
Means of transportation	mit dem Flugzeug	*by airplane*
Vicinity	bei München	*near Munich*
Somebody's place	bei den Eltern	*(staying) with parents*
Place of employment	bei McDonald's	*at McDonald's*

Übung 9 Im Haus und im Garten

Womit machen Sie die folgenden Sachen?

MODELL S1: Womit mähst du den Rasen?
S2: Mit dem Rasenmäher.

der Besen
das Bügeleisen
der Gartenschlauch
die Gießkanne
das Handtuch
die Kaffeemaschine
der Putzlappen
der Computer
der Staubsauger
die Zahnbürste

1. Kaffee kochen
2. staubsaugen
3. die Zähne putzen
4. den Boden fegen
5. bügeln
6. die Hände abtrocknen
7. einen Brief tippen
8. die Blumen im Garten gießen
9. den Boden wischen
10. die Blumen in der Wohnung gießen

Übung 10 Minidialoge

Ergänzen Sie die Sätze mit den Präpositionen **mit** oder **bei.**

1. FRAU KÖRNER: Fahren Sie _____[a] dem Bus oder _____[b] dem Fahrrad zur Arbeit?
   MICHAEL PUSCH: _____[c] dem Bus. Ich arbeite jetzt _____[d] Siemens. Das ist am anderen Ende von München.
2. PETER: Wohnst du in Krefeld _____[a] deinen Eltern?
   ROLF: Ja, sie haben ein wunderschönes Haus _____[b] einem riesigen Garten.
   PETER: Liegt Krefeld eigentlich _____[c] Dortmund?
   ROLF: Nein, nach Dortmund fährt man über eine Stunde _____[d] dem Auto.
3. JÜRGEN: Oh je, jetzt habe ich deinen Gummibaum[1] umgeworfen[2]! Soll ich die Erde[3] _____[a] dem Staubsauger aufsaugen?
   SILVIA: Mach es lieber _____[b] dem Besen. Er steht dahinten _____[c] der Kellertür.

---

[1]*rubber plant* [2]*knocked over* [3]*dirt*

KAPITEL 7

Im Bahnhof von München. Wohin geht die Reise?

Kapitel 7 is about geography and transportation. You will learn more about the geography of the German-speaking world and about the kinds of transportation used by people who live there.

Unterwegs

THEMEN
Geographie
Transportmittel
Das Auto
Reiseerlebnisse

LEKTÜRE
Wie bezahlen Sie Ihr neues Auto?
Wo—vielleicht dort
Die Welt aus den Augen einer Katze

KULTURELLES
Die Sage von der Lorelei
Zugfahren
Autofahren
Kulturprojekt: Österreich
Porträt: Caspar David Friedrich und Greifswald
Videoecke: Ein futuristischer Personenzug

STRUKTUREN
7.1 Relative clauses
7.2 The superlative of adjectives and adverbs
7.3 Referring to and asking about things and ideas: **da**-compounds and **wo**-compounds
7.4 The perfect tense (review)

SPRECHSITUATIONEN

Geographie

➤ **Grammatik 7.1–7.2**

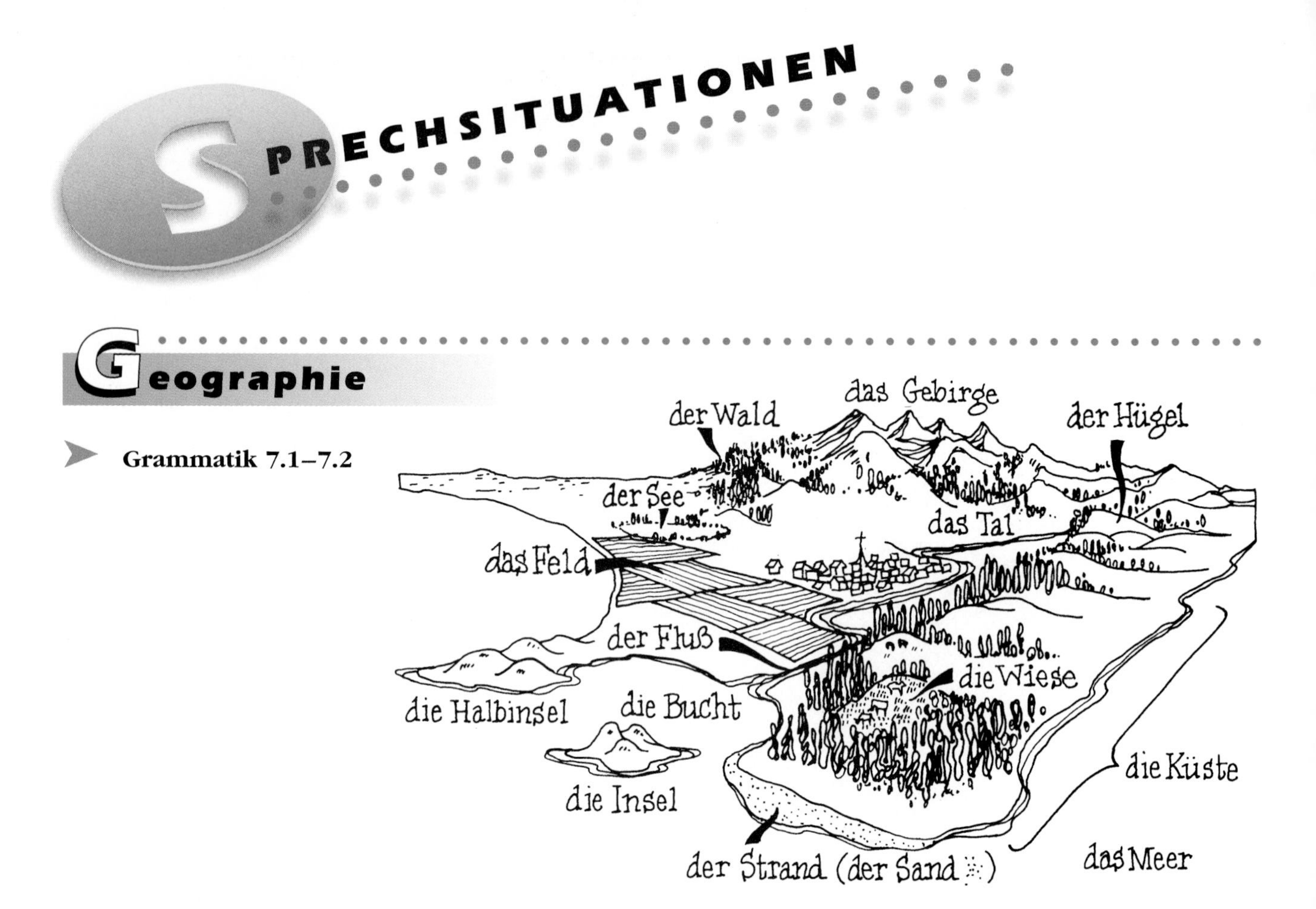

Situation 1 Erdkunde: Wer weiß—gewinnt

1. Fluß, der durch Wien fließt
2. Wald, in dem die Germanen[1] die Römer[2] besiegt haben
3. Insel in der Ostsee, auf der weiße Kreidefelsen[3] sind
4. Berg, auf dem sich die Hexen treffen
5. See, der zwischen Deutschland, Österreich und der Schweiz liegt
6. Meer, das Europa von Afrika trennt
7. Gebirge in Österreich, in dem man sehr gut Ski fahren kann
8. Berühmte Wüste, die in Ostasien liegt
9. Inseln, die vor der Küste von Ostfriesland liegen
10. Fluß, an dem die Lorelei ihr Haar kämmt

a. das Mittelmeer
b. der Brocken im Harz (1142 Meter hoch)
c. die Kitzbühler Alpen
d. der Teutoburger Wald
e. der Bodensee
f. die Wüste Gobi
g. der Rhein
h. die Donau
i. Rügen
j. die Ostfriesischen Inseln

[1] *Teutons* [2] *Romans* [3] *chalk cliffs*

Kultur ... Landeskunde ... Informationen

Die Sage von der Lorelei

Die Lorelei

von Heinrich Heine

Ich weiß nicht, was soll es bedeuten,
daß ich so traurig bin;
ein Märchen aus alten Zeiten,
das kommt mir nicht aus dem Sinn.[1]

Die Luft ist kühl und es dunkelt,[2]
und ruhig fließt der Rhein;
der Gipfel[3] des Berges funkelt[4]
im Abendsonnenschein.

Die schönste Jungfrau[5] sitzet
dort oben wunderbar;
ihr goldnes Geschmeide[6] blitzet,
sie kämmt ihr goldenes Haar.

Sie kämmt es mit goldenem Kamme[7]
und singt ein Lied dabei;
das hat eine wundersame,
gewaltige[8] Melodei.

Den Schiffer im kleinen Schiffe
ergreift[9] es mit wildem Weh;[10]
er schaut nicht die Felsenriffe,[11]
er schaut nur hinauf in die Höh'.

Ich glaube, die Wellen[12] verschlingen[13]
am Ende Schiffer und Kahn;[14]
und das hat mit ihrem Singen
die Lore-Ley getan.

Bringen Sie die Sätze in die richtige Reihenfolge.

_____ Unten auf dem Rhein hört ein Schiffer ihr Singen.
_____ Eine schöne Frau sitzt oben auf einem Berg am Rhein.
_____ Er schaut fasziniert nach oben zu der Frau.
_____ Ihr Schmuck funkelt in der Abendsonne.
_____ Sein Schiff sinkt, und er ertrinkt.[15]
_____ Sie kämmt sich und singt ein Lied dabei.
_____ Weil er nicht aufpaßt, fährt er auf einen Felsen.

[1] das ... *that I can't forget* [2] *is growing dark* [3] *peak* [4] *is sparkling* [5] *virgin; young woman* [6] *jewelry* [7] *comb* [8] *powerful* [9] *seizes* [10] *pain, longing* [11] *cliffs* [12] *waves* [13] *devour, swallow up* [14] *boat* [15] *drowns*

Situation 2 Ratespiel: Stadt, Land, Fluß

1. Wie heißt der tiefste See der Schweiz?
2. Wie heißt der höchste Berg Österreichs?
3. Wie heißt der längste Fluß Deutschlands?
4. Wie heißt das salzigste Meer der Welt?
5. Wie heißt der größte Gletscher der Alpen?
6. Wie heißt die nördlichste Millionenstadt Deutschlands?
7. Was ist die heißeste Wüste der Welt?
8. Wie heißt die älteste Universitätsstadt Deutschlands?
9. Wie heißt das kleinste Land, in dem man Deutsch spricht?
10. Wie heißt die berühmteste Höhle in Österreich?

a. die Dachstein-Mammuthöhle
b. das Tote Meer
c. der Genfer See
d. der Großglockner
e. die Libysche Wüste
f. der Rhein
g. Hamburg
h. Liechtenstein
i. der Große Aletschgletscher
j. Heidelberg

Situation 3 Informationsspiel: Deutschlandreise

Wo liegen die folgenden Städte? Hannover, Flensburg, Erfurt, Dresden, Magdeburg, Bayreuth, Heidelberg, Aachen, Freiburg, Wiesbaden. Schreiben Sie die Namen der Städte auf die Landkarte.

MODELL S1: Wo liegt Bremen?
S2: Bremen liegt im Norden.
S1: Wo genau?
S2: Westlich von Hamburg.

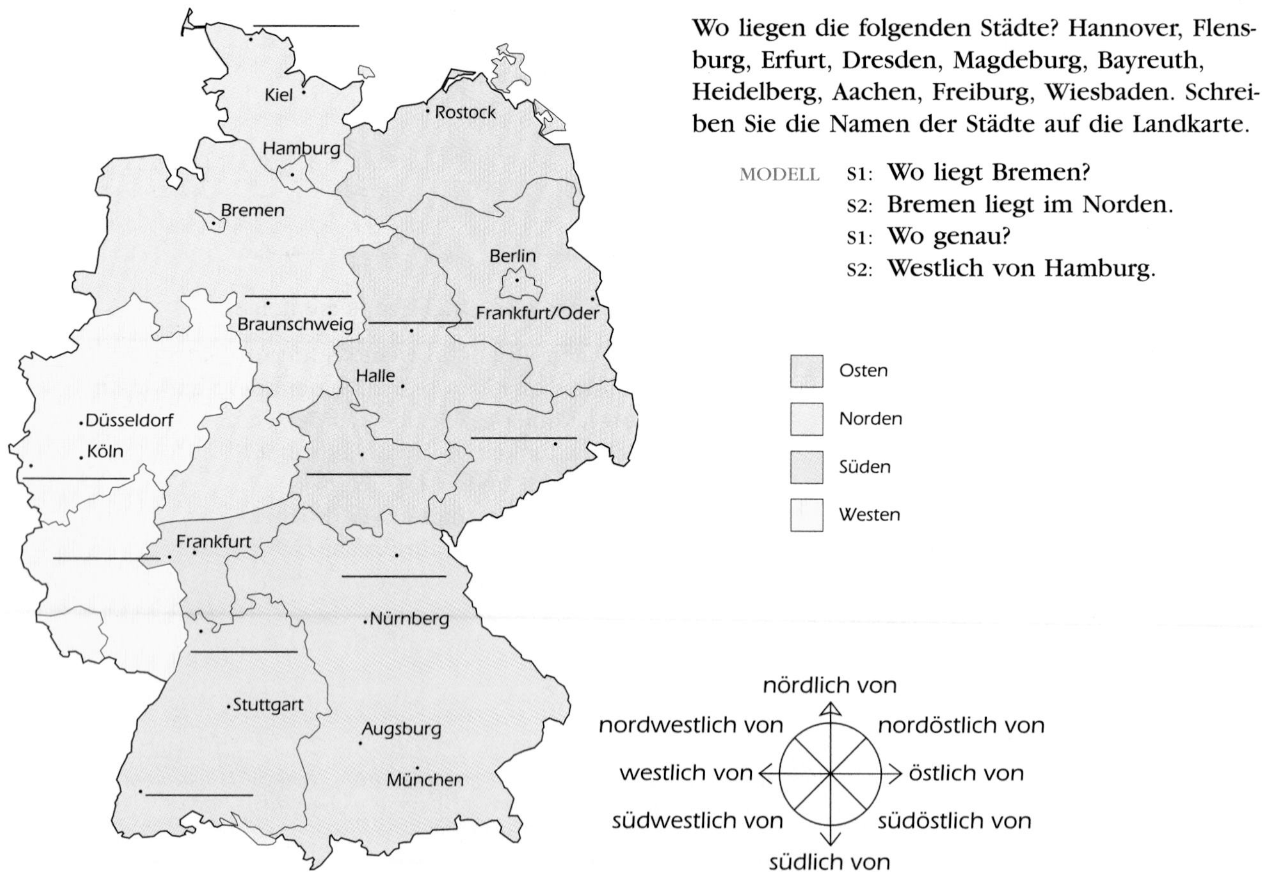

Situation 4 Interview: Urlaub

1. Warst du schon mal im Gebirge? Wo? Was hast du da gemacht? Wie heißt der höchste Berg, den du gesehen (oder bestiegen) hast?
2. Warst du schon einmal am Meer? Wo und wann war das? Hast du gebadet? Was hast du sonst noch gemacht?
3. Wohnst du in der Nähe von einem großen Fluß? Wie heißt er? Wie heißt der größte Fluß, an dem du schon warst? Was hast du da gemacht?
4. Wie heißt die interessanteste Stadt, in der du schon warst? Was hast du dort gemacht?
5. Warst du schon einmal in der Wüste oder im Dschungel? Wie war das Wetter? Welche Tiere hat es da gegeben?
6. Wohin fährst du am liebsten? Warum?

Transportmittel

Grammatik 7.1, 7.4

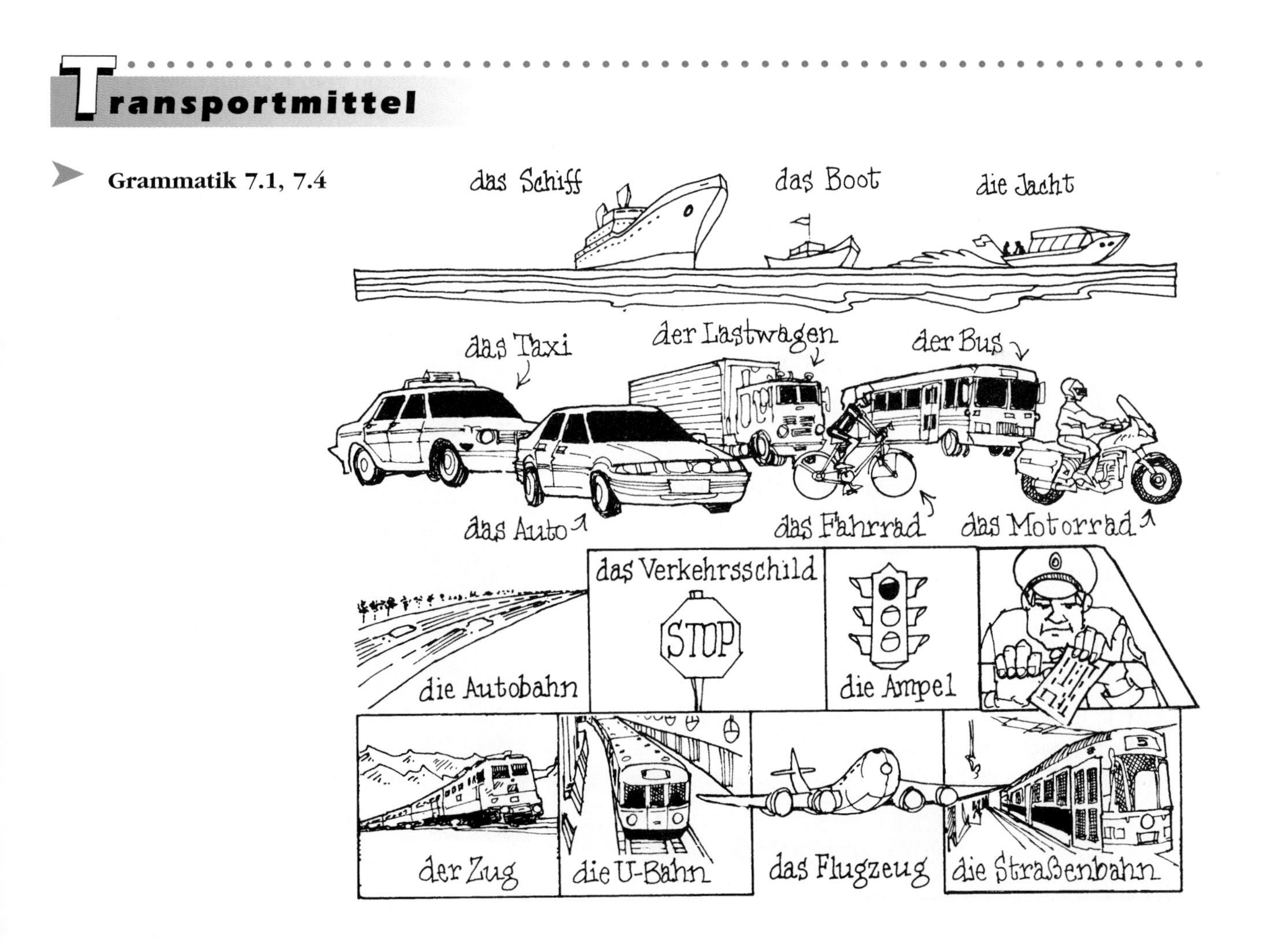

Situation 5 Definitionen: Transportmittel

1. das Flugzeug
2. die Rakete
3. das Kamel
4. die Jacht
5. das Fahrrad
6. der Kinderwagen
7. der Zeppelin
8. der Zug
9. das Taxi

a. Transportmittel, das Waggons und eine Lokomotive hat
b. Transportmittel, das fliegt
c. Transportmittel, das im Wasser schwimmt
d. Tier, das Araber als Transportmittel benutzen
e. Transportmittel, mit dem man zum Mond fliegen kann
f. Auto, das in Deutschland ein gelbes Schild auf dem Dach hat
g. Transportmittel in der Luft, das wie eine Zigarre aussieht
h. Transportmittel mit zwei Rädern, das ohne Benzin fährt
i. Wagen, in dem man Babys transportiert

Situation 6 Interview

1. Welche Transportmittel hast du schon benutzt?
2. Fährst du oft mit der U-Bahn oder mit dem Bus? Warum (nicht)?
3. Fährst du gern mit dem Zug (oder möchtest du gern mal mit dem Zug fahren)? Welche Vorteile/Nachteile hat das Reisen mit dem Zug?
4. Fliegst du gern? Warum (nicht)? Welche Vorteile/Nachteile hat das Reisen mit dem Flugzeug?
5. Bist du schon mal mit dem Schiff gefahren? Wo war das? Wirst du leicht seekrank?
6. Fährst du lieber mit dem Auto oder mit öffentlichen Verkehrsmitteln? Warum? Womit fährst du am liebsten?

Kultur ... Landeskunde ... Informationen

Zugfahren

- Wie heißt die Eisenbahnlinie in Ihrem Land?
- Fahren viele Leute mit dem Zug?
- Wie reisen Geschäftsleute und Touristen meistens?
- Warum ist das Flugzeug ein wichtiges Transportmittel in Nordamerika?

Sie hören einen Text über Zugfahren in Deutschland. Hören Sie gut zu, und beantworten Sie die Fragen.

- Wie heißt der neue superschnelle Zug?
- Wie schnell fährt er im Durchschnitt[1]?
- Welche Vorteile hat er?

Unsere Bahn.

[1] im . . . *on average*

Der Inter-City-Express (ICE). Alles einsteigen, bitte!

Situation 7 Dialog: Im Reisebüro in Berlin

RENATE: Guten Tag.
ANGESTELLTE: Guten Tag. ________?
RENATE: Ich möchte ________ nach Zürich fahren.
ANGESTELLTE: ___ möchten Sie denn fahren?
RENATE: Montagmorgen _ früh __ möglich.
ANGESTELLTE: Der erste InterCity geht ______________. Ist das früh genug?
RENATE: Wann ist er denn in Zürich?
ANGESTELLTE: ______________________.
RENATE: Sehr gut. Reservieren Sie mir bitte einen Platz ______________.

Situation 8 Rollenspiel: Am Fahrkartenschalter

S1: Sie stehen am Fahrkartenschalter im Bahnhof von Bremen und wollen eine Fahrkarte nach München kaufen. Sie wollen billig fahren, müssen aber vor 16.30 Uhr am Bahnhof in München ankommen. Fragen Sie, wann und wo der Zug abfährt und über welche Städte der Zug fährt.

Das Auto

➤ **Grammatik 7.3**

1. Damit kann man hupen.
2. Daran sieht man, woher das Auto kommt.
3. Darin kann man seine Koffer verstauen.
4. Damit wischt man die Scheiben.

Situation 9 Definitionen: Die Teile des Autos

1. die Bremsen
2. die Scheibenwischer
3. das Autoradio
4. das Lenkrad
5. die Hupe
6. das Nummernschild
7. die Sitze
8. die Türen
9. das Benzin
10. der Tank

a. Man setzt sich darauf.
b. Man braucht sie, wenn man bei Regen fährt.
c. Damit lenkt man das Auto.
d. Damit warnt man andere Fahrer oder Fußgänger.
e. Man öffnet sie, wenn man ins Auto einsteigen will.
f. Daran sieht man, woher das Auto kommt.
g. Damit hört man Musik und Nachrichten.
h. Damit fährt das Auto.
i. Darin ist das Benzin.
j. Damit hält man den Wagen an.

Situation 10 Rollenspiel: Ein Auto kaufen

Sie wollen einen Gebrauchtwagen kaufen und lesen deshalb die Anzeigen in der Zeitung. Die Anzeigen für einen Opel Astra und einen Ford Fiesta sind interessant. Rufen Sie an, und stellen Sie Fragen.

Sie haben auch eine Anzeige in die Zeitung gesetzt, weil Sie Ihren alten Wagen, einen VW Golf, verkaufen wollen. Antworten Sie auf die Fragen der Leute, die Ihr Auto kaufen wollen.

MODELL Guten Tag, ich rufe wegen des Opel Astra an.
Wie alt ist der Wagen?
Welche Farbe hat er?
Wie ist der Kilometerstand?
Wie lange hat er noch TÜV?
Was kostet der Wagen?

Modell	VW Golf	Opel Corsa	Opel Astra	Ford Fiesta
Baujahr	1992	1995		
Farbe	rot	graugrün		
Kilometerstand	65 000 km	25 000 km		
TÜV	noch 1 Jahr	neu		
Benzin pro 100 km	6 Liter	5,5 Liter		
Preis	18 900 DM	15 700 DM		

Situation 11 Interview: Das Auto

1. Hast du einen Führerschein? Wann hast du ihn gemacht?
2. Was für ein Auto möchtest du am liebsten haben? Warum?
3. Welche Autos findest du am schönsten?

4. Welche Autos findest du am praktischsten (unpraktischsten)? Warum?
5. Wer von deinen Freunden hat das älteste Auto? Wie alt ist es ungefähr? Und wer hat das häßlichste (schnellste, interessanteste)?
6. Mit was für einem Auto möchtest du am liebsten in Urlaub fahren?
7. Was glaubst du: Was ist das teuerste Auto der Welt?
8. Was glaubst du: In welchem Land fährt man am schnellsten?
9. Was glaubst du: Was ist das kleinste Auto der Welt?

Situation 12 Verkehrsschilder

a.
b. STOP
c. Einbahnstraße
d.
e.
f. P
g.
h.
i.
j.

Kennen Sie diese Verkehrsschilder? Was bedeuten sie?

1. Dieses Verkehrsschild bedeutet „Halt".
2. Hier darf man nicht halten.
3. Wer von rechts kommt, hat Vorfahrt.
4. Hier darf man nur in eine Richtung fahren.
5. Hier darf man nur mit dem Rad fahren.
6. Hier darf man auf dem Fußgängerweg parken.
7. Hier dürfen keine Autos fahren.
8. Achtung Radfahrer!
9. Dieser Weg ist nur für Fußgänger.
10. Hier dürfen keine Motorräder fahren.

Situation 13 Zum Schreiben: Eine Anzeige

Sie wollen ein Fahrzeug (Auto, Boot, Motorrad, Fahrrad usw.) verkaufen. Schreiben Sie eine Anzeige. Machen Sie sie interessant!

Kultur ... Landeskunde ... Informationen

Autofahren

Was meinen Sie? Warum sind die USA die Autofahrer-Nation Nr. 1? Kreuzen Sie an.

- ☐ Weil Amerikaner gern Auto fahren.
- ☐ Weil die Massenproduktion von Autos in den USA begonnen hat.
- ☐ Weil das Land so groß ist.
- ☐ Weil Autos so billig sind.
- ☐ Weil es ein Tempolimit gibt.
- ☐ Weil das Benzin so billig ist.
- ☐ Weil es wenig öffentliche Verkehrsmittel gibt.
- ☐ Weil die Straßen so gut sind.

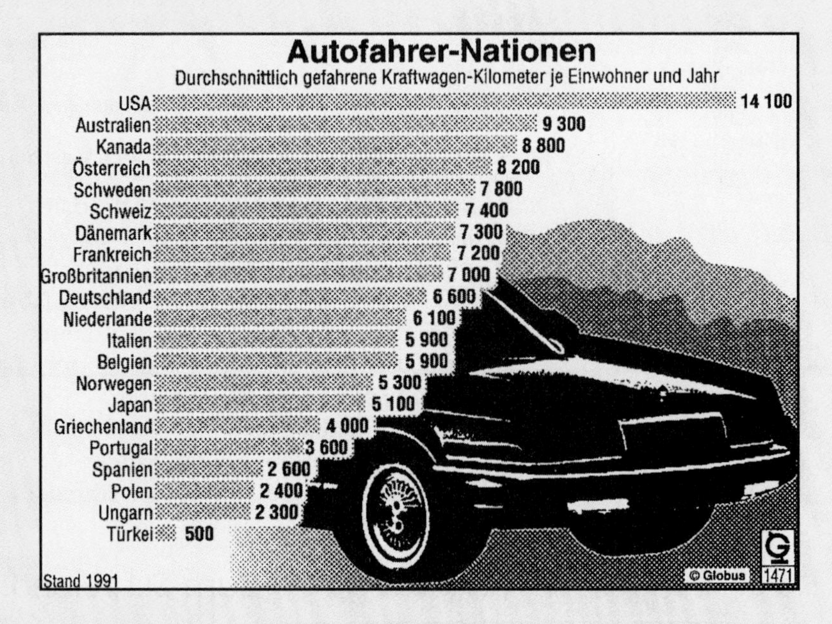

Nach[1] der Statistik wird am meisten in den USA Auto gefahren. Hinter den USA folgen[2] die beiden riesigen[3] Länder Australien und Kanada. Die Deutschen liegen mit 6 000 gefahrenen Kilometern je[4] Einwohner[5] und Jahr im Mittelfeld.[6] Im Durchschnitt[7] fahren die Autofahrer der alten Bundesländer jährlich rund 7 000 Kilometer, in den neuen Bundesländern sind es dagegen[8] nur 4 500 Kilometer.

- Auf welchen Plätzen liegen die deutschsprachigen Länder?
- Wie viele Kilometer fahren die Autofahrer durchschnittlich im Jahr in den alten Bundesländern?
- Wie viele Kilometer fahren sie in den neuen Bundesländern?
- Warum, glauben Sie, sind es in den neuen Bundesländern weniger?

[1] *according to* [2] *follow* [3] *huge* [4] *per* [5] *resident* [6] *middle of the scale* [7] *on average* [8] *in comparison*

Reiseerlebnisse

➤ **Grammatik 7.4**

Im letzten Urlaub waren Maria und Michael in Marokko.

Zuerst ist Maria auf einem Kamel geritten.

Dann hat sie mit Michael einen Basar besucht.

Michael hat sich dort einen Hut gekauft.

Leider hat jemand dabei Michaels Brieftasche gestohlen.

Die Polizei ist gekommen und hat alles genau notiert.

Um auf andere Gedanken zu kommen, haben Maria und Michael einem Schlangenbeschwörer[1] zugesehen.

Dann sind sie zurück zu ihrem Zelt gegangen.

Situation 14 Umfrage: Wer in der Klasse . . . ?

1. war noch nie in Österreich ____________
2. war schon in Chicago ____________
3. war schon auf einem Oktoberfest ____________
4. hat schon Sauerkraut in einem Restaurant gegessen ____________
5. ist noch nie mit dem Zug gefahren ____________
6. war schon in einem deutschen Film ____________
7. hat noch nie einen Liechtensteiner kennengelernt ____________
8. ist schon auf einen hohen Berg gestiegen ____________
9. hat noch nie Schweizer Fondue probiert ____________
10. ist noch nie ins Ausland gereist ____________

[1] *snake charmer*

Situation 15 Bildgeschichte: Stefans Reise nach Österreich

Kulturprojekt Österreich

Suchen Sie die Informationen zu Österreich auf einer Landkarte und in einer Enzyklopädie.

- Wie viele Bundesländer hat Österreich?
- Wie heißen die Bundesländer?
- Wie heißt die Hauptstadt von Österreich?
- Wie heißen die Hauptstädte der Bundesländer?
- Wie heißen die Nachbarländer Österreichs?
  Im Norden: ______________
  Im Osten: ______________
  Im Süden: ______________
  Im Westen: ______________
- Deutschland hat eine Fläche von ungefähr 360 000 km^2. Wie groß ist Österreich?
- Deutschland hat ungefähr 80 Millionen Einwohner. Wie viele hat Österreich?
- Womit bezahlt man in Österreich? Kreuzen Sie an.
  - ☐ mit der österreichischen Mark
  - ☐ mit dem Alpendollar
  - ☐ mit dem österreichischen Franken
  - ☐ mit dem österreichischen Schilling

Hints for working with the Kulturprojekt

You will find most of the information requested here in any good world atlas. In addition to maps, most atlases will provide information about specific countries in a section towards the back of the atlas. A reference work such as *The Universal Almanac* is also a quick source of information about specific countries.

- Welches Nationalitätskennzeichen[1] hat Österreich? □ Ö □ AU □ A
- Welche der folgenden Skizzen stellt Österreich dar?

a. b. c. d.

Porträt

Caspar David Friedrich, „Kreidefelsen auf Rügen" (Ölgemälde 1818)

Caspar David Friedrich (1774 - 1840) ist ein Maler[1] der Romantik. Er wurde in Greifswald an der Ostsee geboren und lebte in Dresden. In Caspar David Friedrichs Landschaften[2] sieht man oft das Meer mit großen Wellen,[3] Felsen und manchmal einem Schiff, oder er malt Gebirge im Schnee. Oft stehen Menschen im Bild, aber dann relativ klein im Verhältnis zur[4] Natur, und man sieht meistens nur den Rücken. So hat man den Eindruck,[5] daß diese Menschen dasselbe Bild betrachten. Caspar David Friedrich ist als einer der größten romantischen Maler Deutschlands bekannt.

Greifswald ist eine Stadt an der Ostsee in Mecklenburg-Vorpommern. Es hat eine der ältesten Universitäten in Deutschland. Die Ernst-Moritz-Arndt-Universität wurde 1456 gegründet. Greifswald ist ungefähr 750 Jahre alt und schon seit 1281 Mitglied der Hanse. In der Innenstadt zeugen[6] Kirchen und alte Bürgerhäuser vom früheren Reichtum[7] der Stadt.

Marktplatz in Greifswald mit alten Bürgerhäusern

[1]*painter* [2]*landscapes* [3]*waves* [4]im . . . *with respect to* [5]*impression* [6]*testify* [7]*wealth*

[1]*national abbreviation*

Ein futuristischer Personenzug

Die Magnetbahn *Transrapid* soll das Verkehrsmittel des 21. Jahrhunderts sein. Der Clip zeigt, worum es sich hier handelt.[1]

- Wie schnell fährt die Magnetbahn?
- Wo soll die 1. Strecke gebaut werden?
- Wann soll diese Strecke fertig sein?
- Wie lange soll dann die Fahrt dauern?

[1] worum . . . *what it's all about*

Transrapid ist eine völlig neue Bahntechnik. Es ist eine Hochtechnologie, in der Deutschland weltweit führend ist.

Wortschatz

Geographie — Geography

die **Bucht, -en** (R)	bay
die **Insel, -n**	island
die **Halbinsel, -n**	peninsula
die **Millionenstadt, ¨e**	city with a million or more inhabitants
die **Nähe**	proximity; vicinity
in der Nähe	in the vicinity
die **Richtung, -en**	direction
die **Wiese, -n**	meadow, pasture
die **Wüste, -n**	desert
der **Fluß, Flüsse**	river
der **Gipfel, -**	mountaintop
der **Gletscher, -**	glacier
der **Hügel, -**	hill
der **See, -n** (R)	lake
der **Strand, ¨e** (R)	shore, beach
der **Wald, ¨er** (R)	forest, woods
das **Feld, -er**	field
das **Gebirge, -**	(range of) mountains
das **Meer, -e** (R)	sea
das **Tal, ¨er**	valley

Ähnliche Wörter

die **Küste, -n**; die **Landkarte, -n** der **Dschungel, -** **die Alpen** (*pl.*) **nördlich (von); nordöstlich (von); nordwestlich (von); östlich (von); südlich (von); südöstlich (von); südwestlich (von); westlich (von)**

Auto — Car

die **Bremse, -n**	brake
die **Hupe, -n**	horn
die **Motorhaube, -n**	hood
die **Reifenpanne, -n**	flat tire
der **Gang, ¨e**	gear
der **Gebrauchtwagen, -**	used car
der **Kilometerstand**	mileage
der **Kofferraum, ¨e**	trunk
der **Reifen, -**	tire
der **Scheibenwischer, -**	windshield wiper
der **Sicherheitsgurt, -e**	safety belt
der **Sitz, -e**	seat
das **Lenkrad, ¨er**	steering wheel
das **Nummernschild, -er**	license plate
das **Rad, ¨er**	wheel
hupen	to honk
verstauen	to stow

Ähnliche Wörter

der **Tank, -s** das **Autoradio, -s**

Verkehr und Transportmittel — Traffic and Means of Transportation

die **Ampel, -n**	traffic light
die **Bahn, -en**	railroad
die **Autobahn, -en**	interstate highway; freeway

die **Seilbahn, -en**	cable railway
die **Straßenbahn, -en**	street car
die **U-Bahn, -en (Untergrundbahn)**	subway
die **Kreuzung, -en**	intersection
die **Parklücke, -n**	parking space
die **Radfahrerin, -nen**	(female) bicyclist
die **Rakete, -n**	rocket
die **Straße, -n** (R)	street
die **Einbahnstraße, -n**	one-way street
die **Landstraße, -n**	rural highway
die **Vorfahrt, -en**	right-of-way
der **Fahrkartenschalter, -**	ticket window
der **Flug, ¨e**	flight
der **Fußgänger, -**	pedestrian
der **Fußgängerweg, -e**	sidewalk
der **Radfahrer, -**	(male) bicyclist
der **Radweg, -e**	bicycle path
der **Stau, -s**	traffic jam
der **Strafzettel, -**	(parking or speeding) ticket
der **Wagen, -**	car
der **Kinderwagen, -**	baby carriage
der **Lastwagen, -**	truck
der **Waggon, -s**	train car
der **Zug, ¨e**	train
der **Personenzug, ¨e**	passenger train
das **Flugzeug, -e**	airplane
das **Motorrad, ¨er** (R)	motorcycle
das **Schild, -er**	sign
das **Verkehrsschild, -er**	traffic sign
das **Verbot, -e**	prohibition
das **Halteverbot, -e**	no-stopping zone
die **öffentlichen Verkehrsmittel** (*pl.*)	public transportation
ab·fahren, fährt ab, ist abgefahren	to depart
an·halten, hält an, angehalten	to stop
halten, hält, gehalten	to stop

Ähnliche Wörter

die **Fahrerin, -nen**; die **Jacht, -en**; die **Lokomotive, -n** der **Bus, Busse** (R); der **Fahrer, -**; der **Zeppelin, -e** das **Boot, -e**; das **Schiff, -e**; das **Taxi, -s** (R) **parken; transportieren**

Reiseerlebnisse — Travel Experiences

die **Reise, -n**	trip, journey
auf Reisen sein	to be on a trip
die **Geschäftsreise, -n**	business trip
die **Stadtrundfahrt, -en**	tour of the city
die **Wanderung, -en**	hike
die **Welt, -en**	world
der **Reisescheck, -s**	traveler's check
besichtigen	to visit, sightsee
besteigen	to climb

Ähnliche Wörter

der **Paß, Pässe** das **Visum, Visa** **buchen; packen; planen; reservieren**

Sonstige Substantive — Other Nouns

die **Achtung**	attention
die **Angestellte, -n**	female clerk
die **Brieftasche, -n**	wallet
die **Fläche, -n**	surface
die **Hexe, -n**	witch
die **Luft**	air
die **Million, -en**	million
die **Scheibe, -n**	windowpane
der **Angestellte, -n**	male clerk
der **Gedanke, -n** (*wk. masc.*)	thought
auf andere Gedanken kommen	to keep one's mind off something
der **Regen**	rain
bei Regen	in rainy weather
der **Teil, -e**	part
der **Nachteil, -e**	disadvantage
der **Vorteil, -e**	advantage
das **Tier, -e**	animal
die **Leute** (*pl.*)	people
die **Geschäftsleute** (*pl.*)	businesspeople
die **Nachrichten** (*pl.*)	news

Ähnliche Wörter

die **Mark, -**; die **Zigarre, -n** der **Basar, -e**; der **Dollar, -s; zwei Dollar**; der **Franken, -**; der **Liter, -**; der **Preis, -e**; der **Sand**; der **Schilling, -e; zwei Schilling** das **Baby, -s**; das **Fondue**; das **Kamel, -e**; das **Oktoberfest, -e**; das **Sauerkraut**

Sonstige Verben — Other Verbs

benutzen	to use
besiegen	to conquer
denken, gedacht	to think
ein·schlafen, schläft ein, ist eingeschlafen	to fall asleep
erlauben	to permit
fließen, ist geflossen	to flow
nach·denken (über + *akk.*)**, nachgedacht**	to think (about), consider

rufen, gerufen — to call, shout
schwimmen, ist geschwommen — to swim; to float
setzen — to put, place, set
sparen — to save (money)
trennen — to separate
verlieren, verloren — to lose
versprechen, verspricht, versprochen — to promise
warten — to wait
wischen — to wipe
zu·sehen, sieht zu, zugesehen — to observe, look on

Ähnliche Wörter

beantworten, notieren, stehlen, warnen

Adjektive und Adverbien / Adjectives and Adverbs

berühmt — famous
lieb — dear
  am liebsten — like (*to do something*) best

Ähnliche Wörter

exotisch, graugrün, interessant, pünktlich, salzig, seekrank, superschnell, tief

Sonstige Wörter und Ausdrücke / Other Words and Expressions

bitte schön? — yes please?; may I help you?
deshalb — therefore; that's why
dort — there
durch — through
rechts — to the right
schließlich — finally
ungefähr — approximately
zuerst — first
zwischen — between

LESEECKE

LEKTÜRE 1

Vor dem Lesen

A. Newspaper and magazine articles must capture their readers' attention quickly before they flip to another article; therefore, you will usually find the main point in the title or somewhere in the first paragraph.

Lesen Sie zuerst den Titel und den ersten Absatz des Artikels. Wovon handelt er?

B. Wie bezahlen die meisten Leute in Deutschland ein neues Auto? Sehen Sie sich dazu die Grafik an, und suchen Sie im kurzen Text darüber die Antworten auf folgende Fragen.

1. Wieviel Prozent vom Preis des neuen Autos kommen vom Sparkonto[1]?
2. Wieviel Prozent kommen vom Verkauf des alten Autos, und wieviel sind ein Kredit[2]?
3. Wieviel Prozent vom Preis sind ein Geschenk von Verwandten?

C. Lesen Sie den Text. Unterstreichen und numerieren Sie die drei Fragen, die im Text erscheinen.

---

[1]*savings account* [2]*loan*

Wie bezahlen Sie Ihr neues Auto?

Das Geld für einen Neuwagen
kommt zum größten Teil vom Sparkonto: 55% des Autopreises werden vom Ersparten bezahlt. Der Verkauf des Vorwagens bringt weitere 29%. Kredite werden weniger in Anspruch genommen: 15%. Fehlt noch 1%: Dieses Geld haben die Käufer von Verwandten geschenkt bekommen.

Autos sind ganz schön teuer geworden. Durchschnittlich[1] 28 000 Mark bezahlt der deutsche Autokäufer für einen Neuwagen. Infratest* untersuchte für die *ADAC motorwelt,* wie die Bundesbürger ihr neues Auto finanzieren.

Warum nehmen nur relativ wenige Neuwagenkäufer einen Kredit auf? Erstes Motiv: „Dann gehört der Wagen der Bank und nicht mir." Zweiter Grund: „Die Zinsen[2] machen das Auto teurer, als wenn ich es bar[3] kaufe. Und wenn ich Bargeld hinlege, dann kann man beim Händler[4] einen besseren Preis rausholen."

Eine weitere Finanzierungsform ist das „Familien-Darlehen":[5] 2% der deutschen Autokäufer leihen sich Geld bei Verwandten. Erwartungsgemäß[6] pumpen junge Käufer doppelt so häufig ihre lieben Verwandten an[7] wie die älteren.

Vati und Mutti, Opa und Oma sind auch gefragt, wenn es um Geldgeschenke fürs neue Auto geht. 4% der Käufer kommen in den Genuß[8] eines kostenlosen Geldsegens (durchschnittlich 5 000 DM).

Nach wie vor die beliebteste Finanzierungsart ist jedoch der Sparstrumpf.[9] Laut Infratest stecken 87% der deutschen PKW-Besitzer ihre Ersparnisse in das neue Auto, und zwar[10] im Durchschnitt 18 500 DM.

Wie lange sparen die Käufer für ein neues Auto? Ganz unterschiedlich.[11] Der Angestellte Michael Rieger: „Meine Autos sind immer Neuwagen und werden bar bezahlt. Zehn Jahre spare ich für ein neues Auto." Schneller geht es bei dem Architekten Horst Koppensteiner: „Das Geld für mein neues Auto kommt in etwa zwei bis drei Jahren auf meinem Sparkonto zusammen." Fünf Jahre hat es bei Silvia Hohenadl gedauert, bis sie das Geld zusammen hatte, aber „das lief eigentlich mehr nebenbei,[12] und ich mußte mich nicht einschränken.[13]"

Für das neue Auto auf Hobbys oder den Urlaub verzichten[14]? Das will praktisch keiner. Dann lieber einen Gebrauchten kaufen.

[1]*on average* [2]*interest (on a bank balance)* [3]*in cash* [4]*dealer* [5]*loan from a family member* [6]*Not surprisingly* [7]pumpen . . . an *ask (someone) for money* [8]kommen . . . *enjoy* [9]*lit.: savings stocking* [10]*namely* [11]ganz . . . *it varies* [12]*incidentally* [13]mich . . . einschränken *tighten my belt* [14]*give up*
*Infratest is an opinion research institute.

Arbeit mit dem Text

A. Zu welchen Fragen gehören diese Antworten aus dem Text? Schreiben Sie **1**, **2** oder **3** davor. (Siehe *Vor dem Lesen C.*)

_____ Ganz unterschiedlich. Manche Leute sparen zwei oder drei, andere zehn Jahre.
_____ Kein Mensch will für ein neues Auto auf Hobbys verzichten.
_____ Das Auto gehört dann der Bank und nicht dem Käufer.
_____ Silvia hat fünf Jahre gespart.
_____ Das Auto ist teurer, weil man Zinsen bezahlen muß.
_____ Wenn man bar bezahlt, bekommt man vom Händler einen besseren Preis.

B. Noch ein paar Einzelheiten:

1. Was ist ein „Familien-Darlehen"?
2. Wieviel bekommen Autokäufer durchschnittlich von ihren Eltern und Großeltern geschenkt?
3. Wieviel Geld vom Sparkonto stecken die Käufer durchschnittlich ins neue Auto?

LEKTÜRE 2

Wo—vielleicht dort

von Jürgen Becker

Wo vielleicht dort
wohin
mal sehen
warum
nur so (5)
was dann
dann vielleicht da
wie lange
mal sehen
mit wem (10)
nicht sicher
wie
nicht sicher
wer
mal sehen (15)
was noch
sonst nichts

Arbeit mit dem Text

1. Unterstreichen Sie alle Fragepronomen.
2. Dieses Gedicht ist eigentlich ein Dialog. Schreiben Sie die ganzen Fragen auf, und erfinden Sie neue Antworten dazu.

LEKTÜRE 3

Die Welt aus den Augen einer Katze

Ach, diese Langeweile ... Herrchen und Frauchen haben nie Zeit für mich und spielen nie mit mir. Sie haben es immer eilig[1] und sind immer beschäftigt. Was für ein Leben diese Menschen führen. Frauchen steht morgens sehr früh auf, geht in die Küche und kocht dieses seltsame[2] schwarze Zeug,[3] das sie den ganzen Tag trinken. Dann weckt sie Herrchen. Er möchte eigentlich noch ein bißchen schlafen, aber sie macht die Fenster auf und dreht das Radio ganz laut. Herrchen stöhnt[4] und zieht die Decke[5] über den Kopf, aber es hat alles keinen Sinn.[6]

Schließlich[7] steht er auf, duscht und trinkt dieses stinkende schwarze Zeug, liest die Zeitung und geht zur Arbeit.

Frauchen bleibt noch etwas länger zu Hause, und manchmal darf ich noch ein bißchen am Fußende vom Bett liegen. Aber nicht lange, dann setzt sie mich vor die Tür und sagt: „Los, fang[8] Mäuse!" Ich will aber morgens nicht draußen sein. Es ist kalt und ungemütlich, also sitze ich vor dem Fenster und mache ein unglückliches Gesicht. Aber Frauchen geht dann auch weg, und ich muß bis nachmittags warten. Dann kommen beide nach Hause und machen etwas zu essen. Es riecht immer sehr gut—diese Menschen essen nicht schlecht!—, aber ich bekomme leider nur die Reste.[9]

Manchmal spielt Herrchen noch ein bißchen mit mir, aber dann sitzen sie den ganzen Abend vor diesem komischen Ding, das solchen Krach[10] macht, und sehen die Bilder von anderen Menschen an. Sie beachten[11] mich nicht mehr. Schließlich gehen sie ins Bett, und ich suche mir auch ein Plätzchen zum Schlafen.

Am schlimmsten ist es aber, wenn sie verreisen. Dann kommt nur einmal am Tag ein anderer Mensch vorbei, der mir etwas zu fressen[12] hinstellt, und ich muß in der Garage schlafen. Ein schreckliches Leben ist das!

[1]haben ... *are always in a hurry* [2]*strange* [3]*stuff* [4]*groans* [5]*blanket* [6]es ... *it's pointless* [7]*finally* [8]*catch* [9]*leftovers* [10]*racket, loud noise* [11]*pay attention to* [12]*eat (said of animals)*

Arbeit mit dem Text

A. Die Menschen oder die Katze?

Ordnen Sie die Stichwörter in die Tabelle ein.

Herrchen	Frauchen	die Katze
	steht sehr früh auf	

möchte noch ein bißchen schlafen
kocht Kaffee
weckt Herrchen
zieht die Decke über den Kopf
macht die Fenster auf
darf am Fußende des Bettes liegen
bekommt nur die Reste
sitzt vor dem Fenster
spielt noch ein bißchen mit der Katze
muß in der Garage schlafen
hat es immer eilig
liest die Zeitung
will morgens nicht draußen sein

B. Die Welt aus den Augen . . . Suchen Sie sich ein Tier, und beschreiben Sie die Welt und ihre Bewohner aus den Augen dieses Tieres.

STRUKTUREN UND ÜBUNGEN

7.1 Relative clauses

Relative clauses add information about a person, place, thing, or idea already mentioned in the sentence. The relative pronoun begins the relative clause, which usually follows the noun it describes. The relative pronoun corresponds to the English words *who, whom, that,* and *which.* The conjugated verb is in the end position.

RELATIVE CLAUSE

Der Atlantik ist das Meer, **das** Europa und Afrika von Amerika trennt.

VERB IN END POSITION

The Atlantic is the ocean that separates Europe and Africa from America.

Do not omit the relative pronoun in the German sentence.

While relative pronouns may sometimes be omitted in English, they cannot be omitted from German sentences.

Das ist der Mantel, **den** ich letzte Woche gekauft habe.
That is the coat (that) I bought last week.

Relative clauses are preceded by a comma.

Likewise, the comma is not always necessary in an English sentence, but it must precede a relative clause in German. If the relative clause comes in the middle of a German sentence, it is followed by a comma as well.

Der See, **der** zwischen Deutschland, Österreich und der Schweiz **liegt,** heißt Bodensee.
The lake that lies between Germany, Austria, and Switzerland is called Lake Constance.

A. Relative Pronouns in the Nominative Case

In the nominative (subject) case, the forms of the relative pronoun are the same as the forms of the definite article **der, das, die.**

Der Fluß, **der** durch Wien fließt, heißt Donau.
Gobi heißt **die** Wüste, **die** in Innerasien liegt.

The relative pronoun and the noun it refers to have the same number and gender.

The relative pronoun has the same gender and number as the noun it refers to.

Masculine	der Mann, **der** . . .	*the man who* . . .
Neuter	das Auto, **das** . . .	*the car that* . . .
Feminine	die Frau, **die** . . .	*the woman who* . . .
Plural	die Leute, **die** . . .	*the people who* . . .

B. Relative Pronouns in the Accusative and Dative Cases

The case of a relative pronoun depends on its function within the relative clause.

When the relative pronoun functions as an accusative object or as a dative object within the relative clause, then the relative pronoun is in the accusative or dative case, respectively.

ACCUSATIVE

Nur wenige Menschen haben **den Mount Everest** bestiegen. — *Only a few people have climbed Mount Everest.*

Mount Everest ist ein Berg, **den** nur wenige Menschen bestiegen haben. — *Mount Everest is a mountain that only a few people have climbed.*

DATIVE

Ich habe **meinem Vater** nichts davon erzählt. — *I haven't told my father anything about it.*

Mein Vater ist der einzige Mensch, **dem** ich nichts davon erzählt habe. — *My father is the only person whom I haven't told anything about it.*

As in the nominative case, the accusative and dative relative pronouns have the same forms as the definite article, except for the dative plural, **denen.**

	Masculine	*Neuter*	*Feminine*	*Plural*
Accusative	den	das	die	die
Dative	dem	dem	der	denen

C. Relative Pronouns Following a Preposition

The case of the relative pronoun depends on the preposition that precedes it.

When a relative pronoun follows a preposition, the case is determined by that preposition. The gender and number of the pronoun are determined by the noun.

Ich spreche am liebsten **mit meinem** Bruder. — *Most of all I like to talk with my brother.*

Mein Bruder ist der Mensch, **mit dem** ich am liebsten spreche. — *My brother is the person (whom) I like to talk with most of all.*

Auf der Insel Rügen sind weiße Kreidefelsen.	*There are white chalk cliffs on the island of Rügen.*
Rügen ist eine Insel in der Ostsee, **auf der** weiße Kreidefelsen sind.	*Rügen is an island in the Baltic sea on which there are white chalk cliffs.*

Preposition + relative pronoun = inseparable unit.

The preposition and the pronoun stay together as a unit in German.

Wer war die Frau, **mit der** ich dich gestern gesehen habe?	*Who was the woman (whom) I saw you with yesterday?*

Übung 1 Das mag ich, das mag ich nicht!

Bilden Sie Sätze!

MODELL Ich mag Leute, die spät ins Bett gehen.

nett sein	betrunken sein	langweilig sein
laut lachen	interessant aussehen	gern verreisen
Spaß machen	exotisch sein	viel sprechen
schnell fahren		?

1. Ich mag Leute, die . . .
2. Ich mag keine Leute, die . . .
3. Ich mag eine Stadt, die . . .
4. Ich mag keine Stadt, die . . .
5. Ich mag einen Mann, der . . .
6. Ich mag keinen Mann, der . . .
7. Ich mag eine Frau, die . . .
8. Ich mag keine Frau, die . . .
9. Ich mag einen Urlaub, der . . .
10. Ich mag ein Auto, das . . .

Übung 2 Risiko[1]

Hier sind die Antworten. Stellen Sie die Fragen!

MODELL Amerika: Den Kontinent hat Kolumbus entdeckt. →
Wie heißt der Kontinent, den Kolumbus entdeckt hat?

1. Europa
2. Mississippi
3. San Francisco
4. die Alpen
5. Washington
6. das Tal des Todes
7. Ellis
8. der Pazifik
9. die Sahara
10. der Große Salzsee

a. Auf diesem See in Utah kann man segeln.
b. Diese Insel sieht man von New York.
c. Diese Stadt liegt an einer Bucht.
d. Diese Wüste kennt man aus vielen Filmen.
e. Diesem Staat in den USA hat ein Präsident seinen Namen gegeben.
f. In diesem Tal ist es sehr heiß.
g. In diesen Bergen kann man sehr gut Ski fahren.
h. Dieser Kontinent ist eigentlich eine Halbinsel von Asien.
i. Über dieses Meer fliegt man nach Hawaii.
j. Von diesem Fluß erzählt Mark Twain.

[1]*Jeopardy*

7.2 The superlative of adjectives and adverbs

A. Formation of the Superlative

To express the superlative in German, use the contraction **am** with a predicate adjective or adverb plus the ending **-sten.**

Ein Porsche ist schnell, ein Flugzeug ist schneller, eine Rakete ist am schnellsten.	*A Porsche is fast, an airplane is faster, a rocket is the fastest.*

Superlatives: **am** + **-sten**

Unlike the English superlative, which has two forms, all German adjectives and adverbs form the superlative in this way.

Hans ist **am jüngsten.**	*Hans is the youngest.*
Jens ist **am tolerantesten.**	*Jens is the most tolerant.*

When the adjective or adverb ends in **d** or **t,** or an **s**-sound such as **s, ß, sch, x,** or **z,** an **e** is inserted between the stem and the ending.

frisch	→	am frischesten	heiß	→	am heißesten
gesund	→	am gesündesten	intelligent	→	am intelligentesten

Um die Mittagzeit ist es oft am heißesten.	*The hottest (weather) is often around noontime.*

Groß is an exception to the rule: **am größten.**

Irregular superlatives, like their comparative counterparts, have an umlaut whenever possible.

B. Irregular Superlative Forms

The following one-syllable adjectives have an umlaut in the superlative as well as in the comparative.

alt	älter	am ältesten
groß	größer	am größten
jung	jünger	am jüngsten
kalt	kälter	am kältesten
krank	kränker	am kränksten
kurz	kürzer	am kürzesten
lang	länger	am längsten
warm	wärmer	am wärmsten

Im März ist es oft wärmer als im Januar. Im August ist es am wärmsten.	*In March it's often warmer than in January. It's warmest in August.*

As in English, some superlative forms are very different from their base forms:

gern	lieber	am liebsten
gut	besser	am besten
hoch	höher	am höchsten
nah	näher	am nächsten
viel	mehr	am meisten

Ich spreche Deutsch, Englisch und Spanisch. Englisch spreche ich am besten, und Deutsch spreche ich am liebsten.

I speak German, English, and Spanish. I speak English the best, and I like to speak German the most.

C. Superlative Forms Preceding Nouns

Superlatives before nouns in the nominative:
der/das/die + **-(e)ste**
die (*pl.*) + **-(e)sten**

When the superlative form of an adjective is used with a definite article (**der, das, die**) directly *before* a noun, it has an -(**e**)**ste** ending in all forms of the nominative singular and an -(**e**)**sten** ending in the plural. You will get used to the **-e/-en** distribution as you have more experience listening to and reading German. (A more detailed description of adjectives that precede nouns will follow in **Kapitel 9**.)

	Fluß (m.)	*Tal (n.)*	*Wüste (f.)*	*Berge (pl.)*
Nominative	der längst**e**	das tiefst**e**	die größt**e**	die höchst**en**

—Wie heißt der längste Fluß Europas?
—Wolga.

What is the name of the longest river in Europe?
The Volga.

—In welchem Land wohnen die meisten Menschen?
—In China.

What country has the most people?
China.

Übung 3 Geographie und Geschichte

MODELL Das Tal des Todes (−86 m) liegt tiefer als das Kaspische Meer (−28 m). →
Das Tote Meer (−396 m) liegt am tiefsten.

1. In Rom (25,6°C) ist es im Sommer heißer als in München (17,2°C).
2. In Wien (−1,4°C) ist es im Winter kälter als in Paris (3,5°C).
3. Liechtenstein (157 km²)* ist kleiner als Luxemburg (2 586 km²).
4. Deutschland (911) ist älter als die Schweiz (1291).
5. Kanada (1840) ist jünger als die USA (1776).
6. Der Mississippi (6 021 km) ist länger als die Donau (2 850 km).
7. Philadelphia (40° nördl. Breite) liegt nördlicher als Kairo (30° nördl. Breite).
8. Der Mont Blanc (4 807 m) ist höher als der Mount Whitney (4 418 m).
9. Österreich (83 849 km²) ist größer als die Schweiz (41 288 km²).

a. Athen (27,6°C)
b. das Tote Meer (−396 m)
c. Deutschland (357 050 km²)
d. Frankfurt (50° nördl. Breite)
e. Frankreich (498)
f. Monaco (1,49 km²)
g. Moskau (−9,9°C)
h. Mount Everest (8 848 m)
i. Nil (6 671 km)
j. Südafrika (1 884)

*km² = Quadratkilometer

Übung 4 Vergleiche

Vergleichen Sie. [(+) = Superlativ]

MODELL alt / Thomas / Heidi → Thomas ist **älter** als Heidi.
alt (+) → Monika ist am ältesten.

	Thomas	Heidi	Stefan	Monika
Alter	20	19	18	21
Größe	1,89 m	1,75 m	1,82 m	1,69 m
Gewicht	75 kg	65 kg	75 kg	57 kg
Haarlänge	20 cm	15 cm	5 cm	25 cm
Note in Deutsch	A	A	C	B

1. schwer / Monika / Heidi
2. schwer (+)
3. gut in Deutsch / Thomas / Monika
4. gut in Deutsch (+)
5. klein / Heidi / Stefan
6. klein (+)
7. jung / Thomas / Stefan
8. jung (+)
9. lang / Heidis Haare / Thomas' Haare
10. lang (+)
11. kurz / Monikas Haare / Heidis Haare
12. kurz (+)
13. schlecht in Deutsch / Heidi / Monika
14. schlecht in Deutsch (+)

7.3 Referring to and asking about things and ideas: *da*-compounds and *wo*-compounds

In both German and English, personal pronouns are used directly after prepositions when these pronouns refer to people or animals.

Ich werde bald **mit ihr** sprechen.	*I'll talk to her soon.*
—Bist du mit Josef gefahren?	*Did you go with Josef?*
—Ja, ich bin **mit ihm** gefahren.	*Yes, I went with him.*

da- or **dar-** + preposition

When the object of the preposition is a thing or concept, it is common in English to use the pronoun *it* or *them* with a preposition: *with it, for them,* and so on. In German, it is preferable to use compounds that begin with **da-** (or **dar-** if the preposition begins with a vowel).*

*Note that the following prepositions cannot be preceded by **da(r)-**: **ohne, außer, seit.**

daraus *out of it/them*	darin *in it/them*
damit *with it/them*	daran *on it/them*
davon *from it/them*	darauf *on top of it/them*
dazu *to it/them*	dahinter *behind it/them*
dadurch *through it/them*	davor *in front of it/them*
dafür *for it/them*	darüber *over it/them*
dagegen *against it/them*	darunter *underneath it/them*
	daneben *next to it/them*
	dazwischen *between it/them*

—Was macht man mit einer Hupe? — *What do you do with a horn?*
—Man warnt andere Leute **damit.** — *You warn other people with it.*

—Hast du etwas gegen das Rauchen? — *Do you have something against smoking?*
—Nein, ich habe nichts **dagegen.** — *No, I don't have anything against it.*

Some **da**-compounds are idiomatic.

dabei *on me/you . . .* — darum *that's why*

Hast du Geld **dabei**? — *Do you have any money on you?*

Darum hast du auch kein Glück. — *That's why you don't have any luck.*

Use a preposition + **wem** or **wen** to ask about people.

Questions about people begin with **wer** (*who*) or **wen/wem** (*whom*). If a preposition is involved, it precedes the question word.

—Mit **wem** gehst du ins Theater? — *Who will you go to the theater with? (With whom . . . ?)*
—Mit Melanie. — *With Melanie.*

—In **wen** hast du dich diesmal verliebt? — *Who did you fall in love with this time? (With whom . . . ?)*

Use **wo-** + preposition to ask about things or ideas.

Questions about things and concepts begin with **was** (*what*). If a preposition is involved, German speakers use compound words that begin with **wo-** (or **wor-** if the preposition begins with a vowel).

—**Womit** fährst du nach Berlin? — *How are you getting to Berlin?*
—Mit dem Bus. — *By bus.*

—**Worüber** sprichst du? — *What are you talking about?*
—Ich spreche über den neuen Film von Wim Wenders. — *I'm talking about Wim Wenders' new film.*

People	*Things and Concepts*
mit wem	womit
von wem	wovon
zu wem	wozu
an wen	woran
für wen	wofür
über wen	worüber
auf wen	worauf
um wen	worum

—**Von wem** ist die Oper „Parsifal“? *Who is the opera "Parzival" by?*
—Von Richard Wagner. *By Richard Wagner.*
—**Wovon** handelt diese Oper? *What is the opera about?*
—Von der Suche nach dem Gral. *About the search for the Holy Grail.*

Übung 5 Bildbeschreibung: Juttas Zimmer

Ergänzen Sie **darin, daran, darauf, davor, dahinter, darüber, darunter, daneben, dazwischen.**

Links[1] ist eine Kommode. Eine Lampe steht _____[a]. Rechts _____[b] steht der Schreibtisch. _____[c] steht Juttas Tasche. An der Wand steht ein Schrank. _____[d] hängen Juttas Sachen. Links an der Wand steht Juttas Bett. _____[e] liegt die Katze auf dem Teppich. An der Wand _____[f] hängt ein Bild. Auf dem Bild ist eine Wiese mit einem Baum. _____[g] hängen Äpfel. Mitten im Zimmer steht ein Sessel. _____[h] sieht man Juttas Schuhe, und _____[i] hat sich Hans versteckt.[2]

Übung 6 Ein Interview mit Richard Augenthaler

Das folgende Interview ist nicht vollständig. Es fehlen die Fragen. Rekonstruieren Sie die Fragen aus den Antworten.

---

[1] *to the left* [2] hat . . . versteckt *has hidden himself*

1. Ins Theater gehe ich am liebsten allein.
2. Am meisten freue ich mich auf die Ferien.
3. Ich muß immer auf meinen Freund warten. Er kommt immer zu spät.
4. In letzter Zeit habe ich mich am meisten über meinen Physiklehrer geärgert.
5. Wenn ich „USA" höre, denke ich an Wolkenkratzer und Ghettos, an den Grand Canyon und die Rocky Mountains und natürlich an Iowa.
6. Zur Schule fahre ich meistens mit dem Fahrrad, manchmal auch mit dem Bus.
7. Ich schreibe nicht gern über Sachen, die mich nicht interessieren, wie zum Beispiel die Vorteile und Nachteile des Kapitalismus.
8. Meinen letzten Brief habe ich an einen alten Freund von mir geschrieben. Der ist vor kurzem nach Graz gezogen, um dort Jura zu studieren.
9. Ich halte nicht viel von meinen Lehrern. Die tun nur immer so, als wüßten sie alles; in Wirklichkeit wissen die gar nichts.
10. Ich träume von einer Welt, in der alle Menschen genug zu essen haben und in der sich niemand fürchten muß.

7.4 The perfect tense (review)

As you remember from **Kapitel 4**, it is preferable to use the perfect tense in oral communication when talking about past events.

Ich **habe** im Garten Äpfel **gepflückt.**	*I picked apples in the garden.*

perfect tense = **haben/sein** + past participle

To form the perfect tense, use **haben** or **sein** as an auxiliary with the past participle of the verb.

A. haben or sein

Use **haben** with most verbs.
Use **sein** if the verb:
- cannot take an accusative object
- indicates change of location or condition.

Haben is by far the more commonly used auxiliary. **Sein** is normally used only when both of the following conditions are met: (1) The verb does not have an accusative object. (2) The verb implies a change of location or condition.

Bert Brecht **ist** 1956 in Berlin **gestorben.**	*Bert Brecht died in Berlin in 1956.*
Ernst **ist** mit seinem Hund **spazierengegangen.**	*Ernst went for a walk with his dog.*

In spite of the fact that there is no change of location or condition, the following verbs also take **sein** as an auxiliary: **sein, bleiben,** and **passieren.**

Letztes Jahr **bin** ich in St. Moritz **gewesen.**	*Last year I was in St. Moritz.*
Was **ist passiert**?	*What happened?*

See the appendix for a list of verbs that take **sein** as their auxiliary.

B. Forming the Past Participle

Strong verbs end in **-en**; weak verbs end in **-t** or **-et.**

There are basically two ways to form the past participle. Strong verbs add the prefix **ge-** and the ending **-en** to the stem. Weak verbs add the prefix **ge-** and the ending **-t** or **-et.**

rufen	hat **ge**ruf**en**	*to shout, call*
reisen	ist **ge**reis**t**	*to travel*
arbeiten	hat **ge**arbeit**et**	*to work*

In the past-participle form, most, but not all, strong verbs have a changed stem vowel or stem.

bleiben	ist gebl**ie**ben	*to stay*
gehen	ist geg**ang**en	*to walk*
werfen	hat gew**o**rfen	*to throw*
but: laufen	ist gelaufen	*to run*

Very few weak verbs have a change in the stem vowel. Here are some common weak verbs that do change.

dürfen	hat ged**u**rft	*to be allowed to*
können	hat gek**o**nnt	*to be able to*
müssen	hat gem**uß**t	*to have to*
bringen	hat gebr**ach**t	*to bring*
denken	hat ged**ach**t	*to think*
kennen	hat gek**a**nnt	*to know, be acquainted with*
wissen	hat gew**uß**t	*to know (as a fact)*

C. Past Participles with and without ge-

no **ge-** with
- verbs ending in **-ieren**
- inseparable prefix verbs

Another group of verbs forms the past participle without **ge-.** You will recognize them because, unlike most verbs, they are not pronounced with an emphasis on the first syllable. These verbs fall into two major groups: those that end in **-ieren** and those that have inseparable prefixes.

passieren	ist passiert	*to happen*
studieren	hat studiert	*to study, go to college*
verlieren	hat verloren	*to lose*
erlauben	hat erlaubt	*to allow*

common inseparable prefixes
- **be-**
- **ent-**
- **er-**
- **ge-**
- **ver-**

The most common inseparable prefixes are **be-**, **ent-**, **er-**, **ge-**, and **ver-**.

besuchen	hat besucht	*to visit*
entdecken	hat entdeckt	*to discover*
erzählen	hat erzählt	*to tell*
gewinnen	hat gewonnen	*to win*
versprechen	hat versprochen	*to promise*

The past participle of separable-prefix verbs is formed by adding the prefix to the past participle of the base verb.

anfangen	hat angefangen	*to begin*
aufstehen	ist aufgestanden	*to get up*
einschlafen	ist eingeschlafen	*to fall asleep*
nachdenken	hat nachgedacht	*to think something over*

Übung 7 Renate

Ergänzen Sie **haben** oder **sein.**

1. In meiner Schulzeit _____ ich nie gern aufgestanden.
2. Meine Mutter _____[a] mich immer geweckt, denn ich _____[b] nie von allein aufgewacht.
3. Ich _____[a] ganz schnell etwas gegessen und _____[b] zur Schule gerannt.
4. Meistens hatte es schon zur Stunde geklingelt, wenn ich angekommen _____.
5. In der Schule war es oft langweilig; in Biologie _____ ich sogar einmal eingeschlafen.
6. Einmal in der Woche hatten wir nachmittags Sport. Am liebsten _____[a] ich Basketball gespielt und _____[b] geschwommen.
7. Auf dem Weg nach Hause _____[a] ich einmal einen Autounfall gesehen. Zum Glück _____[b] nichts passiert.
8. Aber viele Leute _____[a] herumgestanden, bis die Polizei gekommen _____[b] .
9. Sie _____[a] geblieben, bis eine Autowerkstatt die kaputten Autos abgeholt _____[b].
10. Ich _____ nicht so lange gewartet, denn ich mußte viele Hausaufgaben machen.

Übung 8 Ernst

Ernst war heute fleißig. Er ist früh aufgestanden und hat schon alles gemacht. Übernehmen Sie seine Rolle.

MODELL Steh endlich auf! → Ich bin schon aufgestanden.

1. Mach Frühstück!
2. Trink deine Milch!
3. Mach den Tisch sauber!
4. Lauf mal schnell zum Bäcker!
5. Bring Brötchen mit!
6. Nimm Geld mit!
7. Füttere den Hund!
8. Mach die Tür zu!

KAPITEL 8

Märchenfiguren im Schloßgarten von Ludwigsburg

Kapitel 8 deals with memories and past events. You will have the opportunity to talk about your childhood, and you will learn more about the tales that are an important part of childhood in the German-speaking world.

Kindheit und Jugend

THEMEN
Kindheit
Jugend
Geschichten
Märchen

LEKTÜRE
Der Mann, der nie zu spät kam
Ich habe zwei Heimatländer
Juttas neue Frisur

KULTURELLES
Jugend in den 90er Jahren
Jung sein in Österreich
Lesen
Kulturprojekt: Bücher und Filme
Porträt: Johann Heinrich Pestalozzi und Zürich
Videoecke: Die Sonne und die Frösche

STRUKTUREN

8.1 The conjunction **als** with dependent-clause word order
8.2 The simple past tense of **haben, sein, werden,** the modal verbs, and **wissen**
8.3 Time: **als, wenn, wann**
8.4 The simple past tense of strong and weak verbs (receptive)
8.5 Sequence of events in past narration: the past perfect tense and the conjunction **nachdem** (receptive)

SPRECHSITUATIONEN

Kindheit

➤ **Grammatik 8.1**

Jens hat seinem Onkel den Rasen gemäht.

Uli hat im Garten Äpfel gepflückt.

Richard hat mit seiner Mutter Kuchen gebacken.

Bernd hat staubgesaugt und saubergemacht.

Willi hat seiner Oma die Blumen gegossen.

Jochen hat seinem kleinen Bruder Geschichten vorgelesen.

Situation 1 Die Kindheit berühmter Personen

Was haben diese berühmten Leute in ihrer Kindheit gemacht? Ordnen Sie die Sätze den folgenden Leuten zu.

Elizabeth Taylor, amerikanische Schauspielerin
Bertolt Brecht, deutscher Dramatiker
Marie Curie, französische Wissenschaftlerin
Lothar Matthäus, deutscher Fußballnationalspieler[1]
Steffi Graf, deutsche Tennisspielerin

1. Sie ist in London geboren.
2. Er hat die Fensterscheiben der Nachbarn eingeworfen.
3. Sie hat viel über Naturwissenschaft nachgedacht.
4. Er hat in Schwaben gelebt.
5. Er hat Gedichte geschrieben.
6. Sie hat in Frankreich gelebt.
7. Sie hat jeden Tag Tennis gespielt.
8. Sie hat Französisch gesprochen.
9. Er hat täglich Fußball gespielt.
10. Er hat viel gelesen.

[1] *player on the national soccer team*

11. Die besten Fußballspieler der Welt waren seine Vorbilder.
12. Sie hat von Wimbledon geträumt.
13. Sie hat in einem Kino gearbeitet.
14. Sie hat Deutsch gesprochen.
15. Sie hat tanzen gelernt.
16. Sie hat eine Schauspielschule besucht.
17. Er ist mit seinem Vater Fußball spielen gegangen.
18. Er hat gern Geschichten erzählt.

Situation 2 Umfrage

MODELL S1: Hast du als Kind Karten gespielt?
S2: Ja.
S1: Unterschreib bitte hier.

	UNTERSCHRIFT
1. Karten gespielt	______________
2. viel ferngesehen	______________
3. dich mit den Geschwistern gestritten	______________
4. oft die Hosen zerrissen	______________
5. manchmal die Leute geärgert	______________
6. einen Hund oder eine Katze gehabt	______________
7. in einer Baseballmannschaft gespielt	______________
8. Ballettunterricht genommen	______________
9. Fensterscheiben eingeworfen	______________
10. am 31. Oktober ein Kostüm getragen	______________

Situation 3 Interaktion: Als ich 12 Jahre alt war . . .

Wie oft haben Sie das gemacht, als Sie 12 Jahre alt waren: **oft, manchmal, selten** oder **nie**?

1. mein Zimmer aufgeräumt
2. Kuchen gebacken
3. Liebesromane gelesen
4. Videos angeschaut
5. heimlich jemanden geliebt
6. spät aufgestanden
7. Freunde eingeladen
8. allein verreist
9. zu einem Fußballspiel gegangen
10. meine Hausaufgaben vergessen

Situation 4 Interview

Als du acht Jahre alt warst . . .

1. Wo hast du gewohnt? Hattest du Geschwister? Freunde? Wo hat dein Vater gearbeitet? deine Mutter? Was hast du am liebsten gegessen?
2. In welche Grundschule bist du gegangen? Wann hat die Schule angefangen? Wann hat sie aufgehört? Welchen Lehrer / Welche Lehrerin hattest du am liebsten? Welche Fächer hattest du am liebsten? Was hast du in den Pausen gespielt? Was hast du nach der Schule gemacht?
3. Hast du viel ferngesehen? Was hast du am liebsten gesehen? Hast du gern gelesen? Was? Hast du Sport getrieben? Was? Was hast du gar nicht gern gemacht?

Kultur ... Landeskunde ... Informationen

Jugend in den 90er Jahren

Tobias Klapp, 23, Tischlergeselle.
Lebensziel: sich täglich neu verändern.

Welche verbotenen Dinge tun Sie manchmal? Wie sieht der ideale Freitagabend aus? Diese und viele andere Fragen haben 2 034 deutsche Jugendliche zwischen 14 und 29 Jahren für eine repräsentative Umfrage im Jahr 1994 beantwortet. Die Antworten zeigen das Selbstporträt einer eigensinnigen,[1] illusionslosen[2] Generation.

Beantworten Sie die folgenden Fragen zuerst für sich selbst. Vergleichen Sie dann ihre Antworten mit den Antworten der anderen Studenten in Ihrem Deutschkurs und dann mit denen der deutschen Jugendlichen.

1. Wie sind Sie erzogen worden?

liebevoll	40 %
liberal	26 %
streng	19 %
antiautoritär	6 %
nachlässig[3]	5 %
mit Prügel[4] und Hausarrest	4 %
gar nicht	2 %

2. Wo sind Sie aufgewachsen?

bei beiden Elternteilen[5]	85 %
bei einem Elternteil	14 %
bei Verwandten	1 %

3. Wo wohnen Sie zur Zeit?

bei den Eltern	50 %
mit meinem Lebenspartner	24 %
allein	18 %
in einer Wohngemeinschaft	6 %
im Wohnheim	1 %

4. Wie viele Stunden sehen Sie jeden Tag fern?

gar nicht	3 %
unter 1 Stunde	21 %
1 bis 2 Stunden	42 %
2 bis 4 Stunden	28 %
4 bis 6 Stunden	5 %
mehr als 6 Stunden	1 %

5. Wie viele Videos sehen Sie pro Woche?

keines	46 %
ein bis zwei	42 %
drei bis fünf	10 %
mehr als zehn	1 %

6. Wie häufig sehen Sie die Nachrichten im Fernsehen?

fast jeden Tag	39 %
oft	32 %
selten	23 %
nie	4 %

7. Wie oft lesen Sie eine Tageszeitung?

fast jeden Tag	42 %
oft	25 %
selten	26 %
nie	7 %

8. Wie viele Bücher haben Sie in den letzten drei Monaten gelesen?

keines	41 %
ein bis zwei	33 %
drei oder mehr	25 %

[1] *stubborn* [2] *without illusions* [3] *lax* [4] *beatings* [5] *parents*

Jugend

Grammatik 8.2–8.3

1. Sybille Gretter war sehr begabt. In der Schule wußte sie immer alles.

2. Sie brauchte für die Prüfungen nicht viel zu lernen.

3. Sie konnte auch sehr gut tanzen und wollte Ballerina werden.

4. Dreimal in der Woche mußte sie zum Ballettunterricht.

5. Als sie in der letzten Klasse war, hatte sie einen Freund.

6. Ihr Vater durfte nichts davon wissen, denn er war sehr streng.

7. Eines Tages hat sie ihren Freund ihren Eltern vorgestellt.

8. Aber ihr Vater mochte ihn nicht, und sie mußten sich trennen.

Situation 5 Interaktion: Wann war das?

MODELL S1: Wann bist du auf dein erstes Fest gegangen?
S2: Als ich 14 Jahre alt war.

1. auf das erste Fest gehen
2. die erste Schallplatte[1] oder Kassette bekommen
3. das erste Mal ins Kino gehen
4. das erste Footballspiel sehen
5. die erste Ferienreise allein machen
6. das erste Glas Bier trinken
7. das erste Mal in ein Konzert gehen

---

[1]*phonograph record*

Kultur ... Landeskunde ... Informationen

Jung sein in Österreich

„Freizeit ist normalerweise das, wo man machen kann, was man will. Aber das stimmt hinten und vorn nicht. . . ."

Sind Sie derselben Meinung? Warum? Was machen Sie gern in Ihrer Freizeit? Was macht Ihnen keinen Spaß? Beantworten Sie die folgenden Fragen.

- Welche Freizeitaktivität macht mir Spaß?
- Was brauche ich dazu?
- Wohin muß ich dazu gehen?
- Wieviel Zeit verbringe ich pro Woche mit dieser Aktivität?
- Sollen andere Leute dabei sein?
- Ist diese Freizeitaktivität teuer, billig oder gratis[1]?

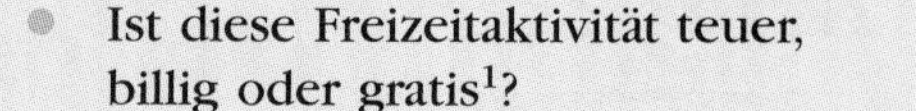

So ist es in Österreich . . .

mit den Eltern zusammen sein
lesen
basteln[2]/handarbeiten[3]
im Café/Lokal sitzen
träumen, nachdenken
mit Freunden zusammensein
allein Radio hören
fernsehen/Video
Tätigkeit am Computer
Vereinsteilnahme[4]
kulturelle Ausbildung
Sport
ein Instrument lernen
(Stunden) 1 2 3 4 5 6 7

Junge Österreicher in Bregenz

Was würden Sie mit einem gleichaltrigen[5] österreichischen Jugendlichen in Ihrer Stadt machen? Stellen Sie Freizeitangebote Ihrer Stadt in einem Führer zusammen!

[1] *free* [2] *building things* [3] *needlework* [4] *membership in a club* [5] *of the same age*

Situation 6 Interview

1. Mußtest du früh aufstehen, als du zur Schule gegangen bist? Wann?
2. Wann mußtest du von zu Hause weggehen?
3. Mußtest du zur Schule, wenn du krank warst?
4. Durftest du abends lange fernsehen, wenn du morgens früh aufstehen mußtest?
5. Konntest du zu Fuß zur Schule gehen?
6. Wolltest du manchmal lieber zu Hause bleiben? Warum?
7. Was wolltest du werden, als du ein Kind warst?
8. Durftest du abends ausgehen? Wann mußtest du zu Hause sein?

Situation 7 Geständnisse

Sagen Sie, was in diesen Situationen passiert ist, oder was Sie gemacht haben.

MODELL Als ich zum ersten Mal allein verreist bin, habe ich meinen Teddy mitgenommen.

1. Als ich einmal mit einem Jungen / einem Mädchen im Kino war
2. Als ich zum ersten Mal einen Kaffee getrunken habe
3. Wenn ich zu spät nach Hause gekommen bin
4. Als ich mein erstes F bekommen habe
5. Wenn ich keine Hausaufgaben gemacht habe
6. Wenn ich total verliebt war
7. Als ich zum ersten Mal verliebt war
8. Als ich einmal meinen Hausschlüssel verloren habe
9. Wenn ich eine schlechte Note bekommen habe
10. Wenn ich eine neue Hose kaputt gemacht habe

Situation 8 Rollenspiel: Das Klassentreffen

S1: Sie sind auf dem fünften Klassentreffen Ihrer alten High-School-Klasse. Sie unterhalten sich mit einem alten Schulfreund / einer alten Schulfreundin. Fragen Sie: was er/sie nach Abschluß der High School gemacht hat, was er/sie jetzt macht und was seine/ihre Pläne für die nächsten Jahre sind.

Geschichten

➤ **Grammatik 8.4**

Als Willi mal allein zu Hause war . . .

Situation 9 Und dann?

Suchen Sie für jede Situation eine logische Folge.

MODELL Jutta konnte ihren Hausschlüssel nicht finden und kletterte durchs Fenster.

1. Ernst warf die Fensterscheibe ein
2. Jens reparierte sein Fahrrad
3. Richard sparte ein ganzes Jahr
4. Claire kam in Innsbruck an
5. Michael bekam ein neues Fahrrad
6. Rolf lernte sechs Jahre Englisch
7. Josef arbeitete drei Monate im Krankenhaus
8. Silvia wohnte zwei Semester allein
9. Melanie bekam ihren ersten Kuß

a. machte dann Urlaub in Spanien.
b. fuhr gleich gegen einen Baum.
c. kaufte sich ein Motorrad.
d. kaufte sich einen neuen Pulli.
e. lief weg.
f. machte eine Radtour.
g. flog dann nach Amerika.
h. sagte leise: „Ach du lieber Gott!"
i. zog dann in eine Wohngemeinschaft.
j. ?

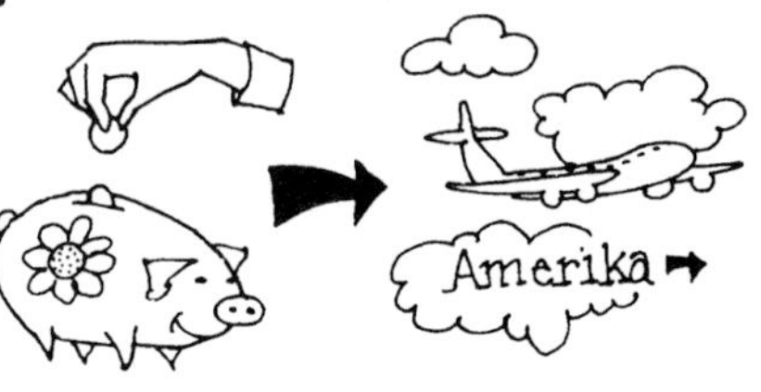

Situation 10 Bildgeschichte: Beim Zirkus

Kultur ... Landeskunde ... Informationen

Lesen

Lesen Sie eigentlich gern? Untersuchen Sie Ihre Lesegewohnheiten!

- Wie viele Bücher lesen Sie pro Jahr in Ihrer Freizeit?

  0-12 ☐ 13-30 ☐ mehr als 30 ☐

- Wie viele fremdsprachige Bücher lesen Sie pro Jahr?

  keins ☐ 1-2 ☐ mehr als 3 ☐

- Welche Bücher lesen Sie in Ihrer Freizeit? Kreuzen Sie an.

	OFT	SELTEN	NIE
Kriminalromane	☐	☐	☐
Sach- und Fachbücher[1]	☐	☐	☐
Science Fiction	☐	☐	☐
Liebesromane	☐	☐	☐
Reiseberichte	☐	☐	☐
Biographien großer Persönlichkeiten	☐	☐	☐
Unterhaltungsromane	☐	☐	☐
Literarisches[2]	☐	☐	☐

- Warum lesen Sie? (mehrere Antworten möglich)

  ☐ Weil es mir Spaß macht.
  ☐ Aus Langeweile.
  ☐ Weil ich mich informieren will.
  ☐ Weil ich mehr wissen und meinen Horizont erweitern[3] will.
  ☐ Weil ich mich mit den Helden identifizieren will.
  ☐ Weil ich Ratschläge fürs Leben erhalten[4] möchte.
  ☐ _____

- Welches Buch haben Sie zuletzt gelesen (Titel, Autor, Art des Buches)? Was halten Sie von dem Buch?

  ☐ Es hat mir sehr gut gefallen. ☐ Ich fand es interessant.
  ☐ Ich fand es langweilig. ☐ _____

Lesen Sie, welche Bücher 1994 in Deutschland am beliebtesten waren.

- Welche Sachbuchautoren kennen Sie? Wie heißen die Titel auf englisch?
- Welche Sachbücher sind wahrscheinlich Übersetzungen?
- Welche Romanautoren kennen Sie? Welche Art Roman schreiben diese Autoren (z.B. Krimi, Liebesroman usw.)?
- Welche Romane sind wahrscheinlich Übersetzungen?
- Haben Sie Sachbücher oder Romane von dieser Liste gelesen? Welche?
- Möchten Sie Sachbücher oder Romane von dieser Liste lesen? Welche?

SACHBUCH-JAHRESHITS

1. N.E. Thing Enterprises: Das magische Auge
2. N.E. Thing Enterprises: Das magische Auge II
3. Ogger: Nieten in Nadelstreifen
4. Carnegie: Sorge dich nicht, lebe!
5. Ogger: Das Kartell der Kassierer
6. Ditzinger/Kuhn: Phantastische Bilder
7. Kelder: Die Fünf „Tibeter"
8. Thomas: Ein ganz besonderer Saft – Urin
9. 3D – Die dritte Dimension
10. N.E. Thing Enterprises: Das magische Auge III

LITERATUR-JAHRESHITS

1. Gaarder: Sofies Welt
2. Høeg: Frl. Smillas Gespür für Schnee
3. Grisham: Der Klient
4. Grisham: Die Akte
5. Gordon: Der Schamane
6. Crichton: Enthüllung
7. Pilcher: Wilder Thymian
8. Pirinçi: Francis — Felidae II
9. Pilcher: Das blaue Zimmer
10. Pilcher: Die Muschelsucher

[1]Sach- . . . *nonfiction and specialty books* [2]*belles lettres* [3]*expand* [4]*to get*

Märchen

➤ **Grammatik 8.4–8.5**

Situation 11 Schneewittchen

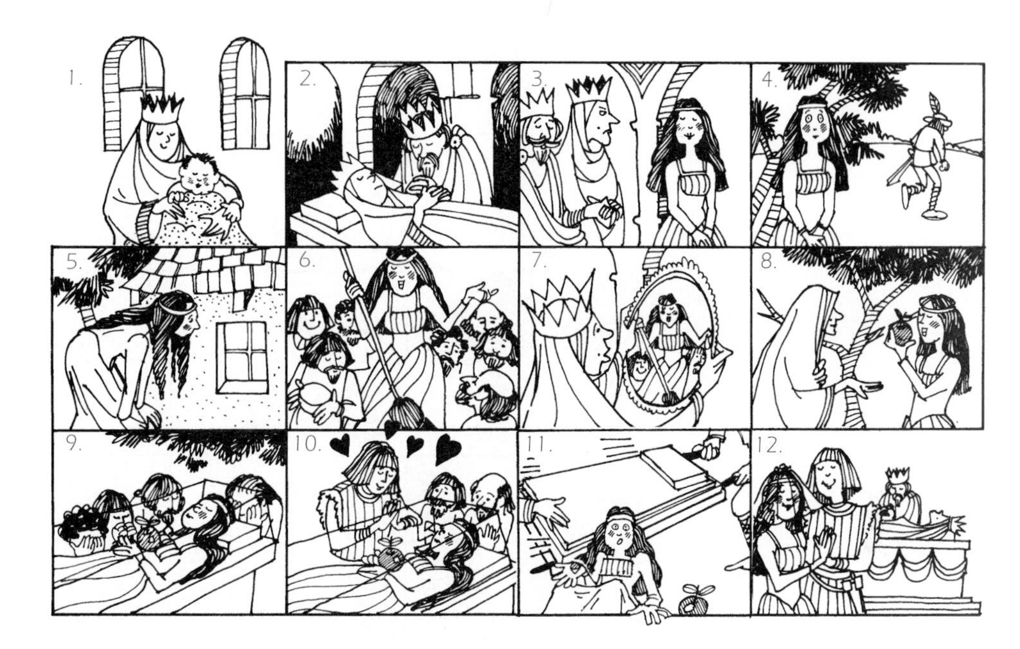

Bringen Sie die Sätze in die richtige Reihenfolge.

_____ Die Königin starb bald darauf, und der König heiratete wieder.
_____ Der Prinz und Schneewittchen heirateten, aber die böse Stiefmutter mußte sterben.
_____ Ein Jäger brachte Schneewittchen in den dunklen Wald.
_____ Eines Tages kam ein Königssohn. Als er Schneewittchen sah, verliebte er sich in sie und wollte sie mit nach Hause nehmen.
_____ Die böse Stiefmutter haßte Schneewittchen, weil sie so schön war.
_____ Schneewittchen blieb bei den Zwergen und führte ihnen den Haushalt.
_____ Es war einmal eine Königin, die bekam eine Tochter, die so weiß war wie Schnee, so rot wie Blut und so schwarzhaarig wie Ebenholz.[1]
_____ Die Stiefmutter hörte bald von ihrem Spiegel, daß Schneewittchen noch am Leben war.
_____ Schneewittchen lief durch den Wald und kam zu den sieben Zwergen.
_____ Die Zwerge weinten und legten sie in einen gläsernen Sarg.
_____ Als seine Diener den Sarg wegtrugen, stolperte ein Diener. Das giftige Apfelstück rutschte aus Schneewittchens Hals, und sie wachte auf.
_____ Die Stiefmutter verkaufte Schneewittchen einen giftigen Apfel, Schneewittchen biß hinein und fiel tot um.

---

[1] *ebony*

Situation 12 Bildgeschichte: Dornröschen

Situation 13 Wer weiß—gewinnt.

Aus welchem Märchen ist das?

Dornröschen

Rumpelstilzchen

Aschenputtel

Der Froschkönig

Rotkäppchen

Hänsel und Gretel

Schneewittchen

1. „Knusper, knusper, knäuschen,
   wer knuspert an meinem Häuschen?"
   „Der Wind, der Wind, das himmlische Kind."

2. „Spieglein, Spieglein an der Wand, wer ist die Schönste im ganzen Land?"
„Frau Königin, Ihr seid die Schönste hier, aber die junge Königin ist tausendmal schöner als Ihr."
3. „Ei, Großmutter, was hast du für große Ohren!"
„Daß ich dich besser hören kann."
„Ei, Großmutter, was hast du für große Augen!"
„Daß ich dich besser sehen kann."
„Ei, Großmutter, was hast du für ein großes Maul!"
„Daß ich dich besser fressen kann."
4. „Die Königstochter soll an ihrem fünfzehnten Geburtstag in einen tiefen Schlaf fallen, der hundert Jahre dauert."
5. „Wenn ich am Tisch neben dir sitzen und von deinem Teller essen und aus deinem Becher trinken und in deinem Bett schlafen darf, dann will ich deinen goldenen Ball aus dem Brunnen heraufholen."
6. „Rucke di guh, rucke di guh,
Blut ist im Schuh:
Der Schuh ist zu klein,
die rechte Braut sitzt noch daheim."
7. „Heute back ich, morgen brau ich,
übermorgen hol' ich der Königin ihr Kind:
ach, wie gut, daß niemand weiß,
daß ich _____ heiß!"

Situation 14 Was ist passiert?

1. Nachdem Schneewittchen den giftigen Apfel gegessen hatte,
2. Nachdem Hänsel und Gretel durch den dunkeln Wald gelaufen waren,
3. Nachdem die Prinzessin den Frosch geküßt hatte,
4. Nachdem die Müllerstochter keinen Schmuck mehr hatte,
5. Nachdem Aschenputtel alle Linsen[1] eingesammelt[2] hatte,
6. Nachdem der Wolf die Großmutter gefressen hatte,
7. Nachdem der Prinz Dornröschen geküßt hatte,
8. Nachdem Rumpelstilzchen seinen Namen gehört hatte,

a. legte er sich in ihr Bett.
b. wurde er sehr wütend.
c. wachte sie auf.
d. fiel sie tot um.
e. verwandelte er sich in einen Prinzen.
f. ging sie auf den Ball.
g. kamen sie zum Haus der Hexe.
h. versprach sie Rumpelstilzchen ihr erstes Kind.

---

[1]*lentils* [2]*gathered*

Situation 15 Zum Schreiben: Es war einmal . . .

Schreiben Sie ein Märchen. Wählen Sie aus den vier Kategorien etwas aus, oder erfinden Sie etwas.

DIE GUTEN	DIE BÖSEN	DIE AUSGANGSLAGE	DIE AUFGABE
eine schöne Prinzessin	eine böse Hexe	frißt Menschen und Tiere	drei Rätsel lösen
ein armer Student	eine grausame Professorin	ist von zu Hause weggelaufen	mit einem Riesen kämpfen
eine tapfere Königin	ein hungriger Drache	hat lange Zeit geschlafen	etwas Verlorenes wiederfinden
ein treuer Diener	ein böser Stiefvater	bekommt immer nur Fs	eine List erfinden
ein König ohne Land	ein ekliger Frosch	vergiftet das Wasser	die Hexe verjagen[1]
?	?	?	?

Hints for working with the Kulturprojekt

In addition to the sources mentioned, you may want to consult a reference work such as the *Encyclopedia Britannica.* Information on writers and film stars can be found in its articles on the various German-speaking countries (look up, e.g., "Austria" and then read the section on "cultural life").

Kulturprojekt Bücher und Filme

BÜCHER

- Kennen Sie deutschsprachige Bücher, die ins Englische übersetzt sind? Welche?
- Kennen Sie deutschsprachige Schriftsteller/Schriftstellerinnen? Welche?

Wenn Sie keine deutschsprachigen Bücher oder Schriftsteller/Schriftstellerinnen kennen, fragen Sie Ihren Lehrer / Ihre Lehrerin, oder fragen Sie in der Bibliothek oder in einem Buchladen.

Wählen Sie einen Schriftsteller / eine Schriftstellerin aus Deutschland, Österreich oder der Schweiz. Schreiben Sie eine kurze Biographie (Geburtsdatum, Geburtsort, Werke, Sonstiges) zu seinem/ihrem Leben. Benutzen Sie *Who's Who* oder eine Enzyklopädie.

FILME

- Kennen Sie deutschsprachige Filme, die ins Englische übersetzt sind? Welche?
- Kennen Sie deutschsprachige Regisseure/Regisseurinnen? Welche? Welche Filme haben sie gemacht?
- Kennen Sie deutschsprachige Schauspieler/Schauspielerinnen? Welche? In welchen Filmen haben sie mitgespielt?

Wenn Sie keine deutschsprachigen Filme oder Regisseure/Regisseurinnen (Schauspieler/Schauspielerinnen) kennen, fragen Sie Ihren Lehrer / Ihre Lehrerin, oder fragen Sie in der Bibliothek oder in einem Videoladen.

Wählen Sie einen Regisseur / eine Regisseurin (Schauspieler/Schauspielerin) aus Deutschland, Österreich oder der Schweiz. Schreiben Sie eine kurze Biographie (Geburtsdatum, Geburtsort, Filme, Sonstiges) zu seinem/ihrem Leben. Benutzen Sie *Who's Who* oder eine Enzyklopädie.

---

[1] *to chase away*

Porträt

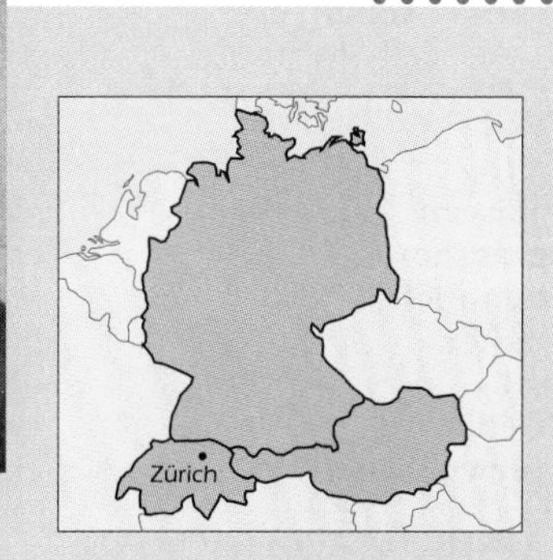

Der Pädagoge und Sozialreformer Johann Heinrich Pestalozzi (1746–1827) wurde in Zürich geboren. Er war zuerst Landwirt,[1] engagierte sich aber bald für[2] die Erziehung[3] und Betreuung[4] von armen Kindern und Waisenkindern.[5] Seine reformerischen Ideen wirkten weit über die Schweiz und Europa hinaus[6] und machten ihn zum geistigen[7] Schöpfer[8] der modernen Grundschule.

Blick auf Zürich von der Limmat

Zürich liegt an der Limmat, einem Fluß, der aus dem Zürichsee entspringt,[9] und ist die größte Stadt der Schweiz. Zürich ist eins der wirtschaftlichen und kulturellen Zentren des Landes und schon sehr alt. Die Ursprünge[10] der Stadt gehen auf die vorrömische[11] Zeit zurück. Im 16. Jahrhundert ging die Reformation in der deutschen Schweiz von Zürich aus. Der Reformator Ulrich Zwingli führte 1525 die Reformation in Zürich ein.[12]

[1] *farmer* [2] engagierte sich ... für *got involved in* [3] *upbringing* [4] *care* [5] *orphans* [6] wirkten ... hinaus *had an effect* [7] *intellectual* [8] *creator* [9] *originates from* [10] *origins* [11] *pre-Roman* [12] führte ... ein *introduced*

VIDEOECKE

Die Sonne und die Frösche

Warum quaken die Frösche, wenn sie den Mond sehen? Der Videoclip beschreibt, wie es dazu kam.

- Was sollte mit dem Mond geschehen?
- Warum fürchteten sich die Frösche davor[1]?
- Auf welchen Plan verfielen[2] die Frösche?
- Was bewirkte[3] dieser Plan?

[1] fürchteten sich ... davor *were afraid of it* [2] *came up (with)* [3] *caused*

Habt ihr denn nicht gehört? Die Sonne will Hochzeit machen!

WORTSCHATZ

Kindheit und Jugend — Childhood and Youth

die **Ausbildung, -en** — education
die **Klasse, -n** — grade (level)
die **Note, -n** — grade
die **Puppe, -n** — doll

der **Abschluß, Abschlüsse** — graduation
der **Unterricht** (R) — class, instruction
  der **Ballettunterricht** — ballet class

das **Klassentreffen, -** — class reunion
das **Mädchen, -** — girl
das **Vorbild, -er** — role model, idol

Ähnliche Wörter

der **Clown, -s;** der **Spielplatz, ¨-e;** der **Teddy, -s;** der **Zirkus, -se** das **Kostüm, -e**

Märchen — Fairy Tales

die **Braut, ¨-e** — bride
die **Fee, -n** — fairy
die **Hexe, -n** (R) — witch
die **Königin, -nen** — queen
die **List, -en** — deception, trick

der **Brunnen, -** — well; fountain
der **Diener, -** — servant
der **Drache, -n** (*wk. masc.*) — dragon
der **Jäger, -** — hunter
der **König, -e** — king
der **Riese, -n** (*wk. masc.*) — giant
der **Sarg, ¨-e** — coffin
der **Schatz, ¨-e** — treasure
der **Zwerg, -e** — dwarf

das **Rätsel, -** — puzzle, riddle
  ein Rätsel lösen — to solve a puzzle/riddle
das **Schloß, Schlösser** (R) — castle

erlösen — to rescue, free
kämpfen — to fight
klettern, ist geklettert — to climb
küssen — to kiss
sterben, stirbt, ist gestorben — to die
töten — to kill
träumen — to dream
um·fallen, fällt um, ist umgefallen — to fall over
vergiften — to poison
sich verwandeln in (+ *akk.*) — to change (into)
verwünschen — to curse, cast a spell on

böse — evil, mean
eklig — gross, loathsome
giftig — poisonous
gläsern — glass
grausam — cruel
heimlich — secret
tapfer — brave
tot — dead
treu — loyal, true
verwunschen — cursed

Ähnliche Wörter

die **Stiefmutter, ¨-;** die **Prinzessin, -nen** der **Stiefvater, ¨-;** der **Prinz, -en** (*wk. masc.*) das **Blut;** das **Feuer**

Natur und Tiere — Nature and Animals

der **Baum, ¨-e** — tree
der **Frosch, ¨-e** — frog
der **Schnee** — snow

das **Maul, ¨-er** — mouth (of an animal)
das **Pferd, -e** — horse

beißen, gebissen — to bite
fressen, frißt, gefressen — to eat (*said of an animal*)
füttern — to feed
pflücken — to pick

Ähnliche Wörter

der **Busch, ¨-e;** der **Elefant, -en** (*wk. masc.*); der **Dorn, -en;** der **Wind, -e;** der **Wolf, ¨-e** das **Schwein, -e**

Sonstige Substantive — Other Nouns

die **Einbrecherin, -nen** — female burglar
die **Feier, -n** — celebration, party
die **Fensterscheibe, -n** — windowpane
die **Ferienreise, -n** — holiday trip, vacation
die **Fremdsprache, -n** — foreign language
die **Freude, -n** — joy, pleasure
die **Mannschaft, -en** — team
  die **Baseballmannschaft, -en** — baseball team
die **Naturwissenschaft, -en** — natural science
die **Radtour, -en** — bicycle tour
die **Regisseurin, -nen** — female director
die **Schauspielerin, -nen** — actress
die **Süßigkeit, -en** — sweet, candy
die **Taschenlampe, -n** — flashlight
die **Wissenschaftlerin, -nen** — female scientist

der **Becher, -**	cup, mug
der **Einbrecher, -**	male burglar
der **Hals, ¨e**	neck; throat
der **Liebesroman, -e**	romance novel
der **Regisseur, -e**	male director
der **Schatten, -**	shadow, shade
der **Schauspieler, -**	actor
der **Schlüssel, -**	key
der **Hausschlüssel, -**	house key
der **Wissenschaftler, -**	male scientist
das **Geräusch, -e**	sound, noise
das **Leben, -**	life
am Leben sein	to be alive

Ähnliche Wörter

die **Ballerina, -s**; die **Dramatikerin, -nen**; die **Fußballspielerin, -nen**; die **Tennisspielerin, -nen** der **Dramatiker, -**; der **Fußballspieler, -**; der **Haushalt**; der **Schlaf**; der **Tennisspieler, -** das **Französisch**; das **Glas, ¨er**; das **Rockkonzert, -e**; das **Video, -s**; das **Werk, -e**

Sonstige Verben / Other Verbs

ändern	to change
an·fangen, fängt an, angefangen	to begin
bitten (**um** + *akk.*), **gebeten**	to ask (for)
ein·schlafen, schläft ein, ist eingeschlafen	to fall asleep
ein·werfen, wirft ein, eingeworfen	to break (a window)
hassen	to hate
holen	to fetch, (go) get
legen	to lay, put, place
los·fahren, fährt los, ist losgefahren	to drive/ride off
rutschen, ist gerutscht	to slide, slip
schimpfen	to cuss; to scold
stolpern, ist gestolpert	to trip
streiten, gestritten	to argue, quarrel
sich trennen	to separate, break up (*people*)
übersetzen	to translate
sich unterhalten, unterhält, unterhalten	to converse
sich verlieben (**in** + *akk.*)	to fall in love (with)
verlieren, verloren	to lose
versprechen, verspricht, versprochen	to promise
sich verstecken	to hide
versuchen	to try, attempt
vor·lesen, liest vor, vorgelesen	to read aloud
vor·stellen	to introduce
wachsen, wächst, ist gewachsen	to grow
zerreißen, zerrissen	to tear

Ähnliche Wörter

fallen, fällt, ist gefallen; helfen, hilft, geholfen; wecken; weg·tragen, trägt weg, weggetragen

Adjektive und Adverbien / Adjectives and Adverbs

arm	poor
begabt	gifted
naß	wet
streng	strict

Ähnliche Wörter

deutschsprachig, hungrig, schwarzhaarig, täglich

Sonstige Wörter und Ausdrücke / Other Words and Expressions

bald	soon
bald darauf	soon thereafter
daheim	at home
denn	for, because
endlich	finally
gar nicht	not at all
gegen (+ *akk.*)	against
hinein	into
leise	quietly
mitten	in the middle
mitten in der Nacht	in the middle of the night
nachdem	afterward
neben	next to
neulich	recently
nichts	nothing
niemand	no one, nobody
plötzlich	suddenly
Sonstiges	other things
trotzdem	in spite of that
übermorgen	the day after tomorrow
unterwegs	on the road
vorbei	past, over
zurück	back

LESEECKE

LEKTÜRE 1

Vor dem Lesen

1. Wann sind Sie pünktlich, wann kommen Sie etwas früher oder etwas später? Schreiben Sie die Uhrzeit genau auf.

- **a.** Die Schule fängt um halb neun an. ________
- **b.** Sie haben um Viertel nach drei einen Termin beim Arzt. ________
- **c.** Ein Freund hat Sie zu einer Party eingeladen. Es geht um acht los. ________
- **d.** Sie sind bei Bekannten um sieben Uhr zum Abendessen eingeladen. ________
- **e.** In Ihrem Ferienjob bei K-mart fangen Sie morgens um halb acht an. ________

2. Entschuldigungen. Wenn man zu einem wichtigen Termin, zur Schule oder zum Kurs an der Uni zu spät kommt, sollte man sich entschuldigen. Welche Gründe würden Sie akzeptieren? Kreuzen Sie an.

- ☐ Bus (Bahn, U-Bahn usw.) verpaßt
- ☐ verschlafen
- ☐ Auto/Fahrrad kaputt
- ☐ Verkehrsstau
- ☐ Termin (z.B. beim Arzt) gehabt
- ☐ sich verlaufen
- ☐ Autoschlüssel nicht gefunden
- ☐ Uhr verloren
- ☐ abends zu viel getrunken
- ☐ schlechtes Wetter
- ☐ Wecker hat nicht geklingelt
- ☐ Bauchschmerzen
- ☐ mußte noch Hausaufgaben machen
- ☐ keine Lust

Der Mann, der nie zu spät kam

von Paul Maar

(1) Ich will von einem Mann erzählen, der immer sehr pünktlich war. Er hieß Wilfried Kalk und war noch nie in seinem Leben zu spät gekommen. Nie zu spät in den Kindergarten, nie zu spät zur Schule, nie zu spät zur Arbeit, nie zu spät zum Zug. Der Mann war sehr stolz[1] darauf.

[1]*proud*

Schon als Kind war Wilfried regelmäßig eine halbe Stunde vor dem Weckerklingeln aufgewacht. Wenn seine Mutter hereinkam, um ihn zu wecken, saß er angezogen in seinem Zimmer und sagte: „Guten Morgen, Mama. Wir müssen uns beeilen.[2]" Jeden Werktag, wenn der Hausmeister in der Frühe gähnend[3] über den Schulhof schlurfte,[4] um das große Schultor aufzuschließen, stand Wilfried bereits davor. Andere Kinder spielten nach der Schule Fußball und schauten sich auf dem Heimweg die Schaufenster an. Das tat Wilfried nie. Er rannte sofort nach Hause, um nicht zu spät zum Essen zu kommen.

Später arbeitete Wilfried in einem großen Büro in der Nachbarstadt. Er mußte mit dem Zug zur Arbeit fahren. Trotzdem[5] kam er nie zu spät. Er nahm den frühesten Zug und stand immer zwanzig Minuten vor der Abfahrt auf dem richtigen Bahnsteig. Kein Arbeitskollege konnte sich erinnern, daß er jemals[6] ins Büro gekommen wäre und Wilfried Kalk nicht an seinem Schreibtisch gesessen hätte. Der Chef stellte ihn gern als gutes Beispiel hin. „Die Pünktlichkeit von Herrn Kalk, die lobe[7] ich mir", sagte er. „Da könnte sich mancher hier eine Scheibe abschneiden.[8]" Deswegen sagten die Arbeitskollegen oft zu Wilfried: „Könntest du nicht wenigstens einmal zu spät kommen? Nur ein einziges Mal!"

Aber Wilfried schüttelte den Kopf und sagte: „Ich sehe nicht ein,[9] welchen Vorteil es bringen soll, zu spät zu kommen. Ich bin mein ganzes Leben pünktlich gewesen."

Wilfried verabredete sich[10] nie mit anderen und ging nie zu einer Versammlung.[11] „Das alles sind Gelegenheiten,[12] bei denen man zu spät kommen könnte", erklärte er. „Und Gefahren[13] soll man meiden.[14]"

Einmal glaubte ein Arbeitskollege, er habe Wilfried bei einer Unpünktlichkeit ertappt.[15] Er saß im Kino und schaute sich die Sieben-Uhr-Vorstellung an. Da kam Wilfried während des Films herein und tastete sich[16] im Dunkeln durch die Reihe.

„Hallo, Wilfried! Du kommst ja zu spät", sagte der Arbeitskollege verwundert.[17] Aber Wilfried schüttelte unwillig den Kopf und sagte: „Unsinn! Ich bin nur etwas früher gekommen, um rechtzeitig zur Neun-Uhr-Vorstellung hier zu sein."

Ins Kino ging Wilfried sowieso[18] sehr selten. Lieber saß er zu Hause im Sessel und studierte den Fahrplan. Er kannte nicht nur alle Ankunfts- und Abfahrtszeiten auswendig,[19] sondern auch die Nummern der Züge und den richtigen Bahnsteig.

Als Wilfried 25 Jahre lang nie zu spät zur Arbeit gekommen war, veranstaltete[20] der Chef ihm zu Ehren[21] nach Dienstschluß eine Feier. Er öffnete eine Flasche Sekt[22] und überreichte Wilfried eine Urkunde.[23] Es war das erste Mal, daß Wilfried Alkohol trank. Schon nach einem Glas begann er zu singen. Nach dem zweiten fing er an zu schwanken,[24] und als der Chef ihm ein drittes Glas eingegossen hatte, mußten zwei Arbeitskollegen den völlig betrunkenen Wilfried heimbringen und ins Bett legen.

[2]Wir . . . *We must hurry.* [3]*yawning* [4]*dragged his feet* [5]*In spite of that* [6]*ever* [7]*praise* [8]Da . . . *Some of you could take a cue (from him).* [9]sehe . . . ein *understand* [10]verabredete . . . *made a date* [11]*gathering* [12]*occasions* [13]*dangers* [14]*avoid* [15]*caught (in the act)* [16]tastete . . . *groped his way* [17]*surprised* [18]*anyway* [19]*by heart* [20]*arranged* [21]ihm . . . *in his honor* [22]*sparkling wine* [23]*certificate (of merit)* [24]*sway*

(5) Am nächsten Morgen wachte er nicht wie üblich eine halbe Stunde vor dem
45 Weckerklingeln auf. Als der Wecker längst geläutet hatte, schlief er immer noch tief. Er erwachte erst,[25] als ihm die Sonne ins Gesicht schien. Entsetzt[26] sprang er aus dem Bett, hastete zum Bahnhof. Die Bahnhofsuhr zeigte 9 Uhr 15. Viertel nach neun, und er saß noch nicht hinter seinem Schreibtisch! Was würden die Kollegen sagen? Was der Chef? „Herr Kalk, Sie kommen zu spät, nachdem Sie erst
50 gestern eine Urkunde bekamen?!"

Kopflos rannte er den Bahnsteig entlang. In seiner Hast stolperte[27] er über einen abgestellten Koffer, kam zu nahe an die Bahnsteigkante,[28] trat ins Leere[29] und stürzte hinunter auf die Schienen.[30]

. . .

[25] *not until* [26] *Horrified* [27] *stumbled* [28] *edge of the train platform* [29] *emptiness* [30] *train tracks*

Arbeit mit dem Text

1. Kombinieren Sie die Überschriften mit den richtigen Abschnitten.

_____ Der Chef veranstaltete Wilfried zu Ehren eine Feier.
_____ Wilfried verbrachte seine Freizeit am liebsten zu Hause.
_____ Schon als Kind war Wilfried immer pünktlich.
_____ Wilfried verschläft zum ersten Mal in seinem Leben.
_____ Wilfried kam nie zu spät zur Arbeit.

2. Was wissen Sie über die Hauptperson?

Vorname und Nachname		*Familie*	
Alter		*Hobbys*	
Wo arbeitet er?		*Rauchen*	
Wie lange schon?		*Trinken*	
Wie kommt er zur Arbeit?		*Und was noch?*	

3. Wie endet wohl diese Geschichte? Schreiben Sie sie zu Ende.

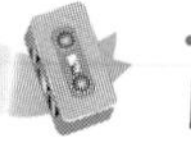

LEKTÜRE 2

Vor dem Lesen

Das folgende Gedicht ist von einem türkischen Dichter. Es heißt „Ich habe zwei Heimatländer".

1. Welche Länder sind das wohl?
2. Warum ist Sabri Çakir wahrscheinlich in Deutschland?

Ich habe zwei Heimatländer

von Sabri Çakir

Ich habe zwei Sprachen
die eine spreche ich zu Hause
Sie verstehen mich so besser
meine Frau und mein Sohn
5 Die andere spreche ich auf der Arbeit
beim Einkaufen im Ausländeramt

Ich habe zwei Gesichter
Das eine benutze ich für die Deutschen
Dieses Gesicht kann alles
10 lachen und weinen
Das andere halte ich
für meine Landsleute[1] bereit[2]

Ich habe zwei Heimatländer
Eins in dem ich geboren wurde
15 Das andere in dem ich satt werde[3]
Das Land meiner Väter liebe ich mehr
Aber erdulden[4] muß ich
Die Schmerzen[5] beider

[1] *countrymen* [2] halte . . . *keep ready* [3] satt . . . *become full* [4] *suffer, endure* [5] *pains*

Arbeit mit dem Text

1. Der Dichter hat nicht nur zwei Heimatländer, er hat auch zwei Sprachen und zwei Gesichter. Tragen Sie in die Tabelle ein, wie er sie charakterisiert.

Sprache 1	Sprache 2	Gesicht 1	Gesicht 2	Heimatland 1	Heimatland 2
zu Hause					
mit seiner Frau / seinem Sohn					

2. Daß der Dichter zwei Gesichter hat, ist bildlich[1] gemeint. Welches der folgenden Wörter ist hier ein Synonym für Gesicht?

☐ Persönlichkeit[2] ☐ Laune[3] ☐ Miene[4] ☐ Erziehung

[1] *figurative* [2] *personality* [3] *mood* [4] *facial expression*

LEKTÜRE 3

Vor dem Lesen

1. Was wissen Sie von Jutta Ruf?
2. Lesen Sie den Cartoon. Welche „Haarmoden" (Frisuren) sind noch „kontrovers"? Zeichnen Sie eine „kontroverse" Haarmode oder bringen Sie Fotos mit in den Kurs.

Juttas neue Frisur

Jutta Ruf hat einen neuen Freund, Billy. Eigentlich heißt er nicht Billy, sondern Paul, aber sein Vorbild ist Billy Idol, und so nennt er sich nach ihm. Er hat sich auch die Haare ganz kurz geschnitten und hellblond gebleicht und trägt immer alte, kaputte Jeans, zerrissene[1] T-Shirts und eine Lederjacke mit Ketten.[2] Auf dem Oberarm hat er einen Totenkopf[3] tätowiert,[4] und auf seiner linken Hand steht „no future". Auf beiden Wangen hat er je drei parallele Narben.[5] Die hat er sich auf einer Fete nach einem Billy-Idol-Konzert mit einer Rasierklinge[6] geschnitten . . . Jutta findet ihn toll! Sie trägt jetzt immer zerrissene, schwarze Strumpfhosen,[7] Turnschuhe, die sie silbern gesprüht[8] hat, ein T-Shirt, auf dem „I love Billy" steht, und eine alte Jeansjacke.

Es ist Mittwochabend nach acht Uhr. Jutta steht vor der Tür und traut sich nicht hinein.[9] Sie hat Angst, daß ihre Eltern ihre neue Frisur nicht so toll finden wie ihre Freunde, besonders Billy.

Am Morgen ist sie nicht zur Schule gegangen, sondern hat sich mit Billy in einer Kneipe getroffen. Da haben sie noch eine Stunde über die neue Frisur gesprochen, und dann sind sie zum Friseur gegangen. Jutta hatte darauf gespart, denn so eine Frisur ist nicht billig. Nach drei Stunden war alles fertig, und Billy war begeistert.[10] Allerdings[11] hat es dann auch 95,- DM gekostet, wegen der neuen Farbe und so.

[1]*torn* [2]*chains* [3]*skull* [4]*tattooed* [5]*scars* [6]*razor blade* [7]*stockings* [8]*spray painted*
[9]traut . . . *is afraid to go inside* [10]*thrilled* [11]*of course*

20 Jutta hat jetzt einen ziemlich ungewöhnlichen Haarschnitt. In der Mitte steht ein zehn Zentimeter breiter Haarstreifen, der von der Stirn[12] bis in den Nacken[13] läuft. Die Haare sind fünfzehn Zentimeter lang, stehen fest und gerade nach oben und sind violett und grün. Der Rest des Kopfes ist kahl.[14] Billy wollte dann noch mit ihr zu einem Tätowierer gehen und ihr „Billy" auf die rechte Seite des Kopfes 25 tätowieren lassen, aber sie hatten kein Geld mehr. Alle Freunde fanden es toll . . . aber jetzt steht sie allein vor der Tür. Sie will warten, bis ihre Eltern ins Bett gegangen sind.

Plötzlich hört sie jemanden.

„Mensch, das bist ja du, Jutta!" Es ist ihr Bruder Hans, der aus dem Fenster 30 schaut. „Wie siehst du denn aus?" Hans kann vor Lachen[15] kaum[16] sprechen. „Das sieht ja unmöglich aus!"

„Ach, du hast doch keine Ahnung!"

„Mutti und Papi finden es sicher toll. Komm schnell herein!"

„Nein, ich will noch warten, bis sie ins Bett gegangen sind."

35 „Da kannst du lange warten, es ist doch erst acht Uhr! Komm, das will ich sehen, wie die reagieren!"

[12] *forehead* [13] *neck* [14] *bald* [15] vor . . . *from laughing (so hard)* [16] *hardly*

Arbeit mit dem Text

A. Wie sehen sie aus?

	Haarschnitt	Haarfarbe	Kleidung
Billy			
Jutta			

B. Mittwochmorgen oder Mittwochabend? Schreiben Sie ein **M** oder ein **A** vor die Sätze, und bringen Sie sie in die richtige Reihenfolge.

_____ Billy hat geklatscht.[1]
_____ Jutta steht vor der Tür und hat Angst.
_____ Hans will sehen, wie die Eltern reagieren.
_____ Jutta ist nicht in die Schule gegangen.
_____ Jutta hat Billy in einer Kneipe getroffen.
_____ Hans schaut aus dem Fenster.
_____ Jutta ist zum Friseur gegangen.
_____ Billy wollte mit Jutta zu einem Tätowierer gehen.

C. Fragen:

1. Warum sind Jutta und Billy nicht mehr zum Tätowieren gegangen?
2. Wie findet Hans Juttas Frisur?
3. Was, glauben Sie, werden Juttas Eltern sagen?

[1] *clapped his hands*

STRUKTUREN UND ÜBUNGEN

8.1 The conjunction *als* with dependent-clause word order

The conjunction **als** (*when*) is commonly used to express that two events or circumstances happened at the same time. The **als**-clause establishes a point of reference in the past for an action or event described in the main clause.

Als ich zwölf Jahre alt war, bin ich zum ersten Mal allein verreist.	*When I was twelve years old, I traveled alone for the first time.*

When an **als**-clause introduces a sentence, it occupies the first position. Consequently, the conjugated verb in the main clause occupies the second position and the subject of the main clause the third position. Note that the conjugated verb in the **als**-clause appears at the end of the clause.

[1: Als ich 12 Jahre alt **war,**] [2: **bin**] [3: **ich**] zum ersten Mal allein verreist.

Übung 1 Meilensteine

Schreiben Sie 10–15 Sätze über Ihr Leben. Beginnen Sie jeden Satz mit **als.**

MODELL Als ich eins war, habe ich laufen gelernt.
Als ich zwei war, habe ich sprechen gelernt.
Als ich fünf war, bin ich in die Schule gekommen.

8.2 The simple past tense of *haben, sein, werden,* the modal verbs, and *wissen*

Use the simple past tense of **haben, sein, werden, wissen,** and the modal verbs in both writing and conversation.

The simple past tense is preferred over the perfect tense with some frequently used verbs, even in conversational German. These verbs include **haben, sein, werden,** the modal verbs, and the verb **wissen.** The conjugations appear below; notice that the **ich-** and the **er/sie/es**-forms are the same.

Frau Gretter **war** sehr begabt.	*Mrs. Gretter was very talented.*
In der Schule **wußte** sie immer alles.	*In school she always knew everything.*
Sie **hatte** viele Freundinnen und Freunde.	*She had many friends.*

A. The verbs **sein** and **haben**

sein			
ich	war	wir	waren
du	warst	ihr	wart
Sie	waren	Sie	waren
er / sie / es	war	sie	waren

haben			
ich	hatte	wir	hatten
du	hattest	ihr	hattet
Sie	hatten	Sie	hatten
er / sie / es	hatte	sie	hatten

B. The verb **werden**

Michael **wurde** Tierpfleger. — *Michael became an animal caretaker.*

Im August **wurde** er sehr krank. — *In August he became very sick.*

werden			
ich	wurde	wir	wurden
du	wurdest	ihr	wurdet
Sie	wurden	Sie	wurden
er / sie / es	wurde	sie	wurden

C. Modal Verbs

To form the simple past tense of modal verbs, use the stem, drop any umlauts, and add **-te-** plus the appropriate ending.

können → könn → konn → konnte → du konntest

Gestern **wollten** wir ins Kino gehen. — *Yesterday, we wanted to go to the movies.*

Mehmet **mußte** jeden Tag um sechs aufstehen. — *Mehmet had to get up at six every morning.*

Helga und Sigrid **durften** mit sechs Jahren noch nicht fernsehen. — *When they were six, Helga and Sigrid weren't yet allowed to watch TV.*

Here are the simple past-tense forms of the modal verbs.

	können	**müssen**	**dürfen**	**sollen**	**wollen**	**mögen**
ich	konnte	mußte	durfte	sollte	wollte	mochte
du	konntest	mußtest	durftest	solltest	wolltest	mochtest
Sie	konnten	mußten	durften	sollten	wollten	mochten
er / sie / es	konnte	mußte	durfte	sollte	wollte	mochte
wir	konnten	mußten	durften	sollten	wollten	mochten
ihr	konntet	mußtet	durftet	solltet	wolltet	mochtet
Sie	konnten	mußten	durften	sollten	wollten	mochten
sie	konnten	mußten	durften	sollten	wollten	mochten

Note the consonant change in the past tense of **mögen: mo*ch*te.**

D. The verb **wissen**

The forms of the verb **wissen** are similar to those of the modal verbs.

Ich **wußte** nicht, daß du keine Erdbeeren magst.	*I didn't know that you don't like strawberries.*

Here are the simple past-tense forms.

wissen			
ich	wußte	wir	wußten
du	wußtest	ihr	wußtet
Sie	wußten	Sie	wußten
er / sie / es	wußte	sie	wußten

Übung 2 Fragen und Antworten

Hier sind die Fragen. Was sind die Antworten?

MODELL Lydia, warum bist du nicht mit ins Kino gegangen? (nicht können) → Ich konnte nicht.

1. Ernst, warum bist du nicht mit zum Schwimmen gekommen? (nicht dürfen)
2. Maria, warum bist du nicht gekommen? (nicht wollen)

3. Jens, gestern war Juttas Geburtstag! (das/nicht wissen)
4. Jutta, warum hast du eine neue Frisur? (eine/wollen)
5. Jochen, warum hast du das Essen nicht gekocht? (das/nicht sollen)

Übung 3 Minidialoge

Setzen Sie Modalverben oder **wissen** ein.

1. SILVIA: Was hast du gemacht, wenn du nicht zur Schule gehen _____[a], Jürgen?
   JÜRGEN: Ich habe gesagt: „Ich bin krank."
   SILVIA: Haben deine Eltern das geglaubt?
   JÜRGEN: Nein, meine Mutter _____[b] immer, was los war.
2. ERNST: Hans, warum bist du gestern nicht auf den Spielplatz gekommen?
   HANS: Ich _____[a] nicht. Ich habe eine Fünf in Mathe geschrieben und _____[b] zu Hause bleiben.
   ERNST: Schade. Wir _____[c] Fußball spielen, aber dann _____[d] wir nicht genug Spieler finden.
3. HERR RUF: Guten Tag, Frau Gretter. Tut mir leid, daß ich neulich nicht zu Ihrer kleinen Feier kommen _____[a]. Aber ich _____[b] meine alte Tante in Würzburg besuchen.
   FRAU GRETTER: Ja, wirklich schade. Ich _____[c] gar nicht, daß Sie eine Tante in Würzburg haben.
   HERR RUF: Sie zieht diese Woche nach Düsseldorf zu ihrer Tochter, und ich _____[d] sie noch einmal besuchen.

8.3 Time: *als, wenn, wann*

Als refers to a circumstance (time period) in the past or to a single event (point in time) in the past or present, but never in the future.

TIME PERIOD

Als ich 15 Jahre alt war, sind meine Eltern nach Texas gezogen.
When I was 15 years old my parents moved to Texas.

POINT IN TIME

Als wir in Texas angekommen sind, war es sehr heiß.
When we arrived in Texas, it was very hot.

Als Veronika ins Zimmer kommt, klingelt das Telefon.
When (As) Veronika comes into the room, the phone rings.

Wenn has three distinct meanings: a conditional meaning and two temporal meanings. In conditional sentences, **wenn** means *if.* In the temporal sense, **wenn** may be used to describe events that happen or happened one or more times (*when*[*ever*]) or to describe events that will happen in the future (*when*).

CONDITION

Wenn man auf diesen Knopf drückt, öffnet sich die Tür.
If you press this button, the door will open.

REPEATED EVENTS

Wenn Herr Wagner nach Hause kam, freuten sich die Kinder.
When(ever) Mr. Wagner came home, the children would be happy.

Wenn Herr Wagner nach Hause kommt, freuen sich die Kinder.
When(ever) Mr. Wagner comes home, the children are happy.

FUTURE EVENT

Wenn ich in Frankfurt ankomme, rufe ich dich an.
When I arrive in Frankfurt, I'll call you.

In the simple past, **wenn** refers to a habit or an action or event that happened repeatedly or customarily; **als** refers to a specific action or event that happened once, over a particular time period or at a particular point in time in the past.

Wenn ich nicht zur Schule gehen wollte, habe ich gesagt, ich bin krank. — *When(ever) I didn't want to go to school, I said that I was sick.*

Als ich mein erstes F bekommen habe, habe ich geweint. — *When I got my first F, I cried.*

Wann is an adverb of time meaning *at what time.* It is used in both direct and indirect questions.

Wann hast du deinen ersten Kuß bekommen? — *When did you get your first kiss?*

Ich weiß nicht, **wann** der Zug kommt. — *I don't know when the train is coming.*

Note that, when **wann** is used in an indirect question, the conjugated verb comes at the end of the clause.

When	
Single event in past or present (*at one time*) Circumstance in the past	**als**
Condition (*if*) Repeated event in past, present, or future (*whenever*) Single event in the future (*when*)	**wenn**
Adverb of time (*at what time?*)	**wann**

Übung 4 Minidialoge

Wann, wenn oder **als**?

1. ERNST: _____[a] darf ich fernsehen?
   FRAU WAGNER: _____[b] du deine Hausaufgaben gemacht hast.
2. ROLF: Oma, _____[a] hast du Opa kennengelernt?
   SOFIE: _____[b] ich siebzehn war.
3. STEFAN: Was habt ihr gemacht, _____ ihr in München wart?
   NORA: Wir haben sehr viele Filme gesehen.
4. MARTHA: _____[a] hast du Sofie getroffen?
   WILLI: Gestern, _____[b] ich an der Uni war.
5. ALBERT: _____[a] fliegst du nach Europa?
   PETER: _____[b] ich genug Geld habe.
6. MONIKA: Du spielst sehr gut Tennis. _____[a] hast du das gelernt?
   HEIDI: _____[b] ich noch klein war.

Übung 5 Ein Brief

Wann, wenn oder **als**?

Liebe Tina,

gestern nachmittag mußte ich meiner Oma mal wieder Kuchen und Wein bringen. Immer _____[a] ich mich mit meinen Freunden verabredet,[1] will mein Vater irgendetwas[2] von mir. Ich war ganz schön wütend. _____[b] ich den Korb[3] zusammengepackt habe, habe ich leise geschimpft. _____[c] ich meine Oma besuche, muß ich immer ein bißchen dableiben und mich mit ihr unterhalten. Das ist langweilig und anstrengend,[4] denn die Oma hört nicht mehr so gut. Außerdem wohnt sie am anderen Ende der Stadt. Auch _____[d] ich mit dem Bus fahre, dauert es mindestens zwei Stunden.

_____[e] ich aus dem Haus gekommen bin, habe ich an der Ecke Billy auf seinem Moped gesehen. _____[f] ich ihn zum letzten Mal gesehen habe, haben wir uns prima unterhalten.

„_____[g] kommst du mal wieder ins Jugendzentrum?" hat Billy gerufen.

„Vielleicht heute gegen Abend", habe ich geantwortet. _____[h] ich mich auf den Weg gemacht habe, hat es auch noch angefangen zu regnen. Und natürlich . . . wie immer . . . _____[i] es regnet, habe ich keinen Regenschirm dabei. Soviel für heute.

Tausend Grüße

Deine Jutta

---

[1] *made a date* [2] *something* [3] *basket* [4] *strenuous*

8.4 The simple past tense of strong and weak verbs (receptive)

In written texts, the simple past tense is frequently used instead of the perfect to refer to past events.

Jutta **fuhr** allein in Urlaub.	*Jutta went on vacation alone.*
Ihr Vater **brachte** sie zum Bahnhof.	*Her father took her to the train station.*

In the simple past tense, just as in the present tense, separable-prefix verbs are separated in independent clauses but joined in dependent clauses.

Rolf **stand** um acht Uhr **auf.** Es war selten, daß er so früh **aufstand.**	*Rolf got up at eight. It was rare that he got up so early.*

A. Weak Verbs

weak verbs = **-(e)te**

You can recognize the simple past of weak verbs by the **-(e)te-** that is inserted between the stem and the ending.

PRESENT	SIMPLE PAST	PRESENT	SIMPLE PAST
du sagst :	du sag**te**st	sie arbeitet :	sie arbeit**ete**

Wir bad**ete**n, bau**te**n Sandburgen und spiel**te**n Volleyball.	*We went swimming, built sand castles, and played volleyball.*

Like modal verbs, simple past-tense forms do not have an ending in the **ich-** and the **er/sie/es**-forms: **ich sagte, er sagte.** Here are the simple past-tense forms of the verb **machen.**

machen			
ich	machte	wir	machten
du	machtest	ihr	machtet
Sie	machten	Sie	machten
er / sie / es	machte	sie	machten

irregular weak verbs = **-te** + stem vowel change

For a few weak verbs, the stem of the simple past is the same as the one used to form the past participle.

PRESENT	SIMPLE PAST	PERFECT	
bringen	brachte	hat gebracht	*to bring*
denken	dachte	hat gedacht	*to think*
kennen	kannte	hat gekannt	*to know, be acquainted with*
wissen	wußte	hat gewußt	*to know (as a fact)*

B. Strong Verbs

strong verbs = stem vowel change

All strong verbs have a different stem in the simple past: **schwimmen/schwamm, singen/sang, essen/aß.** Since English also has a number of verbs with irregular stems in the past (*swim/swam, sing/sang, eat/ate*), you will usually have no trouble recognizing simple past stems. You will recognize the **ich**- and **er/sie/es**-forms of strong verbs easily, because they do not have an ending.

Through practice reading texts in the simple past, you will gradually become familiar with the various patterns of stem change that exist. Here are some common past-tense forms you are likely to encounter in your reading.* A complete list of stem-changing verbs can be found in Appendix E.

bleiben	blieb	*to stay*	rufen	rief	*to call*
essen	aß	*to eat*	schlafen	schlief	*to sleep*
fahren	fuhr	*to drive*	schreiben	schrieb	*to write*
fliegen	flog	*to fly*	sehen	sah	*to see*
geben	gab	*to give*	sprechen	sprach	*to speak*
gehen	ging	*to go*	stehen	stand	*to stand*
lesen	las	*to read*	tragen	trug	*to carry*
nehmen	nahm	*to take*	waschen	wusch	*to wash*

Der Bus fuhr um sieben Uhr ab.	*The bus left at seven o'clock.*
Sechs Kinder schliefen in einem Zimmer.	*Six children were sleeping in one room.*
Jutta aß frische Krabben.	*Jutta ate fresh shrimp.*

Übung 6 Die Radtour

Setzen Sie die Verben ein:

aßen	gingen	kamen	schwammen	standen
fuhren	hielten	schliefen	sprangen	

Richard und Franz wollten eine Radtour machen, aber ihre Räder waren kaputt. Sie mußten sie reparieren, bevor sie losfahren konnten. Am Morgen der Tour _____[a] sie um sechs Uhr auf, _____[b] in die Garage, wo die Räder waren und machten sich an die Arbeit. Gegen acht waren sie fertig, sie frühstückten noch, und dann _____[c] sie ab. Gegen elf _____[d] sie an einen kleinen See. Sie _____[e] an und setzten sich ins Gras. Richards Mutter hatte ihnen Essen eingepackt. Sie waren hungrig und _____[f] alles auf. Sie _____[g] im See und legten sich dann in den Schatten und _____[h]. Am späten Nachmittag _____[i] sie noch mal ins Wasser und radelten dann zurück nach Hause. Die Rückfahrt dauerte eine Stunde länger als die Hinfahrt.

---

*It is fairly easy to make an educated guess about the form of the infinitive when encountering new simple past-tense forms. The following vowel correspondences are the most common.

SIMPLE PAST	INFINITIVE	EXAMPLES
a	e/i	gab-geben, fand-finden
i/ie	a/ei	ritt-reiten, hielt-halten, schrieb-schreiben

Übung 7 Hänsel und Gretel

Ergänzen Sie die Verben.

1. brachten gaben hieß kamen liefen machten schliefen wohnte

Vor einem großen Wald _____[a] ein armer Mann mit seiner Familie. Der Junge _____[b] Hänsel und das Mädchen Gretel. Als sie eines Tages nichts mehr zu essen hatten, _____[c] die Eltern die Kinder in den Wald. Sie _____[d] ihnen ein Feuer und _____[e] jedem noch ein Stück Brot. Die Kinder _____[f] ein, und als sie wieder aufwachten, waren sie allein. Sie _____[g] durch den Wald, bis sie an ein kleines Haus _____[h].

2. fanden kochte lief saß sahen schloß tötete trug

Durch das Fenster _____[a] sie eine alte Frau, die vor dem Kamin[1] _____[b] und strickte. Als die Alte die Kinder bemerkte,[2] holte sie sie herein und _____[c] ihnen etwas zu essen. Die Kinder _____[d] die Frau sehr freundlich, aber leider war sie eine böse Hexe. Sie packte[3] Hänsel, _____[e] ihn in den Stall und _____[f] die Tür. Sie wollte, daß er dick wird, damit sie ihn essen konnte. Gretel weinte und versuchte, Hänsel zu helfen. Sie _____[g] die Hexe und _____[h] mit Hänsel weg.

8.5 Sequence of events in past narration: the past perfect tense and the conjunction *nachdem* (receptive)

A. Uses of the Past Perfect Tense

The past perfect tense is used to describe past actions and events that were completed before other past actions and events.

Nachdem Jochen zwei Stunden **ferngesehen hatte,** ging er ins Bett.	*After Jochen had watched TV for two hours, he went to bed.*
Nachdem Jutta mit ihrer Freundin **telefoniert hatte,** machte sie ihre Hausaufgaben.	*After Jutta had talked with her friend on the phone, she did her homework.*

The past perfect tense is often used in the clause with **nachdem.** The simple past tense is then used in the concluding (main) clause.

The past perfect tense often occurs in a dependent clause with the conjunction **nachdem** (*after*); the verb of the main clause is in the simple past or the perfect tense.

Nachdem Jens seine erste Zigarette **geraucht hatte, wurde** ihm schlecht.	*After Jens had smoked his first cigarette, he got sick.*

[1]*hearth* [2]*noticed* [3]*grabbed*

A dependent clause introduced by **nachdem** usually precedes the main clause. This results in the pattern "verb, verb."

DEPENDENT CLAUSE	MAIN CLAUSE
1	2

Nachdem ich die Schule **beendet hatte, machte** ich eine Lehre.
After I had finished school, I learned a trade.

The conjugated verb of the dependent clause is at the end of the clause; and the conjugated verb of the main clause is at the beginning of that clause. Because the entire dependent clause holds the first position in the sentence, the verb-second rule applies here.

B. Formation of the Past Perfect Tense

past perfect tense:
hatte/war + past participle

The past perfect tense of a verb consists of the simple past tense of the auxiliary **haben** or **sein** and the past participle of the verb.

Ich **hatte** schon **bezahlt,** und wir konnten gehen.	*I had already paid, and we could go.*
Als wir ankamen, **waren** sie schon **weggegangen.**	*When we arrived, they had already left.*

Übung 8 Was ist zuerst passiert?

Bilden Sie logische Sätze mit Satzteilen aus beiden Spalten.

MODELL Nachdem Jutta den Schlüssel verloren hatte, kletterte sie durchs Fenster.

1. Nachdem Jutta den Schlüssel verloren hatte,
2. Nachdem Ernst die Fensterscheibe eingeworfen hatte,
3. Nachdem Claire angekommen war,
4. Nachdem Hans seine Hausaufgaben gemacht hatte,
5. Nachdem Jens sein Fahrrad repariert hatte,
6. Nachdem Michael die Seiltänzerin[1] gesehen hatte,
7. Nachdem Richard ein ganzes Jahr gespart hatte,
8. Nachdem Silvia zwei Semester allein gewohnt hatte,
9. Nachdem Willi ein Geräusch gehört hatte,

a. flog er nach Australien.
b. ging er ins Bett.
c. kletterte sie durchs Fenster.
d. lief er weg.
e. machte er eine Radtour.
f. rief er den Großvater an.
g. rief sie Melanie an.
h. war er ganz verliebt.
i. zog sie in eine Wohngemeinschaft.

[1] *tightrope walker*

KAPITEL 9

Ein Schnellimbiß in Düsseldorf

In **Kapitel 9**, you will learn to talk about shopping for food and cooking and about the kinds of foods you like. You will also talk about household appliances and about dining out.

Essen und Einkaufen

THEMEN

Essen und Trinken
Haushaltsgeräte
Einkaufen und Kochen
Im Restaurant

LEKTÜRE

Die 20 gesündesten Lebensmittel
Mord im Café König?

KULTURELLES

Essen in Deutschland, Österreich und der Schweiz
Eßgewohnheiten
Stichwort „Restaurant"
Kulturprojekt: Deutsche Restaurants und deutsches Essen
Porträt: Elly Ney und Düsseldorf
Videoecke: Wie gesund ist das Schulbrot?

STRUKTUREN

9.1 Adjectives: an overview
9.2 Attributive adjectives in the nominative and accusative cases
9.3 Destination vs. location: **stellen/stehen, legen/liegen, setzen/sitzen, hängen/hängen**
9.4 Adjectives in the dative case
9.5 Being polite: the subjunctive form of modal verbs

SPRECHSITUATIONEN

Essen und Trinken

➤ **Grammatik 9.1–9.2**

Meistens esse ich ein frisches Brötchen, ein gekochtes Ei und selbstgemachte Marmelade zum Frühstück. Außerdem brauche ich einen starken Kaffee.

Zum Mittagessen esse ich am liebsten einen gemischten Salat, gebratenes Fleisch oder gegrillten Fisch mit gekochten Kartoffeln.

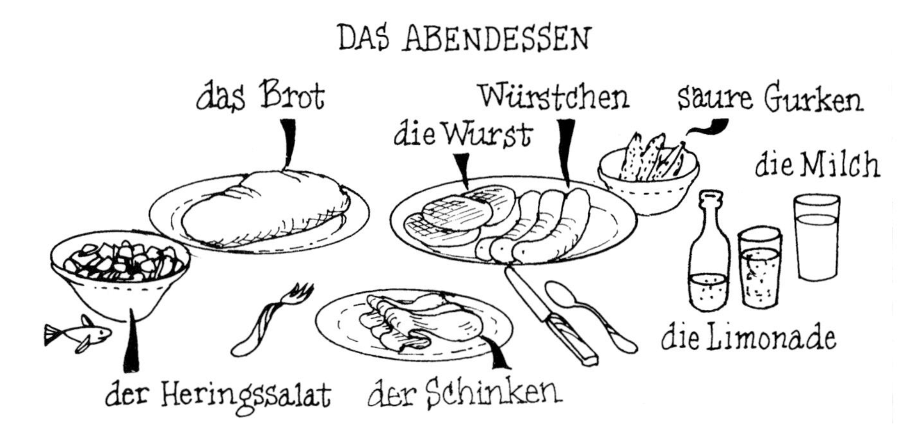

Heiße Würstchen? Die mag ich heute nicht. Kauf doch mal wieder den guten Heringssalat.

Situation 1 Informationsspiel: Mahlzeiten und Getränke

MODELL S1: Was ißt Stefan zum Frühstück?
S2: ______
S1: Was ißt du zum Frühstück?
S2: ______

	Frau Gretter	Stefan	Andrea	mein(e) Partner(in)
zum Frühstück essen	frische Brötchen			
zum Frühstück trinken	schwarzen Kaffee		heißen Kakao	
zum Mittagessen essen		belegte Brote und Kartoffelchips		
zum Abendessen essen	nichts, sie will abnehmen		Brot mit Honig	
nach dem Sport trinken			Apfelsaft	
auf einem Fest trinken		mexikanisches Bier		
essen, wenn er/sie groß ausgeht	etwas für kalorienbewußte		den schönsten Kinderteller	

Kultur ... Landeskunde ... Informationen

Essen in Deutschland, Österreich und der Schweiz

- Welche deutschen (österreichischen, schweizerischen) Speisen oder Gerichte kennen Sie? Zu welcher Mahlzeit ißt man sie?
- Welche Getränke sind Ihrer Meinung nach typisch für Deutschland (Österreich, die Schweiz)? Gibt es dabei regionale Unterschiede?

EINE SACHE, VIELE NAMEN

MODELL S1: Wo sagt man die Bulette?
S2: In Berlin.

die Frikadelle	Standardsprache
die Bulette	_____
das Fleischpflanzerl	_____
das Fleischchüechli	_____

Bayern Berlin Schweiz

Berliner Bulette

das Brötchen	Standardsprache
das Mutschli/Semmeli	_____
die Semmel	_____
die Schrippe	_____

Süddeutschland und Österreich Berlin Schweiz

Bayrische Semmeln

die Schlagsahne	Standardsprache
der Schlagrahm	_____
Gschwungne Nidel	_____
der Schlagobers	_____

Schweiz Süddeutschland Österreich

Österreichische Sachertorte mit Schlagobers

Kartoffelpfannkuchen	Standardsprache
Reiberdatschi	_____
Kartoffelpuffer	_____
Gromperekichelcher	_____
Reibeplätzchen	

Österreich und Bayern Westfalen Westdeutschland Luxemburg

Luxemburgische Gromperekichelcher

Situation 2 Wer in der Klasse . . .?

1. ißt nie fettige Hamburger?
2. ißt oft Japanisch?
3. ißt fast jeden Tag frisches Obst?
4. frühstückt fast nie?
5. ißt gebratene Eier mit Speck zum Frühstück?
6. ißt fast immer im Studentenheim?
7. ißt manchmal gegrilltes Hähnchen?
8. würzt sein Essen mit viel Pfeffer?
9. ißt selten zu Hause?
10. hat für heute Mittag ein belegtes Brot dabei?

Situation 3 Interview: Die Mahlzeiten

1. Was ißt du normalerweise zum Frühstück? Was zum Mittagessen?
2. Ißt du viel zum Abendessen? Was?
3. Ißt du immer eine Nachspeise? Was ißt du am liebsten als Nachspeise?
4. Trinkst du viel Kaffee?
5. Ißt du zwischen den Mahlzeiten? Warum (nicht)?
6. Was ißt du, wenn du mitten in der Nacht großen Hunger hast?
7. Was trinkst du, wenn du auf Feste gehst?
8. Was hast du heute morgen gegessen und getrunken?
9. Was ißt du heute zum Mittagessen?
10. Was ißt du heute zum Abendessen?

Haushaltsgeräte

➤ **Grammatik 9.3**

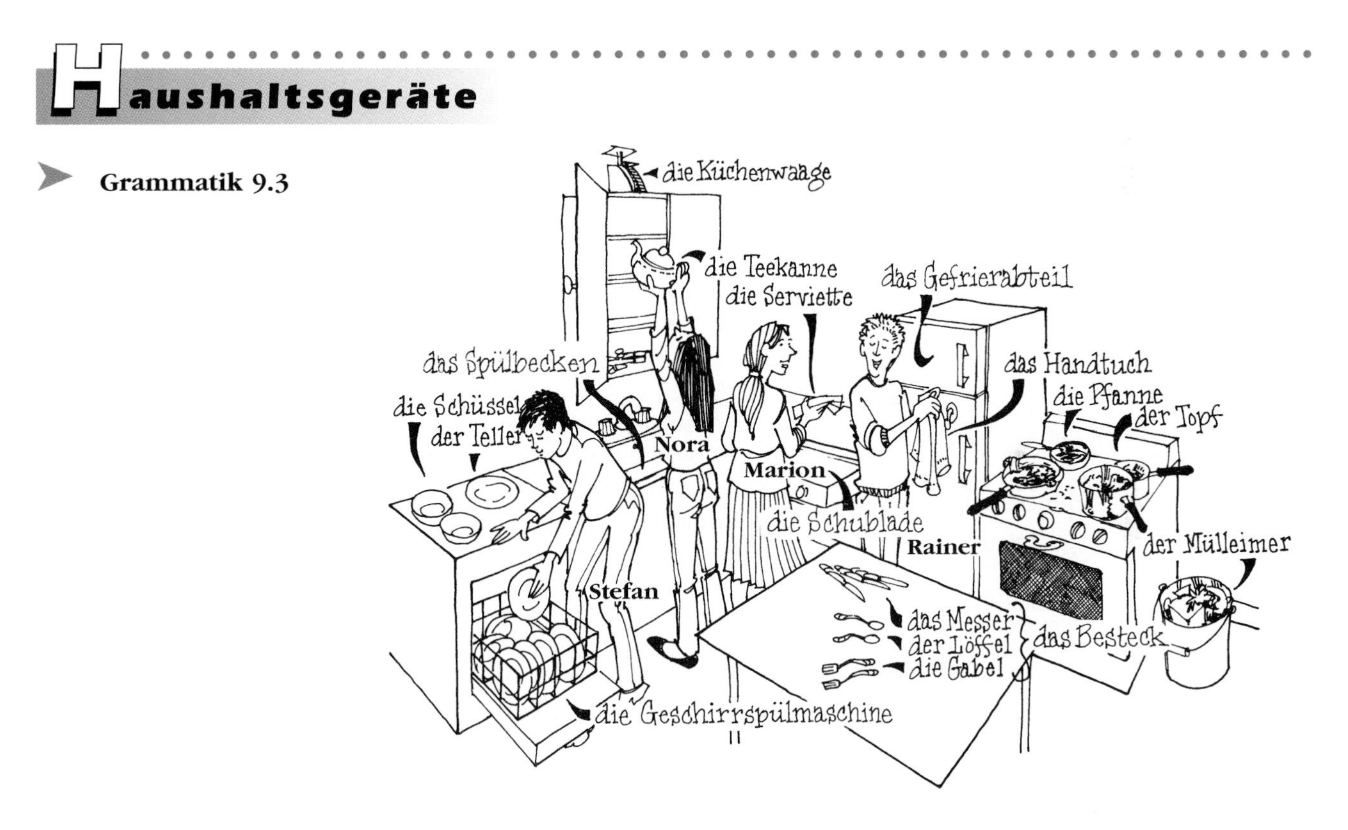

Stefan stellt die Schüsseln und Teller in die Geschirrspülmaschine.

Die Messer, Gabeln und Löffel liegen noch auf dem Tisch.

Die schmutzigen Töpfe und Pfannen stehen auf dem Herd.

Nora stellt die Teekanne in den Schrank.

Marion legt die Servietten in die Schublade.

Rainer hängt das Handtuch an den Haken.

Situation 4 Was kosten diese Geräte?

Listen Sie die Geräte in jeder Gruppe dem Preis nach. Beginnen Sie mit dem teuersten Gerät. Wählen Sie dann aus jeder Gruppe die vier Geräte aus, auf die Sie am wenigsten verzichten[1] könnten.

GRUPPE A

1. eine Kaffeemaschine
2. ein elektrischer Dosenöffner
3. eine Küchenmaschine
4. ein Korkenzieher
5. eine Kaffeemühle
6. ein Bügeleisen
7. eine Küchenwaage
8. ein Toaster

GRUPPE B

1. ein Mikrowellenherd
2. ein Kühlschrank
3. eine Geschirrspülmaschine
4. eine Waschmaschine
5. ein Wäschetrockner
6. ein Grill
7. ein Staubsauger
8. eine Gefriertruhe

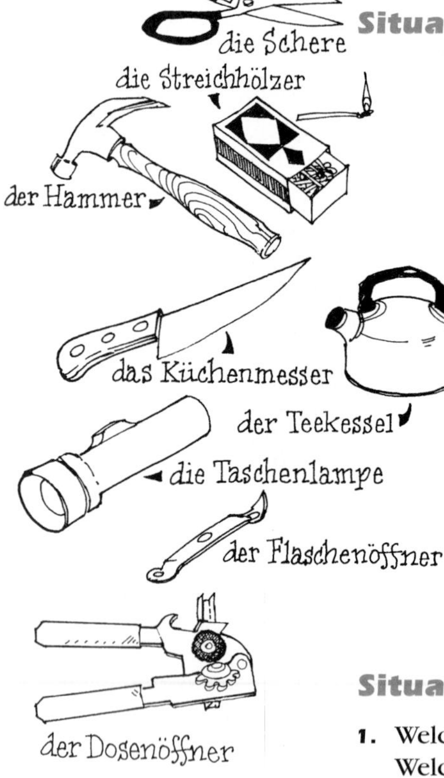

Situation 5 Was brauchen Sie dazu?

1. Sie bekommen ein Paket, das mit einer Schnur zugebunden ist. Sie wollen die Schnur durchschneiden.
2. Sie wollen sich ein belegtes Brot machen und eine Scheibe Wurst abschneiden.
3. Sie wollen sich eine Dose Suppe heiß machen und müssen die Dose aufmachen.
4. Sie haben Gäste und wollen ein paar Flaschen Bier aufmachen.
5. Sie wollen eine Kerze anzünden.
6. Sie wollen Tee kochen und müssen Wasser heiß machen.
7. Sie haben eine Reifenpanne und müssen einen rostigen Nagel aus einem Autoreifen ziehen.
8. Sie wollen ein Bild aufhängen und müssen einen Nagel in die Wand schlagen.
9. Beim Gewitter ist der Strom ausgefallen. Es ist total dunkel in Ihrem Zimmer.

die Zange

Situation 6 Diskussion: Haushaltsgeräte

1. Welche elektrischen Haushaltsgeräte haben Sie, Ihre Eltern oder Freunde? Welches Gerät finden Sie am wichtigsten?
2. Stellen Sie sich vor, Sie dürfen nur ein Gerät im Haus haben. Welches wählen Sie und warum?

---

[1] *do without*

3. Welche Werkzeuge sollte es in jedem Haushalt geben?
4. Sie wollen übers Wochenende zum Zelten. Machen Sie eine Liste, welche Geräte Sie zum Essen und Kochen brauchen.
5. Sie planen ein elegantes Picknick. Was packen Sie alles ein?

Einkaufen und Kochen

➤ **Grammatik 9.4**

Situation 7 Was kostet das?

Sie gehen in Göttingen zum All-Kauf-Markt. Das ist ein großer Supermarkt, der recht billig ist und viele Sonderangebote[1] hat. Sehen Sie sich die drei Einkaufslisten an, und rechnen Sie den Preis für jede Liste aus.

LISTE 1

200 g geräucherter Speck
2 Dosen Tomatensuppe
1 kg Hackfleisch
3 Zitronen
1 Packung Haferflocken

LISTE 2

1 kg Hackfleisch
1 Glas Mayonnaise
1 kg Zwiebeln
1 kg frische Karotten
2 kg Äpfel

LISTE 3

400 g frische Krabben
1 kg Pfirsiche
500 g Schnitzelfleisch
2 Salatgurken
1 kg Tomaten
1 Flasche Salatsoße

Situation 8 Einkaufsliste

Sie wollen heute abend kochen. Was wollen Sie kochen? Was brauchen Sie? (Sie finden Ideen im Wortkasten auf Seite 313.) Machen Sie für jedes Gericht eine Einkaufsliste. Denken Sie auch an Salat, Gemüse und Gewürze, an Vorspeise und Nachspeise und an Getränke.

1. ein italienisches Gericht
2. ein amerikanisches Gericht
3. ein chinesisches Gericht
4. ein deutsches Gericht
5. ein französisches Gericht

[1]*sale items*

Fisch Nudeln Salz Bohnen
Paprika Bambussprossen Oliven
Zwiebeln Erbsen Gurken
Schnitzel Knoblauch
Pfeffer Kopfsalat Pilze
Tomaten Tomatensoße
Kartoffeln Sojasoße
Karotten Essig und Öl
Hackfleisch

In einem Berliner Feinkostladen. Guten Appetit!

Situation 9 Bildgeschichte: Michaels bestes Gericht

Michael kocht heute wieder sein bestes Gericht: Omelette à la haute cuisine . . .

Situation 10 Zum Schreiben: Ein Rezept

Ein Austauschstudent aus Deutschland möchte ein Rezept für ein typisch amerikanisches Gericht. Geben Sie ihm/ihr Ihr persönliches Lieblingsrezept. Schreiben Sie zuerst auf, was man alles braucht und wieviel. Dann beschreiben Sie, wie man es zubereitet. Machen Sie auch kleine Zeichnungen dazu. (Keine Mikrowellenmahlzeit, bitte!)

ZUTATEN	ZUBEREITUNG
______________	______________________________
______________	______________________________
______________	______________________________

Kultur ... Landeskunde ... Informationen

Eßgewohnheiten

- Gibt es typisch amerikanisches Essen? Wenn ja, was?
- Welche Art von ausländischem Essen ist in den USA besonders beliebt? Stellen Sie eine Rangliste von eins (am wenigsten beliebt) bis zehn (am meisten beliebt) auf.

_____ italienisch	_____ französisch	_____ deutsch	_____ koreanisch	_____ japanisch
_____ griechisch	_____ mexikanisch	_____ spanisch	_____ chinesisch	_____ indisch

- Welche Art von ausländischem Essen ist in Deutschland am beliebtesten? Raten Sie!

□ chinesisch □ türkisch □ italienisch □ griechisch □ französisch

Lesen Sie den Text, und suchen Sie Antworten auf die Fragen.

Eine Studie über Eßgewohnheiten zeigt: Am Kochtopf sind die Deutschen besonders ausländerfreundlich

Das morgendliche Croissant zum Cappuccino, die Pizza und die Frühlingsrolle animierten unlängst[1] das SZ-Magazin[2] zu der Frage: „Wie konnten wir früher satt werden,[3] ohne Mozzarella und Basilikum zu kennen?"

Der Deutsche, so belegt[4] ein Rundgang durch Supermärkte und Restaurants, serviert Grünkohl, Schweinebraten und Eisbein anscheinend[5] nur noch auf Volksfesten und für Touristenmenüs. Er aber wendet sich statt dessen[6] liebevoll griechischem Fetakäse, Curry und Couscous zu.[7] Und ohne Pasta kann er schon gar nicht mehr leben.

- Welche ausländischen Speisen und Getränke können Sie im Text indentifizieren? Aus welchen Ländern kommen sie ursprünglich?
- Welche deutschen Speisen und Getränke können Sie identifizieren?
- Wo und für wen servieren die Deutschen anscheinend nur noch deutsches Essen?

Schauen Sie sich die Graphik genau an, und beantworten Sie die Fragen.

- Wer ißt zu Hause öfter ausländisch, Leute unter 35 oder über 55?
- Wieviel Prozent der Deutschen unter 35 gehen sehr häufig in ein ausländisches Restaurant?
- Wieviel Prozent der Deutschen über 55 gehen nie in ein ausländisches Restaurant?

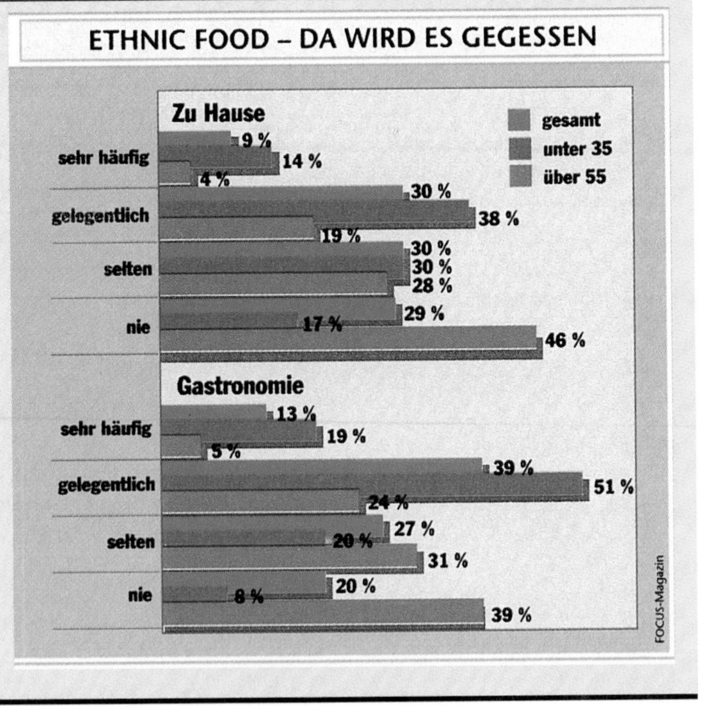

[1]*not long ago, lately* [2]*magazine supplement to the „Süddeutsche Zeitung"* [3]satt ... *get sated, full* [4]*verifies* [5]*apparently* [6]statt ... *instead (of that)* [7]wendet sich ... zu *turns to*

Eine Münchner Metzgerei. Nichts für Vegetarier.

Situation 11 Interview: Einkaufen und Kochen

1. Kannst du kochen? Was zum Beispiel?
2. Kochst du oft? Wer kocht in deiner Familie?
3. Was kochst du am liebsten? Welche Zutaten braucht man dazu? Wie macht man das?
4. Kaufst du jeden Tag ein? Wenn nicht, wie oft in der Woche? An welchen Tagen? Wo kaufst du meistens ein? Was kaufst du meistens ein?

Im Restaurant

Grammatik 9.5

—Ist hier noch frei?
—Ja, bitte schön.

—Was darf ich Ihnen bringen?
—Könnte ich bitte die Speisekarte haben?
—Ja, gern, einen Moment, bitte.

—Ein Wasser, bitte.
—Ein Mineralwasser. Kommt sofort!

—Wir würden gern zahlen.
—Gern. Das waren zwei Schnitzel Natur, ein Glas Wein und eine Limo . . .

—38,80 Franken bitte schön.
—Das stimmt so.
—Vielen Dank.
—Könnten Sie mir dafür eine Quittung geben?
—Selbstverständlich.

—Darf ich Sie noch zu einem Kaffee einladen?
—Das ist nett, aber leider muß ich mich jetzt beeilen.

Situation 12 Was sagen Sie?

Wählen Sie zu jeder Situation einen passenden Ausdruck.

1. Sie sitzen an einem Tisch im Restaurant. Sie haben Hunger, aber noch keine Speisekarte. Sie sehen die Kellnerin und sagen: _____
2. Sie haben mit Ihren Freunden im Restaurant gegessen. Sie haben es eilig und möchten zahlen. Sie rufen den Kellner und sagen: _____
3. Sie sind allein essen gegangen. Das Restaurant ist voll. Es gibt keine freien Tische mehr. Plötzlich kommt jemand, den Sie nicht kennen, und fragt, ob er sich an Ihren Tisch setzen kann. Sie sagen: _____
4. Ihr Essen und Trinken hat 19 Mark 20 gekostet. Sie haben der Kellnerin einen Zwanzigmarkschein gegeben. 80 Pfennig sind Trinkgeld. Sie sagen: _____
5. Sie essen mit Ihren Eltern in einem feinen Restaurant. Da stellen Sie fest, daß eine Fliege in der Suppe schwimmt. Sie rufen den Kellner und sagen: _____
6. Sie haben einen Sauerbraten mit Knödeln bestellt. Die Kellnerin bringt Ihnen einen Schweinebraten. Sie sagen: _____

a. Das kann nicht stimmen. Ich habe doch einen Sauerbraten bestellt.
b. Das stimmt so.
c. Die Speisekarte, bitte.
d. Herr Kellner, bitte, sehen Sie sich das mal an.
e. Ich liebe Schweinebraten.
f. Ja, bitte sehr.
g. Leider habe ich kein Geld.
h. Morgen fliege ich in die USA.
i. Nein, danke.
j. Zahlen, bitte.

Situation 13 Dialog: Melanie und Josef gehen aus.

Melanie und Josef haben sich einen Tisch ausgesucht und sich hingesetzt. Der Kellner kommt an ihren Tisch.

KELLNER: Bitte schön?
MELANIE: Könnten wir die ________ haben?
KELLNER: Natürlich. Möchten Sie etwas trinken?
MELANIE: Für mich ein _________ bitte.
JOSEF: Und _____ ein Bier.
KELLNER: Gern.

KELLNER: ____________, was Sie essen möchten?
MELANIE: Ich möchte das Rumpsteak mit Pilzen und Kroketten.
JOSEF: Und _________ die Forelle „blau“ mit Kräuterbutter, _____ Salat und Salzkartoffeln. Dazu noch ein Bier bitte.
KELLNER: Gern. Darf ich ____ auch noch etwas zu trinken bringen?
MELANIE: Nein, danke, im Moment nicht.

Kultur ... Landeskunde ... Informationen

Stichwort „Restaurant"

- Gehen Sie oft ins Restaurant?
- Haben Sie ein Lieblingsrestaurant?
- Was machen Sie, wenn alle Tische besetzt sind?
- Sitzen Sie lieber im Raucher- oder im Nichtraucherteil?
- Wie lange bleiben Sie normalerweise im Restaurant sitzen, nachdem Sie gegessen haben?

Wie verhalten sich die Deutschen im Restaurant? Hören Sie zu.

Mini-Wörterbuch zum Hörtext

die **Anerkennung** acknowledgment
aufmerksam attentive
die **Bewirtung** service
die **Geselligkeit** sociability, social life
je nach Betrag depending on the amount
der **Umsatz** sales, returns
die **Vorschrift** regulation

Vergleichen Sie! Deutschland (D) oder USA (A)?

_____ Platz selbst aussuchen
_____ auf einen freien Tisch warten
_____ nach dem Essen bald gehen
_____ nach dem Essen noch eine Weile sitzen bleiben
_____ Raucher- und Nichtraucherteile
_____ nur selten Nichtraucherteile
_____ weniger Trinkgeld geben
_____ 15%–20% Trinkgeld geben

Lesen Sie aus der Statistik, wo man in Deutschland unbeschränkt rauchen darf. Wo darf man in den USA noch unbeschränkt rauchen? Wo darf man überhaupt nicht rauchen?

FOCUS-FRAGE

„Wo fühlen Sie sich durch Passivrauchen besonders belästigt?"[1]

NIKOTIN STÖRT BEIM ESSEN

Die 71 Prozent Nichtraucher unter den 1300 Befragten* antworteten

in Restaurants	40 %
in Reisebussen	29 %
in Warteräumen	26 %
bei Veranstaltungen[2]	25 %
am Arbeitsplatz	21 %
auf Behörden[3]	20 %
in der Öffentlichkeit[4]	15 %
im Flugzeug	14 %

32 Prozent der Nichtraucher fühlen sich durch Passivrauchen überhaupt nicht belästigt

* Repräsentative Umfrage des Sample-Instituts für FOCUS im Juli. Mehrfachnennung möglich

[1] *bothered, disturbed* [2] *public events* [3] auf . . . *in public buildings* [4] in . . . *in public*

Situation 14 Rollenspiel: Im Restaurant

S1: Sie sind im Restaurant und möchten etwas zu essen und zu trinken bestellen. Wenn Sie mit dem Essen fertig sind, bezahlen Sie und geben Sie der Bedienung ein Trinkgeld.

Situation 15 Bildgeschichte: Herr und Frau Wagner waren gestern im Restaurant

Situation 16 Interview

1. Gehst du oft essen? Wie oft in der Woche ißt du nicht zu Hause?
2. Gehst du oft in die Mensa? Schmeckt dir das Essen da?
3. Gehst du oft zu McDonald's oder ähnlichen Restaurants? Was ißt du da meistens?
4. Magst du japanisches Essen oder chinesisches?
5. Warst du schon mal in einem deutschen Restaurant? Wenn ja, was hast du dort gegessen? Wenn nein, was würdest du dort bestellen?
6. Welche Restaurants magst du am liebsten? Gibt es ein Restaurant, in dem du oft ißt? Wie heißt es, und welches Essen gibt es da?
7. Welches ist das feinste Restaurant in deiner Gegend? Wieviel muß man da für ein gutes Essen bezahlen?
8. Was würdest du da bestellen, wenn Geld keine Rolle spielen würde?

Kulturprojekt Deutsche Restaurants und deutsches Essen

- Gibt es in Ihrer Stadt oder in der Nähe ein Restaurant mit deutscher Küche? Wenn ja, wie heißt es? Schauen Sie in den Gelben Seiten oder in einem Stadtführer nach. Was kann man dort essen? Gehen Sie ins Restaurant und schauen Sie sich die Speisekarte an oder rufen Sie das Restaurant an.
- Gehen Sie zu Ihrem Supermarkt oder zu einem Feinkostladen.[1] Gibt es dort Produkte aus Deutschland, Österreich oder der Schweiz? Wenn ja, was für Produkte? Welche Markennamen[2] haben sie?
- Suchen Sie ein Kochbuch für deutsche oder internationale Küche. Schreiben Sie ein deutsches, österreichisches oder schweizerisches Rezept auf. Wenn Sie Lust dazu haben, bereiten Sie das Gericht zu, und bringen Sie es mit in den Unterricht.

[1]*delicatessen, specialty foods store* [2]*brand names*

Porträt

Elly Neys (1882 - 1968) großes Vorbild war Clara Wieck (1819 - 1896), die Ehefrau[1] von Robert Schumann. Sie war wie Elly Ney Pianistin und Musiklehrerin. Beide Frauen arbeiteten in einem Bereich,[2] der vollkommen[3] von Männern dominiert war. Elly Ney wurde weltberühmt für ihre Interpretationen von Ludwig van Beethoven und Johannes Brahms und gab bis ins hohe Alter Konzerte. Sie lehrte am Mozarteum[4] in Salzburg und gab ihr Können[5] und ihre Begeisterung[6] für Musik an die nächste Generation weiter.

Düsseldorf, die Geburtsstadt von Elly Ney und die Hauptstadt von Nordrhein-Westfalen, ist Wirtschaftszentrum und Kulturmetropole zugleich.[7] An der Kunstakademie lehren und lehrten so berühmte Leute wie Joseph Beuys. Die Deutsche Oper am Rhein, das Theater und exzellente Kunstausstellungen[8] gehören zu den Attraktionen von Düsseldorf. Außerdem ist Düsseldorf die Modestadt Deutschlands, wo jedes Jahr wichtige Modenschauen stattfinden.

[1]*wife* [2]*area* [3]*completely* [4]*famous music school named after Mozart* [5]*skill, talent* [6]*enthusiasm* [7]*at the same time* [8]*art exhibitions*

Düsseldorf am Rhein mit der Lambertuskirche

VIDEOECKE

Zwischen Mathe und Englisch, die große Pause. Zeit für das zweite Frühstück.[2]

Wie gesund ist das Schulbrot?

Sie erfahren, was deutsche Schüler in den Schulpausen essen und trinken und wie gesund das ist.

- Wie viele Schüler wurden befragt?
- Was wurde eingesammelt[1]?
- Wieviel Prozent der Schüler kommt ohne Frühstück in die Schule?
- Wieviel Prozent der Schüler bekommt ein Pausenbrot von zu Hause mit?
- Wieviel Prozent der Schüler trinkt in der großen Pause Milch?

[1]*collected* [2]das . . . *mid-morning snack*

WORTSCHATZ

Frühstück — Breakfast

die **Wurst, ̈-e** — sausage

der **Käse** — cheese
der **Quark** — *type of creamy cottage cheese*
der **Schinken** — ham
der **Speck** — bacon

das **Brötchen, -** — roll
das **Ei, -er** — egg
gekochte Eier — boiled eggs
das **Hörnchen, -** — croissant
das **Würstchen, -** — frank(furter); hot dog

die **Haferflocken** (*pl.*) — rolled oats (*for oatmeal*)

Ähnliche Wörter

die **Marmelade, -n**   der **Honig**   das **Omelett, -s**

Mittagessen und Abendessen — Lunch and Dinner

die **Beilage, -n** — side dish
die **Forelle, -n** — trout
die **Mahlzeit, -en** — meal
die **Nachspeise, -n** — dessert
die **Vorspeise, -n** — appetizer

der **Braten, -** — roast
der **Sauerbraten** — sauerbraten (marinated beef roast)
der **Schweinebraten** — pork roast
der **Eisbecher, -** — dish of ice cream
der **Hummer, -** — lobster
der **Knödel, -** — dumpling
der **Pilz, -e** — mushroom

das **Brot, -e** (R) — bread
das **belegte Brot**, die **belegten Brote** — open-face sandwich
das **Fleisch** — meat
das **Hackfleisch** — ground beef (or pork)
das **Rindfleisch** — beef
das **Schweinefleisch** — pork
das **Geflügel** — poultry

die **Krabben** (*pl.*) — shrimp
die **Pommes frites** (*pl.*) — french fries

Ähnliche Wörter

die **Krokette, -n**; die **Muschel, -n**; die **Nudel, -n**   der **Fisch, -e**; der **Reis**   das **Rumpsteak, -s**; das **Schnitzel, -**

Obst und Nüsse — Fruit and Nuts

die **Birne, -n** — pear
die **Erdbeere, -n** — strawberry
die **Kirsche, -n** — cherry
die **Weintraube, -n** — grape
die **Zitrone, -n** — lemon

der **Pfirsich, -e** — peach

Ähnliche Wörter

die **Nuß, Nüsse**; die **Orange, -n**; die **Pflaume, -n**   der **Apfel, ̈** (R)

Gemüse — Vegetables

die **Bohne, -n**	bean
grüne Bohnen	green beans
die **Erbse, -n**	pea
die **Gurke, -n**	cucumber
saure Gurken	pickles
die **Kartoffel, -n**	potato
die **Salzkartoffeln**	boiled potatoes
die **Zwiebel, -n**	onion
der **Kohl**	cabbage
der **Blumenkohl**	cauliflower
der **Rosenkohl**	brussel sprouts
die **Bambussprossen** (*pl.*)	bamboo shoots

Ähnliche Wörter

die **Karotte, -n;** die **Olive, -n;** die **Tomate, -n** der **Salat, -e** (R); der **Heringssalat;** der **Kopfsalat;** der **Spinat**

Getränke — Beverages

der **Saft, ¨-e**	juice
der **Apfelsaft**	apple juice
der **Orangensaft**	orange juice

Ähnliche Wörter

die **Milch** der **Kaffee,** der **Kakao** das **Mineralwasser**

Zutaten — Condiments and Ingredients

der **Essig**	vinegar
der **Knoblauch**	garlic
der **Senf**	mustard
das **Gewürz, -e**	spice; seasoning

Ähnliche Wörter

die **Butter;** die **Kräuterbutter;** die **Mayonnaise;** die **Soße, -n;** die **Salatsoße, -n;** die **Tomatensoße** **der Pfeffer;** der **Zucker** das **Öl** (R); das **Salz**

Küche und Zubereitung — Cooking and Preparation

auf·schneiden, schnitt auf, aufgeschnitten	to chop
bestreuen	to sprinkle
braten, brät, briet, gebraten	to fry
bräunen	to brown, fry
erhitzen	to heat
geben, gibt, gab, gegeben (in + *akk.*)	to put (into)
gießen, goß, gegossen	to pour
schlagen, schlägt, schlug, geschlagen	to beat
vermischen	to mix
würzen	to season

Im Restaurant — At the Restaurant

die **Bedienung**	service; waiter, waitress
die **Quittung, -en**	receipt, check
die **Speisekarte, -n**	menu
der **Teller, -**	plate
der **Kinderteller, -**	child's plate
der **Schein, -e**	bill, note (*of currency*)
der **Zwanzigmarkschein, -e**	twenty-mark note
das **Gericht, -e**	dish
das **Stück, -e**	slice; piece

Ähnliche Wörter

das **Trinkgeld, -er** die **Öffnungszeiten** (*pl.*)

Im Haushalt — In the Household

die **Dose, -n**	can
die **Gabel, -n**	fork
die **Gefriertruhe, -n**	freezer
die **Küchenmaschine, -n**	mixer
die **Schere, -n**	scissors
die **Schnur, ¨-e**	string
die **Schublade, -n** (R)	drawer
die **Schüssel, -n**	bowl
die **Serviette, -n**	napkin
die **Zange, -n**	pliers, tongs
der **Dosenöffner, -**	can opener
der **Haken, -**	hook
der **Löffel, -**	spoon
der **Mülleimer, -**	garbage can
der **Nagel, ¨**	nail
der **Strom**	electricity, power
der **Wäschetrockner, -**	clothes dryer
das **Gerät, -e**	appliance
das **Messer, -**	knife
das **Küchenmesser, -**	kitchen knife
das **Paket, -e**	package
das **Streichholz, ¨-er**	match
das **Werkzeug, -e**	tool

Ähnliche Wörter

die **Kaffeemühle, -n;** die **Teekanne, -n** der **Flaschenöffner, -;** der **Grill, -s;** der **Hammer, ¨;** der **Korkenzieher, -;** der **Teekessel, -;** der **Toaster, -** das **Handtuch, ¨-er** (R)

Sonstige Substantive — Other Nouns

die **Zeichnung, -en**	drawing
der **Beutel, -**	bag
das **Gewitter, -**	thunderstorm

Ähnliche Wörter

die **Einkaufsliste, -n;** die **Flamme, -n;** die **Fliege, -n;** die **Packung, -en** der **Autoreifen, -** das **Rezept, -e**

Sonstige Verben	Other Verbs
ab·nehmen, nimmt ab, nahm ab, abgenommen	to lose weight
ab·schneiden, schnitt ab, abgeschnitten	to cut off
aus·fallen, fällt aus, fiel aus, ist ausgefallen	to go out (*power*)
aus·rechnen	to figure, total (up)
aus·wählen	to select
sich beeilen	to hurry
bestellen	to order (*food*)
durch·schneiden, schnitt durch, durchgeschnitten	to cut through
hängen, hing, gehangen	to hang, be (*hanging*)
hängen, hängte, gehängt	to hang, place (*in a hanging position*)
legen	to lay, put, place (*in a horizontal position*)
liegen, lag, gelegen	to lie, be (*in a horizontal position*)
setzen (R)	to set, place (*in a sitting position*)
sitzen, saß, gesessen (R)	to sit, be in a sitting position
stehen, stand, gestanden	to stand, be (*in a vertical position*)
stellen	to stand up, place (*in a vertical position*)
stimmen	to be right
das stimmt so	that's right; keep the change
ziehen, zog, gezogen	to pull
zu·bereiten	to prepare (*food*)

Adjektive und Adverbien	Adjectives and Adverbs
fettig	fat; greasy
gebraten	roasted; broiled; fried
geräuchert	smoked
kalorienarm	low in calories
kalorienbewußt	calorie-conscious
leer	empty
verschieden	different, various
zart	tender
zugebunden	tied shut

Ähnliche Wörter

eiskalt, elegant, elektrisch, fein, frisch, gegrillt, gekocht, gemischt, gesalzen, holländisch, mexikanisch, rostig, sauer, verboten

Sonstige Wörter und Ausdrücke	Other Words and Expressions
dazu	in addition
meistens	usually, mostly
nebeneinander	next to each other
normalerweise	normally
selten	rare(ly), seldom
am wenigsten	the least
wofür	what for?

LESEECKE

LEKTÜRE 1

Vor dem Lesen

1. Welche Vitamine kennen Sie? In welchen Lebensmitteln sind sie enthalten[1]?
2. Welche Mineralien kennen Sie? In welchen Lebensmitteln sind sie enthalten?

[1] *contained*

3. Welche verschiedenen Gruppen von Lebensmitteln soll man jeden Tag essen?
4. Lesen Sie zuerst nur die Namen der Lebensmittel, die im Artikel im Fettdruck[1] erscheinen. Ordnen Sie sie den folgenden Kategorien zu.

Obst und Gemüse	Fleisch und ähnliche[2] Produkte	Milchprodukte	Getreideprodukte[3]	Sonstiges

[1] *boldface type* [2] *similar* [3] *cereals and grains*

Die 20 gesündesten Lebensmittel

Essen Sie sich gesund und schön!

Wer sich kalorienbewußt und vitaminreich ernährt,[1] fühlt sich wohler, kann mehr leisten und hat ein besser funktionierendes Immunsystem. **Kontakte** stellt Ihnen 20 Lebensmittel vor, die Sie mit Vitaminen, Mineralien und anderen Gesundmachern versorgen.[2]

1. Tomaten: die Vitamine A und C sind wichtig für besseres Sehen und glatte, schöne Haut.

2. Salatgurken (ungesalzen): exzellente Schlankmacher, die den Körper entwässern.[3]

3. Hähnchenbrust (ohne Haut): enthält wertvolle Proteine und B-Vitamine, kräftigt[4] die Haare und gibt ihnen Glanz.

4. Joghurt (fettarm): hilft mit Vitamin B gegen schuppige[5] Haut und rauhe Lippen.

5. Möhren: mit ihrer Hilfe bekommen Sie eine gesunde Gesichtsfarbe – dank Carotin.

6. Bananen: bringen verbrauchte Energien durch viele Kohlehydrate und Kalium zurück.

7. Vollkornbrot: dieses ballastreiche[6] Nahrungsmittel ist gut für die Verdauung.[7]

8. Vollkornnudeln: machen mit Eisen,[8] vielen Spurenelementen[9] und Kohlehydraten schnell fit.

9. Sonnenblumenkerne: ideal für spröde[10] Fingernägel wegen ihres Eisengehalts, ihrer ungesättigten Fettsäuren[11] und ihrer B-Vitamine.

10. Paprika: macht müde Augen wieder munter durch viel Vitamin C.

11. Bierhefe:[12] macht mit viel Vitamin B1 das Gehirn[13] wieder fit.

12. Fisch: hilft gegen Herzinfarkt.[14]

13. Soja: stark eiweißhaltig,[15] senkt den Cholesterinspiegel.

14. Weizenkeime:[16] mit Ballaststoffen und den Vitaminen E und B wirken sie gegen Schlafstörungen[17] und Nervosität.

15. Eier: helfen gegen schlecht Heilende Haut und bei Haarausfall.

16. Leber: enthält Vitamin A – das Schutz-vitamin für Haut und Schleimhäute.[18]

17. Kiwi: ihr hoher Vitamin-C-Gehalt sorgt für festes Bindegewebe[19] und stabilen Knochenbau.[20]

18. Maiskeimöl:[21] fördert[22] durch seinen hohen Vitamin-E-Gehalt die Durchblutung der Haut.

19. Milch: ihr Kalzium sorgt für gesunde Zähne.

20. Spinat: enthält viel Eisen und regelt den Sauerstofftransport[23] im Blut.

[1] sich . . . *eats* [2] *provide* [3] *rid of excess water* [4] *strengthens* [5] *scaly* [6] *high in fiber* [7] *digestion* [8] *iron* [9] *trace elements* [10] *brittle* [11] ungesättigt . . . *unsaturated fatty acids* [12] *brewer's yeast* [13] *brain* [14] *heart attack* [15] *protein-rich* [16] *wheat germ* [17] *sleep disorders* [18] *mucous membranes* [19] *connective tissues* [20] *bone structure* [21] *corn oil* [22] *promotes* [23] *oxygenation*

Arbeit mit dem Text

1. Welche Lebensmittel sind gut für . . . ?

   die Haut:
   die Augen:
   die Nägel:
   das Gehirn:
   das Herz:
   die Haare:
   die Knochen:
   die Zähne:
   die Verdauung:

2. Welche Lebensmittel sind „Fitmacher"?

3. In welchen Lebensmitteln finden Sie folgende Vitamine und Mineralien?

   Vitamin A:
   Vitamin B_1 und B_6:
   Vitamin C:
   Vitamin E:
   Eisen:
   Kalzium:

4. Wovon bekommen Sie eine gesunde Gesichtsfarbe?

LEKTÜRE 2

Vor dem Lesen

Der Titel der Geschichte ist „Mord im Café König". Welche Möglichkeiten gibt es bei einem typischen Mord? Füllen Sie die Tabelle aus, ohne den Text zu lesen.

Tat	*Mord*
Tatort	______
Täter[1]	______
Mordwaffe[2]	______
Motiv	______
Augenzeugen[3]	______
Beweise[4]	______

[1] *person(s) who did it, the perpetrator(s)* [2] *murder weapon* [3] *eyewitnesses* [4] *pieces of evidence*

Mord im Café König?

Ein Mann steigt auf der Königsallee in Düsseldorf aus einem Taxi, zahlt und geht zu einem Kiosk. Er wirkt[1] nervös, sieht sich mehrmals um.

„Er hat mir über zwei Mark Trinkgeld gegeben“, sagte der Taxifahrer nachher[2] aus.[3]

Am Kiosk[4] kauft der Mann eine *Süddeutsche Zeitung* und eine *International Herald Tribune.* Wieder sieht er sich mehrere Male um und beobachtet[5] die Straße.

„Ich glaube, er hörte nicht gut, er hat mich dreimal nach dem Preis gefragt“, sagte der Kioskbesitzer aus.

Ein dunkelgrauer Mercedes 450 SL mit drei Männern und einer Frau am Steuer[6] parkt gegenüber. Die vier beobachten den Mann. Der sieht sie und geht schnell in die Köpassage, ein großes Einkaufszentrum mit vielen Geschäften, Restaurants und Cafés. Zwei der Männer steigen aus und folgen ihm.

„Sie trugen graue Regenmäntel“, sagte ein Passant, als Inspektor Schilling ihm die Fotos der Männer zeigte.

Der Mann mit den beiden Zeitungen betritt[7] das Café König, setzt sich in eine Ecke, schlägt sehr schnell eine der Zeitungen auf[8] und versteckt sich dahinter.

„Er wirkte sehr nervös“, sagte die Kellnerin.

Er bestellt einen Kaffee und einen Cognac und zahlt sofort.

„Er verschüttete[9] die Milch, als er sie in den Kaffee goß, aber er gab mir ein sehr gutes Trinkgeld“, sagte die Kellnerin weiter aus.

Die beiden Männer in den Regenmänteln betreten das Café und sehen sich um. Als sie den Mann hinter der aufgeschlagenen *Herald Tribune* erkennen, gehen sie hinüber und setzen sich an den Nachbartisch.

„Sie waren sehr unfreundlich und bestellten beide Mineralwasser“, meinte die Kellnerin, die sie bediente.

Eine attraktive Frau, Mitte dreißig, betritt das Café, sieht sich um, lächelt, als sie den Mann mit der Zeitung sieht, wird bleich,[10] als ihr Blick auf die beiden Männer fällt. Sie setzt sich in eine andere Ecke und beobachtet alles.

„Sie war sehr elegant gekleidet“, sagte der Kellner, der an ihrem Tisch bediente.

Schließlich geht einer der Männer zu dem Mann mit der Zeitung hinüber, er beugt sich zu ihm hinunter[11] und hinter die Zeitung. Plötzlich fällt der Mann mit der Zeitung mit dem Kopf auf den Tisch. Er bewegt sich nicht mehr. Der andere nimmt ihm die *Herald Tribune* aus der Hand, faltet sie schnell zusammen. Die ersten Leute werden unruhig, weil sie merken,[12] daß etwas passiert ist. Die beiden Männer rennen aus dem Café, über die Königsallee und springen in den parkenden Wagen.

[1]*looks* [2]*afterward* [3]sagte . . . aus *stated* [4]*newsstand* [5]*observes* [6]*steering wheel* [7]*enters* [8]schlägt . . . auf *opens up* [9]*spilled* [10]*pale* [11]beugt . . . *bends over him* [12]*notice*

„Sie sind mit quietschenden[13] Reifen davongefahren", berichtete ein Polizist,
40 der gerade Streife ging.[14]

Die Gäste des Cafés laufen jetzt laut schreiend durcheinander. Keiner beachtet[15] die Frau, die zu dem Toten hinübergeht und die *Süddeutsche Zeitung* nimmt, sie unter den Arm steckt und schnell das Café verläßt.[16]

„Ich erinnere mich[17] so gut an sie, weil sie nicht bezahlt hat", sagte der
45 Kellner.

Die Polizei ist sehr schnell da. Immer noch laufen alle Leute durcheinander, keiner kümmert sich um[18] den Toten. Als die Polizei den Toten sehen will, ist der verschwunden.[19]

Inspektor Schilling fragt: Was ist passiert?

[13] *screeching* [14] Streife . . . *was on patrol* [15] *notices* [16] *leaves* [17] erinnere . . . *remember* [18] kümmert . . . *pays attention to* [19] *disappeared*

Arbeit mit dem Text

A. Wer hat das gesagt? Suchen Sie die Namen der Personen im Text.

„Der Mann hat mir mehr als zwei Mark Trinkgeld gegeben."
„Er hat bei mir zwei Zeitungen gekauft."
„Die Männer trugen graue Regenmäntel."
„Weil der Mann sehr nervös war, verschüttete er die Milch."
„Sie bestellten Mineralwasser und waren sehr unfreundlich."
„Die Frau war sehr elegant gekleidet."
„Die Männer sind mit quietschenden Reifen weggefahren."
„Die Frau hat nicht bezahlt, deshalb erinnere ich mich an sie."

B. Dieser Text hat zwei Teile: 1. Einen Bericht der Fakten im Präsens. 2. Zitate von Augenzeugen in der direkten Rede.

Kennzeichnen Sie, was zum Bericht (B) oder zu den Zitaten (Z) gehört.

C. In dieser Geschichte bleiben viele Fragen offen. Welche von den drei möglichen Antworten finden Sie am logischsten? Oder haben Sie eine logischere Antwort?

1. Wer war der Mann mit den Zeitungen?
- **a.** Ein Spion.
- **b.** Ein Politiker.
- **c.** Ein Genforscher.[1]
- **d.** Ein _____ .

2. Warum war der Mann nervös?
- **a.** Weil er gefährliche[2] Feinde[3] hatte.
- **b.** Weil er an dem Tag eine Prüfung in Deutsch hatte.
- **c.** Weil er nur noch kurze Zeit zu leben hatte.
- **d.** Weil _____ .

[1] *geneticist* [2] *dangerous* [3] *enemies*

3. Warum hörte er nicht gut?
- **a.** Weil er erkältet war.[1]
- **b.** Weil er sehr unkonzentriert war.
- **c.** Weil er ein Mikrophon im Ohr hatte.
- **d.** Weil _____ .

4. Wer waren die Leute im Mercedes?
- **a.** Spione vom KGB.
- **b.** Seine Leibwächter.[2]
- **c.** Seine Freunde.
- **d.** _____ .

5. Warum geht der Mann ins Café König?
- **a.** Weil er dort eine Verabredung[3] hat.
- **b.** Weil er noch einen Kaffee trinken will.
- **c.** Weil er sich verstecken will.
- **d.** Weil _____.

6. Wer ist die Frau?
- **a.** Seine Sekretärin.
- **b.** Seine Partnerin.
- **c.** Eine Spionin.
- **d.** _____ .

7. Was passiert, als der Mann im grauen Regenmantel zu dem Mann hinter der Zeitung geht?
- **a.** Der Mann stirbt vor Angst.
- **b.** Tödliche Viren bringen ihn um.[4]
- **c.** Der Mann wird erstochen.[5]
- **d.** _____ .

8. Warum nimmt der Mann im grauen Regenmantel die Zeitung mit?
- **a.** Weil das verabredet war.
- **b.** Weil geheime Informationen darin versteckt sind.
- **c.** Weil er die Polizei auf eine falsche Spur[6] locken will.
- **d.** Weil _____ .

9. Warum nimmt die Frau die andere Zeitung mit?
- **a.** Weil sie unbedingt die Wohnungsanzeigen lesen will.
- **b.** Weil sie ein Andenken[7] von ihm haben möchte.
- **c.** Weil sie weiß, daß das die richtige Zeitung ist.
- **d.** Weil _____ .

10. Was passiert mit dem Toten?
- **a.** Der KGB transportiert ihn ab.
- **b.** Der Cafébesitzer schafft ihn weg.[8]
- **c.** Leute vom Gesundheitsamt[9] nehmen ihn mit.
- **d.** _____ .

D. Erklären Sie jetzt Inspektor Schilling, was passiert ist. Schreiben Sie ihm einen Brief.

---

[1]erkältet . . . *had a cold* [2]*bodyguards* [3]*appointment* [4]bringen . . . *kill him* [5]*stabbed* [6]*track* [7]*souvenir* [8]schafft . . . *disposes of him* [9]*health department*

STRUKTUREN UND ÜBUNGEN

9.1 Adjectives: an overview

A. Attributive and predicate adjectives

Attributive adjectives precede nouns and have endings.
Predicate adjectives follow the verb **sein** and have no endings.

Adjectives that precede nouns are called *attributive adjectives* and have endings similar to the forms of the definite article: **kalter, kaltes, kalte, kalten, kaltem.** Adjectives that follow the verb **sein** and a few other verbs are called *predicate adjectives* and do not have any endings.

VERKÄUFER:	**Heiße** Würstchen! Ich verkaufe **heiße** Würstchen!	VENDOR:	*Hot dogs! I'm selling hot dogs!*
KUNDE:	Verzeihung, sind die Würstchen auch wirklich **heiß**?	CUSTOMER:	*Excuse me, are the hot dogs really hot?*
VERKÄUFER:	Natürlich, was denken Sie denn?!	VENDOR:	*Of course, what do you think?!*

B. Attributive adjectives with and without preceding article

If *no* article or article-like word (**mein, dein,** or **dieser,** and the like) precedes the adjective, then the adjective itself has the ending of the definite article **(der, das, die).** This means, the adjective provides the information about the gender, number, and case of the noun that follows.

Ich esse gern gegrill**ten** Fisch.
I like to eat grilled fish.
den Fisch = masculine accusative

Stefan ißt gern frisch**es** Müsli.
Stefan likes to eat fresh cereal.
das Müsli = neuter accusative

If an article or article-like word precedes the adjective but does not have an ending, the adjective—again—has the ending of the definite article. **Ein**-words (the indefinite article **ein,** the negative article **kein,** and the possessive adjectives **mein, dein,** etc.) do *not* have an ending in the masculine nominative and in the neuter nominative and accusative. In these instances, as expected, the adjective gives the information about the gender, number, and case of the noun that follows.

Ein groß**er** Topf steht auf dem Herd.
There is a large pot on the stove.
der Topf = masculine nominative

Ich esse ein frisch**es** Brötchen.
I am eating a fresh roll.
das Brötchen = neuter accusative

If an article or article-like word with an ending precedes the adjective, the adjective ends in either **-e** or **-en.** (See Sections 9.2 and 9.4.)

Ich nehme das holländisch**e** Bier. — *I'll take the Dutch beer.*
Ich nehme die deutsch**en** Äpfel. — *I'll take the German apples.*

9.2 Attributive adjectives in the nominative and accusative cases

As described in Section 9.1, adjective endings vary according to the gender, number, and case of the noun they describe and according to whether this information is already indicated by an article or article-like word. In essence, however, there are only a very limited number of possibilities. Study the following chart carefully and try to come up with some easy rules of thumb that will help you remember the adjective endings.

	Masculine	*Neuter*	*Feminine*	*Plural*
Nom.	der kalt**e** Tee ein kalt**er** Tee kalt**er** Tee	das kalt**e** Bier ein kalt**es** Bier kalt**es** Bier	die kalt**e** Limo eine kalt**e** Limo kalt**e** Limo	die kalt**en** Getränke kalt**e** Getränke
Acc.	den kalt**en** Tee einen kalt**en** Tee kalt**en** Tee	das kalt**e** Bier ein kalt**es** Bier kalt**es** Bier	die kalt**e** Limo eine kalt**e** Limo kalt**e** Limo	die kalt**en** Getränke kalt**e** Getränke

Rules of thumb:
1. *In many instances, the adjective ending is the same as the ending of the definite article.*
2. *But: after* **der** *(nominative masculine) and* **das,** *the adjective ending is* **-e.***
3. *But: after* **die** *(plural), the adjective ending is* **-en.**

Übung 1 Spezialitäten!

Jedes Land hat eine Spezialität, ein Gericht oder ein Getränk, das aus diesem Land einfach am besten schmeckt. An welche Länder denken Sie bei den folgenden Gerichten oder Getränken? Nützliche Wörter:

amerikanisch	griechisch	neuseeländisch
deutsch	holländisch	norwegisch
dänisch	italienisch	polnisch
englisch	japanisch	russisch
französisch	kolumbianisch	ungarisch

MODELL Salami → Italienische Salami!

1. Steak (n.)	**5.** Champagner (m.)	**9.** Paprika (m.)
2. Kaviar (m.)	**6.** Wurst (f.)	**10.** Marmelade (f.)
3. Oliven (pl.)	**7.** Käse (m.)	**11.** Kaffee (m.)
4. Sojasoße (f.)	**8.** Spaghetti (pl.)	**12.** Kiwi (pl.)

*Remember this rule as "**der** (nominative masculine)" because, as you will learn in Section 9.4, **der** may also refer to dative feminine, in which case the adjective ending will be **-en.**

Übung 2 Der Gourmet

Michael ist etwas Besseres, oder glaubt es zumindest zu sein, und ißt und trinkt daher nicht alles, sondern nur, was er für fein hält. Übernehmen Sie Michaels Rolle.

MODELL Magst du Kognak (m.)? / französisch → Ja, aber nur französischen Kognak!

1. Magst du Brot (n.)? / deutsch
2. Magst du Kaviar (m.)? / russisch
3. Magst du Salami (f.)? / italienisch
4. Magst du Kaffee (m.)? / kolumbianisch
5. Magst du Kiwis (pl.)? / neuseeländisch
6. Magst du Wein (m.)? / französisch
7. Magst du Bier (n.)? / belgisch
8. Magst du Muscheln (pl.)? / spanisch
9. Magst du Marmelade (f.)? / englisch
10. Magst du Thunfisch (m.)? / japanisch

Übung 3 Im Geschäft

Michael hat kein Geld, aber er möchte alles kaufen. Maria muß ihn immer bremsen.

MODELL der schicke Anzug / teuer →
MICHAEL: Ich möchte den schicken Anzug da.
MARIA: Nein, dieser schicke Anzug ist viel zu teuer.

1. der graue Wintermantel / schwer
2. die gelbe Hose / bunt
3. das schicke Hemd / teuer
4. die roten Socken / warm
5. der schwarze Schlafanzug / dünn
6. die grünen Schuhe / groß
7. der modische Hut / klein
8. die leichten Winterstiefel / leicht
9. die elegante Sonnenbrille / bunt
10. die roten Tennisschuhe / grell

Übung 4 Minidialoge

Ergänzen Sie die Adjektivendungen.

1. HERR RUF: Na, wie ist denn Ihr neu_____[a] Auto?
   FRAU WAGNER: Ach, der alt_____[b] Mercedes war mir lieber.
   HERR RUF: Dann hätte ich mir aber keinen neu_____[c] Wagen gekauft!
2. KELLNER: Wie schmeckt Ihnen denn der italienisch_____[a] Wein?
   MICHAEL: Sehr gut. Ich bestelle gleich noch eine weiter_____[b] Flasche.
3. MICHAEL: Heute repariere ich mein kaputt_____[a] Fahrrad.
   MARIA: Prima! Dann kannst du meinen blöd_____[b] Kassettenrecorder auch reparieren. Er ist schon wieder kaputt.
   MICHAEL: Na gut, aber dann habe ich wieder kein frei_____[c] Wochenende.

9.3 Destination vs. location: *stellen/stehen, legen/liegen, setzen/sitzen, hängen/hängen*

destination = accusative
location = dative

Destination implies accusative case; location implies dative case.

DESTINATION	LOCATION
Verbs of action and direction used with two-way prepositions followed by the accusative.	Verbs of condition and location used with two-way prepositions followed by the dative.

Maria stellt eine Flasche Wein **auf den** Tisch.

Die Flasche Wein steht **auf dem** Tisch.

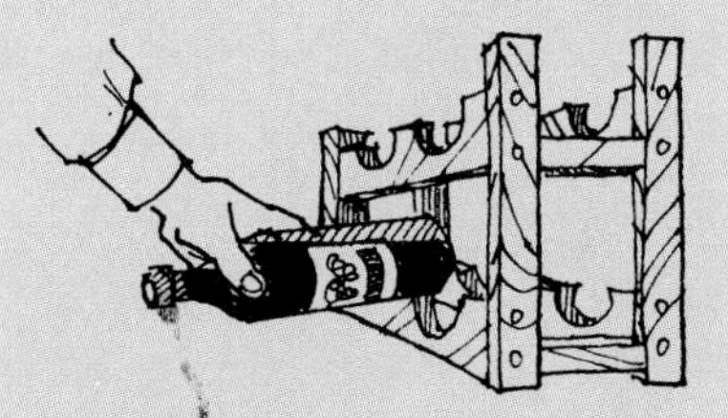

Michael legt eine Flasche Wein **ins** Weinregal.

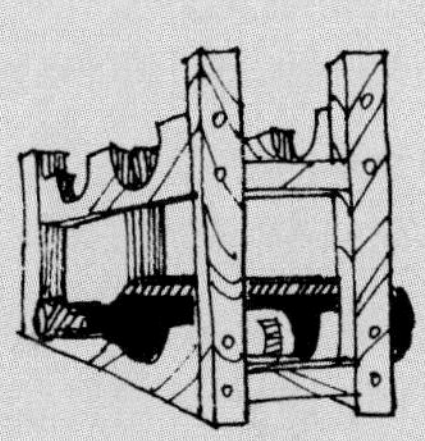

Die Flasche Wein liegt **im** Weinregal.

stellen/stehen = vertical position
legen/liegen = horizontal position

Stellen and **stehen** designate vertical placement or position. They are used with people and animals, as well as with objects that have a base and can "stand" without falling over. **Legen** and **liegen** designate horizontal placement or position. They are used with people and animals, as well as with objects that do not have a base and cannot "stand" without falling over.

DESTINATION

LOCATION

Frau Wagner setzt Paula **in den** Hochstuhl.

Paula sitzt **im** Hochstuhl.

Andrea hängt das Handtuch **an den** Haken.

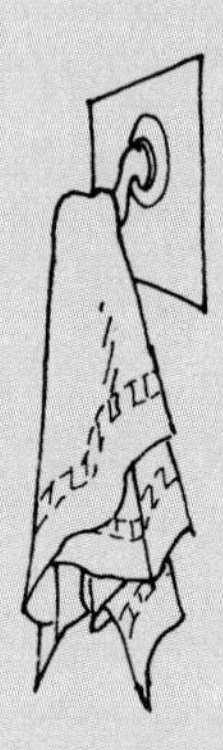

Das Handtuch hängt **am** Haken.

sitzen/setzen = sitting position (people and certain animals)
hängen/hängen = hanging position

Setzen designates the act of being seated; **sitzen** the state of sitting. These verbs are used only with people and with animals that are capable of sitting. **Hängen (hängte, gehängt)** designates the act of being hung; **hängen (hing, gehangen)** the state of hanging.

The verbs **stellen, legen, setzen,** and **hängen** are weak verbs that require an accusative object. The two-way preposition is used with the accusative case.

stellen	hat gestellt
legen	hat gelegt
setzen	hat gesetzt
hängen	hat gehängt

The verbs **stehen, liegen, sitzen, hängen** are strong verbs that cannot take an accusative object. The two-way preposition is used with the dative case.

stehen	hat gestanden
liegen	hat gelegen
sitzen	hat gesessen
hängen	hat gehangen

Übung 5 Minidialoge

Ergänzen Sie die Artikel, die Präposition plus Artikel, oder das Pronomen. Nützliche Wörter:

das Bett	das Regal	das Sofa
die Gläser	der Schrank	die Tasche
der Herd	der Schreibtisch	der Tisch

1. SILVIA: Wohin stellst du die Blumen?
JÜRGEN: Auf _____ Tisch.

2. JOSEF: Warum setzt du dich nicht an _____[a] Tisch?
MELANIE: Ich sitze hier auf _____[b] Sofa bequemer.

3. MARIA: Meine Bücher liegen auf _____[a] Tisch. Bitte stell sie auf _____[b] Regal.
MICHAEL: Okay.

4. ALBERT: Ich kann Melanie nicht finden.
STEFAN: Sie sitzt auf _____ Bank im Garten.

5. MONIKA: Hast du die Weinflaschen in _____[a] Schrank gestellt?
HEIDI: Ja, sie stehen neben _____[b] Gläsern.

6. SOFIE: (*am Telefon*) Was machst du heute?
MARTA: Nichts! Ich lege mich (in) _____[a] Bett.
SOFIE: Liegst du schon (in) _____[b] Bett?
MARTA: Nein, jetzt sitze ich noch (an) _____[c] Schreibtisch.

7. KATRIN: Darf ich mich neben _____[a] (du) setzen?
STEFAN: Ja, bitte setz _____[b].

8. FRAU RUF: Hast du die Suppe auf _____[a] Herd gestellt?
HERR RUF: Sie steht schon seit einer Stunde auf _____[b] Herd.

9. HERR RUF: Wo ist der Stadtplan?
FRAU RUF: Er liegt unter _____ Tasche.

Übung 6 Vor dem Abendessen

Beschreiben Sie die Bilder. Nützliche Wörter:

legen/liegen	der Küchenschrank	das Sofa
setzen/sitzen	der Schrank	der Teller
stehen/stellen	die Schublade	der Tisch
	die Serviette	

MODELL: Die Schuhe → Die Schuhe liegen auf dem Boden.

Peter → Peter stellt die Schuhe vor die Tür.

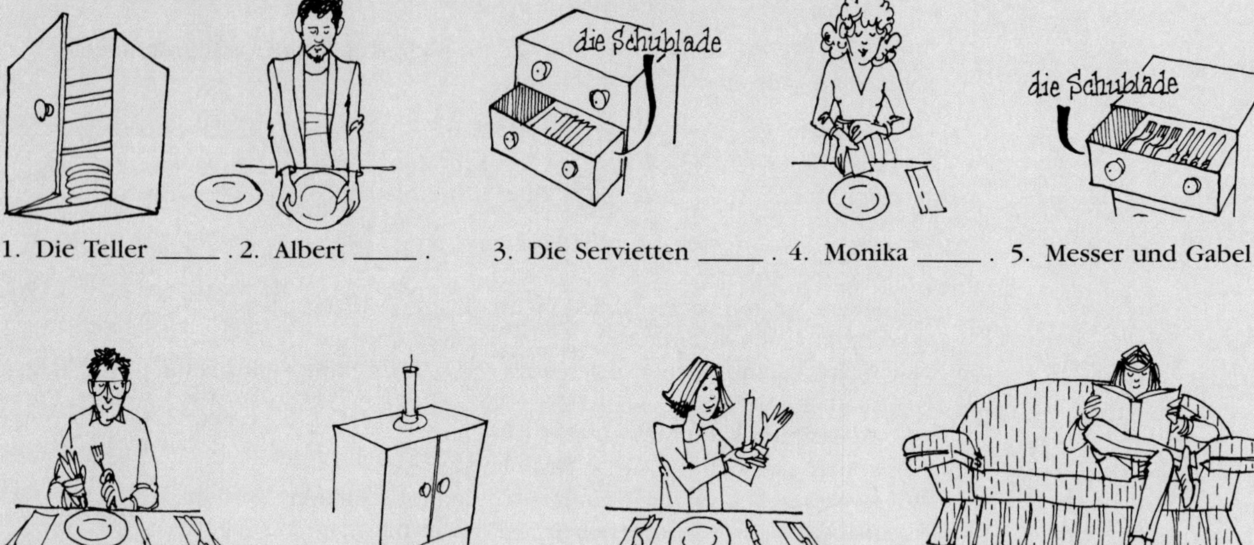

1. Die Teller _____ . 2. Albert _____ . 3. Die Servietten _____ . 4. Monika _____ . 5. Messer und Gabel _____

6. Stefan _____ . 7. Die Kerze _____ . 8. Heidi _____ . 9. Thomas _____ .

9.4 Adjectives in the dative case

In the dative case, nouns are usually preceded by an article **(dem, der, den; einem, einer)** or an article-like word **(diesem, dieser, diesen; meinem, meiner, meinen).** When adjectives occur before such nouns they end in **-en.***

Jutta geht mit ihr**em** neu**en** Freund spazieren.	*Jutta is going for a walk with her new friend.*
Jens gießt sein**er** krank**en** Tante die Blumen.	*Jens is watering the flowers for his sick aunt.*
Ich spreche nicht mehr mit die**sen** unhöflich**en** Menschen.	*I'm not talking with these impolite people any more.*

	Masculine	*Neuter*	*Feminine*	*Plural*
Dat.	dies**em** lieb**en** Vater mein**em** lieb**en** Vater	dies**em** lieb**en** Kind mein**em** lieb**en** Kind	dies**er** lieb**en** Mutter mein**er** lieb**en** Mutter	dies**en** lieb**en** Eltern mein**en** lieb**en** Eltern

*Unpreceded adjectives in the dative case follow the same pattern as in the nominative and accusative case, that is, they have the ending of the definite article. For example, **mit frischem Honig** (*with fresh honey*), **mit kalter Milch** (*with cold milk*).

Achtung!

All nouns have an **-n** in the dative plural unless their plural ends in **-s.**

Nominative: die Freunde *Dative:* den Freunde**n** *but:* den Hobbys

Übung 7 Was machen diese Leute?

Schreiben Sie Sätze.

MODELL Jens / seine alte Tante / einen Brief schreiben →
Jens schreibt sein**er** alt**en** Tante einen Brief.

1. Jutta / ihr neuer Freund / ihre Lieblings-CD leihen
2. Jens / der kleine Bruder von Jutta / eine Ratte verkaufen
3. Ernst / nur seine besten Freunde / die Ratte zeigen
4. Jutta / ihre beste Freundin / ein Buch schenken
5. Jens / sein wütender Lehrer / eine Krawatte kaufen
6. Ernst / seine große Schwester / einen Witz erzählen
7. Jutta / die netten Leute von nebenan / Kaffee kochen
8. Ernst / das süße Baby von nebenan / einen Kuß geben

9.5 Being polite: the subjunctive form of modal verbs

Use the subjunctive form of modal verbs to be more polite.

Könnten Sie mir bitte dafür eine Quittung geben? — *Could you please give me a receipt for that?*

Ich **müßte** mal telefonieren. **Dürfte** ich Ihr Telefon benutzen? — *I have to make a phone call. Could I use your phone?*

The subjunctive is formed from the simple past-tense stem. Add an umlaut if there is an umlaut in the infinitive.

To form the subjunctive of a modal verb, add an umlaut to the simple past form if there is also one in the infinitive. If the modal verb has no umlaut in the infinitive (**sollen** and **wollen**), the subjunctive form is the same as the simple past form.

Present	*Past*	*Subjunctive*
dürfen	ich durfte	ich d**ü**rfte
können	ich konnte	ich k**ö**nnte
mögen	ich mochte	ich m**ö**chte
müssen	ich mußte	ich m**ü**ßte
sollen	ich sollte	ich sollte
wollen	ich wollte	ich wollte

Here are the subjunctive forms of **können** and **wollen.**

können			
ich	könnte	wir	könnten
du	könntest	ihr	könntet
Sie	könnten	Sie	könnten
er / sie / es	könnte	sie	könnten

wollen			
ich	wollte	wir	wollten
du	wolltest	ihr	wolltet
Sie	wollten	Sie	wollten
er / sie / es	wollte	sie	wollten

In modern German, **möchte,** the subjunctive form of **mögen,** has become almost a synonym of **wollen.**

—Wohin wollen Sie fliegen? *Where do you want to go (fly)?*
—Wir möchten nach Kanada fliegen. *We want to fly to Canada.*

Another polite form, **hätte gern,** is now used more and more, especially in conversational exchanges involving goods and services.

Ich hätte gern eine Cola, bitte. *I'd like a coke, please.*
Wir hätten gern die Speisekarte, bitte. *We'd like the menu, please.*

Übung 8 Überredungskünste

Versuchen Sie, jemanden zu überreden,[1] etwas anderes zu machen als das, was er/sie machen will.

MODELL S1: Ich fahre jetzt. (bleiben)
S2: Ach, könntest du nicht bleiben?

1. Ich koche Kaffee. (Tee, Suppe, ?)
2. Ich lese jetzt. (später, morgen, ?)
3. Ich sehe jetzt fern. (etwas Klavier spielen, mit mir sprechen, ?)
4. Ich rufe meine Mutter an. (deinen Vater, deine Tante, ?)
5. Ich gehe nach Hause. (noch eine Stunde bleiben, bis morgen bleiben, ?)

[1]*convince*

MODELL S1: Wir fahren nach Spanien. (Italien)
S2: Könnten wir nicht mal nach Italien fahren?

6. Wir übernachten im Zelt. (Hotel, Campingbus, ?)
7. Wir kochen selbst. (essen gehen, fasten, ?)
8. Wir gehen jeden Tag wandern. (schwimmen, ins Kino, ?)
9. Wir schreiben viele Briefe. (nur einen Brief, nur Postkarten, ?)
10. Wir sehen uns alle Museen an. (in der Sonne liegen, viel schlafen, ?)

Übung 9 Eine Autofahrt

Sie wollen mit einem Freund ausgehen und fahren in seinem Auto mit. Stellen Sie Fragen. Versuchen Sie, besonders freundlich und höflich zu sein.

MODELL wir / jetzt nicht fahren können → Könnten wir jetzt nicht fahren?

1. du / nicht noch tanken müssen
2. wir / nicht Jens abholen sollen
3. zwei Freunde von mir / auch mitfahren können
4. wir / nicht zuerst in die Stadt fahren sollen
5. du / nicht zur Bank wollen
6. du / etwas langsamer fahren können
7. ich / das Autoradio anmachen dürfen
8. ich / das Fenster aufmachen dürfen

KAPITEL 10

Schloß Neuschwanstein in Oberbayern, eine der bekanntesten Touristenattraktionen in Deutschland

Kapitel 10 focuses on travel. You will also learn to get around in the German-speaking world by following directions and reading maps.

Auf Reisen

THEMEN
Reisepläne
Nach dem Weg fragen
Die große weite Welt
Kleider und Aussehen

LEKTÜRE
Wem Gott will rechte Gunst erweisen
Vornehme Leute, 1200 Meter hoch

KULTURELLES
Reiseziele
Reisen und Urlaub
Stichwort „Mode"
Kulturprojekt: Reisen
Porträt: Bertolt Brecht und Augsburg
Videoecke: Die deutsche Weinstraße

STRUKTUREN
10.1 Prepositions to talk about places: **aus, bei, nach, von, zu**
10.2 Indirect questions: **Wissen Sie, wo . . . ?**
10.3 Prepositions for giving directions: **an . . . vorbei, bis zu, entlang, gegenüber von, über**
10.4 Expressing possibility: **würde** + infinitive
10.5 Dative verbs

SPRECHSITUATIONEN

Reisepläne

➤ **Grammatik 10.1–10.2**

—Wir möchten einen Flug buchen.
—Touristenklasse oder erster Klasse?

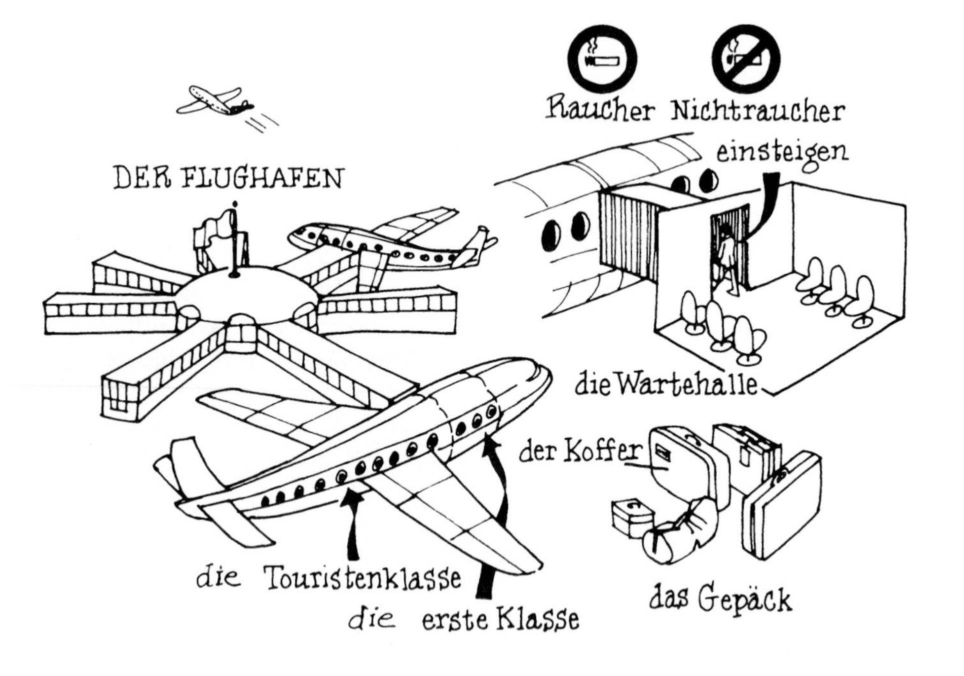

Situation 1 Eine Reise machen

Bringen Sie die folgenden Aktivitäten in eine logische Reihenfolge.

_____ ins Reisebüro gehen und die Fahrkarten kaufen
_____ ins Flugzeug einsteigen
_____ Kleidung und andere Sachen kaufen
_____ die Reise planen
_____ zum Flughafen fahren
_____ Paß und Visum besorgen
_____ die Koffer packen
_____ auf der Bank Reiseschecks kaufen
_____ Geld für die Reise sparen
_____ den Flug buchen

Barocke Häuser in der Altstadt von Erfurt

Kultur ... Landeskunde ... Informationen

Reiseziele

- Welche amerikanischen Bundesstaaten oder Städte sind für Sie beliebte Reiseziele? Warum?
- Was mögen Touristen an den USA besonders? Wohin fahren sie am liebsten? Warum?
- Welche Andenken (Souvenirs) bringen sie mit nach Hause? Spekulieren Sie!
- Welches sind beliebte Urlaubsländer für Amerikaner? Warum?

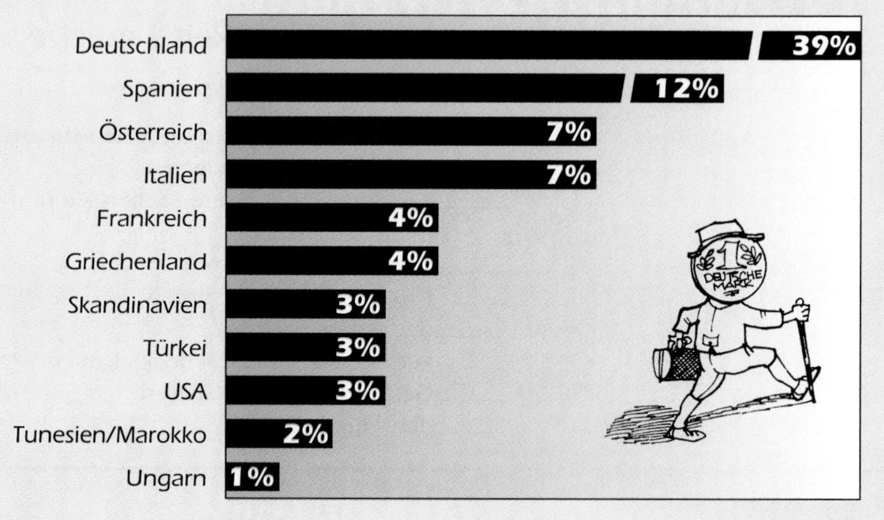

Schauen Sie sich die Graphik an.

- Wo machen Deutsche am liebsten Urlaub?
- Was macht Spanien, Österreich und Italien attraktiv für deutsche Urlauber?

  - ☐ Man spricht dort deutsch.
  - ☐ Spanier und Italiener sind besonders deutschfreundlich.
  - ☐ Der Urlaub ist relativ preisgünstig.
  - ☐ Man kann mit dem Auto hinfahren.
  - ☐ Es ist warm, und die Sonne scheint.
  - ☐ Das Essen schmeckt sehr gut.
  - ☐ ?

Situation 2 Informationsspiel: Reisen

MODELL

S1: Woher kommt Sofie? S2: Aus _____ .
S1: Wohin fährt sie in den Ferien? S2: Nach/In _____ .
S1: Wo wohnt sie? S2: Bei _____ .
S1: Was macht sie da? S2: Sie _____ .
S1: Wann kommt sie zurück? S2: In _____ .

	Richard	Sofie	Mehmet	Peter	Jürgen	mein(e) Partner(in)
Woher?	aus Innsbruck		aus Izmir		aus Bad Harzburg	
Wohin?	nach Frankreich		nach Italien		in die Alpen	
Wo?	bei einer Gastfamilie			bei seiner Schwester		
Was?		Bücher kaufen; Verwandte besuchen		einen Vulkan besteigen		
Wann?	in drei Monaten				in zwei Wochen	

Situation 3 Dialog: Am Fahrkartenschalter

Silvia steht am Fahrkartenschalter und möchte mit dem Zug von Göttingen nach München fahren.

BAHNBEAMTER: Bitte schön?
SILVIA: Können Sie mir sagen, wann morgen der erste Zug nach München ___?
BAHNBEAMTER: Moment, da muß ich nachsehen . . . ______________.
SILVIA: Das ist __ ein bißchen zu früh. Wann geht der nächste?
BAHNBEAMTER: Um acht Uhr fünf geht ein InterCity ___________________.
SILVIA: Gut. Eine Fahrkarte zweiter Klasse bitte.
BAHNBEAMTER: _____ oder Hin- und Rückfahrt?
SILVIA: Hin und zurück bitte. Wissen Sie, wo der Zug ____?
BAHNBEAMTER: Gleis vierzehn. Das macht dann _______________ Mark bitte.
SILVIA: Wissen Sie auch, wie lange die Fahrt ____?
BAHNBEAMTER: ___ Stunden und . . . Moment . . . ______ Minuten genau.
SILVIA: Vielen Dank.

Situation 4 Interview

1. Verreist du gern?
2. Warst du schon mal in Europa (in Mexiko oder Kanada, in einem anderen US-Staat)? Wo warst du? Wann warst du da? Was hast du da gemacht?
3. Wohin fährst du, wenn du Ski fahren möchtest?
4. Wohin fährst du, um Sonne, Strand und Meer zu erleben?
5. Wohin würdest du am liebsten reisen? Was würdest du da machen? Wie lange würdest du bleiben?
6. Wo und wie kann man billig Urlaub machen?
7. Welche deutsche Stadt interessiert dich am meisten? Warum?
8. Würdest du gern jemanden aus einem anderen Land heiraten? Wenn ja, aus welchem?
9. Aus welchem Land sind deine Vorfahren gekommen? Warst du schon einmal da? Wenn ja, wann? Wie lange? Hast du noch Verwandte dort? Möchtest du einmal dorthin?

Nach dem Weg fragen

Grammatik 10.3

Biegen Sie an der Ampel nach links ab.

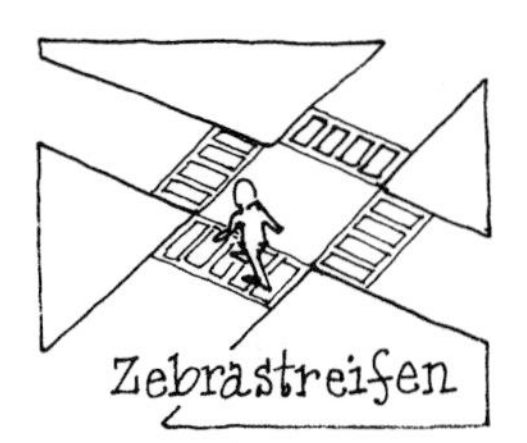

Gehen Sie über den Zebrastreifen.

Gehen Sie geradeaus, bis Sie eine Kirche sehen.

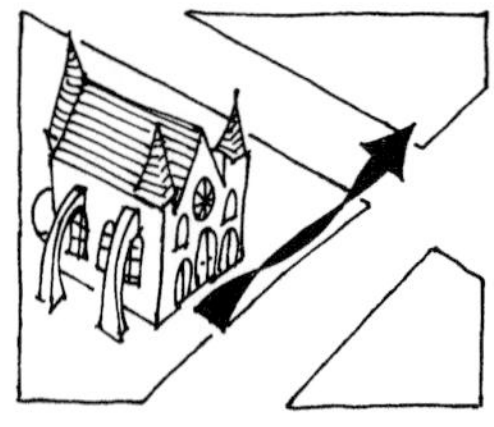
Gehen Sie an der Kirche vorbei, immer geradeaus.

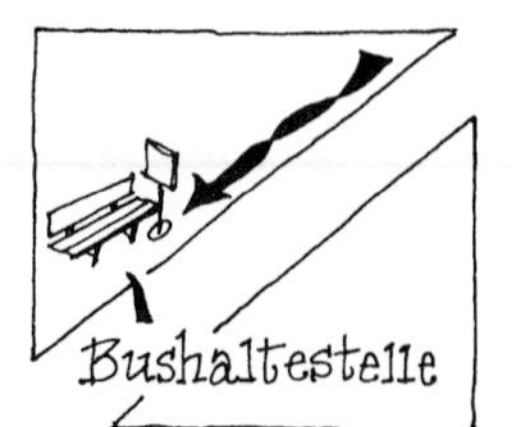

Gehen Sie die Goetheallee entlang bis zur Bushaltestelle.

Gehen Sie über die Brücke. Auf der linken Seite ist dann das Rathaus.

Die U-Bahnhaltestelle ist gegenüber vom Markthotel.

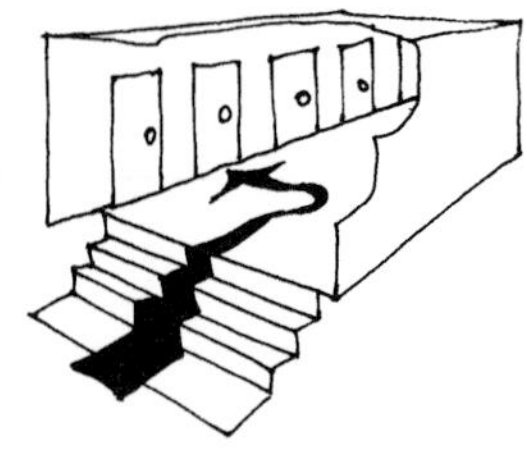
Gehen Sie die Treppe hinauf, und dann ist es die zweite Tür links.

Situation 5 Dialoge

1. Jürgen ist bei Silvias Mutter zum Geburtstag eingeladen.

JÜRGEN: Wie komme ich denn zu eurem Haus?
SILVIA: Das ist ganz einfach. Wenn du _____ Bahnhofsgebäude herauskommst, siehst du rechts _____ anderen Seite der Straße ein Lebensmittelgeschäft. Geh _____ Straße, links __ Lebensmittelgeschäft vorbei, und wenn du einfach geradeaus weitergehst, kommst du __ __ Bismarckstraße. Die mußt du nur ganz hinaufgehen, bis du __ ____ Kreisverkehr kommst. Direkt _____ anderen Seite ist unser Haus.

2. Claire und Melanie sind in Göttingen und suchen die Universitätsbibliothek.

MELANIE: Entschuldige, kannst du uns sagen, wo die Universitätsbibliothek ist?
STUDENT: Ach, da seid ihr aber ganz schön falsch. Also, geht erst mal wieder zurück ______ großen Kreuzung. _____ Kreuzung _____ und ___ Fußgängerzone ___. Immer geradeaus ______ Fußgängerzone ____ Prinzenstraße. Da rechts. ____ rechten Seite seht ihr dann die Post. Direkt ___________ Post ist die Bibliothek. Könnt ihr gar nicht verfehlen.
MELANIE UND CLAIRE: Danke.

3. Frau Frisch findet ein Zimmer im Rathaus nicht.

FRAU FRISCH: Entschuldigen Sie, ich suche Zimmer 204.
SEKRETÄRIN: Das ist __ dritten Stock. Gehen Sie den Korridor entlang _____ Treppenhaus. Dann eine Treppe ____ und oben links. Zimmer 204 ist die zweite Tür _____ rechten Seite.
FRAU FRISCH: Vielen Dank. Da hätte ich ja lange suchen können . . .

Situation 6 Mit dem Stadtplan unterwegs in Regensburg

Suchen Sie sich ein Ziel in Regensburg aus dem Stadtplan. Beschreiben Sie Ihrem Partner / Ihrer Partnerin den Weg, ohne das Ziel zu verraten.[1] Wenn er/sie dort richtig ankommt, bekommen Sie einen Punkt, und es wird gewechselt. Achtung: Ausgangspunkt[2] und Ziel dürfen nicht im selben Quadrat liegen!

---

[1] *give away* [2] *starting point*

NÜTZLICHE AUSDRÜCKE

links/rechts die (Goliath)straße entlang
links/rechts in die (Kram)gasse hinein
geradeaus über den (Krauterer)markt / über die (Kepler)straße
weiter bis zum/zur _____
an der (Steinernen Brücke) vorbei

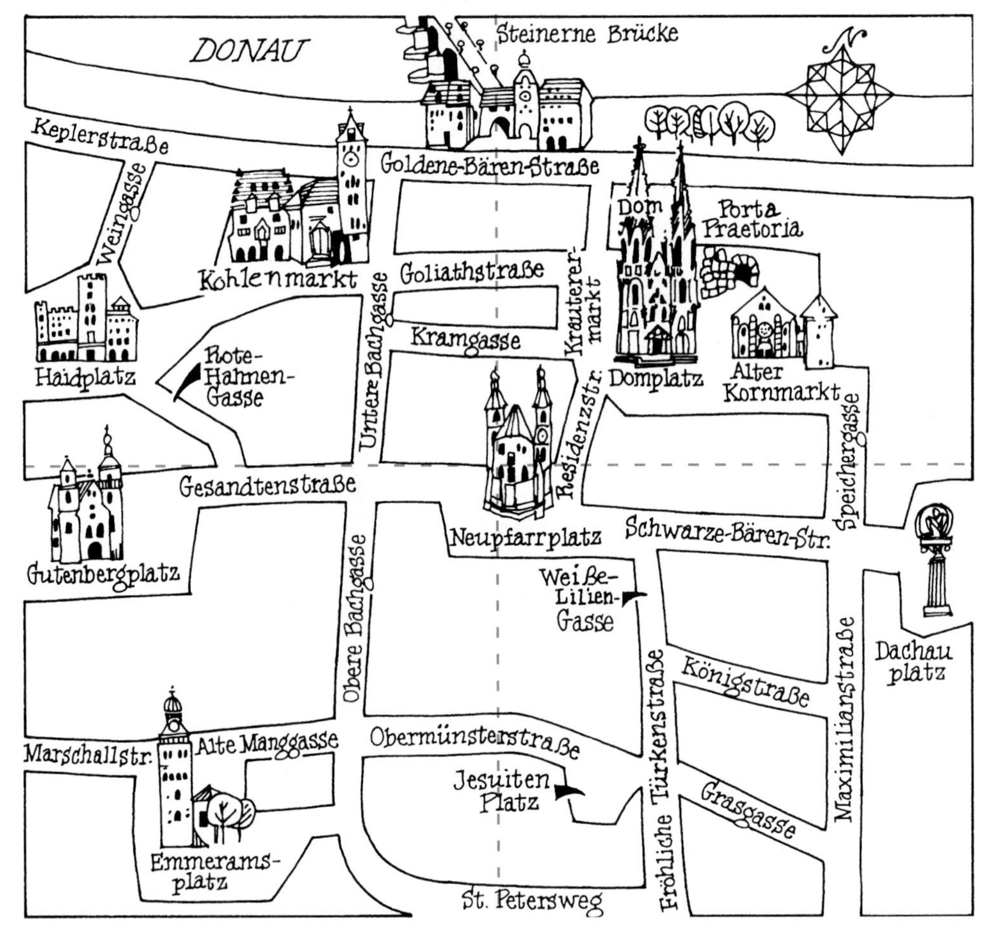

1. vom Dachauplatz zum/zur . . .
2. vom Domplatz . . .
3. von der Ecke Grasgasse/Maximilianstraße . . .
4. vom Gutenbergplatz . . .
5. von der Porta Praetoria . . .
6. vom Haidplatz . . .
7. vom Alten Kornmarkt . . .
8. vom Emmeramsplatz . . .

der Dom
die Fröhliche Türkenstraße
die Goliathstraße
die Keplerstraße
der Krauterermarkt
die Marschallstraße
die Steinerne Brücke
die Weingasse

Situation 7 Wie komme ich . . . ?

Beschreiben Sie Ihrem Partner / Ihrer Partnerin,

1. wie man zu Ihrem Haus oder zu Ihrer Wohnung kommt.
2. wo die nächste Post ist, und wie man dahinkommt.
3. wo die beste Kneipe/Disko in der Stadt ist, und wie man dahinkommt.
4. wie man zum Schwimmbad kommt.
5. wie man zur Bibliothek kommt.
6. wo der nächste billige Kopierladen ist, und wie man dahinkommt.
7. wie man zum Büro von Ihrem Lehrer / Ihrer Lehrerin kommt.
8. wo der nächste Waschsalon ist, und wie man dahinkommt.

Die große weite Welt

➤ **Grammatik 10.4**

—Haben Sie noch zwei Betten für eine Nacht frei?
—Ja. Haben Sie einen Jugendherbergsausweis?

—Guten Tag, was kostet der Campingplatz?
—Fünf Mark für das Auto und neun Mark pro Person. Kinder die Hälfte.

—Guten Tag, ich habe ein Einzelzimmer mit Dusche und Toilette bestellt.
—Auf welchen Namen bitte?
—Röder, Renate Röder.

—Wir suchen ein Zimmer mit Frühstück. Haben Sie noch etwas frei?
—Wie lange möchten Sie denn bleiben?

—Wir suchen eine Ferienwohnung.
—Für wie viele Personen sollte sie denn sein?

—Ich glaube, wildes Camping ist in Deutschland verboten.
—Ach, glaubst du, daß uns hier jemand erwischt?

Situation 8 Informationsspiel: Wo wollen wir übernachten?

MODELL Wieviel kostet _____?
Haben die Zimmer im (in der) _____ eine eigene Dusche und Toilette?
Gibt es im (in der) _____ Einzelzimmer?
Gibt es im (in der, auf dem) _____ einen Fernseher?
Ist das Frühstück im (in der, auf dem) _____ inbegriffen?
Ist die Lage von dem (von der) _____ zentral/ruhig?
Gibt es im (in der, auf dem) _____ Telefon?

	das Hotel am Stadtpark	das Gästehaus Radaublick	die Jugendherberge	der Campingplatz
Preis pro Person	78,- DM		6,50 DM	9,- DM
Dusche/Toilette	ja	nicht in allen Zimmern		
Einzelzimmer	ja	ja	nein	
Fernseher			im Aufenthaltsraum	
Frühstück		inbegriffen		
zentrale Lage	ja	ja	im Wald	am Stadtrand
ruhige Lage	ja	ja	ja	
Telefon				

Situation 9 Dialog: Auf Zimmersuche

Herr und Frau Ruf suchen ein Zimmer.

HERR RUF: Guten Tag, haben Sie noch ein Doppelzimmer mit Dusche frei?
WIRTIN: Wie lange möchten Sie denn _____?
HERR RUF: _______.
WIRTIN: Ja, da habe ich ein Zimmer _______ und Toilette.
FRAU RUF: Ist das Zimmer auch ruhig?
WIRTIN: Natürlich. Unsere Zimmer sind alle ruhig.
FRAU RUF: _______ das Zimmer denn?
WIRTIN: 54 Mark ______.
HERR RUF: Ist Frühstück dabei?
WIRTIN: Selbstverständlich ist Frühstück dabei.
FRAU RUF: Gut, wir nehmen das Zimmer.

HERR RUF: Und wann können wir _______?
WIRTIN: __________ im Frühstückszimmer.

Kultur ... Landeskunde ... Informationen

Reisen und Urlaub

- Was ist für Amerikaner im Urlaub besonders wichtig? Stellen Sie eine Rangliste auf.

  _____ Abenteuer erleben
  _____ Land und Leute kennenlernen
  _____ ausschlafen
  _____ gut essen
  _____ flirten
  _____ mit dem Partner/der Partnerin/der Familie zusammensein
  _____ einkaufen
  _____ etwas für die Gesundheit tun
  _____ Sport treiben
  _____ sich erholen

- Was ist für Sie im Urlaub besonders wichtig? Nennen Sie drei Dinge.

Schauen Sie sich die folgende Statistik an.

- Was ist für Deutsche im Urlaub besonders wichtig?
- Auf welchem Platz in dieser Statistik stehen Ihre Präferenzen?

FOCUS-FRAGE

„Was ist für Sie im Urlaub besonders wichtig?"

FERIEN MIT DER FAMILIE

von 1300 Befragten* antworteten

46%	mit dem Partner, der Familie zusammensein
31%	Ausschlafen
31%	Land und Leute kennenlernen
25%	etwas für die Gesundheit tun
20%	Abenteuer erleben
10%	Flirten

* Repräsentative Umfrage des Sample-Instituts für FOCUS im Mai 1993

Situation 10 Rollenspiel: Im Hotel

S1: Sie sind im Hotel und möchten ein Zimmer mit Dusche und Toilette. Außerdem möchten Sie ein ruhiges Zimmer. Fragen Sie auch nach Preisen, Frühstück, Telefon und wann Sie morgens abreisen müssen.

Situation 11 Zum Schreiben: Ein Brief an ein Gästehaus

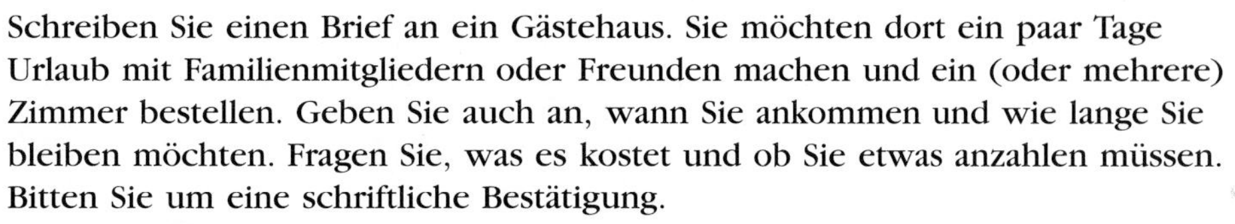

Schreiben Sie einen Brief an ein Gästehaus. Sie möchten dort ein paar Tage Urlaub mit Familienmitgliedern oder Freunden machen und ein (oder mehrere) Zimmer bestellen. Geben Sie auch an, wann Sie ankommen und wie lange Sie bleiben möchten. Fragen Sie, was es kostet und ob Sie etwas anzahlen müssen. Bitten Sie um eine schriftliche Bestätigung.

Geschäftsbriefe beginnt man mit „Sehr geehrte(r) Frau/Herr" oder mit „Sehr geehrte Damen und Herren", wenn man den Namen nicht weiß. Am Ende schreibt man „Hochachtungsvoll" oder etwas weniger distanziert „Mit freundlichen Grüßen" und dann seinen Namen.

Situation 12 Interview

1. Warst du schon einmal auf einem Campingplatz? Wo war das und mit wem?
2. Warst du schon einmal in einer Jugendherberge? Wann, wo und mit wem?
3. Hast du schon einmal in einem Hotel übernachtet? Wo? Wie war das Zimmer? Was gab es alles?
4. Wo hast du übernachtet, als du zuletzt verreist bist? Wie war es dort? Wo hast du gefrühstückt?
5. Stell dir vor, du würdest eine Reise nach Deutschland machen. Wo würdest du übernachten?
6. Stell dir vor, du würdest mit dem Zug in Wien ankommen und eine Unterkunft suchen. Was würdest du machen?

Kleider und Aussehen

➤ **Grammatik 10.5**

—Kann ich Ihnen helfen?
—Vielen Dank, aber ich möchte mich noch ein bißchen umsehen.

—Die Hose steht dir aber gut.
—Sie paßt mir auch genau und ist sehr bequem.

—Die gestreifte Bluse gefällt mir.
—Sie paßt gut zu dem grauen Rock.

—Wie gefallen Ihnen diese Stiefel?
—Ich hätte gern welche mit flachen Absätzen.

Situation 13 Definitionen

1. Man trägt sie, um keine kalten Füße zu bekommen.
2. Man benutzt ihn, wenn es regnet oder schneit.
3. Man trägt ihn im Bett.
4. Man trägt ihn um den Hals, wenn es kalt ist.
5. Man trägt sie, wenn die Hände kalt sind.
6. Man trägt sie unter der Kleidung.
7. Eine Art Schuhe; man trägt sie oft im Sommer.
8. Man trägt ihn oft nach dem Duschen.

a. der Regenschirm
b. der Schlafanzug
c. der Schal
d. die Socken
e. die Unterhose
f. die Handschuhe
g. der Bademantel
h. die Sandalen

Kultur ... Landeskunde ... Informationen

Stichwort „Mode"

- Kennen Sie Modeschöpfer? Welche? Aus welchem Land kommen sie?
- Welche Länder sind wegen der Mode bekannt?
- Welche Städte sind als Modestädte bekannt?

Beim Stichwort „Mode" denkt man an Paris oder Mailand,[1] aber einer der bekanntesten Modeschöpfer ist ein Deutscher. Karl Lagerfeld wurde 1938 in Hamburg geboren. Er arbeitete für verschiedene französische Modehäuser, bis er 1984 eigene Studios in Paris und New York eröffnete. Jil Sanders ist eine andere deutsche Modeschöpferin, die man auch in den USA kennt.

Düsseldorf hat auch den Spitznamen „Klein-Paris", weil es die Modestadt Deutschlands ist. Jedes Jahr findet in Düsseldorf eine Modemesse statt, wo die neusten Trends vorgestellt werden.

Karl Lagerfeld, Modeschöpfer, im Kreise seiner Schönen

- In welchen Ländern liegen Paris und Mailand?
- In welchem Bundesland liegt Düsseldorf?
- Düsseldorf ist nicht nur die „Modestadt" Deutschlands, es ist auch die _____ von Nordrhein-Westfalen.

[1] *Milan*

Situation 14 Informationsspiel: Gespräche im Kaufhaus

MODELL S1: Welche Farbe gefällt Jutta am besten?
S2: ______ .
S1: Welche Farbe gefällt dir am besten?
S2: ______ .

	Jutta	Juttas Mutter	mein(e) Partner(in)
Welche Farbe gefällt ... am besten?		hellgrün	
Welches Kleidungsstück fehlt ... noch?	eine schwarze Lederjacke		
Was steht ... gut?	ihr Irokesenschnitt		
Paßt ... Größe M?		ja	
Hilf(s)t ... gern anderen beim Kleiderkauf?	nur ihren Freundinnen		
Was gehört ... seit mindestens drei Jahren?		ein Goldring	

Situation 15 Interview

1. Welche Farben gefallen dir besonders gut?
2. Trägst du gern einen Anzug (einen Rock)?
3. Was ziehst du zu einem eleganten Fest an?
4. Was trägst du in deiner Freizeit?
5. Was für Schuhe trägst du am liebsten?
6. Trägst du gern modische Kleidung?
7. Wieviel Geld gibst du im Monat für Kleidung aus?
8. Du bekommst einen Gutschein (1 500 Dollar) von einem teuren Geschäft. Wofür gibst du das Geld aus?
9. Trägst du gern Hüte oder Mützen?

Kulturprojekt Reisen

Planen Sie eine Reise in ein deutschsprachiges Land. Wählen Sie eine Stadt oder Gegend aus. Sammeln Sie Informationen aus Reiseführern oder Prospekten aus dem Reisebüro.

- Wo wollen Sie Urlaub machen?
- Mit wem reisen Sie?
- Wie kommen Sie dahin? (Genaue Reiseroute!)
- Bleiben Sie an einem Ort, oder reisen Sie in andere Gegenden?
- Wo übernachten Sie? (Campingplatz, Jugendherberge, Pension, Hotel) Wie ist/sind die Adresse/n?
- Was machen Sie an Ihrem Urlaubsort? Planen Sie Besichtigungen, Unternehmungen und Ausflüge.
- Kalkulieren Sie die ungefähren Kosten.

Porträt

Bertolt Brecht (1898–1956) ist einer der bekanntesten deutschen Dramatiker dieses Jahrhunderts. Er ist nicht nur bekannt als Schöpfer[1] eines neuen modernen Theaters, sondern auch als Frauenheld.[2] Das Bänkellied „Mack the Knife" aus seinem größten Hit *„Die Dreigroschenoper"* die er zusammen mit dem Komponisten Kurt Weill schrieb, ist auch heute noch in den Staaten bekannt. Er lebte in den USA kurze Zeit im Exil, da sein Name wegen seiner Verbindung[3] zu der kommunistischen Partei auf Hitlers Schwarzer Liste stand. Auch in den USA wurde er verfolgt[4] und mußte sich vor dem Committee Against Anti-American Activities verteidigen.[5] Er ging deshalb zurück nach Europa und führte ein internationales Leben: Er hatte seinen Wohnsitz in der DDR, besaß die österreichische Staatsbürgerschaft[6] und ein Schweizer Bankkonto.

In Augsburg, der Geburtsstadt Brechts, lebten im 16. Jahrhundert die Fugger. Sie waren eine reiche Bankiers- und Kaufmannsfamilie, die—wie Brecht—ein Verständnis[7] für Geld und für sozialistische Gedanken hatten. Sie waren so reich, daß der Kaiser[8] zu ihnen kam, um Geld zu leihen.[9] Sie waren auch die ersten „Sozialisten". Sie schufen[10] die sogenannte Fuggerei. Es sind Häuser, in denen Arme[11] wohnen konnten. Die Miete war sehr niedrig: jeden Tag ein Gebet[12] für die Seele der Fugger.

Die Fuggerei in Augsburg

[1] *creator* [2] *Don Juan* [3] *connection* [4] *persecuted* [5] *defend* [6] *citizenship* [7] here: *sense* [8] *emperor* [9] *borrow* [10] here: *initiated* [11] *the poor* [12] *prayer*

VIDEOECKE

Die deutsche Weinstraße

Wer feste schafft,[1] soll auch feste feiern

Die deutsche Weinstraße in der Pfalz ist ein beliebtes Urlaubs- und Reiseziel in Deutschland. In diesem Clip sehen Sie warum.

- Wo liegt die Pfalz?
- Was gibt es in der Pfalz?
- Wofür ist diese Region besonders bekannt?
- Wie ist hier meistens das Wetter?

[1] feste . . . *works hard*

WORTSCHATZ

Reisen und Tourismus / Travel and Tourism

die **Bahnbeamtin, -nen**	female train agent
die **Bestätigung, -en**	confirmation
die **Fahrt, -en**	trip
die **einfache Fahrt**	one-way trip
die **Hin- und Rückfahrt**	round trip
die **Ferienwohnung, -en**	vacation apartment/condo
die **Führung, -en**	guided tour
die **Haltestelle, -n**	stop
die **Bushaltestelle, -n**	bus stop
die **U-Bahnhaltestelle, -n**	subway stop
die **Jugendherberge, -n**	youth hostel
die **Klasse, -n** (R)	class
erster Klasse fliegen/fahren	to fly/travel first class
die **Lage, -n**	place; position
die **Reisende, -n**	female traveler
die **Schiene, -n**	train track
die **Unterkunft, ¨-e**	lodging
der **Aufenthaltsraum, ¨-e**	lounge, recreation room
der **Ausweis, -e** (R)	identification card
der **Jugendherbergsausweis, -e**	youth hostel ID card
der **Bahnbeamte, -n** (*wk. masc.*)	male train agent
der **Bahnhof, ¨-e** (R)	train station
der **Fahrkartenschalter, -** (R)	ticket counter
der **Flugschein, -e**	plane ticket
der **Hafen, ¨**	harbor, port
der **Flughafen, ¨** (R)	airport
der **Koffer, -** (R)	suitcase
der **Nichtraucher, -**	nonsmoker
der **Raucher, -**	smoker
der **Reisende, -n** (*wk. masc.*)	male traveler
der **Reisepaß, Reisepässe**	passport
der **Spaziergang, ¨-e**	walk
der **Vulkan, -e**	volcano
der **Wirt, -e**	host, innkeeper; barkeeper
der **Zug, ¨-e** (R)	train
das **Andenken, -**	souvenir
das **Fremdenverkehrsamt, ¨-er**	tourist bureau
das **Gästehaus, ¨-er**	bed and breakfast inn
das **Gepäck**	luggage, baggage
das **Gleis, -e**	(set of) train tracks
das **Ziel, -e**	destination
die **Herbergseltern** (*pl.*)	owners/managers of a youth hostel

Ähnliche Wörter

die **Rezeption, -en;** die **Touristenklasse;** die **Wartehalle, -n** der **Campingplatz, ¨-e** das **Camping, wildes Camping;** das **Doppelzimmer, -;** das **Fernsehzimmer, -;** das **Frühstückszimmer, -;** das **Reisebüro, -s** (R)

Den Weg beschreiben / Giving Directions

ab·biegen, bog ab, ist abgebogen	to turn

entlang·gehen, ging entlang, ist entlanggegangen	to go along
verfehlen	to miss, not notice
vorbei·gehen (an + *dat.*), **ging vorbei, ist vorbeigegangen**	to go by
weiter·fahren, fährt weiter, fuhr weiter, ist weitergefahren	to keep on driving
weiter·gehen, ging weiter, ist weitergegangen	to keep on walking
dorthin	there, to a specific place
entlang	along
gegenüber von (R)	across from
geradeaus	straight ahead
her(·kommen)	(to come) this way (*toward the speaker*)
heraus(·kommen)	(to come) out this way (*toward the speaker*)
herein(·kommen)	(to get/go) in this way (*toward the speaker*)
hin(·gehen)	(to go) that way (*away from the speaker*)
hinauf(·gehen)	(to go) up that way (*away from the speaker*)
hinüber(·gehen)	(to go) over that way (*away from the speaker*)
links	left
oben	above
rechts	right

In der Stadt — In the City

die **Brücke, -n**	bridge
die **Gasse, -n**	narrow street; alley
die **Gegend, -en**	area
der **Dom, -e**	cathedral
der **Kopierladen, ¨**	copy shop
der **Kreisverkehr, -**	traffic roundabout
der **Waschsalon, -s**	laundromat
der **Zebrastreifen, -**	crosswalk

Ähnliche Wörter

die **Altstadt, ¨e**; die **Fußgängerzone, -n**; die **Linie, -n** der **Markt, ¨e**; der **Stadtpark, -s**; der **Stadtplan, ¨e**; der **Zoo, -s** das **Einkaufszentrum, Einkaufszentren**; das **Fußballstadion, Fußballstadien**

Im Kleidungsgeschäft — At the Clothing Store

die **Größe, -n** (R)	size
die **Strumpfhose, -n**	pantyhose
die **Tasche, -n** (R)	pocket; purse, pocketbook
die **Unterwäsche**	underwear
der **Absatz, ¨e**	heel
der **Mantel, ¨** (R)	coat
der **Bademantel, ¨**	bathrobe
der **Pelzmantel, ¨**	fur coat
der **Regenschirm, -e** (R)	umbrella
der **Schal, -s**	scarf
das **Kleidungsstück, -e**	article of clothing
das **Unterhemd, -en**	undershirt
an·probieren	to try on
sich um·sehen, sieht um, sah um, umgesehen	to look around
um·tauschen	to exchange

Ähnliche Wörter

die **Lederjacke, -n**; die **Sandale, -n**; die **Socke, -n**; die **Unterhose, -n** der **Handschuh, -e**; der **Schlafanzug, ¨e** das **Nachthemd, -en**

Sonstige Substantive — Other Nouns

die **Bürgerin, -nen**	female citizen
der **Bürger, -**	male citizen
der **Geschäftsbrief, -e**	business letter
der **Gruß, ¨e**	greeting
mit freundlichen Grüßen	regards
der **Irokesenschnitt, -e**	mohawk haircut
der **Vorfahre, -n**	ancestor
das **Familienmitglied, -er**	family member
das **Treppenhaus, ¨er**	stairwell

Ähnliche Wörter

die **Hälfte, -n**; die **Sandburg, -en** der **Goldring, -e**; der **Staat, -en**; der **Walkman, Walkmen**

Sonstige Verben — Other Verbs

ab·reisen, ist abgereist	to depart
an·zahlen	to pay in advance
sich aus·ruhen	to rest
bauen	to build
begegnen (+ *dat.*), **ist begegnet**	to meet, encounter
ein·steigen (R), **stieg ein, ist eingestiegen**	to board
entscheiden, entschied, entschieden	to decide
sich erkundigen nach	to ask about, get information about
erleben	to experience
erwischen	to catch (*person, train*)

fehlen (+ *dat.*) (R)	to lack, be missing
fest·stellen	to establish
gefallen (+ *dat.*), **gefällt, gefiel, gefallen**	to please, be pleasing to; to like, be to one's liking
es gefällt mir	I like it, it pleases me
gehören (+ *dat.*)	to belong (to)
gratulieren (+ *dat.*) (R)	to congratulate
sich informieren über (+ *akk.*)	to inform oneself about
mit·machen	to participate
nach·sehen, sieht nach, sah nach, nachgesehen	to look up
passen (+ *dat.*)	to fit
schaden (+ *dat.*)	to harm, hurt
schmecken (+ *dat.*)	to taste good (to)
stehen (+ *dat.*), **stand, gestanden**	to suit
sich (*dat.*) **vor·stellen**	to imagine
wiederholen	to repeat
zu·hören (+ *dat.*) (R)	to listen (to)

Ähnliche Wörter

antworten (+ *dat.*) (R); **helfen** (+ *dat.*) (R), **hilft, half, geholfen**

Adjektive und Adverbien — Adjectives and Adverbs

auffällig	conspicuous
flach	flat
geehrt	honored; dear
sehr geehrte Damen und Herren	to whom it may concern, dear Madames and Sirs
sehr geehrter Herr	dear Mr.
sehr geehrte Frau	dear Ms.
gestreift	striped
herzlich	hearty
kariert	plaid
lieb	sweet; lovable
mehrere (*pl.*)	several
modisch	fashionable
nützlich	useful
schriftlich	written
wunderschön	exceedingly beautiful

Ähnliche Wörter

extra, schick, voll, zentral

Sonstige Wörter und Ausdrücke — Other Words and Expressions

an . . . vorbei	by
aus	of; from; out of
außerdem	besides
bei (R)	at; with; near
bis zu	as far as; up to
danach	afterward
eilig	rushed
es eilig haben	to be in a hurry
hin und zurück	there and back; round trip
inbegriffen	included
nach	to (*a place*)
nach Hause	(to) home
ob (R)	whether
selbstverständlich	of course
vielen Dank	many thanks
von (R)	of; from
zu (R)	to (*a place*)
zu Hause	at home
zuletzt	finally

LESEECKE

LEKTÜRE 1

Vor dem Lesen

1. Wohin fahren Sie, wenn Sie die „weite Welt" erleben wollen?
2. Welche „Naturwunder" gibt es in den USA? Wo befinden sie sich?

3. Wie stellen Sie sich eine idyllische Landschaft vor? Zeichnen Sie ein Bild. (Ideen: Wald, Wiese, Berg, Tal, Bach oder Fluß, Vögel, Schmetterlinge,[1] Tiere)
4. Was machen die Leute auf dem Bild unten?
5. Wo ist das? in der Stadt oder in der Natur?

---

[1]*butterflies*

Wem Gott will rechte Gunst[1] erweisen[2]

von Joseph von Eichendorff (1788–1857)

Wem Gott will rechte Gunst erweisen,
Den schickt er in die weite Welt,
Dem will er seine Wunder weisen[3]
In Berg und Tal und Strom und Feld.

5 Die Trägen,[4] die zu Hause liegen,
Erquicket[5] nicht das Morgenrot,
Sie wissen nur von Kinderwiegen,[6]
Von Sorgen,[7] Last[8] und Not[9] um Brot.

Die Bächlein von den Bergen springen,
10 Die Lerchen[10] schwirren hoch vor Lust,
Was sollt' ich nicht mit ihnen singen
Aus voller Kehl'[11] und frischer Brust[12]?

Den lieben Gott laß ich nur walten;[13]
Der Bächlein,[14] Lerchen, Wald und Feld
15 Und Erd' und Himmel will erhalten,[15]
Hat auch mein Sach' aufs best' bestellt![16]

[1]*favor* [2]*show* [3]*show* [4]*idle people* [5]*enlivens* [6]*cradles* [7]*worries* [8]*burdens* [9]*need* [10]*larks* [11]*throat* [12]*chest* [13]*rule* [14]*brooks* [15]*preserve* [16]Hat . . . *is taking good care of me too!*

Arbeit mit dem Text

1. Wie erlebt man in dem Lied die „weite Welt"? Per Zug, per Auto, oder per Fuß? Spekulieren Sie.
2. In dem Lied ist vieles in Bewegung. Ergänzen Sie die Verben.

   a. die Bäche ______________
   b. die Lerchen ______________
   c. der Wanderer ______________

3. Was ist zu Hause? Was ist in der weiten Welt? Ergänzen Sie die Tabelle.

zu Hause	weite Welt

4. Wer spricht?

- ☐ ein Junggeselle[1]
- ☐ ein verheirateter Mann
- ☐ eine verheiratete Frau mit Kindern
- ☐ ein junges Mädchen
- ☐ eine ledige Frau

LEKTÜRE 2

Vor dem Lesen

1. Dieses Gedicht von Kurt Tucholsky hat den Titel „Vornehme[2] Leute, 1200 Meter hoch“. Wie sind vornehme Leute? Kreuzen Sie an.

Österreichisches Luxushotel in Kitzbühel

VORNEHME LEUTE

- ☐ sind reich
- ☐ haben viel Zeit
- ☐ haben einen guten Geschmack
- ☐ haben viel Arbeit
- ☐ sind Aristokraten
- ☐ haben gute Manieren
- ☐ haben Kultur
- ☐ haben eine große Familie
- ☐ treiben viel Sport
- ☐ sind elegant gekleidet

2. Schauen Sie sich das Foto an. Das ist ein „Grandhotel“ in den österreichischen Alpen. Was kann man dort im Urlaub machen?

[1]*bachelor* [2]*refined*

Vornehme Leute, 1200 Meter hoch

von Kurt Tucholsky (1890–1935)

Sie sitzen in den Grandhotels.
Ringsum[1] sind Eis und Schnee.
Ringsum sind Berge und Wald und Fels.
Sie sitzen in den Grandhotels
und trinken immer Tee. (5)

Sie haben ihren Smoking[2] an.
Im Walde klirrt[3] der Frost.
Ein kleines Reh[4] hüpft durch den Tann.[5]
Sie haben ihren Smoking an
und lauern auf[6] die Post. (10)

Sie tanzen Blues im Blauen Saal,
wobei es draußen schneit.
Es blitzt und donnert manches Mal,
Sie tanzen Blues im Blauen Saal
und haben keine Zeit. (15)

Sie schwärmen sehr für[7] die Natur
und heben[8] den Verkehr.
Sie schwärmen sehr für die Natur
und kennen die Umgebung nur
von Ansichtskarten[9] her. (20)

Sie sitzen in den Grandhotels
und sprechen viel von Sport.
Doch einmal treten sie, im Pelz,
sogar vors Tor der Grandhotels—
und fahren wieder fort![10] (25)

[1]*all around* [2]*tuxedo* [3]*is rattling* [4]*deer* [5]*forest of fir trees* [6]lauern . . . *lie in wait for*
[7]schwärmen . . . *rave about* [8]*increase* [9]*picture postcards* [10]fahren . . . fort *depart*

Arbeit mit dem Text

1. Schreiben Sie auf: Was machen die Leute im Grandhotel? Was ist draußen los?

im Grandhotel	draußen

2. Schreiben Sie das Gedicht um. Stellen Sie sich vor, das „Grandhotel" ist in Aspen im US-Bundestaat Colorado oder auf Maui. Was machen prominente Urlauber dort?

STRUKTUREN UND ÜBUNGEN

10.1 Prepositions to talk about places: *aus, bei, nach, von, zu*

Use the prepositions **aus** and **von** to indicate origin; **bei** to indicate a fixed location; and **nach** and **zu** to indicate destination. These five prepositions are always used with nouns and pronouns in the dative case.

Woher (kommt sie?)	*Wo (ist sie?)*	*Wohin (geht/fährt sie?)*
aus Spanien		nach Spanien
aus dem Zimmer		nach Hause
von rechts		nach links
von Erika	bei Erika	zu Erika
vom Strand		zum Strand

A. The Prepositions **aus** and **von**

aus: enclosed spaces
countries
towns
buildings

1. Use **aus** to indicate that someone or something comes from an enclosed or defined space, such as a country, a town, or a building.

Diese Fische kommen aus der Donau. — *These fish come from the Danube river.*
Jens kam aus seinem Zimmer. — *Jens came from his room.*

Most country and city names are neuter; no article is used with these names.

Josef kommt **aus Deutschland.**
Silvia kommt **aus Göttingen.**

However, the article is included when the country name is masculine, feminine, or plural.

Richards Freund Ali kommt **aus dem Iran.**
Mehmets Familie kommt **aus der Türkei.**
Ich komme **aus den USA.**

von: open spaces
directions
persons

2. Use **von** to indicate that someone or something comes not from an enclosed space but from an open space, from a particular direction, or from a person.

Achtung!

von + dem = vom
bei + dem = beim
zu + dem = zum
zu + der = zur

Melanie kommt gerade **vom Markt** zurück.	*Melanie's just returning from the market.*
Das rote Auto kam **von rechts.**	*The red car came from the right.*
Michael hat es mir gesagt. Ich weiß es **von ihm.**	*Michael told me. I know it through (from) him.*

B. The Preposition **bei**

bei: place of work
residence

Use **bei** before the name of the place where someone works or the place where someone lives or is staying.

Albert arbeitet **bei McDonald's.**	*Albert works at McDonald's.*
Rolf wohnt **bei einer Gastfamilie.**	*Rolf is staying with a host family.*
Treffen wir uns **bei Katrin.**	*Let's meet at Katrin's.*

C. The Prepositions **nach** and **zu**

nach: cities
countries without articles
direction
nach Hause (idiom)

Use **nach** with neuter names of cities and countries (no article), to indicate direction, and in the idiom **nach Hause** ([*going*] *home*).

Wir fahren morgen **nach Salzburg.**	*We'll go to Salzburg tomorrow.*
Biegen Sie an der Ampel **nach links ab.**	*Turn left at the light.*
Gehen Sie **nach Westen.**	*Go west.*
Ich muß jetzt **nach Hause.**	*I have to go home now.*

zu: places
persons
zu Hause (idiom)

Use **zu** to indicate movement toward a place or a person, and in the idiom **zu Hause** (*at home*).

Wir fahren heute **zum Strand.**	*We'll go to the beach today.*
Wir gehen morgen **zu Tante Julia.**	*We'll go to Aunt Julia's tomorrow.*

Übung 1 Die Familie Ruf

Kombinieren Sie Fragen und Antworten.

1. Hier kommt Herr Ruf. Er hat seine Hausschuhe an. Woher kommt er gerade?
2. Hans hat noch seine Schultasche auf dem Rücken. Woher kommt er?
3. Frau Ruf kommt mit zwei Taschen voll Obst und Gemüse herein. Woher kommt sie?
4. Jutta kommt herein. Sie hat eine neue Frisur. Woher kommt sie?
5. Gestern abend war Jutta nicht zu Hause. Wo war sie?
6. Ihre Mutter war auch nicht zu Hause. Wo war sie?
7. Morgen geht Herr Ruf aus. Wohin geht er?
8. Hans fährt am Wochenende weg. Wohin fährt er?
9. Frau Ruf ist am Wochenende geschäftlich unterwegs. Wohin fährt sie?
10. Jutta möchte im Sommer mit Billy Urlaub machen. Wohin wollen sie?

a. Aus der Schule.
b. Aus seinem Zimmer.
c. Bei Billy.
d. Bei ihrer Freundin.
e. Nach England.
f. Nach Frankfurt.
g. Vom Friseur.
h. Vom Markt.
i. Zu Herrn Thelen, Karten spielen.
j. Zu seiner Tante.

Übung 2 Melanies Reise nach Dänemark

Beantworten Sie die Fragen. Verwenden Sie die Präpositionen **aus, bei, nach, von** oder **zu.**

MODELL CLAIRE: Wohin bist du gefahren? (Dänemark) →
MELANIE: Nach Dänemark.

1. Wohin genau? (Kopenhagen)
2. Wohin bist du am ersten Tag gegangen? (der Strand)
3. Und deine Freundin Fatima? Wohin ist sie gegangen? (ihre Tante Sule)
4. Woher kommt die Tante deiner Freundin? (die Türkei)
5. Kommt deine Freundin auch aus der Türkei? (nein / der Iran)
6. Am Strand hast du Peter getroffen, nicht? Woher ist der plötzlich gekommen? (das Wasser)
7. Sein Freund war auch dabei, nicht? Woher ist der gekommen? (der Markt)
8. Weißt du, wo die beiden übernachten wollten? (ja / uns)
9. Und wo haben sie übernachtet? (Fatimas Tante)
10. Wohin seid ihr am nächsten Morgen gefahren? (Hause)

10.2 Indirect questions: *Wissen Sie, wo . . . ?*

Indirect questions are dependent clauses that are commonly preceded by an introductory clause such as **Wissen Sie, . . .** or **Ich weiß nicht, ...** Recall that the conjugated verb is in last position in a dependent clause.

Wissen Sie, **wo** die Bibliothek **ist**?	*Do you know where the library is?*
Können Sie mir sagen, **wann** der Zug in München **ankommt**?	*Can you tell me when the train arrives in Munich?*

Indirect questions:
- dependent clause begins with a question word or **ob**
- conjugated verb in the dependent clause appears at the end of the clause

The question word of the direct question functions as a subordinating conjunction in an indirect question.

DIRECT QUESTION: Wie **komme** ich zum Bahnhof?
INDIRECT QUESTION: Ich weiß nicht, **wie** ich zum Bahnhof **komme.**

Use the conjunction **ob** (*whether, if*) when the corresponding direct question does not begin with a question word but with a verb.

DIRECT QUESTION: **Kommt** Michael heute abend?
INDIRECT QUESTION: Ich weiß nicht, **ob** Michael heute abend **kommt.**

Übung 3 Bitte etwas freundlicher!

A. Verwandeln Sie die folgenden direkten Fragen in etwas höflichere indirekte Fragen. Beginnen Sie mit **Wissen Sie, . . .** oder **Können Sie mir sagen, ...**

MODELL Wo ist der Bahnhof? →
Wissen Sie, wo der Bahnhof ist?
oder Können Sie mir sagen, wo der Bahnhof ist?

1. Wann fährt der nächste Zug nach Kassel?
2. Wie lange fährt man nach Kassel?
3. Wie groß ist Kassel?
4. Was gibt es in Kassel zu sehen?
5. Kann man dort gut essen gehen?
6. Gibt es in Kassel eine Universität?
7. Wie groß ist die Universität?
8. Ist es eine gute Universität?
9. Was kann man in Kassel abends machen?
10. Wann fährt der letzte Zug zurück?

B. Ersetzen Sie „Kassel" mit einer Stadt, die Sie kennen, und beantworten Sie jetzt Ihre Fragen.

10.3 Prepositions for giving directions: *an . . . vorbei, bis zu, entlang, gegenüber von, über*

ACCUSATIVE:
entlang (follows the noun)
über (precedes the noun)

A. **entlang** (*along*) and **über** (*over*) + Accusative

Use the prepositions **entlang** and **über** with nouns in the accusative case. Notice that **entlang** follows the noun.

Fahren Sie **den Fluß entlang.** — *Drive along the river.*
Gehen Sie **über den Zebrastreifen.** — *Walk across the crosswalk.*

The preposition **über** may also be used as the equivalent of English *via.*

Der Zug fährt **über** Frankfurt und Hannover nach Hamburg. — *The train goes to Hamburg via Frankfurt and Hanover.*

DATIVE:
an . . . vorbei (encloses the noun)
bis zu (precedes the noun)
gegenüber von (precedes the noun)

B. **an . . . vorbei** (*past*), **bis zu** (*up to, as far as*), **gegenüber von** (*across from*) + Dative

Use **an . . . vorbei, bis zu,** and **gegenüber von** with the noun in the dative case. Notice that **an . . . vorbei** encloses the noun.

Gehen Sie **am Lebensmittelgeschäft vorbei.** — *Go past the grocery store.*
Fahren Sie **bis zur Fußgängerzone** und biegen Sie links ab. — *Drive to the pedestrian mall and turn left.*
Die U-Bahnhaltestelle ist **gegenüber vom Markthotel.** — *The subway station is across from the Markthotel.*

Übung 4 Wie komme ich dahin?

Ein Ortsfremder[1] fragt Sie nach dem Weg. Antworten Sie! Nützliche Wörter:

entlang	an . . . vorbei	gegenüber von
über	bis . . . zu	

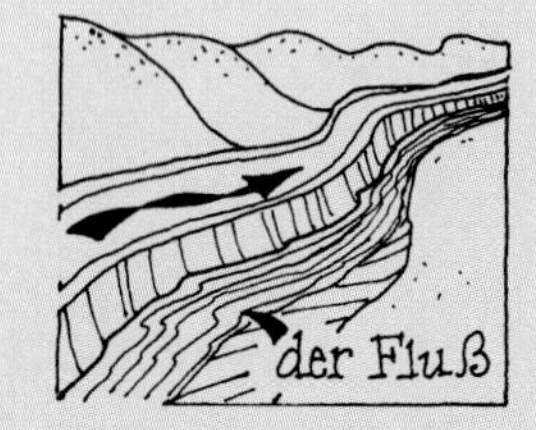

1. Wie muß ich fahren?

2. Wie muß ich gehen?

3. Wie muß ich gehen?

4. Wie muß ich fahren?

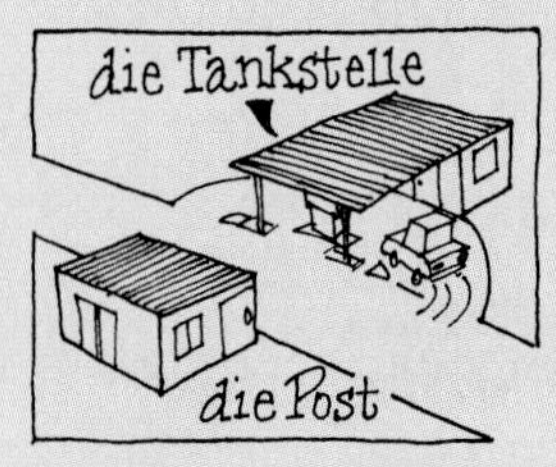

5. Wo ist die Tankstelle?

6. Wie komme ich zum Zug?

7. Immer geradeaus?

8. Vor dem Rathaus links?

9. Das Hotel „Patrizier"?

10. Wie komme ich nach Nürnberg?

10.4 Expressing possibility: *würde* + infinitive

würde = *would*

Use the construction **würde** + infinitive to talk about possibilities: things you would do, if you were in that particular situation.

Stell dir vor, du würdest nach Deutschland fliegen.	*Imagine you were flying to Germany.*
Wo würdest du übernachten?	*Where would you stay for the night?*

Here are the forms of **würde,** which are the subjunctive forms of the verb **werden.**

[1] *stranger*

werden			
ich	würde	wir	würden
du	würdest	ihr	würdet
Sie	würden	Sie	würden
er / sie / es	würde	sie	würden

Übung 5 Eine Deutschlandreise

Stellen Sie sich vor, Sie würden nach Deutschland reisen! Was würden Sie tun?

MODELL wie nach Deutschland / fliegen, schwimmen, mit dem Schiff →
Ich würde nach Deutschland fliegen.

1. wo übernachten / Zelt, Jugendherberge, bei Freunden, _____
2. welche Stadt zuerst / Berlin, München, Regensburg, _____
3. wohin zuerst / ins Museum, in eine Kneipe, in eine Kirche, _____
4. wo essen / in der Mensa, in einem griechischen Restaurant, bei meinen Freunden, _____
5. was am Abend / durch die Stadt bummeln,[1] ins Kino gehen, schlafen, _____
6. was kaufen / ein Stück der Berliner Mauer, einen Bierkrug, eine Trachtenjacke,[2] _____
7. wem Postkarten schreiben / meinen Eltern, allen meinen Freunden, meinem Deutschlehrer / meiner Deutschlehrerin, _____
8. wie lange bleiben / ein paar Tage, eine Woche, ein Jahr, _____

Übung 6 Kein Problem!

Was würden Sie in diesen Situationen machen? Beantworten Sie die Fragen!

Was würden Sie machen,

1. wenn Sie Ihr Deutschbuch verlieren würden?
2. wenn Sie eine sehr schlechte Note bekommen würden?
3. wenn Sie vergessen hätten, was Ihre Hausaufgaben sind?
4. wenn Ihre Eltern Sie morgen plötzlich besuchen würden?
5. wenn Ihre Eltern Ihnen kein Geld geben würden?
6. wenn Sie im Sommer keine Arbeit finden würden?
7. wenn Ihr Freund / Ihre Freundin betrunken Auto fahren wollte?
8. wenn Ihr Freund / Ihre Freundin nicht mehr Ihr Freund / Ihre Freundin sein wollte?
9. wenn ein Filmstar Sie auf seine / ihre Jacht einladen würde?
10. wenn Sie jemand um Ihr Autogramm bitten würde?

---

[1] *to stroll* [2] *traditional folk jacket*

10.5 Dative verbs

The dative object usually indicates the person to whom or for whom something is done. The dative case can be seen as the partner case. The "something" that is done (or given) is in the accusative case (it is the direct object).

Ich schenke **dir ein Buch.**	*I'll give you a book. (I'll give a book to you.)*
Ich kaufe **meinem Bruder ein Buch.**	*I'll buy my brother a book. (I'll buy a book for my brother.)*

"Dative" verbs are verbs that require a dative object.

Certain verbs, called "dative verbs," require only a subject and a dative object; there is no accusative object. These verbs fall into two groups.

In Group 1, both the subject and the dative object are persons.

antworten (*to answer*)	Er antwortete mir nicht.	*He didn't answer me.*
begegnen (*to meet*)	Wir begegneten einem alten Mann.	*We met an old man.*
gratulieren (*to congratulate*)	Ich gratuliere dir zum Geburtstag.	*Happy Birthday! (I congratulate you on your birthday.)*
helfen (*to help*)	Soll ich dir helfen?	*Do you want me to help you?*
zuhören (*to listen*)	Ich höre dir genau zu.	*I'm listening to you carefully.*

In Group 2, the subject is usually a thing; the dative object is the person who experiences or owns the thing.

gehören (*to belong to*)	Diese Schallplatten gehören mir.	*These records belong to me.*
passen (*to fit*)	Diese Hose paßt mir nicht.	*These pants don't fit me.*
schaden (*to be harmful to*)	Rauchen schadet der Gesundheit.	*Smoking is bad for (damages) your health.*
schmecken (*to taste good to*)	Schmeckt Ihnen der Fisch?	*Does the fish taste good to you?*
stehen (*to suit*)	Blau steht dir gut.	*Blue suits you well.*

Note that the following Group 2 verbs express ideas that are rendered very differently in English.

fehlen (*to be missing*)	Mir fehlt ein Buch.	*I'm missing a book.*
gefallen (*to be to one's liking, to please*)	Gefällt Ihnen dieses Bild?	*Do you like this picture? (Does this picture please you?)*

Übung 7 Minidialoge

Ergänzen Sie das Verb. Nützliche Wörter:

antworten	gehören	schaden
begegnen	gratulieren	schmecken
fehlen	helfen	stehen
gefallen	passen	zuhören

1. MONIKA: Schau, ich habe mir eine neue Bluse gekauft.
   KATRIN: Die ist aber schön! Die _____ mir gut!
2. MARTA: Hallo, Willi. Ich habe gehört, du hast deine Prüfung bestanden. Ich _____ dir ganz herzlich.
   WILLI: Danke. Das ist aber lieb von dir.
3. FRAU RUF: Jochen, kannst du mir bitte _____ ? Ich kann nicht alles allein tragen.
   HERR RUF: Ja, ich komme.
4. FRAU GRETTER: _____ Ihnen der Salat?
   HERR SIEBERT: Ja, sehr gut, die Soße ist ausgezeichnet.
5. FRAU KÖRNER: Dieser Rock _____ mir nicht. Ich glaube, ich brauche doch eine Nummer größer.
   VERKÄUFER: Ich seh mal nach, ob wir noch eine Nummer größer haben.
6. JÜRGEN: Weißt du, wem dieser Schal _____ ? Jemand hat ihn gestern hier liegengelassen.
   SILVIA: Aber Jürgen, das ist doch dein Schal! Ich habe ihn dir gestern geschenkt!
7. FRAU SCHULZ: Was suchst du Albert? _____ dir etwas?
   ALBERT: Ja, ich kann mein Heft nicht finden.
8. FRAU KÖRNER: Wissen Sie, wer mir gestern _____ ist, Herr Siebert?
   HERR SIEBERT: Nein, wer denn?
   FRAU KÖRNER: Die Mutter von Maria. Und wissen Sie, was die mir erzählt hat?
   HERR SIEBERT: Nein, was denn?
   FRAU KÖRNER: Also, . . .
9. ARZT: Also, Herr Ruf, Sie müssen jetzt wirklich mit dem Rauchen aufhören. Nikotin _____ Ihrer Gesundheit!
   HERR RUF: Aber, Herr Doktor, dann habe ich ja gar keine Freude mehr im Leben.
10. STEFAN: Entschuldigung, Frau Schulz, ich habe Ihnen nicht _____ . Können Sie das nochmal wiederholen?
    FRAU SCHULZ: Na, gut.

Übung 8 Interview

1. Wem haben Sie neulich zum Geburtstag gratuliert?
2. Wem sind Sie neulich begegnet?
3. Welches Essen schmeckt Ihnen am besten?
4. Wie steht Ihnen Ihr Lieblingshemd?
5. Wie gefällt Ihnen der Deutschkurs?

Alte Apotheke in Salzburg

Kapitel 11 focuses on health and fitness. You will talk about how to stay fit and about illness and accidents.

Gesundheit und Krankheit

THEMEN
Krankheit
Körperteile und Körperpflege
Arzt, Apotheke, Krankenhaus
Unfälle

LEKTÜRE
„Montagmorgengeschichte"
„Warten auf die Seuche"

KULTURELLES
Hausmittel
Körperpflege
Die Krankenkasse
Kulturprojekt: Naturwissenschaft und Medizin
Porträt: Karl Landsteiner und Wien
Videoecke: Charly hat Masern

STRUKTUREN
11.1 Accusative reflexive pronouns
11.2 Dative reflexive pronouns
11.3 Word order of accusative and dative objects
11.4 Requests and instructions: the imperative (summary review)
11.5 Word order in dependent and independent clauses (summary review)

SPRECHSITUATIONEN

Krankheit

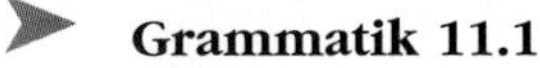

➤ **Grammatik 11.1**

Stefan hat sich erkältet.

Er fühlt sich nicht wohl.

Er hat Husten.

Er hat Schnupfen.

Er hat Kopfschmerzen.

Er hat Halsschmerzen.

Und er hat Fieber.

Er darf sich nicht aufregen.

Er muß sich ins Bett legen.

Er muß sich ausruhen.

Situation 1 Hausmittel[1]

Was machen Sie immer (manchmal, nie)?

1. Wenn ich Fieber habe,

- **a.** lege ich mich ins Bett.
- **b.** nehme ich zwei Aspirin.
- **c.** gehe ich zum Arzt.
- **d.** rege ich mich auf.

2. Wenn ich Husten habe,

- **a.** nehme ich Hustensaft.
- **b.** trinke ich heißen Tee mit Zitrone.
- **c.** rauche ich eine Zigarette.
- **d.** lutsche ich Hustenbonbons.

3. Wenn ich mich erkältet habe,

- **a.** gehe ich schwimmen.
- **b.** ruhe ich mich aus.
- **c.** gehe ich in die Sauna.
- **d.** ärgere ich mich furchtbar.

4. Wenn ich Kopfschmerzen habe,

- **a.** gehe ich zum Friseur.
- **b.** nehme ich zwei Aspirin.
- **c.** bleibe ich im Bett.
- **d.** nehme ich ein heißes Bad.

---

[1]*home remedies*

5. Wenn ich Zahnschmerzen habe,
   - a. trinke ich heißen Kaffee.
   - b. gehe ich zum Zahnarzt.
   - c. nehme ich Tabletten.
   - d. setze ich mich aufs Sofa.
6. Wenn ich mich verletzt habe,
   - a. desinfiziere ich die Wunde.
   - b. falle ich in Ohnmacht.
   - c. hole ich ein Pflaster.
   - d. ziehe ich mich aus.
7. Wenn ich Halsschmerzen habe,
   - a. trinke ich heißen Tee mit Zitrone.
   - b. lutsche ich Halsbonbons.
   - c. gehe ich zum Zahnarzt.
   - d. fahre ich ins Krankenhaus.
8. Wenn ich mich in den Finger geschnitten habe,
   - a. ärgere ich mich furchtbar.
   - b. hole ich ein Pflaster.
   - c. nehme ich Hustensaft.
   - d. desinfiziere ich die Wunde.
9. Wenn ich mich nicht wohl fühle,
   - a. gehe ich ins Kino.
   - b. lege ich mich ins Bett.
   - c. gehe ich zum Arzt.
   - d. gehe ich in die Sauna.
10. Wenn ich Magenschmerzen habe,
    - a. lege ich mich aufs Sofa.
    - b. trinke ich Kamillentee.
    - c. ziehe ich mich aus.
    - d. esse ich einen Salat.

Kultur ... Landeskunde ... Informationen

Hausmittel

- Welche von diesen Hausmitteln kennen Sie? Wogegen helfen sie?

  - ☐ Eisbeutel
  - ☐ grüner Tee
  - ☐ Hühnersuppe
  - ☐ Kamillentee
  - ☐ Knoblauch
  - ☐ heißer Tee mit Zitrone
  - ☐ warme Umschläge
  - ☐ Salzwasser

- Benutzen Sie Hausmittel, wenn Sie sich nicht wohl fühlen? Wenn ja, welche?

Schauen Sie sich die Bilder an, und lesen Sie den Text.

- Was tut die Frau gegen ihre Erkältung?
- Wieviel grünen Tee muß man jeden Tag trinken, um die Cholesterinwerte zu senken?
- Wann beginnt dieses Hausmittel zu wirken?

[1] *cholesterol level* [2] *exclusively* [3] *dependent on* [4] *just* [5] *however* [6] *not until* [7] treten . . . auf *happen, take place* [8] *level of fat in one's blood*

Grüner Tee ist gut gegen Cholesterin

Wer Probleme mit erhöhten Cholesterinwerten[1] hat, ist nun nicht länger ausschließlich[2] auf Medikamente angewiesen.[3] Auch grüner Tee kann den Spiegel von Fetten im Blut senken. Dies ergaben Studien japanischer Wissenschaftler.

Bereits[4] ein täglicher Konsum von fünf Gramm senkt den Cholesterin- und Triglyceridspiegel im Blut wieder auf Normalniveau. Allerdings[5] treten diese Wirkungen erst[6] nach sieben Monaten Teegenuß auf.[7]

Gesund: Grüner Tee senkt den Blutfettspiegel[8]

Situation 2 Was tut dir weh?

MODELL Du warst in einem Rockkonzert. → Ich habe Ohrenschmerzen.

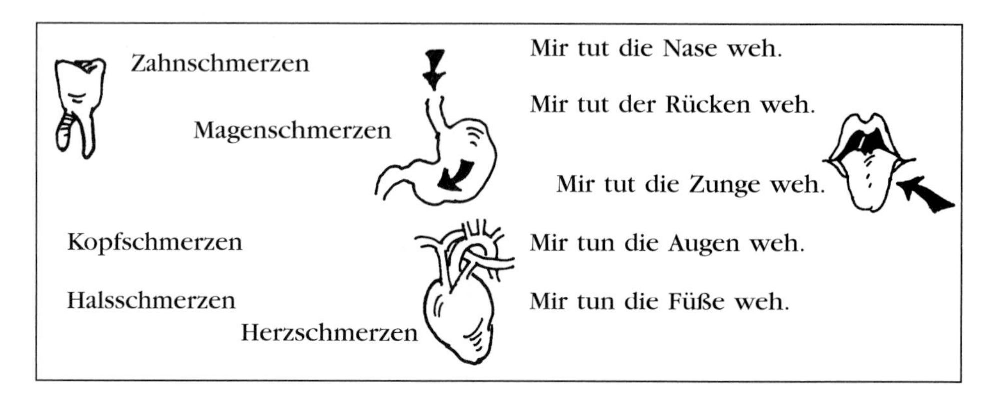

1. Du hast den ganzen Tag in der Bibliothek gesessen und Bücher gelesen.
2. Du hast zwei große Teller Chili gegessen.
3. Jemand hat dich auf die Nase geschlagen.
4. Du bist 20 Kilometer gewandert.
5. Du hast gestern abend zuviel Kaffee getrunken.
6. Du warst in einem Footballspiel und hast viel geschrien.
7. Du hast zu viele Bonbons gegessen.
8. Du hast furchtbaren Liebeskummer.
9. Du hast zwei Stunden Schnee geschaufelt.
10. Der Kaffee, den du getrunken hast, war zu heiß.

Situation 3 Umfrage

MODELL S1: Legst du dich ins Bett, wenn du dich erkältet hast?
S2: Ja.
S1: Unterschreib bitte hier.

	UNTERSCHRIFT
1. Ruhst du dich aus, wenn du Kopfschmerzen hast?	________
2. Ärgerst du dich, wenn du in den Ferien krank wirst?	________
3. Legst du dich ins Bett, wenn du eine Grippe hast?	________
4. Bist du gegen Katzen allergisch?	________
5. Hast du einen niedrigen Blutdruck?	________
6. Freust du dich, wenn dein Professor / deine Professorin krank ist?	________
7. Regst du dich auf, wenn du dich verletzt hast?	________
8. Nimmst du Aspirin, wenn du Kopfschmerzen hast?	________
9. Erkältest du dich oft?	________
10. Nimmst du Tabletten, wenn du dich nicht wohl fühlst?	________

Körperteile und Körperpflege

➤ **Grammatik 11.2–11.3**

Ich wasche mich.

Ich wasche mir die Haare.

Ich trockne mich ab.

Ich trockne mir die Hände ab.

Ich kämme mir die Haare.

Ich schminke mich.

Ich rasiere mich.

Ich putze mir die Zähne.

Ich ziehe mich an.

Situation 4 Körperteile

MODELL S1: Was macht man mit den Augen?
S2: Mit den Augen sieht man.

1. mit den Ohren
2. mit den Händen
3. mit dem Gehirn
4. mit der Nase
5. mit der Lunge
6. mit den Zähnen
7. mit den Lippen
8. mit den Beinen
9. mit dem Mund
10. mit dem Herzen

Situation 5 Körperpflege

1. Wenn meine Haut trocken ist,
   - a. kreme ich sie ein.
   - b. gehe ich schwimmen.
   - c. gehe ich zum Arzt.
2. Wenn meine Fingernägel lang sind,
   - a. bade ich mich.
   - b. schneide ich sie mir.
   - c. kaue ich sie ab.
3. Wenn meine Haare fettig sind,
   - a. putze ich mir die Zähne.
   - b. schneide ich sie mir.
   - c. wasche ich sie mir.
4. Wenn ich ins Theater gehe,
   - a. schminke ich mich.
   - b. rasiere ich mich.
   - c. schneide ich mir die Haare.
5. Wenn ich ins Bett gehe,
   - a. ziehe ich mir warme Schuhe an.
   - b. putze ich mir die Zähne.
   - c. schneide ich mir die Fingernägel.
6. Wenn ich mich geduscht habe,
   - a. ziehe ich mich aus.
   - b. trockne ich mich ab.
   - c. föne ich mir die Haare.
7. Wenn ich mich erholen will,
   - a. gehe ich in die Sauna.
   - b. rasiere ich mir die Beine.
   - c. nehme ich Tabletten.
8. Wenn es draußen kalt ist,
   - a. dusche ich mich heiß.
   - b. ziehe ich mir eine warme Hose an.
   - c. ziehe ich mich aus.
9. Wenn ich eine Verabredung habe,
   - a. schminke ich mich.
   - b. wasche ich mir die Haare.
   - c. esse ich viel Knoblauch.

Situation 6 Bildgeschichte: Maria hat eine Verabredung.

Kultur ... Landeskunde ... Informationen

Körperpflege

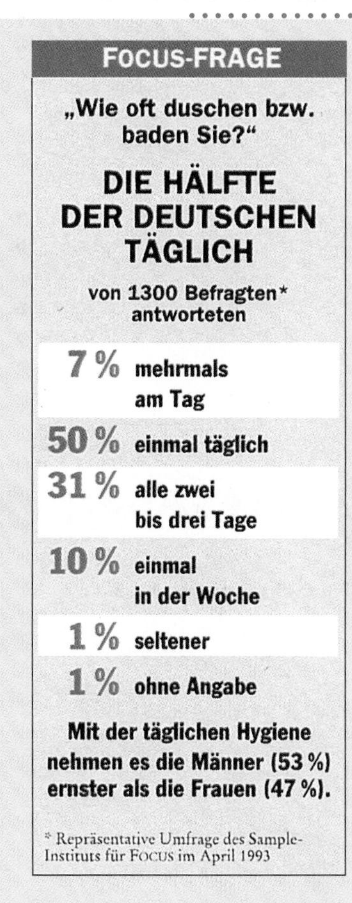

- Wie oft duscht oder badet der typische Amerikaner? Kreuzen Sie an.

  □ jeden Tag □ alle zwei bis drei Tage □ einmal pro Woche

- Die Hälfte der Deutschen duscht täglich. Was meinen Sie, wieviel Prozent der Amerikaner duschen täglich?
- Wer in Deutschland achtet nach Statistik mehr auf Hygiene, Männer oder Frauen? Wie ist das in den USA? Begründen Sie Ihre Antwort.
- Lesen Sie die Werbung für den Rasierapparat. Wer sagt: „Ich dachte, du verschenkst nichts Praktisches."

„Ich dachte, du verschenkst nichts Praktisches."

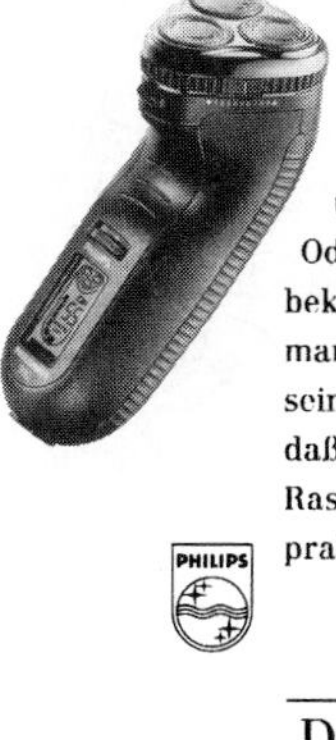

Da nimmt man sich etwas vor und bricht dann wieder seine Prinzipien. Weil man Wert darauf legt, daß er sich gründlich und zugleich hautschonend rasiert. Oder daß er den leisesten Philishave bekommt, den es je gab. Oder weil man selbst etwas davon spüren möchte: seine sanfte Haut nämlich. Übrigens, daß ihm der meistgekaufte Elektro-Rasierer Europas nicht gefällt, ist praktisch unmöglich.

PHILIPS

- Ergänzen Sie die Lücken mit folgenden Wörtern aus der Anzeige:

  Elektro-Rasierer, gründlich, leiseste, sanfte.

  Der Mann soll sich _____ und hautschonend rasieren.
  Die Frau möchte seine _____ Haut spüren.
  Dieser Rasierapparat ist der _____ Philishave, den es je gab.
  Der Philishave ist der meistgekaufte _____ Europas.

Situation 7 Interview: Körperpflege

1. (für Frauen) Schminkst du dich jeden Tag? Was machst du?
2. (für Männer) Rasierst du dich jeden Tag? Hattest du schon mal einen Bart? Was für einen? Wie war das? Wenn du einen Bart hast: Seit wann hast du einen Bart?
3. Wäschst du dir jeden Tag die Haare? Fönst du sie dir auch? Was für Haar hast du (trockenes, fettiges, normales Haar)?
4. Putzt du dir jeden Tag die Zähne? Gehst du oft zum Zahnarzt?
5. Wie oft gehst du zum Friseur? Hattest du mal eine Dauerwelle? Wie hast du ausgesehen?
6. Hast du trockene Haut? Kremst du dich oft ein?
7. Treibst du regelmäßig Sport? Was machst du? Wie oft? Gehst du manchmal in die Sauna oder ins Solarium?

Arzt, Apotheke, Krankenhaus

➤ **Grammatik 11.4**

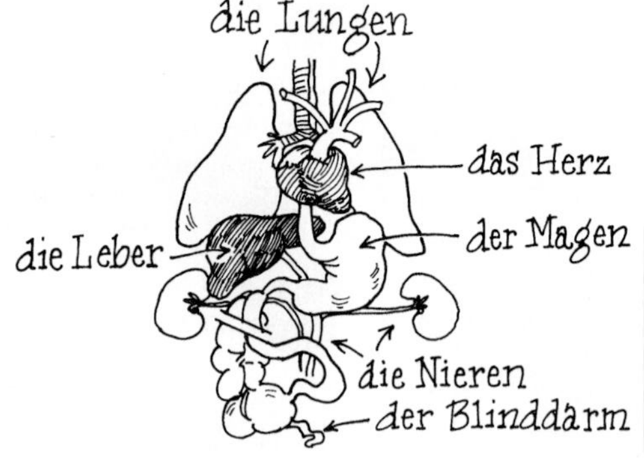

Jürgen hat sich das Bein gebrochen. Jetzt muß er einen Gips tragen.

Silvia bekommt eine Spritze.

Josef bekommt einen Verband.

Der Zahnarzt zieht Melanie einen Zahn.

Die Ärztin gibt Claire ein Rezept.

Situation 8 Medizinische Berufe

Wohin gehen Sie?

ins Krankenhaus	zum Hausarzt	zum Psychiater	in die Apotheke
in die Drogerie	zum Zahnarzt	zum Augenarzt	zum Tierarzt

1. Sie haben sich erkältet und brauchen Hustensaft.
2. Sie haben schon seit zwei Wochen eine schlimme Halsentzündung und wollen Antibiotika.
3. Ihr Freund / Ihre Freundin hat sich in den Finger geschnitten. Der Finger blutet stark.
4. Ihr Freund / Ihre Freundin hat Sie verlassen, und Sie sind sehr deprimiert.
5. Ihr Goldfisch frißt schon seit mehreren Tagen nicht mehr.
6. Sie haben furchtbare Zahnschmerzen.
7. Sie können im Unterricht nicht lesen, was an der Tafel steht.
8. Ihr Arzt hat Ihnen ein Rezept geschrieben, und Sie wollen sich das Medikament abholen.

Situation 9 Interaktion: Ich bin krank.

Ein Mitstudent / Eine Mitstudentin ist krank. Was raten Sie ihm/ihr?

MODELL S1: Ich habe Fieber.
S2: Leg dich ins Bett.

1. Ich habe Fieber.
2. Ich habe Kopfschmerzen.
3. Ich fühle mich nicht wohl.
4. Ich habe starken Husten.
5. Ich habe mich in den Finger geschnitten.
6. Ich habe mich erkältet.
7. Ich habe Zahnschmerzen.
8. Ich bin allergisch gegen Katzen.
9. Mir tun die Augen weh.
10. Ich habe Magenschmerzen.

a. Geh zum Arzt.
b. Nimm Hustensaft.
c. Leg dich ins Bett.
d. Geh nach Hause.
e. Kauf dir Kopfschmerztabletten.
f. Ruh dich aus.
g. Nimm ein warmes Bad.
h. Zieh dich warm an.
i. Verkauf deine Katze.
j. Geh zum Zahnarzt.
k. Kauf dir eine Brille.
l. _____ ?

Kultur... Landeskunde... Informationen

Die Krankenkasse

- Haben Sie eine Krankenversicherung?
- Müssen Sie nach einem Arztbesuch etwas bezahlen?
- Wissen Sie, wieviel der Arzt für die Behandlung[1] bekommt?

AOK - Die Gesundheitskasse.
AOK
Franz Mustermann
VERSICHERTEN KARTE
1234567 123456789012 1234 5 1096
Kasse Versichertennummer Status gültig bis

Diese Karte geben die Patienten beim Arzt ab. Die Informationen werden elektronisch gespeichert,[2] und der Arzt rechnet nach der Behandlung mit der Krankenkasse ab.[3] Der Patient muß nichts bezahlen und erfährt auch nicht, was die Behandlung gekostet hat.

Sie hören jetzt einen kurzen Text über die Krankenkasse. Hören Sie gut zu, und ergänzen Sie die Sätze.

- „Krankenkasse" ist ein anderes Wort für _____ .
- Der monatliche Beitrag[4] ist _____% vom Verdienst.[5]
- Die Krankenkasse bezahlt _____ .
- Für Arbeitnehmer, die weniger als _____ Mark im Monat verdienen, ist die Krankenversicherung Pflicht.[6]

[1]*treatment* [2]*stored* [3]rechnet . . . ab *settles* [4]*contribution* [5]*earnings* [6]*mandatory*

Situation 10 Informationsspiel: Krankheitsgeschichte

MODELL Hat Claire sich (Hast du dir) schon mal etwas gebrochen? Was?
Ist Claire (Bist du) schon mal im Krankenhaus gewesen? Warum?
Hat Herr Thelen (Hast du) schon mal eine Spritze bekommen? Gegen was?
Erkältet sich Herr Thelen (Erkältest du dich) oft?
Ist Claire (Bist du) gegen etwas allergisch? Gegen was?
Hat man Claire (Hat man dir) schon mal einen Zahn gezogen?
Hatte Herr Thelen (Hattest du) schon mal hohes Fieber? Wie hoch?
Ist Claire (Bist du) schon mal in Ohnmacht gefallen?

	Claire	Herr Thelen	mein(e) Partner(in)
sich etwas brechen		das Bein	
im Krankenhaus sein		Lungenentzündung	
eine Spritze bekommen	Diphtherie		
oft erkältet sein	ja		
gegen etwas allergisch sein		Katzen	
einen Zahn gezogen haben		ja	
hohes Fieber haben	104° F		
in Ohnmacht fallen		nein	

Situation 11 Dialoge

1. Herr Thelen möchte einen Termin beim Arzt.

HERR THELEN: Guten Tag, ich hätte gern ________ für nächste Woche.
SPRECHSTUNDENHILFE: Gern, vormittags oder nachmittags?
HERR THELEN: Das ist mir eigentlich ___.
SPRECHSTUNDENHILFE: Mittwochmorgen um neun?
HERR THELEN: Ja, ________. Vielen Dank.

2. Frau Körner geht in die Apotheke.

FRAU KÖRNER: Ich habe schon seit Tagen ___________. Können Sie mir etwas ______ geben?
APOTHEKERIN: Wir haben gerade etwas ganz Neues bekommen, Magenex.
FRAU KÖRNER: Hauptsache, _________.
APOTHEKERIN: Es soll sehr gut ____. Hier ist es.

3. Frau Frisch ist bei ihrem Hausarzt.

HAUSARZT: Guten Tag, Frau Frisch, wie geht es Ihnen?
FRAU FRISCH: Ich fühle mich gar nicht wohl. ______________ . . . alles tut mir weh.
HAUSARZT: Das klingt nach ____. Sagen Sie mal bitte „Ah".

Situation 12 Rollenspiel: Anruf beim Arzt

S1: Sie fühlen sich nicht gut. Wahrscheinlich haben Sie Grippe. Rufen Sie beim Arzt an, und lassen Sie sich einen Termin geben. Es ist dringend, aber Sie haben einen vollen Stundenplan.

Situation 13 Interview

1. Warst du schon mal schwer krank? Wann? Was hat dir gefehlt?
2. Warst du schon mal im Krankenhaus? Wann? Warum? Wie lange? Hat man dich untersucht? Hat man dir Blut abgenommen? Hast du eine Spritze bekommen?
3. Hast du dir schon mal was gebrochen? Was? Hattest du einen Gips? Wie lange?
4. Hat man dich schon mal geröntgt? Wann? Warum?
5. Erkältest du dich oft? Was machst du, wenn du eine Erkältung hast?
6. Bist du gegen etwas allergisch? Gegen was?

Unfälle

➤ **Grammatik 11.5**

Zwei Autos sind zusammengestoßen. Eine Frau ist schwer verletzt.

Situation 14 Ein Autounfall

Eine Polizistin spricht mit einem Zeugen über einen Unfall. Bringen Sie die Sätze in eine logische Reihenfolge.

_____ Wie spät war es ungefähr?
_____ Also, heute morgen war ich auf dem Weg zur Uni.
__1__ Bitte erzählen Sie genau, was passiert ist.
_____ Ein Auto ist aus einer Einfahrt gekommen.
_____ Ich glaube nicht, er hat jedenfalls nicht gebremst, bevor er auf die Straße gefahren ist.
_____ Hat der Fahrer auf den Verkehr geachtet?
_____ Ja, ein anderes Auto kam von rechts, und dann sind sie zusammengestoßen.
_____ So zwischen halb und Viertel vor neun.
_____ Was haben Sie da gesehen?
_____ Und dann?
_____ Vielen Dank für Ihre Hilfe.

Situation 15 Unfälle

Welcher Satz paßt zu welchem Bild?

1. Michael und Maria waren beim Segeln, als das Boot umkippte.
2. Sofie schnitt gerade Tomaten, als plötzlich vor ihrem Haus ein Mann von einem Auto überfahren wurde.
3. Melanie und Josef waren auf dem Weg ins Konzert, als Melanie ausrutschte und hinfiel.
4. Jürgen saß gerade in der Bibliothek, als auf der Straße zwei Autos zusammenstießen.
5. Herr Frisch fuhr gerade zur Arbeit, als ihm ein Hund vors Auto lief.
6. Als Ernst mit seinen Freunden Fußball spielte, brach er sich das Bein.
7. Marta und ihr Freund liefen Schlittschuh, als ein Kind ins Eis einbrach.
8. Rolf wollte gerade nach Hawaii fliegen, als ein Flugzeug abstürzte.

Situation 16 Notfälle

Was machen Sie, wenn . . .

1. Sie einen Unfall sehen?
2. der Verletzte einen Schock hat?
3. der Fahrer von dem anderen Auto flüchtet?
4. Sie im Fahrstuhl steckenbleiben?
5. Sie ausrutschen und hinfallen?
6. Sie sich den Arm gebrochen haben?
7. Sie ins Wasser fallen?
8. es im Nachbarhaus brennt?
9. Sie sich die Zunge verbrannt haben?

a. den Krankenwagen rufen
b. die Feuerwehr rufen
c. die Autonummer aufschreiben
d. die Polizei rufen
e. eine Decke holen und den Verletzten zudecken
f. fluchen
g. liegenbleiben und warten, daß jemand kommt
h. schwimmen
i. um Hilfe rufen
j. _____ ?

Situation 17 Paulas Unfall

Situation 18 Zum Schreiben: So ist das passiert.

Beschreiben Sie einen Unfall, den Sie einmal hatten oder gesehen haben. Was ist passiert? Wer war dabei? Was haben Sie gemacht?

Kulturprojekt Naturwissenschaft und Medizin

A. Suchen Sie Informationen zu zwei der folgenden Wissenschaftler und Wissenschaftlerinnen.

Emil von Behring
Hans Berger
Paul Ehrlich
Sigmund Freud
Felix Hoffmann
Albert Hofmann
Robert Koch
Konrad Lorenz
Lise Meitner
Gregor Johann Mendel
Margarete Mitscherlich
Wilhelm Conrad Röntgen

- Wann haben sie gelebt? / Wann sind sie geboren?
- Aus welchem Land stammen/stammten sie?
- Was sind/waren sie von Beruf?
- Was haben sie entdeckt oder entwickelt? Woran haben sie gearbeitet?

B. Kennen Sie diese deutschsprachigen Hersteller von Medikamenten und Kosmetika? Welche Produkte von diesen Firmen sind Ihnen bekannt? In welcher Stadt haben diese Firmen Ihren Hauptsitz?

BASF
Bayer
Beiersdorf
Chemie Linz AG
Ciba-Geigy
Hoechst
Sandoz
Weleda
Schering

Porträt

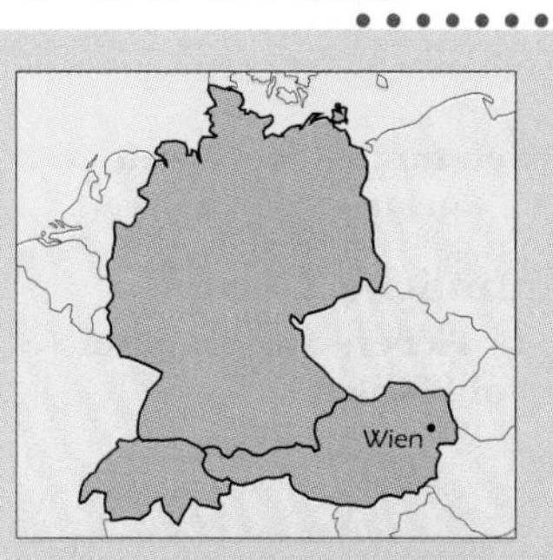

Der Arzt Karl Landsteiner (1868–1943) wurde in Wien geboren und begann dort seine Karriere als Bakteriologe. 1919 wanderte er zuerst nach Holland und später in die USA aus. Von 1922 bis 1943 war er Mitglied des „Rockefeller Institute for Medical Research". Für die Entdeckung der Blutgruppen erhielt[1] er 1930 den Nobelpreis. Zusammen mit dem Amerikaner Alexander S. Wiener entdeckte er 1940 den Rhesusfaktor.

Wien, die Hauptstadt von Österreich, liegt an der Donau und ist das politische, wirtschaftliche, administrative und kulturelle Zentrum des Landes. Seit dem Sieg[2] über die Türken, die 1683 Wien belagerten,[3] wurde die Stadt unter den Habsburgern zur Kaiserstadt[4] und zum Zentrum der österreich-ungarischen Monarchie. Die Komponisten Haydn, Mozart und Beethoven wurden als Wiener Klassiker weltberühmt. (Keiner der drei wurde übrigens[5] in Wien geboren.) Zu den bekanntesten Wahrzeichen[6] der Stadt gehören der Stephansdom und der Prater, ein berühmter Vergnügungspark auf der ehemaligen[7] Donauinsel.

[1] *received* [2] *victory* [3] *laid siege to* [4] *imperial city* [5] *by the way* [6] *landmarks* [7] *former*

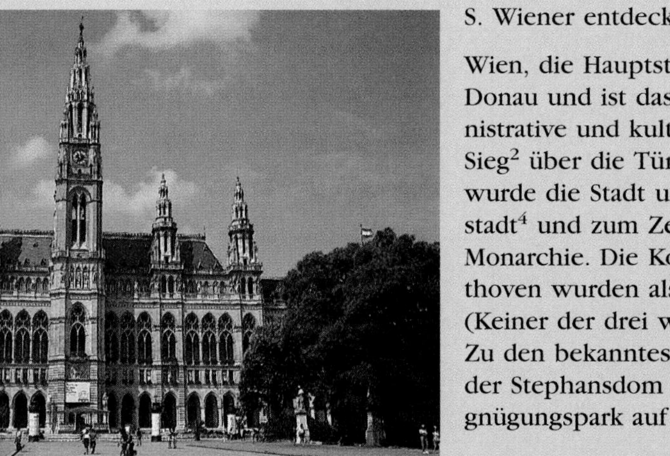

Das Wiener Rathaus

VIDEOECKE

Charly hat Masern[1]

Oje, irgendjemand muß mich heute nacht angemalt[3] haben.

Der arme Charly! Er hat die Masern. Der Zeichentrickfilm[2] erzählt, wie man aussieht und was passieren kann, wenn man die Masern hat.

- Wie fühlt sich Charly?
- Wie lange dauert seine Krankheit?
- Warum darf er nicht mehr in die Schule gehen?
- Warum dürfen seine Freunde ihn besuchen?

[1] *measles* [2] *cartoon* [3] *painted*

WORTSCHATZ

Krankheit und Gesundheit — Illness and Health

die **Entzündung, -en**	infection
die **Lungenentzündung**	pneumonia
die **Nierenentzündung**	kidney infection
die **Erkältung, -en**	(head) cold
die **Gesundheit**	health
die **Grippe**	influenza, flu
die **Krankheit, -en**	illness, sickness
die **Ohnmacht**	unconsciousness
in Ohnmacht fallen	to faint
der **Blutdruck**	blood pressure
niedrigen/hohen Blutdruck haben	to have low/high blood pressure
der **Husten**	cough
der **Hustensaft, ¨e**	cough syrup
der **Liebeskummer**	lovesickness
der **Schmerz, -en**	pain
die **Halsschmerzen**	sore throat
die **Herzschmerzen**	heartache
die **Kopfschmerzen**	headache
die **Magenschmerzen**	stomachache
die **Ohrenschmerzen**	earache
die **Zahnschmerzen**	toothache
der **Schnupfen, -**	cold (*with a runny nose*), sniffles
das **Bonbon, -s**	drop, lozenge
das **Halsbonbon, -s**	throat lozenge
das **Hustenbonbon, -s**	cough drop
sich auf·regen	to get excited, get upset
sich ärgern (R)	to get angry
sich erkälten	to catch a cold
fehlen (+ *dat.*) (R)	to be wrong with, be the matter with (*a person*)
weh tun, tat weh, weh getan	to hurt

Ähnliche Wörter

das **Fieber**; das **Symptom, -e** (**sich) fühlen; sich wohl·fühlen**

Der Körper — The Body

die **Haut, ¨e**	skin
die **Niere, -n**	kidney
die **Zunge, -n**	tongue
der **Blinddarm**	appendix
der **Magen, ¨**	stomach
der **Zahn, ¨e**	tooth
das **Gehirn, -e**	brain
atmen	to breathe
greifen, griff, gegriffen	to grab, grasp
kauen	to chew
lutschen	to suck
riechen, roch, gerochen	to smell

Ähnliche Wörter

die **Leber, -n**; die **Lippe, -n**; die **Lunge, -n**; die **Nase, -n** der **Finger, -**; der **Fingernagel, ¨** das **Haar, -e**; das **Herz, -en**

Apotheke und Krankenhaus — Pharmacy and Hospital

die **Apothekerin, -nen**	female pharmacist
die **Ärztin, -nen** (R)	female doctor, physician
die **Augenärztin, -nen**	eye doctor
die **Hausärztin, -nen**	family doctor
die **Arztpraxis, Arztpraxen**	doctor's office
die **Psychiaterin, -nen**	female psychiatrist
die **Spritze, -n**	vaccine, shot
die **Tierärztin, -nen**	female veterinarian
der **Apotheker, -**	male pharmacist
der **Arzt, ¨e** (R)	male doctor, physician
der **Augenarzt, ¨e**	eye doctor
der **Hausarzt, ¨e**	family doctor
der **Gips**	cast (*plaster*)
der **Psychiater, -**	male psychiatrist
der **Tierarzt, ¨e**	male veterinarian
der **Verband, ¨e**	bandage
das **Medikament, -e**	medicine
ein **Medikament gegen**	medicine for
das **Pflaster, -**	adhesive bandage (Band-Aid)
das **Rezept, -e**	prescription
ab·nehmen, nimmt ab, nahm ab, abgenommen	to remove; to lose weight
Blut ab·nehmen	to take blood
röntgen	to X-ray
wirken	to work, take effect

Ähnliche Wörter

die **Diphtherie**; die **Tablette, -n**; die **Kopfschmerztablette, -n**; die **Wunde, -n** der **Schock**; der **Tetanus** das **Aspirin**; das **Blut** die **Antibiotika** (*pl.*) **bluten; desinfizieren**

Unfälle — Accidents

die **Feuerwehr**	fire department
die **Unfallstelle, -n**	scene of the accident
die **Zeugin, -nen**	female witness
der **Schaden, ¨**	damage
der **Unfallbericht, -e**	accident report
der/die **Verletzte, -n** (*wk. masc.*)	injured person
der **Zeuge, -n** (*wk. masc.*)	male witness
ab·stürzen, ist abgestürzt	to crash
aus·rutschen, ist ausgerutscht	to slip
bremsen	to brake
brennen, brannte, gebrannt	to burn
hin·fallen, fällt hin, fiel hin, ist hingefallen	to fall down
schlagen, schlägt, geschlagen	to hit
stecken·bleiben, blieb stecken, ist steckengeblieben	to get stuck
überfahren, überfährt, überfuhr, überfahren	to run over
um·kippen	to knock over
verbrennen, verbrannte, verbrannt	to burn
sich (die Zunge) verbrennen	to burn (one's tongue)
sich verletzen	to injure oneself
zu·decken	to cover
zusammen·stoßen, stieß zusammen, ist zusammengestoßen	to crash

Ähnliche Wörter

der **Krankenwagen, -** **brechen, bricht, brach, gebrochen; sich (den Arm) brechen**

Körperpflege — Personal Hygiene

die **Dauerwelle, -n**	perm
das **Solarium, Solarien**	tanning salon
sich ab·trocknen	to dry oneself off
sich an·ziehen, zog an, angezogen (R)	to get dressed
sich aus·ruhen	to rest
sich aus·ziehen, zog aus, ausgezogen (R)	to get undressed
(sich) duschen	to shower (take a shower)
sich ein·kremen	to put lotion on
sich erholen	to recuperate
sich (die Haare) fönen	to blow-dry (one's hair)
sich (die Zähne) putzen	to brush (one's teeth)
sich rasieren	to shave
sich schminken	to put makeup on
(sich) schneiden, schnitt, geschnitten	to cut (oneself)
sich sonnen	to sunbathe

Ähnliche Wörter

die **Sauna, -s** **(sich) baden; sich (die Haare) kämmen; (sich) waschen, wäscht, gewaschen**

Sonstige Substantive — Other Nouns

die **Anschrift, -en**	address
die **Decke, -n**	blanket
die **Einfahrt, -en**	driveway
die **Perücke, -n**	wig
die **Tüte, -n**	(paper or plastic) bag
die **Verabredung, -en**	appointment; date

der **Termin, -e**	appointment
der **Terminkalender, -**	appointment calendar
der **Verkehr**	traffic
das **Fahrzeug, -e**	vehicle

Ähnliche Wörter

die **Autonummer, -n** der **Chili, -s;** der **Goldfisch, -e**

Sonstige Verben — Other Verbs

achten auf (+ *akk.*)	to watch out for; to pay attention to
auf·schreiben, schrieb auf, aufgeschrieben	to write down
auf·stellen	to set up
beschreiben, beschrieb, beschrieben	to describe
ein·schalten	to turn on
fluchen	to curse, swear
flüchten	to flee
sich freuen über (+ *akk.*)	to be happy about
sich gewöhnen an (+ *akk.*)	to get used to
grüßen	to greet, say hi to
herunter·klettern, ist heruntergeklettert	to climb down
sich hin·legen	to lie down
klingen (wie), klang, geklungen	to sound (like)
lassen, läßt, ließ, gelassen	to let
einen Termin geben lassen	to get an appointment
passen (R)	to fit
das paßt gut	that fits well
rufen, rief, gerufen	to call
schaufeln	to shovel
verlassen, verläßt, verließ, verlassen	to leave; to abandon
versuchen	to try, attempt

Ähnliche Wörter

markieren, sich setzen (R)

Adjektive und Adverbien — Adjectives and Adverbs

fettig (R)	greasy
deprimiert	depressed
gesund	healthy
regelmäßig	regularly
schlimm	bad
sichtbar	visible
stark	heavy
trocken	dry
ungeduldig	impatient
verletzt	injured
schwer verletzt	critically injured

Ähnliche Wörter

allergisch, medizinisch

Sonstige Wörter und Ausdrücke — Other Words and Expressions

aber (R)	but
als (R)	when (*conj.*)
bevor	before (*conj.*)
bis (R)	until (*prep., conj.*)
damit	so that
daß	that (*conj.*)
denn (R)	for, because
dagegen	*here:* for it
haben Sie etwas dagegen?	do you have something for it (*illness*)?
draußen	outside
gemeinsam	together; common
herunter	down (*toward the speaker*)
Hilfe!	help!
jedenfalls	in any case
mal	(*word used to soften commands*)
komm mal vorbei!	come on over
nachdem (R)	afterward
ob (R)	whether
obwohl	although
oder (R)	or
seit	since, for (*prep.*)
seit mehreren Tagen	for several days
sondern (R)	on the contrary
und (R)	and
während	during
wahrscheinlich	probably
weil (R)	because
wenn (R)	if; whenever

LESEECKE

LEKTÜRE 1

Vor dem Lesen

A. Schreiben Sie mit den folgenden Stichwörtern und Ausdrücken eine kleine Geschichte: Was ist an diesem Montagmorgen passiert?

Autofahrer	Unfall
Adresse	schnell laufen
Schultasche	Krankenhaus
Bremsenquietschen[1]	Kreidestriche auf der Straße
Konferenz	nicht aufgepaßt[2]
neunjähriger Junge	Polizeirevier[3]

B. Orientierung. Sehen Sie sich jetzt den Text an; lesen Sie zuerst nur das **Fettgedruckte** und das *Kursivgedruckte.* Aus welchen Teilen besteht die Geschichte?

[1]*squealing of brakes* [2]*paid attention* [3]*police station*

Montagmorgengeschichte

von Susanne Kilian

So stand es in der Zeitung:

Nicht aufgepaßt

Nicht genügend aufgepaßt hatte ein neunjähriger Junge, der . . .

5 *So ist es passiert:*

7 Uhr 30

Herr Langen hat in Ruhe gefrühstückt. Um 8 Uhr 10 hat er eine Vertreterkonferenz. Er ist ausgeruht und gut vorbereitet. Er hat keine Eile. Sorgfältig und in 10 Ruhe startet er seinen Wagen.

7 Uhr 42

Lothar Bernich hat um 8 Uhr Schule. Heute ist alles verquer. Nicht mal Zeit zum Frühstücken hat er. Das Brot ißt er auf dem Schulweg. Das geht doch auch mal! 15

7 Uhr 44

Herr Langen fährt die stille Seitenstraße auf dem Weg zu seinem Büro entlang. Zum x-ten Mal. Er kennt diese Straße genau.

Lothar Bernich rast:[1] Ihm fällt ein, daß er sich 20 heute mit dem Martin verabredet hat.[2] Er will mit ihm zusammen zur Schule gehen.

Er rennt aus der Tür. Er rennt zwischen den parkenden Autos einfach durch. Er rennt direkt in das Auto von Herrn Langen. 25

[1]*is rushing* [2]verabredet . . . *agreed to meet*

7 Uhr 46
Lothar liegt auf der Straße. Das Auto von Herrn Langen hat ihn erwischt. Herr Langen kann das nicht begreifen.[3] Er hat das Kind nicht gesehen. Als er es sah, hat er gebremst. Das Auto stand sofort. Lothar tut alles weh. Er denkt an die Schule. An den Martin. Wieso liegt er jetzt auf der Straße? Wie ging das so schnell? Ihm tut alles weh.

7 Uhr 47
Herr Hartmann hat das Bremsenquietschen gehört. Er rennt ans Fenster. Sieht das Kind vor dem Auto auf der Straße liegen. Sofort ruft er das Unfallkommando an.

7 Uhr 49
Das Unfallkommando der Polizei hat die Arbeitersamariter verständigt. Lothar weiß nicht, was überhaupt mit ihm passiert. Leute starren ihn an. Die Sanitäter heben ihn schnell und vorsichtig[4] hoch. An den Beinen und am Kopf. Er spürt eine weiche Bahre[5] unter sich. „Meine Mama, wo ist bloß meine Mama . . .“ jammert er.

7 Uhr 55
Lothar wird ins Krankenhaus gefahren. Die Polizei trifft an der Unfallstelle ein. Sie untersucht Lothars Ranzen.[6] Findet seine Adresse im Ranzendeckel stehen—sie wird per Funk zum Revier durchgegeben. Von dort wird Lothars Mutter verständigt. Herr Langen wird zum Unfall vernommen. Wo der Junge lag, wird mit Kreidestrichen eine Skizze auf die Straße gemalt. Herr Langen hat das nicht gewollt. Er ist nervös. Er zittert. Er hat den Jungen nicht zwischen den Autos hervorrennen sehen. Er gibt der Polizei seine Papiere.

Die Zeugen:

Alte Frau:
Klar. Der Mann ist doch gerast[7] wie verrückt. Heute ist man doch auf der Straße wie Freiwild. Rasen einfach. Für Fußgänger ist kein Platz mehr. Das arme Kind, das kleine!

Mann:
Na, also der Bub[8] ist doch zwischen den Autos nur so rausgeschossen.[9] Den konnte der im Auto doch gar nicht sehen. Das war ganz unmöglich. Der hat überhaupt nicht aufgepaßt . . . hat sicher an ganz was anderes gedacht . . .

Mädchen:
Ich weiß nicht. Also, ich weiß nicht . . . das ging alles so schnell. Eben hab ich noch den Jungen rennen gesehen, da lag er schon auf der Straße. Ich weiß wirklich nicht. Bremsenquietschen hab ich gehört.

Später auf dem Polizeirevier:

Der Unfallbericht wird angefertigt.[10]

Ist Lothar schuld,[11] der es so eilig hatte? Weil er ein paar Sekunden nicht aufgepaßt hat?

Ist Herr Langen schuld, der gar nicht wußte, was geschah, bis Lothar vor seinem Auto lag? Wer ist schuld? Feststeht: das kann jedem jeden Tag passieren.

[3]verstehen [4]*carefully* [5]*stretcher* [6]*schoolbag* [7]ist . . . *was speeding* [8]*boy* [9]*shot out* [10]*prepared* [11]*at fault*

Arbeit mit dem Text

A. Was ist zu dieser Zeit passiert? Ordnen Sie die Sätze aus dem Berichtteil der richtigen Zeit zu. Achtung: Meistens gehören mehrere Sätze zu einer Zeit.

7 Uhr 30
7 Uhr 42
7 Uhr 44
7 Uhr 46
7 Uhr 47
7 Uhr 49
7 Uhr 55

7 Uhr _____: Lothar rennt zwischen den parkenden Autos durch auf die Straße.

7 Uhr ____: Herr Langen ist auf dem Weg in sein Büro.
7 Uhr ____: Die Polizei kommt an die Unfallstelle.
7 Uhr ____: Die Sanitäter kommen und legen Lothar auf eine Bahre.
7 Uhr ____: Lothar rast, weil er sich mit Martin verabredet hat.
7 Uhr ____: Lothar hat keine Zeit, weil er schon um 8 Uhr da sein muß.
7 Uhr ____: Die Sanitäter bringen Lothar ins Krankenhaus.
7 Uhr ____: Lothar ist vor ein Auto gelaufen und liegt jetzt auf der Straße.
7 Uhr _30_: Herr Langen muß erst um 8 Uhr 10 zu einer Konferenz und hat keine Eile.
7 Uhr ____: Die Polizei ruft Lothars Mutter an.
7 Uhr ____: Herr Langen ist sehr nervös und schockiert, als er der Polizei seine Papiere gibt.
7 Uhr ____: Lothar weiß gar nicht, was los ist.
7 Uhr ____: Herr Hartmann ruft das Unfallkommando der Polizei an.
7 Uhr ____: Die Polizei malt mit Kreide eine Skizze auf die Straße.

B. Wer sagt was? (die alte Frau, der Mann, das Mädchen)

„Ich weiß nicht, wer schuld ist. Es ging alles viel zu schnell."
„Der Autofahrer ist schuld, weil er viel zu schnell gefahren ist."
„Der Junge ist schuld, weil er nicht aufgepaßt hat."

C. Was glauben Sie? Ist der Junge schuld, der Autofahrer oder jemand anderes? Was könnte man machen, damit so was nicht passiert?

D. Lesen Sie wieder die ersten vier Zeilen. Wobei hat der Junge nicht aufgepaßt? Schreiben Sie den Relativsatz (Zeile 4) zu Ende.

LEKTÜRE 2

Vor dem Lesen

1. Vorbeugung[1] gegen Schnupfen. Was hilft? Kreuzen Sie an.

- ☐ jeden Tag spazierengehen
- ☐ Hände waschen
- ☐ im Winter zu Hause bleiben
- ☐ Vitamin-C-Tabletten nehmen
- ☐ kleine Räume mit vielen Menschen meiden[2]
- ☐ bei offenem Fenster schlafen

2. Was hilft, wenn Sie bereits verschnupft sind?
3. Was muß man bei Grippe tun?

[1]*prevention* [2]*avoid*

4. Typisch für Grippe (G) oder Erkältung (E)? Ordnen Sie die Symptome zu.

Fieber	______	Niesen[4]	______
Kopfschmerzen	______	Müdigkeit[5]	______
Muskelschmerzen[1]	______	Entkräftung[6]	______
Schüttelfrost[2]	______	trockener, stoßweiser[7] Husten	______
Halsschmerzen	______	dauert höchstens eine Woche	______
laufende oder verstopfte[3] Nase	______	dauert ein bis zwei Wochen oder länger	______

5. Vergleichen Sie Ihre Tabelle mit der Tabelle im Text (Seite 391).
6. In Zeitschriftenartikeln ist der Anfang eines neuen Absatzes oft **fett gedruckt,** damit die Leser sich leicht orientieren können und wissen, daß ein neues Thema folgt. Lesen Sie den Titel mit Untertitel und jeweils den ersten Satz nach den fettgedruckten Wörtern. Was ist das Thema des Artikels? Welche Unterthemen gibt es?

[1] *muscle pain* [2] *chills* [3] *stuffy* [4] *sneezing* [5] *fatigue* [6] *weakness* [7] *hacking*

Warten auf die Seuche

Ein Virusforscher warnt: Mit Grippe ist nicht zu spaßen. In Schweinen lauert schon heute das Virus für die nächste tödliche Epidemie

„Die nächste weltweite Grippeepidemie steht vor der Tür", warnt Christoph Scholtissek, Virologe an der Universität Gießen. Ein Aufruf gegen die weitverbreitete Impfmüdigkeit. Denn die Grippe ist – neben Aids – die letzte große Seuche der Menschheit, die immer wieder Tausende von Toten hinterläßt: 20 bis 30 Millionen starben im Winter 1918/19 an der „Spanischen Grippe" – mehr als wenige Jahre zuvor im Ersten Weltkrieg. Die Hongkong-Grippe kostete noch 1968/69 allein in Deutschland 50 000 Menschenleben.

Das Virus kommt jedes Jahr in neuem Design: So wie die Haute Couture mit immer neuen Modellen aufwartet, so überlistet auch die Grippe in immer neuen Variationen die menschliche Immunabwehr.

Schmarotzer: Ein Virus hat keinen eigenen Stoffwechsel. Es kann sich nur vermehren, indem es lebende Zellen befällt. In die Erbsubstanz dieser Zellen schleust es seine eigene DNA ein. Dann zwingt es die Zelle, von dieser DNA millionenfach Kopien herzustellen und so neue Viren zu bilden.

Wie entsteht ein neues Grippevirus? Beim Vergleich menschlicher Viren mit denen von Vögeln und Schweinen kam Christoph Scholtissek zusammen mit dem US-Virologen Robert Webster einem erstaunlichen Zusammenhang auf die Spur:

Der Ursprung vieler neuer Viren liegt in Wasservögeln, vor allem in Wildenten. Die Vögel werden selbst nicht krank, sie können auch Menschen nicht direkt anstecken. Über ihren Kot infizieren sie jedoch Schweine. Diese Hausschweine sind aber bereits mit einem menschlichen Virus infiziert. Schuld daran: Der Bauer, der im Schweinestall hustet, hat es angesteckt.

Idealer Nährboden: Im Schwein tauschen die beiden verschiedenen Grippeviren ihr Erbmaterial aus und bilden immer wieder neue Kombinationen.

Das doppelt infizierte Schwein hustet, während der Bauer den Stall saubermacht, und gibt so das neu entstandene Virus an den Menschen weiter. Dessen Immunsystem hat kaum eine Chance gegen den neuen, noch unbekannten Erreger.

Grippe oder Erkältung: Eine Erkältung bringt eine verstopfte Nase, Halsschmerzen und vielleicht Husten. Aber nach einer Woche ist alles wieder vorbei, egal ob mit oder ohne Doktor, ob mit oder ohne Tabletten oder Vitamin C. Hausmittel wie auch Rezeptfreies aus der Apotheke lindern zwar die Symptome, schneller gesund wird man damit jedoch nicht.

Antibiotika helfen nicht, auch wenn mancher Arzt schnell das Rezept zur Hand hat: Sie töten lediglich Bakterien, gegen Schnupfen oder Grippeviren haben sie keine Chance.

Die echte Grippe ist gefährlicher als eine banale Erkältung. Innerhalb weniger Stunden kann sich hohes Fieber entwickeln, es folgen Muskelschmerzen, heftige Kopfschmerzen, manchmal Erbrechen. Deutlichstes Kennzeichen: Wer Grippe hat, ist schlapp und müde. Bei einer Virusgrippe kann das Immunsystem so geschwächt werden, daß der Körper die Kontrolle verliert: Andere Erreger können sich breitmachen, etwa die von Lungenentzündung oder sogar Hirnhautentzündung.

	SCHNUPFEN	GRIPPE
SYMPTOME Fieber	selten	tritt plötzlich auf, hohe Temperatur, dauert drei bis vier Tage
Kopfschmerzen	leicht	stark
Muskelschmerzen	wenig	oft, oft sehr stark
Müdigkeit	kaum	extrem, kann bis zu zwei bis drei Wochen dauern
Entkräftung	nie	stark
Laufende oder verstopfte Nase	oft	manchmal
Niesen	üblich	manchmal
Halsschmerzen	oft	oft
Husten	leicht bis mäßig, trockener, stoßweiser Husten	oft, kann sehr heftig werden
KOMPLIKATIONEN	Neben- oder Stirnhöhlenentzündung, Mittelohrentzündung	Bronchitis, Neben- oder Stirnhöhlenentzündung, Lungenentzündung, kann lebensgefährlich werden
VORBEUGUNG	persönliche Hygiene wie Händewaschen, beim Husten/Niesen ein Verbreiten der Keime vermeiden (Taschentuch)	jährliche Impfung gegen die Influenzaviren vom Typ A und B
BEHANDLUNG	nur begrenzte Linderung der Symptome	Bettruhe, viel Flüssigkeit, u. U.[1] antivirales Medikament

Thema: ______________________

Unterthemen: ______________________

____

____

____

____

[1]unter Umständen *if need be*

Arbeit mit dem Text

1. Welcher der folgenden Sätze faßt welchen Absatz im Text zusammen? Schreiben Sie die Buchstaben neben die Absätze.

   A. Neue Viren werden oft von Wasservögeln auf Schweine und von Schweinen dann auf Menschen übertragen.[1]
   B. Ein Virus kann sich nur mit Hilfe lebender Zellen[2] vermehren, weil es keinen eigenen Stoffwechsel[3] hat.
   C. Die Grippe ist zusammen mit Aids die letzte große Seuche,[4] an der immer wieder Tausende von Menschen sterben.
   D. Ein neues Virus entsteht, indem Grippeviren von Vögeln und Grippeviren von Schweinen ihr Erbmaterial[5] kombinieren.
   E. Erkältung und Grippe werden durch Viren verursacht[6] und haben ähnliche Symptome, aber eine Grippe ist eine viel gefährlichere Krankheit.

2. Die Sätze oben liefern den Anfang für eine Zusammenfassung des Textes. Schreiben Sie die Sätze in die richtige Reihenfolge und fügen Sie aus der Liste unten je ein interessantes Detail aus dem Text dazu. Dann haben Sie eine Zusammenfassung von „Warten auf die Seuche".

DETAILS

- Das Schwein ist der ideale Nährboden[7] für das Virus, das dann wieder auf den Menschen übertragen wird.
- Es befällt[8] die Zelle und zwingt[9] sie, das DNA des Virus zu kopieren.
- Grippe macht müde und schlapp, und Komplikationen wie Lungenentzündung[10] oder sogar Hirnhautentzündung[11] können dazukommen.
- Jedes Jahr gibt es neue Virusvariationen, die eine Epidemie verursachen können.
- Trotzdem lassen sich viele Leute nicht gegen Grippe impfen.
- Viele Hausschweine sind aber schon mit einem menschlichen Grippevirus infiziert.

---

[1]*transmitted* [2]*cells* [3]*metabolism* [4]*plague* [5]*genetic material* [6]*caused* [7]*culture medium* (lit.: *fertile soil*) [8]*infests* [9]*forces* [10]*pneumonia* [11]*meningitis*

STRUKTUREN UND ÜBUNGEN

11.1 Accusative reflexive pronouns

Reflexive pronouns are generally used to express the fact that someone is doing something to or for himself or herself.

Ich lege das Baby ins Bett.	*I'm putting the baby to bed.*
Ich lege mich ins Bett.	*I'm putting myself to bed (lying down).*

Some verbs are always used with a reflexive pronoun in German, whereas their English counterparts may not be.

Ich habe mich erkältet.	*I caught a cold.*
Warum regst du dich auf?	*Why are you getting excited?*

Here are some common reflexive verbs.

sich ärgern	*to get angry*	sich freuen	*to be happy*
sich aufregen	*to get excited*	sich (wohl) fühlen	*to feel (well)*
sich ausruhen	*to rest*	sich hinlegen	*to lie down*
sich erkälten	*to catch a cold*	sich verletzen	*to get hurt*

In most instances the forms of the reflexive pronoun are the same as those of the personal object pronouns. The only reflexive form that is distinct is **sich,** which corresponds to **er, sie** (*she*), **es, sie** (*they*), and **Sie*** (*you*).

Accusative Reflexive Pronouns	
ich → mich	wir → uns
du → dich	ihr → euch
Sie → sich	Sie → sich
er / sie / es → sich	sie → sich

Ich fühle mich nicht wohl.	*I don't feel well.*
Michael hat sich verletzt.	*Michael hurt himself.*

*Even when it refers to the polite form of *you,* **Sie, sich** is not capitalized.

Verbs with reflexive pronouns use the auxiliary **haben** in the perfect and past perfect tenses.

Heidi hat sich in den Finger geschnitten.	*Heidi cut her finger.*

Übung 1 Minidialoge

Ergänzen Sie das Verb und das Reflexivpronomen.

sich ärgern (geärgert)	sich fühlen (gefühlt)
sich aufregen (aufgeregt)	sich legen (gelegt)
sich ausruhen (ausgeruht)	sich schneiden (geschnitten)
sich erkälten (erkältet)	sich verletzen (verletzt)
sich freuen (gefreut)	

1. SILVIA: Ich _____ _____[a] gar nicht wohl.
   JÜRGEN: Warum denn?
   SILVIA: Ich glaube, ich habe _____ _____[b].
   JÜRGEN: Du Ärmste! Du mußt _____ gleich ins Bett _____[c].
2. MICHAEL: Du, weißt du, daß Herr Thelen einen Herzinfarkt[1] hatte?
   MARIA: Kein Wunder, er hat _____ auch immer so furchtbar _____[a].
   MICHAEL: Na, jetzt muß er _____ erst mal ein paar Wochen _____[b].
3. FRAU RUF: Du blutest ja! Hast du _____ _____[a]?
   HERR RUF: Ja, ich habe _____ in den Finger _____[b].
4. HEIDI: Warum _____ du _____[a], Stefan?
   STEFAN: Ich habe in meiner Prüfung ein D bekommen.
   HEIDI: Du solltest _____ _____[b], daß du kein F bekommen hast.

11.2 Dative reflexive pronouns

When a clause contains another object in addition to the reflexive pronoun, then the reflexive pronoun is in the dative case; the other object, usually a thing or a part of the body, is in the accusative case.

Ich ziehe mir (DAT.) den Mantel (ACC.) aus.	*I'm taking off my coat.*

Notice that the accusative object (the piece of clothing or part of the body) is preceded by the definite article.

Wäschst du dir **die** Haare jeden Tag?	*Do you wash your hair every day?*
Natalie hat sich **den** Arm gebrochen.	*Natalie broke her arm.*

[1] *heart attack*

Only the reflexive pronouns that correspond to **ich** and **du** have different dative and accusative forms.

Reflexive Pronouns

	SINGULAR		PLURAL		
	Accusative	*Dative*	*Accusative*	*Dative*	
ich	**mich**	**mir**	**uns**		wir
du	**dich**	**dir**	**euch**		ihr
Sie	**sich**				Sie
er/sie/es					sie

Übung 2 Meine Morgentoilette

In welcher Reihenfolge machen Sie das?

MODELL Erst stehe ich auf. Dann dusche ich mich. Dann . . .

sich abtrocknen
aufstehen
sich anziehen
sich duschen
frühstücken
sich rasieren
sich schminken
sich die Fingernägel putzen
sich das Gesicht waschen
sich die Haare fönen
sich die Haare kämmen
sich die Haare waschen
zur Uni gehen
sich die Zähne putzen

Übung 3 Körperpflege

Wer macht das? Sie, Ihre Freundin, Ihr Vater . . . ?

1. sich jeden Morgen rasieren
2. sich zu sehr schminken
3. sich nicht oft genug die Haare waschen
4. sich nach jeder Mahlzeit die Zähne putzen
5. sich immer verrückt anziehen
6. sich jeden Tag duschen
7. sich nie kämmen
8. sich nie die Haare fönen
9. sich nicht gern baden
10. sich immer elegant anziehen

ich
meine Freundin
mein Freund
mein Vater
meine Mutter
meine Schwester
meine Oma
mein Onkel
_____ ?

11.3 Word order of accusative and dative objects

When the accusative object and the dative object are both *nouns,* then the dative object precedes the accusative object.

DAT. ACC.

Ich schenke **meiner Mutter einen Ring.** *I'm giving my mother a ring.*

When either the accusative object or the dative object is a *pronoun* and the other object is a *noun,* then the pronoun precedes the noun regardless of case.

DAT. ACC.

Ich schenke **ihr einen Ring.** *I'm giving her a ring.*

ACC. DAT.

Ich schenke **ihn meiner Mutter.** *I'm giving it to my mother.*

The dative object precedes the accusative object, unless the accusative object is a pronoun.

When the accusative object and the dative object are both *pronouns,* then the accusative object precedes the dative object.

ACC. DAT.

Ich schenke **ihn ihr.** *I'm giving it to her.*

Note that English speakers use a similar word order. Remember that German speakers do *not* use a preposition to emphasize the dative object as English speakers often do (*to my mother, to her*).

Übung 4 Im Hotel

Sie sind mit Ihrem Partner / Ihrer Partnerin in einem Hotel. Sie sind gerade aufgestanden und packen Ihre gemeinsame Toilettentasche aus.

MODELL S1: Brauchst du den Lippenstift?
S2: Ja, kannst du ihn mir geben?
oder Nein, ich brauche ihn nicht.

1. Brauchst du das Shampoo?
2. Brauchst du den Spiegel?
3. Brauchst du den Rasierapparat?
4. Brauchst du die Seife?
5. Brauchst du das Handtuch?
6. Brauchst du den Fön?
7. Brauchst du die Kreme?
8. Brauchst du das Rasierwasser?
9. Brauchst du den Kamm?

Übung 5 Gute Ratschläge!

Geben Sie Ihrem Partner/Ihrer Partnerin Rat.

NÜTZLICHE WÖRTER

einkremen
fönen
putzen
schneiden
waschen

MODELL S1: Meine Hände sind schmutzig.
S2: Warum wäschst du sie dir nicht?

1. Mein Bart ist zu lang.
2. Meine Füße sind schmutzig.
3. Meine Fingernägel sind zu lang.
4. Meine Haut ist ganz trocken.
5. Meine Haare sind naß.
6. Mein Hals ist schmutzig.
7. Meine Nase läuft.
8. Meine Haare sind zu lang.
9. Mein Gesicht ist ganz trocken.
10. Meine Haare sind fettig.

11.4 Requests and instructions: the imperative (summary review)

As you have already learned, the imperative (command form) in German is used to make requests, to give instructions and directions, and to issue orders. To soften requests or to make them more polite, words such as **doch, mal,** and **bitte** are often included in imperative sentences.

Mach mal das Fenster **zu**! — *Close the window!*
Bringen Sie mir **bitte** noch einen Kaffee! — *Bring me another cup of coffee, please.*

The imperative has four forms: the familiar singular (**du**), the familiar plural (**ihr**), the polite (**Sie**), and the first-person plural (**wir**).

A. Sie and wir

In both the **Sie**- and **wir**-forms, the verb begins the sentence, and the pronoun follows.

Kontrollieren **Sie** bitte das Öl! — *Please check the oil.*
Gehen wir doch heute ins Kino! — *Let's go to the movies today.*

B. ihr

The familiar plural imperative consists of the present-tense **ihr**-form of the verb but does not include the pronoun **ihr.**

Lydia und Rosemarie, **kommt her** und **hört** mir **zu**! — *Lydia and Rosemarie, come here and listen to me.*
Sagt immer die Wahrheit! — *Always tell the truth.*

C. du

The familiar singular imperative consists of the present-tense **du**-form of the verb without the -(**s**)**t** ending and without the pronoun **du.**

du kommst	**Komm!**
du tanzt	**Tanz!**
du arbeitest	**Arbeite!**
du ißt	**Iß!**

In written German, you will sometimes see a final **-e** (**komme, gehe**), but this **-e** is usually omitted in the spoken language for all verbs except those for which the present-tense **du**-form ends in **-est.**

du arbeitest	**Arbeite!**
du öffnest	**Öffne!**

Verbs that have a stem-vowel change from **a** to **ä** or **au** to **äu** do not have an umlaut in the **du**-imperative.

du fährst	**Fahr!**
du läufst	**Lauf!**
du hältst	**Halt!**

D. sein

The verb **sein** has irregular imperative forms.

du → **Sei** leise!	*Be quiet!* (*Paul!*)
ihr → **Seid** leise!	*Be quiet!* (*You two!*)
Sie → **Seien Sie** leise!	*Be quiet!* (*Mrs. Smith!*)
wir → **Seien wir** leise!	*Let's be quiet!*
Sei so gut und gib mir die Butter, Andrea.	*Be so kind and pass me the butter, Andrea.*
Seid keine Egoisten!	*Don't be such egotists!*

Übung 6 Was rätst du mir?

Was raten Sie in den folgenden Situationen?

MODELL S1: Ich sehe nicht mehr gut.
S2: Geh zum Augenarzt!
oder Kauf dir eine neue Brille!

1. Es ist kalt.	**a.** sich einen Pullover anziehen
2. Es ist heiß.	**b.** sich nicht ärgern
3. Es regnet.	**c.** sich ausruhen
4. Mein Auto ist kaputt.	**d.** sich die Jacke ausziehen
5. Ich bin blaß.	**e.** mit dem Bus fahren
6. Meine Haare sind naß.	**f.** sich fönen
7. Meine Fingernägel sind zu lang.	**g.** den Regenschirm mitnehmen
8. Ich habe Hunger.	**h.** sich schneiden
9. Ich bin so wütend.	**i.** sich sonnen
10. Ich bin so müde.	**j.** etwas essen
	k. _____?

Übung 7 Aufforderungen!

Sie sind die erste Person in jeder Zeile. Was sagen Sie?

MODELL Frau Wagner: Jens und Ernst / Zimmer aufräumen →
Jens und Ernst, räumt euer Zimmer auf!

1. Herr Wagner: Jens und Ernst / nicht so laut sein
2. Frau Körner: Michael und Maria / pünktlich sein
3. Frau Wagner: Uli / nicht so viel rauchen
4. Herr Ruf: Jutta / mehr Obst essen
5. Herr Siebert: Herr Pusch / nicht so schnell fahren
6. Michael: Frau Körner / an der Ecke warten
7. Frau Frisch: Natalie und Rosemarie / nicht ungeduldig sein
8. Herr Thelen: Andrea und Paula / Vater von mir grüßen
9. Frau Ruf: Hans / sich waschen und sich die Zähne putzen
10. Oma Schmitz: Helga und Sigrid / jeden Tag die Zeitung lesen

Übung 8 Minidialoge

Verwenden Sie die folgenden Verben.

helfen	sprechen	warten
machen	vergessen	

1. FRAU RUF: Ich sitze jetzt schon wieder sechs Stunden vor dem Computer.
   HERR RUF: Du arbeitest zu viel. _____ mal eine Pause.
2. HERR SIEBERT: _____ bitte lauter, ich verstehe Sie nicht.
   MARIA: Ja, wie laut soll ich denn sprechen? Wollen Sie, daß ich schreie?
3. MICHAEL: Na, was ist? Kommen Sie nun oder kommen Sie nicht?
   FRAU KÖRNER: Ich bin ja gleich fertig. Bitte _____ doch noch einen Moment.
4. HANS: Kann ich mit euch zum Schwimmen gehen?
   JENS: Ja, komm und _____ deine Badehose nicht.
5. OMA SCHMITZ: _____ mir bitte, ich kann die Koffer nicht allein tragen.
   HELGA UND SIGRID: Aber natürlich, Großmutter, wir helfen dir doch gern.

11.5 Word order in dependent and independent clauses (summary review)

To connect thoughts more effectively, two or more clauses may be combined in one sentence. There are essentially two kinds of combinations:

1. Coordination: both clauses are equally important and do not depend on each other structurally.
2. Subordination: one clause depends on the other one; it does not make sense when it stands alone.

COORDINATION

Heute ist ein kalter Tag, und es schneit.	*Today is a cold day, and it is snowing.*

SUBORDINATION

Gestern war es wärmer, weil die Sonne schien.	*Yesterday was warmer because the sun was shining.*

A. Coordination

These are the five most common coordinating conjunctions.

und	*and*
oder	*or*
aber	*but*
sondern	*but, on the contrary*
denn	*because*

In clauses joined with these conjunctions, the conjugated verb is in second position in both statements.

CLAUSE 1	CONJ.	CLAUSE 2
I II		I II
Ich muß noch viel lernen,	denn	ich habe morgen eine Prüfung.

(*I have to study a lot, since I have a test tomorrow.*)

B. Subordination

Clauses joined by subordinating conjunctions follow one of two word order patterns.

1. When the sentence begins with the main clause, that clause has regular word order (verb second in statements) and the dependent clause introduced by the conjunction has dependent word order (verb last).

CLAUSE 1	CONJ.	CLAUSE 2
I II		I LAST
Ich muß noch viel lernen,	weil	ich morgen eine Prüfung habe.

(*I have to study a lot because I have a test tomorrow.*)

2. When a sentence begins with a dependent clause, the entire dependent clause is considered the first part of the main clause and occupies first position. The verb-second rule applies, then, moving the subject of the main clause after the verb.

CLAUSE 1	CLAUSE 2
I	II SUBJECT
Weil ich morgen eine Prüfung habe,	muß ich noch viel lernen.

(*Because I have a test tomorrow, I have to study a lot.*)

Here are the most commonly used subordinating conjunctions.

als	*when*	ob	*whether, if*
bevor	*before*	obwohl	*although*
bis	*until*	während	*while*
damit	*so that*	weil	*because, since*
daß	*that*	wenn	*if, when*
nachdem	*after*		

Übung 9 Opa Schmitz ist im Garten.

Ergänzen Sie **daß, ob, weil, damit** oder **wenn.**

1. OMA SCHMITZ: Weißt du, _____[a] Opa schon den Rasen gemäht hat?
   HELGA: Ich weiß nur, _____[b] er schon seit zwei Stunden im Garten ist.
   OMA SCHMITZ: _____[c] Opa schon so lange im Garten ist, liegt er bestimmt in der Sonne.
2. HELGA: Du, Opi, was machst du denn im Gras?
   OPA SCHMITZ: Ich habe mich nur kurz hingelegt, _____[a] mich die Nachbarn nicht sehen.
   HELGA: Aber warum sollen die dich denn nicht sehen?
   OPA SCHMITZ: _____[b] ich mich heute noch nicht rasiert habe.

Übung 10 Minidialoge

Ergänzen Sie **obwohl, als, nachdem, bevor** oder **während.**

1. HERR THELEN: Was hat denn deine Tochter gesagt, _____[a] du mit deiner neuen Frisur nach Hause gekommen bist?
   HERR SIEBERT: Zuerst gar nichts. Erst _____[b] sie ein paar Mal um mich herumgegangen war, hat sie angefangen zu lachen und gesagt: „Aber, Papi, erst fast eine Glatze und jetzt so viele Haare. Das sieht aber komisch aus!"
2. FRAU ROWOHLT: Guten Tag, Herr Frisch! Kommen Sie doch bitte erst zu mir, _____ Sie mit Ihrer Arbeit beginnen.
   HERR FRISCH: Aber natürlich, Frau Direktorin.
3. JOSEF: Ja, seid ihr denn immer noch nicht fertig? Was habt ihr eigentlich die ganze Zeit gemacht?
   MELANIE: _____ du dich stundenlang geduscht hast, haben wir die ganze Wohnung aufgeräumt.
4. MARIA: Aber, Herr Wachtmeister, könnten Sie nicht mal ein Auge zudrücken? Die Ampel war doch schon fast wieder grün.
   POLIZIST: Nein, leider nicht, _____ ich es gern tun würde, meine gnädige[1] Frau. Aber Sie wissen ja, Pflicht ist Pflicht.

---

[1]*dear*

KAPITEL 12

Zusammen leben
und lernen

In **Kapitel 12,** you will discuss social relationships and some of the issues that arise in modern multicultural societies. In addition, you will learn to express your expectations for the future, and you will listen to and tell stories about our four-legged friends and foes.

Partner

THEMEN

Familie, Ehe, Partnerschaft
Multikulturelle Gesellschaft
Was die Zukunft wohl bringt?
Tiere

LEKTÜRE

„Deutsche Kastanien"
„Frauen kommen langsam, aber gewaltig"

KULTURELLES

Gleichberechtigung im Haushalt und im Beruf
Multikulturelle Gesellschaft
Zukunft
Tiere in Sprichwörtern
Kulturprojekt: Fremde in Deutschland
Porträt: Hedwig Dohm und Berlin
Videoecke: Krawalle in Magdeburg

STRUKTUREN

12.1 The genitive case
12.2 Causality and purpose: **weil, damit, um . . . zu**
12.3 Talking about the future: the present and future tenses
12.4 The passive voice

Familie, Ehe, Partnerschaft

➤ **Grammatik 12.1**

Die gute alte Zeit: der Herr im Haus

Eine mögliche Rolle des modernen Mannes

Die alte Rolle der Frau: Hausfrau und Mutter

Das neue Bild der Frau, die im Berufsleben steht

Verliebt, verlobt, verheiratet

Er kümmert sich um die Kinder, sie kümmert sich um das Geld.

Situation 1 Wer in der Klasse . . . ?

1. ist verheiratet
2. ist verlobt
3. hat einen Sohn oder eine Tochter
4. war noch nie verliebt

5. möchte einen Arzt / eine Ärztin heiraten
6. möchte keine Hausfrau / kein Hausmann sein
7. will mehr als drei Kinder haben
8. wird leicht eifersüchtig
9. findet gemeinsame Hobbys wichtig
10. ist gerade glücklich verliebt

Situation 2 Informationsspiel: Der ideale Partner

MODELL Wie soll Rolfs ideale Partnerin aussehen?
Was für einen Charakter soll sie haben?
Welchen Beruf soll Heidis idealer Partner haben?
Welche Interessen sollte er haben?
Wie alt sollte dein idealer Partner / deine ideale Partnerin sein?
Welche Konfession sollte er/sie haben?
Welcher Nationalität sollte Rolfs Partnerin angehören?
Welche politische Einstellung sollte sie haben?

	Rolf	Heidi	mein(e) Partner(in)
Aussehen		groß und stark	
Charakter		fleißig und geduldig	
Beruf	egal		
Interessen	Kunst und Kultur		
Alter	so alt wie er		
Konfession	egal		
Nationalität		egal	
politische Einstellung		liberal	

Situation 3 Interview

1. Willst du heiraten? (Bist du verheiratet?)
2. Wie sollte dein Partner sein? Welche Eigenschaften findest du wichtig an deinem Partner?
3. Sind Aussehen und Beruf wichtig für dich? Was ist sonst noch wichtig?
4. Willst du Kinder haben? Wie viele? (Hast du Kinder? Wie viele?)
5. Würdest du zu Hause bleiben, wenn du Kinder hättest?
6. Was hältst du von einem Ehevertrag vor der Ehe?
7. Was würdest du tun, wenn du dich mit deinem Partner nicht mehr verstehst?
8. Was wäre für dich ein Grund zur Scheidung?
9. Sollte sich vor allem die Mutter um die Kinder kümmern? Warum (nicht)?
10. Welche Eigenschaften hat ein guter Vater?

Kultur ... Landeskunde ... Informationen

Gleichberechtigung im Haushalt und im Beruf

- Haben sich Ihr Vater (V), Ihre Mutter (M) oder beide zusammen (b) um die folgenden Aufgaben im Alltag[1] gekümmert?

_____ einkaufen
_____ Auto warten[2]
_____ Geschirr spülen
_____ Kinder betreuen[3]
_____ kochen
_____ putzen
_____ Rasen mähen
_____ Rechnungen bezahlen
_____ Reparaturen im Haus
_____ waschen

Berufstätige Frauen arbeiten doppelt — am Arbeitsplatz und zu Hause, denn Hausarbeit ist immer noch meistens Frauensache.[4] Zwar[5] wollen 27% der Männer ihren Frauen grundsätzlich[6] helfen, aber Sache der Frauen ist es: zu waschen (90%), zu kochen (88%), zu putzen (80%), einzukaufen (75%) und zu spülen (71%). Ebenso[7] gibt es immer noch traditionelle Männeraufgaben: Reparaturen (80%) und das Auto (66%). Die Berufstätigkeit von Frauen hat an der alten Rollenteilung wenig geändert. Auch gleicher Lohn[8] für gleiche Arbeit ist leider immer noch eine Utopie. Frauen verdienen durchschnittlich ein Drittel weniger als ihre männlichen Kollegen. Auch von der Arbeitslosigkeit werden Frauen stärker betroffen,[9] vor allem in den neuen Bundesländern. 1993 waren 21% der ostdeutschen Frauen im Vergleich zu 11% der Männer arbeitslos gemeldet. Durch die sogenannte „Stille Reserve", das sind Frauen, die arbeiten würden, wenn sie die Möglichkeit hätten, liegt die Zahl der arbeitslosen Frauen weit höher.

- Vergleichen Sie die Angaben im Text mit Ihren eigenen. Hatte Ihre Familie eine ähnliche[10] Arbeitsteilung? Wo gibt es Unterschiede?
- Machen Sie eine Umfrage im Kurs, und vergleichen Sie die Prozentzahlen.
- Haben beide Eltern oder hat nur ein Elternteil gearbeitet? Wer hat mehr verdient, Ihr Vater oder Ihre Mutter?

[1]im . . . *day-to-day* [2]*do maintenance on* [3]*take care of* [4]*a woman's job* [5]*to be sure* [6]*in principle* [7]*likewise* [8]*pay* [9]stärker . . . *harder hit* [10]*similar*

Multikulturelle Gesellschaft

➤ **Grammatik 12.2**

Mehmets Onkel und Tante leben seit 25 Jahren in Berlin.

Mehr als zwei Millionen Ausländer und Ausländerinnen arbeiten in Deutschland.

In Mölln steckten Neonazis zwei Wohnhäuser an. Drei Türkinnen verbrannten.

In Hoyerswerda griffen Rechtsradikale ein Wohnheim an, in dem vor allem Sinti und Roma lebten.

In München protestierten Bürger und Bürgerinnen mit einer Lichterkette gegen Ausländerhaß.

Ausländer, die sich diskriminiert fühlen, können das antirassistische Telefon benutzen.

Die ganze Welt am Ende der Skala: 106,8 Die Welle für die Weltstadt

24 Stunden Non-stop-Programm für Berliner aller Couleur, von überall her

Unsere Musik schillert in allen Farben: Trommeln aus Simbabwe, Chöre vom Balkan, Rababe aus Ägypten und Samba aus Brasilien. Wir bringen Nachrichten aus aller Herren Länder in 16 Muttersprachen. Wir sprechen mit Akzent und senden Deutsch als Fremdsprache. Wir holen Moderatoren aus Pamplona und St. Petersburg. Und reden Tacheles mit Fürsten und Fans, mit Spree-Athenern und Stadt-Indianern. Wer versteht, kann sich verständigen. Wir sprechen türkisch, russisch, polnisch, arabisch, bosnisch-kroatisch-mazedonisch-serbisch-slowenisch, italienisch, griechisch, spanisch, kurdisch, vietnamesisch, albanisch, persisch, romanes, deutsch als Fremdsprache.

Situation 4 Bildgeschichte: Mehmet erzählt

Situation 5 Warum wandern Menschen aus?

Jedes Jahr wandern viele Menschen in Deutschland ein, aber jedes Jahr wandern auch viele Deutsche aus Deutschland aus, z.B. nach Australien oder nach Kanada. Was glauben Sie: Was sind Gründe dafür, in ein Land wie Deutschland einzuwandern? Was sind Gründe dafür, aus einem Land wie Deutschland auszuwandern? Ordnen Sie die Stichpunkte in zwei Spalten.

um Arbeit zu bekommen
damit die Familie besser leben kann
damit die Kinder eine gute Schule besuchen können
um nicht zu verhungern
um nicht ins Gefängnis zu kommen
um weniger Steuern zu zahlen
weil Verwandte dort wohnen
weil man freier leben will
um mehr Geld zu verdienen
weil Deutschland zu eng ist
damit die Kinder studieren können
weil es in Europa Krieg geben könnte
weil die Leute mit der Politik nicht einverstanden sind
weil es in Deutschland zu wenig Natur gibt
um nicht politisch oder religiös verfolgt zu werden
weil man da billiger ein Haus kaufen kann

GRÜNDE FÜR EINWANDERUNG	GRÜNDE FÜR AUSWANDERUNG
______________________	______________________
______________________	______________________

Situation 6 Informationsspiel: Ausländische Mitbürger

MODELL S1: Aus welchem Land kommt . . . ?
S2: Aus der Türkei.
S1: Was ist . . . von Beruf?
S2: Das weiß ich nicht.
S1: Wofür ist . . . bekannt?
S2: Für . . . / Als . . .

Name	Nationalität	Beruf	bekannt
Renan Demirkan	türkisch		für Fernsehfilme
Giovanni di Lorenzo		Journalist	
Lew Kopelew	russisch		als Schriftsteller und Übersetzer von Heinrich Böll
Şinasi Dikmen		Krankenpfleger	
Yilmaz Karahasan	türkisch		als erstes ausländisches Vorstandsmitglied
Katharina Oguntoye		—	
Akif Pirinçci	türkisch		für seinen Bestseller „Felidae“
Yüksel Pazarkaya		Schriftsteller	

Situation 7 Diskussion: Rechtsradikale

1. Gibt es Rechtsradikale in Ihrem Land? Wo? Was für Ziele haben sie? Was machen sie?
2. Kennen Sie einen Rechtsradikalen / eine Rechtsradikale? Wie denkt er/sie? Was halten Sie davon?
3. Was ist, Ihrer Meinung nach, ein typischer deutscher Neonazi?

□ Mann	□ Frau
□ jung	□ alt
□ gut ausgebildet	□ schlecht ausgebildet
□ arm	□ reich
□ sympathisch	□ unsympathisch
□ konservativ	□ progressiv

4. Finden Sie es richtig, Gewalt anzuwenden, wenn man seine Ziele anders nicht erreichen kann?
5. Warum gibt es Rechtsradikale/Neonazis?
6. Was wollen sie?
7. Was soll man mit ihnen machen?

Kultur ... Landeskunde ... Informationen

Multikulturelle Gesellschaft

Fast jedes Land hat in seiner Geschichte verschiedene kulturelle Einflüsse erfahren. Die USA sind sogar ein besonders gemischtes Land.

- Welche ethnischen Gruppen sind in Ihrer Stadt oder Gegend zu finden?
- Die folgende Broschüre ist eine Antwort auf den rechtsradikalen Slogan „Ausländer raus". Aus welcher Stadt kommt sie?
- Man versteht den Text besser, wenn man die Stadt kennt. Wo liegt sie? Was ist der Roland? Was ist die Hanse[1]? Wer sind die Bremer Stadtmusikanten?
- Welche „Ausländer" haben in Bremen ihre Spuren[2] hinterlassen?
- Wie sieht es in Ihrer Stadt oder Gegend aus? Schreiben Sie einen ähnlichen Text über den eigenen Ort.

Ausländer rein.

„Unsere" bremische Geschichte.

„Unser" Roland war **Franzose.**
Vielleicht auch **Spanier.**
„Unser" Rathaus haben **Holländer** gebaut.
Genauso wie „unseren" ersten Hafen,
„unsere" Hansekogge und „unseren" Wall.
„Unser" Wahrzeichen sind **Flüchtlinge,**
die Bremer Stadtmusikanten.
„Unsere" Textilindustrie in Bremen-Nord
haben **Tschechen, Polen** und **Russen** aufgebaut.
Für „unser" Wirtschaftswunder wurden
Italiener, Griechen, Jugoslawen,
Portugiesen und **Türken** angeworben.

Wer würde „uns" eigentlich kennen
ohne „unser" Rathaus, „unseren" Roland
und „unsere" Stadtmusikanten?
Was wären wir eigentlich
ohne „unseren" Hafen und „unsere" Wirtschaft?
Was wären wir eigentlich ohne **Ausländer?**

Die Ausländerbeauftragte
des Landes Bremen
Zentralstelle für die Integration von Zugewanderten

Protestmarsch gegen Ausländerhaß in Innsbruck

[1] *Hanseatic league* [2] *tracks, traces*

Was die Zukunft wohl bringt?

➤ **Grammatik 12.3**

Wenn Silvia mit ihrem Studium fertig ist, wird sie erst für ein Jahr nach Amerika gehen, um dort als Deutschlehrerin zu arbeiten.

Sofie plant, an einer Universität im westlichen Teil Deutschlands weiterzustudieren, um bessere Chancen im Beruf zu haben.

Richard wird nach dem Wehrdienst nach Frankreich ziehen, um dort mit seiner Freundin zu leben.

Heidi arbeitet neben dem Studium, um Geld für eine Reise durch Europa zu sparen.

Rolf wird nach seinem Austauschjahr in Berkeley mit seiner Diplomarbeit anfangen.

Helga geht noch aufs Gymnasium und arbeitet sehr fleißig, um gute Noten zu bekommen.

Situation 8 Diskussion: Karriere und Glück

1. Was wollen Sie werden? Warum?
2. Glauben Sie, daß man auch ohne konkrete Pläne glücklich sein kann?
3. Was erwarten Sie von Ihrem Beruf? Geld, persönliche Befriedigung, Abenteuer?
4. Wollen Sie Ihr ganzes Leben im gleichen Beruf arbeiten? Warum (nicht)?
5. Wollen Sie sich selbständig machen? Warum (nicht)?
6. Wie stellen Sie sich ein glückliches Leben vor?
7. Gibt es eine Art von „Glück", das man kaufen kann? Erklären Sie Ihre Antwort.
8. Welche Art von Glück kann man nicht kaufen?
9. Was sind Ihre Ziele im Leben? Können Sie die ohne Geld erreichen?
10. Was machen Sie, um glücklich zu sein?

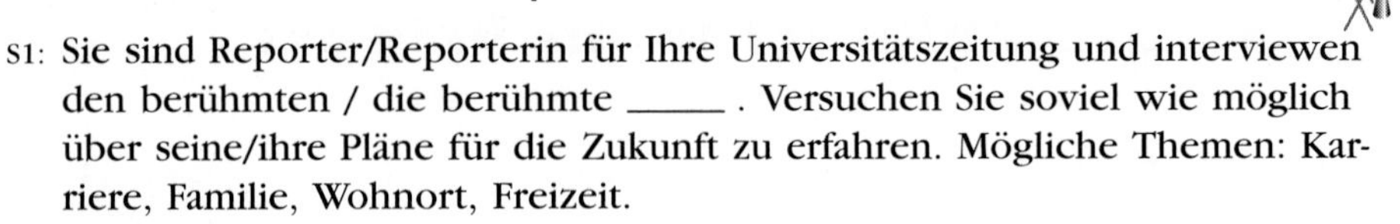

Situation 9 Rollenspiel: Ein besonderes Interview

S1: Sie sind Reporter/Reporterin für Ihre Universitätszeitung und interviewen den berühmten / die berühmte _____ . Versuchen Sie soviel wie möglich über seine/ihre Pläne für die Zukunft zu erfahren. Mögliche Themen: Karriere, Familie, Wohnort, Freizeit.

Kultur ... Landeskunde ... Informationen

Zukunft

Bald beginnt ein neues Jahrtausend.

- Machen Sie sich viel Gedanken[1] um die Zukunft?
- Haben Sie Angst vor der Zukunft?
- Wird in der Zukunft das Leben für die Menschen lebenswerter sein?
- Welche der folgenden Themen halten Sie in der Zukunft für sehr wichtig? Stellen Sie eine Rangliste auf.

_____ Medien und Computer
_____ Berufsausbildung
_____ Gesundheitsversorgung[2]
_____ Persönliche Sicherheit
_____ Drogen und Sucht[3]
_____ Ehe und Familie
_____ Richtige Ernährung[4]
_____ Urlaub und Freizeit
_____ Kirche und Glauben[5]
_____ Umweltverschmutzung[6]

Das deutsche Nachrichtenmagazin „FOCUS" wollte wissen, wie die Menschen ihre Zukunft sehen. Ein Meinungsforschungsinstitut befragte die Deutschen und stellte fest, daß 78% sich viel oder sehr viel Gedanken über die Zukunft machen. Aber sie sind optimistisch dabei. Zwei Drittel haben keine Angst vor dem, was in den

Berufsausbildung, Altersversorgung, Gesundheit sind die Top-Themen der Zukunft. Weit unten: Urlaub, Verteidigung, Kirche und Glauben

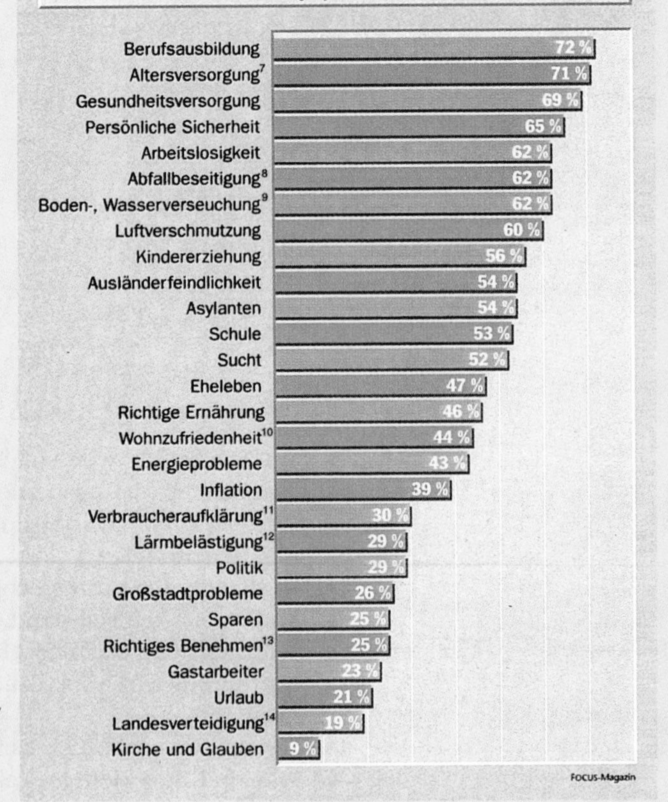

[1] *thoughts, concerns* [2] *health care* [3] *addiction* [4] *nutrition* [5] *faith* [6] *environmental pollution* [7] *retirement plan* [8] *garbage removal* [9] Boden-, ... *ground and water pollution* [10] *satisfaction with one's living arrangements* [11] *consumer education* [12] *noise pollution* [13] Richtiges ... *proper behavior* [14] *national defense*

nächsten Jahren auf sie zukommt; im Gegenteil, sie glauben, daß die Zukunft lebenswerter sein wird als die Gegenwart. Die Grafik zeigt, welche Themen Deutsche in der Zukunft für sehr wichtig halten.

- Welche der Themen halten Sie *nicht* für wichtig?
- Welche wichtigen Themen sind nicht auf der Liste?
- Machen Sie eine Umfrage im Kurs (oder im Studentenwohnheim) zu den vier Fragen oben. Unterscheiden sich Ihre Ergebnisse von denen in Deutschland?

Schreinerlehrling in Freiburg in der praktischen Ausbildung

Tiere

Grammatik 12.4

Juttas Ratte wird gegen Tollwut geimpft.

Ernsts Meerschweinchen wird oft gebadet.

Schildkröten werden oft als Haustiere gehalten.

In der Wüste muß man aufpassen, daß man nicht von einer Schlange gebissen wird.

Gestern wurde Silvia von einer Biene gestochen.

Als Josef und Melanie gestern beim Baden waren, wurden sie von tausend Mücken gestochen.

Situation 10 Ratespiel

1. Das größte Landsäugetier: Es hat einen Rüssel und zwei Stoßzähne aus Elfenbein; wegen des Elfenbeins wird es oft illegal gejagt.
2. Die schnellste Katze der Welt: Sie läuft mindestens 80 Kilometer in der Stunde.
3. Das schwerste Tier: Es lebt im Wasser, aber es ist kein Fisch.
4. Das langsamste Tier: Es trägt oft ein Haus auf seinem Rücken und hat keine Beine.
5. Es sieht aus wie ein Hund, ist aber nicht so zahm.
6. Dieses Tier lebt länger als der Elefant.
7. Das ist die giftigste Schlange in Nordamerika.
8. Dieser Wasservogel hat eine Spannweite von mehr als drei Metern.
9. Dieses Tier hat die höchste Herzfrequenz, zirka 1 000 Schläge pro Minute.
10. Dieses Tier hört schärfer als ein Delphin.

a. der Kolibri
b. der Elefant
c. die Riesenschildkröte
d. die Schnecke
e. die Fledermaus
f. der Blauwal
g. der Gepard
h. die Klapperschlange
i. der Albatros
j. der Wolf

Situation 11 Informationsspiel: Tiere

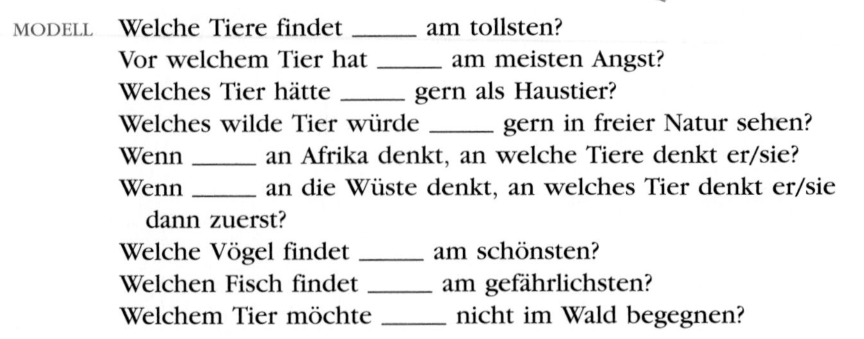

MODELL Welche Tiere findet _____ am tollsten?
Vor welchem Tier hat _____ am meisten Angst?
Welches Tier hätte _____ gern als Haustier?
Welches wilde Tier würde _____ gern in freier Natur sehen?
Wenn _____ an Afrika denkt, an welche Tiere denkt er/sie?
Wenn _____ an die Wüste denkt, an welches Tier denkt er/sie dann zuerst?
Welche Vögel findet _____ am schönsten?
Welchen Fisch findet _____ am gefährlichsten?
Welchem Tier möchte _____ nicht im Wald begegnen?

	Ernst	Maria	mein(e) Partner(in)
Lieblingstier		eine Katze	
Angst	vor dem Hund von nebenan		
Haustier	eine Schlange		
wildes Tier		eine Giraffe	
Afrika	an Löwen		
Wüste		an ein Kamel	
Vögel		Eulen	
Fisch	den weißen Hai		
Wald	einem Wolf		

Situation 12 Interview: Tiere

1. Was ist dein Lieblingstier? Warum?
2. Hast du oder hattest du ein Haustier? Was für eins? Wie heißt oder wie hieß es? Beschreib es. Erzähl eine Geschichte von ihm!
3. Vor welchen Tieren fürchtest du dich?
4. Welches Tier findest du am interessantesten?
5. Welches Tier findest du am häßlichsten?
6. Welches Tier wärst du am liebsten? Warum?
7. Findest du es wichtig, daß Kinder mit Tieren aufwachsen? Wenn ja, mit welchen? Warum?

Situation 13 Bildgeschichte: Lydias Hamster

Kultur ... Landeskunde ... Informationen

Tiere in Sprichwörtern

In vielen Sprachen gibt es Sprichwörter, in denen Tiere vorkommen. Welche Sprichwörter fallen Ihnen auf englisch ein? Ordnen Sie jeder Zeichnung ein passendes Sprichwort zu.

1. Wenn dem Esel zu wohl ist, geht er aufs Eis.
2. Einem geschenkten Gaul (= Pferd) sieht man nicht ins Maul.
3. Wenn die Katze nicht zu Hause ist, tanzen die Mäuse.
4. Den letzten beißen die Hunde.
5. In der Not[1] frißt der Teufel Fliegen.
6. Ein blindes Huhn findet auch ein Korn.

Was bedeuten die Sprichwörter? Kombinieren Sie die Definitionen mit den Sprichwörtern.

a. Wenn man etwas geschenkt bekommt, sollte man nicht zu kritisch damit sein.
b. Wenn man etwas nötig braucht, muß man nehmen, was da ist.
c. Wenn der Chef nicht da ist, machen die Angestellten, was sie wollen.
d. Jemandem, der sonst wenig Erfolg hat, kann auch mal etwas gelingen.
e. Wenn man sich nicht beeilt, ergeht es einem schlecht.
f. Leute, die zuviel Erfolg oder Glück haben, werden übermütig.[2]

[1] *need* [2] *cocky*

Situation 14 Zum Schreiben: Eine Tiergeschichte

Salzburg. Ein vierbeiniger Freund wird Gassi geführt.

1. Hatten Sie oder Freunde von Ihnen ein Haustier? Schreiben Sie über dieses Haustier eine lustige, peinliche oder traurige Geschichte.
2. Schreiben Sie eine Geschichte über ein Erlebnis mit einem Haustier oder mit einem freilebenden Tier.

Machen Sie zuerst eine Liste mit Stichwörtern. Schreiben Sie dann eine Einleitung. Beenden Sie die Geschichte mit einem Schlußsatz.

Kulturprojekt Fremde in Deutschland

Lesen Sie in einem Geschichtsbuch oder in einer Enzyklopädie nach:

- Im 17. und 18. Jahrhundert kamen Franzosen nach Deutschland. Wer waren sie? Warum kamen sie? Wie wurden sie aufgenommen?
- Im 19. Jahrhundert kamen billige Arbeitskräfte[1] für den Bergbau[2] ins Ruhrgebiet. Aus welchem Land kamen sie?
- Nach 1945 kamen viele deutsche Flüchtlinge aus früher deutschen Gebieten in die Bundesrepublik. Wie viele waren es ungefähr und aus welchen Ländern wurden sie vertrieben?
- Zwischen 1955 und 1973, in der Zeit des Wirtschaftswunders,[3] wurden „Gastarbeiter" nach Deutschland geholt. Aus welchen Ländern kamen sie? Welche Gruppe ist am größten?
- Mit den neuen Reisemöglichkeiten in den früher sozialistischen Ländern kommen Deutsche aus osteuropäischen Ländern nach Deutschland. Man nennt sie Aussiedler[4] und Aussiedlerinnen. Woher kommen sie? Warum kommen sie nach Deutschland? Welche Probleme haben sie?
- Wie viele Ausländer und Ausländerinnen leben zur Zeit in Deutschland?

[1] *workers* [2] *mining* [3] *"economic miracle" (refers to the post-war reconstruction of West Germany)* [4] *expatriates*

Porträt

Die Frauenrechtlerin[1] Hedwig Dohm (1833-1919) war in der bürgerlichen Frauenbewegung aktiv, die nach der Revolution von 1848 in Deutschland begann. Hedwig Dohm protestierte gegen das Leitbild[2] der „guten deutschen Hausfrau" und die Reduzierung der Frau auf die Mutterrolle. Sie forderte[3] bessere Bildungschancen für Mädchen, unter anderem in wissenschaftlichen Berufen, das Wahlrecht[4] für Frauen, absolute Gleichberechtigung[5] und Mutterschutz:[6] „Lernt eure Kraft kennen, meine sanften[7] Schwestern. . . ." Hedwig Dohm gehört neben Helene Lange (1848-1930), Louise Otto-Peters (1819-1895) und der Sozialistin Clara Zetkin (1857-1933) zu den prominentesten Mitgliedern der Frauenbewegung in Deutschland.

Berlin, die Heimat- und Geburtsstadt von Hedwig Dohm, war jahrzehntelang das Symbol der deutschen Teilung. Die frühere und jetzige Hauptstadt von Deutschland war das Zentrum des Kalten Krieges zwischen den westlichen Siegermächten[8] und der Sowjetunion. Die Berliner Mauer, die am 13. August 1961 von der DDR gebaut wurde, machte die Gegensätze[9] zwischen Ost und West deutlicher als alles andere. Die Mauer fiel am 9. November 1989 nach einer friedlichen[10] Revolution in der DDR. Ein neues Kapitel in der 750 Jahre alten Stadt hat begonnen.

Die Berliner Mauer fällt

[1]*women's rights advocate* [2]*ideal* [3]*demanded* [4]*right to vote* [5]*equal rights* [6]*protection of pregnant women and new mothers* [7]*gentle* [8]*victorious powers* [9]*contrasts* [10]*peaceful*

VIDEOECKE

Krawalle[1] in Magdeburg

Ausländerfeindlichkeit und Rechtsradikalismus: eins der vielen Probleme des wiedervereinigten Deutschlands. Der Clip zeigt, wieviel Terror von einigen wenigen gewaltbereiten[2] rechtsradikalen Jugendlichen ausgehen kann und was man dagegen machen muß.

- Wie viele rechte Jugendliche haben Jagd[3] auf Ausländer gemacht?
- Was hat die Polizei gemacht?
- Wer hat gegen die Krawalle protestiert?
- Welcher Politiker hat diese Krawalle kommentiert?

Viele Menschen aus Magdeburg haben spontan Demonstrationen organisiert

[1]*riots* [2]*violent* [3]*hunt, attack*

Partner und Familie — Partners and Family

Partner und Familie	Partners and Family
die **Ehe, -n**	marriage
die **Konfession, -en**	religious denomination, church
die **Scheidung, -en**	divorce
die **Verantwortung, -en**	responsibility
der **Beschützer, -**	protector
der **Vertrag, ¨e**	contract
der **Ehevertrag, ¨e**	prenuptial agreement
das **Berufsleben**	career, professional life
sich kümmern um	to take care of
mit·versorgen	to be equally responsible for taking care of
sorgen für	to take care of
übernehmen, übernimmt, übernahm, übernommen	to take on (responsibility)
sich verheiraten mit	to get married to
verheiratet sein	to be married
sich verlieben in (+ *akk.*)	to fall in love with
verliebt sein	to be in love
sich verloben mit	to get engaged to
verlobt sein	to be engaged

Ähnliche Wörter

die **Hausfrau, -en**; die **Partnerin, -nen**; die **Ehepartnerin, -nen**; die **Partnerschaft, -en** der **Hausmann, ¨er**; der **Partner, -**; der **Ehepartner, -**

Multikulturelle Gesellschaft — Multicultural Society

Multikulturelle Gesellschaft	Multicultural Society
die **Ausländerin, -nen**	female foreigner
die **Türkin, -nen**	female Turk
der **Ausländer, -**	male foreigner
der **Ausländerhaß**	hostility toward foreigners
der **Flüchtling, -e**	refugee
der **Türke, -n**	male Turk
das **Vorurteil, -e**	prejudice
aus·wandern, ist ausgewandert	to emigrate
ein·wandern, ist eingewandert	to immigrate
verfolgen	to persecute

Ähnliche Wörter

der **Neonazi, -s**; der **Rechtsradikale, -n** (*wk. masc.*)
diskriminieren

Berufe — Professions

Berufe	Professions
die **Gewerkschaftssekretärin, -nen**	female union secretary
die **Herausgeberin, -nen**	female editor
die **Übersetzerin, -nen**	female translator
der **Gewerkschaftssekretär, -e**	male union secretary
der **Herausgeber, -**	male editor
der **Übersetzer, -**	male translator
das **Vorstandsmitglied, -er**	committee member

Ähnliche Wörter

die **Germanistin, -nen**; die **Journalistin, -nen**; die **Kabarettistin, -nen**; die **Krimiautorin, -nen**; die **Zoodirektorin, -nen** der **Germanist, -en** (*wk. masc.*); der **Journalist, -en** (*wk. masc.*); der **Kabarettist, -en** (*wk. masc.*); der **Krimiautor, -en** (*wk. masc.*); der **Rockstar, -s**; der **Zoodirektor, -en** (*wk. masc.*) das **Fotomodell, -e**

Tiere — Animals

Tiere	Animals
die **Biene, -n**	bee
die **Fledermaus, ¨e**	bat
die **Mücke, -n**	mosquito
die **Schildkröte, -n**	turtle
die **Schlange, -n**	snake
die **Klapperschlange, -n**	rattlesnake
die **Riesenschlange, -n**	boa constrictor; python
die **Schnecke, -n**	snail
der **Adler, -**	eagle
der **Gepard, -e**	cheetah
der **Hai, -e**	shark
der **Kolibri, -s**	hummingbird
der **Löwe, -n** (*wk. masc.*)	lion
der **Papagei, -en**	parrot
der **Rüssel, -**	trunk (*of an elephant*)
der **Stoßzahn, ¨e**	tusk
der **Vogel, ¨**	bird
der **Wasservogel, ¨**	water fowl
das **Meerschweinchen, -**	guinea pig
das **Tier, -e**	animal
das **Haustier, -e**	pet
das **Landsäugetier, -e**	land mammal

Ähnliche Wörter

die **Giraffe, -n;** die **Maus, ¨-e;** die **Ratte, -n** der **Albatros, -se;** der **Blauwal, -e;** der **Delphin, -e;** der **Hamster, -** der **Piranha, -s;** der **Skorpion, -e** das **Krokodil, -e;** das **Wildschwein, -e;** das **Zebra, -s**

Sonstige Substantive — Other Nouns

die **Diplomarbeit, -en** — thesis (*for an advanced degree*)
die **Eigenschaft, -en** — trait, characteristic
die **Einstellung, -en** — attitude
die **Gewalt** — violence
  Gewalt an·wenden — to use violence
die **Lichterkette, -n** — candlelight march
die **Pension** — retirement
  in Pension gehen — to retire
die **Steuer, -n** — tax
die **Tollwut** — rabies
die **Zukunft** — future

der **Bauernhof, ¨-e** — farm
der **Grund, ¨-e** — reason
der **Käfig, -e** — cage
der **Sinn (für)** — sense (of, for)
der **Stichpunkt, -e** — main point
der **Träger, -** — recipient (*of a prize*)
der **Unsinn** — nonsense
der **Wehrdienst** — military service

das **Elfenbein** — ivory
das **Glück** (R) — happiness; luck
das **Loch, ¨-er** — hole
das **Wohnhaus, ¨-er** — apartment building
das **Wohnheim, -e** — state-subsidized apartment building

Ähnliche Wörter

die **Chance, -n;** die **Intelligenz;** die **Karriere, -n;** die **Krise, -n;** die **Natur; in freier Natur;** die **Steinzeit;** die **Technik** der **Bestseller, -s;** der **Charakter;** der **Chauvi, -s;** der **Fanatiker, -;** der **Fernsehfilm, -e;** der **Preis, -e;** der **Text, -e** das **Nest, -er**

Sonstige Verben — Other Verbs

an·gehören — to belong to (*an organization*)
an·greifen, griff an, angegriffen — to attack
auf·wachsen, wächst auf, wuchs auf, ist aufgewachsen — to grow up
binden an (+ *akk.*) — to tie to
erreichen — to reach
erwarten — to expect
fördern — to promote
sich fürchten vor (+ *dat.*) — to be afraid of
halten von, hält, hielt, gehalten — to think of
impfen gegen — to vaccinate for
stechen, sticht, stach, gestochen — to sting; to bite (*of insects*)
verbrennen (R) — to burn; incinerate
verhungern — to starve
verschwinden, verschwand, ist verschwunden — to disappear

Ähnliche Wörter

auf·hängen, interviewen, protestieren

Adjektive und Adverbien — Adjectives and Adverbs

ausgebildet — educated
eng — tight; narrow; small
fleißig — industrious
geborgen — protected
geduldig — patient
gefährlich — dangerous
handwerklich — handy
komisch — funny, strange
lustig — fun, funny
minderwertig — inferior
neugierig — curious
peinlich — embarrassing
rechzeitig — timely, on time
selbständig — independent
unbegabt — untalented
zahm — tame

Ähnliche Wörter

afro-deutsch, antirassistisch, dominant, gemütlich, ideal, illegal, konkret, logisch, russisch

Sonstige Wörter und Ausdrücke — Other Words and Expressions

anstatt (+ *gen.*) — instead of
außerhalb (+ *gen.*) — outside of
damit (R) — so that
eher — rather
einverstanden — in agreement
  einverstanden sein mit — to be in agreement with
statt (+ *gen.*) — instead of
trotz (+ *gen.*) — in spite of
überall — everywhere
um . . . zu — in order to
während (+ *gen.*) — during
wegen (R) (+ *gen.*) — because of
wohl — probably

LESEECKE

LEKTÜRE 1

Vor dem Lesen

1. Die USA sind eines der traditionellen Einwandererländer der Welt. Welche Gründe haben Menschen, ihr Heimatland zu verlassen?
2. Was für Probleme haben Fremde in den USA?
3. Was wissen Sie über ausländische Arbeitnehmer oder „Gastarbeiter" in der Bundesrepublik? Welche Probleme könnten sie haben?
4. Der Schriftsteller hat die folgende Kurzgeschichte in zwei Sprachen geschrieben, auf deutsch und auf türkisch. Warum?

Deutsche Kastanien[1]

von Yüksel Pazarkaya

„Du bist kein Deutscher!" sagte Stefan zu Ender in der Pause auf dem Schulhof. Weshalb[2] nur wollte er heute mit Ender nicht Fangen[3] spielen? Um eben einen Grund dafür zu nennen, sagte er einfach: „Du bist doch kein Deutscher." Ender war verdutzt[4] und betroffen.[5] Stefan war sein liebster Klassen- 5 kamerad, sein bester Spielfreund.

„Wieso[6]?" konnte er nur fragen.

Stefan verstand ihn nicht. Was heißt da „wieso"? Oder hält sich[7] Ender wohl für einen Deutschen? „Du bist eben kein Deutscher", sagte er. „Du bist kein Deutscher wie ich." Enders schöne dunkle Augen wurden traurig. Sein Inneres[8] 10 sträubte sich,[9] als hätte er sich etwas zuschulden kommen lassen.[10] In seinem Herzen zerbrach[11] etwas. Er schwieg.[12] Er ließ den Kopf hängen. Er ging weg. An diesem Tag sprach er mit Stefan kein Wort mehr. Dem Unterricht konnte er nicht folgen. Dem Lehrer konnte er nicht zuhören. Sein Kopf wurde immer schwerer.

Auch im letzten Herbst war es ihm einmal so ergangen. In dem Wohnviertel 15 gibt es einen hübschen kleinen Park, voll Blumen und Bäume. Im Herbst ist er am schönsten. Dann ziehen die Kastanien alle Kinder in der Umgebung an. Die Kinder werfen die Kastanien mit Steinen herunter. Wer viel sammelt,[13] verkauft

[1]*chestnuts* [2]*why* [3]*tag* [4]*taken aback* [5]*stunned* [6]*Why* [7]hält . . . *consider himself* [8]*inside* [9]sträubte . . . *stood on end* [10]als . . . *as if he had done something wrong* [11]*broke to pieces* [12]*became silent* [13]*collects*

sie an den Zoo als Futter für die Elefanten und Kamele. Andere bringen sie in die Schule mit. Man kann sie nämlich im Mathematikunterricht brauchen. Und die
20 kleinen, die noch nicht zur Schule gehen, spielen mit den Kastanien wie mit Murmeln.[14]

Der Lehrer sagte: „Jedes Kind bringt zehn Stück mit." Sie sind 34 Kinder in der Klasse. Wenn jedes Kind zehn Kastanien mitbringt, macht es genau 340 Stück. Und damit lassen sich ganz gut Mengenlehre[15] und die vier Rechenarten[16] üben.

25 Am Nachmittag ging Ender in den Park. Zwei Kinder warfen mit Steinen nach den Kastanien. Sie waren zwar[17] keine Freunde von ihm, aber er kannte sie. Er sah sie öfters in diesem Wohnviertel.

Ender näherte sich[18] ihnen. Er bückte sich[19] nach einer Kastanie, die auf dem Boden lag. Eines von den beiden Kindern sagte zu ihm: „Finger weg!" — „Ich will
30 auch Kastanien sammeln", sagte Ender. Das zweite Kind rief: „Du darfst sie nicht sammeln, das sind deutsche Kastanien." Ender verstand nichts. Das erste Kind fügte hinzu:[20] „Du bist kein Deutscher." Dann sagte das andere: „Du bist Ausländer." Sie stellten sich herausfordernd[21] vor Ender hin. Er verharrte gebückt[22] und mit ausgestreckter Hand. Wenn er sich noch ein bißchen bückte, könnte er die
35 Kastanie fassen.[23] Doch er konnte sie nicht erreichen. Den Kopf nach oben, den Kindern zugewandt,[24] erstarrte[25] er eine Weile in gebückter Haltung. Dann richtete er sich auf.[26] Natürlich ohne Kastanie. Verstummt.[27] Er wollte zwar sagen: „Der Park gehört allen, jeder kann Kastanien sammeln", doch er brachte kein Wort heraus. Dafür waren die anderen um so lauter: „Du bist Ausländer. Das sind deut-
40 sche Kastanien. Wenn du sie anfaßt,[28] kannst du was erleben", wollten sie ihm Angst einjagen.[29]

Ender war völlig durcheinander. „Soll ich mit denen kämpfen?" schoß[30] es ihm durch den Kopf. Dann sah er mal den einen, mal den anderen an. „Gegen zwei zu kämpfen ist unklug", dachte er. Er rannte fort,[31] ohne die beiden noch einmal
45 anzusehen.

Als er an jenem Tag nach Hause kam, stellte Ender seiner Mutter einige Fragen. Aber seine Mutter ging nicht darauf ein.[32] Sie lenkte ab.[33]

Nun war Ender entschlossen,[34] nach dem, was heute zwischen Stefan und ihm passiert war, die Frage endlich zu lösen, die den ganzen Tag wieder in seinem
50 Kopf herumschwirrte.[35] Sobald er den Fuß über die Türschwelle[36] setzte, schleuderte[37] er der Mutter seine Frage ins Gesicht: „Mutti, was bin ich?"

Das war eine unerwartete Frage für seine Mutter. Ebenso unerwartet war ihre Antwort: „Du bist Ender."

„Ich weiß, ich heiße Ender. Das habe ich nicht gefragt. Aber was bin ich?"
55 blieb Ender hartnäckig.[38]

[14]*marbles* [15]*set theory* [16]*mathematical functions* [17]*to be sure* [18]näherte . . . *approached* [19]bückte . . . *bent down* [20]fügte . . . *added* [21]*challenging* [22]Er . . *he stayed bent forward* [23]*grab* [24]*turned toward* [25]*stood paralyzed* [26]richtete . . . auf *got back up* [27]*speechless* [28]*touch* [29]ihm . . . *scare him* [30]*shot* [31]*away* [32]ging . . . *didn't get into it* [33]lenkte . . . *got off the subject* [34]*determined* [35]*was buzzing around* [36]*threshold* [37]*hurled* [38]*obstinate*

„Komm erstmal herein. Nimm deinen Ranzen[39] ab, zieh die Schuhe aus", sagte seine Mutter.

„Gut", sagte Ender. „Aber sag du mir auch, was ich bin."

Daraufhin dachte Enders Mutter, daß er mit ihr einen Jux machte[40] oder ihr
60 vielleicht ein Rätsel aufgab. „Du bist ein Schüler", sagte sie.

Ender ärgerte sich.[41] „Du nimmst mich auf den Arm",[42] sagte er. „Ich frage dich, was ich bin. Bin ich nun Deutscher oder Türke, was bin ich?"

Hoppla![43] Solche Fragen gefielen Enders Mutter gar nicht. Denn die Antwort darauf fiel ihr schwer. Was sollte sie da sagen? Im Grunde[44] war das keine schwere
65 Frage. Sie kannte auch die genaue Antwort auf diese Frage. Aber würde Ender sie auch verstehen können? Würde er sie akzeptieren, akzeptieren können? Wenn er sie auch annahm,[45] würde ihm das überhaupt nützen?[46]

Seine Mutter und sein Vater sind Türken. In der Türkei sind sie geboren, aufgewachsen und in die Schule gegangen. Nach Deutschland sind sie nur gekom-
70 men, um zu arbeiten und Geld verdienen zu können. Sie können auch gar nicht gut Deutsch. Wenn sie Deutsch sprechen, muß Ender lachen. Denn sie sprechen oft falsch. Sie können nicht alles richtig sagen.

Bei Ender ist es aber ganz anders. Er ist in Deutschland geboren. Hier ist er in den Kindergarten gegangen. Jetzt geht er in die erste Klasse, in eine deutsche
75 Schule. Deutsche Kinder sind seine Freunde. In seiner Klasse sind auch einige ausländische Kinder. Ender macht aber zwischen ihnen keinen Unterschied,[47] er kann keinen machen, dieser Deutscher, dieser nicht oder so, denn außer einem sprechen sie alle sehr gut Deutsch. Da gibt es nur einen, Alfonso. Alfonso tut Ender etwas leid. Alfonso kann nicht so gut Deutsch sprechen wie die anderen
80 Kinder. Ender denkt, daß Alfonso noch gar nicht sprechen gelernt hat. Die kleinen Kinder können doch auch nicht sprechen: so wie ein großes Baby kommt ihm Alfonso vor.

Ender spricht auch Türkisch, aber nicht so gut wie Deutsch. Wenn er Türkisch spricht, mischt er oft deutsche Wörter hinein. Wie eine Muttersprache hat er
85 Deutsch gelernt. Nicht anders als die deutschen Kinder. Manchmal hat er das Gefühl, daß zwischen ihnen doch ein Unterschied ist, weil deutsche Kinder nicht Türkisch können. Doch wenn in der Klasse der Unterricht oder auf dem Schulhof das Spielen beginnt, vergeht dieses Gefühl wieder ganz schnell. Gerade wenn er mit Stefan spielt, ist es unmöglich, daß ihm ein solches Gefühl kommt.

90 Deshalb war sein Staunen[48] so groß über die Worte Stefans. Und wenn Stefan nie wieder mit ihm spielte? Dann wird er sehr allein sein. Er wird sich langweilen.

Am Abend kam Enders Vater von der Arbeit nach Hause. Noch bevor die Tür sich richtig öffnete, fragte Ender: „Vati, bin ich Türke oder Deutscher?"

Sein Vater war sprachlos.

[39] *school bag* [40] einen . . . *was joking* [41] ärgerte . . . *got angry* [42] Du . . . *You're teasing me* [43] *Oops!* [44] Im . . . *In principle* [45] *accepted* [46] würde . . . *what good would it do him anyway?* [47] *difference, distinction* [48] *amazement*

95 „Warum fragst du?“ sagte er nach kurzem Überlegen.[49]
„Ich möchte es wissen“, sagte Ender entschlossen.
„Was würdest du lieber sein, ein Türke oder ein Deutscher?“ fragte sein Vater.
„Was ist besser?“ gab Ender die Frage wieder zurück.
„Beides ist gut, mein Sohn“, sagte sein Vater.
100 „Warum hat dann Stefan heute nicht mit mir gespielt?“
So kam Ender mit seinem Kummer[50] heraus, der ihn den ganzen Tag gequält[51] hatte.
„Warum hat er nicht mit dir gespielt?“ fragte sein Vater.
„‚Du bist kein Deutscher!‘ hat er gesagt. Was bin ich, Vati?“
105 „Du bist Türke, mein Sohn, aber du bist in Deutschland geboren“, sagte darauf sein Vater hilflos.
„Aber die Namen der deutschen Kinder sind anders als mein Name.“
Sein Vater begann zu stottern.
„Dein Name ist ein türkischer Name“, sagte er. „Ist Ender kein schöner Name?“
110 Ender mochte seinen Namen. „Doch! Aber er ist nicht so wie die Namen anderer Kinder“, sagte er.
„Macht nichts, Hauptsache, es ist ein schöner Name!“ sagte sein Vater.
„Aber Stefan spielt nicht mehr mit mir.“
Enders Vater schnürte es den Hals zu.[52] Ihm war, als ob er ersticken[53] müßte.
115 „Sei nicht traurig“, sagte er nach längerem Schweigen zu Ender. „Ich werde morgen mit Stefan sprechen. Er wird wieder mit dir spielen. Er hat sicher Spaß gemacht.“
Ender schwieg.

[49] *consideration* [50] *trouble* [51] *tormented* [52] schnürte . . . *constricted his throat* [53] *suffocate*

Arbeit mit dem Text

1. Deutsche oder Ausländer? Ordnen Sie die Personen in der Geschichte den zwei Kategorien zu.

2. Wer sagt das im Text?

Ender	Enders Mutter	Stefan
Enders Vater	Enders Lehrer	Kinder im Park

a. „Du bist kein Deutscher wie ich.“ ________
b. „Jedes Kind bringt zehn Stück mit.“ ________
c. „Ich will auch Kastanien sammeln.“ ________
d. „Das sind deutsche Kastanien.“ ________
e. „Du bist Ausländer.“ ________
f. „Du bist Ender.“ ________
g. „Du bist ein Schüler.“ ________
h. „Bin ich nun Deutscher oder Türke, was bin ich?“ ________
i. „Was würdest du lieber sein, ein Türke oder ein Deutscher?“ ________
j. „Dein Name ist ein türkischer Name.“ ________

3. Kombinieren Sie die Satzteile.

a. Stefan wollte nicht mit Ender spielen,	aber er kannte sie.
b. Ender ging weg,	damit er wieder mit Ender spielt.
c. Alle Kinder sammeln im Herbst Kastanien,	denn man kann sie gut gebrauchen.
d. Die Kinder im Park waren keine Freunde von Ender,	denn sie wußte keine Antwort.
e. Ender sammelte keine Kastanien,	mischt er oft deutsche Wörter hinein.
f. Als Ender nach Hause kam,	nachdem er mit den Kindern gesprochen hatte.
g. Die Fragen gefielen der Mutter nicht,	stellte er seiner Mutter Fragen.
h. Wenn Ender Türkisch spricht,	weil er kein Deutscher war.
i. Deutsche Kinder sind anders,	weil er traurig war.
j. Der Vater will mit Stefan sprechen,	weil sie kein Türkisch können.

4. Wie finden Sie Ender? Wie finden Sie die deutschen Kinder?

5. Der Schluß ist offen. Schreiben Sie auf, wie es weitergeht.

LEKTÜRE 2

Vor dem Lesen

Was assoziieren Sie mit Frauen?

Frauen

Frauen kommen langsam, aber gewaltig[1]

Songtext von Ina Deter

Schlaue Frauen sind verdächtig,[2] nehmen alles in die Hand[3]
Schlaue Frauen beweisen[4] täglich ihren Verstand
Schlaue Frauen schlagen auf den Magen, müssen immer besser sein
Schlaue Frauen jagen Männern Ängste ein

5 Frauen machen ständig[5] klar
Frauen lieben sich sonderbar[6]
Frauen setzen alles dran[7]
Frauen nehmen es wie'n Mann

Starker Mann, was nun?
10 *Keine Zeit mehr, was zu tun.*
Frauen kommen langsam, aber gewaltig

[1] *powerfully* [2] *suspicious* [3] nehmen . . . *take control of everything* [4] *prove* [5] *always* [6] *peculiarly* [7] setzen . . . *leave no stone unturned*

Starke Frauen haben schwache Nerven, müssen wie ein Wunder sein
Starke Frauen trinken heimlich,[8] ganz allein
Starke Frauen sind wie Kinder, wollen Komplimente hören
15 Starke Frauen lassen sich schnell irreführen[9]

Frauen sind wie im Roman
Rufen immer zuerst an
Frauen suchen Zärtlichkeit[10]
Wollen was auf Ewigkeit[11]

20 *Starker Mann, was nun . . .*

Frauen gibt man immer Küsse
Hassen ihre Kompromisse
Frauen hab'n 'nen Schlankheitstick[12]
Finden sich immer zu dick
25 Frauen macht die Liebe blind
Wünschen sich heimlich ein Kind
Frauen fragen sich immer was
Kriegen ohne Männer Spaß[13]

Starker Mann, was nun . . .

30 Schöne Frauen haben's leichter, hab'n die alten Trickse drauf[14]
Schöne Frauen fängt man vor dem Fallen auf
Schöne Frauen werden blöd angequatscht[15] und billig angemacht[16]
Schöne Frauen muß man 'rumkriegen[17] für 'ne Nacht

Starker Mann, was nun . . .

[8]*secretly* [9]lassen . . . *let themselves be quickly led astray* [10]*tenderness* [11]auf . . . *for eternity* [12]*obsession with being thin* [13]kriegen . . . Spaß *have fun* [14]haben . . . *are up to their old tricks* [15]blöd . . . *hit on feeble-mindedly* [16]*hit on* [17]*round up, win over*

Arbeit mit dem Songtext

1. Von welchen Frauen singt Ina Deter? Setzen Sie die Adjektive ein.

	________ Frauen	________ Frauen	________ Frauen
Wie sind sie?			
Was machen sie?			
Was macht man mit ihnen?			

2. Schreiben Sie in die Tabelle oben, was im Text über diese Frauen vorkommt.
3. Schreiben Sie fünf Aussagen über Frauen im allgemeinen auf, die Sie besonders interessant, witzig oder stereotyp finden.
4. Welche Stereotype über schöne Frauen kommen vor?

STRUKTUREN UND ÜBUNGEN

12.1 The genitive case

Spoken German: Possession may be indicated by **von.**

As you have learned, the preposition **von** followed by the dative case is commonly used in spoken German to express possession.

Das ist das Haus **von meinen Eltern.**	*This is my parents' house.*

Written German: Use the genitive case to indicate possession.

In writing, and sometimes in speech, this relationship between two noun phrases may also be expressed with the genitive case. The genitive case in German is equivalent to both the *of*-phrase and the possessive with *'s* in English.

Kennst du den Freund **meiner Schwester**?	*Do you know my sister's friend?*
Die Farbe **des Mantels** gefällt mir nicht.	*I don't like the color of the coat.*

English tends to use the possessive *'s* with nouns denoting people (for example: *the girl's mother*). In German, **s** (without the apostrophe) is added only to *proper names* of people and places.

Nora**s** Vater	*Nora's father*
England**s** Rettung	*England's salvation*

A. Nouns in the Genitive

Feminine nouns and plural nouns do not add any endings in the genitive case. In the singular genitive, masculine and neuter nouns of more than one syllable add **-s** and those of one syllable add **-es: die Farbe des Vogel*s*, die Größe des Haus*es*.**

Masculine	*Neuter*	*Feminine*	*Plural*
des Vater**s**	des Kind**es**	der Mutter	der Eltern

B. Articles and Article-like Words in the Genitive

In the genitive case, all determiners—**der**-words and **ein**-words—end in **es** in the masculine and neuter singular, and in **er** in the feminine singular and all plural forms.

Masculine	*Neuter*	*Feminine*	*Plural*
d**es** Mannes	d**es** Kindes	d**er** Frau	d**er** Eltern
ein**es** Mannes	ein**es** Kindes	ein**er** Frau	
mein**es** Mannes	mein**es** Kindes	mein**er** Frau	mein**er** Eltern
dies**es** Mannes	dies**es** Kindes	dies**er** Frau	dies**er** Eltern

C. Adjectives in the Genitive

In the genitive, all adjectives end in **en** when preceded by a determiner.*

Masculine and Neuter	*Feminine and Plural*
des arm**en** Mannes	der arm**en** Frau
des arm**en** Kindes	der arm**en** Leute

Eine mögliche Rolle des moder**nen** Mannes ist es, zu Hause zu bleiben und auf die Kinder aufzupassen.

A possible role for a modern man is to stay home and take care of the children.

Übung 1 Minidialoge

Ergänzen Sie die Wörter in Klammern.

1. KATRIN: Ist das dein Auto?
   ALBERT: Nein, das ist das Auto _____ Bruders. (mein)
2. BEAMTER: Was ist das Alter _____ Kinder? (Ihr)
   FRAU FRISCH: Natalie ist fünf, Rosemarie ist sechs und Lydia ist neun Jahre alt.
3. FRAU SCHULZ: Ist es wichtig, daß der Partner einen guten Beruf hat?
   THOMAS: Also, ich muß sagen, der Beruf _____ zukünftigen Partnerin ist mir ziemlich egal. (mein)
4. MONIKA: Möchtest du mit mir in die Berge fahren? Meine Eltern haben da ein Wochenendhaus.
   ROLF: Wo ist denn das Wochenendhaus _____ Eltern? (dein)
   MONIKA: In der Nähe von Lake Tahoe.
5. HEIDI: Kennst du den Film „M — Mörder unter uns“?
   ROLF: Ja.
   HEIDI: Wie heißt doch noch mal der Regisseur _____ Films? (dies-)

*Unpreceded masculine and neuter adjectives also end in **en;** unpreceded feminine and plural adjectives end in **er.** Unpreceded adjectives, however, rarely occur in the genitive.

6. ROLF: Brauchst du denn kein neues Nummernschild?
   PETER: Ach, ich nehme einfach das Nummernschild meines _____ Autos. (alt)
7. FRAU GRETTER: Wer ist denn das?
   FRAU KÖRNER: Das ist die zweite Frau meines _____ Mannes. (erst-)
8. FRAU AUGENTHALER: 24352—was ist denn das für eine Telefonnummer?
   RICHARD: Das ist die Telefonnummer meiner _____ Freundin. (neu)

Übung 2 Worüber sprechen sie?

Bilden Sie Sätze.

MODELL Albert sagt, daß sein Auto rot ist. →
Albert spricht über die Farbe seines Autos.

das Alter	die Kleidung	die Situation
der Beruf	die Länge	die Sprache
das Bild	die Qualität	

1. Monika sagt, daß ihre Schwester als Lehrerin arbeitet.
2. Thomas sagt, daß sein Vater einen Picasso besitzt.
3. Frau Schulz sagt, daß ihre Nichten fünf und acht Jahre alt sind.
4. Stefan sagt, daß sein Studium insgesamt fünf Jahre dauert.
5. Albert sagt, daß seine Großeltern nur Spanisch sprechen.
6. Nora sagt, daß ihr Freund gern Jeans und lange Pullover trägt.
7. Thomas sagt, daß das Leitungswasser in Berkeley sehr gut ist.
8. Katrin sagt, daß Frauen für die gleiche Arbeit immer noch weniger verdienen als Männer.

12.2 Causality and purpose: *weil, damit, um . . . zu*

weil = reason for action
damit = goal of action
um . . . zu = goal of action

Use **weil** + dependent clause to express the reason for a particular action. Use **damit** or **um . . . zu** to express the goal of an action.

Viele Deutsche wanderten nach Australien aus, **weil ihnen Deutschland zu eng war.**	*Many Germans emigrated to Australia because Germany was too crowded for them.*
Sie wanderten nach Australien aus, **um dort eine bessere Arbeit zu finden.**	*They emigrated to Australia in order to find a better job there.*

Weil and **damit** introduce a dependent clause. Recall that the conjugated verb is in last position in a dependent clause.

Albert steht auf, damit Frau Schulz sich setzen **kann.**	*Albert gets up so that Frau Schulz can sit down.*

Um . . . zu clauses have no expressed subjects.

Damit and **um . . . zu** both express the aim or goal of an action. But whereas **damit** introduces a dependent clause complete with subject and conjugated verb, **um . . . zu** introduces a dependent infinitive without a subject and without a conjugated verb. Use **damit** when the subject of the main clause is different from the subject of the dependent clause; use **um . . . zu** when the understood subject of the dependent infinitive is the same as the subject of the main clause.

Heidi macht das Fenster zu, **damit** Stefan nicht friert.
Heidi closes the window so that Stefan won't be cold.

Heidi macht das Fenster zu, **damit** sie nicht friert. → Heidi macht das Fenster zu, **um** nicht **zu** frieren.

Heidi closes the window so that she won't be cold. → *Heidi closes the window so as not to be cold.*

Übung 3 Erfolgsgeschichten

Was muß man tun, um Erfolg an der Universität zu haben?

MODELL Um gute Noten zu bekommen, muß man fleißig lernen.

1. morgens munter[1] sein
2. die Professoren kennenlernen
3. die Mitstudenten kennenlernen
4. am Wochenende nicht allein sein
5. die Kurse bekommen, die man will
6. in vier Jahren fertig werden
7. nicht verhungern
8. einen Freund / eine Freundin finden
9. ein A in Deutsch bekommen
10. nicht ins Sprachlabor gehen müssen

a. Deutsch belegen
b. sich die Kassetten kaufen oder ausleihen
c. früh ins Bett gehen
d. in die Sprechstunde gehen
e. jeden Tag zum Unterricht kommen
f. Leute einladen
g. regelmäßig essen
h. sich so früh wie möglich einschreiben
i. viel Gruppenarbeit machen
j. viel lernen und wenig Feste feiern

Übung 4 Gute Gründe?

Verbinden Sie Sätze aus der ersten Gruppe mit Sätzen aus der zweiten Gruppe mit Hilfe der Konjunktionen **weil, damit, um . . . zu.** Wenn Ihnen ein Grund nicht gefällt, suchen Sie einen besseren Grund.

MODELL Ich möchte immer in den USA leben. Die USA sind das beste Land der Welt. →
Ich möchte immer in den USA leben, weil die USA das beste Land der Welt sind.

---

[1] *wide awake*

GRUPPE 1

Ich möchte immer in den USA leben.
Ich möchte für ein paar Jahre in Deutschland leben.
Ausländer haben oft Probleme.
Wenn ich Kinder habe, möchte ich in den USA leben.
Viele Ausländer kommen in die USA.
Englisch sollte die einzige offizielle Sprache der USA sein.

GRUPPE 2

Ausländer verstehen die Sprache und Kultur des Gastlandes nicht.
Ich möchte richtig gut Deutsch lernen.
Die USA sind das beste Land der Welt.
In den USA kann man gut Geld verdienen.
Meine Kinder sollen als Amerikaner aufwachsen.
Aus der multikulturellen Bevölkerung soll eine homogene Gemeinschaft werden.

12.3 Talking about the future: the present and future tenses

You already know that **werden** is the equivalent of English *to become.*

Ich möchte Ärztin werden. — *I'd like to become a physician.*

future tense = **werden** + infinitive

You can also use a form of **werden** plus infinitive to talk about future events.

Im Jahr 2000 **wird** der Liter Benzin 5,- DM **kosten.** — *In the year 2000, a liter of gas will cost 5 marks.*
Dann **werde** ich wahrscheinlich nicht mehr Auto **fahren.** — *Then I probably won't drive anymore.*

When an adverb of time is present or when it is otherwise clear that future actions or events are indicated, German speakers normally use the present tense rather than the future tense to talk about what will happen in the future.

Nächstes Jahr **fahren** wir nach Schweden. — *Next year we're going to Sweden.*
Was **machst** du, wenn du in Schweden bist? — *What are you going to do when you're in Sweden?*

Use **wohl** with the future tense to express present or future probability.

The future tense with **werden** can express present or future probability. In such cases, the sentence often includes an adverb such as **wohl** (*probably*).

Mein Freund wird jetzt **wohl** zu Hause sein. — *My friend should be home now.*
Morgen abend werden wir **wohl** zu Hause bleiben. — *Tomorrow evening, we'll probably stay home.*

Don't forget to put **werden** at the end of the dependent clause.

Ich weiß nicht, ob ich einmal heiraten **werde.**	*I don't know if I'm ever going to get married.*

Übung 5 Morgen ist Samstag

Was machen Frau Schulz und ihre Studenten morgen?

MODELL Katrin geht morgen ins Kino.

Katrin

1. Frau Schulz 2. Heidi 3. Peter 4. Monika

5. Stefan 6. Nora 7. Albert 8. Thomas

12.4 The passive voice

A. Uses of the Passive Voice

The passive voice is used in German to focus on the action of the sentence itself rather than on the person or thing performing the action.

ACTIVE

Der Arzt impft die Kinder.	*The physician inoculates the children.*

PASSIVE

Die Kinder **werden geimpft.**	*The children are (being) inoculated.*

Notice that the object of the active sentence, **die Kinder,** becomes the subject of the passive sentence.

In passive sentences, the agent of the action is often unknown or unspecified. In the following sentences, there is no mention of who performs each action.

Schildkröten werden oft als Haustiere gehalten.	*Turtles are often kept as pets.*
1088 wurde die erste Universität gegründet.	*The first university was founded in 1088.*

B. Forming the Passive Voice

passive = **werden** + past participle

The passive voice is formed with the auxiliary **werden** and the past participle of the verb. The present-tense and simple past-tense forms are the tenses you will encounter most frequently in the passive voice.

Passive Voice: **fragen**

Present Tense

ich	werde gefragt	wir	werden gefragt
du	wirst gefragt	ihr	werdet gefragt
Sie	werden gefragt	Sie	werden gefragt
er / sie / es	wird gefragt	sie	werden gefragt

Past Tense

ich	wurde gefragt	wir	wurden gefragt
du	wurdest gefragt	ihr	wurdet gefragt
Sie	wurden gefragt	Sie	wurden gefragt
er / sie / es	wurde gefragt	sie	wurden gefragt

C. Expressing the Agent in the Passive Voice

Passive agents are indicated by **von** + noun.

In most passive sentences in German, the agent (the person or thing performing the action) is not mentioned. When the agent is expressed, the construction **von** + dative is used.

ACTIVE VOICE

Die Kinder füttern die Tiere. — *The children are feeding the animals.*

PASSIVE VOICE

AGENT: **von** + DATIVE

Die Tiere werden **von den Kindern** gefüttert. — *The animals are being fed by the children.*

Übung 6 Frühjahrsputz bei den Wagners

Was wird alles gemacht?

MODELL Die Lampen werden abgestaubt.

1. die Fenster
2. das Silber
3. die Lampen
4. die Fußböden
5. die Schränke
6. die Gardinen
7. die Sessel
8. der Hof
9. die Teppiche

a. staubsaugen
b. fegen
c. putzen
d. polieren
e. waschen
f. aufräumen
g. aufwischen
h. reinigen[1]
i. abstauben

---

[1] *to clean*

Übung 7 Geschichte

Hier sind die Antworten. Was sind die Fragen?

MODELL 1492 → Wann wurde Amerika entdeckt?

1. um 2500 v. Chr.[1]
2. 44 v. Chr.
3. 800 n. Chr.[2]
4. 1088
5. 1661
6. 1789
7. 1867
8. 1945
9. 1963
10. 1990

a. Deutschland vereinigen
b. John F. Kennedy erschießen
c. die amerikanische Verfassung unterschreiben
d. die erste Universität (Bologna) gründen
e. die Atombomben auf Hiroshima und Nagasaki werfen
f. die ersten Pyramiden bauen
g. Cäsar ermorden
h. Alaska an die USA verkaufen
i. Karl den Großen zum Kaiser krönen
j. das erste Thanksgiving-Fest feiern

---

[1] vor Christus [2] nach Christus

APPENDICES

APPENDIX A
Informationsspiele: 2. Teil

Einführung B

Situation 6 Familie

MODELL S1: Wie heißt Claires Mutter?
S2: Sie heißt ______ .
S1: Wie schreibt man das?
S2: ______ .
S1: Wie alt ist Sofies Vater?
S2: Er ist ______ Jahre alt.
S1: Wo wohnt Mehmets Vater?
S2: Er wohnt in ______ .

		Claire	Richard	Sofie	Mehmet
Vater	*Name*	Bill			Kenan
	Alter		39		
	Wohnort			Dresden	
Mutter	*Name*		Maria		
	Alter	40	38	47	54
	Wohnort	New York			Izmir
Bruder	*Name*	—		Erwin	
	Alter	—			
	Wohnort	—	Innsbruck	Leipzig	Istanbul
Schwester	*Name*		Elisabeth	—	Fatima
	Alter	17	16	—	31
	Wohnort			—	

Situation 9 Temperaturen

MODELL S1: Wieviel Grad Fahrenheit sind 18 Grad Celsius?
S2: _____ Grad Fahrenheit.

F	90		32		−5	
C	32	18	0	−18	−21	−39

Kapitel 1

Situation 2 Freizeit

MODELL S1: Wie alt ist Richard?
S2: _____ .
S1: Woher kommt Rolf?
S2: Aus _____ .
S1: Was macht Jürgen gern?
S2: Er _____ .

S1: Wie alt bist du?
S2: _____ .
S1: Woher kommst du?
S2: _____ .
S1: Was machst du gern?
S2: _____ .

	Alter	Wohnort	Hobby
Richard		Innsbruck	geht gern in die Berge
Rolf	20		spielt gern Tennis
Jürgen		Göttingen	
Sofie			kocht gern
Jutta	16	München	
Melanie		Regensburg	
mein Partner / meine Partnerin			

Situation 7 Juttas Stundenplan

MODELL S1: Was hat Jutta am Montag um acht Uhr?
S2: Sie hat Latein.

Uhr	Montag	Dienstag	Mittwoch	Donnerstag	Freitag
8.00-8.45	Latein			Biologie	
8.50-9.35		Englisch	Englisch		Physik
9.35-9.50	←		Pause		→
9.50-10.35			Mathematik		Religion
10.40-11.25	Geschichte	Französisch		Mathematik	
11.25-11.35	←		Pause		→
11.35-12.15		Musik		Sport	
12.20-13.00	Erdkunde		Kunst		

Situation 10 Diese Woche

MODELL S1: Was macht Silvia am Montag?
S2: Sie steht um sechs Uhr auf.

	Silvia Mertens	Renate Röder	Mehmet Sengün
Montag	Sie steht um 6.00 Uhr auf.		
Dienstag		Sie spielt Tennis.	
Mittwoch	Sie schreibt eine Prüfung.		Er singt im Männerchor.
Donnerstag	Sie spielt mit Jürgen Squash.		
Freitag		Sie geht tanzen.	Er hört um 15 Uhr mit der Arbeit auf.
Samstag		Sie räumt ihre Wohnung auf.	Er räumt seine Wohnung auf.
Sonntag		Sie besucht ihre Eltern.	

Kapitel 2

Situation 3 Was machen sie morgen?

MODELL S1: Schreibt Silvia morgen einen Brief?
S2: Ja.
S1: Schreibst du morgen einen Brief?
S2: Ja. (Nein.)

	Jürgen	Silvia	mein(e) Partner(in)
einen Brief schreiben		+	
ein Buch kaufen		+	
einen Film anschauen	–	–	
eine Freundin anrufen			
die Hausaufgaben machen		+	
den Computer reparieren	–	+	
einen Freund besuchen			
das Zimmer aufräumen		–	

Situation 15 Was machen sie gern?

MODELL S1: Was trägt Richard gern?
S2: Pullis.
S1: Was trägst du gern?
S2: ______

	Richard	Josef und Melanie	mein(e) Partner(in)
fahren		Zug	
tragen	Pullis		
essen		Pizza	
sehen		Gruselfilme	
vergessen	seine Hausaufgaben		
waschen		ihr Auto	
treffen		ihre Lehrer	
einladen		ihre Eltern	
sprechen	Italienisch		

Kapitel 3

Situation 2 Kann Katrin kochen?

MODELL S1: Kann Peter kochen?
S2: Ja, fantastisch.
S1: Kannst du kochen?
S2: Ja, aber nicht so gut.

[+] ausgezeichnet, fantastisch, sehr gut, gut
[0] ganz gut
[−] nicht so gut, nur ein bißchen, gar nicht, kein bißchen

	Katrin	Peter	mein(e) Partner(in)
kochen		fantastisch	
zeichnen	sehr gut		
tippen		ganz gut	
Witze erzählen		ganz gut	
tanzen	fantastisch		
stricken	gar nicht		
Skateboard fahren		nicht so gut	
Geige spielen		nur ein bißchen	
schwimmen		nur ein bißchen	
ein Auto reparieren	nicht so gut		

Situation 14 Was machen sie, wenn . . . ?

MODELL S1: Was macht Renate, wenn sie müde ist?
S2: Sie trinkt Kaffee.
S1: Was machst du, wenn du müde bist?
S2: Ich gehe ins Bett.

	Renate	Mehmet	Ernst	mein(e) Partner(in)
traurig sein		hört Musik		
müde sein	trinkt Kaffee		geht ins Bett	
in Eile sein		geht sehr schnell		
wütend sein		trinkt ein Bier		
krank sein	geht zum Arzt		geht ins Bett	
glücklich sein		tanzt		
Hunger haben		ißt ein Stück Brot		
Langeweile haben	liest ein Buch		ärgert seine Schwester	

Kapitel 4

Situation 7 Wochenende

MODELL S1: Was hat Frau Ruf am Freitag gemacht?
S2: Sie ist nach Augsburg gefahren.
S1: Was hast du am Samstag gemacht?
S2: Ich _____ .

	am Freitag	am Samstag	am Sonntag
Frau Ruf	ist nach Augsburg gefahren		
Herr Ruf		hat die Wäsche gewaschen	hat im Garten gearbeitet
Jutta			hat den Hund gebadet
Hans		hat einen Roman gelesen	hat bis mittags geschlafen
Michael	hat mit Maria zu Abend gegessen		
Maria	hat am Abend viel Wein getrunken	hat in der Stadt eine Freundin getroffen	
mein Partner / meine Partnerin			

Situation 12 Das Wochenende der Nachbarn

MODELL S1: Was hat Herr Siebert am Samstag gemacht?
S2: Er hat seinen Keller aufgeräumt.

	am Freitag	am Samstag	am Sonntag
Herr Siebert		hat seinen Keller aufgeräumt	
Herr Thelen	hat seine neue Nachbarin kennengelernt		hat ein neues graues Haar entdeckt
Frau Gretter	ist mit ihrer Freundin ausgegangen		hat am Telefon ihren Namen buchstabiert
mein Partner / meine Partnerin			

Kapitel 6

Situation 16 Haus- und Gartenarbeit

MODELL S2: Was macht Thomas am liebsten?
S1: Er _____ am liebsten _____ .
S2: Was hat Nora letztes Wochenende gemacht?
S1: Sie hat _____ .

S1: Was muß Thomas diese Woche noch machen?
S2: Er muß _____ .
S1: Was machst du am liebsten?
S2: Ich _____ am liebsten _____ .

	Thomas	Nora	mein(e) Partner(in)
am liebsten		einkaufen gehen	
am wenigsten gern	das Bad putzen		
jeden Tag	nichts von alledem		
einmal in der Woche		die Wäsche waschen	
letztes Wochenende	das Geschirr spülen		
gestern	die Blumen gießen		
diese Woche		den Boden aufwischen	
bald mal wieder		staubwischen	

Kapitel 7

Situation 3 Deutschlandreise

Wo liegen die folgenden Städte? Braunschweig, Kiel, Bremen, Rostock, Frankfurt/Oder, Halle, Augsburg, Nürnberg, Stuttgart, Düsseldorf. Schreiben Sie die Namen der Städte auf die Landkarte.

MODELL S1: Wo liegt Hannover?
S2: Hannover liegt im Norden.
S1: Wo genau?
S2: Südlich von Hamburg.

Kapitel 9

Situation 1 Mahlzeiten und Getränke

MODELL S1: Was ißt Frau Gretter zum Frühstück?
S2: ______ .
S1: Was ißt du zum Frühstück?
S2: ______ .

	Frau Gretter	Stefan	Andrea	mein(e) Partner(in)
zum Frühstück essen		frisches Müsli	Brot mit selbstgemachter Marmelade	
zum Frühstück trinken		kalten Orangensaft		
zum Mittagessen essen	kalorienarmes Gemüse und Hähnchen		heiße Würstchen	
zum Abendessen essen		italienische Spaghetti		
nach dem Sport trinken	nichts, sie treibt keinen	kalten Tee mit Zitrone		
auf einem Fest trinken	deutschen Sekt		eiskalte Limonade	
essen, wenn er/sie groß ausgeht		frischen Fisch mit französischer Soße		

Kapitel 10

Situation 2 Reisen

MODELL

S1:	Woher kommt Richard?	S2:	Aus ______ .
S1:	Wohin fährt er in den Ferien?	S2:	Nach/In ______ .
S1:	Wo wohnt er?	S2:	Bei ______ .
S1:	Was macht er da?	S2:	Sie ______ .
S1:	Wann kommt er zurück?	S2:	In ______ .

	Richard	Sofie	Mehmet	Peter	Jürgen	mein(e) Partner(in)
Woher?		aus Dresden		aus Berkeley		
Wohin?		nach Düsseldorf		nach Hawaii		
Wo?		bei ihrer Tante	bei alten Freunden		bei einem Freund	
Was?	Französisch lernen		am Strand liegen; schwimmen		Ski fahren natürlich	
Wann?		in einer Woche	in zwei Wochen	nächstes Wochenende		

Situation 8 Wo wollen wir übernachten?

MODELL Wieviel kostet _____ ?
Haben die Zimmer im (in der) _____ eine eigene Dusche und Toilette?
Gibt es im (in der) _____ Einzelzimmer?
Gibt es im (in der, auf dem) _____ einen Fernseher?
Ist das Frühstück im (in der, auf dem) _____ inbegriffen?
Ist die Lage von dem (von der) _____ zentral/ruhig?
Gibt es im (in der, auf dem) _____ Telefon?

	das Hotel am Stadtpark	das Gästehaus Radaublick	die Jugendherberge	der Campingplatz
Preis pro Person		42,- DM		
Dusche/Toilette			nein	nein
Einzelzimmer				natürlich nicht
Fernseher	in jedem Zimmer	im Fernsehzimmer		natürlich nicht
Frühstück	inbegriffen		kostet extra	nein
zentrale Lage				
ruhige Lage				in der Nähe der Autobahn
Telefon	in jedem Zimmer	im Telefonzimmer	bei den Herbergseltern	Telefonzelle

Situation 14 Gespräche im Kaufhaus

MODELL S1: Welche Farbe gefällt Juttas Mutter am besten?
S2: _____ .
S1: Welche Farbe gefällt dir am besten?
S2: _____ .

	Jutta	Juttas Mutter	mein(e) Partner(in)
Welche Farbe gefällt ... am besten?	schwarz		
Welches Kleidungsstück fehlt ... noch?		ein schicker Pelzmantel	
Was steht ... gut?		ihr neues Kostüm	
Paßt ... Größe M?	nein, zu groß		
Hilf(s)t ... gern anderen beim Kleiderkauf?		allen, außer Jutta	
Was gehört ... seit mindestens drei Jahren?	ihr Walkman		

Kapitel 11

Situation 10 Krankheitsgeschichte

MODELL Hat Herr Thelen sich (Hast du dir) schon mal etwas gebrochen? Was?
Ist Herr Thelen (Bist du) schon mal im Krankenhaus gewesen? Warum?
Hat Claire (Hast du) schon mal eine Spritze bekommen? Gegen was?
Erkältet sich Claire (Erkältest du dich) oft?
Ist Herr Thelen (Bist du) gegen etwas allergisch? Gegen was?
Hat man Herrn Thelen (Hat man dir) schon mal einen Zahn gezogen?
Hatte Claire (Hattest du) schon mal hohes Fieber? Wie hoch?
Ist Herr Thelen (Bist du) schon mal in Ohnmacht gefallen?

	Claire	Herr Thelen	mein(e) Partner(in)
sich etwas brechen	den Arm		
im Krankenhaus sein	Nierenentzündung		
eine Spritze bekommen		Tetanus	
oft erkältet sein		nein	
gegen etwas allergisch sein	Sonne		
einen Zahn gezogen haben	nein		
hohes Fieber haben		41.2° C	
in Ohnmacht fallen	nein		

Kapitel 12

Situation 2 Der ideale Partner

MODELL Wie soll Heidis idealer Partner aussehen?
Was für einen Charakter soll er haben?
Welchen Beruf soll Rolfs ideale Partnerin haben?
Welche Interessen sollte sie haben?
Wie alt sollte dein idealer Partner/deine ideale Partnerin sein?
Welche Konfession sollte er/sie haben?
Welcher Nationalität sollte Heidis Partner angehören?
Welche politische Einstellung sollte er haben?

	Rolf	Heidi	mein(e) Partner(in)
Aussehen	schlank und sportlich		
Charakter	lustig und neugierig		
Beruf		Rechtsanwalt	
Interessen		Sport und Reisen	
Alter		ein paar Jahre jünger als sie	
Konfession		kein Fanatiker	
Nationalität	deutsch		
politische Einstellung	eher konservativ		

Situation 6 Ausländische Mitbürger

MODELL S1: Aus welchem Land kommt . . . ?
S2: Aus der Türkei.
S1: Was ist . . . von Beruf?
S2: Das weiß ich nicht.
S1: Wofür ist . . . bekannt?
S2: Für . . . / Als . . .

Name	Nationalität	Beruf	bekannt
Renan Demirkan		Schauspielerin	
Giovanni di Lorenzo	italienisch		als politischer Reporter für die „Süddeutsche Zeitung“
Lew Kopelew		Germanist	
Şinasi Dikmen	türkisch		als Kabarettist und Satiriker
Yilmaz Karahasan		Gewerkschaftssekretär der IG-Metall	
Katharina Oguntoye	afro-deutsch		als Mitherausgeberin von Texten afro-deutscher Frauen
Akif Pirinçci		Krimiautor	
Yüksel Pazarkaya	türkisch		als Träger des Adalbert-von-Chamisso-Preises

Situation 11 Tiere

MODELL Welche Tiere findet _____ am tollsten?
Vor welchem Tier hat _____ am meisten Angst?
Welches Tier hätte _____ gern als Haustier?
Welches wilde Tier würde _____ gern in freier Natur sehen?
Wenn _____ an Afrika denkt, an welche Tiere denkt er/sie?
Wenn _____ an die Wüste denkt, an welches Tier denkt er/sie dann zuerst?
Welche Vögel findet _____ am schönsten?
Welchen Fisch findet _____ am gefährlichsten?
Welchem Tier möchte _____ nicht im Wald begegnen?

	Ernst	Maria	mein(e) Partner(in)
Lieblingstier	ein Krokodil		
Angst		vor Mäusen	
Haustier		einen Papagei	
wildes Tier	einen Elefanten		
Afrika		an Zebras	
Wüste	an einen Skorpion		
Vögel	Adler		
Fisch		den Piranha	
Wald		einem Wildschwein	

APPENDIX B
Rollenspiele: 2. Teil

Kapitel 1

Situation 16 Im Auslandsamt

S2: Sie arbeiten im Auslandsamt der Universität. Ein Student / Eine Studentin kommt zu Ihnen und möchte ein Stipendium für Österreich.

- Fragen Sie nach den persönlichen Daten und schreiben Sie sie auf: Name, Adresse, Telefon, Geburtstag, Studienfach.
- Sagen Sie „Auf Wiedersehen".

Kapitel 2

Situation 14 Am Telefon

S2: Das Telefon klingelt. Ein Freund / Eine Freundin ruft an. Er/Sie lädt Sie ein. Fragen Sie: **wo, wann, um wieviel Uhr, wer ist da.** Sagen Sie „ja" oder „nein", und sagen Sie „tschüs".

Kapitel 3

Situation 12 In der Mensa

S2: Sie sind Student/Studentin an der Uni in Regensburg und sind in der Mensa. Jemand möchte sich an Ihren Tisch setzen. Fragen Sie, wie er/sie heißt, woher er/sie kommt und was er/sie studiert.

Kapitel 4

Situation 15 Das Studentenleben

S2: Sie sind Student/Studentin an einer Uni in Nordamerika. Ein Reporter / Eine Reporterin aus Österreich fragt Sie viel, und Sie antworten gern. Sie wollen aber auch wissen, was der Reporter / die Reporterin gestern alles gemacht hat: am Vormittag, am Mittag, am Nachmittag und am Abend.

Kapitel 5

Situation 12 Bei der Berufsberatung

S2: Sie sind Student/Studentin und gehen zur Berufsberatung, weil Sie nicht wissen, was Sie nach dem Studium machen sollen. Beantworten Sie die Fragen des Berufsberaters / der Berufsberaterin.

Kapitel 6

Situation 13 Zimmer zu vermieten

S2: Sie möchten ein Zimmer in Ihrem Haus vermieten. Das Zimmer ist 25 Quadratmeter groß und hat Zentralheizung. Es kostet warm 510 DM im Monat. Es hat große Fenster und ist sehr ruhig. Das Zimmer hat keine Küche und auch kein Bad, aber der Mieter / die Mieterin darf Ihre Küche und Ihr Bad benutzen. Der Mieter / Die Mieterin darf Freunde einladen, aber sie dürfen nicht zu lange bleiben. Sie haben kleine Kinder, die früh ins Bett müssen. Fragen Sie, was der Student / die Studentin studiert, ob er/sie raucht, ob er/sie oft laute Musik hört, ob er/sie Haustiere hat, ob er/sie Möbel hat.

Kapitel 7

Situation 8 Am Fahrkartenschalter

S2: Sie arbeiten am Fahrkartenschalter im Bahnhof von Bremen. Ein Fahrgast möchte eine Fahrkarte nach München kaufen. Hier ist der Fahrplan.

	Abfahrt	Ankunft	2. Kl.	1. Kl.
D-Zug	4.25	15.40	160,- DM	195,- DM
InterCity	7.15	16.05	175,-	210,-
D-Zug	7.30	20.45	160,-	195,-

Alle Züge fahren über Hannover und Würzburg.

Situation 10 Ein Auto kaufen

S2: Sie wollen einen Gebrauchtwagen kaufen und lesen deshalb die Anzeigen in der Zeitung. Die Anzeigen für einen VW Golf und einen Opel Corsa sind interessant. Rufen Sie an, und stellen Sie Fragen.

Sie haben auch eine Anzeige in die Zeitung gesetzt, weil Sie Ihren alten Wagen, einen Opel Astra, verkaufen wollen. Antworten Sie auf die Fragen der Leute, die Ihr Auto kaufen wollen.

MODELL Guten Tag, ich rufe wegen des VW Golf an.
Wie alt ist der Wagen?
Welche Farbe hat er?
Wie ist der Kilometerstand?
Wie lange hat er noch TÜV?
Was kostet der Wagen?

Modell	VW Golf	Opel Corsa	Opel Astra	Ford Fiesta
Baujahr			1992	1995
Farbe			braun	blau
Kilometerstand			90 000 km	45 000 km
TÜV			6 Monate	fast 2 Jahre
Benzin pro 100 km			7 Liter	6 Liter
Preis			17 900 DM	14 500 DM

Kapitel 8

Situation 8 Das Klassentreffen

S2: Sie sind auf dem fünften Klassentreffen Ihrer alten High-School-Klasse. Sie unterhalten sich mit einem alten Schulfreund / einer alten Schulfreundin. Fragen Sie: was er/sie nach Abschluß der High School gemacht hat, was er/sie jetzt macht und was seine/ihre Pläne für die nächsten Jahre sind.

Kapitel 9

Situation 14 Im Restaurant

S2: Sie arbeiten als Kellner/Kellnerin in einem Restaurant. Ein Gast setzt sich an einen freien Tisch. Bedienen Sie ihn.

Kapitel 10

Situation 10 Im Hotel

S2: Sie arbeiten an der Rezeption von einem Hotel. Alle Zimmer haben Dusche und Toilette. Manche haben auch Telefon. Frühstück ist inklusive. Das Hotel ist im Moment ziemlich voll. Ein Reisender / Eine Reisende kommt herein und erkundigt sich nach Zimmern. Denken Sie zuerst darüber nach: Was für Zimmer sind noch frei? Was kosten die Zimmer? Bis wann müssen die Gäste abreisen?

Kapitel 11

Situation 12 Anruf beim Arzt

S2: Sie arbeiten in einer Arztpraxis. Ein Patient / Eine Patientin ruft an und möchte einen Termin. Fragen Sie, was er/sie hat und wie dringend es ist. Der Terminkalender für diesen Tag ist schon sehr voll.

Kapitel 12

Situation 9 Ein besonderes Interview

S2: Sie sind der/die berühmte _____ , und Sie geben ein Exklusivinterview. Ein Reporter / Eine Reporterin der Universitätszeitung stellt Ihnen Fragen zu Ihren Plänen für die Zukunft. Mögliche Themen: Karriere, Familie, Wohnort, Freizeit.

APPENDIX C
Ending to Story: Der Mann, der nie zu spät kam

Kapitel 8, S. 288–290.

Noch während des Sturzes[1] wußte er: Alles ist aus. Dies ist der Bahnsteig vier, folglich[2] fährt hier in diesem Augenblick der 9-Uhr-16-Zug ein, Zugnummer 1072, 55 planmäßige[3] Weiterfahrt 9 Uhr 21. Ich bin tot[4]!

Er wartete eine Weile, aber nichts geschah.[5] Und da er offensichtlich[6] noch lebte, stand er verdattert[7] auf, kletterte auf den Bahnsteig zurück und suchte einen Bahnbeamten. Als er ihn gefunden hatte, fragte er atemlos:[8] „Der 9-Uhr-16! Was ist mit dem 9-Uhr-16-Zug?"

60 „Der hat sieben Minuten Verspätung", sagte der Beamte im Vorbeigehen.

„Verspätung", wiederholte Wilfried und nickte begreifend.[9]

An diesem Tag ging Wilfried überhaupt nicht ins Büro. Am nächsten Morgen kam er erst um zehn Uhr und am übernächsten um halb zwölf. „Sind Sie krank, Herr Kalk?" fragte der Chef erstaunt.[10] „Nein", sagte Wilfried. „Ich habe 65 inzwischen[11] nur festgestellt,[12] daß Verspätungen von Vorteil sein können."

[1] *fall* [2] *consequently* [3] *according to schedule* [4] *dead* [5] *happened* [6] *apparently* [7] *bewildered* [8] *breathlessly* [9] *understandingly* [10] *astonished* [11] *in the meantime* [12] *observed*

APPENDIX D
Grammar Summary Tables

I. Personal Pronouns

Nominative	*Accusative*	*Accusative Reflexive*	*Dative*	*Dative Reflexive*
ich	mich	mich	mir	mir
du Sie	dich Sie	dich sich	dir Ihnen	dir sich
er sie es	ihn sie es	sich sich sich	ihm ihr ihm	sich sich sich
wir	uns	uns	uns	uns
ihr Sie	euch Sie	euch sich	euch Ihnen	euch sich
sie	sie	sich	ihnen	sich

II. Definite Articles / Pronouns Declined Like Definite Articles

dieser/dieses/diese	*this*
mancher/manches/manche	*some, many a*
welcher/welches/welche	*which*
jeder/jedes/jede (*singular*)	*each, every*
alle (*plural*)	*all*

(See declensional chart on next page.)

	Singular			*Plural*
	MASCULINE	NEUTER	FEMININE	
Nominative	der dieser	das dieses	die diese	die diese
Accusative	den diesen	das dieses	die diese	die diese
Dative	dem diesem	dem diesem	der dieser	den diesen
Genitive	des dieses	des dieses	der dieser	der dieser

III. Indefinite Articles / Negative Articles / Possessive Adjectives

mein/meine	*my*
dein/deine	*your (familiar singular)*
Ihr/Ihre	*your (polite singular)*
sein/seine	*his, its*
ihr/ihre	*her, its*
unser/unsere	*our*
euer/eure	*your (familiar plural)*
Ihr/Ihre	*your (polite plural)*
ihr/ihre	*their*

	Singular			*Plural*
	MASCULINE	NEUTER	FEMININE	
Nominative	ein kein mein	ein kein mein	eine keine meine	 keine meine
Accusative	einen keinen meinen	ein kein mein	eine keine meine	 keine meine
Dative	einem keinem meinem	einem keinem meinem	einer keiner meiner	 keinen meinen
Genitive	eines keines meines	eines keines meines	einer keiner meiner	 keiner meiner

IV. Relative Pronouns

	Singular			*Plural*
	MASCULINE	NEUTER	FEMININE	
Nominative	der	das	die	die
Accusative	den	das	die	die
Dative	dem	dem	der	denen
Genitive	dessen	dessen	deren	deren

V. Question Pronouns

	People	*Things and Concepts*
Nominative	wer	was
Accusative	wen	was
Dative	wem	
Genitive	wessen	

VI. Attributive Adjectives

		Masculine	*Neuter*	*Feminine*	*Plural*
Nominative	*strong*	guter	gutes	gute	gute
	weak	gute	gute	gute	guten
Accusative	*strong*	guten	gutes	gute	gute
	weak	guten	gute	gute	guten
Dative	*strong*	gutem	gutem	guter	guten
	weak	guten	guten	guten	guten
Genitive	*strong*	guten	guten	guter	guter
	weak	guten	guten	guten	guten

Nouns declined like adjectives: Angestellte, Beamte, Deutsche, Geliebte, Verletzte, Verwandte

VII. Comparative and Superlative Adjectives and Adverbs

A. *Regular Patterns*

schnell	schneller	am schnellsten
intelligent	intelligenter	am intelligentesten
heiß	heißer	am heißesten
teuer	teurer	am teuersten
dunkel	dunkler	am dunkelsten

B. *Irregular Patterns*

alt	älter	am ältesten
groß	größer	am größten
jung	jünger	am jüngsten

Similarly: arm, hart, kalt, krank, lang, scharf, schwach, stark, warm, oft, dumm, kurz

gern	lieber	am liebsten
gut	besser	am besten
hoch	höher	am höchsten
nah	näher	am nächsten
viel	mehr	am meisten

VIII. Weak Masculine Nouns

These nouns add **-(e)n** in the accusative, dative, and genitive.

A. *International nouns ending in* ***-t*** *denoting male persons:* Dirigent, Komponist, Patient, Polizist, Präsident, Soldat, Student, Tourist
B. *Nouns ending in* ***-e*** *denoting male persons or animals:* Drache, Junge, Kunde, Löwe, Neffe, Riese, Vorfahre, Zeuge
C. *The following nouns:* Elefant, Herr, Mensch, Nachbar, Name[1]

	Singular	*Plural*
Nominative	der Student der Junge	die Studenten die Jungen
Accusative	den Studenten den Jungen	die Studenten die Jungen
Dative	dem Studenten dem Jungen	den Studenten den Jungen
Genitive	des Studenten des Jungen	der Studenten der Jungen

[1] *Genitive:* des Namens

IX. Prepositions

Accusative	*Dative*	*Accusative/Dative*	*Genitive*
durch	aus	an	(an)statt
für	außer	auf	trotz
gegen	bei	hinter	während
ohne	mit	in	wegen
um	nach	neben	
	seit	über	
	von	unter	
	zu	vor	
		zwischen	

X. Dative Verbs

antworten	*to answer*
begegnen	*to meet*
danken	*to thank*
erlauben	*to allow*
fehlen	*to be missing*
folgen	*to follow*
gefallen	*to please, be pleasing to*
gehören	*to belong to*
glauben	*to believe*
gratulieren	*to congratulate*
helfen	*to help*
leid tun	*to be sorry; to feel sorry for*
passen	*to fit*
passieren	*to happen*
raten	*to advise*
schaden	*to be harmful*
schmecken	*to taste (good)*
stehen	*to suit*
weh tun	*to hurt*
zuhören	*to listen to*

XI. Reflexive Verbs

sich anziehen	*to get dressed*
sich ärgern	*to get angry*
sich aufregen	*to get excited*

sich ausruhen	*to rest*
sich ausziehen	*to get undressed*
sich beeilen	*to hurry*
sich erholen	*to relax, recover*
sich erkälten	*to catch a cold*
sich erkundigen	*to ask*
sich (die Haare) fönen	*to blow-dry (one's hair)*
sich fragen (ob)	*to wonder (if)*
sich freuen	*to be happy*
sich (wohl) fühlen	*to feel (well)*
sich fürchten	*to be afraid*
sich gewöhnen an	*to get used to*
sich hinlegen	*to lie down*
sich infizieren	*to get infected*
sich informieren	*to get information*
sich interessieren für	*to be interested in*
sich kümmern um	*to take care of*
sich rasieren	*to shave*
sich schminken	*to put on makeup*
sich setzen	*to sit down*
sich umsehen	*to look around*
sich unterhalten	*to have a conversation*
sich verletzen	*to get hurt*
sich verloben	*to get engaged*
sich vorstellen	*to imagine*

XII. Verbs + Prepositions

Accusative

bitten um	*to ask for*
denken an	*to think about*
glauben an	*to believe in*
nachdenken über	*to think about; to ponder*
schreiben an	*to write to*
schreiben/sprechen über	*to write/talk about*
sorgen für	*to care for*
verzichten auf	*to renounce, do without*
warten auf	*to wait for*

sich + *Accusative*

sich ärgern über	*to be angry at/about*
sich erinnern an	*to remember*
sich freuen über	*to be happy about*
sich gewöhnen an	*to get used to*

sich kümmern um	*to take care of*
sich interessieren für	*to be interested in*
sich verlieben in	*to fall in love with*
Dative	
fahren/reisen mit	*to go/travel by*
halten von	*to think of; to value*
handeln von	*to deal with*
träumen von	*to dream of*
sich + *Dative*	
sich erkundigen nach	*to ask about*
sich fürchten vor	*to be afraid of*

XIII. Inseparable Prefixes of Verbs

A. *Common*

be-	bedeuten, bekommen, bestellen, besuchen, bezahlen usw.
er-	erfinden, erkälten, erklären, erlauben, erreichen usw.
ver-	verbrennen, verdienen, vergessen, verlassen, verletzen usw.

B. *Less Common*

ent-	entdecken, entscheiden, entschuldigen
ge-	gefallen, gehören, gewinnen, gewöhnen
zer-	zerreißen, zerstören

APPENDIX E
Verbs

I. Conjugation Patterns

A. *Simple tenses*

		Present	*Simple Past*	*Subjunctive*	*Past Participle*
Strong	ich	komme	kam	käme	bin gekommen
	du	kommst	kamst	kämst	bist gekommen
	er/sie/es	kommt	kam	käme	ist gekommen
	wir	kommen	kamen	kämen	sind gekommen
	ihr	kommt	kamt	kämt	seid gekommen
	sie, Sie	kommen	kamen	kämen	sind gekommen
Weak	ich	glaube	glaubte	glaubte	habe geglaubt
	du	glaubst	glaubtest	glaubtest	hast geglaubt
	er/sie/es	glaubt	glaubte	glaubte	hat geglaubt
	wir	glauben	glaubten	glaubten	haben geglaubt
	ihr	glaubt	glaubtet	glaubtet	habt geglaubt
	sie, Sie	glauben	glaubten	glaubten	haben geglaubt
Irregular Weak	ich	weiß	wußte	wüßte	habe gewußt
	du	weißt	wußtest	wüßtest	hast gewußt
	er/sie/es	weiß	wußte	wüßte	hat gewußt
	wir	wissen	wußten	wüßten	haben gewußt
	ihr	wißt	wußtet	wüßtet	habt gewußt
	sie, Sie	wissen	wußten	wüßten	haben gewußt
Modal	ich	kann	konnte	könnte	habe gekonnt
	du	kannst	konntest	könntest	hast gekonnt
	er/sie/es	kann	konnte	könnte	hat gekonnt
	wir	können	konnten	könnten	haben gekonnt
	ihr	könnt	konntet	könntet	habt gekonnt
	sie, Sie	können	konnten	könnten	haben gekonnt
haben	ich	habe	hatte	hätte	habe gehabt
	du	hast	hattest	hättest	hast gehabt
	er/sie/es	hat	hatte	hätte	hat gehabt
	wir	haben	hatten	hätten	haben gehabt
	ihr	habt	hattet	hättet	habt gehabt
	sie, Sie	haben	hatten	hätten	haben gehabt

(continued)

		Present	*Simple Past*	*Subjunctive*	*Past Participle*
sein	ich	bin	war	wäre	bin gewesen
	du	bist	warst	wärst	bist gewesen
	er/sie/es	ist	war	wäre	ist gewesen
	wir	sind	waren	wären	sind gewesen
	ihr	seid	wart	wärt	seid gewesen
	sie, Sie	sind	waren	wären	sind gewesen
werden	ich	werde	wurde	würde	bin geworden
	du	wirst	wurdest	würdest	bist geworden
	er/sie/es	wird	wurde	würde	ist geworden
	wir	werden	wurden	würden	sind geworden
	ihr	werdet	wurdet	würdet	seid geworden
	sie, Sie	werden	wurden	würden	sind geworden

B. *Compound tenses*

1. *Active voice*

	Perfect	*Past perfect*	*Future*	*Subjunctive*
Strong	ich habe genommen ich bin gefahren	hatte genommen war gefahren	werde nehmen werde fahren	würde nehmen würde fahren
Weak	ich habe gekauft ich bin gesegelt	hatte gekauft war gesegelt	werde kaufen werde segeln	würde kaufen würde segeln
Irr. Weak	ich habe gewußt	hatte gewußt	werde wissen	würde wissen
Modal	ich habe gekonnt	hatte gekonnt	werde können	würde können
haben	ich habe gehabt	hatte gehabt	werde haben	würde haben
sein	ich bin gewesen	war gewesen	werde sein	würde sein
werden	ich bin geworden	war geworden	werde werden	würde werden

2. *Passive voice*

	Present	*Simple past*	*Perfect*
Strong	es wird genommen	wurde genommen	ist genommen worden
Weak	es wird gekauft	wurde gekauft	ist gekauft worden

II. Strong and Irregular Weak Verbs

backen (backt)	backte	hat gebacken	*to bake*
beginnen (beginnt)	begann	hat begonnen	*to begin*
beißen (beißt)	biß	hat gebissen	*to bite*
bekommen (bekommt)	bekam	hat bekommen	*to get, receive*
beschreiben (beschreibt)	beschrieb	hat beschrieben	*to describe*
besitzen (besitzt)	besaß	hat besessen	*to own, possess*
besteigen (besteigt)	bestieg	hat bestiegen	*to climb*
bitten (bittet)	bat	hat gebeten	*to ask for*
bleiben (bleibt)	blieb	ist geblieben	*to stay*
braten (brät)	briet	hat gebraten	*to roast, fry*
brechen (bricht)	brach	hat gebrochen	*to break*
brennen (brennt)	brannte	hat gebrannt	*to burn*
bringen (bringt)	brachte	hat gebracht	*to bring*
denken (denkt)	dachte	hat gedacht	*to think*
dürfen (darf)	durfte	hat gedurft	*to be allowed to*
essen (ißt)	aß	hat gegessen	*to eat*
empfehlen (empfiehlt)	empfahl	hat empfohlen	*to recommend*
entscheiden (entscheidet)	entschied	hat entschieden	*to decide*
erfinden (erfindet)	erfand	hat erfunden	*to invent*
fahren (fährt)	fuhr	ist gefahren	*to go, drive*
fallen (fällt)	fiel	ist gefallen	*to fall*
fangen (fängt)	fing	hat gefangen	*to catch*
finden (findet)	fand	hat gefunden	*to find*
fliegen (fliegt)	flog	ist geflogen	*to fly*
fliehen (flieht)	floh	ist geflohen	*to flee*
fließen (fließt)	floß	ist geflossen	*to flow*
fressen (frißt)	fraß	hat gefressen	*to eat*
geben (gibt)	gab	hat gegeben	*to give*
gefallen (gefällt)	gefiel	hat gefallen	*to please, be pleasing to*
gehen (geht)	ging	ist gegangen	*to go, walk*
gewinnen (gewinnt)	gewann	hat gewonnen	*to win*
gießen (gießt)	goß	hat gegossen	*to water*
haben (hat)	hatte	hat gehabt	*to have*
halten (hält)	hielt	hat gehalten	*to hold*
hängen (hängt)	hing	hat gehangen	*to hang, be suspended*
heben (hebt)	hob	hat gehoben	*to lift*
heißen (heißt)	hieß	hat geheißen	*to be called*
helfen (hilft)	half	hat geholfen	*to help*
kennen (kennt)	kannte	hat gekannt	*to know*
klingen (klingt)	klang	hat geklungen	*to sound*

kommen (kommt)	kam	ist gekommen	*to come*
können (kann)	konnte	hat gekonnt	*to be able*
laden (lädt)	lud	hat geladen	*to invite*
lassen (läßt)	ließ	hat gelassen	*to let, leave*
laufen (läuft)	lief	ist gelaufen	*to run*
leihen (leiht)	lieh	hat geliehen	*to lend, borrow*
lesen (liest)	las	hat gelesen	*to read*
liegen (liegt)	lag	hat gelegen	*to lie*
mögen (mag)	mochte	hat gemocht	*to like*
müssen (muß)	mußte	hat gemußt	*to have to*
nehmen (nimmt)	nahm	hat genommen	*to take*
nennen (nennt)	nannte	hat genannt	*to name*
raten (rät)	riet	hat geraten	*to advise*
reiten (reitet)	ritt	ist geritten	*to ride*
riechen (riecht)	roch	hat gerochen	*to smell*
rufen (ruft)	rief	hat gerufen	*to call*
scheiden (scheidet)	schied	hat geschieden	*to leave, divorce*
schießen (schießt)	schoß	hat geschossen	*to shoot*
schlafen (schläft)	schlief	hat geschlafen	*to sleep*
schlagen (schlägt)	schlug	hat geschlagen	*to strike, beat*
schließen (schließt)	schloß	hat geschlossen	*to shut, close*
schneiden (schneidet)	schnitt	hat geschnitten	*to cut*
schreiben (schreibt)	schrieb	hat geschrieben	*to write*
schwimmen (schwimmt)	schwamm	ist geschwommen	*to swim*
sehen (sieht)	sah	hat gesehen	*to see*
sein (ist)	war	ist gewesen	*to be*
senden (sendet)	sandte	hat gesandt	*to send*
singen (singt)	sang	hat gesungen	*to sing*
sinken (sinkt)	sank	ist gesunken	*to sink*
sitzen (sitzt)	saß	hat gesessen	*to sit*
sprechen (spricht)	sprach	hat gesprochen	*to speak*
springen (springt)	sprang	ist gesprungen	*to spring, jump*
stehen (steht)	stand	hat gestanden	*to stand*
steigen (steigt)	stieg	ist gestiegen	*to climb*
sterben (stirbt)	starb	ist gestorben	*to die*
stoßen (stößt)	stieß	hat gestoßen	*to shove, push*
streiten (streitet)	stritt	hat gestritten	*to quarrel, fight*
tragen (trägt)	trug	hat getragen	*to wear, carry*
treffen (trifft)	traf	hat getroffen	*to meet, hit*
treiben (treibt)	trieb	hat getrieben	*to do sports*
trinken (trinkt)	trank	hat getrunken	*to drink*
tun (tut)	tat	hat getan	*to do*

verbrennen (verbrennt)	verbrannte	hat verbrannt	*to burn; to incinerate*
verbringen (verbringt)	verbrachte	hat verbracht	*to spend (time)*
vergessen (vergißt)	vergaß	hat vergessen	*to forget*
verlassen (verläßt)	verließ	hat verlassen	*to leave (a place)*
verlieren (verliert)	verlor	hat verloren	*to lose*
verschwinden (verschwindet)	verschwand	ist verschwunden	*to disappear*
versprechen (verspricht)	versprach	hat versprochen	*to promise*
wachsen (wächst)	wuchs	ist gewachsen	*to grow*
waschen (wäscht)	wusch	hat gewaschen	*to wash*
werden (wird)	wurde	ist geworden	*to become*
wissen (weiß)	wußte	hat gewußt	*to know*

APPENDIX F
Answers to Grammar Exercises

Einführung A
Übung 1: 1. Hören Sie zu! 2. Geben Sie mir die Hausaufgabe! 3. Öffnen Sie das Buch! 4. Schauen Sie an die Tafel! 5. Nehmen Sie einen Stift! 6. Sagen Sie „Guten Tag"! 7. Schließen Sie das Buch! 8. Schreiben Sie „Tschüs"! **Übung 2:** 1.a. heißt b. heiße c. heiße 2.a. heißen b. heiße 3.a. heiße b. heiße c. heißt **Übung 3:** 1.a. bist b. bin c. sind 2.a. ist b. sind 3.a. seid b. bin c. ist. 4.a. bin b. bin **Übung 4:** 1.a. haben b. habe 2.a. hast 3.a. Habt b. hat c. haben d. habe **Übung 5:** 1. S1: Welche Farbe hat die Jacke? S2: Sie ist blau. 2. S1: Welche Farbe hat der Hut? S2: Er ist schwarz. 3. S1: Welche Farbe hat der Rock? S2: Er ist orange. 4. S1: Welche Farbe hat das Hemd? S2: Es ist gelb. 5. S1: Welche Farbe hat das Sakko? S2: Es ist rot. 6. S1: Welche Farbe hat die Hose? S2: Sie ist grün. 7. S1: Welche Farbe haben die Schuhe? S2: Sie sind braun. 8. S1: Welche Farbe haben die Schuhe? S2: Sie sind rosa. 9. S1: Welche Farbe hat die Bluse? S2: Sie ist weiß. **Übung 6:** 1. Sie 2. Es 3. Er 4. Sie 5. Es 6. Er 7. Er 8. Sie 9. Sie 10. Er **Übung 7:** 1. du 2. Sie 3. du 4. ihr 5. Sie 6. Sie 7. Sie 8. ihr

Einführung B
Übung 1: 1.a. ein b. der Stift c. rot 2.a. eine b. die Uhr c. braun 3.a. ein b. der Stuhl c. grün 4.a. ein b. das Buch c. orange 5.a. eine b. die Tafel c. grau 6.a. eine b. die Brille c. schwarz **Übung 2:** 1. Nein, das ist eine Lampe. 2. Nein, das ist eine Tafel. 3. Nein, das ist ein Fenster. 4. Nein, das ist ein Kind. 5. Nein, das ist ein Heft. 6. Nein, das ist eine Uhr. 7. Nein, das ist ein Tisch. 8. Nein, das ist eine Tür. 9. Nein, das ist ein Stuhl. **Übung 3:** 1. Hosen 2. Lampe 3. Freundin 4. Uhren 5. Hefte 6. Autos 7. Kleider 8. Stuhl 9. Tische 10. Rock **Übung 4:** 1. Der Mensch hat zwei Arme, zwei Augen, zwei Beine, zehn Finger, zwei Füße, viele Haare, zwei Hände, eine Nase, zwei Ohren, zwei Schultern. 2. *(Numbers will vary.)* In meinem Zimmer sind viele Bücher, ein Fenster, zwei Lampen, zwei Stühle, ein Tisch, eine Tür, eine Uhr, vier Wände. **Übung 5:** 1. Er ist schwarz. 2. Es ist weiß. 3. Sie ist blau. 4. Sie ist gelb. 5. Sie sind weiß. 6. Es ist rot. 7. Er ist lila. 8. Sie sind braun. 9. Sie ist grün. 10. Er ist rosa. **Übung 6:** 1.a. kommst b. komme 2.a. kommt b. aus c. Woher d. kommen e. ich f. aus 3.a. sie b. kommen 4.a. ihr b. wir **Übung 7:** 1.a. deine b. Sie 2.a. dein b. mein 3.a. mein b. mein c. Dein 4.a. Ihre b. Meine c. mein **Übung 8:** *(Answers will vary.)* 1. Ich komme aus ______ . 2. Meine Mutter kommt aus ______ . 3. Mein Vater kommt aus ______ . 4. Meine Großeltern kommen aus ______ . / Mein Großvater kommt aus ______ , und meine Großmutter kommt aus ______ . 5. Mein Professor / Meine Professorin kommt aus ______ . 6. Ein Student aus meinem Deutschkurs heißt ______ , und er kommt aus ______ . 7. Eine Studentin aus meinem Deutschkurs heißt ______ , und sie kommt aus ______ .

Kapitel 1
Übung 1: *(Answers may vary.)* 1. Ich besuche Freunde. 2. Ihr geht ins Kino. 3. Jutta und Jens lernen Spanisch. 4. Du spielst gut Tennis. 5. Melanie studiert in Regensburg. 6. Ich lese ein Buch. 7. Wir reisen nach Deutschland. 8. Richard hört gern Musik. 9. Jürgen und Silvia kochen Spaghetti. **Übung 2:** 1. sie 2. Sie 3.a. du b. Ich 4.a. ihr b. Wir 5.a. Ich b. ihr c. Wir **Übung 3:** 1.a. (tanz)t b. (tanz)e c. (tanz)t 2.a. (geh)t b. (mach)en c. (reis)t d. (arbeit)et 3.a. (koch)en b. (mach)t c. (besuch)en **Übung 4:** 1. Monika und Albert spielen gern Schach. 2. Heidi arbeitet gern. 3. Stefan besucht gern Freunde. 4. Nora geht gern ins Kino. 5. Peter hört gern Musik. 6. Katrin macht gern Fotos. 7. Monika zeltet gern. 8. Albert trinkt gern Tee. **Übung 5:** 1. Frau Ruf liegt gern in der Sonne. Jutta liegt auch gern in der Sonne, aber Herr Ruf liegt nicht gern in der Sonne. 2. Jens reitet gern. Ernst reitet auch gern, aber Jutta reitet nicht gern. 3. Jens kocht gern. Jutta kocht auch gern, aber Andrea kocht nicht gern. 4. Michael und Maria spielen gern Karten. Die Rufs spielen auch gern Karten, aber die Wagners spielen nicht gern Karten. **Übung 6:** 1. Es ist halb acht. 2. Es ist elf Uhr. 3. Es ist Viertel vor fünf. 4. Es ist halb eins. 5. Es ist zehn vor sieben. 6. Es ist Viertel nach zwei. 7. Es ist fünfundzwanzig nach fünf. 8. Es ist halb elf. **Übung 7:** 1. (Rolf) nach 2. (er) vor 3. (Seine Großmutter) nach 4. (Rolf) vor 5. (er) vor 6. (er) vor 7. (er) vor 8. (Er) nach **Übung 8:** *(Answers will vary.)* 1. Ich studiere ______ . 2. Im Moment wohne ich in ______ . 3. Heute koche ich ______ . 4. Manchmal trinke ich ______ . 5. Ich spiele gern ______ . 6. Mein Freund (Meine Freundin) heißt ______ . 7. Jetzt wohnt er (sie) in ______ . 8. Manchmal spielen wir ______ . **Übung 9:** 1. auf 2. auf 3. ein 4. an 5. aus 6. ab 7. ein 8. aus 9. auf 10. spazieren **Übung 10:** 1. Rolf kommt in San Francisco an. 2. Katrin lernt Rolf kennen. 3. Thomas räumt das Zimmer auf. 4. Heidi ruft Thomas an. 5. Albert füllt das Formular aus. 6. Peter holt Monika ab. 7. Peter und Monika gehen aus. 8. Frau Schulz packt die Bücher ein. 9. Stefan steht um halb elf auf. **Übung 11:** 1. Wann bist du geboren? 2. Woher kommst du? 3. Wo wohnst du? 4. Welche Augenfarbe hast du? 5. Wie groß bist du? 6. Studierst du? 7. Welche Fächer studierst du? 8. Wie viele Stunden arbeitest du? 9. Was machst du gern? **Übung 12:** *(Answers may vary.)* 1. Wie heißt du? 2. Kommst du aus München? 3. Woher kommst du? 4. Was studierst du? 5. Wie heißt dein Freund? 6. Wo wohnt

er? 7. Spielst du Tennis? 8. Tanzt du gern? 9. Trinkst du Bier? 10. Trinkt Willi gern Bier?

Kapitel 2

Übung 1: Ernst kauft die Tasche, die Stühle und den Schreibtisch. Melanie kauft die Tasche, das Regal und den Schreibtisch. Jutta kauft den Pullover, die Lampe und den Videorecorder. Ich kaufe . . . *(Answers will vary.)* **Übung 2:** *(Answers will vary.)* Ich habe ein Bett, Bilder, Bücher, einen Fernseher, eine Lampe, ein Telefon und einen Sessel. **Übung 3:** *(Sentences may vary.)* 1. Heidi hat einen Computer, aber keinen Fernseher. Sie hat eine Gitarre, aber kein Fahrrad. Sie hat ein Telefon und einen Teppich, aber sie hat keine Bilder. 2. Peter hat einen Computer, aber er hat keinen Fernseher und keine Gitarre. Er hat ein Fahrrad und ein Telefon, aber er hat keine Bilder. Er hat einen Teppich. 3. Monika hat keinen Computer, keinen Fernseher und keine Gitarre. Aber sie hat ein Fahrrad, ein Telefon, Bilder und einen Teppich. 4. Ich habe ______. **Übung 4:** *(Answers will vary.)* 1. Ich möchte ein Auto und eine Sonnenbrille. 2. Mein bester Freund möchte eine Katze. 3. Meine Eltern möchten einen Videorecorder. 4. Meine Mitbewohnerin möchte einen Fernseher. 5. Mein Nachbar möchte ein Motorrad. 6. Meine Professorin möchte einen Koffer. 7. Mein Bruder möchte einen Hund. **Übung 5:** Seine Haare; Seine Augen; Seine Kette; Seine Schuhe; Seine Gitarre; Sein Zimmer; Sein Fenster; Ihre Haare; Ihre Augen; Ihre Kette ist kurz. Ihre Schuhe sind sauber. Ihre Gitarre ist neu. Ihr Zimmer ist klein. Ihr Fenster ist groß. **Übung 6:** 1. Ihren 2. Deine 3. eure 4. Deine 5. Ihr 6. deine 7. Euren **Übung 7:** *(Answers will vary.)* **Übung 8:** 1.a. ihr b. wir 2.a. Sie b. Ich 3.a. sie b. er 4.a. du b. Ich c. ihr d. Wir **Übung 9:** a. machen b. fährt c. sieht d. Ißt e. ißt f. ißt g. macht h. lese i. schläft j. fahren **Übung 10:** *(Answers will vary.)* 1. Wir sprechen (nicht) gern Deutsch. Sprecht ihr auch (nicht) gern Deutsch? 2. Ich lade (nicht) gern Freunde ein. Lädst du auch (nicht) gern Freunde ein? 3. Ich laufe (nicht) gern im Wald. Läufst du auch (nicht) gern im Wald? 4. Ich trage (nicht) gern Pullis. Trägst du auch (nicht) gern Pullis? 5. Wir sehen (nicht) gern fern. Seht ihr auch (nicht) gern fern? 6. Ich fahre (nicht) gern Fahrrad. Fährst du auch (nicht) gern Fahrrad? 7. Wir vergessen (nicht) gern die Hausaufgabe. Vergeßt ihr auch (nicht) gern die Hausaufgabe? 8. Ich schlafe (nicht) gern. Schläfst du auch (nicht) gern? **Übung 11:** 1. Schlaf nicht den ganzen Tag! 2. Lieg nicht den ganzen Tag in der Sonne! 3. Vergiß nicht deine Hausaufgaben! 4. Lies deine Bücher! 5. Sieh nicht den ganzen Tag fern! 6. Trink nicht zu viel Cola! 7. Sprich nicht mit vollem Mund! 8. Trag deine Brille! 9. Geh spazieren! 10. Treib Sport! **Übung 12:** 1. Trag heute ein T-Shirt! 2. Spiel keine laute Musik! 3. Lern den Wortschatz! 4. Ruf deine Freunde an! 5. Lauf nicht allein im Park! 6. Lieg nicht zu lange in der Sonne! 7. Räum dein Zimmer auf! 8. Iß heute abend in einem Restaurant! 9. Geh nicht zu spät ins Bett! 10. Steh früh auf!

Kapitel 3

Übung 1: *(Predicates will vary.)* A.1. Mein Freund / Meine Freundin kann ______. 2. Meine Eltern können ______. 3. Ich kann / Wir können ______. 4. Mein Bruder / Meine Schwester kann ______. 5. Der Professor / Die Professorin kann ______. B.1. Kannst du / Könnt ihr Gedichte schreiben? 2. Kannst du / könnt ihr Auto fahren. 3. Kannst du / Könnt ihr tippen? 4. Kannst du / Könnt ihr stricken? 5. Kannst du / Könnt ihr zeichnen? **Übung 2:** *(Answers will vary.)* 1. Heute abend will ich ______. 2. Morgen kann ich nicht ______. 3. Mein Freund / Meine Freundin kann gut ______. 4. Am Samstag will mein Freund / meine Freundin ______. 5. Mein Freund / Meine Freundin und ich wollen ______. 6. Im Winter wollen meine Eltern / meine Freunde ______. 7. Meine Eltern / Meine Freunde können gut ______. **Übung 3:** 1. Sie darf nicht mit Jens zusammen lernen. 2. Sie darf nicht viel fernsehen. 3. Sie muß in der Klasse aufpassen und mitschreiben. 4. Sie darf nicht jeden Tag tanzen gehen. 5. Sie muß jeden Tag ihren Wortschatz lernen. 6. Sie muß amerikanische Filme im Original sehen. 7. Sie muß ihren Englischlehrer zum Abendessen einladen. 8. Sie muß für eine Woche nach London fahren. 9. Sie muß die englische Grammatik fleißig lernen. **Übung 4:** 1.a. Willst b. will c. kann d. muß 2.a. darf b. mußt c. kann d. darfst e. könnt 3.a. sollst b. kann c. mußt **Übung 5:** 1.a. dich 2.a. mich b. dich 3.a. uns 4.a. euch 5.a. dich b. dich 6.a. mich b. Sie 7.a. Sie **Übung 6:** 1. Nein, sie liest ihn nicht, sie schreibt ihn. 2. Nein, er ißt sie nicht, er trinkt sie. 3. Nein, sie macht ihn nicht an, sie macht ihn aus. 4. Nein, er kauft es nicht, er verkauft es. 5. Nein, er zieht sie nicht aus, er zieht sie an. 6. Nein, sie trägt ihn nicht, sie kauft ihn. 7. Nein, er bestellt es nicht, er ißt es. 8. Nein, er besucht ihn nicht, er ruft ihn an. 9. Nein, sie kämmt es nicht, sie wäscht es. 10. Nein, er bläst sie nicht aus, er zündet sie an. **Übung 7:** 1. Weil ich krank bin. 2. Weil er müde ist. 3. Weil wir Hunger haben. 4. Weil sie keine Zeit hat. 5. Weil sie Langeweile hat. 6. Weil ich traurig bin. 7. Weil sie Durst haben. 8. Weil ich Angst habe. 9. Weil er glücklich ist. 10. Weil ich lernen muß. **Übung 8:** *(Answers will vary.)* 1. S1: Was macht Albert, wenn er müde ist? S2: Wenn Albert müde ist, geht er nach Hause. S1: Und du? S2: Wenn ich müde bin, ______. 2. S1: Was macht Maria, wenn sie glücklich ist? S2: Wenn Maria glücklich ist, trifft sie Michael. S1: Und du? S2: Wenn ich glücklich bin, ______. 3. S1: Was macht Herr Ruf, wenn er Durst hat? S2: Wenn Herr Ruf Durst hat, trinkt er eine Cola. S1: Und du? S2: Wenn ich Durst habe, ______. 4. S1: Was macht Frau Wagner, wenn sie in Eile ist? S2: Wenn Frau Wagner in Eile ist, fährt sie mit dem Taxi. S1: Und du? S2: Wenn ich in Eile bin, ______. 5. S1: Was macht Heidi, wenn sie Hunger hat? S2: Wenn Heidi Hunger hat, kauft sie einen Hamburger. S1: Und du? S2: Wenn ich Hunger habe, ______. 6. S1: Was macht Frau Schulz, wenn sie Ferien hat? S2: Wenn Frau Schulz Ferien hat, fliegt sie nach Deutschland. S1: Und du? S2: Wenn ich Ferien habe, ______. 7. S1: Was macht Hans, wenn er Angst hat? S2: Wenn Hans Angst hat, ruft er „Mama, Mama". S1: Und du? S2: Wenn ich Angst habe, ______. 8. S1: Was macht Stefan, wenn er krank ist? S2: Wenn Stefan krank ist, geht er zum Arzt. S1: Und du? S2: Wenn ich krank bin, ______. **Übung 9:** 1. Jürgen ist wütend, weil er immer so früh aufstehen muß. 2. Silvia ist froh, weil sie heute nicht arbeiten muß. 3. Claire ist in Eile, weil sie noch einkaufen muß. 4. Josef ist traurig, weil Melanie ihn nicht anruft. 5. Thomas geht nicht zu Fuß, weil seine Freundin ihn zur Uni mitnimmt. 6. Willi hat selten Langeweile, weil er immer fernsieht. 7. Marta hat Angst vor Wasser, weil sie nicht schwimmen kann. 8. Mehmet fährt in die Türkei, weil er seine Eltern besuchen will.

Kapitel 4

Übung 1: a. hat b. ist c. hat d. hat e. ist f. sind g. ist h. hat i. hat **Fragen:** 1. Rosemarie ist um 7 Uhr aufgestanden. 2. Sie sind zur Schule gegangen. 3. Frau Dehne ist die Lehrerin. 4. Sie hat „Herzlich Willkommen" an die Tafel geschrieben. **Übung 2:** a. haben b. sind c. haben d. sind e. sind f. haben g. haben h. sind i. haben j. sind **Fragen:** 1. Josef und Melanie sind mit dem Taxi zum Bahnhof gefahren. 2. Sie sind um 5:30 mit dem Zug abgefahren. 3. Sie haben im Speisewagen gefrühstückt. 4. Nachts haben sie schlecht geschlafen. **Übung 3:** a. aufgestanden b. geduscht c. gefrühstückt d. gegangen e. gehört f. getroffen g. getrunken h. gearbeitet i. gegessen **Übung 4:** 1. Hast du schon gefrühstückt? 2. Bist du schon geschwommen? 3. Hast du schon eine Geschichte gelesen? 4. Hast du schon Klavier gespielt? 5. Hast du schon geschlafen? 6. Hast du schon gegessen? 7. Hast du schon Geschirr gespült? 8. Hast du den Brief schon geschrieben? 9. Bist du schon ins Bett gegangen? **Übung 5:** 1. Katrin hat bis 9 Uhr im Bett gelegen. 2. Sie hat einen Rock getragen. 3. Sie hat mit Frau Schulz gesprochen. 4. Sie hat ein Referat gehalten. 5. Sie hat Freunde getroffen. 6. Sie hat gearbeitet. 7. Es hat geregnet. 8. Sie ist nach Hause gekommen. 9. Sie hat ihre Wäsche gewaschen. 10. Sie ist abends zu Hause geblieben. **Übung 6:** 1. *(Answers will vary.)* 2. *(Answers will vary.)* 3. Am fünfundzwanzigsten Dezember. 4. Am vierten Juli. 5. Am ersten Januar. 6. Am vierzehnten Februar. 7. *(Answers will vary.)* 8. *(Answers will vary.)* 9. Am einundzwanzigsten März. 10. Am dreiundzwanzigsten Juni. **Übung 7:** a. im b. im c. — d. am e. Am f. um g. um h. Am i. im j. am **Übung 8:** *(Answers will vary.)* **Übung 9:** A: 1. R 2. F 3. R 4. R 5. R B: Partizipien mit **ge-**:

aufgestanden	aufstehen
gehört	hören
gegangen	gehen
gekocht	kochen
gefahren	fahren
geparkt	parken
zurückgekommen	zurückkommen
gewaschen	waschen
aufgeräumt	aufräumen
gefallen	fallen
eingelaufen	einlaufen
abgebrannt	abbrennen

Partizipien ohne **ge-**:

verschlafen	verschlafen
bekommen	bekommen
bezahlt	bezahlen
zerbrochen	zerbrechen

Übung 10: a. ist . . . angekommen b. hat . . . begrüßt c. getrunken d. ist . . . gegangen e. hat . . . geschlafen f. ist . . . gegangen g. haben . . . gefragt h. hat . . . gesprochen i. haben . . . getrunken j. sind . . . gegangen **Übung 11:** *(Answers will vary.)* 1. —Bist du gestern früh aufgestanden? —Ja. —Wann? —Um 6 Uhr. 2. —Hast du gestern jemanden fotografiert? —Ja. —Wen? —Jane. 3. —Hast du gestern jemanden besucht? —Ja. —Wen? —Alan. 4. —Bist du gestern ausgegangen? —Ja. —Wohin? —Ins Kino. 5. —Hast du gestern etwas bezahlt? —Ja. —Was? —Die Rechnung. 6. —Hast du gestern etwas repariert? —Ja. —Was? —Mein Auto. 7. —Hast du gestern etwas Neues probiert? —Ja. —Was? —Segeln. 8. —Hast du gestern ferngesehen? —Ja. —Wie lange? —Eine Stunde. 9. —Hast du gestern etwas nicht verstanden? —Ja. —Was? —Sophies Referat. 10. —Hast du gestern dein Zimmer aufgeräumt? —Ja. —Wann? —Um 4 Uhr.

Kapitel 5

Übung 1: *(Answers will vary.)* Ich backe meiner Tante einen Kuchen. Ich erkläre meinem Partner eine Geschichte. Ich erzähle meiner Kusine einen Witz. Ich gebe meinem Freund einen Kuß. Ich kaufe meinem Vater eine Krawatte. Ich koche meiner Mitbewohnerin Kaffee. Ich leihe meinem Bruder fünfzig Dollar. Ich schenke meiner Großmutter ein Buch. Ich schreibe meiner Mutter einen Brief. Ich verkaufe meinem Zimmerkameraden mein Deutschbuch. **Übung 2:** *(Answers will vary.)* Heidi erklärt ihrer Freundin die Grammatik. Peter erzählt seinem Vetter ein Märchen. Thomas gibt seiner Mutter ein Armband. Katrin kauft ihrem Mann einen Rucksack. Stefan kocht seinem Freund eine Suppe. Albert leiht seinen Eltern einen Regenschirm. Monika schenkt ihrer Schwester einen Bikini. Frau Schulz schreibt ihrer Tante eine Karte. Nora verkauft ihrem Professor ein Zelt. **Übung 3:** 1. Wer 2. Wen 3. Wem 4. Wen 5. Wem 6. wer **Übung 4:** 1. Was passiert am Abend? Es wird dunkel. 2. Was passiert, wenn man Bücher schreibt? Man wird bekannt. 3. Was passiert, wenn man Fieber bekommt? Man wird krank. 4. Was passiert im Frühling? Die Tage werden länger. 5. Was passiert im Herbst? Die Blätter werden bunt. 6. Was passiert, wenn Kinder älter werden? Sie werden größer. 7. Was passiert, wenn man in der Lotterie gewinnt? Man wird reich. 8. Was passiert, wenn man Medizin studiert? Man wird Arzt. 9. Was passiert am Morgen? Es wird hell. 10. Was passiert im Sommer? Es wird heiß. **Übung 5:** 1. Vielleicht wird sie Köchin. 2. Vielleicht wird sie Apothekerin. 3. Vielleicht wird er Pilot. 4. Vielleicht wird er Lehrer. 5. Vielleicht wird sie Architektin. 6. Vielleicht wird sie Bibliothekarin. 7. Vielleicht wird er Krankenpfleger. 8. Vielleicht wird sie Dirigentin. **Übung 6:** 1. Was macht man im Kino? Man sieht einen Film 2. Was macht man auf der Post? Man kauft Briefmarken. 3. Was macht man an der Tankstelle? Man tankt Benzin. 4. Was macht man in der Disko? Man tanzt. 5. Was macht man in der Kirche? Man betet. 6. Was macht man auf der Bank? Man wechselt Geld. 7. Was macht man im Meer? Man schwimmt. 8. Was macht man in der Bibliothek? Man liest ein Buch. 9. Was macht man im Park? Man geht spazieren. **Übung 7:** 1. Monika ist in der Kirche. 2. Albert schwimmt im Meer. 3. Heidi ist auf der Polizei. 4. Nora ist in einem Hotel. 5. Katrin ist im Schwimmbad. 6. Thomas ist auf der Post. 7. Frau Schulz ist in der Küche. 8. Das Poster ist an der Wand. 9. Der Topf ist auf dem Herd. 10. Der Wein ist im Kühlschrank. **Übung 8:** 1. mir 2. dir 3. euch 4. Ihnen 5. uns **Übung 9:** 1. Er hat ihr einen Regenschirm geschenkt. 2. Sie hat ihm ihr Auto geliehen. 3. Er hat ihm tausend Mark geliehen. 4. Sie hat ihr einen Witz erzählt. 5. Er hat ihnen eine Geschichte erzählt. 6. Sie hat ihr ihre Sonnenbrille verkauft. 7. Er hat ihnen seinen Fernseher verkauft. 8. Sie hat ihm ihr Büro gezeigt. 9. Er hat ihm seine Wohnung gezeigt. 10. Sie hat ihr eine neue Brille gekauft. 11. Er hat ihr einen Kinderwagen gekauft.

Kapitel 6

Übung 1: *(Some answers will vary.)* 1. Berlin ist größer als Zürich. 2. München ist älter als San Francisco. 3. Athen ist wärmer als Hamburg. 4. Mount Everest ist höher als das Matterhorn. 5. Der Mississippi ist länger als der Rhein. 6. Liechtenstein ist kleiner als die Schweiz. 7. Leipzig ist kälter als Kairo. 8. Ein Fernseher ist billiger als eine Waschmaschine. 9. Schnaps ist stärker als Bier. 10. Ein Haus auf dem Land ist schöner als ein Haus in der Stadt. 11. Zehn Dollar ist mehr als zehn Mark. 12. Ein Appartement ist teurer als eine Wohnung in einem Studentenheim. 13. Ein Motorrad ist schneller als ein Fahrrad. 14. Ein Sofa ist schwerer als ein Stuhl. 15. Bier ist besser als Milch. **Übung 2:** 1. Herr Thelen ist älter als Herr Wagner. 2. Frau Gretter ist so groß wie Herr Thelen. 3. Frau Gretter ist größer als Frau Ruf. 4. Frau Ruf ist kleiner als Herr Thelen. 5. Frau Gretter ist leichter als Herr Thelen. 6. Herr Wagner ist schwerer als Frau Ruf. 7. Frau Ruf ist intelligenter als Herr Wagner. 8. Frau Gretter ist so intelligent wie Herr Wagner. 9. Frau Ruf ist progressiver als Herr Wagner. 10. Herr Thelen ist so progressiv wie Frau Gretter. 11. Herr Wagner ist konservativer als Herr Thelen. **Übung 3:** *(Answers may vary.)* 1. Die Katze liegt unter dem Bett. 2. Der Spiegel hängt an der Wand. 3. Der Kühlschrank steht neben dem Fernseher. 4. Das Deutschbuch liegt im Kühlschrank. 5. Die Lampe hängt über dem Tisch. 6. Der Computer steht auf dem Schreibtisch. 7. Die Schuhe liegen auf dem Bett. 8. Die Hose liegt auf dem Tisch. 9. Das Poster von Berlin hängt über dem Fernseher. 10. Albert ist unter der Dusche. **Übung 4:** *(Answers will vary.)* **Übung 5:** *(Answers may vary).* 1. Ich bin heute abend in der Bibliothek. 2. Ich bin am Nachmittag in der Mensa. 3. Ich bin um 16 Uhr bei Freunden. 4. Ich bin in der Nacht im Bett. 5. Ich bin am frühen Morgen am Frühstückstisch. 6. Ich bin am Montag in der Klasse. 7. Ich bin am 1. August im Urlaub. 8. Ich bin an Weihnachten auf einer Party. 9. Ich bin im Winter bei meinen Eltern. 10. Ich bin am Wochenende auf einer Party. **Übung 6:** 1. Er geht zum Arzt. 2. Er geht zum Fußballplatz. 3. Sie geht ins Hotel. 4. Er fährt zur Tankstelle. 5. Er geht zum Supermarkt. 6. Er geht auf die Post. 7. Sie gehen in den Wald. 8. Sie geht zu ihrem Freund. 9. Er fährt zum Flughafen. 10. Sie geht ins Theater. **Übung 7:** 1.a. aufstehst 2.a. mache b. aus c. fernsiehst 3.a. kommt b. an 4.a. zieht b. um 5. einladen 6.a. räumt b. auf 7.a. mitkommen b. mitnimmst 8.a. rufst b. an **Übung 8:** Herr und Frau Ruf sind spazierengegangen. Sofie und Willi sind radgefahren. Andrea hat ferngesehen. Katrin und Peter sind ausgegangen. Heidi hat Frau Schulz angerufen. Herr Ruf hat das Geschirr abgetrocknet. Jürgen ist ausgezogen. Jutta hat ihr Abendkleid angezogen. Maria ist aus Bulgarien angekommen. Herr Thelen ist aufgewacht. **Übung 9:** 1. Womit kochst du Kaffee? Mit der Kaffeemaschine. 2. Womit saugst du staub? Mit dem Staubsauger. 3. Womit putzt du dir die Zähne? Mit der Zahnbürste. 4. Womit fegst du den Boden? Mit dem Besen. 5. Womit bügelst du? Mit dem Bügeleisen. 6. Womit trocknest du dir die Hände ab? Mit dem Handtuch. 7. Womit tippst du einen Brief? Mit dem Computer. 8. Womit gießt du die Blumen im Garten? Mit dem Gartenschlauch. 9. Womit wischst du den Boden? Mit dem Putzlappen. 10. Womit gießt du die Blumen in der Wohnung? Mit der Gießkanne. **Übung 10:** 1.a. mit b. mit c. Mit d. bei 2.a. bei b. mit c. bei d. mit 3.a. mit b. mit c. bei.

Kapitel 7

Übung 1: *(Answers will vary.)* 1. Ich mag Leute, die laut lachen. 2. Ich mag keine Leute, die viel sprechen. 3. Ich mag eine Stadt, die Spaß macht. 4. Ich mag keine Stadt, die langweilig ist. 5. Ich mag einen Mann, der gern verreist. 6. Ich mag keinen Mann, der interessant aussieht. 7. Ich mag eine Frau, die nett ist. 8. Ich mag keine Frau, die betrunken ist. 9. Ich mag einen Urlaub, der exotisch ist. 10. Ich mag ein Auto, das schnell fährt. **Übung 2:** 1. Europa → Wie heißt der Kontinent, der eigentlich eine Halbinsel von Asien ist? 2. Mississippi → Wie heißt der Fluß, von dem Mark Twain erzählt? 3. San Francisco → Wie heißt die Stadt, die an einer Bucht liegt? 4. die Alpen → Wie heißen die Berge, in denen man sehr gut Ski fahren kann? 5. Washington → Wie heißt der Staat in den USA, dem ein Präsident seinen Namen gegeben hat? 6. das Tal des Todes → Wie heißt das Tal, in dem es sehr heiß ist? 7. Ellis → Wie heißt die Insel, die man von New York sieht? 8. der Pazifik → Wie heißt das Meer, über das man nach Hawaii fliegt? 9. die Sahara → Wie heißt die Wüste, die man aus vielen Filmen kennt? 10. der Große Salzsee → Wie heißt der See in Utah, auf dem man segeln kann? **Übung 3:** 1. In Athen ist es am heißesten. 2. In Moskau ist es am kältesten. 3. Monaco ist am kleinsten. 4. Frankreich ist am ältesten. 5. Südafrika ist am jüngsten. 6. Der Nil ist am längsten. 7. Frankfurt liegt am nördlichsten. 8. Der Mount Everest ist am höchsten. 9. Deutschland ist am größten. **Übung 4:** 1. Heidi ist schwerer als Monika. 2. Thomas und Stefan sind am schwersten. 3. Thomas ist besser in Deutsch als Monika. 4. Thomas und Heidi sind am besten. 5. Heidi ist kleiner als Stefan. 6. Monika ist am kleinsten. 7. Stefan ist jünger als Thomas. 8. Stefan ist am jüngsten. 9. Thomas' Haare sind länger als Heidis. 10. Monikas Haare sind am längsten. 11. Heidis Haare sind kürzer als Monikas. 12. Stefans Haare sind am kürzesten. 13. Monika ist schlechter in Deutsch als Heidi. 14. Stefan ist in Deutsch am schlechtesten. **Übung 5:** a. darauf b. daneben c. Dazwischen d. Darin e. Davor f. darüber g. Daran h. Darunter i. dahinter **Übung 6:** 1. Mit wem gehen Sie am liebsten ins Theater? 2. Worauf freuen Sie sich am meisten? 3. Auf wen müssen Sie immer warten? 4. Über wen haben Sie sich in letzter Zeit am meisten geärgert. 5. Woran denken Sie, wenn Sie „USA" hören? 6. Womit fahren Sie zur Schule? 7. Worüber schreiben Sie nicht gern? 8. An wen haben Sie Ihren letzten Brief geschrieben? 9. Von wem halten Sie nicht viel? 10. Wovon träumen Sie? **Übung 7:** 1. bin 2.a. hat b. bin 3.a. habe b. bin 4. bin 5. bin 6.a. habe b. bin 7.a. habe b. ist 8.a. haben b. ist 9.a. ist / sind b. hat 10. habe **Übung 8:** 1. Ich habe schon Frühstück gemacht. 2. Ich habe meine Milch schon getrunken. 3. Ich habe den Tisch schon saubergemacht. 4. Ich bin schon zum Bäcker gelaufen. 5. Ich habe schon Brötchen mitgebracht. 6. Ich habe schon Geld mitgenommen. 7. Ich habe den Hund schon gefüttert. 8. Ich habe die Tür schon zugemacht.

Kapitel 8

Übung 1: *(Answers will vary.)* **Übung 2:** 1. Ich durfte nicht. 2. Ich wollte nicht. 3. Das wußte ich nicht. 4. Ich wollte eine. 5. Ich sollte das nicht. **Übung 3:** 1.a. wolltest b. wußte 2.a. durfte b. mußte c. wollten d. konnten 3.a. konnte b. mußte c. wußte d. wollte **Übung 4:** 1.a. Wann b. Wenn 2.a. wann b. Als 3. als 4.a. Wann

b. als 5.a. Wann b. Wenn 6.a. Wann b. Als **Übung 5:** a. wenn b. Als c. Wenn d. wenn e. Als f. Als g. Wann h. Als i. wenn **Übung 6:** a. standen b. gingen c. fuhren d. kamen e. hielten f. aßen g. schwammen h. schliefen i. sprangen **Übung 7:** (1) a. wohnte b. hieß c. brachten d. machten e. gaben f. schliefen g. liefen h. kamen (2) a. sahen b. saß c. kochte d. fanden e. trug f. schloß g. tötete h. lief **Übung 8:** 1. Nachdem Jutta den Schlüssel verloren hatte, kletterte sie durchs Fenster. 2. Nachdem Ernst die Fensterscheibe eingeworfen hatte, lief er weg. 3. Nachdem Claire angekommen war, rief sie Melanie an. 4. Nachdem Hans seine Hausaufgaben gemacht hatte, ging er ins Bett. 5. Nachdem Jens sein Fahrrad repariert hatte, machte er eine Radtour. 6. Nachdem Michael die Seiltänzerin gesehen hatte, war er ganz verliebt. 7. Nachdem Richard ein ganzes Jahr gespart hatte, flog er nach Australien. 8. Nachdem Silvia zwei Semester allein gewohnt hatte, zog sie in eine Wohngemeinschaft. 9. Nachdem Willi ein Geräusch gehört hatte, rief er den Großvater an.

Kapitel 9

Übung 1: *(Answers will vary.)* Amerikanisches Steak! 2. Russischer Kaviar! 3. Griechische Oliven! 4. Japanische Sojasoße! 5. Französischer Champagner! 6. Deutsche Wurst! 7. Dänischer Käse! 8. Italienische Spaghetti! 9. Ungarischer Paprika! 10. Englische Marmelade! 11. Kolumbianischer Kaffee! 12. Neuseeländische Kiwi! **Übung 2:** 1. Ja, aber nur deutsches Brot. 2. Ja, aber nur russischen Kaviar. 3. Ja, aber nur italienische Salami. 4. Ja, aber nur kolumbianischen Kaffee. 5. Ja, aber nur neuseeländische Kiwis. 6. Ja, aber nur französischen Wein. 7. Ja, aber nur belgisches Bier. 8. Ja, aber nur spanische Muscheln. 9. Ja, aber nur englische Marmelade. 10. Ja, aber nur japanischen Thunfisch. **Übung 3:** 1. Michael: Ich möchte den grauen Wintermantel da. Maria: Nein, der graue Wintermantel ist viel zu schwer. 2. Michael: Ich möchte die gelbe Hose da. Maria: Nein, die gelbe Hose ist viel zu bunt. 3. Michael: Ich möchte das schicke Hemd da. Maria: Nein, das schicke Hemd ist viel zu teuer. 4. Michael: Ich möchte die roten Socken da. Maria: Nein, die roten Socken sind viel zu warm. 5. Michael: Ich möchte den schwarzen Schlafanzug da. Maria: Nein, der schwarze Schlafanzug ist viel zu dünn. 6. Michael: Ich möchte die grünen Schuhe da. Maria: Nein, die grünen Schuhe sind viel zu groß. 7. Michael: Ich möchte den modischen Hut da. Maria: Nein, der modische Hut ist viel zu klein. 8. Michael: Ich möchte die leichten Winterstiefel da. Maria: Nein, die leichten Winterstiefel sind viel zu leicht. 9. Michael: Ich möchte die elegante Sonnenbrille da. Maria: Nein, die elegante Sonnenbrille ist viel zu bunt. 10. Michael: Ich möchte die roten Tennisschuhe da. Maria: Nein, die roten Tennisschuhe sind viel zu grell. **Übung 4:** 1.a. Ihr neues Auto b. der alte Mercedes c. keinen neuen Wagen 2.a. der italienische Wein b. eine weitere Flasche 3.a. mein kaputtes Fahrrad b. meinen blöden Kassettenrecorder c. kein freies Wochenende **Übung 5:** 1. den 2.a. den b. dem 3.a. dem b. das 4. der 5.a. den b. den 6.a. ins b. im c. am 7.a. dich b. dich 8.a. den b. dem 9. der **Übung 6:** 1. Die Teller stehen im Küchenschrank. 2. Albert stellt die Teller auf den Tisch. 3. Die Servietten liegen in der Schublade. 4. Monika legt die Servietten auf den Tisch. 5. Messer und Gabeln liegen in der Schublade. 6. Stefan legt Messer und Gabeln auf den Tisch. 7. Die Kerze steht auf dem Schrank. 8. Heidi stellt die Kerze auf den Tisch. 9. Thomas sitzt auf dem Sofa. **Übung 7:** 1. Jutta leiht ihrem neuen Freund ihre Lieblings-CD. 2. Jens verkauft dem kleinen Bruder von Jutta eine Ratte. 3. Ernst zeigt die Ratte nur seinen besten Freunden. 4. Jutta schenkt ihrer besten Freundin ein Buch. 5. Jens kauft seinem wütenden Lehrer eine Krawatte. 6. Ernst erzählt seiner großen Schwester einen Witz. 7. Jutta kocht den netten Leuten von nebenan Kaffee. 8. Ernst gibt dem süßen Baby von nebenan einen Kuß. **Übung 8:** 1. Ach, könntest du nicht Suppe kochen? 2. Ach, könntest du nicht später lesen? 3. Ach, könntest du nicht etwas Klavier spielen? 4. Ach, könntest du nicht deinen Vater anrufen? 5. Ach, könntest du nicht noch eine Stunde bleiben? 6. Ach, könnten wir nicht mal im Hotel übernachten? 7. Ach, könnten wir nicht mal essen gehen? 8. Ach, könnten wir nicht mal schwimmen gehen? 9. Ach, könnten wir nicht mal nur einen Brief schreiben. 10. Ach, könnten wir nicht mal in der Sonne liegen? **Übung 9:** 1. Müßtest du nicht noch tanken? 2. Sollten wir nicht Jens abholen? 3. Könnten zwei Freunde von mir nicht auch mitfahren? 4. Sollten wir nicht zuerst in die Stadt fahren? 5. Wolltest du nicht zur Bank? 6. Könntest du nicht etwas langsamer fahren? 7. Dürfte ich das Autoradio anmachen? 8. Dürfte ich das Fenster aufmachen?

Kapitel 10

Übung 1: 1. Aus seinem Zimmer. 2. Aus der Schule. 3. Vom Markt. 4. Vom Friseur. 5. Bei Billy. 6. Bei ihrer Freundin. 7. Zu Herrn Thelen, Karten spielen. 8. Zu seiner Tante. 9. Nach Frankfurt. 10. Nach England. **Übung 2:** 1. Nach Kopenhagen. 2. Zum Strand. 3. Zu ihrer Tante Sule. 4. Aus der Türkei. 5. Nein, sie kommt aus dem Iran. 6. Aus dem Wasser. 7. Vom Markt. 8. Ja, bei uns. 9. Bei Fatimas Tante. 10. Nach Hause. **Übung 3:** 1. Können Sie mir sagen, wann der nächste Zug nach Kassel fährt? 2. Wissen Sie, wie lange man nach Kassel fährt? 3. Können Sie mir sagen, wie groß Kassel ist? 4. Wissen Sie, was es in Kassel zu sehen gibt? 5. Können Sie mir sagen, ob man dort gut essen gehen kann? 6. Wissen Sie, ob es in Kassel eine Universität gibt? 7. Können Sie mir sagen, wie groß die Universität ist. 8. Wissen Sie, ob es eine gute Universität ist? 9. Können Sie mir sagen, was man abends in Kassel machen kann? 10. Wissen Sie, wann der nächste Zug zurückfährt? **Übung 4:** 1. Fahren Sie den Fluß entlang. 2. Gehen Sie über die Brücke. 3. Gehen Sie an der Kirche vorbei. 4. Fahren Sie links vor dem Bahnhof. 5. Die Tankstelle ist gegenüber von der Post. 6. Gehen Sie über die Schienen. 7. Ja, und dann biegen Sie in die dritte Straße rechts ein. 8. Nein, gehen Sie an dem Rathaus vorbei und dann links. 9. Das Hotel „Patrizier" ist gegenüber von dem Rathaus. 10. Fahren Sie 10 km die Straße entlang. **Übung 5:** *(Answers will vary.)*1. Ich würde bei Freunden übernachten. 2. Ich würde zuerst nach Berlin fahren. 3. Ich würde zuerst ins Museum gehen. 4. Ich würde bei meinen Freunden essen. 5. Ich würde am Abend ins Kino gehen. 6. Ich würde ein Stück der Berliner Mauer kaufen. 7. Ich würde allen meinen Freunden Postkarten schreiben. 8. Ich würde ein Jahr bleiben. **Übung 6:** *(Answers will vary.)* **Übung 7:** 1. steht 2. gratuliere 3. helfen 4. Schmeckt 5. paßt 6. gehört 7. Fehlt 8. begegnet 9. schadet 10. zugehört **Übung 8:** *(Answers will vary.)*

Kapitel 11

Übung 1: 1.a. fühle mich b. mich erkältet c. dich legen 2.a. sich aufgeregt b. sich ausruhen 3.a. dich verletzt b. mich geschnitten 4.a. ärgerst dich b. dich freuen **Übung 2:** *(Answers will vary.)* Erst stehe ich auf. Dann dusche ich mich. Dann wasche ich mir das Gesicht. Dann wasche ich mir die Haare. Dann trockne ich mich ab. Dann putze ich mir die Fingernägel. Dann rasiere ich mich. Dann kämme ich mir die Haare. Dann ziehe ich mich an. Dann frühstücke ich. Dann putze ich mir die Zähne und gehe zur Uni. **Übung 3:** *(Answers will vary.)* 1. Ich rasiere mich jeden Morgen. 2. Meine Oma schminkt sich zu sehr. 3. Mein Freund wäscht sich nicht oft genug die Haare. 4. Mein Vater putzt sich nach jeder Mahlzeit die Zähne. 5. Mein Onkel zieht sich immer verrückt an. 6. Meine Schwester duscht sich jeden Tag. 7. Meine Freundin kämmt sich nie. 8. Mein Bruder föont sich nie die Haare. 9. Meine Kusine badet sich nicht gern. 10. Meine Mutter zieht sich immer elegant an. **Übung 4:** 1. Ja, kannst du es mir geben?/Nein, ich brauche es nicht. 2. Ja, kannst du ihn mir geben?/Nein, ich brauche ihn nicht. 3. Ja, kannst du ihn mir geben?/ Nein, ich brauche ihn nicht. 4. Ja, kannst du sie mir geben?/Nein, ich brauche sie nicht. 5. Ja, kannst du es mir geben?/Nein, ich brauche es nicht. 6. Ja, kannst du ihn mir geben?/Nein, ich brauche ihn nicht. 7. Ja, kannst du sie mir geben?/Nein, ich brauche sie nicht. 8. Ja, kannst du es mir geben?/ Nein, ich brauche es nicht. 9. Ja, kannst du ihn mir geben?/Nein, ich brauche ihn nicht. **Übung 5:** 1. Warum schneidest du ihn dir nicht? 2. Warum wäschst du sie dir nicht? 3. Warum schneidest du sie dir nicht? 4. Warum kremst du sie dir nicht ein? 5. Warum fönst du sie dir nicht? 6. Warum wäschst du ihn dir nicht? 7. Warum putzt du sie dir nicht? 8. Warum läßt du sie dir nicht schneiden? 9. Warum kremst du es dir nicht ein? Warum wäschst du sie dir nicht? **Übung 6:** 1. Zieh dir einen Pullover an! 2. Zieh dir die Jacke aus! 3. Nimm einen Regenschirm mit! 4. Fahr mit dem Bus! 5. Sonn dich! 6. Fön dir die Haare! 7. Schneide sie dir! 8. Iß etwas! 9. Ärger dich nicht! 10. Ruh dich aus! **Übung 7:** 1. Jens und Ernst, seid nicht so laut! 2. Michael und Maria, seid pünktlich! 3. Uli, rauche nicht so viel! 4. Jutta, iß mehr Obst! 5. Herr Pusch, fahren Sie nicht so schnell! 6. Frau Körner, warten Sie an der Ecke! 7. Natalie und Rosemarie, seid nicht so ungeduldig! 8. Andrea und Paula, grüßt euren Vater von mir! 9. Hans, wasch dich und putz dir die Zähne! 10. Helga und Sigrid, lest jeden Tag die Zeitung! **Übung 8:** 1. Mach 2. Sprechen 3. warte 4. vergiß 5. Helft **Übung 9:** 1.a. ob b. daß c. Wenn 2.a. damit b. weil **Übung 10:** 1.a. als b. nachdem 2. bevor 3. Während 4. obwohl

Kapitel 12

Übung 1: 1. meines 2. Ihrer 3. meiner 4. deiner 5. dieses 6. alten 7. ersten 8. neuen **Übung 2:** 1. Monika spricht über den Beruf ihrer Schwester. 2. Thomas spricht über das Bild seines Vaters. 3. Frau Schulz spricht über das Alter ihrer Nichten. 4. Stefan spricht über die Länge seines Studiums. 5. Albert spricht über die Sprache seiner Großeltern. 6. Nora spricht über die Kleidung ihres Freundes. 7. Thomas spricht über die Qualität des Leitungswassers in Berkeley. 8. Katrin spricht über die Situation der Frauen. **Übung 3:** 1. Um morgens munter zu sein, muß man früh ins Bett gehen. 2. Um die Professoren kennenzulernen, muß man in die Sprechstunde gehen. 3. Um die Mitstudenten kennenzulernen, muß man viel Gruppenarbeit machen. 4. Um am Wochenende nicht allein zu sein, muß man Leute einladen. 5. Um die Kurse zu bekommen, die man will, muß man sich so früh wie möglich einschreiben. 6. Um in vier Jahren fertig zu werden, muß man viel lernen und wenig Feste feiern. 7. Um nicht zu verhungern, muß man regelmäßig essen. 8. Um einen Freund/eine Freundin zu finden, muß man Deutsch belegen. 9. Um ein A in Deutsch zu bekommen, muß man jeden Tag zum Unterricht kommen. 10. Um nicht ins Sprachlabor gehen zu müssen, muß man sich Kassetten kaufen oder ausleihen. **Übung 4:** *(Answers may vary.)* 1. Ich möchte immer in den USA leben, weil die USA das beste Land der Welt sind. 2. Ich möchte für ein Paar Jahre in Deutschland leben, um richtig gut Deutsch zu lernen. 3. Ausländer haben oft Probleme, weil sie die Sprache und Kultur des Gastlandes nicht verstehen. 4. Wenn ich Kinder habe, möchte ich in den USA leben, damit meine Kinder als Amerikaner aufwachsen. 5. Viele Ausländer kommen in die USA, weil man gut Geld verdienen kann. 6. Englisch sollte die einzige offizielle Sprache der USA sein, damit eine homogene Gemeinschaft aus der multikulturellen Bevölkerung wird. **Übung 5:** 1. Frau Schulz repariert morgen das Auto. 2. Heidi fährt morgen aufs Land. 3. Peter spielt morgen Fußball. 4. Monika schreibt morgen einen Brief. 5. Stefan geht morgen einkaufen. 6. Nora heiratet morgen. 7. Albert geht in den Supermarkt. 8. Thomas räumt morgen sein Zimmer auf. **Übung 6:** 1. Die Fenster werden geputzt. 2. Das Silber wird poliert. 3. Die Lampen werden abgestaubt. 4. Die Fußböden werden aufgewischt. 5. Die Schränke werden aufgeräumt. 6. Die Gardinen werden gewaschen. 7. Die Sessel werden gereinigt. 8. Der Hof wird gefegt. 9. Die Teppiche werden staubgesaugt. **Übung 7:** 1. um 2500 v. Chr. → Wann wurden die ersten Pyramiden gebaut? 2. 44 v. Chr. → Wann wurde Cäsar ermordet? 3. 800 n. Chr. → Wann wurde Karl der Große zum Kaiser gekrönt? 4. 1088 → Wann wurde die erste Universität (Bologna) gegründet? 5. 1661 → Wann wurde das erste Thanksgiving-Fest gefeiert? 6. 1789 → Wann wurde die amerikanische Verfassung unterschrieben? 7. 1867 → Wann wurde Alaska an die USA verkauft? 8. 1945 → Wann wurden die Atombomben auf Hiroshima und Nagasaki geworfen? 9. 1963 → Wann wurde John F. Kennedy erschossen? 10. 1990 → Wann wurde Deutschland vereinigt?

VOKABELN
Deutsch-Englisch

Note to Students: The definitions in this vocabulary are based on the words as used in this text. For additional meanings, please refer to a dictionary.

Proper nouns are given only if the name is feminine or masculine, or if the spelling is different from that in English.

The letters or numbers in parentheses following the entries refer to the chapters in which the words first occur in the chapter vocabulary list.

ABBREVIATIONS

acc.	accusative	*neut.*	neuter
adj.	adjective	*nom.*	nominative
adv.	adverb	*n.*	noun
coll.	colloquial	*o.s.*	oneself
coord. conj.	coordinating conjunction	*pl.*	plural
dat.	dative	*p.p.*	past participle
def. art.	definite article	*prep.*	preposition
dem. pron.	demonstrative pronoun	*pron.*	pronoun
fem.	feminine	*rel. pron.*	relative pronoun
for.	formal	*sg.*	singular
for. pl.	formal plural	*s.o.*	someone
for. sg.	formal singular	*s.th.*	something
gen.	genitive	*subord. conj.*	subordinate conjunction
infor. pl.	informal plural	*v.*	verb
infor. sg.	informal singular	*wk.*	weak masculine noun
masc.	masculine		

A

ab (+ *dat.*) as of, effective

ab·bekommen (bekommt . . . ab), bekam . . . ab, abbekommen to get s.th.

ab·biegen (biegt . . . ab), bog . . . ab, ist abgebogen to turn (10)

ab·brennen (brennt . . . ab), brannte . . . ab, ist abgebrannt to burn down

der **Abend, -e** evening (1); **am Abend** at night, in the evening (4); **gegen Abend** toward evening; **gestern abend** last night; **guten Abend!** good evening; **der Heilige Abend** Christmas Eve; **heute abend** tonight; **zu Abend essen** to dine, have dinner (4)

das **Abendessen, -** supper, evening meal, dinner (1, 9); **beim Abendessen** during dinner; **zum Abendessen** for dinner

das **Abendkleid, -er** evening dress

die **Abendnachrichten** (*pl.*) evening news

abends evenings, in the evening (4)

die **Abendsonne** evening sun, setting sun

der **Abendsonnenschein** evening sunlight

der **Abendverkauf** *permission to keep stores open at night*

das **Abenteuer, -** adventure; **Abenteuer erleben** to have adventures

aber (*coord. conj.*) but (A, 11)

ab·fahren (fährt . . . ab), fuhr . . . ab, ist abgefahren to leave, depart (4, 7)

die **Abfahrt, -en** departure

die **Abfahrtszeit, -en** time of departure

die **Abfallbeseitigung** waste disposal

ab·geben (gibt . . . ab), gab . . . ab, abgegeben to hand over (to); to deliver (to)

abgenutzt worn

ab·holen, abgeholt to pick (*s.o.*) up (from a place) (1)

das **Abitur** college-prep-school degree (5)

ab·nehmen (nimmt . . . ab), nahm . . . ab, abgenommen to lose weight; to take off/away; to remove (9); **Blut abnehmen** to take blood (11)

ab·räumen, abgeräumt to clear; to remove (3)

ab·reisen, ist abgereist to depart (10)

der **Absatz, ⸚e** heel (10); paragraph

der **Abschied** farewell; **zum Abschied** when leaving

ab·schließen (schließt . . . ab), schloß . . . ab, abgeschlossen to finish

der **Abschluß, Abschlüsse** completion; final examination; graduation (8)

ab·schneiden (schneidet . . . ab), schnitt . . . ab, abgeschnitten to cut off (9); to slice

der **Abschnitt, -e** segment, section

ab·schreiben (schreibt . . . ab), schrieb . . . ab, abgeschrieben to copy (from another person)

die **Absicht, -en** intention
absolut absolute
die **Abstammung** origin; extraction
ab·stauben, abgestaubt to dust (off)
ab·stellen, abgestellt to put, set down
ab·stürzen, ist abgestürzt to crash (11)
ab·transportieren, abtransportiert to carry away; to cart off
(sich) **ab·trocknen, abgetrocknet** to dry (*o.s.*) off (6, 11)
ab·waschen (wäscht . . . ab), wusch . . . ab, abgewaschen to wash (dishes)
abwechselnd alternately; taking turns
ab·wischen, abgewischt to wipe off; to wipe clean (6)
ab·ziehen (zieht . . . ab), zog . . . ab, abgezogen to subtract
ach: ach oh; ach ja? oh really; **ach wie nett** how nice; **ach so** I see
acht eight (A, 4)
achten auf (+ *acc.*) to watch out for; to pay attention to (11)
achtunddreißig thirty-eight
achtundzwanzig twenty-eight (A)
die **Achtung** attention (7)
achtzehn eighteen (A)
achtzig eighty (A)
der **ADAC** = **Allgemeiner Deutscher Automobilclub** *German automobile club*
adaptiert adapted
addieren, addiert to add
das **Adjektiv, -e** adjective
die **Adjektivendung, -en** adjective ending
der **Adler, -** eagle (12)
administrativ administrative
die **Adresse, -n** address (1)
der **Advent** Advent (*period beginning four Sundays before Christmas*); **der erste/zweite/dritte/vierte Advent** the first/second/third/fourth Sunday in Advent
die **Adventsdekoration, -en** decoration for Advent
der **Adventskalender, -** calendar counting the days of Advent
das **Adverb, -ien** adverb
(das) **Afrika** Africa (B)
afro-deutsch Afro-German (*adj.*) (12)
aggressiv aggressive
(das) **Ägypten** Egypt (B)
der **Ahnenforscher, -** genealogist
die **Ahnenforschung, -en** genealogy
ähnlich similar(ly)
ähnliches: etwas ähnliches something similar

die **Ahnung, -en** idea; suspicion; **keine Ahnung** no idea (4)
das **Akkordeon, -s** accordion (4)
der **Akkusativ, -e** accusative
die **Akte, -n** file; record
die **Aktiengesellschaft (AG)** (stock) corporation
aktiv active
die **Aktivität, -en** activity
aktuell current; present-day
akzeptabel acceptable
akzeptieren, akzeptiert to accept; to agree to
der **Alarm, -e** alarm
(das) **Albanien** Albania (B)
der **Albatros, -se** albatross (12)
(das) **Algier** Algiers
(das) **Algerien** Algeria (B)
der **Alkohol** alcohol
alkoholfrei nonalcoholic
alle (*pl.*) everybody; **nichts von alledem** none of this; **vor allem** above all
allein(e) alone; by oneself (3); **von allein** on one's own; by oneself
allerdings however; nevertheless; of course
allergisch (gegen + *acc.*) allergic (to) (11)
alles everything; **alles in Ordnung** everything (is) okay; **alles Mögliche** everything possible (2)
alles zusammen all together; one check (*restaurant*)
allgemein general(ly); **im allgemeinen** generally
der **Alltag, -e** everyday life
die **Alpen** (*pl.*) the Alps (7)
das **Alphabet** alphabet (3)
alpin alpine
als (*after comparative*) than; (*subord. conj.*) when; as (11); **als was?** as what? (5)
also well; so; thus (2)
alt old (A)
der **Altbau, Altbauten** *building built before June 20, 1948*
das **Alter** age (1)
die **Älteren** (*pl.*) the elderly
alternativ alternative
die **Altersversorgung** old-age pension
die **Altstadt, ¨e** old part of town (10)
das **Alugestell, -e** aluminum frame
am = **an dem** at/on the
(das) **Amerika** the USA, America (B)
der **Amerikaner, -** / die **Amerikanerin, -nen** American (*person*) (B)

amerikanisch American (*adj.*) (3)
amerikanisieren, amerikanisiert to Americanize
die **Ampel, -n** traffic light
das **Amt, ¨er** public office
an (+ *acc./dat.*) at; on; to; **am Abend** in the evening (4); **am ersten Oktober** on the first of October (4); **am Samstag** on Saturday (2); **am Telefon** on the phone (2); **an der Uni** at the university; **ans Meer** to the sea (2); **an welchem Tag?** on what day? (4); **an . . . vorbei** by (10)
das **Andenken, -** souvenir (10); memento
die **Analphase, -n** anal phase
analysieren, analysiert to analyze
ander- other; different; **alles andere** everything else; **anders** different; **unter anderem** among other things
der/die **Andere, -n** (ein **Anderer**) other (person)
(sich) **ändern, geändert** to change (8)
die **Anerkennung, -en** acknowledgment; appreciation
der **Anfang, ¨e** beginning
an·fangen (fängt . . . an), fing . . . an, angefangen to begin (4), start; (**zu** + *inf.*) to begin
an·fassen, angefaßt to touch
an·fertigen, angefertigt to prepare (a report)
an·fressen (frißt . . . an), fraß . . . an, angefressen to nibble (at)
die **Angabe, -n** statement; information
an·gehören, angehört to belong to (an organization) (12)
der/die **Angestellte, -n (ein Angestellter)** employee; clerk (7)
angewiesen sein (auf + *acc.*) to depend on
die **Anglistik** English language and literature
an·greifen (greift . . . an), griff . . . an, angegriffen to attack (12)
die **Angst, ¨e** fear; **Angst bekommen** to become afraid; **Angst haben (vor** + *dat.*) to be afraid (of) (3); **keine Angst!** don't be afraid!
an·halten (hält . . . an), hielt . . . an, hat/ist angehalten to stop
animieren, animiert to encourage; animate
an·kommen (kommt . . . an), kam . . . an, ist angekommen to arrive (1)
an·kreuzen, angekreuzt to mark with a cross

die **Ankunft, ¨-e** arrival
die **Ankunftszeit, -en** time of arrival
die **Anlage, -en** set; equipment
an·machen, angemacht to turn on, switch on (3)
an·nehmen (nimmt . . . an), nahm . . . an, angenommen to accept; to take
anonym anonymous
an·probieren, anprobiert to try on (10)
an·pumpen, angepumpt (*coll.*) to borrow money from (*s.o.*)
an·quatschen, angequatscht (*coll.*) to speak to; to babble at
der **Anruf, -e** phone call
der **Anrufbeantworter, -** answering machine
an·rufen (ruft . . . an), rief . . . an, angerufen to call up (on the telephone) (1)
der **Anrufer, -** person calling on the phone
ans = an das to the
an·schauen, angeschaut to look at (2); to watch
anscheinend apparently
die **Anschrift, -en** address (11)
an·sehen (sieht . . . an), sah . . . an, angesehen to look at; to watch (3)
die **Ansichtskarte, -n** postcard
der **Anspruch, ¨-e** claim; **in Anspruch nehmen** lay claim to
an·starren, angestarrt to stare at
anstatt (+ *gen.*) instead of (12)
sich **an·stecken (mit + *acc.*), angesteckt** to infect (with)
sich **an·stellen, angestellt** to get in line
anstrengend stressful; tiring
antiautoritär antiauthoritarian
die **Antibiotika** (*pl.*) antibiotics (11)
antirassistisch antiracist (*adj.*) (12)
antiviral antiviral
der **Antrag, ¨-e** application
der **Antragsteller, -** applicant
der **Antrieb, -e** motivation
die **Antwort, -en** answer (A)
antworten (+ *dat.*), **geantwortet** to answer (4, 10)
der **Anwalt, ¨-e** / die **Anwältin, -nen** lawyer (5)
an·wenden (wendet . . . an), wandte . . . an, angewandt to use, apply; **Gewalt anwenden** to use force (12)
an·werben (wirbt . . . an), warb . . . an, angeworben to recruit
an·zahlen, angezahlt to pay in advance (10)
die **Anzeige, -n** ad (6)
sich **an·ziehen (zieht . . . an), zog . . . an, angezogen** to get dressed; to put on (*clothes*) (3, 11)
der **Anzug, ¨-e** suit (A)
an·zünden, angezündet to light (3); to set on fire
der **Apfel, ¨** apple (3, 9)
der **Apfelsaft, ¨-e** apple juice (9)
der **Apfelstrudel, -** apple pie
das **Apfelstück, -e** piece of apple
die **Apotheke, -n** drug store; pharmacy (6, 11)
der **Apotheker, -** / die **Apothekerin, -nen** pharmacist (11)
der **Apparat, -e** telephone; apparatus
das **Appartement, -s** apartment
das **Appartementhaus, ¨-er** apartment complex
(der) **April** April (B)
der **Araber, -** / die **Araberin, -nen** Arabian (*person*)
arabisch Arabian (*adj.*) (B)
die **Arbeit, -en** work; **zur Arbeit gehen** to go to work (1)
arbeiten, gearbeitet to work (1)
der **Arbeiter, -** / die **Arbeiterin, -nen** worker (5)
der **Arbeitgeber, -** / die **Arbeitgeberin, -nen** employer
der **Arbeitnehmer, -** / die **Arbeitnehmerin, -nen** employee
das **Arbeitsamt, ¨-er** employment office
das **Arbeitsbuch, ¨-er** workbook (3)
der **Arbeitskollege, -n** (*wk.*) / die **Arbeitskollegin, -nen** co-worker
die **Arbeitskraft, ¨-e** employee (*sg.*), work force (*pl.*)
arbeitslos unemployed (5)
die **Arbeitslosigkeit** unemployment
der **Arbeitsplatz, ¨-e** work place
die **Arbeitsstelle, -n** work place
die **Arbeitsteilung, -en** division of labor
die **Arbeitszeit, -en** working hours
der **Archäologe, -n** (*wk.*) / die **Archäologin, -nen** archeologist
der **Architekt, -en** (*wk.*) / die **Architektin, -nen** architect (5)
die **Architektur, -en** architecture
archivieren, archiviert to archive
ärgerlich angry; annoyed
ärgern, geärgert to annoy; to tease (3); to bother; **sich ärgern (über + *acc.*)** to get angry (about) (11)
das **Argument, -e** argument
der **Aristokrat, -en** (*wk.*) aristocrat
arm poor (8)
der **Arm, -e** arm (A)
das **Armband, ¨-er** bracelet (2)
die **Armbanduhr, -en** watch (A)
der / die **Arme, -n** (ein **Armer**) poor person
die **Art, -en** kind, type (2)
der **Artikel, -** article
der **Arzt, ¨-e** / die **Ärztin, -nen** doctor; physician (3, 5, 11)
der **Arztbesuch, -e** doctor visit
die **Arztkosten, -** bill from physician
ärztlich medical
die **Arztpraxis, Arztpraxen** doctor's office (11)
(das) **Aschenputtel** Cinderella
(das) **Asien** Asia (B)
die **Asphaltschindeln** shingles made of asphalt
das **Aspirin** aspirin (3, 11)
assoziieren (mit + *acc.*), assoziiert to associate (with)
der **Asylant, -en** (*wk.*) asylum-seeker
atemlos out of breath
(das) **Athen** Athens
(der) **Atlantik** Atlantic Ocean
atlantisch Atlantic
atmen, geatmet to breathe (11)
die **Atombombe, -n** atomic bomb
die **Attraktion, -en** attraction
attraktiv attractive (6)
auch also; too (A); **auch noch** on top of it all; **auch wenn** (*subord. conj.*) even if
auf (+ *dat./acc.*) on; upon; onto; to; at; **auf die Bank gehen** to go to the bank; **auf dem Land** in the country; **auf und ab** back and forth, up and down; **auf** (+ *acc.*) **. . . zu** toward
auf Wiedersehen! good-bye! (A)
auf·bauen, aufgebaut to build
der **Aufenthaltsraum, ¨-e** lounge, recreation room (10)
auffällig conspicuous(ly) (10)
die **Aufforderung, -en** request; command; instructions (A)
die **Aufgabe, -n** task; homework; job; assignment (4)
auf·geben (gibt . . . auf), gab . . . auf, aufgegeben to give up; to resign
auf·haben (hat . . . auf), hatte . . . auf, aufgehabt to be assigned (as homework) (4)
auf·hängen (hängt . . . auf), hing . . . auf, aufgehängt to hang up (12)
auf·hören (mit + *dat.*), aufgehört to quit; to end; to stop (*doing s.th.*) (1)

auf·machen, aufgemacht to open (3)
aufmerksam attentive
auf·nehmen (nimmt . . . auf), nahm . . . auf, aufgenommen to accept; to offer lodging; to obtain; to take down (notes); (**in** + *acc.*) to include, incorporate (into); **Kredit aufnehmen** to take out a loan
auf·passen, aufgepaßt to pay attention; to watch out (3)
auf·räumen, aufgeräumt to clean (up) (1), tidy up
sich **auf·regen, aufgeregt** to get upset; to get excited (11)
auf·schneiden (schneidet . . . auf), schnitt . . . auf, aufgeschnitten to chop (9)
der **Aufruf, -e** call; appeal
aufs = **auf das** upon/onto/to the
auf·saugen, aufgesaugt to absorb
auf·schlagen (schlägt . . . auf), schlug . . . auf, aufgeschlagen to open up; to beat
auf·schließen (schließt . . . auf), schloß . . . auf, aufgeschlossen to unlock; to open
auf·schreiben (schreibt . . . auf), schrieb . . . auf, aufgeschrieben to write down (11)
auf·stehen (steht . . . auf), stand . . . auf, ist aufgestanden to get up; to rise; to stand up (A, 1)
auf·stellen, aufgestellt to place; to set up (11)
auf·wachen, ist aufgewacht to wake up (4)
auf·wachsen (wächst . . . auf), wuchs . . . auf, ist aufgewachsen to grow up (12)
auf·warten (mit + *dat.*), **aufgewartet** to come up with
der **Aufzug, ¨-e** elevator (6)
das **Auge, -n** eye (A, 11)
der **Augenarzt, ¨-e** / die **Augenärztin, -nen** eye doctor (11)
der **Augenblick, -e** moment
die **Augenfarbe, -n** eye color (1)
der **Augenzeuge, -n** eye witness
(das) **Augsburg** Augsburg
(der) **August** August (B)
aus out of; from; of (10); **aus Stein** made (out) of stone
die **Ausbildung, -en** education; training; **praktische Ausbildung** practical (career) training (5)
die **Ausbildungsdaten** (*pl.*) educational data
die **Ausbildungszeit, -en** period of training
der **Ausblick, -e** view
aus·bürgern, ist ausgebürgert to denaturalize
der **Ausdruck, ¨-e** expression
die **Ausdrucksform, -en** mode of expression
aus·fallen (fällt . . . aus), fiel . . . aus, ist ausgefallen to fail, break down; to go out (*power*) (9)
aus·füllen, ausgefüllt to fill in (1); to fill out
der **Ausflug, ¨-e** excursion
die **Ausgabe, -n** expenditure
der **Ausgang, ¨-e** exit
die **Ausgangslage, -n** starting position; initial situation
der **Ausgangspunkt, -e** starting point
aus·geben (gibt . . . aus), gab . . . aus, ausgegeben to spend (*money*) (3)
ausgebildet educated (12)
aus·gehen (geht . . . aus), ging . . . aus, ist ausgegangen to go out (1)
ausgewaschen faded
ausgewogen well-balanced
ausgezeichnet excellent (3)
das **Ausland** foreign country; **im Ausland** abroad (6)
der **Ausländer, -** / die **Ausländerin, -nen** foreigner (12)
das **Ausländeramt, ¨-er** center/office for foreigners/foreign students
der/die **Ausländerbeauftragte, -n** (ein **Ausländerbeauftragter**) *officer working on behalf of foreigners*
die **Ausländerfeindlichkeit** xenophobia
ausländerfreundlich friendly/open to foreigners
der **Ausländerhaß** hatred of foreigners (12)
ausländisch foreign
das **Auslandsamt, ¨-er** center for study abroad (1)
aus·leeren, ausgeleert to empty (3)
aus·leihen (leiht . . . aus), lieh . . . aus, ausgeliehen to lend; to loan
aus·machen, ausgemacht to turn off (3)
die **Ausnahme, -n** exception
aus·nutzen, ausgenutzt to use; to take advantage of
aus·packen, ausgepackt to unpack
aus·rechnen, ausgerechnet to figure; to calculate; to total (9)
ausreichend sufficient; adequate; passing (*grade*)
sich **aus·ruhen, ausgeruht** to rest (11); to relax (10)
aus·rutschen, ist ausgerutscht to slip (11)
aus·sagen, ausgesagt to testify; to state
aus·schlafen (schläft . . . aus), schlief . . . aus, ausgeschlafen to sleep in
ausschließlich exclusive(ly)
aus·sehen (sieht . . . aus), sah . . . aus, ausgesehen to look (2); to appear; **aussehen wie** to look like
der **Aussiedler, -** / die **Aussiedlerin, -nen** resettler
aus·steigen (steigt . . . aus), stieg . . . aus, ausgestiegen to get out/off
die **Ausstellung, -en** exhibition
aus·strecken, ausgestreckt to stretch out
aus·suchen, ausgesucht to choose; to pick out
das **Austauschjahr, -e** year of exchange study
der **Austauschstudent, -en** (*wk.*) / die **Austauschstudentin, -nen** exchange student
aus·tragen (trägt . . . aus), trug . . . aus, ausgetragen to deliver; **Zeitungen austragen** to deliver newspapers (5)
(das) **Australien** Australia (B)
der **Australier, -** / die **Australierin, -nen** Australian (*person*) (B)
aus·treiben (treibt . . . aus), trieb . . . aus, ausgetrieben to chase away
aus·üben, ausgeübt to practice (*a profession*)
ausverkauft sold out (5)
aus·wählen, ausgewählt to choose; to select (9)
die **Auswandererfamilie, -n** family of emigrants
aus·wandern, ist ausgewandert to emigrate (4, 12)
die **Auswanderung, -en** emigration
der **Ausweis, -e** I.D. card (10)
aus·weisen (weist . . . aus), wies . . . aus, ausgewiesen to expel; to deport
auswendig by heart
aus·werten, ausgewertet to evaluate
sich **aus·ziehen (zieht . . . aus), zog . . . aus, ausgezogen** to take off (*clothes*) (3); to get undressed (11)
der/die **Auszubildende, -n** (ein **Auszubildender**) trainee
außer (+ *dat.*) except, besides
außerdem besides (5, 10)
außerhalb (+ *gen.*) out of; outside of (12)
das **Auto, -s** car (A); **Auto fahren**

(fährt . . . Auto), fuhr . . . Auto, ist Auto gefahren to drive (*a car*)
die **Autobahn, -en** interstate highway (7); freeway
das **Autofahren** driving
der **Autofahrer, -** / die **Autofahrerin, -nen** driver
die **Autofahrt, -en** drive
der **Autokäufer, -** / die **Autokäuferin, -nen** car buyer
das **Autokennzeichen, -** license plate
der **Automechaniker, -** / die **Automechanikerin, -nen** car mechanic (5)
die **Automobilfirma, -firmen** car manufacturer
die **Autonummer, -n** license plate number (11)
der **Autopreis, -e** price of a car
der **Autor, -en** / die **Autorin, -nen** author
das **Autoradio, -s** car radio (7)
der **Autoreifen, -** tire
der **Autoschlüssel, -** car key
das **Autotelefon, -e** car phone (2)
der **Autounfall, ¨-e** car accident
die **Autowerkstatt, ¨-en** car repair shop

B

das **Baby, -s** baby (7)
der **Babysitter, -** / die **Babysitterin, -nen** babysitter
das **Babysitting** babysitting
der **Bach, ¨-e** creek
das **Bächlein, -** small creek
backen (bäckt), backte, gebacken to bake (5)
die **Bäckerei, -en** bakery (6); **in der Bäckerei** at the bakery (5)
der **Bäckergehilfe, -n** (*wk.*) / die **Bäckergehilfin, -nen** baker's aid
der **Backofen, ¨-** oven (5)
die **Backsteingotik** Gothic architecture in brick
das **Bad, ¨-er** bathroom (6)
der **Badeort, -e** bathing resort
der **Badeanzug, ¨-e** bathing suit (5)
die **Badehose, -n** swimming trunks (5)
der **Bademantel, ¨-** bathrobe (10)
der **Bademeister, -** / die **Bademeisterin, -nen** lifeguard; swimming pool attendant (5)
baden, gebadet to bathe; to swim (3) **sich baden** to bathe (*o.s.*) (11)
die **Badewanne, -n** bathtub (6)
(der) **Baedeker, -** *travel guide in a series of guidebooks named after Karl Baedecker*
die **Bahn, -en** railroad (7); **mit der Bahn** by train
der **Bahnbeamte, -n** (ein **Bahnbeamter**) / die **Bahnbeamtin, -nen** train agent (10)
die **Bahnhaltestelle, -n** train stop
der **Bahnhof, ¨-e** train station (building) (4, 5, 6, 10)
das **Bahnhofsgebäude, -** train station (building)
die **Bahnhofsuhr, -en** clock in the train station
der **Bahnpreis, -e** price for train ticket
der **Bahnsteig, -e** railroad platform
die **Bahnsteigkante, -n** edge of railroad platform
die **Bahnstrecke, -n** railway segment; railway route
die **Bahre, -n** stretcher
das **Bakterium, Bakterien** bacterium
der **Bakteriologe, -n** (*wk.*) / die **Bakteriologin, -nen** bacteriologist
bald soon (8); **bis bald** so long; **bald darauf** soon thereafter (8)
baldmöglichst as soon as possible
der **Balkon, -e** balcony (6)
der **Ball, ¨-e** ball (A, 1)
ballastreich full of roughage
der **Ballaststoff, -e** roughage
die **Ballerina, -s** ballerina (8)
das **Ballett, -e** ballet
der **Ballettunterricht** ballet class (8)
die **Bambussprossen** (*pl.*) bamboo shoots (9)
banal banal
die **Banane, -n** banana
die **Bank, ¨-e** bench
die **Bank, -en** bank (5, 6); **bei einer Bank** at a bank (6)
der/die **Bankangestellte, -n** (ein **Bankangestellter**) bank employee (5)
das **Bargeld** cash
barock baroque
die **Barockstadt, ¨-e** baroque city
der **Bart, ¨-e** beard (A)
der **Basar, -e** bazaar (7)
die **Baseballmannschaft, -en** baseball team (8)
das **Basilikum** basil
der **Basketball, ¨-e** basketball (2)
basteln, gebastelt to tinker; to do handicrafts
der **Bau, Bauten** construction; building
der **Bauch, ¨-e** belly, stomach (A)
die **Bauchschmerzen** (*pl.*) stomach ache
bauen, gebaut to build (10)
das **Bauernbrot, -e** (loaf of) farmer's bread (5)
das **Bauernhaus, ¨-er** farmhouse (6)
der **Bauernhof, ¨-e** farm (12)
die **Bauernmöbel** (*pl.*) rustic furniture
das **Bauhaus** *architectural school and style in the 1920s*
die **Bauhausideen** (*pl.*) ideas of the Bauhaus
der **Bauhausstil** style of the Bauhaus
das **Baujahr, -e** year of construction
der **Baum, ¨-e** tree (8)
der **Baumeister, -** building contractor
das **Baumhaus, ¨-er** tree house (6)
der **Baustil, -e** style of construction
(das) **Bayern** Bavaria
beachten, beachtet to notice; to pay attention to; to consider
der **Beamte, -n** (ein **Beamter**) / die **Beamtin, -nen** civil servant
beantworten, beantwortet to answer (7)
der **Becher, -** cup, mug (8)
bedanken, bedankt to thank
der **Bedarf** need
bedeuten, bedeutet to mean
bedienen, bedient to serve
die **Bedienung, -en** service; waiter, waitress (9)
sich **beeilen, beeilt** to hurry (9)
beeinflussen, beeinflußt to influence
beenden, beendet to end
beerdigen, beerdigt to bury
befallen (befällt), befiel, befallen to attack; to strike
sich **befinden (befindet), befand, befunden** to be situated
befragen, befragt to interview; to interrogate
befreundet sein to be friends with
befriedigend satisfactory
die **Befriedigung, -en** satisfaction
begabt gifted (8)
begegnen (+ *dat.*), **ist begegnet** to meet, encounter (10)
begeistert enthusiastic
die **Begeisterung, -en** enthusiasm
beginnen (beginnt), begann, begonnen to begin; to start (1)
begreifen (begreift), begriff, begriffen to comprehend
begrenzen, begrenzt to limit
die **Begrenzung, -en** limitation
der **Begriff, -e** concept; idea
begründen, begründet to substantiate; to found

der **Begründer, -** / die **Begründerin, -nen** founder
begrüßen, begrüßt to greet
das **Begrüßen** greeting (A)
die **Behandlung, -en** treatment
die **Behörde, -n** public office
bei (+ *dat.*) at; with; near (10); during; upon; **bei dir** at your place (3); **bei einer Bank** at a bank (6); **bei kaltem Wetter** in cold weather; **bei McDonald's** at McDonald's (2); **bei Rudi** at Rudi's place (2)
die **Beilage, -n** side dish (9); condiment
beide both
beim = **bei dem** at/with/near the
das **Bein, -e** leg (A)
das **Beispiel, -e** example; **zum Beispiel (z.B.)** for example (3)
beißen (beißt), biß, gebissen to bite (8)
der **Beitrag, ¨-e** contribution; dues
bekannt well-known; famous
der/die **Bekannte, -n** (ein **Bekannter**) acquaintance
bekennen (bekennt), bekannte, bekannt to admit; to confess
bekommen (bekommt), bekam, bekommen to get, to receive (3); to obtain; **Angst bekommen** to become afraid
belagern, belagert to besiege
belastbar resilient
belästigen, belästigt to bother
belegen, belegt to take (*a course*) (3); **belegtes Brot** sandwich
(das) **Belgien** Belgium (B)
belgisch Belgian (*adj.*)
beliebt popular (3)
bemalen, bemalt to paint; to decorate
bemerken, bemerkt to notice
die **Bemerkung, -en** remark
das **Benimmbuch, ¨-er** book of manners
benutzen, benutzt to use (7)
das **Benzin** gasoline (6)
der **Benzinmotor, -en** gasoline engine
beobachten, beobachtet to observe
bequem comfortable (2)
beraten (berät), beriet, beraten to advise
der **Bereich, -e** area; range
bereit ready; prepared
bereiten, bereitet to prepare
bereit·halten (hält . . . bereit), hielt . . . bereit, bereitgehalten to make available
bereits already
der **Berg, -e** mountain; **in die Berge gehen** to go to the mountains; **in den Bergen wandern** to hike in the mountains (1)
der **Bergbau** mining
der **Bericht, -e** report
berichten, berichtet to report
der **Berichtteil, -e** part of a report
der **Berliner, -** / die **Berlinerin, -nen** person from Berlin
berüchtigt notorious
der **Beruf, -e** profession (1, 5); **was sind Sie von Beruf?** what is your profession? (1)
beruflich professional(ly)
die **Berufsausbildung, -en** professional training
der **Berufsberater, -** / die **Berufsberaterin, -nen** career counselor (5)
die **Berufsberatung, -en** job counseling
das **Berufsleben** career, professional life (12)
die **Berufsschule, -en** vocational school
berufsspezifisch job-specific
der/die **Berufstätige, -n** (ein **Berufstätiger**) employed person
die **Berufstätigkeit, -en** professional activity; employment
berühmt famous (7)
beschäftigt busy (3)
beschenken, beschenkt to give a present
beschreiben (beschreibt), beschrieb, beschrieben to describe (11)
die **Beschreibung, -en** description (A)
der **Beschützer, -** / die **Beschützerin, -nen** protector (12)
der **Besen, -** broom (6)
besetzt occupied, taken
besichtigen, besichtigt to visit (*a landmark*) (7)
die **Besichtigung, -en** viewing
besiegen, besiegt to conquer (7)
der **Besitz** possessions (2)
der **Besitzer, -** / die **Besitzerin, -nen** owner
besonder- special, particular
besonders particularly (3)
besorgt worried (3)
die **Bespannung** strings (of a tennis racket)
besser better (2)
die **Besserung** recovery
die **Bestätigung, -en** confirmation (10)
bester, bestes, beste best (3)
das **Besteck** silverware, cutlery (5)
bestehen (besteht), bestand, bestanden to exist; to last; (**aus** + *dat.*) to consist of
besteigen (besteigt), bestieg, bestiegen to climb (7)
bestellen, bestellt to order (*food*) (9)
bestimmt definitely, certainly (3)
bestreuen, bestreut to sprinkle (9)
der **Bestseller, -** best seller (12)
der **Besuch, -e** visit; **zu Besuch kommen** to visit (3)
besuchen, besucht to visit (1)
beten, gebetet to pray
der **Beton** concrete
der **Betrag, ¨-e** amount (*of money*)
betragen (beträgt), betrug, betragen to amount to
betreten (betritt), betrat, betreten to enter
betreuen, betreut to look after, to care for
die **Betreuung, -en** care
der **Betrieb, -e** business; firm
die **Betriebswirtschaft** business management
betroffen upset; affected
betrunken drunk (3)
das **Bett, -en** bed; **ins Bett gehen** to go to bed (1); **das Bett machen** to make the bed (6)
der **Beutel, -** bag (9)
der **Bettler, -** / die **Bettlerin, -nen** beggar
die **Bettruhe** bed rest
sich **beugen, gebeugt** to bend down
die **Beurteilung, -en** judgment
bevölkern, bevölkert to populate; to inhabit
die **Bevölkerung, -en** population
die **Bevölkerungsstatistik** population statistics
bevor (*subord. conj.*) before (11)
sich **bewegen, bewegt** to move
die **Bewegung, -en** movement
der **Beweis, -e** evidence
beweisen (beweist), bewies, bewiesen to prove
sich **bewerben (um** + *acc.*) **(bewirbt), bewarb, beworben** to apply (for)
bewerten, bewertet to evaluate; to review
die **Bewirtung, -en** service
der **Bewohner, -** / die **Bewohnerin, -nen** inhabitant; tenant
bezahlen, bezahlt to pay (for) (4)
beziehungsweise (bzw.) respectively
die **Bibliothek, -en** library (2)
der **Bibliothekar, -e** / die **Bibliothekarin, -nen** librarian (5)
die **Biene, -n** bee (12)
das **Bier, -e** beer (2, 9)
die **Bierhefe, -n** brewer's yeast
der **Bierkrug, ¨-e** beer mug, stein
der **Bikini, -s** bikini (5)
das **Bild, -er** picture (2)

die **Bildbeschreibung, -en** picture description
bilden, gebildet to form
die **Bildgeschichte, -n** picture story
bildlich figurative(ly)
die **Bildungschancen** (*pl.*) educational opportunities
der **Bildungsreformer, -** educational reformer
billig cheap(ly), inexpensive(ly) (2)
das **Bindegewebe, -** connective tissue
binden (an + *acc.*) **(bindet), band, gebunden** to tie (to) (12)
die **Biographie, -n** biography
biographisch biographical
der **Biologe, -n** (*wk.*) / die **Biologin, -nen** biologist
die **Biologie** biology (1)
die **Birne, -n** pear (9)
bis (*prep., subord. conj.*) until (3, 11); **bis bald!** so long, see you soon! (A); **bis acht Uhr** until eight o'clock (2); **bis um vier Uhr** until four o'clock (4); **bis zu** as far as; up to (10)
bißchen; ein bißchen some; a little (bit) (B); **kein bißchen** not at all (3)
blau blue (A)
bitte please (A)
bitte schön? yes please?; may I help you? (7)
bitten (um + *acc.*) **(bittet), bat, gebeten** to ask (for) (8)
die **Blase, -n** bubble; bladder
das **Blatt, ¨er** leaf
der **Blauwal, -e** blue whale (12)
bleiben (bleibt), blieb, ist geblieben to stay, to remain (1)
der **Bleistift, -e** pencil (A, B)
der **Blick, -e** view; look
blind blind
der **Blinddarm** appendix (11)
blitzen, geblitzt to lighten, flash
blöd(e) stupid
blond blonde (A)
bloß mere(ly); only
die **Blume, -n** flower (3)
der **Blumenkohl** cauliflower (9)
die **Blumenvase, -n** flower vase (5)
die **Bluse, -n** blouse (A)
das **Blut** blood (8, 11)
der **Blutdruck** blood pressure; **niedrigen/hohen Blutdruck haben** to have low/high blood pressure (11)
bluten, geblutet to bleed (11)
der **Blutfettspiegel, -** level of blood fat
die **Blutgruppe, -n** blood type

der **Boden, ¨** floor (B)
der **Bodensee** Lake Constance
die **Bohne, -n** bean; **grüne Bohnen** green beans (9)
das **Bonbon, -s** drop, lozenge (11)
das **Boot, -e** boat (7)
böse evil, mean (8)
(das) **Bosnien** Bosnia (B)
die **Boutique, -n** boutique (6)
die **Box, -en** stereo speaker (6)
boxen, geboxt (1) to box
braten (brät), briet, gebraten to fry (9)
die **Bratwurst, ¨e** (fried) sausage
brauchbar feasible; useful
brauchen, gebraucht to need; to use (1)
das **Brauchtum, ¨er** customs
brauen, gebraut to brew
braun brown (A)
bräunen, gebräunt to brown, to fry (9)
(das) **Braunschweig** Braunschweig
der **Braunschweiger** type of liver sausage, originally from Braunschweig
die **Braut, ¨e** bride (8)
die **BRD = Bundesrepublik Deutschland** FRG = Federal Republic of Germany
brechen (bricht), brach, gebrochen: sich den Arm brechen to break one's arm (11)
die **Bremse, -n** brake (7)
breit wide
die **Breite, -n** (*geographical*) latitude
der **Breitengrad, -e** degree of latitude
sich **breitmachen, breitgemacht** to spread (*o.s.*)
bremisch from the town of Bremen (*adj.*)
bremsen, gebremst to brake (11)
das **Bremsenquietschen** screeching of brakes
brennen (brennt), brannte, gebrannt to burn (11)
das **Brett, -er** board; **das Schwarze Brett** bulletin board
die **Brezel, -n** pretzel
der **Brief, -e** letter (1)
der **Briefkasten, ¨** mailbox
die **Briefmarke, -n** stamp (5)
das **Briefpapier, -e** writing paper, stationery, notepaper (5)
die **Brieftasche, -n** wallet (7)
die **Brille, -n** glasses (A)
bringen (bringt), brachte, gebracht to bring (2)
der **Brocken** *highest mountain in the Harz range*
die **Bronchitis** bronchitis

das **Brot, -e** (loaf of) bread; **belegtes Brot** open-face sandwich (9); **ein Stück Brot** a piece of bread (3)
das **Brötchen, -** roll (9)
die **Brücke, -n** bridge (10)
der **Bruder, ¨** brother (B)
der **Brunnen, -** well; fountain (8)
(das) **Brüssel** Brussels
die **Brust, ¨e** breast
der **Bub, -en** (*wk.*) (*short form of* **Bube**) boy
das **Buch, ¨er** book (A, B, 2)
buchen, gebucht to book, to reserve (7)
das **Bücherregal, -e** bookshelf, book rack
der **Buchhandel** book trade
der **Buchladen, ¨** bookstore (6)
der **Buchleser, -** book reader
der **Buchstabe, -n** (*wk.*) letter
die **Bucht, -en** bay (6, 7)
sich **bücken (nach** + *dat.*), **gebückt** to bend down (toward)
das **Bügeleisen, -** iron (6)
bügeln, gebügelt to iron (6)
(das) **Bukarest** Bucharest
die **Bulette, -n** meatball, hamburger
(das) **Bulgarien** Bulgaria (B)
bummeln (durch + *acc.*), **gebummelt** to stroll (through)
der **Bundesbürger, -** / die **Bundesbürgerin, -nen** German citizen
der **Bundesgerichtshof** federal court of justice
das **Bundesland, ¨er** German state
die **Bundespost** German postal service
die **Bundesrepublik** federal republic
der **Bundesstaat, -en** federal state
die **Bundesverfassung** German constitution
die **Bundeswehr** German armed forces; **bei der Bundeswehr** in the German armed forces (5)
das **Bungee-jumping** bungee jumping; **Bungee-jumping gehen** to go bungee jumping (3)
die **Burg, -en** fortress (6)
bunt colorful
der **Bürger, -** / die **Bürgerin, -nen** citizen (10)
bürgerlich bourgeois, middle-class
das **Büro, -s** office (5)
das **Bürohaus, ¨er** office building (6)
die **Bürohilfskraft, ¨e** clerical office worker
die **Bürste, -n** brush (6)
der **Bus, -se** bus (2, 7)

der **Busch, ¨-e** bush (8)
die **Bushaltestelle, -n** bus stop (6, 10)
die **Butter** butter (9)
bzw. = **beziehungsweise** respectively

C

das **Cabrio, -s** convertible
das **Café, -s** café (4, 6); **im Café** at the café
der **Cafébesitzer, -** / die **Cafébesitzerin, -nen** owner of a café
die **Cafeteria, -s** cafeteria
das **Camping** camping; **wildes Camping** wilderness camping; camping outside designated areas (10)
der **Campingplatz, ¨-e** campsite (10)
(das) **Cannstadt** Cannstadt
der **Cappuccino** cappuccino
das **Carotin** carotene
(der) **Cäsar** Caesar
die **CD, -s** CD, compact disc (3)
der **CD-Spieler, -** CD player (2)
Celsius centigrade; **18 Grad Celsius/Fahrenheit** 18 degrees Celsius/Fahrenheit (B)
der **Champagner, -** champagne
die **Chance, -n** opportunity (12)
der **Charakter, -e** character; personality (12)
charakterisieren, charakterisiert to characterize
charakteristisch sein (für + *acc.*) to be typical, characteristic (of)
der **Chauvi, -s** (*coll.*) chauvinist (12)
die **Checkliste** checklist
der **Chef, -s** / die **Chefin, -nen** boss; director
die **Chemie** chemistry (1)
das **Chemieprodukt, -e** chemical product
der **Chemiker, -** / die **Chemikerin, -nen** chemist
der **Chevignon-Rucksack** Chevignon backpack
das **Chili, -s** chili (11)
(das) **China** China
chinesisch Chinese (*adj.*) (3)
das **Cholesterin** cholesterol
der **Cholesterinspiegel** cholesterol level
die **Cholesterinwerte** (*pl.*) cholesterol values
Chr. = (der) **Christus** (*gen.* **Christi**; *dat.* **Christo**) Christ; **vor/nach Christo** BC/AD
das **Christkind** baby Jesus
christlich Christian
die **Christlich-Soziale Union** (**CSU**) Christian Social Union (*political party*)
chronologisch chronological
circa circa
der **Clown, -s** clown (8)
der **Cognac, -s** cognac
die **Cola, -s** cola (3)
der **Computer, -** computer (2)
die **Computerfirma, -firmen** computer company (4)
die **Computerkenntnis, -se** computer knowledge
das **Computerspiel, -e** computer game (5)
cool cool; fabulous; decent
der **Cord** corduroy
der **Corsa** *an Opel car model*
die **Côte d'Azur** Côte d'Azur
das **Coupé, -s** coupe
der **Cousin, -s** / die **Cousine, -n** cousin
das **Croissant, -s** croissant
die **CSU** = **Christlich-Soziale Union** Christian Social Union

D

da (*adv.*) there (2); **da drüben** over there (B)
dabei in that connection; while doing so; (along) with it; **ist ein/eine . . . dabei?** does it come with . . . ? (6)
dabei·haben (hat . . . dabei), hatte . . . dabei, dabeigehabt to have (*s.th.*) with/on (*s.o.*)
da·bleiben (bleibt . . . da), blieb . . . da, ist dageblieben to stay, to remain (there)
das **Dach, ¨-er** roof (6)
der **Dachauplatz** Dachau Square
dadurch through that; because of that; thereby; by this means
dafür for that; on behalf of it; for that reason; on the other hand
dagegen against it; **haben Sie etwas dagegen?** do you have something against it? (11)
daheim at home (8)
daher from there; from that; therefore
dahin there; to that (*place*)
dahin·kommen (kommt . . . dahin), kam . . . dahin, ist dahingekommen to get there
dahinten over there, in the back
dahinter behind it/that
damals back then, at that time
die **Dame, -n** lady
damit so that (11, 12)
danach afterward (10)
daneben next to it/that; in addition to that
(das) **Dänemark** Denmark (B)
dänisch Danish (*adj.*)
der **Dank** thanks; **vielen Dank** many thanks (10)
danke thank you (A)
dann then (A)
daran of/on/to/in/by it/that
darauf after/for/on it/that; afterward, then; **bald darauf** soon thereafter (8)
daraufhin following that, thereupon
daraus out of it/that
darin in there/that, inside there/that
das **Darlehen, -** (*bank*) loan
dar·stellen, dargestellt to represent, depict
darüber about/above/over it/that
darum therefore, for that reason, that's why
darunter under/below it/that
das (*def. art., neut. nom/acc.*) the; (*rel. pron./dem. pron., neut.*) this/that; **das ist** this/that is; **das sind** these/those are (B)
daß (*subord. conj.*) that (11)
die **Daten** (*pl.*) data; **persönliche Daten** biographical information (1)
der **Dativ, -e** dative
das **Datum, Daten** date; **welches Datum ist heute?** what is today's date? (4)
dauern, gedauert to last (4)
die **Dauerwelle, -n** perm (11)
davon about/from/of it/that
davon·fahren (fährt . . . davon), fuhr . . . davon, ist davongefahren to drive away
davor in front of it/that
dazu in addition (9)
dazwischen in between; between/among them
die **DDR** = **Deutsche Demokratische Republik** German Democratic Republic (former East Germany)
die **Debatte, -n** debate
die **Decke, -n** ceiling (B); blanket (11)
decken, gedeckt to cover; to set; **den Tisch decken** to set the table (3)
defekt defective; **leicht defekt** slightly damaged
die **Definition, -en** definition
dein(e) your (*infor.*) (B)
der **Delphin, -e** dolphin (12)
dem (*def. art., masc./neut. dat.*) the; (*rel. pron./dem. pron., masc./neut. dat.*) this/that
demokratisch democratic
den (*def. art., masc. acc.*) the; (*rel. pron./dem. pron., masc. acc.*) this/that

denen (*rel. pron./dem. pron., dat. pl.*) these, those
denken (denkt), dachte, gedacht to think; (**an** + *acc.*) to think of/about (7)
denn for, because (8, 11)
deprimiert depressed (11)
der (*def. art., masc. nom., fem. dat./gen., pl. gen.*) the; (*rel. pron./dem. pron., masc. nom./fem. dat.*) this/that
deren (*rel. pron.*) whose
derselbe, dasselbe, dieselbe(n) the same
des (*def. art, masc./neut. gen.*) the
deshalb therefore; that's why (7)
das **Design, -s** design
die **Designerklamotten** (*coll., pl.*) designer clothes
desinfizieren, desinfiziert to disinfect (11)
deswegen therefore, for that reason
das **Detail, -s** detail
deutlich distinct, clear, evident
(das) **Deutsch** German (*language*) (B)
das **Deutschbuch, ¨er** German textbook
der/die **Deutsche, -n** (ein **Deutscher**) German (*person*); **ich bin Deutscher / ich bin Deutsche** I am German (B)
der **Deutschkurs, -e** German (*language*) course; German class (A)
deutschfreundlich pro-German
(das) **Deutschland** Germany (B)
die **Deutschlandreise, -n** trip to Germany; tour of Germany
deutschsprachig German-speaking (8)
der **Deutschunterricht** German class
(der) **Dezember** December (B)
der **Dialog, -e** dialogue
dich (*infor. sg. acc.*) you (2)
der **Dichter, -** / die **Dichterin, -nen** poet
die **Dichtung, -en** poem; fictional writing
dick fat
die (*def. art / fem. nom. / acc., pl. nom. / acc.*) the; (*rel. pron./dem. pron.*) this/that
die **Diele, -n** front entryway (6)
dienen, gedient (als) to serve (as)
der **Diener, -** servant (8)
(der) **Dienstag** Tuesday (1)
der **Dienstschluß** end of work
dieser, dies(es), diese this, that, these, those (2, 4)
die **Dimension, -en** dimension
das **Ding, -e** thing (2); **vor allen Dingen** above all
die **Diphtherie** diphtheria (11)
dipl. = **diplomiert** certified
die **Diplomarbeit, -en** thesis (*for an advanced degree*) (12)
dir (*infor. sg. dat.*) you
direkt direct(ly)
der **Direktor, -en** / die **Direktorin, -nen** director, manager
der **Dirigent, -en** (*wk.*) / die **Dirigentin, -nen** (orchestra) conductor (5)
die **Diskothek, -en** discotheque
die **Disko, -s** disco(theque) (3, 6)
diskriminieren, diskriminiert to discriminate (12)
die **Diskussion, -en** discussion
diskutieren, diskutiert to discuss (4)
distanziert reserved
die **DM** = **D-Mark (Deutsche Mark)** German mark (*monetary unit*)
doch! yes (on the contrary)! (4)
der **Doktor, -en** / die **Doktorin, -nen** doctor
dokumentieren, dokumentiert to document, to record
(der) **Dollar, -** dollar (7)
der **Dom, -e** cathedral (10)
dominant domineering (12)
dominieren, dominiert to dominate
der **Domplatz, ¨e** cathedral square
(die) **Donau** Danube (River)
die **Donauinsel** Danube Island
donnern, gedonnert to thunder
(der) **Donnerstag** Thursday (1)
die **Doppelhochzeit, -en** double wedding
doppelt double; twofold; **doppelt so häufig** twice as often
das **Doppelzimmer, -** accommodations for two people, double room (10)
der **Dorn, -en** thorn (8)
(das) **Dornröschen** Sleeping Beauty
dort there (7)
dorthin there, to a specific place (10)
dorthin·fahren (fährt . . . dorthin), fuhr . . . dorthin, ist dorthingefahren to drive/ride there, to get there by car/bus/train
die **Dose, -n** can (9)
der **Dosenöffner, -** can opener (9)
Dr. = **Doktor** Dr.
der **Drache, -n** (*wk.*) dragon (8)
das **Drama, Dramen** drama
der **Dramatiker, -** / die **Dramatikerin, -nen** playwright (8)
dran = **daran** of/on/to/in/by it/that
drauf = **darauf** after/for/on it/that
draußen outside (11)
(sich) **drehen, gedreht** to turn; to twist
die **Drei: eine Drei** satisfactory (*school grade*) (3)
drei three (A)
„Die Dreigroschenoper" *The Threepenny Opera* (*title of play by Bertolt Brecht*)
dreihundert three hundred
dreimal three times (3)
dreißig thirty (A)
dreiundzwanzig twenty-three (A)
dreizehn thirteen (A)
dreizehnt- thirteenth (4)
drin = **darin** in it/that (6)
dringend urgent(ly) (2)
dritt- third (4)
das **Drittel, -** third
drittgrößt- third-largest
die **Droge, -n** drug
der **Drogenhändler, -** drug dealer
die **Drogerie, -n** drugstore (6)
drüben: da drüben over there (B)
drucken, gedruckt to print
der **Dschungel, -** jungle (7)
du (*infor. sg. nom.*) you
dumm stupid (6)
dunkel dark (6)
dunkelbraun dark brown
dunkelgrau dark grey
das **Dunkel** darkness; **im Dunkeln** in the dark; in ignorance
dunkeln, gedunkelt to grow dark
durch through (7)
die **Durchblutung** supply of blood (to)
das **Durcheinander** mess, confusion
durcheinander in confusion
durch·geben (gibt . . . durch), gab . . . durch, durchgegeben to pass on
durch·lesen (liest . . . durch), las . . . durch, durchgelesen to read (all the way) through
durchs = **durch das** through the
durch·schneiden (schneidet . . . durch), schnitt . . . durch, durchgeschnitten to cut through (9)
der **Durchschnitt, -e** average; **im Durchschnitt** on average
durchschnittlich on the average
durch·setzen, durchgesetzt to put through (*s.th.*); **Interessen durchsetzen** to assert/achieve (*one's*) interests
dürfen (darf), durfte, gedurft to be permitted (to), may (3)
der **Durst** thirst; **Durst haben** to be thirsty (3)
die **Duschbenutzung** use of shower
die **Dusche, -n** shower (5, 6)
(sich) **duschen, geduscht** to (take a)

shower (1, 11)
(das) **Düsseldorf** Düsseldorf
die **Dynamomaschine** dynamo machine

E

eben simply, just; just now
ebenfalls also, likewise
das **Ebenholz** ebony
ebenso as well as
echt real(ly) (2)
die **Ecke, -n** corner; **um die Ecke** around the corner (5)
egal equal, same; **das ist mir egal** it doesn't matter to me (6)
die **Ehe, -n** marriage (12)
die **Ehefrau, -en** wife
das **Eheleben** married life
ehemalig former
der **Ehepartner, -** / die **Ehepartnerin, -nen** spouse (12)
eher rather (12)
der **Ehevertrag, ⸚e** prenuptial agreement (12)
die **Ehre, -n** honor
ehren, geehrt to honor
ehrlich honest
das **Ei, -er** egg; **gekochte Eier** soft-boiled eggs (9)
eifersüchtig jealous (3)
eigen own (6)
die **Eigenschaft, -en** trait, characteristic (B, 12)
eigensinnig stubborn
eigentlich actually (3)
die **Eile** hurry; **in Eile sein** to be in a hurry (3)
eilig rushed; **es eilig haben** to be in a hurry (10)
ein(e) a(n); one
ein bißchen a little (bit) (B, 3); **kein bißchen** not at all (3)
ein paar a few (2)
einander one another, each other; **hintereinander** in a row (3); **miteinander** with each other (3)
die **Einbahnstraße, -n** one-way street (7)
ein·brechen (in + *acc.*) **(bricht . . . ein), brach . . . ein, ist eingebrochen** to break into; **ins Eis einbrechen** to go through the ice
der **Einbrecher, -** / die **Einbrecherin, -nen** burglar (8)
einfach simple, simply (2); **die einfache Fahrt** one-way trip (10)
die **Einfahrt, -en** driveway (11)
das **Einfamilienhaus** single-family house
ein·führen, eingeführt to introduce
die **Einführung, -en** introduction (A)
ein·gießen (gießt . . . ein), goß . . . ein, eingegossen to pour
ein·halten (hält . . . ein), hielt . . . ein, eingehalten to observe
einige some; several; a few
die **Einigung, -en** agreement
ein·jagen, eingejagt: jemandem Angst einjagen to give s.o. a fright
ein·kaufen, eingekauft to shop; **einkaufen gehan** to go shopping (1, 5)
die **Einkaufsliste, -n** shopping list (9)
das **Einkaufszentrum, -zentren** shopping center (10)
das **Einkommen, -** income
sich **ein·kremen, eingekremt** to put cream on (11)
ein·laden (lädt . . . ein), lud . . . ein, eingeladen to invite (2)
die **Einladung, -en** invitation (2)
die **Einleitung, -en** introduction
einmal once; **warst du schon einmal?** were you ever? (4)
ein·packen, eingepackt to pack up (1)
ein·räumen, eingeräumt to clear
die **Eins: eine Eins** excellent, very good (*school grade*) (3)
eins one (A)
ein·sammeln, eingesammelt to gather, collect
ein·schalten, eingeschaltet to turn on (11)
ein·schlafen (schläft . . . ein), schlief . . . ein, ist eingeschlafen to fall asleep (7, 8)
ein·schleusen, eingeschleust to infiltrate
sich **ein·schränken, eingeschränkt** to limit (*expenses*), economize; to tighten one's belt
sich **ein·schreiben (schreibt . . . ein), schrieb . . . ein, eingeschrieben** to register, enroll
ein·sehen (sieht . . . ein), sah . . . ein, eingesehen to understand
ein·steigen (steigt . . . ein), stieg . . . ein, ist eingestiegen to board (3, 10)
die **Einstellung, -en** attitude (12)
einstöckig one-story
einteilig one-piece
eintlg. = **einteilig** one-piece
die **Eintopfspezialität, -en** stew specialty
die **Eintrittskarte, -n** admissions ticket (5)
einunddreißig thirty-one
einundzwanzig twenty-one (A)
einundzwanzigst- twenty-first
einverstanden in agreement; **einverstanden sein mit** to be in agreement with (12)
der **Einwanderer, -** / die **Einwanderin, -nen** immigrant (4)
das **Einwandererland, ⸚er** country of immigrants
ein·wandern, ist eingewandert to immigrate (12)
die **Einwanderung, -en** immigration
ein·werfen (wirft . . . ein), warf . . . ein, eingeworfen to break, smash (*a window*)
der **Einwohner, -** / die **Einwohnerin, -nen** inhabitant, resident
das **Einwohnermeldeamt, ⸚er** residents' registration office
die **Einzelbestimmung, -en** individual regulation
die **Einzelheit, -en** detail
die **Einzelstunde, -n** individual lesson
das **Einzelzimmer, -** single room (5)
ein·ziehen (zieht . . . ein), zog . . . ein, ist eingezogen to move in
einzigartig unique(ly)
einzig sole, only
die **Einzimmerwohnung, -en** one-room apartment
der **Einzylinder-Viertakt-Benzinmotor** one-cylinder four-stroke gas engine
das **Eis** ice; ice cream (2); **ins Eis einbrechen** to go through the ice
der **Eisbecher, -** dish of ice cream (9)
das **Eisbein** knuckle of pork
das **Eisen** iron
der **Eisengehalt** iron content
das **Eisenwarengeschäft, -e** hardware store (6)
eisern (*adj.*) iron; **der Eiserne Vorhang** the Iron Curtain
eiskalt ice-cold (9)
das **Eiweiß** protein
eklig gross, loathsome (8)
der **Elefant, -en** (*wk.*) elephant (8)
elegant elegant(ly) (9)
elektrisch electric(al) (9)
das **Elektrogerät, -e** electronic product
der **Elektrorasierer, -** electric shaver
die **Elektrotechnik** electrical engineering
elektrotechnisch electronic
elf eleven (A)
das **Elfenbein** ivory (12)

elft- eleventh (4)
die **Eltern** (*pl.*) parents (B)
der **Elternteil, -e** parent
emanzipiert emancipated, liberated
empfehlen (empfiehlt), empfahl, empfohlen to recommend
das **Ende, -n** end
enden, geendet to end
endlich finally (8)
die **Endung, -en** ending
die **Energie, -n** energy
das **Energieproblem, -e** energy problem
eng tight; narrow; small (12); closely
der **Engel, -** angel
(das) **England** England (B)
der **Engländer, -** / die **Engländerin, -nen** English (*person*) (B)
(das) **Englisch** English (*language*) (B)
der **Englischlehrer, -** / die **Englischlehrerin, -nen** English teacher
entdecken, entdeckt to discover (4)
enthalten (enthält), enthielt, enthalten to contain; to include
die **Enthüllung, -en** disclosure
die **Entkräftung, -en** debility; weakness
entlang along (10)
entlang·gehen (geht . . . entlang), ging . . . entlang, ist entlanggegangen to go along (10)
entscheiden (entscheidet), entschied, entschieden to decide (10)
entschlossen decided
entschuldigen, entschuldigt to excuse; **entschuldigen Sie!** excuse me! (5)
die **Entschuldigung, -en** excuse; **Entschuldigung!** excuse me! (3)
entsetzt horrified
entsprechend corresponding
entspringen (entspringt), entsprang, ist entsprungen to originate from
entstehen (entsteht), entstand, ist entstanden to emerge, arise
entwässern, entwässert to rid of excess water
entweder . . . oder either . . . or
entwerfen (entwirft), entwarf, entworfen to design; to sketch
entwickeln, entwickelt to develop
die **Entzündung, -en** infection (11)
die **Enzyklopädie, -n** encyclopedia
die **Epidemie, -n** epidemic
die **Epoche, -n** era, (time) period
er (*pron., masc. nom.*) he; it
das **Erbmaterial** hereditary material
erbrechen (erbricht), erbrach, erbrochen to vomit
die **Erbse, -n** pea (9)
die **Erbsubstanz** hereditary substance
die **Erdbeere, -n** strawberry (9)
die **Erde, -n** earth; ground; soil
die **Erdkunde** earth science; geography (1)
die **Erdnuß, Erdnüsse** peanut
erdulden, erduldet to suffer, endure
das **Ereignis, -se** event
erfahren (erfährt), erfuhr, erfahren to learn, find out
die **Erfahrung, -en** experience
erfinden (erfindet), erfand, erfunden to invent (4)
die **Erfindung, -en** invention
der **Erfolg, -e** success; **Erfolg haben** to be successful
erfolgreich successful
die **Erfolgsgeschichte, -n** history of success
ergänzen, ergänzt to complete, fill in the blanks (4)
ergeben (ergibt), ergab, ergeben to result in
das **Ergebnis, -se** result
ergreifen, ergriff, ergriffen to seize
erh. = **erhalten** maintained
erhitzen, erhitzt to heat (9)
erhöhen, erhöht to increase, raise
sich **erholen, erholt** to recuperate (11)
das **Erholungsgebiet, -e** holiday area
der **Erholungsort, -e** resort
sich **erinnern (an** + *acc.*), **erinnert** to remember (*s.o./s.th.*)
die **Erinnerung, -en** memory, remembrance (4)
sich **erkälten, erkältet** to catch a cold (11)
die **Erkältung, -en** (head) cold (11)
erkennen (erkennt), erkannte, erkannt to recognize
erklären, erklärt to explain (5)
sich **erkundigen (nach** +*dat.*), **erkundigt** to ask about, get information (about) (10)
erlauben, erlaubt to permit (7)
erleben, erlebt to experience (10); **Abenteuer erleben** to experience adventures
das **Erlebnis, -se** experience (4)
erlösen, erlöst to save (8)
ermorden, ermordet to kill, murder
(sich) **ernähren, ernährt** to feed, nourish (*o.s.*)
die **Ernährung, -en** diet
ernst serious
ernsthaft serious (B)
eröffnen, eröffnet to open; **ein Konto eröffnen** to open a bank account (5)
erreichen, erreicht to reach (12)
erquicken, erquickt to enliven
der **Erreger, -** pathogen
erscheinen (erscheint), erschien, erschienen to appear; to seem
die **Ersparnisse** (*pl.*) savings
das **Ersparte** savings
erst not until; first; **erst um vier Uhr** not until four o'clock (4); **erster Klasse fliegen/fahren** to fly/travel first class; **der erste Oktober** the first of October (4); **zum ersten Mal** for the first time (4)
erstarren, ist erstarrt to be paralysed
erstaunlich amazing, astonishing
erstaunt amazed, astonished
erstechen (ersticht), erstach, erstochen to stab (to death)
ersticken, ist erstickt to suffocate
erstmal for now
ertappen, ertappt to catch (*thief, burglar*)
ertrinken, ertrank, ist ertrunken to drown
erwachen, ist erwacht to wake up
erwachsen grown-up
erwarten, erwartet to expect (12)
die **Erwartung, -en** expectation
erwartungsgemäß as expected, not surprisingly
erweisen (erweist), erwies, erwiesen to show
erweitern, erweitert to widen, expand
erwischen, erwischt to catch (*person, train*) (10)
erzählen, erzählt to tell (3, 5)
die **Erzählung, -en** story
erziehen (erzieht), erzog, erzogen to educate, bring up
die **Erziehung** education, upbringing
der/die **Erziehungsberechtigte** (ein **Erziehungsberechtigter**) parent, legal guardian
die **Erziehungswissenschaft** education (*academic subject*)
erzogen: wie sind sie erzogen worden? how have they been brought up?
es (*pron., neut. nom./acc.*) it
der **Esel, -** donkey
essen (ißt), aß, gegessen to eat (2, 4); **zu Abend essen** to dine, have dinner (4); **essen gehen** to go to a restaurant
der **Essig** vinegar (9)
die **Eßecke, -n** dining area (6)
das **Eßzimmer, -** dining room (6)
ethnisch ethnic

etwa approximately
etwas something, anything (2, 4, 5); **etwas Interessantes/Neues** something interesting/new (4); **sonst noch etwas?** anything else? (5)
(das) **Europa** Europe (B)
die **EU-Länder** countries of the European Union
euch (*infor. pl. pron., dat./acc.*) you; yourselves
euer, eu(e)ren, eu(e)re, (*infor. pl.*) your
der **Europäer,** - / die **Europäerin, -nen** European (*person*)
europäisch European (*adj.*)
die **Ewigkeit, -en** eternity
exakt exact(ly), precise(ly)
das **Exklusivinterview, -s** exclusive interview
exotisch exotic(ally) (7)
der **Exportartikel** export article
das **Exportland, ¨er** export country
extra extra; additional; separate(ly); in addition (10)
extravagant flamboyant (2)
extrem extreme(ly)
exzellent excellent(ly)

F

die **Fabrik, -en** factory (6)
das **Fach, ¨er** academic subject; major (1); specialty
der **Facharbeiter,** - / die **Facharbeiterin, -nen** skilled worker
der **Fachbegriff, -e** technical term
das **Fachbuch, ¨er** specialist book; textbook
die **Fachrichtung** subject, field
das **Fachwerk** half-timbered construction
der **Fachwerkstil** style of half-timbered construction
die **Fähigkeit, -en** capability; ability
die **Fahne, -n** flag
fahren (fährt), fuhr, ist/hat gefahren to drive, ride (2); **erster Klasse fahren** to travel first class (10); **Motorrad fahren** to ride a motorcycle (1)
Fahrenheit Fahrenheit **18 Grad Fahrenheit** 18 degrees Fahrenheit (B)
der **Fahrer,** - / die **Fahrerin, -nen** driver (7)
der **Fährhafen,** ¨ ferry terminal
die **Fahrkarte, -n** ticket (4)
der **Fahrkartenschalter,** - ticket window, ticket counter (7, 10)
der **Fahrplan, ¨e** schedule (*bus, train*)
das **Fahrrad, ¨er** bicycle (2); **Fahrrad fahren (fährt . . . Fahrrad), fuhr . . . Fahrrad, ist Fahrrad gefahren** to ride a bicycle
der **Fahrradhelm, -e** bicycle helmet (5)
die **Fahrradtour, -en** bicycle trip
der **Fahrstuhl, ¨e** lift, elevator
die **Fahrt, -en** trip (10); **eine einfache Fahrt** one-way trip (10)
das **Fahrzeug, -e** vehicle (11)
die **Fahrzeugposition, -en** vehicle position
die **Fakultät, -en** faculty
der **Fall, ¨e** case; **auf jeden Fall** in any case; **auf keinen Fall** by no means; under no circumstances
fallen (fällt), fiel, ist gefallen to fall (8); **in Ohnmacht fallen** to faint (11)
falls (*subord. conj.*) if
falsch wrong (2)
falten, gefaltet to fold
familiär family (*adj.*); familiar; informal
die **Familie, -n** family (B)
das **Familien-Darlehen** family loan
das **Familienfest, -e** family celebration (4)
das **Familienleben** family life
das **Familienmitglied, -er** family member (10)
der **Familienname, -n** (*wk.*) family name (A, 1)
der **Familienstand** marital status (1)
der **Fanatiker,** - fanatic (12)
fangen (fängt), fing, gefangen to catch
fantastisch fantastic, fabulous (3)
die **Farbe, -n** color (A, 1); **welche Farbe hat . . . ?** what color is . . . ? (A)
fast almost (5)
der **Farbfernseher,** - color TV set
fassen, gefaßt to grasp
fasten, gefastet to fast
fasziniert fascinated
faul lazy (3)
faulenzen, gefaulenzt to take it easy, be lazy
das **Fax, -e** fax (2)
das **Faxgerät, -e** fax machine (2)
die **FDP** = **Freie Demokratische Partei** Free Democratic Party
(der) **Februar** February (B)
die **Fee, -n** fairy (8)
fegen, gefegt to sweep (5)
fehlen, gefehlt (+ *dat.*) to lack; to be missing (10); to be wrong with, be the matter with (*a person*) (11); **was fehlt?** what's missing? (A)
die **Feier, -n** celebration, party (8)
feiern, gefeiert to celebrate (5)
(der) **Feiertag, -e** holiday (4)
fein fein (9)
der **Feind, -e** enemy
der **Feinkostladen,** ¨ delicatessen
das **Feld, -er** field (7)
der **Fels, -en** rock
das **Felsenriff, -e** cliff
das **Fenster,** - window (B)
die **Fensterbank, ¨e** windowsill (5)
die **Fensterscheibe, -n** windowpane (8)
die **Ferien** (*pl.*) vacation (1)
der **Ferienjob, -s** vacation job
die **Ferienreise, -n** holiday trip, vacation (8)
die **Ferienwohnung, -en** vacation apartment/condo (10)
die **Fernbedienung** remote control
fern·sehen (sieht . . . fern), sah . . . fern, ferngesehen to watch TV (1, 2)
der **Fernseher,** - TV set (2)
der **Fernsehfilm, -e** TV film (12)
die **Fernsehproduktion** television production
der **Fernsehreporter,** - / die **Fernsehreporterin, -nen** television reporter (5)
das **Fernsehzimmer,** - TV room (10)
fertig ready; finished (3)
fest stiff(ly); steady; fixed
das **Fest, -e** party (2)
fest·stehen (steht . . . fest), stand . . . fest, festgestanden to be definite
fest·stellen, festgestellt to establish (10)
der **Fetakäse** feta cheese
die **Fete, -n** (*coll.*) party
fett fatty
fettarm low-fat
der **Fettdruck** bold print
fettgedruckt in bold print, boldface
fettig fat; greasy (9, 11)
die **Fettsäure, -n** fatty acid
feucht humid (B)
das **Feuer,** - fire (8)
die **Feuerwehr** fire department (11)
„Fidelio“ *title of an opera by Ludwig van Beethoven*
das **Fieber** fever (11)
der **Fiesta** *a Ford car model*
die **Figur, -en** figure; character
der **Film, -e** film, movie (2)
die **Filmgeschichte, -n** film history
der **Filmregisseur, -e**/die **Filmregisseurin, -nen** film director
das **Filmstudio, -s** film studio
finanzieren, finanziert to finance
die **Finanzierungsart, -en** way (or

method) of financing
die **Finanzierungsform, -en** form of financing
finden (findet), fand, gefunden to find (2); **wie findest du das?** how do you like that?
der **Finger, -** finger (11)
der **Fingernagel, ¨** fingernail (11)
(das) **Finnland** Finland (B)
die **Firma, Firmen** company (3)
der **Fisch, -e** fish (9)
fischen, gefischt to fish
der **Fischer, -** fisherman
fit fit
der **Fitmacher, -** healthy food
flach flat (10)
die **Fläche, -n** surface (7)
die **Flagge, -n** flag
die **Flamme, -n** flame (9)
die **Flasche, -n** bottle (5)
der **Flaschenöffner, -** bottle opener (9)
die **Fledermaus, ¨e** bat (12)
das **Fleisch** meat (9)
das **Fleischchuechli** meatball, hamburger
das **Fleischpflanzerl** meatball, hamburger
fleißig industrious (12)
flexibel flexible (5)
die **Fliege, -n** fly (9)
das **Fliegen** fly
fliegen (fliegt), flog, ist/hat geflogen to fly (1); **erster Klasse fliegen** to fly first class (10)
fliehen (flieht), floh, ist geflohen to flee
fließen (fließt), floß, ist geflossen to flow (7)
flirten, geflirtet to flirt
der **Flohmarkt, ¨e** flea market (2)
fluchen, geflucht to curse, swear (11)
flüchten (vor + *dat.***), ist geflüchtet** to flee (from) (11)
der **Flüchtling, -e** refugee (12)
der **Flug, ¨e** flight (7)
der **Flügel, -** wing
der **Flughafen, ¨** airport (6, 10)
die **Fluglinie, -n** airline; air route
der **Flugschein, -e** plane ticket (10)
das **Flugzeug, -e** airplane (7)
der **Flugzeugschalter, -** airplane counter
der **Flur, -e** hallway (6)
die **Flüssigkeit, -en** liquid, fluid
der **Fluß, Flüsse** river (7)
die **Focus-Frage, -n** focus-question
der **Föhn** *warm, dry alpine wind*
die **Folge, -n** consequence; result
folgen (+ *dat.*), **ist gefolgt** to follow
folgend following
folglich consequently; as a result
der **Fön, -e** blow-dryer, hair-dryer
das **Fondue** fondue (7)
fönen, geföont to blow-dry; **sich (die Haare) fönen** to blow-dry (one's hair) (11)
das **Footballspiel, -e** football game
der **Ford** *make of car*
fördern, gefördert to promote (12)
die **Forelle, -n** trout (9)
die **Form, -en** form
das **Formular, -e** form; **ein Formular aus·füllen** to fill out/in a form
die **Forschung, -en** research
das **Forschungszentrum, -zentren** research center
fort·fahren (fährt . . . fort), fuhr . . . fort, ist fortgefahren to drive away, depart
das **Foto, -s** photo (1)
fotografieren, fotografiert to take pictures (4)
das **Fotomodell, -e** model (12)
das **Frühstückszimmer, -** breakfast room (10)
die **Frage, -n** question (A); **Fragen stellen** to ask questions
fragen, gefragt to ask; **(nach +** *dat.***)** to inquire about; **nach dem Weg fragen** to ask for directions
das **Fragepronomen, -** interrogative pronoun
das **Fragespiel, -e** question game
das **Fragewort, ¨er** question word (B)
(der) **Franken, -** franc (7)
fränkisch Franconian (*adj.*)
(das) **Frankreich** France (B)
der **Franzose, -n** (*wk.*) / die **Französin, -nen** French (*person*) (B)
(das) **Französisch** French (*language*) (8)
die **Frau, -en** woman; Mrs., Ms.; wife (A, B)
das **Frauchen, -** *diminutive term for female pet owner*
die **Frauenbewegung** women's movement
die **Frauenrechtlerin, -nen** feminist
die **Frauensache** woman's concern/matter
das Fräulein, - young woman; Miss
frei free(ly); empty; **ist hier noch frei?** is this seat/place taken? (3); **in freier Natur** out in the open (country) (12)
Freie Demokratische Partei (FDP) Free Democratic Party
freilebend living in the wild
(der) **Freitag** Friday (1)
der **Freitagabend, -e** Friday evening
freitags on Friday(s)
das **Freiwild** fair game
freiwillig voluntary; optional
die **Freizeit** leisure time (1)
die **Freizeitaktivität, -en** leisure activity
das **Freizeitangebot, -e** range of activities for leisure time
die **Fremdbestätigung** boost of one's ego
fremd strange; foreign
der/die **Fremde, -n** (ein **Fremder**) foreigner
das **Fremdenverkehrsamt, ¨er** tourist bureau (10)
die **Fremdsprache, -n** foreign language (8)
fremdsprachig foreign-language
fressen (frißt), fraß, gefressen to eat (*said of an animal*) (8)
die **Freude, -n** joy, pleasure (8)
sich **freuen (über +** *acc.***), gefreut** to be happy (about) (11)
der **Freund, -e** / die **Freundin, -nen** friend; boyfriend/girlfriend (A)
freundlich friendly (B); **mit freundlichen Grüßen** regards (10)
der **Friedenspreis** peace prize
friedlich peaceful(ly)
frieren (friert), fror, hat/ist gefroren to be very cold; to freeze
die **Frikadelle, -n** meat patty, hamburger
frisch fresh(ly) (9)
der **Friseur, -e** hair salon (6)
der **Friseur, -e** / die **Friseurin, -nen** hairdresser (5)
die **Frisur, -en** hairstyle
Frl. = **Fräulein** Miss
froh happy; cheerful
fröhlich cheerful; happy; lively
der **Frosch, ¨e** frog (8)
„Der Froschkönig" "The Frog Prince" (*fairy tale*)
der **Frost, ¨e** frost
früh early (1); **bis um vier Uhr früh** until four in the morning (4)
der **Frühjahrsputz** spring cleaning (6)
die **Frühe** early morning; **in der Frühe** in the early morning
früher earlier; former(ly)
der **Frühling, -e** spring; **im Frühling** in the spring (B)
die **Frühlingsrolle, -n** spring roll
der **Frühsommer** early summer
das **Frühstück, -e** breakfast (2, 9)
frühstücken, gefrühstückt to eat breakfast (1)

der **Frühstückstisch, -e** breakfast table
frustriert frustrated (3)
fügen, gefügt to place
der **Fugger** *member of the Fugger merchant family*
(sich) **fühlen, gefühlt** to feel, touch; **wie fühlst du dich?** how do you feel? (3); **ich fühle mich . . .** I feel . . . (3) (11)
der **Führerschein, -e** driver's license (4)
der **Führer, -** leader; guide(book)
die **Führung, -en** guided tour (10)
füllen, gefüllt to fill in
fünf five (A, 3)
die **Fünf: eine Fünf** poor (*school grade*) (3)
fünft- fifth (4)
fünfundvierzig forty-five
fünfundzwanzig twenty-five (A)
fünfzehn fifteen (A)
fünfzehnt- fifteenth
fünfzig fifty (A)
der **Funk** radio; **per Funk** via radio
funkeln, gefunkelt to glitter; to sparkle
funktional functional(ly)
funktionieren, funktioniert to work; **es funktioniert nicht** it's not working (A)
funktionierend functioning, working
funktionstüchtig in (good) working order
für (+ *acc.*) for (2); **was für ein . . . ?** what kind (of) . . . ?; **was für eins?** what kind?
furchtbar terrible (4)
sich **fürchten (vor** + *dat.*), **gefürchtet** to be afraid of (12)
fürs = **für das** for the
der **Fuß, ¨-e** foot (A, 11); **zu Fuß** on foot (3)
der **Fußball, ¨-e** soccer ball; soccer (A, 1)
der **Fußballnationalspieler** member of the national soccer team
der **Fußballspieler, -** / die **Fußballspielerin, -nen** soccer player (8)
das **Fußballstadion, -stadien** soccer stadium (10)
das **Fußballtraining** soccer training
der **Fußboden, ¨** floor
das **Fußende, -n** foot (of the bed)
der **Fußgänger, -** pedestrian (7)
der **Fußgängerweg, -e** sidewalk (7)
die **Fußgängerzone, -n** pedestrian mall (10)
das **Futter** feed; fodder
füttern, gefüttert to feed (8)

G

die **Gabel, -n** fork (9)
gähnend yawning
Galilei Galileo
der **Gang, ¨-e** gear (7)
ganz quite; whole; rather; **ganz gut** quite good; **ganz schön** quite pretty; **ganz schön viel** quite a bit (3); **die ganze Nacht** all night long (3); **eine ganze Menge** a whole lot (4); **ihr ganzes Geld** all her money (3)
gar: gar nicht not at all (3, 8); **gar kein(e/en/er)** no . . . at all; **gar nichts** nothing at all
die **Garage, -n** garage (6)
der **Garçonnière, -n** = **Einzimmerwohnung** one-room apartment
die **Gardine, -n** curtain
der **Garten, ¨** garden; yard (4); **im Garten** in the garden (4)
die **Gartenarbeit, -en** gardening
die **Gartenparty, -s** garden party
der **Gartenschlauch, ¨-e** garden hose (6)
der **Gärtner, -** / die **Gärtnerin, -nen** gardener
die **Gärtnerei** nursery
die **Gasheizung** gas heating
die **Gasse, -n** narrow street; alley (10)
der **Gast, ¨-e** guest; patron, customer
der **Gastarbeiter, -** / die **Gastarbeiterin, -nen** foreign worker
das **Gästehaus, ¨-er** bed and breakfast inn (10)
die **Gastfamilie, -n** host family
das **Gasthaus, ¨-er** inn; restaurant
das **Gastland, ¨-er** host country
die **Gastronomie** restaurant trade; gastronomy
die **Gaststätte, -n** restaurant; **in der Gaststätte** at the restaurant (5)
der **Gaul, ¨-e** horse
(das) **GB** = **Großbritannien** Great Britain
das **Gebäude, -** building (6)
geben (gibt), gab, gegeben to give; **geben Sie mir** give me (A); **es gibt** there is/are; **gibt es . . . ?** is/are there . . . ? (6); **geben (in** + *acc.*) to put (into) (9)
das **Gebirge, -** (range of) mountains (7)
geboren born; **wann sind Sie geboren?** when were you born? (1)
geborgen protected (12)
gebraten roasted; broiled; fried (9)
gebrauchen, gebraucht to use
der **Gebrauchtwagen, -** used car (7)
gebückt: in gebückter Haltung bending forward
gebunden (an + *acc.*) tied, bound (to)
das **Geburtsdatum, -daten** date of birth
der **Geburtsort, -e** place of birth
die **Geburtsstadt, ¨-e** native town/city
der **Geburtstag, -e** birthday (1); **zum Geburtstag** for someone's birthday (2)
das **Geburtstagsgeschenk, -e** birthday present
die **Geburtstagskarte, -n** birthday card
der **Gedanke, -n** (*wk.*) thought; **auf andere Gedanken kommen** to keep one's mind off something (7)
das **Gedicht, -e** poem (3)
das **Gedudel** (*coll.*) tootling
geduldig patient (12)
geehrt honored; dear (10); **sehr geehrte Damen und Herren** dear ladies and gentlemen; **sehr geehrter Herr** dear Mr.; **sehr geehrte Frau** dear Ms.
gefährlich dangerous (12)
geeignet (zu + *dat.*/**für** + *acc.*) suitable (for)
die **Gefahr, -en** danger
gefallen (+ *dat.*) **(gefällt), gefiel, gefallen** to please, be pleasing to; to like, be to one's liking; **es gefällt mir** I like it, it pleases me (10)
die **Gefälligkeit, -en** favor
das **Gefängnis, -se** prison, jail (6)
das **Geflügel** poultry (9)
die **Gefriertruhe, -n** freezer (9)
das **Gefühl, -e** feeling (3)
gegen (+ *acc.*) against (8)
die **Gegend, -en** area (10)
der **Gegensatz, ¨-e** opposite
der **Gegenstand, ¨-e** object
das **Gegenteil, -e** opposite; **im Gegenteil** on the contrary
gegenüber opposite (6); **gleich gegenüber** right across the way (6); **gegenüber (von** + *dat.*) across from (10)
die **Gegenwart** present time
gegrillt broiled; barbecued (9)
der **Gehalt, -e** content
geheim secret
gehen (geht), ging, ist gegangen to go, walk (A); **es geht um** (+ *acc.*) **. . .** the main/important thing is . . . ; **in die Berge gehen** to go to the mountains; **ins Bett gehen** to go to bed (1); **ins Museum gehen** to go to the museum (1); **nach Hause gehen** to go home; **wie geht es dir?** (*infor.*) / **wie geht es Ihnen?** (*for.*) how are you?
das **Gehirn, -e** brain (11)
gehören (zu + *dat.*), **gehört** to belong (to) (10)
die **Geige, -n** violin (3)
die **Geisteswissenschaften** arts;

humanities
geistig mental
gekocht boiled (9)
gelb yellow (A)
das **Geld** money (2); **ihr ganzes Geld** all her money (3)
das **Geldgeschenk, -e** gift of money
der **Geldsegen, -** monetary windfall
die **Gelegenheit, -en** opportunity; occasion
gelegentlich occasional(ly)
der/die **Gelehrte, -n** (ein **Gelehrter**) scholar
der/die **Geliebte, -n** (ein **Geliebter**) lover, beloved (*person*)
gelingen (gelingt), gelang, ist gelungen to succeed
das **Gemälde, -** painting
die **Gemeinde, -n** community
gemeinsam together; common (11)
die **Gemeinschaft, -en** community
gemischt mixed (9)
das **Gemüse, -** vegetable (9)
gemütlich comfortable, cozy (12)
genau exact(ly) (B)
genauso just as
die **Generation, -en** generation
Genfer of/from Geneva; **der Genfer See** Lake Geneva
der **Genforscher, -** / die **Genforscherin, -nen** genetic researcher
genug enough (4)
genügend sufficient(ly)
der **Genuß, Genüsse** enjoyment; **in den Genuß kommen** to acquire unexpectedly
der **Geograph, -en** (*wk.*) / **die Geographin, -nen** geographer
die **Geographie** geography
geographisch geographical(ly)
der **Geologe, -n** (*wk.*) / **die Geologin, -nen** geologist
das **Gepäck** luggage, baggage (10)
der **Gepard, -e** cheetah (12)
gerade right now; just (at the moment); straight, upright
gerade·stellen, geradegestellt to straighten (3); **die Bücher geradestellen** to straighten the books
geradeaus straight ahead (10)
das **Gerät, -e** appliance (9)
geräuchert smoked (9)
das **Geräusch, -e** sound, noise (8)
das **Gericht, -e** dish (9); courthouse; **auf dem Gericht** at the courthouse (5)
der **Germanist, -en** (*wk.*) / die **Germanistin, -nen** *specialist in German language and literature* (12)
die **Germanistik** German studies
gern(e) gladly; willingly; with pleasure; (*with verb*) to like to **ich habe . . . gern** I like (*s.o./s.th.*); **ich hätte gern** I would like to (have) (*s.th.*) (5); **wir singen gern** we like to sing (1)
gesalzen salted (9)
gesamt entire
die **Gesamteinwanderung** entire immigration
das **Geschäft, -e** store (2); shop
geschäftlich (*relating to*) business; **geschäftlich unterwegs sein** to be away on business
der **Geschäftsbrief, -e** business letter (10)
der **Geschäftsführer, -** / die **Geschäftsführerin, -nen** (business) manager
die **Geschäftsleute** (*pl.*) businesspeople (7)
der **Geschäftsmann, -leute** / die **Geschäftsfrau, -en** businessman/businesswoman
die **Geschäftsreise, -n** business trip (7)
die **Geschäftswelt** business world, business life
das **Geschenk, -e** present (2)
die **Geschichte, -n** history (1)
das **Geschichtsbuch, ¨er** history book
das **Geschirr** (*sg.*) dishes (4, 5); **Geschirr spülen** to wash the dishes (4)
der **Geschirrschrank, ¨e** cupboard
die **Geschirrspülmaschine, -n** dishwasher (5, 9)
geschlossen closed (4)
der **Geschmack** taste
die **Geschmacksfrage, -n** question of taste
das **Geschmeide, -** jewelry
die **Geschwister** (*pl.*) brother(s) and sister(s), siblings (B)
der **Gesellenbrief** journeyman's diploma/certificate
die **Gesellenprüfung** journeyman's examination
die **Geselligkeit** sociability; conviviality
die **Gesellschaft, -en** society (12); company; association
gesellschaftlich social
das **Gesicht, -er** face (A)
die **Gesichtsfarbe** complexion
das **Gespräch, -e** conversation
das **Gespür** feel, sense
gestalten, gestaltet to form, fashion
das **Geständnis, -se** confession
gestern yesterday; **gestern abend** last night (4)
gestreift striped
gesund healthy (11)
die **Gesundheit** health (11)
das **Gesundheitsamt, ¨er** public health department
die **Gesundheitsversorgung** health care
der **Gesundmacher, -** healthy food
das **Getränk, -e** beverage (9)
das **Getreideprodukt, -e** grain product
getrennt separate(ly) (5)
die **Gewalt** violence; **Gewalt anwenden** to use violence (12)
gewaltig powerful
der **Gewerkschaftssekretär, -e** / die **Gewerkschaftssekretärin, -nen** union secretary (12)
das **Gewicht, -e** weight
gewinnen (gewinnt), gewann, gewonnen to win; to gain (4)
das **Gewitter, -** thunderstorm (9)
sich **gewöhnen (an** + *acc.*), **gewöhnt** to get used to (11)
die **Gewohnheit, -en** habit
das **Gewürz, -e** spice; seasoning (9)
gießen (gießt), goß, gegossen to water (3); to pour (9); **die Blumen/Pflanzen gießen** to water the flowers/plants
die **Gießkanne, -n** watering can (6)
giftig poisonous (8)
der **Gipfel, -** mountaintop (7)
der **Gips** cast (*plaster*) (11)
die **Giraffe, -n** giraffe (12)
die **Gitarre, -n** guitar (1)
der **Glanz** shine
das **Glas, ¨er** glass (8)
gläsern (*adj.*) (made of) glass (8)
glatt smooth
die **Glatze, -n** bald head
glauben, geglaubt to believe (2)
gleich (*adj.*) same, equal; (*adv.*) right away; directly; in just a moment; just as, exactly; **gleich um die Ecke** right around the corner (6); **gleich gegenüber** right across the way (6)
das **Gleis, -e** (set of) train tracks (10)
gleichaltrig of the same age
die **Gleichberechtigung** equal rights
gleichen (+ *dat.*) **(gleicht), glich, geglichen** to be like, resemble (*s.o./s.th.*)
der **Gletscher, -** glacier (7)
glotzen, geglotzt (*coll.*) to gawk
das **Glück** luck; happiness (3, 12) **viel Glück!** lots of luck!, good luck! (3)
glücklich happy (B, 3)

gnädig gracious, kind; **gnädige Frau** *very formal way of addressing a woman*
golden gold, golden
der **Goldfisch, -e** goldfish (11)
der **Goldring, -e** gold ring (10)
das **Golf** golf (1)
der **Golfplatz, ¨e** golf course
der **Gott, ¨er** god; **Grüß Gott!** Hello!
der **Gourmet, -s** gourmet
das **Grab, ¨er** grave, tomb
das **Grad, -e** degree; **18 Grad Celsius/ Fahrenheit** 18 degrees Celsius/Fahrenheit (B)
die **Grafik, -en** drawing; graphic(s)
der **Grafiker, -** / die **Grafikerin, -nen** (graphic) designer
das **Gramm, -e** gram
die **Grammatik** grammar (A)
das **Grandhotel, -s** luxury or five-star hotel
die **Graphik** = **Grafik**
der **Graphiker** / die **Graphikerin** = der **Grafiker** / die **Grafikerin**
das **Gras, ¨er** grass
gratis free of charge
gratulieren (+ *dat.*), **gratuliert** to congratulate (2, 10)
grau gray (A)
graugrün grayish green (7)
grausam cruel (8)
greifen (greift), griff, gegriffen to grab, grasp (11)
grell gaudy, shrill; *here:* cool, neat (2)
die **Grenze, -n** border
grenzen (an + *acc.*), **gegrenzt** to border (on)
der **Grieche, -n** (*wk.*) / die **Griechin, -nen** Greek (*person*)
(das) **Griechenland** Greece (B)
griechisch Greek (*adj.*)
der **Grill, -s** grill, barbecue (9)
grillen, gegrillt to grill
die **Grippe** influenza, flu (11)
die **Grippeepidemie** influenza epidemic
der **Grippevirus** influenza virus
der **Gromperekichelch** potato pancake
groß large, big; tall (A)
(das) **Großbritannien** Great Britain (B)
die **Größe, -n** height (1); size (10)
die **Großeltern** (*pl.*) grandparents (B)
der **Großglockner** *mountain peak in Austria*
die **Großmutter, ¨** grandmother (B)
das **Großstadtproblem, -e** large-city problem
der **Großvater, ¨** grandfather (B)
grüezi! hi! (*Switzerland*) (A)
grün green (A)
der **Grund, ¨e** reason (12)
gründen, gegründet to found
gründlich thorough(ly)
grundsätzlich fundamental(ly)
die **Grundschule, -n** elementary school (4)
das **Grundstück, -e** property, lot (*land*)
der **Grünkohl** kale
die **Gruppe, -n** group
die **Gruppenarbeit** group work
der **Gruselfilm, -e** horror film (2)
grüß Gott! hi! (*southern Germany, Austria*) (A)
der **Gruß, ¨e** greeting; **mit freundlichen Grüßen** regards (10)
grüßen, gegrüßt to greet, give regards to (11)
die **Gulaschkanone, -n** field kitchen
der **Gummibaum, ¨e** rubber tree
die **Gunst** favor; goodwill
die **Gurke, -n** cucumber; **saure Gurken** pickles (9)
der **Gürtel, -** belt (2)
gut good; well; **ganz gut** very good; quite well; **guten Abend!** good evening! (A); **guten Morgen!** good morning! (A); **guten Tag!** good afternoon! hello! (*for.*) (A)
der **Gutschein, -e** voucher, coupon
der **Gymnasiast, -en** (*wk.*) / die **Gymnasiastin, -nen** pupil at Gymnasium
das **Gymnasium, Gymnasien** college prep school; high school (4, 6)

H

das **Haar, -e** hair (A, 11); **Haare schneiden** to cut hair (3); **sich die Haare fönen** to blow-dry one's hair (11)
der **Haarausfall** hair loss
die **Haarfarbe, -n** hair color (1)
die **Haarmode, -n** hairstyle
der **Haarschnitt, -e** haircut (2), hairstyle
der **Haarstreifen, -** strand of hair
haben (hat), hatte, gehabt to have (A); **gern haben** to like (*s.o.* or *s.th.*); **Heimweh haben** to be homesick (3); **Hunger haben** to be hungry (3); **ich hätte gern** I would like (5)
der **Habsburger, -** *member of the Habsburg royal family*
das **Hackfleisch** ground beef (or pork) (9)
der **Hafen, ¨** harbor (10)
die **Haferflocken** (*pl.*) oats; oatmeal (9)
das **Hähnchen, -** (grilled) chicken
der **Hai, -e** shark (12)
der **Haken, -** hook (9)
halb half; **um halb drei** at two thirty (1)
die **Halbinsel, -n** peninsula (7)
die **Hälfte, -n** half (10)
die **Hallig, -en** *small island(s) on the northwest coast of Germany*
hallo! hi! (*infor.*) (A)
der **Hals, ¨e** neck; throat (8)
das **Halsbonbon, -s** throat lozenge (11)
die **Halsentzündung** throat inflammation
die **Halskette, -n** necklace (5)
die **Halsschmerzen** (*pl.*) sore throat (11)
das **Halstuch, ¨er** scarf (2)
halt! stop!
halten (hält), hielt, gehalten to hold (4); to stop (7); **ein Referat halten** to give a paper/an oral report (4); **halten von** (*dat.*) to think of (12)
die **Haltestelle, -n** stop (10)
die **Haltung, -en** posture
der **Hamburger, -** hamburger (3)
der **Hammer, ¨** hammer (9)
der **Hamster, -** hamster (12)
die **Hand, ¨e** hand (A)
die **Handarbeit, -en** needlework; crafts
handeln (von + *dat.*), **gehandelt** to be about, deal with
das **Handelszentrum, -zentren** trade center
das **Händewaschen** washing one's hands
der **Händler, -** / die **Händlerin, -nen** dealer
der **Handschuh, -e** glove (10)
das **Handtuch, ¨er** hand towel (5, 6, 9)
das **Handwerk, -e** trade; manual labor
handwerklich handy (12)
hängen, (hängt), hing, ist gehangen to hang, be (in a hanging position); **hängen, gehängt** to hang, place (in a hanging position) (3, 9); **das Bild an die Wand hängen** to hang the picture on the wall
(das) **Hannover** Hanover
die **Hansestadt, ¨e** *city that once belonged to the Hanseatic League*
der **Harnstoffwechsel** urea metabolism
harntreibend diuretic
hart hard
hartnäckig stubborn(ly)
(der) **Harz** *mountain range in central Germany*
hassen, gehaßt to hate (8)
der **Haß** hate, hatred
häßlich ugly (2)
häufig often, frequent(ly); **doppelt so häufig** twice as often

das **Hauptfach, ¨-er** major
die **Hauptperson, -en** central figure
die **Hauptsache, -n** main thing
die **Hauptschule, -n** general secondary school
der **Hauptsitz, -e** main office
die **Hauptstadt, ¨-e** capital city (3)
das **Hauptthema, -themen** main topic
das **Haus, ¨-er** house (1, 2, 6); **zu Hause sein** to be at home; **nach Hause gehen** to go home
der/die **Hausangestellte, -n** (ein **Hausangestellter**) domestic servant
die **Hausarbeit, -en** housework, homework
der **Hausarzt, ¨-e** / die **Hausärztin, -nen** family doctor (11)
die **Hausaufgabe, -n** homework assignment (A, 1)
das **Hausboot, -e** houseboat (6)
das **Häuschen, -** small house, cottage
die **Hausfrau, -en** housewife, (*female*) homemaker (12)
der **Haushalt, -e** household (8)
das **Haushaltsgerät, -e** household appliance
der **Hausmann, ¨-er** (*male*) homemaker (12)
der **Hausmeister, -** / die **Hausmeisterin, -nen** custodian (5)
das **Hausmittel, -** homemade remedy
die **Hausnummer, -n** house number (1)
der **Hausschlüssel, -** house key (8)
der **Hausschuh, -e** slipper
das **Hausschwein, -e** domestic pig
das **Haustier, -e** pet (12)
die **Haut, ¨-e** skin (3, 11)
die **Haute Couture** haute couture
hautschonend gentle on the skin
heben (hebt), hob, gehoben to lift
hebräisch Hebrew (*adj.*)
die **Hecke, -n** hedge
das **Heft, -e** notebook (B)
heftig vehement(ly); heatedly
heilen, geheilt to cure, remedy; to heal (5)
heilend healing
der **Heiligabend** Christmas Eve
das **Heim, -e** home
das **Heimatland, ¨-er** homeland
das **Heimatmuseum, -museen** museum of local history
die **Heimatstadt, ¨-e** hometown (6)
heim·bringen (bringt . . . heim), brachte . . . heim, heimgebracht to bring home
heimlich secret(ly) (8)
das **Heimweh** homesickness; **Heimweh haben** to be homesick (3)
die **Heirat, -en** marriage
heiraten, geheiratet to marry (5)
heiß hot (B)
heißen (heißt), hieß, geheißen to be called, to be named; **wie heißen Sie?** (*for.*); **wie heißt du?** (*infor.*) what's your name?; **ich heiße . . .** my name is . . . (A)
die **Heizung, -en** heating
der **Held, -en** (*wk.*) / die **Heldin, -nen** hero/heroine
helfen (+ *dat.*) **(hilft), half, geholfen** to help (8, 10)
hell light (6)
hellblond light blonde
das **Hemd, -en** shirt (A)
her *direction toward*; here; **hin und her** back and forth
her·kommen (kommt . . . her), kam . . . her, ist hergekommen to come this way (*toward the speaker*) (10)
herauf·holen, heraufgeholt to bring up, retrieve (*s.th.*)
heraus (aus + *dat.*) out (of)
heraus·kommen (kommt . . . heraus), kam . . . heraus, ist herausgekommen to come out this way (*toward the speaker*) (10)
herausfordernd provocative(ly); challenging(ly)
der **Herausgeber, -** / die **Herausgeberin, -nen** editor (12); publisher
die **Herbergseltern** (*pl.*) owner/manager of a youth hostel (10)
der **Herbst, -e** fall, autumn (B)
der **Herd, -e** stove (5, 6)
herein in; inside
herein·kommen (kommt . . . herein), kam . . . herein, ist hereingekommen to get/go in this way (*toward the speaker*) (10)
der **Heringssalat, -e** herring salad (9)
die **Herkunft** origin; nationality (B)
der **Herr, -en** (*wk.*) Mr.; gentleman (A)
das **Herrchen, -** *diminutive term for male pet owners*
her·stellen, hergestellt to produce, make; to establish
der **Hersteller, -** manufacturer
die **Herstellung** production, manufacture
herum around, round about
herum·gehen (um + *acc.*) **(geht . . . herum), ging . . . herum, ist herumgegangen** to go around (*s.th.*)
herum·schwirren, ist herumgeschwirrt to buzz around
herum·stehen (steht . . . herum), stand . . . herum, herumgestanden to stand around, loiter
herunter down (*toward the speaker*) (11)
herunter·klettern, heruntergeklettert to climb down (11)
hervor·rennen (rennt . . . hervor), rannte . . . hervor, ist hervorgerannt to dart out from
das **Herz, -en** heart (11)
(das) **Herzegowina** Herzegovina
der **Herzinfarkt, -e** heart attack
herzlich hearty, heartily (10)
die **Herzschmerzen** (*pl.*) heartache (11)
(das) **Hessen** Hessen
hetzen, gehetzt to hunt; to rush
heute today; **heute abend** this evening (2)
die **Hexe, -n** witch (7, 8)
hier here (A)
hilfe! help! (11)
hilflos helpless
der **Hilfsarbeiter, -** laborer; unskilled worker
hilfsbereit ready to help
der **Himmel, -** sky
himmlisch heavenly
die **Hin- und Rückfahrt, -en** round trip (10)
hin *direction away from*; there; **hin und her** back and forth; **wo willst du denn hin?** where are you going? (A)
hin und zurück there and back; round trip (5, 10)
hinauf·gehen (geht . . . hinauf), ging . . . hinauf, ist hinaufgegangen to go up that way (*away from the speaker*) (10)
hinein into (8)
hin·fallen (fällt . . . hin), fiel . . . hin, ist hingefallen to fall down (11)
hin·gehen (geht . . . hin), ging . . . hin, ist hingegangen to go that way (*away from the speaker*) (10)
sich **hin·legen, hingelegt** to lie down (11)
hinüber·gehen (geht . . . hinüber), ging . . . hinüber, ist hinübergegangen to go over that way (*away from the speaker*) (10)
hinunter down, downward; downstairs
sich **hinunter·beugen, hinuntergebeugt** to bend down
hinunter·stürzen, ist hinuntergestürzt to fall down into
der **Hinweis, -e** hint

hinzu·fügen, hinzugefügt to add
die **Hirnhautentzündung** meningitis
die **Hitze** heat
das **Hobby, -s** hobby (1)
hoch high (6)
hochachtungsvoll respectfully
die **Hochschule, -n** college or university
höchst- highest
hochwertig highly nutritious
der **Hocker, -** stool
der **Hof, ⸚e** court; courtyard
hoffen, gehofft to hope (3)
hoffentlich hopefully (3)
die **Hoffnung, -en** hope
höflich polite
die **Höflichkeit, -en** politeness; courtesy
die **Höhe, -n** high altitude
die **Höhle, -n** cave (6)
holen, geholt to fetch, (go) get (8)
(das) **Holland** Holland (B)
der **Holländer, -** / die **Holländerin, -nen** Dutchman/-woman
holländisch Dutch (*adj.*) (9)
(das) **Holländisch** Dutch (*language*)
das **Holz, ⸚er** wood
der **Holzbalken, -** beam
die **Holzschindel, -n** wooden shingle, shake
homogen homogeneous
die **Homosexualität** homosexuality
der **Honda** *make of car*
(das) **Hongkong** Hong Kong
der **Honig** honey (9)
hören, gehört to hear; to listen (1)
horizontal horizontal(ly)
das **Hörnchen, -** croissant (9)
das **Hörspiel, -e** radio play
der **Hörtext, -e** listening text
die **Hose, -n** pants (A), trousers
das **Hotel, -s** hotel (2, 5); **im Hotel** at the hotel (5)
hübsch pretty (2)
der **Hügel, -** hill (7)
das **Huhn, ⸚er** chicken
die **Hühnersuppe, -n** chicken soup
der **Hummer, -** lobster (9)
der **Hund, -e** dog (2)
das **Hundefutter** dog food (5)
hundert hundred (A)
hundertmal a hundred times
hundertst- hundredth (4)
der **Hunger** hunger; **Hunger haben** to be hungry (3)
hungrig hungry (8)
die **Hupe, -n** horn (7)
hupen, gehupt to honk (7)
hüpfen, ist gehüpft to hop
husten, gehustet to cough
der **Husten** cough (11)
das **Hustenbonbon, -s** cough drop (11)
der **Hustensaft, ⸚e** cough syrup (11)
der **Hut, ⸚e** hat (A)
hüten, gehütet to watch
die **Hygiene** hygiene

I

ich I
ideal (*adj.*) ideal, dream (12)
die **Idee, -n** idea; **er ist auf die Idee gekommen** it occurred to him
identifizieren, identifiziert to identify
die **Identität, -en** identity
idyllisch idyllic, pastoral
das **Iglu, -s** igloo (6)
ignorieren, ignoriert to ignore
ihm him (*dat.*)
ihn him (*acc.*) (2)
ihnen them (*dat.*)
ihr you (*infor. pl.*) (1)
ihr, ihre, ihren her, its (2); their
Ihr, Ihre, Ihren your (*for.*) (B)
illegal illegal (12)
illusionslos without illusions
im = in dem in the
immer always (3); **gehen Sie immer geradeaus** keep going straight; **immer mehr** more and more; **immer noch** still; **immer weiter** on and on
die **Immunabwehr** immune resistance
das **Immunsystem** immune system
impfen (gegen + *acc.***), geimpft** to vaccinate (for) (12)
die **Impfmüdigkeit** weariness of vaccination
imponierend impressive
in (+ *dat./acc.*) in, into (B, 4); at (4); **im Café** at the café (4); **im Garten** in the garden (4); **im Restaurant** at the restaurant; **in die Uni / ins Reisebüro gehen** to go to the university/travel agency
inbegriffen included (10); **im Preis inbegriffen** included in the price
indem (*subord. conj.*) while; as
indirekt indirect(ly)
indisch Indian (*adj.*)
indiskret indiscreet, tactless
individualistisch individualistic
die **Industrie, -n** industry
die **Industriemesse, -n** industrial fair
das **Industriezentrum, -zentren** industrial center
der **Infinitiv, -e** infinitive
infizieren, infiziert to infect; **sich infizieren** to get infected
die **Inflation, -en** inflation
der **Influenzavirus, -viren** influenza virus
die **Informatik** computer science (1)
die **Information, -en** information (4)
das **Informationsmaterial, -materialien** informational literature
das **Informationsspiel, -e** information game
(sich) **informieren (über +** *acc.***), informiert** to inform (*o.s. about s.th.*) (10)
der **Ingenieur, -e** / die **Ingenieurin, -nen** engineer (5)
der **Infratest, -e** infratest
inklusive (utilities) included (6)
die **Innenstadt, ⸚e** downtown (6)
(das) **Innerasien** Central Asia
das **Innere** inside
innerhalb (+ *gen.*) within, inside
ins = in das in(to) the
die **Insel, -n** island (7)
insgesamt altogether
der **Inspektor, -en** / die **Inspektorin, -nen** inspector, supervisor
das **Instrument, -e** instrument
die **Integration** integration
intelligent intelligent (B)
die **Intelligenz** intelligence (12)
die **Interaktion, -en** interaction
der **InterCity(-Zug)** intercity (*train*)
der **InterCityExpress** intercity express (train)
interessant interesting (7)
das **Interesse, -n** interest; **Interesse haben (an +** *dat.***)** to be interested in (5); **Interessen durchsetzen** to assert/achieve (*one's*) interests
interessieren, interessiert to interest; **sich interessieren (für +** *acc.***)** to be interested in (5)
international international
die **Interpretation, -en** interpretation
interpretieren, interpretiert to interpret
das **Interview, -s** interview (4)
interviewen, interviewt to interview (12)
die **Invasion, -en** invasion
inzwischen in the meantime, meanwhile
der **IQ** IQ
(der) **Iran** Iran
irgendein any; some
irgendetwas/irgendwas anything;

something
irgendwelcher, irgendwelches, irgendwelche any (+ *noun*) (5)
(das) **Irland** Ireland (B)
der **Irokesenschnitt, -e** mohawk haircut (10)
irre·führen, irregeführt to mislead
isoliert isolated; insulated
(das) **Italien** Italy (B)
der **Italiener, -** / die **Italienerin, -nen** Italian (*person*)
italienisch Italian (*adj.*) (B)
(das) **Italienisch** Italian (*language*)

J

ja yes; **das ist es ja!** that's just it! (4); **wenn ja** if so
die **Jacht, -en** yacht (7)
die **Jacke, -n** jacket (A)
jagen, gejagt to hunt
der **Jäger, -** / die **Jägerin, -nen** hunter (8)
das **Jahr, -e** year (2); **mit sechs Jahren** at the age of six; **zweimal im Jahr** twice a year
der **Jahreshit, -s** hit of the year
der **Jahrestag, -e** anniversary
der **Jahresurlaub, -e** annual leave
der **Jahresverdienst** annual income
die **Jahreszahl, -en** date
die **Jahreszeit, -en** season (B)
das **Jahrhundert, -e** century
-jährig -year-old; -year; **ein dreijähriges Kind** a three-year-old child
jährlich annual(ly)
das **Jahrtausend, -e** millenium
das **Jahrzehnt, -e** decade (4)
jahrzehntelang for decades
jammern, gejammert to whimper, complain
(der) **Januar** January; **im Januar** in January (B)
(das) **Japan** Japan (B)
der **Japaner, -** / die **Japanerin, -nen** Japanese (*person*) (B)
japanisch Japanese (*adj.*)
(das) **Japanisch** Japanese (*language*) (B)
je ever; each; **je nach** according to; **von je** from time immemorial; **von je 100 Jungen** out of 100 young men
die **Jeans** (*pl.*) jeans (2)
die **Jeansjacke, -n** jeans jacket
jedenfalls in any case (11)
jeder, jedes, jede each; every (3, 5); **auf jeden Fall** in any case; **jede Woche** every week (3)
jemand somebody; someone (3)
jemals ever
das **Jenseits** in the afterlife
jetzig present, current
jetzt now (3); **von jetzt an** from now on
jeweils each time; each; every
der **Job, -s** job
jobben, gejobbt to work at temporary jobs
der **Jodelmeister, -** master yodeler
joggen, ist gejoggt to jog
der **Joghurt** yoghurt
der **Journalist, -en** (*wk.*) / die **Journalistin, -nen** journalist (12)
der **Jude, -n** (*wk.*) / die **Jüdin, -nen** Jew/Jewess
jüdisch Jewish
die **Jugend** youth; young people
das **Jugendarbeitsschutzgesetz, -e** law protecting adolescents at work
die **Jugendherberge, -n** youth hostel (10)
der **Jugendherbergsausweis, -e** youth hostel ID card (10)
der/die **Jugendliche, -n** (ein **Jugendlicher**) young person
das **Jugendzentrum, -zentren** youth center
der **Jugoslawe, -n** (*wk.*) / die **Jugoslawin, -nen** Yugoslav (*person*)
(das) **Jugoslawien** Yugoslavia (B)
(der) **Juli** July (B)
jung young (A)
der **Junge, -n** (*wk.*) boy
der **Jungenname, -n** (*wk.*) boy's name
die **Jungfrau, -en** virgin; *name of a mountain*
der **Junggeselle, -n** (*wk.*) bachelor
(der) **Juni** June (B)
der **Jux, -e** joke; **einen Jux machen** to play a joke

K

der **Kabarettist, -en** (*wk.*) / die **Kabarettistin, -nen** cabaret performer (12)
das **Kabelfernsehen** cable TV
der **Kachelofen, ¨** tile stove, hearth (6)
der **Kaffee** coffee (1)
der **Kaffeefilter, -** coffee filter (4)
die **Kaffeemaschine, -n** coffee machine (5)
die **Kaffeemühle, -n** coffee grinder (9)
das **Kaffeetrinken** having coffee
der **Käfig, -e** cage (12)
die **Käfigtür, -en** cage door
kahl bald
der **Kahn, ¨e** boat
(das) **Kairo** Cairo
die **Kaiserstadt, ¨e** imperial town
der **Kakao** cocoa; hot chocolate (9)
(das) **Kalifornien** California
das **Kalium** potassium
der **Kalk, -e** calcium carbonate
kalkulieren, kalkuliert to calculate
kalorienarm low in calories (9)
kalorienbewußt calorie-conscious (9)
kalt cold (B)
das **Kalzium** calcium
das **Kamel, -e** camel (7)
die **Kamera, -s** camera (5)
kämmen, gekämmt: sich die Haare kämmen to comb one's hair (3, 11)
kämpfen, gekämpft to fight (8)
(das) **Kanada** Canada (B)
der **Kanadier, -** / die **Kanadierin, -nen** Canadian (*person*) (B)
der **Kanton, -e** (*Swiss*) canton
das **Kapitel, -** chapter (A)
kaputt broken (3)
kariert plaid (10)
(das) **Kärnten** Carinthia
die **Karotte, -n** carrot (9)
die **Karriere, -n** career (12)
(das) **Karstadt** *department store chain*
die **Karte, -n** card; ticket (1)
das **Kartell, -e** cartel
die **Kartoffel, -n** potato (9)
die **Kartoffelchips** (*pl.*) potato chips
der **Kartoffelpfannkuchen, -** potato pancake
der **Kartoffelpuffer, -** potato pancake (*made from grated raw potatoes*)
der **Käse, -** cheese (9)
das **Käsefondue** cheese fondue
(das) **Kaspische Meer** Caspian Sea
die **Kassette, -n** cassette (A)
der **Kassettenrecorder, -** cassette recorder (2)
der **Kassierer, -** / die **Kassiererin, -nen** cashier (5)
die **Kastanie, -n** chestnut
die **Kategorie, -n** category
die **Katze, -n** cat (2)
der **Katzenkrimi, -s** cat detective story or film
der **Katzenliebhaber, -** / die **Katzenliebhaberin, -nen** cat lover
kauen, gekaut to chew (11)
kaufen, gekauft to buy (1)
das **Kaufhaus, ¨er** department store (5, 6); **im Kaufhaus** at the department store (5)
die **Kaufmannsfamilie, -n** merchant family

kaum hardly
die **Kaution, -en** security deposit (6)
der **Kaviar, -e** caviar
die **Kehle, -n** throat
kehren, gekehrt to sweep
kein(e) no; none (2); **auf keinen Fall** by no means; under no circumstances; **kein bißchen** not at all (3); **kein Wunder** no wonder (4); **keine Ahnung** (I have) no idea (4)
der **Keller,** - basement, cellar (4, 6)
die **Kellertür, -en** basement door
der **Kellner,** - / die **Kellnerin, -nen** waiter/waitress (5)
kennen (kennt), kannte, gekannt to be acquainted with, know (3)
kennen·lernen, kennengelernt to get acquainted with (1)
die **Kenntnisse** (*pl.*) skills; knowledge about a field (5)
das **Kennzeichen,** - sign, mark
die **Kerze, -n** candle (3)
das **Ketchup, -s** ketchup
die **Kette, -n** necklace (2)
kg = das **Kilogramm, -e** kilogram
der **KGB** = **Komitet Gossudarstvennoi Bezopastnosti** Committee of State Security
das **Kilo, -s** kilogram
der **Kilometer,** - kilometer (2)
der **Kilometerstand, ¨-e** mileage (7)
das **Kind, -er** child (B)
die **Kinderarbeit** child labor
der **Kinderarbeiter,** - child worker
die **Kindererziehung** education, bringing up of children
der **Kindergarten, ¨** kindergarten (6)
das **Kinderkriegen** having children
der **Kinderstuhl, ¨-e** child's chair
der **Kinderteller,** - child's plate (9)
der **Kinderwagen,** - baby carriage (7)
die **Kinderwiege, -n** cradle
die **Kindheit** childhood (8)
das **Kino, -s** movie, cinema; **ins Kino gehen** to go to the movies (1)
die **Kinokasse, -n** movie theater ticket booth; **an der Kinokasse** at the movie theater ticket booth (5)
der **Kiosk, -e** newsstand
der **Kioskbesitzer,** - / die **Kioskbesitzerin, -nen** newsstand owner
die **Kippcouch, -en** reclining couch
die **Kirche, -n** church (5, 6); **in der Kirche** at church (5)
die **Kirsche, -n** cherry (9)
der **Kittel,** - overall; smock
(die) **Kitzbühler Alpen** (*pl.*) the Kitzbühlian Alps
die **Kiwi, -s** kiwi
die **Klammer, -n** parenthesis
die **Klamotten** (*pl.*) clothes
die **Klapperschlange, -n** rattlesnake (12)
klar! of course! (2)
die **Klasse, -n** class; classroom (5); grade (level) (8); **erster Klasse fliegen/fahren** to fly/travel first class (10)
das **Klassentreffen,** - class reunion (8)
die **Klassenarbeit, -en** (written) class test
der **Klassenkamerad, -en** (*wk.*) / die **Klassenkameradin, -nen** classmate
der **Klassenlehrer,** - / die **Klassenlehrerin, -nen** homeroom teacher
das **Klassenzimmer,** - classroom (B)
die **Klassik** classical period; **die Wiener Klassik** the Vienna classical period (*music*)
der **Klassiker,** - classical writer/composer
klassizistisch classical
das **Klavier, -e** piano (2); **Klavier spielen** to play the piano
die **Klavierfabrik, -en** piano factory
der **Klaviertischler,** - piano cabinet-maker
das **Kleid, -er** dress (A)
der **Kleiderkauf, ¨-e** clothes shopping
der **Kleiderschrank, ¨-e** clothes closet, wardrobe (6)
die **Kleidung** clothes (A)
das **Kleidungsgeschäft, -e** clothing store (10); **im Kleidungsgeschäft** at the clothing store
das **Kleidungsstück, -e** article of clothing (10)
klein short; small (A)
das **Kleingeld** (small) change
das **Kleinkind, -er** small child
die **Kleinwohnung, -en** small apartment
klettern, ist geklettert to climb (8)
der **Klient, -en** (*wk.*) / die **Klientin, -nen** client
das **Klima, -s** climate
klingeln, geklingelt to ring (2)
klingen (wie) (klingt), klang, geklungen to sound (like) (11)
klirren, geklirrt to clink, rattle
das **Kloster,** - monastery; convent
km = der **Kilometer,** - kilometer
knapp just, barely (6)
die **Kneipe, -n** bar, tavern (3)
der **Knoblauch** garlic (9)
der **Knochen,** - bone
die **Knochenarbeit, -en** back-breaking work
der **Knödel,** - dumpling (9)
der **Knopf, ¨-e** button
knuspern (an + *dat.*), **geknuspert** to nibble (at)
der **Koch, ¨-e** / die **Köchin, -nen** cook, chef (5)
das **Kochbuch, ¨-er** cookbook (2)
kochen, gekocht to cook; to boil (1, 9); **gekochte Eier** soft-boiled eggs (9)
die **Kochgelegenheit** cooking facilities
der **Kochtopf, ¨-e** (cooking) pot
der **Koffer,** - suitcase (2, 10)
das **Kofferradio, -s** portable radio
der **Kofferraum, ¨-e** trunk (7)
der **Kognak, -s** cognac, brandy (9)
der **Kohl** cabbage (9)
das **Kohlehydrat, -e** carbohydrate
das **Kokain** cocaine
der **Kolibri, -s** hummingbird (12)
der **Kollege, -n** (*wk.*) / die **Kollegin, -nen** colleague, co-worker
(das) **Köln** Cologne
kolumbianisch Columbian (*adj.*)
die **Kombination, -en** combination
kombinieren, kombiniert to combine (3)
komisch funny, strange (12)
kommen (aus + *dat.*) **(kommt), kam, ist gekommen** to come (from) (B); **auf andere Gedanken kommen** to keep one's mind off something (7); **in den Genuß kommen** to acquire unexpectedly; **zu Besuch kommen** to visit (3)
die **Kommode, -n** dresser (6)
komplett complete(ly)
die **Komplikation, -en** complication
das **Kompliment, -e** compliment
der **Komponist, -en** (*wk.*) / die **Komponistin, -nen** composer
der **Kompromiß, Kompromisse** compromise
die **Konferenz, -en** conference
die **Konfession, -en** religious denomination, church (12)
die **Konfirmation, -en** confirmation
konfirmiert confirmed
der **Konflikt, -e** conflict
konformistisch conformist; in a conformist way
der **König, -e** / die **Königin, -nen** king/queen (8)
der **Königssohn, ¨-e** prince
die **Königstochter, ¨** princess
konjugieren, konjugiert to conjugate

die **Konjunktion, -en** conjunction
konkret concrete, firm (12)
können (kann), konnte, gekonnt to be able (to), can; may (3)
konservativ conservative(ly) (B)
konstruieren, konstruiert to design; to construct
der **Konsum** consumption
der **Kontakt, -e (zu** + *dat.*) contact (with); **leicht Kontakt bekommen** to connect easily with others
das **Kontinent, -e** continent (B)
das **Kontinentalklima** continental climate
das **Konto, Konten** bank account; **ein Konto eröffnen** to open a bank account (5)
der **Kontostand** balance; state of an/one's account
kontra against
die **Kontrolle, -n** control
kontrollieren, kontrolliert to keep under control
kontrovers conflicting; controversial
das **Konzentrationslager, -** concentration camp
der **Konzern, -e** industrial concern
das **Konzert, -e** concert; **ins Konzert gehen** to go to a concert (1)
konzipieren, konzipiert to conceive
die **Kopassage** *a shopping center*
(das) **Kopenhagen** Copenhagen
der **Kopf, ¨e** head (A)
das **Kopfkissen, -** pillow (6)
kopflos rash(ly)
der **Kopfsalat** lettuce (9)
die **Kopfschmerzen** (*pl.*) headache (11)
die **Kopfschmerztablette, -n** headache pill (11)
kopieren, kopiert to copy
der **Kopierladen, ¨** copy shop (10)
der **Korb, ¨e** basket
der **Korkenzieher, -** corkscrew (9)
das **Korn, ¨er** grain (of corn)
der **Körper, -** body (A)
körperlich physical
die **Körperpflege** personal hygiene (11)
das **Körperteil, -e** body part
der **Korridor, -e** corridor, hall
korrigieren, korrigiert to correct (4)
die **Kosmetik** cosmetics
kosten, gekostet to cost (6)
kostenlos free of charge
das **Kostüm, -e** costume; woman's suit (8)
der **Kot, -e** feces
die **Krabbe, -n** shrimp (9)

der **Krach** loud noise
die **Kraft, ¨e** strength
kräftigen, ist gekräftigt to strengthen
der **Kraftwagen-Kilometer** motor-vehicle kilometer
krank sick (3)
das **Krankenhaus, ¨er** hospital (3, 5, 6, 11)
die **Krankenhauskosten** (*pl.*) hospital cost
die **Krankenkasse** health insurance company
der **Krankenpfleger, -** / die **Krankenpflegerin, -nen** nurse (5)
die **Krankenversicherung, -en** health insurance
der **Krankenwagen, -** ambulance (11)
die **Krankheit, -en** illness (11), sickness
die **Krankheitsgeschichte** medical history
die **Kräuterbutter** herb butter (9)
die **Krawatte, -n** tie (A)
kreativ creative(ly)
die **Kreativität** creativity
der **Krebs** cancer
der **Kredit, -e** credit; loan; **Kredit aufnehmen** to take out a loan
die **Kreide** (piece of) chalk (B)
die **Kreidefelsen** (*pl.*) chalk cliffs
der **Kreidestrich, -e** chalk mark
der **Kreis, -e** circle; (*administrative*) district
der **Kreisverkehr** traffic roundabout (10)
die **Kreme, -s** cosmetic creme
kremen, gekremt to put cream on
kreuzen, gekreuzt to cross
die **Kreuzung, -en** intersection (7)
der **Krieg, -e** war
kriegen, gekriegt to get, receive
der **Krimi, -s** detective story or film
der **Krimiautor, -en** / die **Krimiautorin, -nen** author of a detective story (12)
der **Kriminalroman, -e** detective novel
die **Krise, -n** crisis (12)
die **Kritik, -en** criticism; review
kritisch critical(ly)
(das) **Kroatien** Croatia (B)
die **Krokette, -n** croquette (9)
das **Krokodil, -e** crocodile (12)
krönen, gekrönt to crown; **zum Kaiser krönen** to crown (*s.o.*) emperor
(das) **Kuba** Cuba (B)
die **Küche, -n** kitchen (5, 6)
der **Kuchen, -** cake (5)
die **Küchenarbeit, -en** kitchen work (5)
die **Küchenlampe, -n** kitchen lamp (5)
die **Küchenmaschine, -n** mixer (9)

das **Küchenmesser, -** kitchen knife (9)
der **Küchenschrank, ¨e** kitchen cabinet
der **Küchentisch, -e** kitchen table (5, 6)
die **Küchenuhr, -en** kitchen clock (5)
die **Küchenwaage, -n** kitchen scale (5, 9)
die **Kugel, -n** ball; sphere
das **Kugelhaus, ¨er** round house
der **Kugelschreiber, -** ballpoint pen (4)
kühl cool (B)
der **Kühlschrank, ¨e** refrigerator (5, 6)
die **Kultur, -en** culture
kulturell cultural(ly)
die **Kulturmetropole, -n** cultural metropolis
das **Kulturprojekt, -e** cultural project
der **Kummer** sorrow; grief
sich **kümmern (um** + *acc.*), **gekümmert** to be responsible for (12)
der **Kunde, -n** (*wk.*) / die **Kundin, -nen** customer (5)
die **Kundengespräch, -e** sales pitch
die **Kunst, ¨e** art (1)
die **Kunstakademie, -n** academy (or college) of art
die **Kunstausstellung, -en** art exhibition
die **Kunstgeschichte** art history (1)
der **Künstler, -** / die **Künstlerin, -nen** artist
die **Kunstrichtung, -en** artistic form
der **Kurort, -e** spa, health resort
der **Kurs, -e** (*academic*) course, class (A, 1)
kursivgedruckt printed in italics, italic
kurz short (A); **kurzes Haar** short hair
die **Kurzgeschichte, -n** short story
der **Kurztext, -e** short text
die **Kusine, -n** (*female*) cousin (B)
küssen, geküßt to kiss (8)
die **Küste, -n** coast (7)
der **Kuß, Küsse** kiss (4)

L

die **Labelklamotten** (*coll., pl.*) designer clothes
lächeln, gelächelt to smile
lachen, gelacht to laugh (3)
der **Ladenschluß** store closing time
die **Lage, -n** place; position (10)
die **Lampe, -n** lamp (B)
das **Land, ¨er** country (B); **auf dem Land** in the country (6)
die **Landeshauptstadt, ¨e** capital city; provincial capital
die **Landeskunde** *study of a country's geography and history*
die **Landesverteidigung** national defense

die **Landkarte, -n** map (7)
das **Landsäugetier, -e** land mammal (12)
die **Landschaft, -en** scenery; landscape, region
die **Landsleute** (*pl.*) compatriots
die **Landstraße, -n** country road; rural highway (7)
der **Landwirt,-e** farmer
lang long (A); **am langen Samstag** on the Saturday(s) with extended store hours; **lange Zeit** for a long time; **langes Haar** long hair (A); **schon seit längerer Zeit** for a long time now
lange a long time; **lange dauern** to take a long time; **lange schlafen** to sleep late; **nicht länger** no longer (3)
längerfristig fairly long-term
die **Langeweile** (*also*: **Langweile**) boredom; **Langeweile haben** to be bored (3)
langweilig boring (2)
langsam slow(ly)
längst a long time ago; long since
langweilen, gelangweilt to bore
der **Lärm** noise
die **Lärmbelästigung** disturbance caused by noise
lassen (läßt), ließ, gelassen to let; to have something done; **einen Termin geben lassen** to get an appointment (11)
der **Lastwagen, -** truck (7)
(das) **Latein** Latin (*language*) (1)
lauern (auf + *acc.*), gelauert to wait (for)
der **Lauf: lassen Sie Ihrer Phantasie freien Lauf** let your imagination run wild
laufen (läuft), lief, ist gelaufen to run (2); **laufen Sie** run (A); **der Fernseher läuft** the TV is on; **Schlittschuh laufen** to go ice-skating (3); **was läuft im Kino?** what's playing at the movies? (2)
laufend recurring; runny (*nose*)
die **Laune, -n** mood
laut loud, noisy (3); loudly; (*prep. + gen./dat.*) according to
der **Lautsprecher, -** loudspeaker
die **Lautsprecherbox, -en** (*stereo*) speaker
leben, gelebt to live (3)
das **Leben, -** life; **am Leben sein** to be alive (8)
lebensgefährlich life-threatening
das **Lebensjahr, -e** year (of one's life); **im fünften Lebensjahr** at the age of five
das **Lebensmittel, -** food; groceries
das **Lebensmittelgeschäft, -e** grocery store (6)
der **Lebenslauf, ¨-e** résumé, curriculum vitae
der **Lebenspartner, - /** die **Lebenspartnerin, -nen** companion for life
lebenswert worth living
das **Lebensziel, -e** goal in life
die **Leber, -n** liver (11)
die **Lederjacke, -n** leather jacket (10)
ledig unmarried, single (1)
lediglich only, merely
leer empty, vacant (9)
legal legal(ly)
legen, gelegt to lay, put, place (*in a horizontal position*) (9)
die **Legende, -n** legend
(sich) **lehnen, gelehnt** to lean
die **Lehramtsprüfung, -en** exam for teaching profession
die **Lehre, -n** apprenticeship (5)
lehren, gelehrt to teach
der **Lehrer, - /** die **Lehrerin, -nen** teacher, instructor (A, 1)
die **Lehrwerkstatt, ¨-en** apprentice shop
der **Leibwächter, -** bodyguard
leicht easy; easily; light; slightly (6); **leicht defekt** slightly damaged; **leicht Kontakt bekommen** to connect easily with others
leid tun (tut . . . leid), tat . . . leid, leid getan: tut mir leid! I'm sorry (5)
leider unfortunately (B)
leihen (leiht), lieh, geliehen to lend (5)
leise quiet(ly) (8); silent(ly); soft(ly)
die **Leistung, -en** achievement, accomplishment
das **Leitbild, -er** model
leiten, geleitet to lead
das **Leitungswasser** tap water
die **Lektüre, -n** reading material
lenken, gelenkt to steer; to guide (5)
das **Lenkrad, ¨-er** steering wheel (7)
die **Lerche, -n** lark
lernen, gelernt to learn; to study (1)
die **Leseecke, -n** reading nook
die **Lesegewohnheit, -en** reading habit
lesen (liest), las, gelesen to read (A, 1, 2); **Zeitung lesen** to read the newspaper
der **Leser, - /** die **Leserin, -nen** reader
letzter, letztes, letzte last (4); **das letzte Mal** the last time (4); **letzte Woche** last week; **letzten Montag** last Monday; **letzten Sommer** last summer; **letztes Wochenende** last weekend
der **Leuchtturm, ¨-e** lighthouse (6)
der **Leumund** reputation
die **Leute** (*pl.*) people (7)
die **Levi's** Levi's (jeans)
liberal liberal (6)
libysch Libyan (*adj.*)
das **Licht, -er** light (3)
das **Lichtbild, -er** photograph
die **Lichterkette, -n** candlelight march (12)
lieb dear, beloved; sweet, lovable (10); **am liebsten** like (*to do something*) best (7)
lieben, geliebt to love (2)
lieber rather, preferably; **ich gehe lieber** I'd rather go (2)
der **Liebeskummer** lovesickness (11); **Liebeskummer haben** to be lovesick
der **Liebesroman, -e** romantic novel (8), love story
liebevoll loving(ly)
der **Lieblingsausdruck, ¨-e** favorite expression
die **Lieblings-CD, -s** favorite CDs
das **Lieblingsfach, ¨-er** favorite subject (*in school*) (5)
die **Lieblingsfarbe, -n** favorite color
der **Lieblingsname, -n** (*wk.*) favorite name
das **Lieblingsrestaurant, -s** favorite restaurant
das **Lieblingsrezept, -e** favorite recipe
das **Lieblingstier, -e** favorite animal
(das) **Liechtenstein** Liechtenstein (B)
der **Liechtensteiner, - /** die **Liechtensteinerin, -nen** Liechtensteinian (*person*)
das **Lied, -er** song (3)
liegen, (liegt), lag, ist gelegen to lie, be (in a horizontal position) (1, 9); to recline; to be located; **in der Sonne liegen** to lie in the sun (1)
liegen·bleiben (bleibt . . . liegen), blieb . . . liegen, ist liegengeblieben to remain in a prone position; to stay in bed
der **Lifestyle** lifestyle
lila purple (A)
die **Limmat** Limmat (River)
die **Limo** = **Limonade** soft drink
die **Limonade, -n** soft drink (4, 9); lemonade
die **Linde, -n** linden tree
lindern, gelindert to relieve
die **Linderung** relief
der **Lindwurmbrunnen** dragon fountain
die **Linguistik** linguistics (1)
die **Linie, -n** line (10)
links left (4, 10); on the left; **mit dem linken Fuß auf·stehen** to get up on the wrong side of the bed (4); **nach links** (to the) left
die **Linsen** (*pl.*) lentils

die **Lippe, -n** lip (11)
der **Lippenstift, -e** lipstick
(das) **Lissabon** Lisbon
die **List, -en** deception, trick (8)
die **Liste, -n** list (5)
der **Liter, -** liter (7)
die **Literatur** literature (1)
loben, gelobt to praise
das **Loch, ¨er** hole (12)
locken, gelockt to lure, attract
der **Löffel, -** spoon (9)
logisch logical(ly) (12)
der **Lohn, ¨e** reward; salary
die **Lohnerhöhung** wage or pay increase
die **Lohngruppe, -n** wage group
das **Lokal, -e** restaurant
die **Lokomotive, -n** locomotive (7)
die **Lorelei** Loreley
los loose; away; **los!** go ahead!; **was ist los?** what's happening?; what's the matter?
lösen, gelöst to solve
los·fahren (fährt . . . los), fuhr . . . los, ist losgefahren to drive/ride off (8)
los·kommen (von + *dat.***) (kommt . . . los), kam . . . los, ist losgekommen** to get away (from)
die **Lotterie, -n** lottery; **in der Lotterie gewinnen** to win the lottery (5)
der **Löwe, -n** (*wk.*) lion (12)
die **Lücke, -n** gap; space
die **Luft** air (7)
die **Luftverschmutzung** air pollution
die **Lunge, -n** lung (11)
die **Lungenentzündung** pneumonia (11)
die **Lust** desire; **hast du Lust?** do you feel like it? (2)
lustig fun, funny (12); cheerful
lutschen, gelutscht to suck (11)
(das) **Luxemburg** Luxembourg
(das) **Luzern** Lucerne
die **Lyrik** poetry

M

mach's gut! take care! (*infor.*) (A)
machen, gemacht to make, to do **macht das was?** does it matter? (B); **das Bett machen** to make the bed (6)
das **Mädchen, -** girl (8)
der **Mädchenname, -n** (*wk.*) girl's name; maiden name
der **Magen, ¨** stomach (11)
die **Magenschmerzen** (*pl.*) stomachache (11)
mähen, gemäht to mow (5, 6)
die **Mahlzeit, -en** meal (9)
(der) **Mai** May (B)
der **Main** Main (River)
das **Maiskeimöl** corn oil
das **Mal, -e** time; **das letzte Mal** the last time (4); **zum ersten Mal** for the first time (4)
mal (*word used to soften commands*) **komm mal vorbei!** come on over! (11)
malen, gemalt to paint
der **Maler, -** / die **Malerin, -nen** painter
die **Mama, -s** mama, mom
die **Mami, -s** mommy
man one; people, they
mancher, manches, manche some
manchmal sometimes (B)
mangelhaft deficient, unsatisfactory; grade D (*in school*)
die **Manier, -en** manner
manipulieren, manipuliert to manipulate
der **Mann, ¨er** man; husband (A, B)
die **Männeraufgabe, -n** man's job
der **Männerchor, ¨e** male choir
männlich masculine; male
die **Mannschaft, -en** team (8)
der **Mantel, ¨** coat; overcoat (A, 10)
das **Märchen, -** fairy tale (4)
die **Mark, -** mark (*German monetary unit*) (7)
die **Markenklamotten** (*coll., pl.*) brand-name clothes
der **Markenname, -n** brand name
markieren, markiert to mark (11)
der **Markt, ¨e** market (10)
der **Marktplatz, ¨e** market square (6)
die **Marmelade, -n** jam (9)
der **Marokkaner, -** / die **Marokkanerin, -nen** Moroccan (*person*)
(das) **Marokko** Morocco (B)
(das) **Marrakesch** Marrakesh
der **Marxismus** Marxism
(der) **März** March (B)
der **Maschinenbau** mechanical engineering (1)
die **Massenproduktion** mass production
mäßig moderate
massiv solid(ly)
das **Material, -ien** material, substance
(die) **Mathe** math
die **Mathematik** mathematics (1)
der **Mathematiker, -** / die **Mathematikerin, -nen** mathematician
der **Mathematikunterricht** mathematics class
mathematisch mathematical(ly)
mathematisch-naturwissenschaftlich mathematical(ly); scientific(ally)
die **Matratze, -n** mattress
das **Matterhorn** *mountain in Switzerland*
die **Matura** college entrance exam (*in Austria, Switzerland*)
das **Maul, ¨er** mouth (of an animal) (8)
die **Maus, ¨e** mouse (12)
maximal maximum; at the most
die **Mayonnaise** mayonnaise (9)
der **Mechaniker, -** / die **Mechanikerin, -nen** mechanic
die **Medien** (*pl.*) media
das **Medikament, -e** medicine; **ein Medikament gegen** medicine for (11)
medizinisch medical (11)
die **Medizin** medicine
das **Meer, -e** sea (1, 7); **ans Meer** to the sea (2); **im Meer schwimmen** to swim in the sea (1)
das **Meerschweinchen, -** guinea pig (12)
mehr more (3)
mehrere (*pl.*) several (10)
die **Mehrfachnennung** multiple naming
mehrmals several times (5)
meiden (meidet), mied, gemieden to avoid
der **Meilenstein** milestone
mein, meine my (A, 2)
meinetwegen on my behalf; for my sake
die **Meinung, -en** opinion; **(ganz) anderer Meinung sein** to have a (very) different opinion; to disagree; **der Meinung sein, daß . . .** to be of the opinion that . . . ; **Ihrer Meinung nach** in your opinion
das **Meinungsforschungsinstitut, -e** opinion research institute
meist most(ly); **am meisten** mostly; the most; **die meisten** most (of)
meistens usually, mostly (9)
meistgekauft most-purchased
sich **melden, gemeldet** to report; to check in; to answer the phone
die **Menge, -n** amount; **eine ganze Menge** a whole lot (4)
die **Mengenlehre** set theory
die **Mensa, -s** student cafeteria (2)
der **Mensch, -en** (*wk.*) person; human being (2)
das **Menschenleben** (human) life
das **Menschenrecht, -e** human right
die **Menschheit** humankind
menschlich human
der **Mercedes** *make of car*
merken, gemerkt to notice, realize
die **Messe, -n** trade fair; **auf der Messe** at

the fair
das **Messer,** - knife (9)
die **Messestadt, ¨-e** town well-known for its trade fairs
das **Metall, -e** metal
der **Meter,** - meter
die **Metzgerei, -en** butcher shop (6)
der **Mexikaner,** - / die **Mexikanerin, -nen** Mexican (*person*)(B)
mexikanisch Mexican (*adj.*) (9)
(das) **Mexiko** Mexico (B)
mich me (*accusative case*)
die **Miene, -n** facial expression
mies (*coll.*) crummy
die **Miete, -n** rent (6)
mieten, gemietet to rent (6)
der **Mieter,** - / die **Mieterin, -nen** renter (6)
das **Mietgesuch, -e** rental wanted ad
das **Mikrophon, -e** microphone
der **Mikrowellenherd, -e** microwave oven
die **Mikrowellenmahlzeit, -en** microwave meal
die **Milch** milk (9)
das **Milchprodukt, -e** dairy product
mild mild(ly)
die **Militärmacht, ¨-e** military power
der **Militärdienst** military service
die **Milliarde, -n** billion
die **Million, -en** million (7)
millionenfach millionfold
die **Millionenstadt, ¨-e** city with a million or more inhabitants (7)
das **Minarett, -e** minaret
minderwertig inferior (12)
mindestens at least
die **Mindeststudienzeit** minimum period of study
das **Mineral, Mineralien** mineral
das **Mineralwasser** mineral water (9)
das **Mini-Wörterbuch, ¨-er** mini-dictionary
der **Minidialog, -e** mini-dialogue
minus minus
die **Minute, -n** minute
mir me (*dat.*)
mischen, gemischt to mix
der **Mississippi** Mississippi (River)
mit with (A, 3); **mit mir** with me (3)
der **Mitbewohner,** - / die **Mitbewohnerin, -nen** roommate, housemate (2)
mit·bringen (bringt . . . mit), brachte . . . mit, mitgebracht to bring along (3)
der **Mitbürger,** - / die **Mitbürgerin, -nen** fellow citizen
miteinander with each other
mit·fahren (fährt . . . mit), fuhr . . . mit, ist mitgefahren to ride/travel along
das **Mitglied, -er** member (6)
mit·halten (hält . . . mit), hielt . . . mit, mitgehalten (mit + *dat.*) to keep up (with)
der **Mitherausgeber,** - / die **Mitherausgeberin, -nen** co-editor; co-publisher
mit·kommen (kommt . . . mit), kam . . . mit, ist mitgekommen to come along (2)
mit·machen, mitgemacht to participate (10)
mit·nehmen (nimmt . . . mit), nahm . . . mit, mitgenommen to take along (3)
mit·schreiben (schreibt . . . mit), schrieb . . . mit, mitgeschrieben to write along/at the same time
mit·spielen, mitgespielt to play along, join in
der **Mitstudent, -en** (*wk.*) / die **Mitstudentin, -nen** (A) fellow student
mit·summen, mitgesummt to hum along
der **Mittag, -e** midday, noon (3)
das **Mittagessen,** - midday meal, lunch (9); **zu Mittag essen** to eat lunch (3)
mittags at noon (2)
die **Mittagspause, -n** lunch hour, lunch break
die **Mittagsruhe** after-lunch rest; siesta
die **Mittagszeit** noon; lunchtime
die **Mitte** middle, center; in the middle of; **Mitte dreißig sein** to be in one's mid-thirties; **seit Mitte der 80er Jahre** since the mid-eighties
das **Mittelfeld** middle of the scale
das **Mittelmeer** Mediterranean Sea (B)
die **Mittelohrentzündung** infection of the middle ear
der **Mittelpunkt, -e** center
mitten in the middle; **mitten in der Nacht** in the middle of the night (8)
(der) **Mittwoch** Wednesday (1)
die **Mitternacht** midnight; **um Mitternacht** at midnight
der **Mittwochabend, -e** Wednesday night
der **Mittwochmorgen,** - Wednesday morning
mit·versorgen, mitversorgt to be equally responsible for taking care of (12)
die **Möbel** (*pl.*) furniture (6)
das **Möbelgeschäft, -e** furniture store
möbliert furnished (6)
möchte would like (to) (3)
das **Modalverb, -en** modal verb
die **Mode, -n** fashion
das **Modell, -e** model, example
die **Modemesse, -n** fashion fair
der **Modeschnickschnack** fashionable frills
der **Modeschöpfer,** - / die **Modeschöpferin, -nen** fashion designer
die **Modestadt, ¨-e** fashion town
die **Möglichkeit, -en** possibility (5)
die **Möhre, -n** carrot
modern modern(ly) (6)
modisch fashionable; fashionably
mögen (mag), mochte, gemocht to like, care for (3)
möglich possible; **alles Mögliche** everything possible (2)
möglichst (+ *adv.*) as . . . as possible (6)
(das) **Moldawien** Moldavia (B)
der **Moment, -e** moment; **im Moment** at the moment; right now (1)
die **Monarchie, -n** monarchy
der **Monat, -e** month (B)
monatlich monthly
der **Mond, -e** moon
das **Monopol, -e** monopoly
(der) **Montag** Monday (1)
der **Montagmorgen,** - Monday morning
die **Montagmorgengeschichte, -n** Monday morning story
montags on Monday(s)
das **Moped, -s** moped
der **Mord, -e** murder
morden, gemordet to murder
die **Mordwaffe, -n** murder weapon
der **Morgen,** - morning; **guten Morgen!** good morning! (A)
morgen tomorrow (2)
morgendlich morning
das **Morgenrot** dawn
morgens in the mornings (3)
die **Morgentoilette** morning grooming routine/regimen
die **Mosel** Moselle (River)
(das) **Moskau** Moscow
das **Motiv, -e** motif, theme; motive, reason
der **Motor, -en** motor; engine
die **Motorenfabrik, -en** motor factory
die **Motorhaube, -n** hood (7)
motorisieren, motorisiert to motorize
das **Motorrad, ¨-er** motorcycle (1, 7); **Motorrad fahren** to ride a motorcycle (1)
das **Motorradrennen,** - motorcycle race
die **Motorwelt** motor world
das **Mozarteum** *famous music school named after Mozart*

die **Mozartkugel** *famous chocolate confection named after Mozart*
der **Mozzarella** mozzarella cheese
die **Mücke, -n** mosquito (12)
müde tired (3)
die **Müdigkeit** fatigue, tiredness
der **Mülleimer, -** garbage can (9)
die **Müllerstochter, ¨** miller's daughter
die **Multi-Kulti-Küche** multicultural cuisine
multikulturell multicultural(ly) (12)
multiplizieren, multipliziert multiply
(das) **München** Munich
der **Mund, ¨er** mouth (A)
mündlich oral(ly)
munter cheerful; lively
die **Münze, -n** coin (5)
murmeln, gemurmelt to play marbles
die **Muschel, -n** mussel, shell (9)
der **Muschelsucher, -** mussel finder
das **Museum, Museen** museum; **ins Museum gehen** to go to the museum (1)
die **Musik** music (1)
musikalisch musically gifted
der **Musikant, -en** (*wk.*) / die **Musikantin, -nen** musician
der **Musiklehrer, -** / die **Musiklehrerin, -nen** music teacher
die **Muskelschmerzen** (*pl.*) muscle pain
das **Müsli, -s** granola
müssen (muß), mußte, gemußt to have, must (3)
Mutschli bread roll (*Swiss*)
die **Mutter, ¨** mother (A, B)
die **Mutterrolle, -n** role as a mother
der **Mutterschutz** *laws protecting working pregnant women and mothers of newborn babies*
die **Muttersprache, -n** native language; mother tongue
der **Muttertag** Mother's Day (4)
die **Mutti, -s** mom, mommy
die **Mütze, -n** cap (5)
mysteriös mysterious(ly)
mystisch mythical(ly)

N

na (*interj.*) well, so (3); **na also** now then; **na gut** well, okay; **na klar** of course
nach (+ *dat.*) after; past; according to; toward; to (*a place*) (10); **nach dem Weg fragen** to ask for directions; **nach Hause** (to) home (10); **um zwanzig nach fünf** at twenty after/past five (1)
der **Nachbar, -n** (*wk.*) / die **Nachbarin, -nen** neighbor (4)
das **Nachbarhaus, ¨er** house next door
das **Nachbarland, ¨er** neighboring country
die **Nachbarschaft** neighborhood
die **Nachbarstadt, ¨e** neighboring city/town
der **Nachbartisch, -e** adjacent table
nachdem (*subord. conj.*) afterward (8, 11)
nach·denken (über + *acc.*) **(denkt . . . nach), dachte . . . nach, nachgedacht** to think (about); consider (7)
nachher afterward
die **Nachhilfe** tutoring; **Nachhilfe geben** to tutor (3); **Nachhilfe nehmen** to be tutored (3)
nachlässig lax
der **Nachmieter, -** / die **Nachmieterin, -nen** next tenant
der **Nachmittag, -e** afternoon (4); **am Nachmittag** in the afternoon; **heute nachmittag** this afternoon
nachmittags afternoons, in the afternoon (4)
der **Nachname, -n** (*wk.*) family name
die **Nachrichten** (*pl.*) news (7)
das **Nachrichtenmagazin, -e** news magazine
das **Nachschlagewerk, -e** reference book
nach·sehen (sieht . . . nach), sah . . . nach, nachgesehen to check; to look up (10)
die **Nachspeise, -n** dessert (9)
nächster, nächstes, nächste next
die **Nacht, ¨e** night (3); **die ganze Nacht** all night long; **mitten in der Nacht** in the middle of the night (8)
der **Nachteil, -e** disadvantage (7)
das **Nachthemd, -en** nightshirt (10)
nachts nights, at night (4)
der **Nachttisch, -e** bedside table (6)
der **Nacken, -** neck
der **Nadelstreifen, -** pin-stripe
der **Nagel, ¨** nail (9)
nah close (6); **nah beieinander** close together
die **Nähe** proximity; vicinity (6, 7); **in der Nähe** in the vicinity (6, 7)
sich **nähern, genähert** to approach
der **Nährboden** breeding-ground
das **Nahrungsmittel, -** foodstuff, food
der **Name, -n** (*wk.*) name (A, 1); **auf welchen Namen** under what name
der **Namensvetter, -n** namesake
nämlich namely; actually
die **Narbe, -n** scar
die **Nase, -n** nose (11)
naß wet (3)
die **Nation, -en** nation; **die Vereinten Nationen** the United Nations
der **Nationalfeiertag, -e** national holiday (4)
die **Nationalität, -en** nationality (B)
die **Nationalversammlung, -en** national congress
die **Natur** nature; disposition, temperament; **in freier Natur** out in the open (country) (12)
der **Naturforscher, -** / die **Naturforscherin, -nen** natural scientist
natürlich natural(ly) (2); of course
die **Naturwissenschaft, -en** natural science (8)
das **Naturwunder, -** miracle of nature
das **Nazideutschland** Nazi Germany
neben (+ *dat./acc.*) next to (8), beside; alongside; in addition to
nebenan next door; **von nebenan** from next door (5)
nebenbei on the side; incidentally
nebeneinander next to each other (one another) (9)
das **Nebenfach, ¨er** minor subject
die **Nebenkosten** (*pl.*) extra costs (*e.g., utilities*) (6)
der **Nebensatz, ¨e** subordinate clause
nee (*coll.*) no
der **Neffe, -n** (*wk.*) nephew (B)
negativ negative(ly)
nehmen (nimmt), nahm, genommen to take (A, 3); **in Anspruch nehmen** to make use of; **(etwas) zu sich nehmen** to eat (*s.th.*); **Nachhilfe nehmen** to be tutored (3)
der **Neid** envy
nein no (A)
nennen (nennt), nannte, genannt to name; to call
der **Neonazi, -s** neonazi (12)
der **Nerv, -en** nerve
nervös nervous(ly) (B)
die **Nervosität** nervousness
nervtötend nerve-wracking
das **Nest, -er** nest (12)
nett nice(ly) (B)
das **Netz, -e** (safety) net; network, system; string bag
neu new (A); **etwas Neues** something new; **von neuem** anew, again
neugierig curious(ly) (12); nosy
neulich recently (8)

neun nine (A)
neunjährig nine-year-old (*adj.*)
neunt- ninth (4)
neunundzwanzig twenty-nine (A)
neunzehn nineteen (A)
neunzehnt- nineteenth
neunzig ninety (A)
(das) **Neuseeland** New Zealand (B)
neuseeländisch from New Zealand
der **Neuwagen, -** new (*not used*) car
der **Neuwagenverkäufer, -** / die **Neuwagenverkäuferin, -nen** new car dealer
nicht not (A, B); **nicht mehr** no longer; **nicht (wahr)?** isn't that right?
die **Nichte, -n** niece (B)
der **Nichtraucher, -** / die **Nichtraucherin, -nen** nonsmoker (*person*); (das) **Nichtraucher (abteil)** nonsmoking section (10)
das **Nichtraucherabteil, -e** nonsmoking compartment
nichts nothing (8); **gar nichts** nothing at all; **nichts von alledem** none of this
die **Nickelbrille, -n** metal-rimmed glasses
nicken, genickt to nod
nie never (2); **nie mehr** never again; **noch nie** never (before)
die **Niederlande** (*pl.*) the Netherlands (B)
(das) **Niedersachsen** Lower Saxony
der **Niederschlag, ¨-e** snow, rain
niemand nobody, no one (2)
die **Niere, -n** kidney (11)
die **Nierenentzündung** kidney infection (11)
niesen, geniest to sneeze
die **Niete, -n** rivet
(der) **(Sankt) Nikolaustag** St. Nicholas Day (December 6)
das **Nikotin** nicotine
der **Nil** Nile (River)
der **Nobelpreis, -e** Nobel Prize
noch even, still (B); else; yet; **auch noch** on top of it all; **immer noch** still; **noch ein** another, an additional (one); **noch (ein)mal** once more, again; **noch etwas** something/anything else; **noch nicht** not yet; **noch nie** never (before); **nur noch** only; **sonst noch** otherwise; in addition; else; **sonst noch etwas?** anything/something else? (5); **weder . . . noch** neither . . . nor
nochmal once more, again
das **Nomen, -** noun
nordafrikanisch North African (*adj.*)
(das) **Nordamerika** North America
nordamerikanisch North American (*adj.*)
(das) **Norddeutschland** northern Germany
der **Norden** north
nördlich (von) north (of) (7)
nordöstlich (von) northeast (of) (7)
(das) **Nordrhein-Westfalen** North Rhine-Westphalia
die **Nordsee** North Sea (B)
die **Nordseeinsel, -n** North Sea island
die **Nordseekrabbe, -n** small shrimp caught in the North Sea
die **Nordseeküste, -n** North Sea coast
nordwestlich (von) northwest (of) (7)
normal normal (5)
normalerweise normally (9)
das **Normalniveau, -s** normal level
(das) **Norwegen** Norway (B)
norwegisch Norwegian (*adj.*)
die **Note, -n** grade (*in school*) (8), mark
der **Notfall, ¨-e** emergency
notfalls in case of emergency, if necessary
notieren, notiert to make a note, write down (7)
nötig necessary; **nötig haben** to need; **nötig brauchen** to need urgently
die **Notiz, -en** note
(der) **November** November (B)
Nr. = **Nummer** number
die **Nudel, -n** noodle (9)
null zero
numerieren, numeriert to number
die **Nummer, -n** number (1)
das **Nummernschild, -er** license plate (7)
nun now; well
nur only (3); **nicht nur . . . sondern auch** not only . . . but also; **nur noch** only
(das) **Nürnberg** Nuremberg
die **Nuß, Nüsse** nut (9)
nutzen, genutzt to use
nützlich useful (10)

O

ob (*subord. conj.*) whether, if (6, 10, 11)
oben on top; the top; up high; above; upstairs (10); **ganz oben** way at the top; **von oben** from above
der **Oberarm, -e** upper arm
(das) **Oberbayern** Upper Bavaria
das **Obst** fruit (9)
obwohl (*subord. conj.*) although (11)
die **Ode, -n** ode
oder (*coord. conj.*) or (A, 11)
offen open (3)
offensichtlich apparently
die **Öffentlichkeit** the public
offiziell official(ly)
öffnen, geöffnet to open; **öffnen Sie** open (A)
die **Öffnungszeit, -en** business hours (9)
oft often (B)
öfter frequently
öfters = **öfter** frequently
oh oh
ohne (+ *acc.*) without; **ohne den Text zu lesen** without reading the text
die **Ohnmacht** unconsciousness; **in Ohnmacht fallen** to faint (11)
das **Ohr, -en** ear (A)
die **Ohrenschmerzen** (*pl.*) earache (11)
der **Ohrring, -e** earring (2)
okay (*coll.*) okay; **das geht okay** that's OK
(der) **Oktober** October (B); **am ersten Oktober** on the first of October (4)
das **Oktoberfest, -e** *festival held yearly (in Munich) during late September and early October* (7)
das **Öl** oil (5, 9); **das Öl kontrollieren** to check the oil (5)
die **Ölheizung** oil-fired heating
die **Oldies** oldies
die **Olive, -n** olive (9)
das **Olivenöl** olive oil
die **Oma, -s** grandma (3)
das **Omelett, -s** omelette (9)
der **Onkel, -** uncle (B)
der **Opa, -s** grandpa
der **Opel** *make of car*
der **Opi, -s** grandpa
optimistisch optimistic(ally) (B)
die **Orange, -n** orange (9)
orange orange (*color*) (A)
der **Orangensaft** orange juice (9)
ordentlich orderly; neat
die **Ordinalzahl, -en** ordinal number
ordnen, geordnet to arrange, put in order
die **Ordnung** order; regulation; **alles in Ordnung** everything (is) okay; **nicht in Ordnung sein** to not function properly
organisieren, organisiert to organize
der **Organist, -en** (*wk.*) / die **Organistin, -nen** organist
der **Orientexpress** Orient Express (train)
orientieren, orientiert to orient
die **Orientierung** orientation; guidance
das **Original, -e** original
originell original(ly)
der **Ort, -e** place, town (1, 4)
der/die **Ortsfremde, -n** (ein **Ortsfremder**) nonlocal (person), nonresident; stranger
(das) **Ostasien** East Asia
(das) **Ostberlin** East Berlin

ostdeutsch East German (*adj.*)
der **Osten** east
das **Osterei, -er** Easter egg
(das) **Österreich** Austria (B)
der **Österreicher, -** / die **Österreicherin, -nen** Austrian (*person*) (B)
österreichisch Austrian (*adj.*)
(der) **Ostersonntag** Easter Sunday
osteuropäisch East European (*adj.*)
ostfriesisch East Frisian (*adj.*)
(das) **Ostfriesland** East Friesland (*northwest part of Germany*)
östlich (von) east (of) (7)
die **Ostsee** Baltic Sea (B)
die **Ostseeküste** Baltic coast
der **Ozean, -e** ocean

P

das **Paar, -e** couple; pair (of)
paar: ein paar a few, a couple of
packen, gepackt to pack (7)
die **Packung, -en** package; packet (9)
der **Pädagoge, -n** (*wk.*) / die **Pädagogin, -nen** teacher
die **Pädagogik** pedagogy
pädagogisch pedagogical(ly)
das **Paket, -e** package (9)
der **Paketdienst** parcel service
die **Palme, -n** palm tree (6)
die **Palmenhütte, -n** hut made of palms (6)
der **Papa, -s** daddy, dad
der **Papagei, -en** parrot (12)
der **Papi, -s** daddy
das **Papier, -e** paper (B)
der **Papierkorb, ¨-e** wastepaper basket (3)
das **Papiertuch, ¨-er** paper towel (5)
die **Paprika, -s** bell pepper (9)
die **Parallele, -n** parallel
das **Parfüm, -e** perfume (5)
der **Park, -s** park; **im Park spazierengehen** to walk in the park (1)
parken, geparkt to park (*a car*) (7)
parkende parking
die **Parklücke, -n** parking space (7)
der **Parkplatz, ¨-e** car park, parking lot (6)
die **Partei, -en** (political) party
das **Partizip, -ien** participle
der **Partner, -** / die **Partnerin, -nen** partner (12)
die **Partnerschaft, -en** partnership (12)
die **Party, -s** party (1); **auf eine Party gehen** to go to a party (1)
der **Passant, -en** (*wk.*) / die **Passantin, -nen** passerby
passen, gepaßt (+ *dat.*) to fit (10); to match; to suit; (**zu** + *dat.*) to go with, fit (in with); **das paßt gut** that fits well (11)
passend suitable; appropriate
passieren, ist passiert to happen (4)
das **Passivrauchen** passive smoking
die **Pasta** pasta
der **Paß, Pässe** passport (7)
der **Patient, -en** (*wk.*) / die **Patientin, -nen** patient (5)
der **Patrizier, -** patrician
die **Pause, -n** recess, break (1); **Pause machen** to take a break
peinlich embarrassing (12)
der **Pelz, -e** fur
der **Pelzmantel, ¨-** fur coat (10)
das **Penizillin** penicillin (4)
die **Pension, -en** small hotel; retirement (12); **in Pension gehen** to retire (12)
pensioniert retired
der/die **Pensionierte, -n** (ein **Pensionierter**) retired person
die **Pensionierung, -en** retirement
die **Person, -en** person, individual (A, 1)
der **Personalausweis, -e** (personal) ID card (1)
das **Personalpronomen, -** personal pronoun
der **Personenzug, ¨-e** passenger train (7)
persönlich personal(ly); in person; **persönliche Daten** biographical information (1)
die **Persönlichkeit** personality
die **Perücke, -n** wig (11)
die **Pfanne, -n** (frying) pan (5, 9)
der **Pfeffer** (*black*) pepper (9)
der **Pfennig, -e** pfennig (*German monetary unit*)
das **Pferd, -e** horse (8)
die **Pferderennbahn, -en** horse racing track
der **Pfirsich, -e** peach (9)
die **Pflanze, -n** plant (3, 6); **die Pflanzen gießen** to water the plants
pflanzlich vegetable (*adj.*)
das **Pflaster, -** adhesive bandage (11)
die **Pflaume, -n** plum (9)
pflegen, gepflegt to attend to, to nurse (5); to take care of
die **Pflicht, -en** duty; requirement; obligation (3); **Pflicht sein** to be required/mandatory
das **Pflichtfach, ¨-er** required subject
pflücken, gepflückt to pick (8)
das **Pfund, -e** pound (5)
die **Phantasie, -n** imagination
phantastisch fantastic
das **Phantom, -e** phantom
die **Pharmazie** pharmacy
pharmazeutisch pharmaceutical(ly)
die **Philologie** philology
der **Philosoph, -en** (*wk.*) / die **Philosophin, -nen** philosopher
die **Philosophie** philosophy
philosophisch philosophical(ly)
die **Physik** physics (1)
der **Physiker, -** / die **Physikerin, -nen** physicist
der **Pianist, -en** (*wk.*) / die **Pianistin, -nen** pianist
das **Picknick, -s** picnic (4)
piepe: das ist mir piepe (*coll.*) I don't care
der **Pilot, -en** (*wk.*) / die **Pilotin, -nen** pilot (5)
der **Pilz, -e** mushroom (9)
die **Pinte, -n** bar
der **Piranha, -s** piranha (12)
die **Pizza, -s** pizza (2)
der **Pkw** = der **Personenkraftwagen, -** private car
der **Pkw-Besitzer, -** car owner
der **Plan, ¨-e** plan (3)
planen, geplant to plan (7)
planmäßig according to schedule
der **Plattenspieler, -** record player
der **Platz, ¨-e** place (3), seat; room, space; square; **hier ist kein Platz** there's no room here
das **Plätzchen, -** small place
plötzlich suddenly (8)
(das) **Polen** Poland (B)
polieren, poliert to polish
die **Politik** politics (5)
der **Politiker, -** / die **Politikerin, -nen** politician
die **Politikwissenschaft** political science
politisch political(ly) (4)
der **Politologe, -n** (*wk.*) / die **Politologin, -nen** political scientist
die **Polizei** police station (5); **auf der Polizei** at the police station (5)
das **Polizeirevier, -e** police station
der **Polizist, -en** (*wk.*) / die **Polizistin, -nen** police officer (5)
polnisch Polish (*adj.*)
die **Pommes frites** (*pl.*) french fries (9)
das **Porträt, -s** portrait
(das) **Portugal** Portugal (B)
der **Portugiese, -n** (*wk.*) / die **Portugiesin, -nen** Portuguese (*person*)
positiv positive(ly)

das **Possessivpronomen, -** possessive pronoun
die **Post** post office (5); **auf der Post** at the post office; **auf die Post/zur Post** to the post office
das **Postamt, ¨-er** post office
das **Postauto, -s** mail van
die **Postbank, -en** bank at the post office
der **Postbeamte, -n** (ein **Postbeamter**) / die **Postbeamtin, -nen** postal employee (5)
das **Poster, -** poster (6)
die **Postkarte, -n** postcard (2)
die **Pracht** splendor
die **Präferenz, -en** preference (1)
das **Präfix, -e** prefix
(das) **Prag** Prague
pragmatisch pragmatic(ally)
praktisch practical(ly) (5); **praktische Ausbildung** practical (career) training (5)
die **Präposition, -en** preposition
das **Präsens** presence
der **Präsident, -en** (*wk.*) / die **Präsidentin, -nen** president (5)
der **Prater** *famous amusement park in Vienna*
der **Prediger, -** / die **Predigerin, -nen** preacher
der **Preis, -e** price; prize (7, 12); **im Preis inbegriffen** included in the price
preisgünstig at a favorable price; inexpensive
das **Prestige** prestige (5)
(das) **Preußen** Prussia
der **Priester, -** / die **Priesterin, -nen** priest (5)
prima! great! (6)
der **Prinz, -en** (*wk.*) / die **Prinzessin, -nen** prince/princess (8)
das **Prinzip, Prinzipien** principle
privat private(ly)
pro per; **pro Woche** per week (3)
probieren, probiert to try; to taste (3)
das **Problem, -e** problem
das **Produkt, -e** product
produzieren, produziert to produce
der **Professor, -en** / die **Professorin, -nen** professor (A, B)
programmieren, programmiert to program
progressiv progressive(ly) (B)
das **Projekt, -e** project
prominent prominent(ly)
das **Pronomen, -** pronoun
der **Prospekt, -e** brochure; catalogue
das **Protein, -e** protein
protestieren (gegen + *acc.*), **protestiert** to protest (against) (12)
das **Prozent, -e** percent (4)
der **Prozentsatz, ¨-e** percentage
die **Prozentzahl, -en** percentage number
die **Prüfung, -en** test (1), exam
die **Prügel, -** beatings
der **Psychiater, -** / die **Psychiaterin, -nen** psychiatrist (11)
die **Psychologie** psychology
der **Pudding, -s** pudding
der **Pulli, -s** = der **Pullover**
der **Pullover, -** sweater (2)
pumpen, gepumpt to pump; to borrow
der **Punkt, -e** point (3)
pünktlich punctual(ly); on time (7)
die **Pünktlichkeit** punctuality
die **Puppe, -n** doll (8)
putzen, geputzt to clean (3); **sich die Zähne putzen** to brush one's teeth (11)
der **Putzlappen, -** cloth, rag (for cleaning) (6)
die **Pyramide, -n** pyramid

Q

qm = der **Quadratmeter, -** square meter (m^2)
das **Quadrat, -e** square
der **Quadratkilometer, -** square kilometer
die **Quadratmeile, -n** square mile
der **Quadratmeter, - (qm)** square meter (m^2) (6)
der **Quälgeist, -er** pest, nuisance
die **Qualifikation, -en** capability, qualification
die **Qualität** quality
der **Quark** *type of creamy cottage cheese* (9)
der **Quatsch** baloney, nonsense
die **Quelle, -n** source
quietschend screeching
die **Quittung, -en** receipt, check (9)

R

das **Rad, ¨-er** wheel; bicycle
radeln, ist geradelt to ride a bicycle
rad·fahren (fährt . . . Rad), fuhr . . . Rad, ist radgefahren to bicycle (6)
der **Radfahrer, -** / die **Radfahrerin, -nen** bicyclist (7)
das **Radio, -s** radio (2)
die **Radtour, -en** bicycle tour (8)
der **Radweg, -e** bicycle path; bike lane (7)
die **Rakete, -n** rocket (7)
der **Rand, ¨-er** edge; margin
die **Rangliste, -n** ranking list
der **Ranzen, -** knapsack; satchel
der **Ranzendeckel, -** flap of (a) satchel
rasen, ist gerast to speed, race; to rush
der **Rasen, -** lawn (5)
der **Rasenmäher, -** lawn mower (6)
der **Rasierapparat, -e** shaver, (electric) razor
(sich) **rasieren, rasiert** to shave (11)
die **Rasierklinge, -n** razor blade
das **Rasierwasser** aftershave lotion
das **Raster, -** / grid
der **Rat, Ratschläge** (piece of) advice; **Rat geben** to give advice (5)
raten (+ *dat.*) **(rät), riet, geraten** to advise (a person) (5)
das **Ratespiel, -e** guessing game; quiz
das **Rathaus, ¨-er** town/city hall; city government building (1, 6); **auf dem Rathaus** at the town hall (1)
der **Ratschlag, ¨-e** (piece of) advice
das **Rätsel, -** puzzle, riddle; **ein Rätsel lösen** to solve a puzzle/riddle (8)
die **Ratte, -n** rat (12)
rauchen, geraucht to smoke (3)
der **Raucher, -** / die **Raucherin, -nen** smoker (*person*); **(der) Raucher** smoking section (10)
rauh rough(ly)
der **Raum, ¨-e** room; space
räumlich spatial(ly)
die **Raumstation, -en** space station (6)
raus = **heraus** out
raus·holen, rausgeholt = **heraus·holen** to get *(s.th.)* out of/from *(s.o.)*
raus·schießen (schießt . . . raus), schoß . . . raus, ist rausgeschossen = **heraus·schießen** to shoot out (of/from)
reagieren, reagiert to react
der **Realschulabschluß** graduation from high school
die **Realschule, -n** *type of high school*
die **Rechenart, -en** type of arithmetical operation
rechnen, gerechnet to do arithmetic
die **Rechnung, -en** bill; check (*in restaurant*) (4)
das **Recht, -e (auf** + *acc.*) right (to)
recht right; **du hast recht** you are right (2)
rechts to the right (7, 10); **von rechts** from the right side
der **Rechtsanwalt, ¨-e** / die **Rechtsanwäl-**

tin, -nen lawyer
der/die **Rechtsradikale, -n** (ein **Rechtsradikaler**) right-wing radical (12)
rechtzeitig timely, on time (12)
die **Rede, -n** speech, talk
reden, geredet to speak, talk
die **Reduzierung, -en** reduction
das **Referat, -e** (term) paper; report (3); **ein Referat halten** to give a paper/oral report (4)
das **Reflexivpronomen, -** reflexive pronoun
die **Reformation** (*Luther's*) Reformation
der **Reformator, -en** reformer
reformerisch reforming; of reform
das **Regal, -e** bookshelf, bookcase (2)
die **Regel, -n** rule; **in der Regel** as a rule
regelmäßig regular(ly) (11)
regeln, geregelt to regulate
die **Regelung, -en** regulation
der **Regen** rain; **bei Regen** in rainy weather (7)
der **Regenmantel, ¨** raincoat
der **Regenschirm, -e** umbrella (5, 10)
das **Regime, -** regime
regional regional(ly)
der **Regisseur, -e** / die **Regisseurin, -nen** stage/film director (8)
regnen, geregnet to rain; **es regnet** it's raining (B)
das **Reh, -e** deer
das **Reibeplätzchen** potato pancake
der **Reiberdatschi** potato pancake
reich rich(ly)
reichen, gereicht to pass, hand (to)
der **Reifen, -** tire (7)
die **Reifenpanne, -n** flat tire (7); **eine Reifenpanne haben** to have a flat tire (7)
die **Reihe, -n** row
die **Reihenfolge** sequence, order (2)
rein = **herein** in
reinigen, gereinigt to clean
die **Reinigung, -en** dry cleaner's (6)
der **Reis** rice (9)
die **Reise, -n** trip, journey; **auf Reisen sein** to be on a trip (7)
die **Reiseausgaben** (*pl.*) travel expenditure
der **Reisebericht, -e** report of one's journey; travelogue
das **Reisebüro, -s** travel agency (6, 7, 10); **ins Reisebüro gehen** to go to the travel agency
der **Reisebus, -se** coach
das **Reiseerlebnis, -se** travel experience
der **Reiseführer, -** travel guidebook (5)
die **Reiseküche, -n** mobile kitchen
die **Reisemöglichkeit, -en** travel possibility
reisen, ist gereist to travel (1)
der/die **Reisende, -n** (ein **Reisender**) traveler (10)
der **Reisepaß, Reisepässe** passport (10)
der **Reiseplan, ¨e** travel plan; itinerary; schedule
die **Reiseroute, -n** route
der **Reisescheck, -s** traveler's check (7)
das **Reiseziel, -e** destination
reiten (reitet), ritt, ist geritten to ride horseback; to go horseback riding (1)
das **Reitpferd, -e** saddle horse
relativ relative(ly) (5)
der **Relativsatz, ¨e** relative clause
die **Religion, -en** religion (1)
religiös religious (B); for reasons of religion
die **Renaissance, -n** revival; (*sg.*) Renaissance
rennen (rennt), rannte, ist gerannt to run
renovieren, renoviert to renovate
die **Reparatur, -en** repair
reparieren, repariert to repair (1)
der **Reporter, -** / die **Reporterin, -nen** reporter, journalist (4)
repräsentativ representative
die **Republik, -en** republic
die **Reserve, -n** reserve
reservieren, reserviert to reserve (7)
die **Residenz, -en** residence
respektieren, respektiert to respect; to honor
der **Rest, -e** remainder, rest
das **Restaurant, -s** restaurant (2); **im Restaurant** at the restaurant
das **Resultat, -e** result
die **Rettung, -en** rescue
das **Revier, -e** (police) station
die **Revolution, -en** revolution
das **Rezept, -e** recipe (9); prescription (11)
rezeptfrei without a prescription
die **Rezeption, -en** reception desk (10)
der **Rhein** Rhine (River)
(das) **Rheinland-Pfalz** Rhineland Palatinate
der **Rhesusfaktor** rhesus factor
der **Richter, -** / die **Richterin, -nen** judge (5)
richtig right(ly), correct(ly) (2)
die **Richtung, -en** direction (7)
riechen (riecht), roch, gerochen to smell (11)
der **Riese, -n** (*wk.*) giant (8)
die **Riesenschildkröte, -n** giant tortoise
die **Riesenschlange, -n** boa constrictor; python (12)
riesig gigantic
das **Rinderhackfleisch** ground beef
das **Rindfleisch** beef (9)
der **Ring, -e** ring (2)
ringsum all around
rissig cracked; chapped
der **Rock, ¨e** skirt (A); (*sg.*) rock music
das **Rockkonzert, -e** rock concert (8)
der **Rockstar, -s** rock star (12)
die **Rolle, -n** role; part (4)
das **Rollenspiel, -e** role play
die **Rollenverteilung, -en** distribution/assignment of roles
der **Rollkragenpullover, -** turtleneck sweater
der **Rollschuh, -e** roller skate
(das) **Rom** Rome
der **Roman, -e** novel (3, 5)
der **Romanautor, -en** / die **Romanautorin, -nen** novelist
die **Romanistik** Romance studies
die **Romantik** Romanticism; Romantic movement
romantisch romantic(ally)
die **Römer** (*pl.*) the Romans
römisch Roman (*adj.*)
röntgen, geröntgt to X-ray (11)
rosa pink (A)
der **Rosenkohl** Brussels sprouts (9)
rostig rusty (9)
rot red (A)
(das) **Rotkäppchen** Little Red Riding Hood
die **Rubrik, -en** (*newspaper*) section, column
der **Rücken, -** back (A, 11)
die **Rückfahrt, -en** return trip; **die Hin- und Rückfahrt** round trip
der **Rucksack, ¨e** backpack (2)
der **Rücktritt, -e** resignation
rufen (ruft), rief, gerufen to call, shout (7, 11); **um Hilfe rufen** to call for help
(das) **Rügen** Rügen (Island)
die **Ruhe** silence; peace
ruhig quiet, calm (B)
(das) **Ruhrgebiet** *industrial and metropolitan area on the Ruhr River*
(das) **Rumänien** Romania (B)
(das) **Rumpelstilzchen** Rumpelstiltskin
das **Rumpsteak, -s** steak (9)
rund round; approximately; **rund um die Uhr** around the clock
runden, gerundet to round

der **Rundgang (durch** + *acc.*)**: ein Rundgang durch Supermärkte** a walk around supermarkets
der **Rüssel,** - trunk (*of an elephant*) (12)
russisch Russian (*adj.*) (12)
(das) **Rußland** Russia (B)
der **Rutsch, -e** slide; **guten Rutsch!** happy New Year!
rutschen, ist gerutscht to slide, slip (8)

S

der **Saal, Säle** hall; ballroom
das **Sachbuch, ¨er** nonfiction book
der **Sachbuchautor, -en** / die **Sachbuchautorin, -nen** nonfiction author
die **Sache, -n** thing (2)
(das) **Sachsen-Anhalt** Saxony-Anhalt
der **Saft, ¨e** juice (9)
saftig juicy
die **Sage, -n** legend, saga
sagen, gesagt to say; to tell (A, 5); **sagen Sie** say (A)
das **Sakko, -s** sports jacket (A)
die **Salami,** - salami
der **Salat, -e** salad; lettuce (3, 9)
die **Salatgurke, -n** English cucumber
die **Salatmayonnaise, -n** salad mayonnaise
die **Salatschüssel, -n** salad (mixing) bowl (5)
die **Salatsoße, -n** salad dressing (9)
das **Salz** salt (9)
salzig salty (7)
die **Salzkartoffeln** (*pl.*) boiled potatoes (9)
sammeln, gesammelt to collect, gather
das **Sampleinstitut** polling institute
(der) **Samstag** Saturday (1); **am Samstag** on Saturday (2)
der **Samstagabend, -e** Saturday evening
der **Samstagnachmittag, -e** Saturday afternoon
samstags on Saturday(s)
der **Samstagvormittag, -e** Saturday morning
der **Sand** sand (7)
die **Sandale, -n** sandal (10)
die **Sandburg, -en** sandcastle (10)
der **Sandsturm, ¨e** sandstorm
sanft soft(ly); gentle; gently; peaceful(ly)
der **Sänger,** - / die **Sängerin, -nen** singer
der **Sanitäter,** - paramedic
der **Sarg, ¨e** coffin (8)
das **Satellitenprogramm, -e** satellite channel
der **Satiriker,** - satirist
satt full; well-fed; **satt werden** to get enough to eat
der **Satz, ¨e** sentence (3)
die **Satzklammer, -n** sentence bracket
die **Satzstellung, -en** word order
der **Satzteil, -e** part of sentence, clause
sauber clean (B)
sauber·machen, saubergemacht to clean (3, 6)
sauer sour (9)
der **Sauerbraten,** - sauerbraten (*marinated beef roast*) (9)
das **Sauerkraut** sauerkraut; pickled cabbage (7)
der **Sauerstofftransport** oxygenation
saugen, gesaugt to vacuum
das **Säugetier, -e** mammal
die **Sauna, -s** sauna (11)
das **Schach** chess (1)
schade! too bad! (3)
schaden (+ *dat.*)**, geschadet** to harm, hurt (10)
der **Schaden,** ¨ damage (11)
der **Schal, -s** scarf (10)
die **Schallplatte, -n** record
der **Schalter,** - ticket booth (5); **am Schalter** at the ticket booth
der **Schaltplan, ¨e** circuit diagram
der **Schamane, -n** shaman
scharf sharp(ly); piercing(ly); **scharf hören** to hear extremely well
der **Schatten** shadow, shade (8)
der **Schatz, ¨e** treasure (8)
schauen (an/auf + *acc.*)**, geschaut** to look at; **schauen Sie** look (A)
schaufeln, geschaufelt to shovel (11)
das **Schaufenster,** - shop window
der **Schauspieler,** - / die **Schauspielerin, -nen** actor/actress (8)
die **Schauspielschule, -n** drama school
die **Scheibe, -n** windowpane (7)
der **Scheibenwischer,** - windshield wiper (7)
die **Scheidung, -en** divorce (12)
der **Schein, -e** bill, note (*of currency*) (9)
scheinen (scheint), schien, geschienen to shine; to seem, appear; **es scheint** it seems
schenken, geschenkt to give (as a present) (5)
die **Schere, -n** scissors (9)
schick smart, chic (2, 10)
schicken, geschickt to send (2)
die **Schiene, -n** train track (10)
schießen (schießt), schoß, geschossen to shoot
das **Schiff, -e** ship (7)
der **Schiffer,** - boatsman
das **Schild, -er** sign (7)
die **Schildkröte, -n** turtle (12)
der **Schilling, -e** schilling (7); **zwei Schilling** two schillings
schimpfen, geschimpft to cuss; to scold (8)
die **Schindel, -n** shingle
der **Schinken,** - ham (9)
der **Schlaf** sleep (8)
der **Schlafanzug, ¨e** pajamas (10)
schlafen (schläft), schlief, geschlafen to sleep (2); **lange schlafen** to sleep late
der **Schlafsack, ¨e** sleeping bag (2)
die **Schlafstörung, -en** sleeping disorder
der **Schlafwagen,** - sleeping car (4)
das **Schlafzimmer,** - bedroom (6)
schlagen (schlägt), schlug, geschlagen to beat; to hit (9, 11)
der **Schlag, ¨e** strike (*of a clock*); (heart)beat
das **Schlagobers** whipping cream
der **Schlagrahm** whipping cream
die **Schlagsahne** whipping cream
die **Schlange, -n** snake (12)
der **Schlangenbeschwörer,** - snake charmer
schlank slender, slim (A)
der **Schlankheitstick** obsession with being skinny
der **Schlankmacher,** - low calorie/low fat food
schlapp run-down; listless
schlau clever; smart
schlecht bad(ly) (2)
die **Schleimhaut** mucous membrane
schleudern, geschleudert to hurl
schließen (schließt), schloß, geschlossen to close; **schließen Sie** close, shut (A)
schließlich finally (7)
schlimm bad (11)
der **Schlitten,** - sled (2)
Schlitten fahren (fährt . . . schlitten), fuhr . . . schlitten, ist Schlitten gefahren to go sledding
der **Schlittschuh, -e** ice skate; **Schlittschuh laufen** to go ice-skating (3)
das **Schloß, Schlösser** palace; castle (6, 8)
schlurfen, geschlurft to drag one's feet
der **Schlüssel,** - key (8)
der **Schluß, Schlüsse** end

der **Schlußsatz, ⸚e** final sentence
der **Schmarotzer, -** parasite
schmecken (+ *dat.*), **geschmeckt** to taste good (to) (10)
schmeißen (schmeißt), schmiß, geschmissen to chuck; to sling
der **Schmerz, -en** pain (11)
der **Schmetterling, -e** butterfly
sich **schminken, geschminkt** to put makeup on (11)
der **Schmuck** jewelry (2)
schmutzig dirty (B)
der **Schnaps, ⸚e** spirit; schnapps
die **Schnecke, -n** snail (12)
der **Schnee** snow (8)
das **Schneewittchen** Snow White
schneiden (schneidet), schnitt, geschnitten to cut; **Haare schneiden** to cut hair (3); **sich schneiden** to cut oneself (11)
schneien to snow; **es schneit** it is snowing (B)
schnell quick(ly), fast (3)
das **Schnitzel, -** veal/beef/pork cutlet (9)
das **Schnitzelfleisch** (veal/beef/pork) cutlet meat
der **Schnupfen, -** cold (*with a runny nose*), sniffles (11)
der **Schnuppen** *Low German form for* **Schnupfen**
die **Schnur, ⸚e** string (9)
schnüren, geschnürt to tie up
der **Schnurrbart, ⸚e** moustache (A)
der **Schock** shock (11)
schockiert shocked
die **Schokolade, -n** chocolate (3)
der **Schokoladenpudding** chocolate pudding
schon already; indeed (2, 3); **ich glaube schon** I think so; **warst du schon einmal?** were you ever? (4); **schon wieder** once again (3)
schön pretty, beautiful (B); **ganz schön** quite pretty; **ganz schön viel** quite a bit
die **Schönheit, -en** beauty
der **Schornstein, -e** chimney
der **Schrank, ⸚e** closet; cabinet, wardrobe; cupboard (2, 6); der **Kleiderschrank, ⸚e** clothes closet, wardrobe (6); der **Kühlschrank, ⸚e** refrigerator (6)
schrecklich terrible; terribly; horrible; horribly
schreiben (schreibt), schrieb, geschrieben to write; to spell; (**an** + *acc.*) to write to; (**über** + *acc.*) to write about; (**von** + *dat.*) to write of/about; **schreiben Sie** write; spell (A); **wie schreibt man das?** how do you spell that? (A)
die **Schreibmaschine, -n** typewriter (2)
der **Schreibtisch, -e** desk (2)
das **Schreibwarengeschäft, -e** stationery store (6)
schreien (schreit), schrie, geschrien to scream, yell (3)
die **Schrift, -en** handwriting
schriftlich in writing, written (10)
der **Schriftsteller, -** / die **Schriftstellerin, -nen** writer (5)
die **Schrippe, -n** (bread) roll
der **Schritt, -e** step
die **Schublade, -n** drawer (5, 9)
schüchtern shy (B)
der **Schuh, -e** shoe (A)
das **Schuhgeschäft, -e** shoe store (6)
der **Schulabschluß** *degree received after completing secondary school*
die **Schulbildung** education, schooling (5)
schuld: an etwas (+*def.*) **schuld haben / sein** to be to blame for
schulden, geschuldet to owe
die **Schule, -n** school (A, 1); **in der Schule** at school (5)
der **Schüler, -** / die **Schülerin, -nen** student; pupil (1)
das **Schulfach, ⸚er** subject of study (1)
der **Schulfreund, -e** / die **Schulfreundin, -nen** school friend
der **Schulhof, ⸚e** schoolyard, playground
das **Schuljahr, -e** school year
das **Schulkind, -er** schoolchild
der **Schulleiter, -** / die **Schulleiterin, -nen** principal
die **Schulnote, -n** mark, grade
der **Schultag, -e** school day
die **Schultasche, -n** book bag
die **Schulter, -n** shoulder (A)
das **Schultor, -e** school gate
die **Schulzeit** school days
schuppig scaly
die **Schüssel, -n** bowl (9)
der **Schüttelfrost** chills
schütteln, geschüttelt to shake
das **Schutzvitamin** protective vitamin
(das) **Schwaben** Swabia
schwach weak(ly)
der **Schwager, ⸚** / die **Schwägerin, -nen** brother-/sister-in-law
der **Schwamm, ⸚e** eraser (*for blackboard*) (B)
schwanken, geschwankt to *sway*
schwärmen (für + *acc.*), **geschwärmt** to be crazy about
schwarz black (A)
schwarzhaarig with black hair (8)
der **Schwarzwald** Black Forest
(das) **Schweden** Sweden (B)
(das) **Schwedisch** Swedish (*language*) (B)
schweigen (schweigt), schwieg, geschwiegen to say nothing
das **Schwein, -e** pig (8)
der **Schweinebraten, -** pork roast (9)
das **Schweinefleisch** pork (9)
der **Schweinestall, ⸚e** pigpen
(die) **Schweiz** Switzerland (B)
der **Schweizer, -** / die **Schweizerin, -nen** Swiss (*person*) (B)
schweizerisch Swiss (*adj.*)
schwer heavy; hard, difficult (3)
die **Schwester, -n** sister (B)
schwierig difficult (2)
das **Schwimmbad, ⸚er** swimming pool (1, 5, 6); **ins Schwimmbad fahren** to go to the swimming pool (1); **im Schwimmbad** at the swimming pool (5)
schwimmen (schwimmt), schwamm, ist/hat geschwommen to swim; to float (7); **im Meer schwimmen** to swim in the sea (1); **schwimmen gehen** to go swimming (1)
schwirren, geschwirrt to whir
schwitzen, geschwitzt to sweat
sechs six (A)
sechst- sixth (4)
sechsundzwanzig twenty-six (A)
sechzig sixty (A)
sechzehn sixteen (A)
der **See, -n** lake (7)
seekrank seasick (7)
segeln, gesegelt to sail (1)
sehen (sieht), sah, gesehen to see (2)
sich **sehnen (nach** + *dat.*), **gesehnt** to long (for)
sehr very (B)
sehscharf sharp-sighted
die **Seife, -n** soap (6)
die **Seilbahn, -en** cable railway (7)
der **Seiltänzer, -** / die **Seiltänzerin, -nen** tightrope walker
sein (ist), war, ist gewesen to be (A)
sein(e) his (1)
seit since, for (*prep.*); **seit zwei Jahren** for two years (4); **seit mehreren Tagen** for several days (11)
die **Seite, -n** side; page (6)
der **Seitensprung, ⸚e** affair on the side

die **Seitenstraße, -n** side street
der **Sekretär, -e** fold-out desk (6)
der **Sekretär, -e** / die **Sekretärin, -nen** secretary (5)
der **Sekt** sparkling wine
die **Sekunde, -n** second (1)
selber, selbes, selbe same
selbst even; oneself, myself, himself, herself, itself, yourself; ourselves, yourselves, themselves; by (one)self
selbständig independent (12)
die **Selbsteinschätzung** self-assessment
die **Selbsterkenntnis** knowledge of one's strengths and weaknesses
selbstgemacht homemade
das **Selbstporträt, -s** self-portrait
selbstverständlich of course (10)
selten rare(ly), seldom (9)
seltsam rare(ly), seldom
das **Semester, -** semester (1)
die **Semmel, -n** (bread) roll
das **Semmeli** (bread) roll (*Swiss*)
der **Senf** mustard (9)
senken, gesenkt to reduce
(der) **September** September (B)
seriös serious(ly)
servieren, serviert to serve
die **Serviette, -n** napkin (9)
Servus! hello!; good-bye! (*southern Germany, Austria*) (A)
der **Sessel, -** armchair (2, 6)
setzen, gesetzt to set, put, place (*in a sitting position*) (7, 9); **setzen Sie sich** sit down (A, 11)
die **Seuche, -n** epidemic
das **Shampoo, -s** shampoo
der **Shop, -s** shop
sich oneself, herself, himself, yourself, yourselves, themselves
sicher safe; sure (3)
die **Sicherheit** safety
der **Sicherheitsgurt, -e** safety belt (7)
sicherlich certainly (3)
sichtbar visible (11); visibly
Sie (*for. sg./pl.*) you
sie she; they
sieben seven (A)
siebenundzwanzig twenty-seven (A)
siebt- seventh (4)
siebzehn seventeen (A)
siebzig seventy (A)
der **Sieg, -e** victory
die **Siegermacht, ¨-e** victorious nation
silbern silver, silvery
die **Sinfonie, -n** symphony
singen (singt), sang, gesungen to sing (1)
der **Single, -s** single person
sinken (sinkt), sank, gesunken to sink, drop
der **Sinn (für** + *acc.*) sense (of, for) (12)
sinnvoll useful; sensible
der **Sinto, Sinti** Sinte (Gypsy of German origin)
die **Situation, -en** situation
der **Sitz, -e** seat (7)
sitzen (sitzt), saß, ist gesessen to sit, to be in a sitting position (4, 9)
(das) **Skandinavien** Scandinavia
das **Skateboard, -s** skateboard; **Skateboard fahren (fährt . . . Skateboard), fuhr Skateboard, ist Skateboard gefahren** to skateboard (3)
der **Ski, -er** ski
Ski fahren (fährt . . . Ski), fuhr . . . Ski, ist Ski gefahren to ski (3)
die **Skibrille, -n** ski glasses (5)
der **Skorpion, -e** scorpion (12)
(die) **Slowakei** Slovakia (B)
(das) **Slowenien** Slovenia (B)
so so; such; that way (3)
so oft (*subord. conj.*) whenever (B)
sobald (*subord. conj.*) as soon as
die **Socke, -n** sock (10)
das **Sofa, -s** sofa, couch (6)
sofort immediately (3)
sogar even
sogenannt so-called
der **Sohn, ¨-e** son (B)
das **Soja** soy
die **Sojasoße, -n** soy sauce
das **Solarium, Solarien** tanning salon (11)
solcher, solches, solche such
der **Soldat, -en** (*wk.*) / die **Soldatin, -nen** soldier
sollen (soll), sollte, gesollt to be supposed to (3)
der **Sommer, -** summer (B); **letzten Sommer** last summer (4)
der **Sommerkurs, -e** summer school (3)
die **Sommertemperatur, -en** summer temperature
die **Sonate, -n** sonata
das **Sonderangebot, -e** special sale
sonderbar strange(ly)
die **Sonderbestimmung, -en** special regulation
sondern but (rather/on the contrary) (A, 11)
das **Songbuch, ¨-er** (2) songbook
der **Songtext, -e** song text
die **Sonne, -n** sun; **in der Sonne liegen** to lie in the sun (1)
sich **sonnen, gesonnt** to sunbathe (11)
der **Sonnenblumenkern, -e** sunflower seed
die **Sonnenbrille, -n** (pair of) sunglasses (2)
sonnig sunny (B)
(der) **Sonntag** Sunday (1)
sonntags on Sunday(s)
sonst otherwise (B); **sonst noch etwas?** anything else? (5)
sonstig other; **Sonstiges** other things (8)
sorgen (für + *acc.*), **gesorgt** to take care of (12)
die **Sorgenlast** worry, burden
sorgfältig carefully
die **Soße, -n** gravy; sauce (9); (salad) dressing
soviel so much
sowas something like that; some such thing
sowieso anyway
(die) **Sowjetunion** Soviet Union
sozial social(ly)
die **Sozialdemokratische Partei Deutschlands (SPD)** Social Democratic Party of Germany
der **Sozialist, -en** (*wk.*) / die **Sozialistin, -nen** socialist (*person*)
sozialistisch socialist (*adj.*)
die **Sozialkunde** social studies (1)
der **Sozialreformer, -** / die **Sozialreformerin, -nen** social reformer
die **Soziologie** sociology (1)
der **Soziologe, -n** (*wk.*) / die **Soziologin, -nen** sociologist
die **Spaghetti** (*pl.*) spaghetti (3)
die **Spalte, -n** column
(das) **Spanien** Spain (B)
der **Spanier, -** / die **Spanierin, -nen** Spaniard
(das) **Spanisch** Spanish (*language*) (B)
die **Spannweite** wingspan (12)
sparen, gespart to save (money) (7)
das **Sparkonto, Sparkonten** savings account
der **Sparstrumpf, ¨-e** stocking for one's savings
der **Spaß, ¨-e** fun; **viel Spaß!** have fun! (A)
spät(er) late(r) **wie spät ist es?** what time is it? (1)
die **Spätzle** (*pl.*) spaetzle (*kind of noodles*)
spazieren·gehen (geht . . . spazieren), ging . . . spazieren, ist spazierengegangen to go for a walk (1); **im Park spazierengehen** to walk in the park (1)

der **Spaziergang, ¨e** walk (10)
die **SPD = Sozialdemokratische Partei Deutschlands** Social Democratic Party of Germany
der **Speck** bacon (9)
die **Speditionsfirma, Speditionsfirmen** trucking company
die **Speisekarte, -n** menu (9)
speisen, gespeist to eat; to dine
der **Speisewagen, -** dining car
spekulieren, spekuliert to speculate
die **Spezialität, -en** speciality
speziell special(ly)
der **Spiegel, -** mirror (6)
(das) **Spieglein, -** (*diminutive form of* **der Spiegel**) little mirror
das **Spiel, -e** game; match
die **Spielbank, -en** casino
spielen, gespielt to play (1); **Klavier spielen** to play the piano
der **Spieler, -** / die **Spielerin, -nen** player
der **Spielfreund, -e** / die **Spielfreundin, -nen** playmate
der **Spielplatz, ¨e** playground (8)
die **Spielzeugfabrik, -en** toy factory
der **Spinat** spinach (9)
der **Spion, -e** / die **Spionin, -nen** spy
der **Spitzname, -n** (*wk.*) nickname
der **Sport** sport(s); physical education (1); **Sport treiben** to do sports (2)
die **Sportkleidung** sportswear
der **Sportler, -** / die **Sportlerin, -nen** sportsman/-woman
sportlich athletic (B)
der **Sportplatz, ¨e** sports field; stadium
die **Sportschau** sports show
die **Sportwissenschaft** sports science
die **Sprache, -n** language (B)
die **Sprachkenntnisse** (*pl.*) knowledge of a language/languages
das **Sprachlabor, -s** language laboratory (4)
sprachlos silent(ly)
die **Sprachwissenschaft** linguistics
sprechen (spricht), sprach, gesprochen to speak, talk; (**über** + *acc.*) to talk about; **er/sie spricht** he/she speaks (A)
die **Sprechsituation, -en** conversational situation (A)
die **Sprechstunde, -n** office hour (3)
das **Sprichwort, ¨er** proverb, saying
springen (springt), sprang, ist gesprungen to jump; **springen Sie** jump (A)
die **Spritze, -n** vaccine, shot (11)
spröd(e) brittle
das **Spülbecken, -** sink (5)
spülen, gespült to wash; to rinse (4); **Geschirr spülen** to wash the dishes (4)
die **Spur, -en** trace, track; **auf falscher Spur** on the wrong track
das **Spurenelement, -e** trace element
das **Squash** squash (1)
der **Staat, -en** state; nation (10)
staatlich government (*adj.*); state-owned (*or* operated); with governmental control
die **Staatsangehörigkeit, -en** nationality, citizenship (1)
die **Staatssprache, -n** official language
stabil stable
die **Stadt, ¨e** town, city (2, 6)
die **Stadtbücherei, -en** city library
der **Stadtführer, -** city guidebook
der **Stadtmusikant, -en** (*wk.*) city musician
der **Stadtpark, -s** municipal park (10)
die **Stadtpfarrkirche, -n** city church
der **Stadtplan, ¨e** city street map (10)
das **Stadtproblem, -e** city problem
das **Stadtprofil, -e** city profile
der **Stadtrand, ¨er** city limits (6)
die **Stadtrundfahrt, -en** tour of the city (7)
der **Stadtteil, -e** district, neighborhood (6)
das **Stadtviertel, -** district, neighborhood (6)
der **Stahl** steel
das **Stahlprodukt, -e** steel product
der **Stall, ¨e** barn, stable
der **Stammbaum, ¨e** family tree
stammen (aus + *dat.*), **gestammt** to originate from
die **Standardsprache, -n** standard language
ständig constant(ly)
stark strong; heavy (11)
starten, ist gestartet to take off (*e.g., airplane*)
die **Station, -en** station; stage; **Station machen** to stop over
die **Statistik, -en** statistics
statt (+ *gen.*) instead of (12)
statt·finden (findet . . . statt), fand . . . statt, stattgefunden to take place (5)
das **Statussymbol, -e** status symbol
der **Stau, -s** traffic jam (7)
staub·saugen, staubgesaugt to vacuum (6)
der **Staubsauger, -** vacuum cleaner (6)
staub·wischen, staubgewischt to (wipe) dust
staunen, gestaunt to be astonished
das **Steak, -s** steak
stechen (sticht), stach, gestochen to sting; to bite (*of insects*) (12)
stecken, gesteckt to stick; to put
stecken·bleiben (bleibt . . . stecken), blieb . . . stecken, ist steckengeblieben to get stuck; to stay put (11)
stehen (steht), stand, ist gestanden to stand (*be in a vertical position*) (2, 6, 9); to be (situated); to stop, come to a standstill; (+ *dat.*) to suit (10); **das steht/die stehen dir gut!** that looks/they look good on you! (2); **wie steht's mit . . . ?** how's . . . ?
stehlen (stiehlt), stahl, gestohlen to steal (7)
steigen (steigt), stieg, ist gestiegen to climb; to ascend
der **Stein, -e** stone
steinern (*adj.*) (made of) stone
der **Steinweg, -e** stone path
die **Steinzeit** Stone Age (12)
stellen, gestellt to stand up, put, place (*in a vertical position*) (3, 9); **eine Frage stellen** to ask a question (5)
sterben (stirbt), starb, ist gestorben to die (8)
die **Stereoanlage, -n** stereo system (6)
das **Stereotyp, -en** stereotype
stereotyp stereotypical
die **Steuer, -n** tax (12)
der **Steward, -s** / die **Stewardeß, Stewardessen** flight attendant (5)
der **Stichpunkt, -e** main point (12)
das **Stichwort, ¨er** keyword
der **Stiefel, -** boot (A)
die **Stiefmutter, ¨** stepmother (8)
der **Stiefvater, ¨** stepfather (8)
der **Stift, -e** pen, pencil (A, B)
der **Stil, -e** style
still quiet
stimmen, gestimmt to be right; **das stimmt** that's all right; keep the change (9)
stimmt! that's right! (4)
stinkend smelly
das **Stipendium, Stipendien** scholarship (1)
die **Stirn, -en** forehead
das **Stirnband, ¨er** headband
die **Stirnhöhlenentzündung** frontal sinus inflammation
der **Stock, Stockwerke** floor, story; **im ersten Stock** on the second floor (6)
das **Stockwerk, -e** floor
der **Stoffwechsel** metabolism
stöhnen, gestöhnt to moan, sigh

stolpern, ist gestolpert to trip (8)
der **Stolz** pride
stören, gestört to disturb (3)
stoßen (stößt), stieß, ist gestoßen to hit
der **Stoßzahn, ¨e** tusk (12)
stottern, gestottert to stutter
der **Strafzettel, -** (parking or speeding) ticket (7)
der **Strand, ¨e** beach, shore (4, 7)
die **Straße, -n** street, road (6)
die **Straßenbahn, -en** streetcar (7)
sträuben, gesträubt to bristle; to resist
das **Streichholz, ¨er** match (9)
das **Streichquartett, -e** string quartet
die **Streife, -n** police patrol
streiten (streitet), stritt, gestritten to argue; to quarrel (8)
streng strict (8)
der **Strich, -e** line; stroke
stricken, gestrickt to knit (3)
das **Stroh** straw
der **Strom** electricity, power (9)
die **Struktur, -en** structure
die **Strumpfhose, -n** pantyhose (10)
stubenrein house-trained
das **Stück, -e** slice; piece (9)
der **Student, -en** (*wk.*) / die **Studentin, -nen** student (A, B)
das **Studentenheim, -e** dorm (2)
das **Studentenleben** student life (4)
das **Studentenwohnheim, -e** dormitory
die **Studie, -n** study
der **Studienabschluß** completion of one's studies
das **Studienfach, ¨er** academic subject (1)
die **Studiengebühr, -en** registration fee, tuition
studieren, studiert to study; to attend a university (1)
das **Studio, -s** studio (apartment)
das **Studium** university studies (1)
der **Stuhl, ¨e** chair (B, 2, 6)
die **Stunde, -n** hour (2)
stundenlang for hours
der **Stundenlohn, ¨e** hourly wage
der **Stundenplan, ¨e** schedule (1)
der **Sturz, ¨e** fall
stürzen, ist gestürzt to fall
die **Stussy-Jacke, -n** (*coll.*) Stussy jacket (brand name)
das **Subjekt, -e** subject
das **Substantiv, -e** noun
die **Suchanzeige, -n** housing-wanted ad (6)
suchen, gesucht to look for (1)
der **Süden** south
(das) **Südafrika** South Africa (B)
(das) **Südamerika** South America (B)
süddeutsch southern German (*adj.*)
(das) **Süddeutschland** southern Germany
südlich (von) south (of) (7)
südöstlich (von) southeast (of) (7)
südwestlich (von) southwest (of) (7)
der **Südwind** south wind
summen, gesummt to hum
der **Superlativ, -e** superlative
der **Supermarkt, ¨e** supermarket (5, 6); **im Supermarkt** in the supermarket
superschnell ultra-fast (7)
die **Suppe, -n** soup (3)
surfen, gesurft to surf, go surfing
süß sweet(ly) (4)
die **Süßigkeit, -en** sweet, candy (8)
das **Symbol, -e** symbol
die **Symbolfarbe, -n** symbol color
sympathisch congenial(ly), appealing(ly); sympathetic(ally)
das **Symptom, -e** symptom (11)
das **Synonym, -e** synonym
das ***SZ-Magazin*** = ***Süddeutsche Zeitung Magazin*** magazine section of Sunday edition of *SZ*.
die **Szene, -n** scene

T

das **T-Shirt, -s** T-shirt (2, 5)
tabellarisch tabular, in tabular form
die **Tabelle, -n** table; list
die **Tablette, -n** tablet, pill (11)
die **Tafel, -n** blackboard (A, B)
der **Tag, -e** day; **an welchem Tag?** on what day? (4); **der ganze Tag** all day long, the whole day (1); **guten Tag!** good afternoon!, hello! (*form.*) (A); **welcher Tag ist heute?** what day is today?
das **Tagebuch, ¨er** diary (4)
das **Tageblatt, ¨er** daily newspaper
tagen, getagt to convene
der **Tagesablauf, ¨e** daily routine; course of (one's) day
die **Tageszeitung, -en** daily newspaper
täglich daily (8)
das **Tal, ¨er** valley (7)
das **Talent, -e** talent (3)
(das) **Tanger** Tangier
der **Tank, -s** tank (7)
tanken, getankt to fill up (with gas)
die **Tankstelle, -n** gas station; **an der Tankstelle** at the gas station (5)
der **Tann** forest of fir trees
die **Tante, -n** aunt (B)
tanzen, getanzt to dance (1)
tapfer brave (8)
die **Tasche, -n** (hand)bag; purse; pocket (1, 5, 10)
das **Taschengeld, -er** pocket money, allowance
die **Taschenlampe, -n** flashlight (8, 9)
das **Taschentuch, ¨er** handkerchief (3)
die **Tasse, -n** cup (2, 5)
tasten, getastet to grope one's way
die **Tätigkeit, -en** activity (5)
der **Tatort, -e** scene of a crime
tätowieren, tätowiert to tattoo
tauchen, hat/ist getaucht to dive (3)
tauschen, getauscht to exchange
tausend thousand
tausendmal a thousand times
das **Taxi, -s** taxi (3, 7)
der **Taxifahrer, -** / die **Taxifahrerin, -nen** taxi driver (5)
die **Technik** technology (12)
technisch technical(ly); technological(ly)
der **Technische Überwachungsverein (TÜV)** Technical Control Board (*German agency that checks vehicular safety*)
der **Teddy, -s** / der **Teddybär, -en** (*wk.*) teddy bear (8)
der **Tee, -s** tea (4, 9)
der **Teegenuß, -genüsse** tea consumption
die **Teekanne, -n** teapot (9)
der **Teekessel, -** tea kettle (9)
der **Teich, -e** pond
der **Teil, -e** part, portion (7); **zum größten Teil** for the most part
teilen, geteilt to divide, share
teilmöbliert partially furnished
teil·nehmen (an + *dat.*) **(nimmt . . . teil), nahm . . . teil, teilgenommen** to participate in (*s.th.*)
die **Teilung, -en** division
das **Telefon, -e** telephone (A, 2); **am Telefon** on the phone (2)
der **Telefonanschluß, -anschlüsse** telephone line
das **Telefonbuch, ¨er** telephone book or directory
telefonieren, telefoniert to call (on the telephone) (4)
die **Telefonkarte, -n** telephone card (2)
die **Telefonnummer, -n** telephone number (1)
die **Telefonzelle, -n** telephone booth (2)
das **Telefonzimmer, -** telephone room
das **Telegramm, -e** telegram (2)
die **Telegraphenlinie, -n** telegraph line

der **Teller,** - plate (9)
die **Temperatur, -en** temperature
die **Temperaturschwankung, -en** temperature variation
das **Tempolimit** speed limit
(das) **Tennis** tennis (1); **Tennis spielen** to play tennis
der **Tennisball, ¨-e** tennis ball
der **Tennisschuh, -e** tennis shoe (A)
der **Tennisplatz, ¨-e** tennis court
der **Tennisschläger,** - tennis racket (2)
der **Tennisspieler,** - / die **Tennisspielerin, -nen** tennis player (8)
der **Teppich, -e** carpet, rug (2, 6)
der **Termin, -e** appointment (5, 11)
der **Terminkalender,** - appointment calendar (11)
die **Terrasse, -n** terrace, deck (6)
der **Terror** terrorism
der **Test, -s** test
die **Testfahrt, -en** test drive
der **Tetanus** tetanus (11)
teuer expensive (2)
der **Teufel,** - devil
der **Teutoburger Wald** Teutoburgian Woods
der **Text, -e** text (12)
die **Textilindustrie, -n** textile industry
das **Theater,** - theater (4)
das **Thema, Themen** topic, subject (4)
theoretisch theoretical(ly)
die **Theorie, -n** theory
der **Thunfisch** tuna
(das) **Thüringen** Thuringia
der **Thymian** thyme
der **Tibeter,** - / die **Tibeterin, -nen** Tibetan (*person*)
tief deep (7); deep(ly)
das **Tiefland, ¨-er** lowlands
das **Tiefseekabel,** - underwater cable
das **Tier, -e** animal (7)
der **Tierarzt, ¨-e** / die **Tierärztin, -nen** veterinarian (11)
der **Tip, -s** tip
tippen, getippt to type (6)
der **Tiroler,** - / die **Tirolerin, -nen** Tyrolean (*person*)
der **Tisch, -e** table (B); **den Tisch abräumen** to clear the table (3); **den Tisch decken** to set the table (3)
der **Tischler,** - / die **Tischlerin, -nen** carpenter
(das) **Tischtennis** table tennis (3)
der **Titel,** - title
der **Toaster,** - toaster (9)
die **Tochter, ¨** daughter (B)
der **Tod** death
tödlich fatal(ly)
die **Toilette, -n** toilet (6)
das **Toilettenpapier** toilet paper (4)
die **Toilettentasche, -n** cosmetic bag
tolerant tolerant(ly) (B)
tolerieren, toleriert to tolerate
toll great, neat (2); **einfach toll** simply great
die **Tollwut** rabies (12)
die **Tomate, -n** tomato (9)
die **Tomatensoße, -n** tomato sauce (9)
die **Tomatensuppe, -n** tomato soup
der **Ton, ¨-e** tone, note
das **Tonband, ¨-er** tape
der **Topf, ¨-e** pot, pan (5, 9)
der **Topflappen,** - potholder (5)
das **Tor, -e** gate
tot dead (8)
total total(ly); complete(ly)
totalitär totalitarian; in a totalitarian way
töten, getötet to kill (8)
der **Totenkopf, ¨-e** skull
der/die **Tote, -n** (ein **Toter**) dead person
die **Tour, -en** tour, trip
der **Tourismus** tourism (10)
der **Tourist, -en** (*wk.*) / die **Touristin, -nen** tourist
die **Touristenklasse** tourist class (5, 10)
das **Touristenmenu** (set) meal for tourists
die **Trachtenjacke, -n** *traditional jacket worn in southern Germany or Austria*
die **Tradition, -en** tradition (4)
traditionell traditional(ly)
tragen (trägt), trug, getragen to carry; to wear (A, 2)
der **Träger,** - / die **Trägerin, -nen** recipient (*of a prize*) (12)
der **Trainingsanzug, ¨-e** sweats (2)
trampen, ist getrampt to hitchhike
der **Tramper,** - / die **Tramperin, -nen** hitchhiker
der **Tramper-Rucksack, ¨-e** hitchhiker's backpack
transportieren, transportiert to transport, carry (7)
das **Transportmittel,** - means of transportation; vehicle (7)
sich **trauen, getraut** to dare; **sie traut sich nicht hinein** she doesn't dare go in
die **Trauer** grief
träumen (von + *dat.*), **geträumt** to dream (of, about) (8)
die **Traumküche, -n** kitchen of one's dreams
die **Traumwohnung, -en** apartment of one's dreams
traurig sad (B, 3)
(sich) **treffen (trifft), traf, getroffen** to meet (2); to arrange to meet; **Entscheidungen treffen** to make decisions; **treffen wir uns . . .** let's meet . . . (2)
treiben (treibt), trieb, getrieben to carry out, do; **Sport treiben** to do sports (2)
der Trend, -s trend
trennbar separable
(sich) **trennen, getrennt** to separate, break up (*people*) (7, 8)
die **Treppe, -n** stairway (6)
das **Treppenhaus, ¨-er** stairwell (10)
treten (tritt), trat, ist getreten to step
treu loyal, true (8)
die **Treue** loyalty
der **Trick, -s** trick
der **Triglyceridspiegel** triglyceride level
trimmen, getrimmt to trim (down) (*exercise in order to lose weight*)
trinken (trinkt), trank, getrunken to drink (1)
das **Trinkgeld, -er** tip (9)
trocken dry (11)
trotz (+ *gen.*) in spite of (12)
trotzdem in spite of that (8)
der **Tscheche, -n** (*wk.*) die **Tschechin, -nen** Czech (*person*)
(das) **Tschechien** Czech Republic (B)
(die) **Tschechoslowakei** Czechoslovakia
tschüs! bye-bye (*infor.*) (A), so long
tun (tut), tat, getan to do (A); **(es) tut mir leid** sorry!; **weh tun** to hurt (11)
(das) **Tunesien** Tunisia (B)
die **Tür, -en** door (A)
der **Türke, -n** (*wk.*) / die **Türkin, -nen** Turk (*person*) (12)
(die) **Türkei** Turkey (B)
türkisch Turkish (*adj.*) (B)
der **Turnschuh, -e** gym shoe
die **Türschwelle, -n** threshold
die **Tüte, -n** (paper or plastic) bag (11)
der **TÜV** = **Technischer Überwachungsverein** *agency that checks motor vehicles for safety hazards*
der **Typ, -en** (*coll.*) character, person, guy (B)
typisch typical(ly)

U

die **U-Bahn, -en** = **Untergrundbahn** metro, subway (7)
die **U-Bahnhaltestelle, -n** subway stop (10)

der **U-Bahnpreis, -e** subway fare
u.a. = **unter anderem** among others
üben, geübt to exercise; to practice
über (+ *dat./acc.*) over; above; across; **übers Wochenende** over the weekend (4)
überall everywhere (12)
überfahren (überfährt), überfuhr, überfahren to run over (*s.o.*) (11)
die **Überfahrt (über** + *acc.*) crossing (of)
überfliegen (überfliegt), überflog, überflogen to skim (through)
überhaupt anyway (4); at all; in fact, indeed
überlegen, überlegt to think about
überlisten, überlistet to outwit
übermorgen the day after tomorrow (8)
übermütig in high spirits
übernächsten: am übernächsten Morgen the morning after next
übernachten, übernachtet to stay overnight (6)
übernehmen (übernimmt), übernahm, übernommen to take on (responsibility) (12)
überprüfen, überprüft to check
die **Überraschung, -en** surprise
überreichen, überreicht to present (*s.th.*) to (*s.o.*)
übers = **über das** over the
die **Überschrift, -en** heading
übersetzen, übersetzt to translate (8)
der **Übersetzer, -** / die **Übersetzerin, -nen** translator (12)
die **Übersetzung, -en** translation
übertragen (überträgt), übertrug, übertragen to transfer
überwachen, überwacht to oversee, supervise
üblich usual, customary
übrigens by the way
die **Übung, -en** exercise (A)
die **Uhr, -en** clock (B); **wieviel Uhr ist es?** what time is it? (1); **um wieviel Uhr?** at what time? (1) **bis acht Uhr** until eight o'clock (2); **bis um vier Uhr** until four o'clock (4);
die **Uhrzeit, -en** time
um . . . zu (+ *inf.*) in order to (12)
um: um die Ecke around the corner (5); **um sechs (Uhr)** at six o'clock (1); **um wieviel Uhr?** at what time? (1)
um·fallen (fällt . . . um), fiel . . . um, ist umgefallen to fall over (8)
umfassen, umfaßt to comprise
die **Umfrage, -n** survey (4), poll
der **Umgang** contact
umgeben (umgibt), umgab, umgeben to surrround, enclose
die **Umgebung, -en** surrounding area, environs (5)
um·gehen (mit + *dat.*) **(geht . . . um), ging . . . um, ist umgegangen,** to go around; to associate (with *s.o.*)
um·kippen, ist umgekippt to knock over (11)
die **Umkleidekabine, -n** dressing room (5)
der **Umsatz, ¨-e** sales, returns
sich **um·sehen (sieht . . . um), sah . . . um, umgesehen** to look around (10)
der **Umstand, ¨-e** circumstance
um·steigen (steigt . . . um), stieg . . . um, ist umgestiegen to change (*from one vehicle to another*)
um·tauschen, umgetauscht to exchange (10)
die **Umweltverschmutzung** pollution
um·werfen (wirft . . . um), warf . . . um, umgeworfen to knock over/down
um·ziehen (zieht . . . um), zog . . . um, ist umgezogen to move (*to another apartment/house*); **sich umziehen** (*p.p. with* **haben**) to change clothes
unbedingt at all costs, absolutely
unbegabt untalented (12); **handwerklich unbegabt** not suited for manual labor
unbekannt unknown; unfamiliar
unbeschränkt unlimited
unbestimmt indefinite
und (*coord. conj.*) and (A, 11); **und so weiter (usw.)** and so forth (5)
unentschuldigt without giving any reason
unerwartet unexpected
der **Unfall, ¨-e** accident (4, 11)
der **Unfallbericht, -e** accident report (11)
das **Unfallkommando, -s** ambulance, emergency vehicle
die **Unfallstelle, -n** scene of the accident (11); accident site
unfreundlich unfriendly
ungarisch Hungarian (*adj.*)
(das) **Ungarn** Hungary (B)
ungeduldig impatient(ly) (11)
ungefähr approximately (7)
ungelernt unskilled
ungemütlich uncomfortable
ungenügend unsatisfactory; grade F (*in school*)
ungesalzen unsalted
ungesättigt unsaturated
ungewiß uncertain, unknown
ungewöhnlich unusual(ly)
ungezogen naughty, ill-mannered
unglücklich unhappy; unhappily
unhöflich impolite(ly)
die **Unhöflichkeit** impoliteness
die **Uni, -s** = **Universität -en** (*coll.*) university (B); **auf der Uni** at the university (1); **zur Uni** to the university (1)
die **Universität, -en** university (1, 5); **auf der Universität** at the university (5); **zur Universität gehen** to go to the university
die **Unizeitung, -en** university newspaper (4)
die **Union, -en** union
die **Universitätsbibliothek, -en** university library
die **Universitätsstadt, ¨-e** university town
unklug unwise(ly)
unkonventionell unconventional(ly)
unkonzentriert lacking in concentration
unlängst not long ago; recently
unmöglich impossible
unpraktisch impractical(ly)
die **Unpünktlichkeit** lateness
unrhythmisch unrhythmical(ly)
unruhig restless; agitated; uneasy
uns us (*acc./dat.*)
die **Unschuld** innocence
unser, unsere, unseren our
der **Unsinn** nonsense (12)
unsympathisch uncongenial(ly), disagreeable; disagreeably; unpleasant(ly)
unter (+ *dat./acc.*) among, below, beneath (6); under; **unter anderem** among other things
die **Unterdrückung, -en** suppression, oppression
die **Untergrundbahn, -en (U-Bahn)** metro, subway
der **Unterhalt** living
sich **unterhalten (unterhält), unterhielt, unterhalten** to converse (8)
die **Unterhaltung, -en** conversation; entertainment (3)
der **Unterhaltungsroman, -e** entertainment novel
das **Unterhemd, -en** undershirt (10)
die **Unterhose, -n** underpants, shorts (10)
die **Unterkunft, ¨-e** lodging (10)
das **Unternehmen, -** company
die **Unternehmung, -en** enterprise
der **Unterricht** class, instruction (8)
unterrichten, unterrichtet to teach, in-

struct (5)
die **Unterrichtsveranstaltung, -en** organizing of class
sich **unterscheiden (unterscheidet), unterschied, unterschieden** to be different
der **Unterschied, -e** difference
unterschiedlich different; various
unterschreiben (unterschreibt), unterschrieb, unterschrieben to sign (1)
die **Unterschrift, -en** signature (1)
unterstreichen (unterstreicht), unterstrich, unterstrichen to underline
untersuchen, untersucht to investigate; to examine (5)
das **Unterthema, -themen** subtopic
der **Untertitel, -** subtitle
die **Unterwäsche** underwear (10)
unterwegs on the road (8); in transit; **geschäftlich unterwegs sein** to be away on business
untrennbar inseparable
unveränderlich unchangeable
unwillig reluctant(ly)
der **Uranus** Uranus (4)
der **Urin** urine
die **Urkunde, -n** certificate (*e.g.* of merit)
der **Urlaub** vacation (5); **in Urlaub fahren** to go (away) on vacation; **Urlaub machen** to take a vacation
der **Urlauber, -** vacationer
das **Urlaubsland, ¨er** vacation country
der **Urlaubsort, -e** holiday resort
der **Ursprung, ¨e** origin
ursprünglich original(ly)
(die) **USA** (*pl.*) USA (B)
usw. = und so weiter and so forth / on
die **Utopie, -n** utopia

V

der **Valentinstag** Valentine's Day (4)
die **Variation, -en** variation
die **Vase, -n** vase (3)
der **Vater, ¨** father (B)
der **Vati, -s** dad, daddy
sich **verabreden, verabredet** to make a date
die **Verabredung, -en** appointment; date (11)
das **Verabschieden** leave-taking (A)
sich **verabschieden, verabschiedet** to say good-bye
(sich) **verändern, verändert** to change
veranstalten, veranstaltet to put on (a party)
die **Veranstaltung, -en** public event
die **Verantwortung, -en** responsibility (12)
das **Verb, -en** verb
der **Verband, ¨e** bandage (11)
die **Verbendung, -en** verb ending
verbinden (verbindet), verband, verbunden to connect; to dress (*wounds*)
das **Verbot, -e** prohibition (7)
verboten forbidden (9)
die **Verbraucheraufklärung** consumer information
verbrauchen, verbraucht to use up, consume
verbrennen (verbrennt), verbrannte, verbrannt to burn; incinerate (12); **sich (die Zunge) verbrennen** to burn (one's tongue) (11)
verbringen (verbringt), verbrachte, verbracht to spend (*time*)
verdächtig suspicious
verdattert (*coll.*) bewildered
die **Verdauung** digestion
verdienen, verdient to earn (4)
die **Vereinten Nationen** the United Nations
der **Verdienst, -e** income
verdutzt taken aback
vereinigen, vereinigt to unite
die **Vereinsteilnahme** membership in a club
die **Verfassung, -en** constitution; state (of health or mind); **körperliche und geistige Verfassung** physical and mental state
verfehlen, verfehlt to miss, not to notice (10)
verfilmen, verfilmt to make a movie of
verfolgen, verfolgt to persecute (12)
verfügen (über + *acc.*), verfügt to have (*s.th.*)
vergehen (vergeht), verging, vergangen to elapse, pass; **5 Jahre sind vergangen** five years have passed
vergessen (vergißt), vergaß, vergessen to forget (2)
vergiften, vergiftet to poison (8)
der **Vergleich, -e** comparison
das **Vergnügen** entertainment; pleasure (2)
sich **verhalten (verhält), verhielt, verhalten** to behave, act
das **Verhaltensmuster, -** behavior pattern
verharren, verharrt to remain
sich **verheiraten (mit + *dat.*), verheiratet** to get married to
verheiratet married (1, 12); **frisch verheiratet** newly married
verhelfen (zu + *dat.*) (verhilft), verhalf, verholfen to help to get/achieve (*s.th.*)
verhindern, verhindert to prevent
verhungern, ist verhungert to starve (12)
verjagen, verjagt to chase away
der **Verkauf, ¨e** sale
verkaufen, verkauft to sell (5); **zu verkaufen** for sale
der **Verkäufer, -** / die **Verkäuferin, -nen** salesperson (5)
das **Verkaufsgespräch, -e** sales talk
der **Verkaufstag, -e** day when a store is open for business
der **Verkehr** traffic (11)
das **Verkehrsmittel, -** means of transportation; **die öffentlichen Verkehrsmittel** (*pl.*) public transportation (7)
das **Verkehrsschild, -er** traffic sign (7)
der **Verkehrsstau, -s** traffic jam
der **Verkehrstag, -e** traffic day
verlassen (verläßt), verließ, verlassen to leave; to abandon (11)
sich **verlaufen (verläuft), verlief, verlaufen** to get lost
verlegen, verlegt to move, relocate
verletzen, verletzt to harm, injure; **sich verletzen** to injure oneself (11); **schwer verletzt** critically injured (11)
der/die **Verletzte, -n** (ein **Verletzter**) injured person (11)
die **Verletzung, -en** injury; violation
sich **verlieben (in + *acc.*), verliebt** to fall in love (with) (4, 8, 12)
verlieren (verliert), verlor, verloren to lose (7)
sich **verloben mit, verlobt** to get engaged to (12)
vermieten, vermietet to rent (out) (6)
der **Vermieter, -** / die **Vermieterin, -nen** landlord/landlady (6)
vermischen, vermischt to mix (9)
vernehmen (vernimmt), vernahm, vernommen to interrogate; **vernommen werden** to be interrogated
vernünftig sensible; sensibly
verpassen, verpaßt to miss
verquer: heute ist alles verquer everything is going wrong today
verraten (verrät), verriet, verraten to disclose, give away (*a secret*)
verreisen, ist verreist to go on a trip (3)
verrückt crazy (B); in a zany manner
die **Versammlung, -en** gathering
versäumen, versäumt neglected

verschenken, verschenkt to give away
verschieden different, various (9)
verschlafen (verschläft), verschlief, verschlafen to oversleep
verschlingen (verschlingt), verschlang, verschlungen to devour
verschnupft suffering from a cold; **verschnupft sein** have a cold
verschränken, verschränkt to fold (arms); to cross (legs)
verschütten, verschüttet to spill
verschwinden (verschwindet), verschwand, ist verschwunden to disappear (12)
versetzen, versetzt to go into the next grade
die **Versetzung, -en** advancement (*into the next higher grade*)
die **Versicherung, -en** insurance (5)
versorgen (mit + *dat.*), versorgt to supply (*s.o.*) with (*s.th.*); to take care of
die **Verspätung, -en** lateness
versprechen (verspricht), versprach, versprochen to promise (7)
der **Verstand** reason; mind; sense
verständigen, verständigt to notify
verstauen, verstaut to stow (7)
(sich) **verstecken, versteckt** to hide (8)
verstehen (versteht), verstand, verstanden to understand (4)
verstopft blocked (nose)
verstummen, ist verstummt to fall silent
versuchen, versucht to try, to attempt (8, 11)
die **Verteidigung, -en** defense
der **Vertrag, ⸚e** contract (12)
vertreiben (vertreibt), vertrieb, vertrieben to drive (*s.o./s.th.*) away, expel
die **Vertreterkonferenz, -en** deputy meeting
verursachen, verursacht to cause
die **Verwaltung, -en** administration
sich **verwandeln (in + *acc.*), verwandelt** to change into (8)
der/die **Verwandte, -n** (ein **Verwandter**) relative (2)
verwaltungstätig administrative
verwenden, verwendet to use
verwundert surprised
verwunschen cursed (8)
verwünschen, verwünscht to cast a spell on; to curse (8)
verzaubert bewitched
das **Verzeichnis, -se** list; index
die **Verzeihung** forgiveness
verzichten (auf + *acc.*), verzichtet to do without, renounce (*s.th.*)
der **Vetter, -n** (male) cousin (B)
vgl. = **vergleiche** compare
das **Video, -s** video (8)
der **Videorecorder, -** video recorder (A, 2)
der **Videoladen, ⸚** video shop
viel (*sg.*) much, a lot; **viele** (*pl.*) many (A) **viel Glück!** lots of luck!, good luck! (3); **viel Spaß!** have fun! (A); **vielen Dank!** many thanks! (10)
vielleicht perhaps (2)
die **Vier: eine Vier** unsatisfactory (*school grade*) (3)
vier four (A)
viereckig rectangular
viert- fourth (4)
der **Viertakt-Benzinmotor** four-stroke gas engine
das **Viertel, -** fourth; **um Viertel vor vier** at a quarter to four (1)
die **Viertelstunde, -n** quarter hour (6)
vierundzwanzig twenty-four (A)
vierzehn fourteen (A)
vierzig forty (A)
violett violet
der **Virologe, -n** (*wk.*) / die **Virologin, -nen** virologist
der **Virus, Viren** virus
der **Virusforscher, -** / die **Virusforscherin, -nen** virus researcher
die **Virusgrippe** virus flu
die **Virusvariation, -en** virus variation
das **Visum, Visa** visa (7)
das **Vitamin, -e** vitamin
vitaminreich vitamin-rich
der **Vogel, ⸚** bird (12)
das **Volk, ⸚er** people
das **Volksfest, -e** public festival; fair
voll full (10); full of; fully; **voll Angst** filled with fear
der **Vollbart, ⸚e** beard
das **Völlegefühl** feeling of fullness
der **Volleyball, ⸚e** volleyball (1)
völlig completely
vollkommen perfect(ly), flawless(ly); completely
die **Vollkornnudeln** whole wheat noodles
voll·tanken, vollgetankt to fill up (with gas) (5)
vom = **von dem** of/from the
von (+ *dat.*) from; of; by (*authorship*) (A, 3, 10); **von allein** on one's own; **von der Arbeit** from work (3); **von je** from time immemorial; **von je 100 Jungen** out of 100 young men; **von jetzt an** from now on; **von nebenan** from next door (5)
vor (+ *dat./acc.*) in front of; before; ago; because of; **vor allem** above all; **vor allen Dingen** above all; **vor zwei Tagen** two days ago (4)
die **Voraussetzung, -en** prerequisite
vorbei over, past (8); along
vorbei·kommen (an + *dat.*) (kommt . . . vorbei), kam . . . vorbei, ist vorbeigekommen to come/stop/pass by (3)
vorbei·gehen (an + *dat.*) (geht . . . vorbei), ging . . . vorbei, ist vorbeigegangen to go by (10)
vor·bereiten, vorbereitet to prepare
die **Vorbeugung (gegen + *acc.*)** prevention (of)
das **Vorbild, -er** role model, idol (8)
vorchristlich before Christ
der **Vorfahre, -n** (*wk.*) ancestor (10)
die **Vorfahrt** right-of-way (7)
vorgestern the day before yesterday (4)
der **Vorhang, ⸚e** drapery (6); curtain; **der Eiserne Vorhang** the Iron Curtain
vor·kommen (kommt . . . vor), kam . . . vor, ist vorgekommen to occur
vor·lesen (liest . . . vor), las . . . vor, vorgelesen to read aloud (8)
die **Vorlesung, -en** (*university*) lecture (4)
der **Vormittag, -e** late morning (4); **am Vormittag** in the morning
vormittags in the morning, mornings
das **Vormittagsprogramm, -e** morning program
der **Vorname, -n** (*wk.*) first name (A, 1)
vornehm noble, distinguished
vorrömisch pre-Roman
vors = **vor das** in front of the
der **Vorschlag, ⸚e** suggestion (5)
vor·schlagen (schlägt . . . vor), schlug . . . vor, vorgeschlagen to suggest (5), to propose
die **Vorschrift, -en** rule, regulation; **Vorschriften machen** to dictate
vorsichtig cautious(ly)
vor·singen (singt . . . vor), sang . . . vor, vorgesungen to sing (*s.th.*) to (*s.o.*) (5)
vor·sorgen, vorgesorgt to provide
die **Vorspeise, -n** appetizer (9)
das **Vorstandsmitglied, -er** committee member (12)
vor·stellen, vorgestellt to introduce (8); to present; **sich** (*dat.*) **etwas vorstellen**

to imagine (*s.th.*) (6, 10)
der **Vorteil, -e** advantage (7)
das **Vorurteil, -e** prejudice (12)
der **Vorwagen** previously owned car
das **Vorwort, -e** preface
der **Vulkan, -e** volcano (10)
der **VW** = **Volkswagen** *make of car*

W

wachsen (wächst), wuchs, ist gewachsen to grow (8)
der **Wachtmeister, -** (*police*) constable
der **Wagen, -** car (7)
der **Waggon, -s** train car (7)
die **Wahl, -en** choice; election; **zur Wahl** to choose from
wählen, gewählt to select; to elect
das **Wahlpflichtfach, ¨-er** elective
das **Wahlrecht** right to vote
wahnsinnig insane, crazy
wahr true (3)
während (+ *gen.*) during (11, 12)
wahrhaftig real(ly), truthful(ly)
die **Wahrheit, -en** truth
wahrscheinlich probably (11)
die **Währung, -en** currency
das **Wahrzeichen** symbol, landmark
das **Waisenkind, -er** orphan
der **Wald, ¨-er** forest, woods (2, 7); **im Wald laufen** to run in the woods (2)
der **Walkman, -s** walkman (10)
walten, gewaltet to rule
der **Walzer, -** waltz (3)
die **Wand, ¨-e** wall (B); **das Bild an die Wand hängen** to hang the picture on the wall
der **Wanderer, -** hiker; traveler
wandern, ist gewandert to hike (1)
die **Wanderung, -en** hike (7)
der **Wandervogelrucksack, ¨-e** globetrotter's backpack
die **Wange, -n** cheek
wann when (B, 1); **wann sind Sie geboren?** when were you born? (1)
warm warm (B); hot; (*of room / apartment*) utilities / heat included (6)
die **Warmluftheizung** heating
die **Warnblinkanlage, -n** hazard/warning light, flasher(s) (*on a car*)
das **Warndreieck, -e** warning triangle (*positioned near a disabled car*)
warnen, gewarnt to warn (7)
(das) **Warschau** Warsaw
die **Wartehalle, -n** waiting room (10)
warten (auf + *acc.*), **gewartet** to wait (for) (7)
der **Warteraum, ¨-e** waiting room
warum why (3)
was what (A, B); **was fehlt?** what's missing? (A); **was läuft im Kino?** what's playing at the movies? (2); **was sind Sie von Beruf?** what's your profession? (1)
das **Waschbecken, -** (wash) basin (6)
die **Wäsche** laundry (4)
(sich) **waschen (wäscht), wusch, gewaschen** to wash (*o.s.*) (2, 11)
der **Wäschetrockner, -** clothes dryer (9)
die **Waschküche, -n** laundry room (6)
die **Waschmaschine, -n** washing machine (6)
der **Waschsalon, -s** laundromat (10)
das **Wasser** water
der **Wasserhahn, ¨-e** faucet (5)
die **Wasserverseuchung** water pollution
der **Wasservogel, ¨-** water fowl (12)
wechseln, gewechselt to change; **Geld wechseln** to (ex)change money
wecken, geweckt to wake (*s.o.*) up (8)
der **Wecker, -** alarm clock (2)
das **Weckerklingeln** ringing of an / the alarm clock
weg away; **wie weit weg?** how far away? (6)
der **Weg, -e** way; road; path (10); **den Weg beschreiben** to give directions; **nach dem Weg fragen** to ask for directions; **sich auf den Weg machen** to go on one's way, set off
weg·bringen (bringt . . . weg), brachte . . . weg, weggebracht to take out (5); to take away
wegen (+ *gen.*) on account of; about; because of (6, 12)
weg·fahren (fährt . . . weg), fuhr . . . weg, ist weggefahren to drive off, leave
weg·gehen (geht . . . weg), ging . . . weg, ist weggegangen to leave, to go away (4)
weg·laufen (läuft . . . weg), lief . . . weg, ist weggelaufen to run away
weg·schaffen, weggeschafft to get rid of
weg·stellen, weggestellt to put away (5)
weg·tragen (trägt . . . weg), trug . . . weg, weggetragen to carry away (8)
weh: weh tun, (tut weh), tat weh, weh getan to hurt (11)
der **Wehrdienst** military service (12)
(das) **Weihnachten** Christmas (4)
der **Weihnachtsbrauch, ¨-e** Christmas custom
das **Weihnachtsgeschenk, -e** Christmas present (5)
die **Weihnachtskarte, -n** Christmas card
der **Weihnachtsmann, ¨-er** Santa Claus; Father Christmas
die **Weihnachtstradition, -en** Christmas tradition
weil (*subord. conj.*) because (3, 11, 12)
die **Weile** while; **eine ganze Weile** a good while
die **Weimarer Republik** Weimar Republic
der **Wein, -e** wine
der **Weinberg, -e** vineyard
weinen, geweint to cry (3)
die **Weinflasche, -n** wine bottle
das **Weinglas, ¨-er** wine glass (5)
der **Weinkeller, -** wine cellar (6)
das **Weinregal, -e** wine shelf
die **Weintraube, -n** grape (9)
weisen (weist), wies, gewiesen to show
weiß white (A)
(das) **Weißrußland** Belorussia (B)
weit far; **wie weit weg?** how far away? (6)
weiter (*adj.*) additional; (*adv.*) farther; further; **immer weiter** on and on; **und so weiter** and so forth (5)
weiter·fahren (fährt . . . weiter), fuhr . . . weiter, ist weitergefahren to keep on driving (10), drive farther
die **Weiterfahrt** continuation of one's journey
weiter·gehen (geht . . . weiter), ging . . . weiter, ist weitergegangen to keep on walking (10)
weiter·studieren, weiterstudiert to keep on studying, continue with (*one's*) studies
weitgereist well-traveled
die **Weizenkeime** (*pl.*) wheat germ
welch-: welche Farbe hat . . . ? what color is . . . ? (A); **welche Sprache(n)** what language(s) (B); **welcher Tag** what day (B); **welches Datum ist heute?** what is today's date? (4); **welches Land** what country (B)
die **Welt, -en** world (7); **aus aller Welt** from all over the world
die **Welle, -n** wave
der **Weltatlas** atlas of the world
weltbekannt world famous
weltberühmt world famous
das **Weltbild, -er** world view
der **Weltkrieg, -e** world war; **im Ersten/Zweiten Weltkrieg** in World War I/II
weltweit worldwide
wem whom (*dat.*) (4)

wen whom (*acc.*) (4)
wenig: am wenigsten the least (9)
wenigstens at least (4)
wenn (*subord. conj.*) if; when(ever) (2, 3, 11); **wenn ja** if so
wer who (A, B)
die **Werbeagentur, -en** advertising agency
die **Werbung, -en** advertisement, promotion
werden (wird), wurde, ist geworden to become (5); **was willst du werden?** what do you want to become?
werfen (wirft), warf, geworfen to throw (3)
das **Werk, -e** work; product (8)
die **Werksanlage, -n** factory
die **Werkstatt, ¨-en** repair shop, garage (5)
der **Werkstoff, -e** material
die **Werkswohnung, -en** company-owned apartment
der **Werktag, -e** working day
das **Werkzeug, -e** tool (9)
der **Wert, -e** value
wertvoll valuable, expensive (2)
weshalb why
(das) **Westdeutschland** (*former*) West Germany
der **Westen** west
westlich (*adj.*) western; **(von** + *dat.*) west of (7)
die **Westwindzone** Western zone
der **Wettbewerb, -e** contest
das **Wetter** weather (B); **bei kaltem Wetter** in cold weather
der **Wetterbericht, -e** weather report; weather forecast
wichtig important (2)
wie how; **wie fühlst du dich?** how do you feel? (3); **wie heißen Sie?** (*for.*), **wie heißt du?** (*infor.*) what's your name? (A); **wie schreibt man das?** how do you spell that? (B); **wie spät ist es?** what time is it? (1); **wie viele . . . ?** how many . . . ? (A)
wieder again; **schon wieder** once again (3)
wieder·aufbauen, wiederaufgebaut to reconstruct
wieder·finden (findet . . . wieder), fand . . . wieder, wiedergefunden to find again
wiederholen, wiederholt to repeat (10)
das **Wiederhören: auf Wiederhören!** good-bye, until we talk again (*on the telephone*) (6)
wieder·kommen (kommt . . . wieder), kam . . . wieder, ist wiedergekommen to come back (5)
das **Wiedersehen: auf Wiedersehen!** good-bye!, until we see each other again!
(das) **Wien** Vienna
Wiener Viennese (*adj.*)
die **Wiese, -n** meadow, pasture (7)
wieso why; how is it (that), how come
wieviel: wieviel Uhr ist es? what time is it? (1)
wild wild; **wildes Camping** wilderness camping; camping outside designated areas (10)
die **Wildente, -n** wild duck
das **Wildschwein, -e** wild boar (12)
der **Wind, -e** wind (8)
windig windy (B)
windsurfen gehen (geht . . . windsurfen), ging windsurfen, ist windsurfen gegangen to go windsurfing (1)
der **Winter, -** winter (B)
der **Wintermantel, ¨** winter coat
der **Winterstiefel, -** winter boot
die **Wintertemperatur, -en** winter temperature
wir we
wirken, gewirkt to work, to take effect (11)
wirklich really (B)
die **Wirklichkeit, -en** reality; **in Wirklichkeit** actually
die **Wirkung, -en** effect
der **Wirt, -e** / die **Wirtin, -nen** host/hostess; innkeeper; barkeeper
die **Wirtschaft** economics (1)
wirtschaftlich economical(ly)
die **Wirtschaftskunde** economics
das **Wirtschaftswunder** economic miracle
das **Wirtschaftszentrum, -zentren** economic center
wischen, gewischt to wipe (7)
wissen (weiß), wußte, gewußt to know (2); **ich weiß nicht** I don't know
der **Wissenschaftler, -** / die **Wissenschaftlerin, -nen** scientist (8)
wissenschaftlich scientific
der **Witz, -e** joke; **Witze erzählen** to tell jokes (3)
witzig funny, amusing(ly)
wo where (A, B); **wo willst du denn hin?** where are you going? (A)
wobei with what; where; whereby
die **Woche, -n** week; **in der Woche** during the week (1); **jede Woche** every week (3); **letzte Woche** last week (4)
die **Wochenarbeitszeit** working hours per week
die **Wochenendbeschäftigung, -en** weekend activity
das **Wochenende, -n** weekend; **am Wochenende** over the weekend (1); **letztes Wochenende** last weekend (4); **übers Wochenende** over the weekend
das **Wochenendhaus, ¨-er** weekend cabin/cottage
der **Wochenendheimfahrer, -** one who goes home for the weekend
der **Wochenmarkt, ¨-e** weekly market
wofür what for (9)
woher from where (B)
wohin where to (3)
wohl probably (12)
sich **wohl·fühlen, wohlgefühlt** to feel well (11)
wohnen, gewohnt (in) to live (in) (B)
die **Wohngelegenheit, -en** housing opportunity
die **Wohngemeinschaft, -en** shared housing (6)
das **Wohnhaus, ¨-er** apartment building (12)
das **Wohnheim, -e** state-subsidized apartment building (12)
die **Wohnmöglichkeit, -en** living arrangement
der **Wohnort, -e** place of residence (1)
die **Wohnqualität, -en** living quality
der **Wohntraum, ¨-e** dream about where and how s.o. wants to live
die **Wohnung, -en** apartment (1, 2)
die **Wohnungsanzeige, -n** apartment rental ad
die **Wohnungssuche** search for an apartment; **auf Wohnungssuche** looking for a room/an apartment
die **Wohnungsvermittlung, -en** rental agency; housing office
das **Wohnviertel, -** residential district
der **Wohnwagen, -** mobile home
das **Wohnzimmer, -** living room (6)
der **Wohnzimmertisch, -e** living room table (6)
die **Wohnzufriedenheit** satisfaction with living conditions
der **Wolf, ¨-e** wolf (8)
die **Wolga** Volga (River)
der **Wolkenkratzer, -** skyscraper (6)
wollen, gewollt to want; to intend, to plan (to) (3)

womit with what, by what means
woran at/on/of what; **woran denkst du?** what are you thinking of?
das **Wort, ¨er** word
das **Wörterbuch, ¨er** dictionary (2)
der **Wortschatz, ¨e** vocabulary (A)
worüber about what
wovon about what
die **Wunde, -n** wound (11)
das **Wunder, -** miracle, wonder; **kein Wunder** no wonder (4)
wunderbar wonderful(ly), marvellous(ly)
wundersam strange
wunderschön exceedingly beautiful (10)
der **Wunsch, ¨e** wish
wünschen, gewünscht to wish
der **Wunschtraum, ¨e** wishful dream
der **Wunschzettel, -** wish list (*of things one would like to have*)
die **Wurst, ¨e** sausage; cold cuts (9)
das **Würstchen, -** sausage; frank(furter); hot dog (9)
die **Wurstwaren** (*pl.*) sausages
würzen, gewürzt to season (9)
die **Wüste, -n** desert (7)
wütend angry (3)

X

x-te (*adj.*) (*coll.*) umpteenth; **zum x-ten Mal** for the umpteenth time

Y

die **Yucca-Palme, -n** yucca palm

Z

z.B. = zum Beispiel
die **Zahl, -en** figure, number (A)
zahlen, gezahlt to pay (for) (5); **Miete zahlen** to pay rent; **zahlen, bitte** the check, please
zählen, gezählt to count (A)
zahm tame (12), domesticated
der **Zahn, ¨e** tooth (11); **sich die Zähne putzen** to brush one's teeth (11)
der **Zahnarzt, ¨e** / die **Zahnärztin, -nen** dentist (5)
die **Zahnarztkosten** (*pl.*) dental costs
zahnärztlich dental
die **Zahnbürste, -n** toothbrush
die **Zahnheilkunde** dentistry
die **Zahnmedizin** dentistry
die **Zahnschmerzen** (*pl.*) toothache (11)
die **Zange, -n** pliers; tongs (9)
zart tender(ly) (9)
die **Zärtlichkeit** tenderness
der **Zaun, ¨e** fence
das **Zebra, -s** zebra (12)
der **Zebrastreifen, -** crosswalk (10)
zehn ten (A)
zehnt- tenth (4)
das **Zeichen, -** sign
der **Zeichenkurs, -e** drawing class
zeichnen, gezeichnet to draw, to sketch (3, 5)
die **Zeichnung, -en** drawing (9)
zeigen, gezeigt to show
die **Zeile, -n** line
die **Zeit, -en** time (1); **in kurzer Zeit** in a short time; **in letzter Zeit** lately, recently; **lange Zeit** (for) a long time; **nach einiger Zeit** after a while; **zu dieser Zeit** at this time; **zur Zeit** at present
die **Zeitschrift, -en** magazine
die **Zeitschriftenart, -en** kind of magazine
die **Zeitung, -en** newspaper (2); **Zeitung lesen** to read the newspaper (1)
der **Zeitungskurier, -e** newspaper deliverer
der **Zeitungsladen, ¨** newspaper shop
die **Zelle, -n** cell
das **Zelt, -e** tent (2, 5)
zelten, gezeltet to camp (1), to go camping
der **Zentimeter, -** centimeter
zentral central(ly) (10)
die **Zentralheizung, -en** central heating (6)
der **Zeppelin, -e** zeppelin (7)
zerbrechen (zerbricht), zerbrach, hat / ist zerbrochen to break into pieces
zerreißen (zerreißt), zerriß, zerrissen to tear (8)
zerstören, zerstört to destroy
das **Zeug** stuff
der **Zeuge, -n** (*wk.*) / die **Zeugin, -nen** witness (11)
das **Zeugnis, -se** report card (3)
der **Ziegel, -** clay tile
ziehen (zieht), zog, ist gezogen to move (2); (*p.p. with* **haben**) to pull (9); to draw (*a weapon*); (**aus** + *dat.*) to take out
das **Ziel, -e** destination; goal (10)
ziemlich rather (2)
die **Zigarette, -n** cigarette (4)
die **Zigarre, -n** cigar (7)
das **Zimmer, -** room (2)
die **Zimmerpflanze, -n** indoor plant (6)
die **Zimmersuche** search for a room (*to rent*)
die **Zinsen** (*pl.*) interest
die **Zipfelmütze, -n** pointed cap
zirka circa, about; approximately
der **Zirkus, -se** circus (8)
das **Zitat, -e** quotation
die **Zitrone, -n** lemon (9)
zittern, gezittert to quote
der **Zoo, -s** zoo (10)
der **Zoodirektor, -** / die **Zoodirektorin, -nen** zoo director (12)
zu closed; too; **zu schwer** too heavy (4); too difficult
zu (+ *dat.*) to; for (*an occasion*); for the purpose of; **zu Fuß** on foot (3); **zu Hause** at home (10); **zum Arzt** to the doctor; **zum Geburtstag** for someone's birthday (2); **zum Mittagessen** for lunch; **zur Uni** to the university
zu·bereiten, zubereitet to prepare (*food*) (9)
die **Zubereitung, -en** preparation (9)
zu·binden, zugebunden to tie shut (9)
züchten, gezüchtet to breed
der **Zucker** sugar (9)
die **Zuckerfabrik, -en** sugar factory
zu·decken, zugedeckt to cover (*with a blanket*) (11)
zudem moreover, furthermore
zu·drücken, zugedrückt to squeeze shut; **ein Auge zudrücken** to look the other way
zuerst first (7)
der **Zug, ¨e** train (7, 10)
das **Zugfahren** traveling by train
die **Zugfahrkarte, -n** train ticket (6)
zugleich at the same time
die **Zugnummer, -n** train number
zu·hören (+ *dat.*), **zugehört** to listen (to) (A, 10); **hören Sie zu** listen (A)
zu·kommen (auf + *acc.*) **(kommt . . . zu), kam . . . zu, ist zugekommen** to approach or come up to (*s.o.*)
die **Zukunft** future (12)
zukünftig future (*adj.*)
die **Zukunftsangst, ¨e** fear about the future
zuletzt finally (10)
zum = zu dem to the
zum Beispiel (z.B.) for example (3)
zu·machen, zugemacht to close (3)
zumindest at least
die **Zunge, -n** tongue (11)
zur = zu der to the
(das) **Zürich** Zurich
zurück back (8); **hin und zurück** round trip

zurück·führen (auf + *acc.*), **zurückgeführt** to trace back (to)
zurück·kehren, ist zurückgekehrt to return
zurück·klettern, zurückgeklettert to climb back
zurück·kommen (kommt . . . zurück), kam . . . zurück, ist zurückgekommen to come back, return (6)
zusammen together (2)**: alles zusammen** (everything) together; one check (5)
der **Zusammenhang, ¨-e** connection; coherence
zusammen·falten, zusammengefaltet to fold up
die **Zusammenfassung, -en** summary
zusammen·packen, zusammengepackt to pack up
zusammen·sein (+ *dat.*) **(ist . . . zusammen), war . . . zusammen, ist zusammengewesen** to be together (with)
zusammen·stoßen (stößt . . . zusammen), stieß . . . zusammen, ist zusammengestoßen to crash (11)
zu·schauen, zugeschaut to watch
die **Zuschriften** (*pl.*) application in writing
zuschulden: sich (*dat.*) **etwas zuschulden kommen lassen** do (any) wrong
zu·sehen (sieht . . . zu), sah . . . zu, zugesehen to observe, look on (7)
die **Zutaten** (*pl.*) ingredients (9)
zuviel too much
zuvor before(hand); **so gesund wie nie zuvor** healthier than ever before
zu·wandern, ist zugewandert to immigrate
zu·wenden (wendet . . . zu), wand . . . zu, zugewandt to turn to (*s.o./s.th.*)
zwanzig twenty (A); **um zwanzig nach fünf** at twenty after/past five (1)
der **Zwanzigmarkschein, -e** twenty-mark note (9)
zwanzigst- twentieth (4)
zwar of course; admittedly, to be sure; (while) it's time that . . . ; **und zwar** namely; to be more precise
die **Zwei: eine Zwei** good (*school grade*) (3)
zwei two (A)
der **Zweifel, -** doubt; **im Zweifel** in question
zweifelhaft doubtful
die **Zweigstelle, -n** branch office
zweimal twice (5); **zweimal im Jahr** twice a year
zweit- second (4); **am zweitbesten** second-best
zweiundzwanzig twenty-two (A)
der **Zwerg, -e** dwarf (8)
die **Zwiebel, -n** onion (9)
die **Zwillinge** (*pl.*) twins
zwingen (zwingt), zwang, gezwungen to force
zwischen (+ *dat./acc.*) between (7); among
zwölf twelve (A)
zwölft- twelfth (4)

Englisch-Deutsch

This list contains all the words from the chapter vocabulary sections.

A

to abandon **verlassen (verläßt), verließ, verlassen** (11)
able: to be able **können (kann), konnte, gekonnt** (3)
about **wegen** (+ *gen.*) (6)
above (*adv.*) **oben;** (*prep.*) **über** (+ *acc.* / *dat.*) (10)
abroad **im Ausland** (6)
academic subject **das Fach, ¨er** (1)
accident **der Unfall, ¨e** (4, 11); accident report **der Unfallbericht, -e** (11); scene of the accident **die Unfallstelle, -n** (11)
accordeon **das Akkordeon, -s** (4)
account: bank account **das Konto, Konten** (5); to open a bank account **ein Konto eröffnen** (5); on account of **wegen** (6)
acquainted: to be acquainted with **kennen (kennt), kannte, gekannt** (3); to get acquainted with **kennen·lernen, kennengelernt** (1)
across **gegenüber** (+ *dat.*) (6); across from **gegenüber von** (10); right across the way **gleich gegenüber** (6)
activity **die Tätigkeit, -en** (5)
actor **der Schauspieler, -** (8)
actress **die Schauspielerin, -nen** (8)
actually **eigentlich** (3)
ad **die Anzeige, -n** (6); housing-wanted ad **die Suchanzeige, -n** (6)
addition: in addition **dazu** (9)
address **die Adresse, -n** (1); **die Anschrift, -en** (11)
adhesive bandage (Band-Aid) **das Pflaster, -** (11)
admissions ticket **die Eintrittskarte, -n** (5)
advance: to pay in advance **an·zahlen, angezahlt** (10)
advantage **der Vorteil, -e** (7)
advice **der Rat, Ratschläge** (5)
to advise (*a person*) **raten (rät), riet, geraten** (+ *dat.*) (5)
afraid: to be afraid **Angst haben** (3); to be afraid of **sich fürchten (vor** + *dat.*), **gefürchtet** (12)
Africa **(das) Afrika** (B)
Afro-German **afro-deutsch** (12)
after: at twenty after five **um zwanzig nach fünf** (1)
afternoon **der Nachmittag, -e** (4); good afternoon **guten Tag** (A); afternoons, in the afternoon **nachmittags** (4)
afterward **danach** (10); **nachdem** (*subord. conj.*) (8, 11)
again **wieder** (3); once again **schon wieder** (3)
against **gegen** (+ *acc.*) (8); against it **dagegen** (11); do you have something against it? **haben Sie etwas dagegen?** (11)
age **das Alter** (1); Stone Age **die Steinzeit** (12)
ago **vor** (4); two days ago **vor zwei Tagen** (4)
agreement: in agreement **einverstanden** (12); to be in agreement with **einverstanden sein mit** (12); prenuptial agreement **der Ehevertrag, ¨e** (12)
ahead: straight ahead **geradeaus** (10)
air **die Luft** (7)
airplane **das Flugzeug, -e** (7)
airport **der Flughafen, ¨** (10, 6)
alarm clock **der Wecker, -** (2)
Albania **(das) Albanien** (B)
albatross **der Albatros, -se** (12)
Algeria **(das) Algerien** (B)
alive: to be alive **am Leben sein** (8)
all day long, the whole day **der ganze Tag** (1); all night long **die ganze Nacht** (3); all her money **ihr ganzes Geld** (3); all together **alles zusammen** (5); that's all right **das stimmt** (9)
allergic **allergisch** (11)
alley **die Gasse, -n** (10)
almost **fast** (5)
alone **allein** (3)
along **entlang** (10)
aloud: to read aloud **vor·lesen (liest . . . vor), las . . . vor, vorgelesen** (8)
alphabet **das Alphabet** (3)
Alps **die Alpen** (*pl.*) (7)
already **schon** (2, 3, 4)
also **auch** (A)
although **obwohl** (*subord. conj.*) (11)
always **immer** (3)
ambulance **der Krankenwagen, -** (11)
America **(das) Amerika** (B)
American (*person*) **der Amerikaner, -** / **die Amerikanerin, -nen** (B); (*adj.*) **amerikanisch** (3)
among **unter** (+ *dat.*) (6)
amount **die Menge, -n** (4)
ancestor **der Vorfahre, -n** (*wk.*) (10)
and **und** (A, 11); and so forth **und so weiter** (5)
angry **wütend** (3); to get angry **sich ärgern** (11)
animal **das Tier, -e** (7, 8, 12)
to annoy **ärgern** (3)
answer **die Antwort, -en** (A); to answer **antworten** (+ *dat.*), **geantwortet** (4, 10); **beantworten, beantwortet** (7)
anti-racist **antirassistisch** (12)
antibiotics **die Antibiotika** (*pl.*) (11)
any (+ *noun*) **irgendwelcher, irgendwelches, irgendwelche** (5)
anything **etwas** (5); anything else? **sonst noch etwas?** (5)
anyway **überhaupt** (4)
apartment **die Wohnung, -en** (1, 2); apartment building **das Wohnhaus, ¨er** (12); state-subsidized apartment building **das Wohnheim, -e** (12); vacation apartment **die Ferienwohnung, -en** (10)
appendix **der Blinddarm, ¨e** (11)
appetizer **die Vorspeise, -n** (9)
apple **der Apfel, ¨** (3, 9); apple juice **der Apfelsaft** (9)
appliance **das Gerät, -e** (9)
appointment **der Termin, -e** (5); **die Verabredung, -en** (11); **der Termin, -e** (11); appointment calendar **der Terminkalender, -** (11); to get an appointment **einen Termin geben lassen** (11)
apprenticeship **die Lehre, -n** (5)
approximately **ungefähr** (7)
April **der April** (B)
Arabic (*language*) **das Arabisch** (B)
architect **der Architekt, -en** (*wk.*) / **die Architektin, -nen** (5)
area **die Gegend, -en** (10); surrounding area **die Umgebung, -en** (5)
to argue **streiten (streitet), stritt, gestritten** (8)
arm **der Arm, -e** (A)

armchair **der Sessel, -** (2, 6)
army (German) **die Bundeswehr** (5); in the German army **bei der Bundeswehr** (5)
to arrive **an·kommen (kommt . . . an), kam . . . an, ist angekommen** (1)
art **die Kunst, ¨-e** (1); art history **die Kunstgeschichte** (1)
article of clothing **das Kleidungsstück, -e** (10)
as **als** (5); as far as **bis zu** (+ *dat.*) (10); as . . . possible **möglichst** (+ *adv.*) (6); as well **auch** (A); as what? **als was?** (5)
Asia **(das) Asien** (B)
to ask about **sich erkundigen nach, erkundigt** (10); to ask (for) **bitten (um +** *acc.*) **(bittet), bat, gebeten** (8); to ask a question **eine Frage stellen** (5)
asleep: to fall asleep **ein·schlafen (schläft . . . ein), schlief . . . ein, ist eingeschlafen** (7, 8)
aspirin **das Aspirin** (3, 11)
assigned: to be assigned **auf·haben, aufgehabt** (4)
assignment **die Aufgabe, -n** (4)
at **an** (+ *acc./dat.*) (2); **in** (+ *acc./dat.*) (4); at the café **im café** (4); **bei** (2, 3, 6, 10); at a bank **bei einer Bank** (6); at Rudi's place **bei Rudi** (2); at McDonald's **bei McDonald's** (2); at your place **bei dir** (3); at your parents' **bei deinen Eltern** (6); at seven twenty **um sieben Uhr zwanzig** (1)
athletic **sportlich** (B)
to attack **an·greifen (greift . . . an), griff . . . an, angegriffen** (12)
to attempt **versuchen, versucht** (8, 11), **der Versuch**
to attend to **pflegen, gepflegt** (5)
attention **die Achtung** (7); to pay attention **auf·passen, aufgepaßt** (3); to pay attention to **achten auf** (+ *acc.*), **geachtet** (11)
attitude **die Einstellung, -en** (12)
attractive **attraktiv** (6)
August **der August** (B)
aunt **die Tante, -n** (B)
Australia **(das) Australien** (B)
Australian (*person*) **der Australier, -** / **die Australierin, -nen** (B)
Austria **(das) Österreich** (B)
Austrian (*person*) **der Österreicher, -** / **die Österreicherin, -nen** (B)
automobile **das Auto, -s** (A)
autumn **der Herbst, -e** (B)

B

baby **das Baby, -s** (7); baby carriage **der Kinderwagen, -** (7)
back **der Rücken, -** (A); **zurück** (8); there and back **hin und zurück** (10)
backpack **der Rucksack ¨-e** (2)
bacon **der Speck** (9)
bad **schlecht** (2); **schlimm** (11); too bad! **schade!** (3)
bag **die Tasche, -n** (1); **der Beutel, -** (9); (*paper or plastic bag*) **die Tüte, -n** (11)
baggage **das Gepäck** (10)
to bake **backen (bäckt), backte, gebacken** (5)
bakery **die Bäckerei, -en** (5, 6); at the bakery **in der Bäckerei** (5)
balcony **der Balkon, -e** (6)
ball **der Ball, ¨-e** (A, 1); soccer ball **der Fußball, ¨-e** (A)
ballerina **die Ballerina, -s** (8)
ballet class **der Ballettunterricht** (8)
ballpoint pen **der Kugelschreiber, -** (4)
Baltic Sea **die Ostsee** (B)
bamboo sprouts/shoots **die Bambussprossen** (*pl.*) (9)
bandage **der Verband, ¨-e** (11); adhesive bandage (Band-Aid) **das Pflaster, -** (11)
bank **die Bank, -en** (5, 6); at the bank **auf der Bank** (5): bank account **das Konto, Konten** (5); to open a bank account **ein Konto eröffnen** (5); bank employee **der/die Bankangestellte, -n (ein Bankangestellter)** (5)
bar **die Kneipe, -n** (3)
barely **knapp** (6)
barkeeper **der Wirt, -e** (10)
baseball team **die Baseballmannschaft, -en** (8)
basement **der Keller, -** (4)
basin **das Waschbecken, -** (6)
basketball **der Basketball, ¨-e** (2)
bat **die Fledermaus, ¨-e** (12)
bath **das Bad, ¨-er** (6)
to bathe **baden** (3); **(sich) baden, gebadet** (11)
bathing suit **der Badeanzug, ¨-e** (5)
bathrobe **der Bademantel, ¨** (10)
bathtub **die Badewanne, -n** (6)
bay **die Bucht, -en** (6, 7)
bazaar **der Basar, -e** (7)
to be **sein (ist), war, ist gewesen** (A); to be (*in a horizontal position*) **liegen (liegt), lag, gelegen** (9); to be (*in a vertical position*) **stehen (steht), stand, gestanden** (9)

beach **der Strand, ¨-e** (4, 7)
bean **die Bohne, -n** (9); green beans **grüne Bohnen** (9)
bear: teddy bear **der Teddy, -s** (8)
beard **der Bart, ¨-e** (A)
to beat **schlagen (schlägt), schlug, geschlagen** (9)
beautiful **schön** (B); exceedingly beautiful **wunderschön** (10)
because **weil** (*subord. conj.*) (3, 11, 12); **denn** (*coord. conj.*) (8, 11); because of **wegen** (+ *gen.*) (12)
to become **werden (wird), wurde, ist geworden** (5)
bed **das Bett, -en** (1, 6); bed and breakfast inn **das Gästehaus, ¨-er** (10); to go to bed **ins Bett gehen** (1); to get up on the wrong side of the bed **mit dem linken Fuß auf·stehen** (4); to make one's bed **das Bett machen** (6)
bedroom **das Schlafzimmer, -** (6)
bee **die Biene, -n** (12)
beef **das Rindfleisch** (9); ground beef **das Hackfleisch** (9)
beer **das Bier** (2, 9)
before (*subord. conj.*) **bevor** (11)
to begin **beginnen** (1); **an·fangen (fängt . . . an), fing . . . an, angefangen** (4, 8)
Belgium **(das) Belgien** (B)
to believe **glauben, geglaubt** (2)
belly **der Bauch, ¨-e** (A)
to belong (to) **gehören** (+ *dat.*), **gehört** (10); to belong to (*an organization*) **an·gehören, angehört** (12)
Belorussia **(das) Weißrußland** (B)
below **unter** (+ *dat./acc.*) (6)
belt **der Gürtel, -** (2); safety belt **der Sicherheitsgurt, -e** (7)
beneath **unter** (+ *dat./acc.*) (6)
besides **außerdem** (5, 10)
best **beste, bester, bestes** (3); like (*to do something*) best **am liebsten** (7)
bestseller **der Bestseller, -** (12)
better **besser** (2)
between **zwischen** (+ *dat.* / *acc.*) (7)
beverage **das Getränk, -e** (9)
bicycle **das Fahrrad, ¨-er** (2); bicycle helmet **der Fahrradhelm, -e** (5); bicycle path **der Radweg, -e** (7); bicycle tour **die Radtour, -en** (8); to bicycle **rad·fahren (fährt . . . Rad), fuhr . . . Rad, ist radgefahren** (6)
bicyclist **der Radfahrer, -** / **die Radfahrerin, -nen** (7)

big **groß** (A)

bikini **der Bikini, -s** (5)

bill **die Rechnung, -en** (4); **der Schein, -e** (9)

biographical information **persönliche Daten** (1)

biology **die Biologie** (1)

bird **der Vogel, ¨** (12)

birthday **der Geburtstag, -e** (1, 2); birthday card **die Geburtstagskarte, -n** (2)

to bite **beißen (beißt), biß, gebissen** (8); to bite (*of insects*) **stechen (sticht), stach, gestochen** (12)

black **schwarz** (A); with black hair **schwarzhaarig** (8)

blackboard **die Tafel, -n** (A, B)

blanket **die Decke, -n** (11)

to bleed **bluten, geblutet** (11)

blonde **blond** (A)

blood **das Blut** (8, 11); blood pressure **der Blutdruck** (11); to have low/high blood pressure **niedrigen/hohen Blutdruck haben** (11); to take blood **Blut ab·nehmen** (11)

blouse **die Bluse, -n** (A)

to blow-dry (one's hair) **sich (die Haare) fönen, geföhnt** (11)

blue **blau** (A); blue whale **der Blauwal, -e** (12)

boa constrictor **die Riesenschlange, -n** (12)

boar: wild boar **das Wildschwein, -e** (12)

to board **ein·steigen (steigt . . . ein), stieg . . . ein, ist eingestiegen** (3, 10)

boat **das Boot, -e** (7)

body **der Körper, -** (A, 11)

boiled potatoes **die Salzkartoffeln** (*pl.*) (9)

book **das Buch, ¨er** (A, B, 2); to book **buchen, gebucht** (7); to straighten the books **die Bücher gerade·stellen** (3)

bookcase **das Regal, -e** (2)

bookshelf **das Regal, -e** (2)

bookstore **der Buchladen, ¨** (6)

boot **der Stiefel, -** (A)

booth: movie theater ticket booth **die Kinokasse, -n** (5); ticket booth **der Schalter, -** (5); at the ticket booth **am Schalter** (5)

bored: to be bored **Langeweile haben** (3)

boredom **die Langeweile** (3)

boring **langweilig** (2)

born: to be born **geboren sein** (1); when were you born? **wann sind Sie geboren?** (*for.*) (1)

Bosnia **(das) Bosnien** (B)

bottle **die Flasche, -n** (5); bottle opener **der Flaschenöffner, -** (9)

boutique **die Boutique, -n** (6)

bowl **die Schüssel, -n** (9); salad/mixing bowl **die Salatschüssel, -n** (5)

to box **boxen** (1)

bracelet **das Armband, ¨er** (2)

brain **das Gehirn, -e** (11)

brake **die Bremse, -n** (7); to brake **bremsen, gebremst** (11)

brave **tapfer** (8)

bread (loaf of) **das Brot, -e** (3, 9); farmer's bread **das Bauernbrot, -e** (5); piece of bread **ein Stück Brot** (3)

break **die Pause, -n** (1); to break **brechen (bricht), brach, gebrochen** (11); to break (*a window*) **ein·werfen (wirft . . . ein), warf . . . ein, eingeworfen** (8); to break one's arm **sich den Arm brechen** (11); to break up (*people*) **sich trennen, getrennt** (8)

breakfast **das Frühstück, -e** (2, 9); breakfast room **das Frühstückszimmer, -** (10); to eat breakfast **frühstücken, gefrühstückt** (1)

to breathe **atmen, geatmet** (11)

bride **die Braut, ¨e** (8)

bridge **die Brücke, -n** (10)

to bring **bringen (bringt), brachte, gebracht** (2); to bring along **mit·bringen (bringt . . . mit), brachte . . . mit, mitgebracht** (3)

broiled **gebraten** (9)

broken **kaputt** (3)

broom **der Besen, -** (6)

brother **der Bruder, ¨** (B); brothers and sisters, siblings **die Geschwister** (B)

brown **braun** (A); to brown **bräunen** (9)

brush **die Bürste, -n** (6); to brush (one's teeth) **sich (die Zähne) putzen** (11)

Brussels sprouts **der Rosenkohl** (9)

to build **bauen, gebaut** (10)

building **das Gebäude, -** (6); apartment building **das Wohnhaus, ¨er** (12); office building **das Bürohaus, ¨er** (6); state-subsidized apartment building **das Wohnheim, -e** (12)

Bulgaria **(das) Bulgarien** (B)

bungee-jumping **das Bungee-jumping** (3); to go bungee-jumping **Bungee-jumping machen** (3)

bureau: tourist bureau **das Fremdenverkehrsamt, ¨er** (10); travel bureau **das Reisebüro, -s** (10)

burglar **der Einbrecher, - / die Einbrecherin, -nen** (8)

to burn **brennen (brennt), brannte, gebrannt** (11); **verbrennen (verbrennt), verbrannte, verbrannt** (11); to burn one's tongue **sich die Zunge verbrennen** (11)

bus **der Bus, -se** (2, 7); bus stop **die Bushaltestelle, -n** (6, 10)

bush **der Busch, ¨e** (8)

business hours **die Öffnungszeiten** (*pl.*) (9); business letter **der Geschäftsbrief, -e** (10); businesspeople **die Geschäftsleute** (*pl.*) (7); business trip **die Geschäftsreise, -n** (7)

busy **beschäftigt** (3)

but **aber** (A, 11); but rather **sondern** (A)

butcher shop **die Metzgerei, -en** (6)

butter **die Butter** (9); herb butter **die Kräuterbutter** (9)

to buy **kaufen, gekauft** (1)

by **an . . . vorbei** (10)

bye **tschüs** (*infor.*) (A)

C

cabaret artist **der Kabarettist, -en** (*wk.*) / **die Kabarettistin, -nen** (12)

cabbage **der Kohl** (9)

cable railway **die Seilbahn, -en** (7)

café **das Café, -s** (4, 6)

cafeteria (*student*) **die Mensa, -s** (2)

cage **der Käfig, -e** (12)

cake **der Kuchen, -** (5)

calendar: appointment calendar **der Terminkalender, -** (11)

to call **rufen (ruft), rief, gerufen** (7, 11); to call on the telephone **telefonieren, telefoniert** (4); to call up **an·rufen (ruft . . . an), rief . . . an, angerufen** (1)

called: to be called **heißen (heißt), hieß, geheißen** (A)

calm **ruhig** (B)

calorie-conscious **kalorienbewußt** (9)

calorie: low in calories **kalorienarm** (9)

camel **das Kamel, -e** (7)

camera **die Kamera, -s** (5)

to camp **zelten, gezeltet** (1)

camping **das Camping** (10); camping outside designated areas **wildes Camping** (10)

campsite **der Campingplatz, ¨e** (10)

can (*n.*) **die Dose, -n** (9); can opener **der Dosenöffner, -** (9); garbage can **der Mülleimer, -** (9); watering can **die**

Gießkanne, -n (6); can (*v.*) **können (kann), konnte, gekonnt** (3)
Canada **(das) Kanada** (B)
Canadian (*person*) **der Kanadier, - / die Kanadierin, -nen** (B)
candle **die Kerze, -n** (3)
candlelight march **die Lichterkette, -n** (12)
candy **die Süßigkeit, -en** (8)
cap **die Mütze, -n** (5)
capital city **die Hauptstadt, ¨-e** (3)
car **das Auto, -s** (A, 7); **der Wagen, -** (7); car phone **das Autotelefon, -e** (2); car radio **das Autoradio, -s** (7); streetcar **die Straßenbahn, -en** (7); train car **der Waggon, -s** (7); used car **der Gebrauchtwagen, -** (7)
card **die Karte, -n** (1, 2); birthday card **die Geburtstagskarte, -n** (2); identification card **der Ausweis, -e** (10); postcard **die Postkarte, -n** (2); telephone card **die Telefonkarte, -n** (2); youth hostel ID card **der Jugendherbergsausweis, -e** (10)
to care for **mögen (mag), mochte, gemocht** (3); to take care of **sorgen für, gesorgt** (12)
career **das Berufsleben** (12); **die Karriere, -n** (12); career counselor **der Berufsberater, - / die Berufsberaterin, -nen** (5); career training **praktische Ausbildung** (5)
carpet **der Teppich, -e** (2, 6)
carriage: baby carriage **der Kinderwagen, -** (7)
carrot **die Karotte, -n** (9)
to carry **tragen (trägt), trug, getragen** (A, 2); to carry away **weg·tragen (trägt . . . weg), trug . . . weg, weggetragen** (8); to carry out **treiben (treibt), trieb, getrieben** (2)
case: in any case **jedenfalls** (11)
cashier **der Kassierer, - / die Kassiererin, -nen** (5)
cassette **die Kassette, -n** (A); cassette recorder **der Kassettenrecorder, -** (2)
cast (*plaster*) **der Gips** (11); to cast a spell on **verwünschen** (8)
castle **das Schloß, Schlösser** (8)
cat **die Katze, -n** (2)
to catch (*person, train*) **erwischen, erwischt** (10); to catch a cold **sich erkälten, erkältet** (11)
cathedral **der Dom, -e** (10)
cauliflower **der Blumenkohl** (9)
cave **die Höhle, -n** (6)
CD **die CD, -s** (3); CD player **der CD-Spieler, -** (2)
ceiling **die Decke, -** (B)
to celebrate **feiern, gefeiert** (5)
celebration **die Feier, -n** (8); family celebration **das Familienfest, -e** (4)
cellar **der Keller, -** (4, 6); wine cellar **der Weinkeller, -** (6)
center for study abroad **das Auslandsamt, ¨-er** (1)
central **zentral** (10); central heating **die Zentralheizung** (6)
certainly **bestimmt** (3); **sicherlich** (3)
chair **der Stuhl, ¨-e** (B, 2, 6)
chalk **die Kreide** (B)
to change **ändern, geändert** (8); to change (into) **sich verwandeln in** (+ *acc.*), **verwandelt** (8); to change residence **um·ziehen (zieht . . . um), zog . . . um, ist umgezogen** (2)
chapter **das Kapitel, -** (A)
character **der Typ, -en** (*coll.*) (B); **der Charakter** (12)
characteristic **die Eigenschaft, -en** (B, 12)
cheap **billig** (2)
check **die Quittung, -en** (9); check (*in a restaurant*) **die Rechnung, -en** (4); one check **alles zusammen** (5); separate checks **getrennt** (5); traveler's check **der Reisescheck, -s** (7); to check the oil **das Öl kontrollieren** (5)
cheese **der Käse** (9); *type of creamy cottage cheese* **der Quark** (9)
cheetah **der Gepard, -e** (12)
chemistry **die Chemie** (1)
cherry **die Kirsche, -n** (9)
chess **das Schach** (1)
to chew **kauen, gekaut** (11)
chic **schick** (2, 10)
child **das Kind, -er** (B); child's plate **der Kinderteller, -** (9)
childhood **die Kindheit** (8)
chili **der Chili, -s** (11)
Chinese (*adj.*) **chinesisch** (3)
chips: potato chips **die Kartoffelchips** (*pl.*) (8)
chocolate **die Schokolade** (3); hot chocolate **der Kakao** (9)
to chop **auf·schneiden (schneidet . . . auf), schnitt . . . auf, aufgeschnitten** (9)
Christmas **das Weihnachten** (4); Christmas present **das Weihnachtsgeschenk, -e** (5)
church **die Kirche, -n** (5, 6); **die Konfession, -en** (12); at church **in der Kirche**
cigar **die Zigarre, -n** (7)
cigarette **die Zigarette, -n** (4)
cinema **das Kino, -s** (1)
circus **der Zirkus, -se** (8)
citizen **der Bürger, - / die Bürgerin, -nen** (10)
citizenship **die Staatsangehörigkeit, -en** (1)
city **die Stadt, ¨-e** (2, 6); city limits **der Stadtrand, ¨-er** (6); city park **der Stadtpark, -s** (10); city street map **der Stadtplan, ¨-e** (10); city with a million or more inhabitants **die Millionenstadt, ¨-e** (7); tour of the city **die Stadtrundfahrt, -en** (7)
class **der Kurs, -e** (A, 1); **die Klasse, -n** (5, 10); **der Unterricht** (8); ballet class **der Ballettunterricht** (8); class reunion **das Klassentreffen, -** (8); first class **erster Klasse** (5); tourist class **die Touristenklasse** (5, 10); to fly/travel first class **erster Klasse fliegen/fahren** (10)
classroom **das Klassenzimmer, -** (B)
clean **sauber** (B); to clean **putzen, geputzt** (3, 6); **sauber·machen, saubergemacht** (3, 6); to clean (up) **auf·räumen, aufgeräumt** (1)
cleaner: dry cleaners **die Reinigung, -en** (6)
cleaning: spring cleaning **der Frühjahrsputz** (6)
to clear **ab·räumen, abgeräumt** (3); to clear the table **den Tisch ab·räumen** (3)
clerk **der/die Angestellte, -n (ein Angestellter)** (7)
to climb **besteigen (besteigt), bestieg, bestiegen** (7); **klettern, ist geklettert** (8); to climb down **herunter·klettern, ist heruntergeklettert** (11)
clock **die Uhr, -en** (B); kitchen clock **die Küchenuhr, -en** (5)
close (*adv.*) **nah** (6); to close **schließen (schließt), schloß, geschlossen** (A); to close **zu·machen, zugemacht** (3)
closed **geschlossen** (4)
closet **der Schrank ¨-e** (2, 6); clothes closet **der Kleiderschrank, ¨-e** (6)
cloth **der Putzlappen, -** (6)
clothes **die Kleidung** (A, 2); clothes closet **der Kleiderschrank, ¨-e** (6); clothes dryer **der Wäschetrockner, -** (9)
clothing: article of clothing **das Kleidungsstück, -e** (10); clothing store **das Kleidungsgeschäft, -e** (10)

clown **der Clown, -s** (8)

coach (class) **die Touristenklasse** (5)

coast **die Küste, -n** (7)

coat **der Mantel, ¨** (A, 10); fur coat **der Pelzmantel, ¨** (10)

cocoa **der Kakao** (9)

coffee **der Kaffee** (1, 9); coffee filter **der Kaffeefilter, -** (4); coffee grinder **die Kaffeemühle, -n** (9); coffee machine **die Kaffeemaschine, -n** (5)

coffin **der Sarg, ¨e** (8)

cognac **der Kognak** (9)

coin **die Münze, -n** (5)

cola **die Cola, -s** (3)

cold **kalt** (B); ice cold **eiskalt** (9); cold (head cold) **die Erkältung, -en** (11); cold (*with a runny nose*) **der Schnupfen, -** (11); to catch a cold **sich erkälten, erkältet** (11)

college prep school **das Gymnasium, Gymnasien** (6)

color **die Farbe, -n** (A, 1); color of eyes **die Augenfarbe** (1); color of hair **die Haarfarbe** (1); favorite color **die Lieblingsfarbe, -n** (A); what color is . . . ? **welche Farbe hat . . . ?** (A)

to comb **kämmen, gekämmt** (3); to comb (one's hair) **sich (die Haare) kämmen, gekämmt** (11)

to combine **kombinieren, kombiniert** (3)

to come (from) **kommen (aus) (kommt), kam, ist gekommen** (B); to come back **wieder·kommen (kommt . . . wieder), kam . . . wieder, ist wiedergekommen** (5); **zurück·kommen (kommt . . . zurück), kam . . . zurück, ist zurückgekommen** (6); to come by **vorbei·kommen (kommt . . . vorbei), kam . . . vorbei, ist vorbeigekommen** (3); come on over! **komm mal vorbei!** (11); to come out this way (*toward the speaker*) **heraus·kommen (kommt . . . heraus), kam . . . heraus, ist herausgekommen** (10); to come this way (*toward the speaker*) **her·kommen (kommt . . . her), kam . . . her, ist hergekommen** (10); to come along **mit·kommen (kommt . . . mit), kam . . . mit, ist mitgekommen** (2)

comfortable **bequem** (2); **gemütlich** (12)

committee member **das Vorstandsmitglied, -er** (12)

common **gemeinsam** (11)

company **die Firma, Firmen** (3)

to complete **ergänzen, ergänzt** (4)

computer **der Computer, -** (2); computer company **die Computerfirma, -firmen** (4); computer game **das Computerspiel, -e** (5); computer science **die Informatik** (1)

concert **das Konzert, -e** (1); rock concert **das Rockkonzert, -e** (8); to go to a concert **ins Konzert gehen** (1)

concrete **konkret** (12)

condo: vacation condo **die Ferienwohnung, -en** (10)

conductor (*orchestra*) **der Dirigent, -en** (*wk.*) / **die Dirigentin, -nen** (5)

confirmation **die Bestätigung, -en** (10)

to congratulate **gratulieren** (+ *dat.*), **gratuliert** (2, 10)

to conquer **besiegen, besiegt** (7)

conservative **konservativ** (B)

to consider **nach·denken (über** + *acc.*), **(denkt . . . nach), dachte . . . nach, nachgedacht** (7)

conspicuous **auffällig** (10)

continent **der Kontinent, -e** (B)

contract **der Vertrag, ¨e** (12)

contrary: on the contrary! **doch!** (4); **sondern** (11)

conversational situation **die Sprechsituation, -en** (A)y

to converse **sich unterhalten (unterhält), unterhielt, unterhalten** (8)

cook **der Koch, ¨e / die Köchin, -nen** (5); to cook **kochen, gekocht** (1, 9)

cookbook **das Kochbuch, ¨er** (2)

cooked **gekocht** (9)

cooking **die Küche, -n** (9)

cool **kühl** (B); (neat) **grell** (2)

copy shop **der Kopierladen, ¨** (10)

corkscrew **der Korkenzieher, -** (9)

corner **die Ecke, -n** (5); around the corner **um die Ecke** (5)

correct **richtig** (2); to correct **korrigieren, korrigiert** (4)

to cost **kosten, gekostet** (6)

costume **das Kostüm, -e** (8)

cough **der Husten** (11); cough drop **das Hustenbonbon, -s** (11); cough syrup **der Hustensaft, ¨e** (11)

counselor: career counselor **der Berufsberater, - / die Berufsberaterin, -nen** (5)

to count **zählen, gezählt** (A)

counter: ticket counter **der Fahrkartenschalter, -** (10)

countertop **der Kochplatz, ¨e** (5)

country **das Land, ¨er** (B); country (*rural*) **das Land, ¨er** (6); in the country **auf dem Land** (6); **in freier Natur** (12); foreign countries **das Ausland** (6)

course **der Kurs, -e** (A, 1)

course: of course **klar** (2); **selbstverständlich** (10)

courthouse **das Gericht, -e** (5); at the courthouse **auf dem Gericht** (5)

cousin (*m.*) **der Vetter, -n / die Kusine, -n** (B)

to cover **decken, gedeckt** (3); **zu·decken, zugedeckt** (11)

to crash **ab·stürzen, ist abgestürzt** (11); **zusammen·stoßen (stößt . . . zusammen), stieß . . . zusammen, ist zusammengestoßen** (11)

crazy **verrückt** (B)

cream: to put cream on **sich ein·kremen, eingekremt** (11)

crisis **die Krise, -n** (12)

Croatia **(das) Kroatien** (B)

crocodile **das Krokodil, -e** (12)

croissant **das Hörnchen, -** (9)

croquette **die Krokette, -n** (9)

crosswalk **der Zebrastreifen, -** (10)

cruel **grausam** (8)

to cry **weinen, geweint** (3)

Cuba **(das) Kuba** (B)

cucumber **die Gurke, -n** (9)

cup **die Tasse, -n** (2, 5); **der Becher, -** (8)

cupboard **der Schrank, ¨e** (6)

to cure **heilen, geheilt** (5)

curious **neugierig** (12)

to curse **verwünschen, verwünscht** (8); **fluchen, geflucht** (11)

cursed **verwunschen** (8)

to cuss **schimpfen, geschimpft** (8)

custodian **der Hausmeister, - / die Hausmeisterin, -nen** (5)

customer **der Kunde, -n** (*wk.*) / **die Kundin, -nen** (5)

to cut **schneiden (schneidet), schnitt, geschnitten** (3); to cut oneself **sich schneiden** (11); to cut hair **Haare schneiden** (3); to cut off **ab·schneiden (schneidet . . . ab), schnitt . . . ab, abgeschnitten** (9); to cut through **durch·schneiden (schneidet . . . durch), schnitt . . . durch, durchgeschnitten** (9)

cutlery **das Besteck, e** (5)

cutlet: veal/pork cutlet **das Schnitzel, -** (9)

Czech Republic **(das) Tschechien** (B)

D

daily **täglich** (8)
damage **der Schaden, ̈** (11)
to dance **tanzen, getanzt** (1)
dangerous **gefährlich** (12)
dark **dunkel** (6)
date **das Datum, Daten** (4); **die Verabredung, -en** (11); what is today's date? **welches Datum ist heute?** (4)
daughter **die Tochter, ̈** (B)
day **der Tag, -e** (1); all day long, the whole day **der ganze Tag** (1); on what day? **an welchem Tag?** (4); the day after tomorrow **übermorgen** (8); the day before yesterday **vorgestern** (4); what day is today? **welcher Tag ist heute?** (1)
dead **tot** (8)
dear **lieb** (7); **geehrt** (10); dear ladies and gentlemen **sehr geehrte Damen und Herren** (10); dear Mr. **sehr geehrter Herr** (10); dear Ms. **sehr geehrte Frau** (10)
decade **das Jahrzehnt, -e** (4)
December **der Dezember** (B)
deception **die List, -en** (8)
to decide **entscheiden (entscheidet), entschied, entschieden** (10)
deep(ly) **tief** (7)
definitely **bestimmt** (3)
degree **der Grad, -e** (B); college-prep-school degree **das Abitur** (5)
to deliver **aus·tragen (trägt . . . aus), trug . . . aus, ausgetragen** (5); to deliver newspapers **Zeitungen austragen** (5)
Denmark **(das) Dänemark** (B)
denomination: religious denomination **die Konfession, -en** (12)
dentist **der Zahnarzt, ̈e / die Zahnärztin, -nen** (5)
to depart **ab·fahren (fährt . . . ab), fuhr . . . ab, ist abgefahren** (4, 7); **ab·reisen, ist abgereist** (10)
department store **das Kaufhaus, ̈er** (5, 6); at the department store **im Kaufhaus** (5)
department: fire department **die Feuerwehr** (11)
deposit: security deposit **die Kaution, -en** (6)
depressed **deprimiert** (11)
to describe **beschreiben (beschreibt), beschrieb, beschrieben** (11)
description **die Beschreibung, -en** (A)
desert **die Wüste, -n** (7)
desire **die Lust;** do you feel like it? **hast du Lust?** (2)
desk **der Schreibtisch, -e** (2); fold-out desk **der Sekretär, -e** (6)
dessert **die Nachspeise, -n** (9)
destination **das Ziel, -e** (10)
detective novel writer **der Krimiautor, -en / die Krimiautorin, -nen** (12)
diary **das Tagebuch, ̈er** (4)
dictionary **das Wörterbuch, ̈er** (2)
to die **sterben (stirbt), starb, ist gestorben** (8)
different **verschieden** (9)
difficult **schwierig** (2); **schwer** (3)
dining area **die Eßecke, -n** (6); dining room **das Eßzimmer, -** (6)
dinner **das Abendessen, -** (9)
diphtheria **die Diphtherie** (11)
to direct **lenken, gelenkt** (5)
direction **die Richtung, -en** (7)
directly **gleich** (6)
director **der Regisseur, -e / die Regisseurin, -nen** (8)
dirty **schmutzig** (B)
disadvantage **der Nachteil, -e** (7)
to disappear **verschwinden (verschwindet), verschwand, ist verschwunden** (12)
discotheque **die Disko, -s** (3, 6)
to discover **entdecken, entdeckt** (4)
to discriminate **diskriminieren, diskriminiert** (12)
to discuss **diskutieren, diskutiert** (4)
dish **das Gericht, -e** (9); side dish **die Beilage, -n** (9); dishes **das Geschirr** (4, 5); to wash the dishes **Geschirr spülen** (4)
dishwasher **die Geschirrspülmaschine, -n** (5, 9)
to disinfect **desinfizieren, desinfiziert** (11)
district **das Stadtviertel, -** (6); **der Stadtteil, -e** (6)
to disturb **stören, gestört** (3)
to dive **tauchen, ist getaucht** (3)
divorce **die Scheidung, -en** (12)
to do **tun (tut), tat, getan** (A); **treiben (treibt), trieb, getrieben** (2); to do sports **Sport treiben** (2)
doctor **der Arzt, ̈e / die Ärztin, -nen** (11); eye doctor **der Augenarzt, ̈e / die Augenärztin, -nen** (11); family doctor **der Hausarzt, ̈e / die Hausärztin, -nen** (11); doctor's office **die Arztpraxis, -praxen** (11)
dog **der Hund, -e** (2); dog food **das Hundefutter** (5)
doll **die Puppe, -n** (8)
dollar **der Dollar, -s** (7); two dollars **zwei Dollar** (7)
dolphin **der Delphin, -e** (12)
dominant **dominant** (12)
door **die Tür, -en** (A)
dormitory **das Studentenheim, -e** (2)
double room **das Doppelzimmer, -** (10)
down (*toward the speaker*) **herunter** (11); to fall down **hin·fallen (fällt . . . hin), fiel . . . hin, ist hingefallen** (11)
downtown **die Innenstadt, ̈e** (6)
dragon **der Drache, -n** (*wk.*) (8)
drapery **der Vorhang, ̈e** (6)
to draw **zeichnen, gezeichnet** (3, 5)
drawer **die Schublade, -n** (5, 9)
drawing **die Zeichnung, -en** (9)
to dream **träumen, geträumt** (8)
dress **das Kleid, -er** (A)
dressed: to get dressed **sich an·ziehen (zieht . . . an), zog . . . an, angezogen** (11)
dresser **die Kommode, -n** (6)
dressing room **die Umkleidekabine, -n** (5)
dressing: salad dressing **die Salatsoße, -n** (9)
drink: soft drink **die Limonade, -n** (4, 9); to drink **trinken (trinkt), trank, getrunken** (1, 3)
to drive **fahren (fährt), fuhr, ist gefahren** (2); to drive off **los·fahren (fährt . . . los), fuhr . . . los, ist losgefahren** (8)
driver **der Fahrer, - / die Fahrerin, -nen** (7); driver's license **der Führerschein, -e** (4)
driveway **die Einfahrt, -en** (11)
driving: to keep on driving **weiter·fahren (fährt . . . weiter), fuhr . . . weiter, ist weitergefahren** (10)
drop **das Bonbon, -s** (11); cough drop **das Hustenbonbon, -s** (11)
drugstore **die Drogerie, -n** (6)
drunk **betrunken** (3)
dry **trocken** (11); to dry (dishes) **ab·trocknen, abgetrocknet** (6); to dry oneself off **sich ab·trocknen** (11)
dry cleaners **die Reinigung, -en** (6)
dryer: clothes dryer **der Wäschetrockner, -** (9)
dumb **dumm** (6)
dumpling **der Knödel, -** (9)
during **während** (+ *gen.*) (11, 12)
Dutch (*adj.*) **holländisch** (9)
duty **die Pflicht, -en** (3)
dwarf **der Zwerg, -e** (8)

E

each **jeder, jedes, jede** (3, 5); each other **einander** (3); with each other **miteinander** (3)
eagle **der Adler, -** (12)
ear **das Ohr, -en** (A)
earache **die Ohrenschmerzen** (*pl.*) (11)
early **früh** (1)
to earn **verdienen, verdient** (4)
earring **der Ohrring, -e** (2)
earth science **die Erdkunde** (1)
east (of) **östlich (von)** (7)
to eat **essen (ißt), aß, gegessen** (2, 3, 4); to eat (*said of an animal*) **fressen (frißt), fraß, gefressen** (8); to eat dinner **zu Abend essen** (4); to eat lunch **zu Mittag essen** (3)
economics **die Wirtschaft** (1)
editor **der Herausgeber, - / die Herausgeberin, -nen** (12)
educated **ausgebildet** (12)
education **die Ausbildung, -en** (8)
effect: to take effect **wirken, gewirkt** (11)
egg **das Ei, -er** (9); soft-boiled eggs **gekochte Eier** (9)
Egypt **das Ägypten** (B)
eight **acht** (A)
eighteen **achtzehn** (A)
eighty **achtzig** (A)
eighth **acht-** (4)
electrical(ly) **elektrisch** (9)
electricity **der Strom** (9)
elegant(ly) **elegant** (9)
elementary school **die Grundschule, -n** (4)
elephant **der Elefant, -en** (*wk.*) (8)
elevator **der Aufzug, ¨e** (6)
eleven **elf** (A)
eleventh **elft-** (4)
else: anything else? **sonst noch etwas?** (5)
embarrassing **peinlich** (12)
to emigrate **aus·wandern, ist ausgewandert** (4, 12)
empty **leer** (9); to empty **aus·leeren, ausgeleert** (3); to empty the wastebasket **den Papierkorb aus·leeren** (3)
to encounter **begegnen** (+ *dat.*), **ist begegnet** (10)
engaged **verlobt** (12); to get engaged to **sich verloben** (*mit* + *dat.*), **verlobt** (12)
engineer **der Ingenieur, -e / die Ingenieurin, -nen** (5)
England **(das) England** (B)
English (*language*) **(das) Englisch** (B); English (*person*) **der Engländer, - / die Engländerin, -nen** (B)
enough **genug** (4)
entertainment **die Unterhaltung, -en** (3)
entryway **die Diele, -n** (6)
environs **die Umgebung, -en** (5)
equal **egal** (6)
eraser **der Schwamm, ¨e** (B)
to establish **fest·stellen** (10), **festgestellt**
Europe **(das) Europa** (B)
even **noch** (B)
evening **der Abend, -e** (1, 4); in the evening **am Abend** (4), **abends** (4); evening meal **das Abendessen, -** (1); good evening **guten Abend** (A); this evening **heute abend** (2); evenings **abends** (4)
ever: were you ever? **warst du schon einmal?** (4)
every **jede** (3); every week **jede Woche** (3)
everything **alles** (2); everything possible **alles Mögliche** (2)
everywhere **überall** (12)
evil **böse** (8)
exactly **genau** (B)
to examine **untersuchen, untersucht** (5)
example **das Beispiel, -e** (3); for example **zum Beispiel** (3)
excellent **ausgezeichnet** (3)
exchange **um·tauschen, umgetauscht** (10)
excited: to get excited **sich auf·regen, aufgeregt** (11)
to excuse **entschuldigen, entschuldigt** (5); excuse me! **entschuldigen Sie!** (5)
exercise **die Übung, -en** (A)
exotic **exotisch** (7)
to expect **erwarten, erwartet** (12)
expensive **teuer** (2), **wertvoll** (2)
experience **das Erlebnis, -se** (4); to experience **erleben, erlebt** (10); travel experience **das Reiseerlebnis, -se** (7)
to explain **erklären, erklärt** (5)
expression **der Ausdruck, ¨e** (A)
extra **extra** (10); extra costs **die Nebenkosten** (*pl.*) (6)
extravagant(ly) **extravagant** (2)
eye **das Auge, -n** (A); eye doctor **der Augenarzt, ¨e / die Augenärztin, -nen** (11)

F

face **das Gesicht, -er** (A)
factory **die Fabrik, -en** (6)
faint **in Ohnmacht fallen** (11)
fairy **die Fee, -n** (8)
fairy tale **das Märchen, -** (4, 8)
to fall asleep **ein·schlafen (schläft . . . ein), schlief . . . ein, ist eingeschlafen** (7, 8)
fall **der Herbst, -e** (B)
to fall down **hin·fallen (fällt . . . hin), fiel . . . hin, ist hingefallen** (11)
to fall **fallen (fällt), fiel, ist gefallen** (8)
to fall in love (with) **sich verlieben (in** + *acc.*), **verliebt** (8, 12)
to fall over **um·fallen (fällt . . . um), fiel . . . um, ist umgefallen** (8)
family celebration **das Familienfest, -e** (4)
family **die Familie, -n** (B, 12)
family doctor **der Hausarzt, ¨e / die Hausärztin, -nen** (11)
family member **das Familienmitglied, -er** (10); family name, last name **der Familienname, -n** (*wk.*) (1, A)
famous **berühmt** (7)
fanatic **der Fanatiker, - / die Fanatikerin, -nen** (12)
fantastic(ally) **fantastisch** (3)
far **weit** (6); how far away? **wie weit weg?** (6)
far: as far as **bis zu** (+ *dat.*) (10)
farm **der Bauernhof, ¨e** (12)
farmer's bread (loaf of) **das Bauernbrot, -e** (5)
farmhouse **das Bauernhaus, ¨er** (6)
fashionable **modisch** (10)
fast **schnell** (3); ultra fast **superschnell** (7)
fat **dick** (A); **fettig** (9)
father **der Vater, ¨** (B)
faucet **der Wasserhahn, ¨e** (5)
favorite **Lieblings-** (A)
favorite subject **das Lieblingsfach, ¨er** (5)
fax **das Fax, -e** (2); fax machine **das Faxgerät, -e** (2)
fear **die Angst, ¨e** (3); to be afraid **Angst haben** (3)
February **der Februar** (B)
to feed **füttern, gefüttert** (8)
to feel **fühlen, gefühlt** (3); **(sich) fühlen** (11); how do you feel? **wie fühlst du dich?** (3); I feel . . . **ich fühle mich . . .** (3); to feel well **sich wohl·fühlen, wohlgefühlt** (11)
feeling **das Gefühl, ¨e** (3)
to fetch **holen, geholt** (8)
fever **das Fieber** (11)
few: a few **ein paar** (2)
field **das Feld, -er** (7)
fifteen **fünfzehn** (A)

fifth **fünft-** (4)
fifty **fünfzig** (A)
to fight **kämpfen, gekämpft** (8)
to figure **aus·rechnen, ausgerechnet** (9)
to fill in **aus·füllen, ausgefüllt** (1); to fill in the blanks **ergänzen, ergänzt** (4); to fill up (with gas) **voll·tanken, vollgetankt** (5)
film **der Film, -e** (2); horror film **der Gruselfilm, -e** (2)
filter: coffee filter **der Kaffeefilter, -** (4)
finally **schließlich** (7); **endlich** (8); **zuletzt** (10)
to find **finden (findet), fand, gefunden** (2)
fine **fein** (9)
finger **der Finger, -** (11)
fingernail **der Fingernagel, ¨** (11)
finished **fertig** (3)
Finland **(das) Finnland** (B)
fire **das Feuer, -** (8); fire department **die Feuerwehr** (11)
firm **die Firma, Firmen** (3)
first **erst-** (4); **zuerst** (7); the first of October **der erste Oktober** (4); first name **der Vorname, -n** (A, 1); for the first time **zum ersten Mal** (4); on the first of October **am ersten Oktober** (4)
fish **der Fisch, -e** (9)
to fit **passen** (+ *dat.*), **gepaßt** (10, 11); that fits well **das paßt gut** (11)
five **fünf** (A)
flame **die Flamme, -n** (9)
flashlight **die Taschenlampe, -n** (8)
flat **flach** (10); flat tire **die Reifenpanne, -n** (7)
flea market **der Flohmarkt, ¨e** (2)
to flee from **flüchten vor, ist geflüchtet** (11)
flexible **flexibel** (5)
flight **der Flug, ¨e** (7); flight attendant **der Steward, -s / die Stewardeß, Stewardessen** (5)
to float **schwimmen (schwimmt), schwamm, ist geschwommen** (7)
floor **der Boden, ¨** (B); **der Stock, Stockwerke** (6); on the second floor **im ersten Stock** (6)
to flow **fließen (fließt), floß, ist geflossen** (7)
flower **die Blume, -n** (3); flower vase **die Blumenvase, -n** (5); to water the flowers **die Blumen gießen** (3)
flu **die Grippe** (11)
fly **die Fliege, -n** (9)
to fly **fliegen (fliegt), flog, ist geflogen** (1); to fly first class **erster Klasse fliegen** (10)
fold-out desk **der Sekretär, -e** (6)
fondue **das Fondue** (7)
food: dog food **das Hundefutter** (5)
foot **der Fuß, ¨e** (A)
for **für** (+ *acc.*) (2); **zu** (+ *dat.*) (2, 3); **denn** (*coord. conj.*) (8, 11); **seit** (+ *gen.*) (4, 11); for lunch **zum Mittagessen** (3); for several days **seit mehreren Tagen** (11); for two years **seit zwei Jahren** (4); for someone's birthday **zum Geburtstag** (2)
forbidden **verboten** (9)
foreign countries **das Ausland** (6); foreign language **die Fremdsprache, -n** (8)
foreigner **der Ausländer, - / die Ausländerin, -nen** (12)
forest **der Wald, ¨er** (2, 7)
to forget **vergessen (vergißt), vergaß, vergessen** (2)
fork **die Gabel, -n** (9)
forth: and so forth **und so weiter** (5)
fortress **die Burg, -en** (6)
forty **vierzig** (A)
fountain **der Brunnen, -** (8)
four **vier** (A)
fourteen **vierzehn** (A)
fourth **viert-** (4)
fowl: water fowl **der Wasservogel, ¨** (12)
franc (*Swiss monetary unit*) **der Franken, -** (7)
France **(das) Frankreich** (B)
frankfurter **das Würstchen, -** (9)
free **frei** (3); is this seat free? **ist hier noch frei?** (3)
freeway **die Autobahn, -en** (7)
freezer **die Gefriertruhe, -n** (9)
French (*language*) **(das) Französisch** (8); French (*person*) **der Franzose, -n** (*wk.*) / **die Französin, -nen** (B); French fries **die Pommes frites** (*pl.*) (9)
fresh(ly) **frisch** (9)
Friday **der Freitag** (1)
fried **gebraten** (9)
friend **der Freund, -e / die Freundin, -nen** (A)
friendly **freundlich** (B)
fries: French fries **die Pommes frites** (*pl.*) (9)
frog **der Frosch, ¨e** (8)
from **von** (+ *dat.*) (A, 3, 10); **aus** (+ *dat.*) (10); from work **von der Arbeit** (3)
front entryway **die Diele, -n** (6)
fruit **das Obst** (9)
frustrated **frustriert** (3)
to fry **braten (brät), briet, gebraten** (9); **bräunen, gebräunt** (9)
frying pan **die Pfanne, -n** (5)
full **voll** (10)
fun **lustig** (12); have fun! **viel Spaß!** (A)
funny **komisch** (12); **lustig** (12)
fur coat **der Pelzmantel, ¨** (10)
furnished **möbliert** (6)
furniture **die Möbel** (*pl.*) (6)
future **die Zukunft** (12)

G

game: computer game **das Computerspiel, -e** (5)
garage **die Werkstatt, ¨en** (5); **die Garage, -n** (6)
garbage can **der Mülleimer, -** (9)
garden **der Garten, ¨** (4); garden hose **der Gartenschlauch, ¨e** (6)
garlic **der Knoblauch** (9)
gas station **die Tankstelle, -n** (5); at the gas station **an der Tankstelle** (5)
gasoline **das Benzin** (6)
gaudy **grell** (2)
gear **der Gang, ¨e** (7)
geography **die Erdkunde** (1); **die Geographie** (7)
German (*language*) **(das) Deutsch** (B); German (*person*) **der/die Deutsche, -n (ein Deutscher)** (B); German class/course **der Deutschkurs, -e** (A); German-speaking **deutschsprachig** (8); *specialist in German language and literature* **der Germanist, -en** (*wk.*) / **die Germanistin, -nen** (12); I am German **ich bin Deutscher / Deutsche** (B)
Germany **(das) Deutschland** (B)
to get **bekommen (bekommt), bekam, bekommen** (3); to get (*fetch*) **holen, geholt** (8); to get an appointment **sich einen Termin geben lassen** (11); to get in this way (*toward the speaker*) **herein·kommen (kommt . . . herein), kam . . . herein, ist hereingekommen** (10); to get up **auf·stehen (steht . . . auf), stand . . . auf, ist aufgestanden** (1); to get up on the wrong side of the bed **mit dem linken Fuß auf·stehen** (4); get up **stehen Sie auf** (A)
giant **der Riese, -n** (8)
gifted **begabt** (8)
giraffe **die Giraffe, -n** (12)
girl **das Mädchen, -** (8)
to give **geben (gibt), gab, gegeben** (A, 6);

to give (as a present) **schenken, geschenkt** (5); to give directions **den Weg beschreiben** (10); to give a paper / oral report **ein Referat halten** (4)
glacier **der Gletscher, -** (7)
gladly **gern** (1, 5)
glass **das Glas, ¨er** (8); (of) glass **gläsern** (8); wineglass **das Weinglas, ¨er** (5)
glasses (pair of) **die Brille, -n** (A)
glove **der Handschuh, -e** (10)
to go **gehen (geht), ging, ist gegangen** (A); to go (run) **laufen (läuft), lief, ist gelaufen** (A); to go along **entlang·gehen (geht . . . entlang), ging . . . entlang, ist entlanggegangen** (10); to go away **weg·gehen (geht . . . weg), ging . . . weg, ist weggegangen** (4); to go by **vorbei·gehen (an** + *dat.*) **(geht . . . vorbei), ging . . . vorbei, ist vorbeigegangen** (10); to go in this way (*toward the speaker*) **herein·kommen (kommt . . . herein), kam . . . herein, ist hereingekommen** (10); to go on a trip **verreisen, ist verreist** (3); to go out (*power*) **aus·fallen (fällt . . . aus), fiel . . . aus, ist ausgefallen** (9); to go out **aus·gehen (geht . . . aus), ging . . . aus, ist ausgegangen** (1); to go over that way (*away from the speaker*) **hinüber·gehen (geht . . . hinüber), ging . . . hinüber, ist hinübergegangen** (10); to go that way (*away from the speaker*) **hin·gehen (geht . . . hin), ging . . . hin, ist hingegangen** (10); to go to the mountains **in die Berge gehen** (1); to go to work **zur Arbeit gehen** (1); to go up that way (*away from the speaker*) **hinauf·gehen (geht . . . hinauf), ging . . . hinauf, ist hinaufgegangen** (10); where are you going? **wo willst du denn hin?** (A)
goggles: ski goggles **die Skibrille, -n** (5)
gold ring **der Goldring, -e** (10)
goldfish **der Goldfisch, -e** (11)
golf **das Golf** (1)
good-bye **auf Wiedersehen** (A); **auf Wiederhören!** (6); **Servus** (*southern Germany, Austria*) (A); to say good-bye **wieder·hören, wiedergehört** (6), **sich verabschieden, verabschiedet** (A)
to grab **greifen (greift), griff, gegriffen** (11)
grade **die Note, -n** (3, 8); grade (*level*) **die Klasse, -n** (8)
graduation **der Abschluß, Abschlüsse** (8)
grammar **die Grammatik** (A)
grandfather **der Großvater, ¨** (B)
grandma **die Oma, -s** (3)
grandmother **die Großmutter, ¨** (B)
grandparents **die Großeltern** (*pl.*) (B)
grape **die Weintraube, -n** (9)
to grasp **greifen (greift), griff, gegriffen** (11)
gray **grau** (A)
gray-green **graugrün** (7)
greasy **fettig** (9, 11)
Great Britain **(das) Großbritannien** (B)
great **toll** (2); **prima** (6)
Greece **(das) Griechenland** (B)
green **grün** (A); green beans **grüne Bohnen** (9)
to greet **begrüßen, begrüßt** (A); **grüßen, gegrüßt** (11)
greeting **der Gruß, ¨e** (10)
grill **der Grill, -s** (9)
grilled **gegrillt** (9)
grinder: coffee grinder **die Kaffeemühle, -n** (9)
grocery store **das Lebensmittelgeschäft, -e** (6)
gross **eklig** (8)
ground beef **das Hackfleisch** (9); ground pork **das Hackfleisch** (9)
to grow **wachsen (wächst), wuchs, ist gewachsen** (8); to grow up **auf·wachsen (wächst . . . auf), wuchs . . . auf, ist aufgewachsen** (12)
to guide **lenken, gelenkt** (5)
guidebook: travel guidebook **der Reiseführer, -** (5)
guided tour **die Führung, -en** (10)
guinea pig **das Meerschweinchen, -** (12)
guitar **die Gitarre, -n** (1)
guy **der Typ, -en** (*coll.*) (B)

H

hair **das Haar, -e** (A, 11); hair cut **der Haarschnitt** (2); hair salon **der Friseur, -e** (6); to cut hair **Haare schneiden** (3); with black hair **schwarzhaarig** (8)
haircut: mohawk haircut **der Irokesenschnitt, -e** (10)
hairdresser **der Friseur, -e / die Friseurin, -nen** (5)
half **die Hälfte, -n** (10)
hallway **der Flur, -e** (6)
ham **der Schinken, -** (9)
hamburger **der Hamburger, -** (3)
hammer **der Hammer, -** (9)
hamster **der Hamster, -** (12)
hand **die Hand, ¨e** (A); hand towel **das Handtuch, ¨er** (5, 6, 9)
handbag **die Tasche, -n** (5)
handkerchief **das Taschentuch, ¨er** (3)
handy **handwerklich** (12)
to hang, be in a hanging position **hängen (hängt), hing, gehangen** to hang, place in a hanging position **hängen, gehängt** (3, 9); to hang up **auf·hängen, aufgehängt** (12)
to happen **passieren, ist passiert** (4)
happiness **das Glück** (3, 12)
happy **glücklich** (B, 3); to be happy about **sich freuen über** (+ *acc.*), **gefreut** (11)
harbor **der Hafen, ¨** (10)
hard **schwer** (3)
hardware store **das Eisenwarengeschäft, -e** (6)
to harm **schaden** (+ *dat.*), **geschadet** (10)
hat **der Hut, ¨e** (A)
to hate **hassen, gehaßt** (8)
to have **haben (hat), hatte, gehabt** (A); to have to **müssen (muß), mußte, gemußt** (3)
head **der Kopf, ¨e** (A); head cold **die Erkältung, -en** (11)
headache **die Kopfschmerzen** (*pl.*) (11); headache pill **die Kopfschmerztablette, -n** (11)
to heal **heilen, geheilt** (5)
health **die Gesundheit** (11)
healthy **gesund** (11)
to hear **hören, gehört** (1)
heart **das Herz, -en** (11)
heartache **die Herzschmerzen** (*pl.*) (11)
hearth **der Kachelofen, ¨** (6)
hearty **herzlich** (10)
to heat **erhitzen, erhitzt** (9); heat included **warm** (6)
heated **warm** (6)
heating: central heating **die Zentralheizung** (6)
heavy **schwer** (3); **stark** (11)
heel **der Absatz, ¨e** (10)
height **die Größe, -n** (1)
hello **guten Tag** (*for.*) (A); **Servus** (*southern Germany, Austria*) (A)
helmet: bicycle helmet **der Fahrradhelm, -e** (5)
to help **helfen** (+ *dat.*) **(hilft), half, geholfen** (8, 10); help! **hilfe!** (11); may I help you? **bitte schön?** (7)
her **ihre, ihr, ihren** (1, 2)
herb butter **die Kräuterbutter** (9)
here **hier** (A)

herring salad **der Heringssalat, -e** (9)
hi **hallo** (*infor.*) (A); **grüezi** (*Switzerland*) (A); **grüß Gott** (*southern Germany, Austria*) (A); to say hi to **grüßen, gegrüßt** (11)
to hide **sich verstecken, versteckt** (8)
high **hoch** (6)
high school **das Gymnasium, Gymnasien** (4, 6)
highway: interstate highway **die Autobahn, -en** (7); rural highway **die Landstraße, -n** (7)
hike **die Wanderung, -en** (7); to hike **wandern, ist gewandert** (1); to hike in the mountains **in den Bergen wandern** (1)
hill **der Hügel, -** (7)
him (*acc.*) **ihn** (2); (+ *dat.*) **ihm** (6)
his **seine, sein, seinen** (1, 2)
history **die Geschichte** (1)
to hit **schlagen (schlägt), schlug, geschlagen** (11)
hobby **das Hobby, -s** (1)
to hold **halten (hält), hielt, gehalten** (4)
hole **das Loch, ¨er** (12)
holiday **der Feiertag, -e** (4); holiday trip **die Ferienreise, -n** (8); national holiday **der Nationalfeiertag, -e** (4)
Holland **(das) Holland** (B)
home **das Haus, ¨er** (2); hometown **die Heimatstadt, ¨e** (6); (to) home **nach Hause** (10); at home **zu Hause** (10), **daheim** (8); to be at home **zu Hause sein** (1); to go home **nach Hause gehen** (1)
homesick: to be homesick **Heimweh haben** (3)
homesickness **das Heimweh** (3)
homework (assignment) **die Hausaufgabe, -n** (A, 1); what's our homework? **was haben wir auf?** (4)
honey **der Honig** (9)
honk **hupen, gehupt** (7)
honored **geehrt** (10)
hood **die Motorhaube, -n** (7)
hook **der Haken, -** (9)
to hope **hoffen, gehofft** (3)
hopefully **hoffentlich** (3)
horn **die Hupe, -n** (7)
horror film **der Gruselfilm, -e** (2)
horse **das Pferd, -e** (8)
hose: garden hose **der Gartenschlauch, ¨e** (6)
hospital **das Krankenhaus, ¨er** (3, 5, 6, 11); in the hospital **im Krankenhaus** (5)
host **der Wirt, -e** (10)
hostel: youth hostel **die Jugendherberge, -n** (10); youth hostel ID card **der Jugendherbergsausweis, -e** (10); owner/manager of a youth hostel **die Herbergseltern** (*pl.*) (10)
hot **heiß** (B); hot chocolate **der Kakao** (9); hot dog **das Würstchen, -** (9)
hotel **das Hotel, -s** (2, 5); in the hotel **im Hotel** (5)
hour **die Stunde, -n** (2); business hours **die Öffnungszeiten** (*pl.*) (9); quarter hour **die Viertelstunde, -n** (6)
house **das Haus, ¨er** (1, 2, 6); farmhouse **das Bauernhaus, ¨er** (6); tree house **das Baumhaus, ¨er** (6); house key **der Hausschlüssel, -** (8); house number **die Hausnummer, -n** (1)
houseboat **das Hausboot, -e** (6)
household **der Haushalt** (8)
househusband **der Hausmann, ¨er** (12)
housemate **der Mitbewohner, - / die Mitbewohnerin, -nen** (2)
housewife **die Hausfrau, -en** (12)
housing: shared housing **die Wohngemeinschaft, -en** (6)
housing-wanted ad **die Suchanzeige, -n** (6)
how **wie** (B)
humid **feucht** (B)
hummingbird **der Kolibri, -s** (12)
hundred, one hundred **hundert** (A)
hundredth **hundertst-** (4)
Hungary **(das) Ungarn** (B)
hunger **der Hunger** (3)
hungry **hungrig** (8); to be hungry **Hunger haben** (3)
hunter **der Jäger, -** (8)
hurry **die Eile** (3); to be in a hurry **in Eile sein** (3); **es eilig haben** (10); to hurry **sich beeilen, beeilt** (9)
to hurt **schaden** (+ *dat.*), **geschadet** (10); **weh tun (tut weh), tat weh, weh getan** (11)
husband **der Mann, ¨er** (B)
hut made of palms **die Palmenhütte, -n** (6)
hygiene: personal hygiene **die Körperpflege** (11)

I

ice **das Eis** (2); ice cold **eiskalt** (9); ice cream **das Eis** (2); dish of ice cream **der Eisbecher, -** (9); ice skate **der Schlittschuh, -e** (2)
idea **die Ahnung** (4); (I have) no idea **keine Ahnung** (4)
ideal **ideal** (12)
identification card **der Personalausweis, -e** (1); **der Ausweis, -e** (10); youth hostel ID card **der Jugendherbergsausweis, -e** (10)
idol **das Vorbild, -er** (8)
if **ob** (*subord. conj.*) (6); **wenn** (*subord. conj.*) (2, 3, 11)
igloo **das Iglu, -s** (6)
illegal(ly) **illegal** (12)
illness **die Krankheit, -en** (11)
to imagine **sich etwas vorstellen, vorgestellt** (6); **sich** (+ *dat.*) **vor·stellen, vorgestellt** (10)
immediately **sofort** (3)
immigrant **der Einwanderer, -** (4)
to immigrate **ein·wandern, ist eingewandert** (12)
impatient(ly) **ungeduldig** (11)
important **wichtig** (2)
in **an** (+*acc./dat.*) (4); **in** (+*acc./dat.*) (B, 4); in it **drin/darin** (6); in the evening **am Abend** (4); in the garden **im Garten** (4); in January **im Januar** (B); in the spring **im Frühling** (B); in this way (*toward the speaker*) **herein** (10); to get/go in this way **herein·kommen (kommt . . . herein), kam . . . herein, ist hereingekommen** (10)
to incinerate **verbrennen (verbrennt), verbrannte, verbrannt** (12)
included **inbegriffen** (10); included (*utilities*) **inklusive** (6)
indeed **ja** (4)
independent **selbständig** (12)
industrious **fleißig** (12)
inexpensive **billig** (2)
infection **die Entzündung, -en** (11); kidney infection **die Nierenentzündung, -en** (11)
inferior **minderwertig** (12)
influenza **die Grippe** (11)
to inform oneself about **sich informieren über** (+ *acc.*), **informiert** (10)
information **die Information, -en** (4); to get information about **sich erkundigen nach, erkundigt** (10)
ingredients **die Zutaten** (*pl.*) (9)
to injure oneself **sich verletzen, verletzt** (11)
injured **verletzt** (11); critically injured **schwer verletzt** (11); injured person **der/die Verletzte, -n (ein Verletzter)** (11)
inn: bed and breakfast inn **das Gästehaus, ¨er** (10)
innkeeper **der Wirt, -e** (10)

instead of **statt** (+ *gen.*) (12), **anstatt** (+ *gen.*) (12)
to instruct **unterrichten, unterrichtet** (5)
instruction **die Aufforderung, -en** (A), **der Unterricht** (8)
instructor **der Lehrer, -/die Lehrerin, -nen** (A, 1)
insurance **die Versicherung, -en** (5)
intelligence **die Intelligenz** (12)
intelligent(ly) **intelligent** (B)
to intend **wollen (will), wollte, gewollt** (3)
interest **das Interesse, -n** (5); to interest **interessieren, interessiert** (5)
interested: to be interested in **Interesse haben (an** + *dat.*) (5), **sich interessieren für, interessiert** (5)
interesting **interessant** (7)
intersection **die Kreuzung, -en** (7)
interstate highway **die Autobahn, -en** (7)
interview **das Interview, -s** (4); to interview **interviewen, interviewt** (12)
into **hinein** (8)
to introduce **vor·stellen, vorgestellt** (6, 8)
introduction **die Einführung, -en** (A)
to invent **erfinden (erfindet), erfand, erfunden** (4)
to investigate **untersuchen, untersucht** (5)
invitation **die Einladung, -en** (2)
to invite **ein·laden (lädt . . . ein), lud . . . ein, eingeladen** (2)
Ireland **(das) Irland** (B)
iron **das Bügeleisen, -** (6); to iron **bügeln, gebügelt** (6)
island **die Insel, -n** (7)
Israel **(das) Israel** (B)
it is . . . **es ist . . .** (B)
Italian (*language*) **(das) Italienisch** (B)
Italy **(das) Italien** (B)
its **ihre, ihr, ihren** (2); **seine, sein, seinen** (2)
ivory **das Elfenbein** (12)

J

jacket **die Jacke, -n** (A); leather jacket **die Lederjacke, -n** (10); sports jacket **das Sakko, -s** (A)
jail **das Gefängnis, -se** (6)
jam **die Marmelade, -n** (9); traffic jam **der Stau, -s** (7)
January **der Januar** (B)
Japan **(das) Japan** (B)
Japanese (*language*) **(das) Japanisch** (B); Japanese (*person*) **der Japaner, - / die Japanerin, -nen** (B)
jealous **eifersüchtig** (3)
jeans **die Jeans** (*pl.*) (2)
jewelry **der Schmuck** (2)
job **die Arbeit, -en** (1)
joke **der Witz, -e** (3); to tell jokes **Witze erzählen** (3)
journalist **der Journalist, -en** (*wk.*) / **die Journalistin, -nen** (12)
journey **die Reise, -n** (7)
joy **die Freude, -n** (8)
judge **der Richter, - / die Richterin, -nen** (5)
juice **der Saft, ¨-e** (9); apple juice **der Apfelsaft** (9); orange juice **der Orangensaft** (9)
July **der July** (B)
to jump **springen (springt), sprang, ist gesprungen** (A)
June **der Juni** (B)
jungle **der Dschungel, -** (7)
just **knapp** (6); that's just it! **das ist es ja!** (4)

K

to keep on driving **weiter·fahren (fährt . . . weiter), fuhr . . . weiter, ist weitergefahren** (10); to keep on walking **weiter·gehen (geht . . . weiter), ging . . . weiter, ist weitergegangen** (10); to keep one's mind off something **auf andere Gedanken kommen** (7); keep the change **das stimmt** (9)
kettle: tea kettle **der Teekessel, -** (9)
key **der Schlüssel, -** (8); house key **der Hausschlüssel, -** (8)
kidney **die Niere, -n** (11); kidney infection **die Nierenentzündung, -en** (11)
to kill **töten, getötet** (8)
kilometer **der Kilometer, -** (2)
kind **die Art, -en** (2)
kindergarten **der Kindergarten, ¨** (6)
king **der König, -e** (8)
kiss **der Kuß, Küsse** (4); to kiss **küssen, geküßt** (8)
kitchen **die Küche, -n** (5, 6); kitchen clock **die Küchenuhr, -en** (5); kitchen knife **das Küchenmesser, -** (9); kitchen lamp **die Küchenlampe, -n** (5); kitchen scale **die Küchenwaage, -n** (5, 9); kitchen table **der Küchentisch, -e** (5, 6); kitchen work **die Küchenarbeit, -en** (5)
knife **das Messer, -** (9); kitchen knife **das Küchenmesser, -** (9)
to knit **stricken, gestrickt** (3)
to knock over **um·kippen, umgekippt** (11)
to know **wissen (weiß), wußte, gewußt** (2); **kennen (kennt), kannte, gekannt** (3)
knowledge about a field **die Kenntnisse** (*pl.*) (5)

L

laboratory: language laboratory **das Sprachlabor, -s** (4)
to lack **fehlen** (+ *dat.*), **gefehlt** (10)
lake **der See, -n** (7)
lamp **die Lampe, -n** (B); kitchen lamp **die Küchenlampe, -n** (5); table lamp **die Tischlampe, -n** (9)
land mammal **das Landsäugetier, -e** (12)
landlady **die Vermieterin, -nen** (6)
landlord **der Vermieter, -** (6)
language **die Sprache, -n** (B); foreign language **die Fremdsprache, -n** (8); language laboratory **das Sprachlabor, -s** (4)
large **dick** (A)
last **letzt-** (4); last week **letzte Woche** (4); last Monday **letzten Montag** (4); last summer **letzten Sommer** (4); last weekend **letztes Wochenende** (4); last name **der Familienname, -n** (*wk.*) (A); last night **gestern abend** (4); the last time **das letzte Mal** (4); to last **dauern, gedauert** (4)
late **spät** (1); later **später** (1)
Latin (*language*) **(das) Latein** (1)
to laugh **lachen, gelacht** (3)
laundromat **der Waschsalon, -s** (10)
laundry **die Wäsche** (4); laundry room **die Waschküche, -n** (6)
lawn **der Rasen, -** (5); lawn mower **der Rasenmäher, -** (6)
lawyer **der Anwalt, ¨-e / die Anwältin, -nen** (5)
to lay **legen, gelegt** (8, 9)
lazy **faul** (3)
to learn **lernen, gelernt** (1)
least: at least **wenigstens** (4); the least **am wenigsten** (9)
leather jacket **die Lederjacke, -n** (10)
to leave **weg·gehen (geht . . . weg), ging . . . weg, ist weggegangen** (4); **verlassen (verläßt), verließ, verlassen** (11)
lecture **die Vorlesung, -en** (4)
left **links** (4, 10)
leg **das Bein, -e** (A)

leisure time **die Freizeit, -en** (1)
lemon **die Zitrone, -n** (9)
to lend **leihen (leiht), lieh, geliehen** (5)
to let **lassen (läßt), ließ, gelassen** (11)
letter **der Brief, -e** (1); business letter **der Geschäftsbrief, -e** (10)
lettuce **der Kopfsalat, -e** (9)
liberal(ly) **liberal** (6)
librarian **der Bibliothekar, -e / die Bibliothekarin, -nen** (5)
library **die Bibliothek, -en** (2)
license: driver's license **der Führerschein, -e** (4); license plate **das Nummernschild, -er** (7); license plate number **die Autonummer, -n** (11)
to lie **liegen (liegt), lag, gelegen** (1, 9); to lie down **sich hin·legen, hingelegt** (11); to lie in the sun **in der Sonne liegen** (1)
Liechtenstein **(das) Liechtenstein** (B)
life **das Leben** (8); student life **das Studentenleben** (4)
light **hell** (6); **leicht** (6); light **das Licht, -er** (3); traffic light **die Ampel, -n** (7); to light **an·zünden, angezündet** (3)
lighthouse **der Leuchtturm, ¨e** (6)
like (*to do something*) best **am liebsten** (7)
to like **mögen (mag), mochte, gemocht** (3); **gefallen** (+ *dat.*) **(gefällt), gefiel, gefallen** (10); I like it **es gefällt mir** (10); I would like **ich hätte gern** (5); would like (to) **möchte** (3)
line **die Linie, -n** (10)
linguistics **die Linguistik** (1)
link sausage **das Würstchen, -** (9)
lion **der Löwe, -n** (*wk.*) (12)
lip **die Lippe, -n** (11)
list **die Liste, -n** (5); shopping list **die Einkaufsliste, -n** (9)
to listen (to) **zu·hören** (+ *dat.*), **zugehört** (A, 10)
liter **der Liter, -** (7)
literature **die Literatur** (1)
little: a little bit **ein bißchen** (B, 3)
to live **leben, gelebt** (3); to live (in) **wohnen (in), gewohnt** (B)
liver **die Leber, -n** (11)
living arrangements **die Wohnmöglichkeiten** (*pl.*) (6)
living room **das Wohnzimmer, -** (6); living room table **der Wohnzimmertisch, -e** (6)
loathsome **eklig** (8)
lobster **der Hummer, -** (9)
locomotive **die Lokomotive, -n** (7)
lodging **die Unterkunft, ¨e** (10)
logical(ly) **logisch** (12)
long **lang** (A, 3); no longer **nicht länger** (3)
to look **aus·sehen (sieht . . . aus), sah . . . aus, ausgesehen** (A, 2); it looks good **es sieht gut aus** (2); to look around **sich um·sehen (sieht . . . um), sah . . . um, umgesehen** (10); to look at **an·schauen, angeschaut** (2); to look at **an·sehen (sieht . . . an), sah . . . an, angesehen** (3); to look for **suchen, gesucht** (1); to look on **zu·sehen (sieht . . . zu), sah . . . zu, zugesehen** (7); to look up **nach·sehen (sieht . . . nach), sah . . . nach, nachgesehen** (10); that looks / they look good on you **das steht / die stehen dir gut!** (2)
to lose **verlieren (verliert), verlor, verloren** (7, 8)
to lose weight **ab·nehmen (nimmt . . . ab), nahm . . . ab, abgenommen** (9, 11)
lot: a lot **viel** (A); a whole lot **eine ganze Menge** (4)
lottery **die Lotterie, -n** (5); to win the lottery **in der Lotterie gewinnen** (5)
loud(ly) **laut** (3)
lounge **der Aufenthaltsraum, ¨e** (10)
to love **lieben, geliebt** (2); in love **verliebt** (4, 12); to fall in love (with) **sich verlieben (in** + *acc.*), **verliebt** (8, 12)
lover **der/die Geliebte, -n** (3)
lovesickness **der Liebeskummer** (11)
low in calories **kalorienarm** (9)
loyal **treu** (8)
lozenge **das Bonbon, -s** (11); throat lozenge **das Halsbonbon, -s** (11)
luck **das Glück** (3, 12); lots of luck, good luck! **viel Glück!** (3)
luggage **das Gepäck** (10)
lunch **das Mittagessen, -** (3, 9); to eat lunch **zu Mittag essen** (3)
lung **die Lunge, -n** (11)

M

main point **der Stichpunkt, -e** (12)
makeup: to put makeup on **sich schminken, geschminkt** (11)
mammal: land mammal **das Landsäugetier, -e** (12)
man **der Mann, ¨er** (A, B); man (*coll.*) **der Mensch, -en** (*wk.*) (2)
manager of a youth hostel **die Herbergseltern** (*pl.*) (10)
many **viele** (A)
map **die Landkarte, -n** (7); city street map **der Stadtplan, ¨e** (10)
March **der März** (B)
march: candlelight march **die Lichterkette, -n** (12)
marital status **der Familienstand** (1)
mark (*German monetary unit*) **die Mark, -** (7)
to mark **markieren, markiert** (11)
market **der Markt, ¨e** (10); flea market **der Flohmarkt, ¨e** (2); market square **der Marktplatz, ¨e** (6)
marriage **die Ehe, -n** (12)
married **verheiratet** (1, 12); to get married to **sich verheiraten mit, verheiratet** (12)
to marry **heiraten, geheiratet** (5)
match **das Streichholz, ¨er** (9)
mathematics **die Mathematik** (1)
matter: does it matter? **macht das was?** (B); it doesn't matter to me **das ist mir egal** (6); to be the matter with (*a person*) **fehlen** (+ *dat.*), **gefehlt** (11)
May **der Mai** (B)
may **dürfen (darf), durfte, gedurft** (3); **können (kann), konnte, gekonnt** (3)
mayonnaise **die Mayonnaise** (9)
meadow **die Wiese, -n** (7)
meal **die Mahlzeit, -en** (9); midday meal **das Mittagessen** (3)
mean **böse** (8)
means of transportation **das Transportmittel, -** (7)
meat **das Fleisch** (9)
mechanic **der Automechaniker, - / die Automechanikerin, -nen** (5)
mechanical engineering **der Maschinenbau** (1)
medical(ly) **medizinisch** (11)
medicine **das Medikament, -e** (11); medicine for **ein Medikament gegen** (11)
Mediterranean Sea **das Mittelmeer** (B)
to meet **treffen (trifft), traf, getroffen** (2); let's meet **treffen wir uns . . .** (2); **begegnen** (+ *dat.*), **ist begegnet** (10)
member **das Mitglied, -er** (6); family member **das Familienmitglied, -er** (10)
memory **die Erinnerung, -en** (4)
mental **geistig** (3)
menu **die Speisekarte, -n** (9)
meter: square meter (m^2) **der Quadratmeter (qm)** (6)
Mexican (*adj.*) **mexikanisch** (9); Mexican (*person*) **der Mexikaner, - / die Mexikanerin, -nen** (B)

Mexico **(das) Mexiko** (B)
midday **Mittag** (3)
middle: in the middle **mitten** (8); in the middle of the night **mitten in der Nacht** (8)
mileage **der Kilometerstand** (7)
military service **der Wehrdienst** (12)
milk **die Milch** (9)
million **die Million, -en** (7)
mind: to keep one's mind off something **auf andere Gedanken kommen** (7)
mineral water **das Mineralwasser** (9)
mirror **der Spiegel, -** (6)
to miss **verfehlen, verfehlt** (10)
missing: to be missing **fehlen** (+ *dat.*), **gefehlt** (10); what's missing? **was fehlt?** (A)
to mix **vermischen, vermischt** (9)
mixed **gemischt** (9)
mixer **die Küchenmaschine, -n** (9)
mixing bowl **die Salatschüssel, -n** (5)
model: fashion model **das Fotomodell, -e** (12); role model **das Vorbild, -er** (8)
modern **modern** (6)
mohawk haircut **der Irokesenschnitt, -e** (10)
Moldavia **(das) Moldawien** (B)
moment **der Moment, -e** (1); at the moment **im Moment** (1)
Monday **der Montag** (1)
money **das Geld** (2)
to mop **putzen, geputzt** (6)
more **mehr** (3)
morning: good morning **guten Morgen** (A); in the morning **früh** (4); **morgens** (3); late morning **der Vormittag, -e** (4); until four in the morning **bis um vier Uhr früh** (4)
Morocco **(das) Marokko** (B)
mosquito **die Mücke, -n** (12)
mostly **meistens** (9)
mother **die Mutter, ¨** (A, B); Mother's Day **der Muttertag** (4)
motorcycle **das Motorrad, ¨er** (1, 7); to ride a motorcycle **Motorrad fahren** (1)
mountain **der Berg, -e** (1); mountains **das Gebirge, -** (7); to go to the mountains **in die Berge gehen** (1); to hike in the mountains **in den Bergen wandern** (1)
mountaintop **der Gipfel, -** (7)
mouse **die Maus, ¨e** (12)
mouth **der Mund, ¨er** (A); mouth (*of an animal*) **das Maul, ¨er** (8)
to move **ziehen (zieht), zog, ist gezogen** (2)
movie theater, movies **das Kino, -s** (1); movie theater ticket booth **die Kinokasse, -n** (5); at the movie theater ticket booth **an der Kinokasse** (5); to go to the movies **ins Kino gehen** (1); TV movie **der Fernsehfilm, -e** (12); what's playing at the movies? **was läuft im Kino?** (2)
to mow **mähen, gemäht** (5, 6)
mower: lawn mower **der Rasenmäher, -** (6)
Mr. **der Herr, -en** (*wk.*) (A)
Mrs. **die Frau, -en** (A)
much **viel** (A)
mug **der Becher, -** (8)
multicultural society **multikulturelle Gesellschaft** (12)
museum **das Museum, Museen** (1); to go to a museum **ins Museum gehen** (1)
mushroom **der Pilz, -e** (9)
music **die Musik** (1)
mussel **die Muschel, -n** (9)
must **müssen (muß), mußte, gemußt** (3)
mustard **der Senf** (9)
my **meine, mein, meinen** (A, 2)

N

nail **der Nagel, ¨** (9)
name **der Name, -n** (*wk.*) (A, 1); favorite name **der Lieblingsname, -n** (*wk.*) (A); first name **der Vorname, -n** (*wk.*) (A, 1); my name is . . . **ich heiße . . .** (A); what's your name? **wie heißen Sie?** (*for.*), **wie heißt du?** (*infor.*) (A)
named: to be named **heißen (heißt), hieß, geheißen** (A)
napkin **die Serviette, -n** (9)
narrow **eng** (12); narrow street **die Gasse, -n** (10)
nation **der Staat, -en** (10)
national holiday **der Nationalfeiertag, -e** (4)
nationality **die Herkunft** (B), **die Nationalität, -en** (B), **die Staatsangehörigkeit, -en** (1)
natural science **die Naturwissenschaft, -en** (8)
naturally **natürlich** (2)
nature **die Natur** (8, 12)
near **bei** (10)
neat **grell** (2); **toll** (2)
neck **der Hals, ¨e** (8)
necklace **die Kette, -n** (2), **die Halskette, -n** (5)
to need **brauchen, gebraucht** (1)
neighbor **der Nachbar, -n** (*wk.*) / **die Nachbarin, -nen** (4)
neighborhood **das Stadtviertel, -** (6), **der Stadtteil, -e** (6)
neonazi **der Neonazi, -s** (12)
nephew **der Neffe, -n** (*wk.*) (B)
nervous(ly) **nervös** (B)
nest **das Nest, -er** (12)
Netherlands **(die) Niederlande** (*pl.*) (B)
never **nie** (2)
new(ly) **neu** (A)
New Zealand **(das) Neuseeland** (B)
news **die Nachrichten** (*pl.*) (7)
newspaper **die Zeitung, -en** (2); to deliver newspapers **Zeitungen aus·tragen** (5); university newspaper **die Unizeitung, -en** (4)
next to **neben** (+ *acc./dat.*) (8); next to each other **nebeneinander** (9); next door **nebenan** (5); from next door **von nebenan** (5)
nice(ly) **nett** (B); nice (*weather*) **schön** (B)
niece **die Nichte, -n** (B)
night **die Nacht, ¨e** (3); in the middle of the night **mitten in der Nacht** (8); last night **gestern abend** (4); night table **der Nachttisch, -e** (6); nights **nachts** (4); at night **nachts** (4)
nightshirt **das Nachthemd, -en** (10)
nine **neun** (A)
nineteen **neunzehn** (A)
ninety **neunzig** (A)
ninth **neunt-** (4)
no **nein** (A); **kein(e)** (2)
no one **niemand** (2, 8)
no-stopping zone **das Halteverbot, -e** (7)
nobody **niemand** (2, 8)
noise **das Geräusch, -e** (8)
none **kein(e)** (2)
nonsense **der Unsinn** (12)
nonsmoker **der Nichtraucher, -** (10)
noodle **die Nudel, -n** (9)
noon: at noon **mittags** (2)
normal **normal** (5)
normally **normalerweise** (9)
north (of) **nördlich (von)** (7)
northeast (of) **nordöstlich (von)** (7)
northwest (of) **nordwestlich (von)** (7)
North Sea **die Nordsee** (B)
Norway **(das) Norwegen** (B)
nose **die Nase, -n** (11)
not at all **kein bißchen** (3); **gar nicht** (8)
not **nicht** (A, B); not until **erst** (4)
note (*of currency*) **der Schein, -e** (9); twenty-mark note **der Zwanzigmarkschein, -e** (9)
notebook **das Heft, -e** (B)

nothing **nichts** (8)
to notice **notieren, notiert** (7); to not notice **verfehlen, verfehlt** (10)
noun **das Substantiv, -e** (A)
novel **der Roman, -e** (3, 5); romance novel **der Liebesroman, -e** (8)
November **der November** (B)
now **jetzt** (3)
number **die Zahl, -en** (A); **die Nummer, -n** (1); telephone number **die Telefonnummer, -n** (1)
nurse **der Krankenpfleger, - / die Krankenpflegerin, -nen** (5); to nurse **pflegen, gepflegt** (5)
nut **die Nuß, Nüsse** (9)

O

o'clock: at six o'clock **um sechs (Uhr)** (1)
oats: rolled oats (*for oatmeal*) **die Haferflocken** (*pl.*) (9)
obligation **die Pflicht, -en** (3)
to observe **zu·sehen (sieht . . . zu), sah . . . zu, zugesehen** (7)
October **der Oktober** (B)
Octoberfest (*festival held yearly during late September and early October*) **das Oktoberfest, -e** (7)
of **aus** (+ *dat.*) (10); **von** (+ *dat.*) (A, 3, 10)
of course **klar** (2); **selbstverständlich** (10)
office **das Büro, -s** (5); at the office **im Büro** (5); doctor's office **die Arztpraxis, Arztpraxen** (11); office building **das Bürohaus, ¨-er** (6); office hour **die Sprechstunde, -n** (3)
often **oft** (B), **offen** (3)
oil **das Öl** (5, 9); to check the oil **das Öl kontrollieren** (5)
old **alt** (A); old part of town **die Altstadt, ¨-e** (10)
olive **die Olive, -n** (9)
omelette **das Omelett, -s** (9)
on account of **wegen** (+ *gen.*) (6)
on **an** (+ *acc./dat.*) (2, 4); **bei** (+ *dat.*) (6); on foot **zu Fuß** (3); on Saturday **am Samstag** (2); on the contrary **sondern** (A); on the first of October **am ersten Oktober** (4); on the phone **am Telefon** (2); on what day? **an welchem Tag?** (4)
once **einmal** (4); **schon einmal** (4); once again **schon wieder** (3)
oncle **der Onkel, -** (B)
one **eins** (A); one another **einander** (3)
one-way street **die Einbahnstraße, -n** (7); one-way trip **die einfache Fahrt** (10)
onion **die Zwiebel, -n** (9)
only **nur** (3)
to open **auf·machen, aufgemacht** (3), **öffnen, geöffnet** (A); to open a bank account **ein Konto eröffnen** (5)
open-face sandwich **das belegte Brot, die belegten Brote** (9)
opener: bottle opener **der Flaschenöffner, -** (9); can opener **der Dosenöffner, -** (9)
opportunity **die Chance, -n** (12)
opposite **gegenüber** (6)
optimistic(ally) **optimistisch** (B)
or **oder** (A, 11)
oral report: to give an oral report **ein Referat halten** (4)
orange **orange** (A); **die Orange, -n** (9); orange juice **der Orangensaft, ¨-e** (9)
orchestra conductor **der Dirigent, -en** (*wk.*) / **die Dirigentin, -nen** (5)
order **die Reihenfolge, -n** (2); to order (*food*) **bestellen, bestellt** (9); in order to **um . . . zu** (12)
ordinal number **die Ordinalzahl, -en** (4)
origin **die Herkunft** (B)
other items **das Sonstige** (A); other things **Sonstiges** (8)
otherwise **sonst** (B)
our **unsere, unser, unseren** (2)
out of **aus** (+ *dat.*) (10); out this way (*toward the speaker*) **heraus** (10); to come out this way **heraus·kommen (kommt . . . heraus), kam . . . heraus, ist herausgekommen** (10)
outside **draußen** (11); outside of **außerhalb** (+ *gen.*) (12)
oven **der Backofen, ¨-** (5)
over **über** (+*acc./dat.*) (4); **vorbei** (8); over the weekend **übers Wochenende** (4); over that way (*away from the speaker*) **hinüber** (10); to go over that way **hinüber·gehen (geht . . . hinüber), ging . . . hinüber, ist hinübergegangen** (10); over there **da drüben** (B)
overcoat **der Mantel, ¨-** (A)
overnight: to stay overnight **übernachten, übernachtet** (6)
own **eigen** (6)
owner of a youth hostel **die Herbergseltern** (*pl.*) (10)

P

pack **die Packung, -en** (9); to pack **packen, gepackt** (7); to pack up **ein·packen, eingepackt** (1)
package **das Paket, -e** (9), **die Packung, -en** (9)
packet **die Packung, -en** (9)
page **die Seite, -n** (6)
pain **der Schmerz, -en** (11)
pajamas **der Schlafanzug, ¨-e** (10)
palace **das Schloß, Schlösser** (6)
palm tree **die Palme, -n** (6)
pan **der Topf, ¨-e** (5); **die Pfanne, -n** (5, 9)
pants (pair of) **die Hose, -n** (A)
pantyhose **die Strumpfhose, -n** (10)
paper **das Papier, -e** (B); paper towel **das Papiertuch, ¨-er** (5); toilet paper **das Toilettenpapier** (4); writing paper **das Briefpapier, -e** (5); to give a paper **ein Referat halten** (4)
parents **die Eltern** (*pl.*) (B)
park **der Park, -s** (1); city park **der Stadtpark, -s** (10); to park **parken, geparkt** (7)
parking lot **der Parkplatz, ¨-e** (6); parking space **die Parklücke, -n** (7); parking ticket **der Strafzettel, -** (7)
parrot **der Papagei, -en** (12)
part **der Teil, -e** (7)
to participate **mit·machen, mitgemacht** (10)
particularly **besonders** (3)
partner **der Partner, - / die Partnerin, -nen** (12)
partnership **die Partnerschaft, -en** (12)
party **das Fest, -e** (2); **die Feier, -n** (8); **die Party, -s** (1); to go to a party **auf eine Party gehen** (1)
passenger train **der Personenzug, ¨-e** (7)
passport **der Paß, Pässe** (7); **der Reisepaß, Reisepässe** (10)
past **vorbei** (8)
past: at twenty past five **um zwanzig nach fünf** (1)
pasture **die Wiese, -n** (7)
path: bicycle path **der Radweg, -e** (7)
patient **geduldig** (12); **der Patient, -en** (*wk.*) / **die Patientin, -nen** (5)
to pay **zahlen, gezahlt** (5); to pay (for) **bezahlen, bezahlt** (4); to pay attention **auf·passen, aufgepaßt** (3); to pay attention to **achten auf** (+ *acc.*), **geachtet** (11); to pay in advance **an·zahlen, angezahlt** (10)
pea **die Erbse, -n** (9)
peach **der Pfirsich, -e** (9)
pear **die Birne, -n** (9)
pedestrian **der Fußgänger, -** (7)
pen **der Stift, -e** (A, B)

pencil **der Bleistift, -e** (A, B)
penicillin **das Penizillin** (4)
peninsula **die Halbinsel, -n** (7)
people **die Leute** (*pl.*) (7); businesspeople **die Geschäftsleute** (*pl.*) (7)
pepper **der Pfeffer** (9)
per **pro** (3); per week **pro Woche** (3)
percent **das Prozent, -e** (4)
perfume **das Parfüm, -e** (5)
perhaps **vielleicht** (2)
perm **die Dauerwelle, -n** (11)
to permit **erlauben** (+ *dat.*), **erlaubt** (7)
permitted: to be permitted (to) **dürfen (darf), durfte, gedurft** (3)
to persecute **verfolgen, verfolgt** (12)
person **die Person, -en** (A, 1); **der Mensch, -en** (*wk.*) (2); **der Typ, -en** (*coll.*) (B)
personal hygiene **die Körperpflege** (11)
pet **das Haustier, -e** (12)
pharmacist **der Apotheker, - / die Apothekerin, -nen** (11)
pharmacy **die Apotheke, -n** (6, 11)
photo **das Foto, -s** (1)
to photograph **fotografieren, fotografiert** (4)
physical **körperlich** (3); physical education **der Sport** (1)
physician **der Arzt, ¨-e / die Ärztin, -nen** (3, 5, 11)
physics **die Physik** (1)
piano **das Klavier, -e** (2)
to pick **pflücken, gepflückt** (8); to pick (*s.o.*) up (*from a place*) **ab·holen, abgeholt** (1)
pickles **saure Gurken** (9)
picnic **das Picknick, -s** (4)
picture **das Bild, -er** (2)
piece **das Stück, -e** (9)
pig **das Schwein, -e** (8)
pill **die Tablette, -n** (11); headache pill **die Kopfschmerztablette, -n** (11)
pillow **das Kopfkissen, -** (6)
pilot **der Pilot, -en** (*wk.*) / **die Pilotin, -nen** (5)
pink **rosa** (A)
piranha **der Piranha, -s** (12)
pizza **die Pizza, -s** (2)
place **der Ort, -e** (1, 4); **der Platz, ¨-e** (3); **die Lage, -n** (10); place of residence **der Wohnort, -e** (1); to place (*in a horizontal position*) **legen, gelegt** (8, 9); (*in a sitting position*) **setzen, gesetzt** (7, 9); (*in a vertical/upright position*) **stellen, gestellt** (3, 5, 9)
plaid **kariert** (10)
plan **der Plan, ¨-e** (3); to plan **planen, geplant** (7); to plan (to) **wollen (will), wollte, gewollt** (3)
plane **das Flugzeug, -e** (7); plane ticket **der Flugschein, -e** (10)
plant **die Pflanze, -n** (3, 6); to water the plants **die Blumen gießen** (3)
plate **der Teller, -** (9); child's plate **der Kinderteller, -** (9); license plate **das Nummernschild, -er** (7)
to play **spielen, gespielt** (1); what's playing at the movies? **was läuft im Kino?** (2)
player: soccer player **der Fußballspieler, - / die Fußballspielerin, -nen** (8); tennis player **der Tennisspieler, - / die Tennisspielerin, -nen** (8)
playground **der Spielplatz, ¨-e** (8)
playwright **der Dramatiker, - / die Dramatikerin, -nen** (8)
please **bitte** (A); yes please? **bitte schön?** (7); to please **gefallen** (+ *dat.*) **(gefällt), gefiel, gefallen** (10); it pleases me **es gefällt mir** (10)
pleasing: to be pleasing to **gefallen** (+ *dat.*) **(gefällt), gefiel, gefallen** (10)
pleasure **das Vergnügen** (2); **die Freude, -n** (8); with pleasure **gern** (1)
pliers **die Zange, -n** (9)
plum **die Pflaume, -n** (9)
pneumonia **die Lungenentzündung, -en** (11)
pocket **die Tasche, -n** (1, 5, 10)
pocketbook **die Tasche, -n** (10)
poem **das Gedicht, -e** (3)
point **der Punkt, -e** (3); main point **der Stichpunkt, -e** (12)
to poison **vergiften, vergiftet** (8)
poisonous **giftig** (8)
Poland **(das) Polen** (B)
police officer **der Polizist, -en** (*wk.*) / **die Polizistin, -nen** (5)
police station **die Polizei** (5, 6); at the police station **auf der Polizei** (5)
political(ly) **politisch** (4)
politics **die Politik** (5)
pool: swimming pool **das Schwimmbad, ¨-er** (1, 5, 6); at the swimming pool **im Schwimmbad** (5); to go to the swimming pool **ins Schwimmbad fahren** (1)
poor **arm** (8)
popular **beliebt** (3)
pork **das Schweinefleisch** (9); ground pork **das Hackfleisch** (9); pork cutlet **das Schnitzel, -** (9); pork roast **der Schweinebraten, -** (9)
Portugal **(das) Portugal** (B)
position **die Lage, -n** (10)
possession **der Besitz** (2)
possibility **die Möglichkeit, -en** (5)
possible: everything possible **alles Mögliche** (2)
post office **die Post** (5); at the post office **auf der Post** (5)
postal employee **der Postbeamte, -n** (*wk.*) **/ die Postbeamtin, -nen** (5)
postcard **die Postkarte, -n** (2)
poster **das Poster, -** (6)
pot **der Topf, ¨-e** (5, 9)
potato **die Kartoffel, -n** (9); boiled potatoes **die Salzkartoffeln** (*pl.*) (9); potato chips **die Kartoffelchips** (*pl.*) (8)
potholder **der Topflappen, -** (5)
poultry **das Geflügel** (9)
pound **das Pfund, -e** (5)
to pour **gießen (gießt), goß, gegossen** (9)
power **der Strom** (9)
practical(ly) **praktisch** (5); practical training **praktische Ausbildung** (5)
preference **die Präferenz, -en** (1)
prejudice **das Vorurteil, -e** (12)
prenuptial agreement **der Ehevertrag, ¨-e** (12)
preparation **die Zubereitung** (9)
to prepare (*food*) **zu·bereiten, zubereitet** (9)
prescription **das Rezept, -e** (11)
present **das Geschenk, -e** (2, 5); Christmas present **das Weihnachtsgeschenk, -e** (5); to present **vor·stellen, vorgestellt** (6)
president **der Präsident, -en** (*wk.*) / **die Präsidentin, -nen** (5)
pressure: blood pressure **der Blutdruck** (11); to have low/high blood pressure **niedrigen/hohen Blutdruck haben** (11)
prestige **das Prestige** (5)
pretty **hübsch** (2); **schön** (B); **ziemlich** (*adv.*) (2)
price **der Preis, -e** (7, 12)
priest **der Priester, - / die Priesterin, -nen** (5)
prince **der Prinz, -en** (*wk.*) (8)
princess **die Prinzessin, -nen** (8)
prison **das Gefängnis, -se** (6)
probably **wahrscheinlich** (11); **wohl** (12)
profession **der Beruf, -e** (1, 5); what's your profession? **was sind Sie von Beruf?** (1)
professional life **das Berufsleben** (12)

professor **der Professor, -en / die Professorin, -nen** (A, B)
progressive(ly) **progressiv** (B)
prohibition **das Verbot, -e** (7)
to promise **versprechen (verspricht), versprach, versprochen** (7, 8)
to promote **fördern, gefördert** (12)
protected **geborgen** (12)
protector **der Beschützer, -** (12)
to protest **protestieren, protestiert** (12)
proximity **die Nähe** (7)
psychiatrist **der Psychiater, - / die Psychiaterin, -nen** (11)
public transportation **die öffentlichen Verkehrsmittel** (*pl.*) (7)
to pull **ziehen (zieht), zog, gezogen** (9)
punctual **pünktlich** (7)
pupil **der Schüler, - / die Schülerin, -nen** (1)
purchase **der Einkauf, ¨-e** (5)
purple **lila** (A)
purse **die Tasche, -n** (1, 5, 10)
to put (*in a vertical position*) **stellen, gestellt** (3, 5, 9); (*in a sitting position*) **setzen, gesetzt** (7); (*in a horizontal position*) **legen, gelegt** (8, 9); to put (into) **geben (gibt), gab, gegeben (in + *acc.*)** (9); to put away **weg·stellen, weggestellt** (5); to put on (*clothes*) **an·ziehen, angezogen** (3)
puzzle **das Rätsel, -** (8); to solve a puzzle **ein Rätsel lösen** (8)
python **die Riesenschlange, -n** (12)

Q

to quarrel **streiten (streitet), stritt, gestritten** (8)
quarter: at a quarter to four **um Viertel vor vier** (1); quarter hour **die Viertelstunde, -n** (6)
queen **die Königin, -nen** (8)
question **die Frage, -n** (A); to ask a question **eine Frage stellen** (5)
quick(ly) **schnell** (3)
quiet **ruhig** (B)
quietly **leise** (8)
quite **ganz** (2, 3); quite a bit **ganz schön viel** (3)

R

rabies **die Tollwut** (12)
radio **das Radio, -s** (2); car radio **das Autoradio, -s** (7)
rag (*for cleaning*) **der Putzlappen, -** (6)
railroad **die Bahn, -en** (7)
railway: cable railway **die Seilbahn, -en** (7)
rain **der Regen** (7); to rain **regnen, geregnet** (B)
raining: it's raining **es regnet** (B)
rainy: in rainy weather **bei Regen** (7)
rare(ly) **selten** (9)
rat **die Ratte, -n** (12)
rather **ganz** (3); **eher** (12); **ziemlich** (2); **lieber** (2); I'd rather go . . . **ich gehe lieber . . .** (2)
rattlesnake **die Klapperschlange, -n** (12)
to reach **erreichen, erreicht** (12)
to read **lesen (liest), las, gelesen** (A, 1, 2); to read aloud **vor·lesen (liest . . . vor), las . . . vor, vorgelesen** (8); to read the newspaper **Zeitung lesen** (1)
ready **fertig** (3)
really **wirklich** (B); **echt** (2)
reason **der Grund, ¨-e** (12)
receipt **die Quittung, -en** (9)
to receive **bekommen (bekommt), bekam, bekommen** (3)
recently **neulich** (8)
reception desk **die Rezeption, -en** (10)
recipe **das Rezept, -e** (9)
recipient (*of a prize*) **der Träger, -** (12)
recreation room **der Aufenthaltsraum, ¨-e** (10)
to recuperate **sich erholen, erholt** (11)
red **rot** (A)
refrigerator **der Kühlschrank, ¨-e** (5, 6)
refugee **der Flüchtling, -e** (12)
regards **mit freundlichen Grüßen** (10)
regularly **regelmäßig** (11)
relative(ly) **relativ** (5); relatives **die Verwandten** (*pl.*) (2)
religion **die Religion** (1)
religious **religiös** (B); religious denomination **die Konfession, -en** (12)
to remain **bleiben (bleibt), blieb, ist geblieben** (1)
remembrance **die Erinnerung, -en** (4)
to remove **ab·nehmen (nimmt . . . ab), nahm . . . ab, abgenommen** (11)
rent **die Miete, -n** (6); to rent **mieten, gemietet** (6); to rent out **vermieten, vermietet** (6)
renter **der Mieter, - / die Mieterin, -nen** (6)
to repair **reparieren, repariert** (1)
repair shop **die Werkstatt, ¨-en** (5)
to repeat **wiederholen, wiederholt** (10)
report **das Referat, -e** (3); accident report **der Unfallbericht, -e** (11); report card **das Zeugnis, -se** (3)
reporter **der Reporter, - / die Reporterin, -nen** (4)
requirement **die Pflicht, -en** (3)
to reserve **reservieren, reserviert** (7)
residence **der Wohnort, -e** (1); place of residence **der Wohnort, -e** (1); to change residence **ziehen (zieht), zog, ist gezogen** (2)
responsibility **die Verantwortung, -en** (12)
responsible: to be responsible for **sich kümmern um, gekümmert** (12); to be equally responsible for taking care of **mit·versorgen, mitversorgt** (12)
to rest **sich aus·ruhen, ausgeruht** (10, 11)
restaurant **das Restaurant, -s** (2); **die Gaststätte, -n** (5); at the restaurant **in der Gaststätte** (5)
to retire **in Pension gehen** (12)
retirement **die Pension** (12)
to return **wieder·kommen (kommt . . . wieder), kam . . . wieder, ist wiedergekommen** (5)
reunion: class reunion **das Klassentreffen, -** (8)
rice **der Reis** (9)
riddle **das Rätsel, -** (8); to solve a riddle **ein Rätsel lösen** (8)
to ride **reiten (reitet), ritt, hat/ist geritten** (1); **fahren (fährt), fuhr, ist gefahren** (2); to ride off **los·fahren (fährt . . . los), fuhr . . . los, ist losgefahren** (8)
right **recht** (2); **richtig** (2); **rechts** (10); **gleich** (6); right around the corner **gleich um die Ecke** (6); right away **gleich** (4); right now **im Moment** (1); that's right **stimmt!** (4); to the right **rechts** (7); you are right **du hast recht** (2); to be right **stimmen, gestimmt** (9); that's all right **das stimmt** (9)
right-of-way **die Vorfahrt, -en** (7)
right-wing (extreme) **der / die Rechtsradikale, -n (ein Rechtsradikaler)** (12)
ring **der Ring, -e** (2); gold ring **der Goldring, -e** (10); to ring **klingeln, geklingelt** (2)
to rinse **spülen, gespült** (4)
river **der Fluß, Flüsse** (7)
road **die Straße, -n** (6); on the road **unterwegs** (4, 8)
roast **der Braten, -** (9); sauerbraten (*marinated beef roast*) **der Sauerbraten, -** (9); pork roast **der Schweinebraten, -** (9)
roasted **gebraten** (9)
rock concert **das Rockkonzert, -e** (8)
rock star **der Rockstar, -s** (12)

rocket **die Rakete, -n** (7)
role **die Rolle, -n** (4)
role model **das Vorbild, -er** (8)
roll **das Brötchen, -** (9)
rolled oats (*for oatmeal*) **die Haferflocken** (*pl.*) (9)
romance novel **der Liebesroman, -e** (8)
roof **das Dach, ¨er** (6)
room **das Zimmer, -** (2, 6); dining room **das Eßzimmer, -** (6); bedroom **das Schlafzimmer, -** (6); breakfast room **das Frühstückszimmer, -** (10); double room **das Doppelzimmer, -** (10); dressing room **die Umkleidekabine, -n** (5); living room **das Wohnzimmer, -** (6); recreation room **der Aufenthaltsraum, ¨e** (10); single room **das Einzelzimmer, -** (5); TV room **das Fernsehzimmer, -** (10); waiting room **die Wartehalle, -n** (10)
roommate **der Mitbewohner, - / die Mitbewohnerin, -nen** (2)
roundabout: traffic roundabout **der Kreisverkehr** (10)
round-trip **hin und zurück** (5, 10); round trip **die Hin- und Rückfahrt** (10)
row: in a row **hintereinander** (3)
rug **der Teppich, -e** (6)
Rumania **(das) Rumänien** (B)
rumpsteak **das Rumpsteak, -s** (9)
to run **laufen (läuft), lief, ist gelaufen** (A, 2); to run over **überfahren (überfährt), überfuhr, überfahren** (11); to run in the woods **im Wald laufen** (2)
rural highway **die Landstraße, -n** (7)
rushed **eilig** (10)
rusty **rostig** (9)
Russia **(das) Rußland** (B)
Russian (*adj.*) **russisch** (12)

S

sad **traurig** (B, 3)
safety belt **der Sicherheitsgurt, -e** (7)
to sail **segeln, gesegelt** (1)
salad **der Salat, -e** (3, 9); herring salad **der Heringssalat, -e** (9); salad bowl **die Salatschüssel, -n** (5); salad dressing **die Salatsoße, -n** (9)
salesperson **der Verkäufer, - / die Verkäuferin, -nen** (5)
salon: hair salon **der Friseur, -e** (6)
salt **das Salz** (9)
salted **gesalzen** (9)
salty **salzig** (7)
same **egal** (6)
sand **der Sand** (7)
sandal **die Sandale, -n** (10)
sandcastle **die Sandburg, -en** (10)
sandwich: open-face sandwich **das belegte Brot, die belegten Brote** (9)
Saturday **der Samstag** (1)
sauce **die Soße, -n** (9); tomato sauce **die Tomatensoße, -n** (9)
sauerkraut **das Sauerkraut** (7)
sauna **die Sauna, Saunen** (11)
sausage **die Wurst, ¨e** (9); link sausage **das Würstchen, -** (9)
to save **erlösen, erlöst** (8); to save (*money*) **sparen, gespart** (7)
to say **sagen, gesagt** (A, 5)
scale: kitchen scale **die Küchenwaage, -n** (5, 9)
scarf **das Halstuch, ¨er** (2); **der Schal, -s** (10)
scene of the accident **die Unfallstelle, -n** (11)
schedule **der Stundenplan, ¨e** (1)
schilling (*Austrian monetary unit*) **der Schilling, -e** (7); two schillings **zwei Schilling** (7)
scholarship **das Stipendium, Stipendien** (1)
school **die Schule, -n** (A, 1, 3, 4, 5); at school **in der Schule** (5); elementary school **die Grundschule, -n** (4); high school/ college prep school **das Gymnasium, Gymnasien** (4, 6); summer school **der Sommerkurs, -e** (3)
schooling **die Schulbildung** (5)
shrill **grell** (2)
science: natural science **die Naturwissenschaft, -en** (8)
scientist **der Wissenschaftler, - / die Wissenschaftlerin, -nen** (8)
scissors **die Schere, -n** (9)
to scold **schimpfen, geschimpft** (8)
scorpion **der Skorpion, -e** (12)
to scream **schreien (schreit), schrie, geschrien** (3)
sea **die See, -n** (B); **das Meer, -e** (1, 7)
seasick **seekrank** (7)
season **die Jahreszeit, -en** (B); to season **würzen, gewürzt** (9)
seasoning **das Gewürz, -e** (9)
seat **der Sitz, -e** (7)
second **die Sekunde, -n** (1); second **zweit-** (4)
secret **heimlich** (8)
secretary **der Sekretär, -e / die Sekretärin, -nen** (5); union secretary **der Gewerkschaftssekretär, -e / die Gewerkschaftssekretärin, -nen** (12)
security deposit **die Kaution, -en** (6)
to see **sehen (sieht), sah, gesehen** (2); see you soon **bis bald** (A)
seldom **selten** (9)
to select **aus·wählen, ausgewählt** (9)
to sell **verkaufen, verkauft** (5)
semester **das Semester, -** (1)
to send **schicken, geschickt** (2)
sense (of, for) **der Sinn (für)** (12)
sentence **der Satz, ¨e** (3)
to separate **trennen, getrennt** (7); to separate (*people*) **sich trennen** (8)
separate checks **getrennt** (5)
separately **getrennt** (5)
September **der September** (B)
sequence **die Reihenfolge, -n** (4)
serious **ernsthaft** (B)
servant **der Diener, -** (8)
service **die Bedienung** (9); military service **der Wehrdienst** (12)
to set, **decken gedeckt** (3, 7, 9); to set the table **den Tisch decken** (3); to set up **auf·stellen, aufgestellt** (11)
seven **sieben** (A)
seventeen **siebzehn** (A)
seventh **siebt-** (4)
seventy **siebzig** (A)
several **mehrere** (*pl.*) (10); several times **mehrmals** (5)
shade **der Schatten** (8)
shadow **der Schatten, -** (8)
shared housing **die Wohngemeinschaft, -en** (6)
shark **der Hai, -e** (12)
to shave **sich rasieren, rasiert** (11)
ship **das Schiff, -e** (7)
shirt **das Hemd, -en** (A)
shock **der Schock, -s** (11)
shoe **der Schuh, -e** (A); shoe store **das Schuhgeschäft, -e** (6); tennis shoe **der Tennisschuh, -e** (A)
shoots: bamboo shoots **die Bambussprossen** (*pl.*) (9)
shop: repair shop **die Werkstatt, ¨en** (5); to shop **ein·kaufen, eingekauft** (1)
shopping center **das Einkaufszentrum, Einkaufszentren** (10); shopping list **die Einkaufsliste, -n** (9); to go shopping **einkaufen gehen (geht einkaufen), ging einkaufen, ist einkaufen gegangen** (1, 5)
shore **der Strand, ¨e** (7)
short **klein** (A); **kurz** (A)

shot **die Spritze, -n** (11)
shoulder **die Schulter, -n** (A)
to shout **rufen (ruft), rief, gerufen** (7)
to shovel **schaufeln, geschaufelt** (11)
shower **die Dusche, -n** (5, 6); to shower **(sich) duschen, geduscht** (11); to take a shower **(sich) duschen** (1, 11)
shrimp **die Krabbe, -n** (9)
shut: tied shut **zugebunden** (9); shut **schließen Sie** (A); to shut **schließen (schließt), schloß, geschlossen** (A)
shy **schüchtern** (B)
siblings **die Geschwister** (B)
sick **krank** (3)
sickness **die Krankheit, -en** (11)
side **die Seite, -n** (6); side dish **die Beilage, -n** (9)
sidewalk **der Fußgängerweg, -e** (7)
to sightsee **besichtigen, besichtigt** (7)
sign **das Schild, -er** (7); traffic sign **das Verkehrsschild, -er** (7); to sign **unterschreiben (unterschreibt), unterschrieb, unterschrieben** (1)
signature **die Unterschrift, -en** (1)
sill: window sill **die Fensterbank, ¨e** (5)
silverware **das Besteck, -e** (5, 9)
simply **einfach** (2)
since **seit** (+ *dat.*) (4, 11)
to sing **singen (singt), sang, gesungen** (1); **vor·singen (singt . . . vor), sang . . . vor, vorgesungen** (5)
single room **das Einzelzimmer, -** (5)
sink **das Spülbecken, -** (5); **die Spüle, -n** (9)
sister **die Schwester, -n** (B)
to sit **sitzen (sitzt), saß, gesessen** (4, 9); to sit down **sich setzen, gesetzt** (A, 11)
situation: conversational situation **die Sprechsituation, -en** (A)
six **sechs** (A)
sixteen **sechzehn** (A)
sixth **sechst-** (4)
sixty **sechzig** (A)
size **die Größe, -n** (10)
skate **der Schlittschuh, -e** (3)
skateboard **das Skateboard, -s** (3); to go skateboarding **Skateboard fahren** (3)
skating: to go skating **Schlittschuh laufen** (3)
ski **der Ski, -er** (3); ski goggles **die Skibrille, -n** (5)
skiing: to go skiing **Ski fahren** (3)
skills **die Kenntnisse** (*pl.*) (5)
skin **die Haut, ¨e** (3, 11)
skirt **der Rock, ¨e** (A)
skyscraper **der Wolkenkratzer, -** (6)
sled **der Schlitten, -** (2)
sleep **der Schlaf** (8); to sleep **schlafen (schläft), schlief, geschlafen** (2)
sleeping bag **der Schlafsack, ¨e** (2); sleeping car **der Schlafwagen, -** (4)
slender **schlank** (A)
slice **das Stück, -e** (9)
to slide **rutschen, ist gerutscht** (8)
slim **schlank** (A)
to slip **rutschen, ist gerutscht** (8); **aus·rutschen, ist ausgerutscht** (11)
Slovakia **(die) Slowakei** (B)
Slovenia **(das) Slowenien** (B)
small **klein** (A); **eng** (12)
smart **schick** (2)
smell **riechen (riecht), roch, gerochen** (11)
to smoke **rauchen, geraucht** (3)
smoked **geräuchert** (9)
smoker **der Raucher, -** / die **Raucherin, -nen** (10)
snail **die Schnecke, -n** (12)
snake **die Schlange, -n** (12); rattlesnake **die Klapperschlange, -n** (12)
sniffles **der Schnupfen, -** (11)
snow **der Schnee** (8); to snow **schneien, geschneit** (B)
snowing: it's snowing **es schneit** (B)
so **so** (B, 3); **also** (2); and so forth **und so weiter** (5); so long **bis bald** (A); so that **damit** (*subord. conj.*) (11, 12)
soap **die Seife, -n** (6)
soccer **der Fußball, ¨e** (A, 1); soccer player **der Fußballspieler, -** / die **Fußballspielerin, -nen** (8); soccer stadium **das Fußballstadion, -stadien** (10)
social studies **die Sozialkunde** (1)
society: multicultural society **multikulturelle Gesellschaft** (12)
sociology **die Soziologie** (1)
sock **die Socke, -n** (10)
sofa **das Sofa, -s** (6)
soft drink **die Limonade, -n** (4, 9)
soft-boiled eggs **gekochte Eier** (9)
sold out **ausverkauft** (5)
to solve a puzzle/riddle **ein Rätsel lösen** (8)
somebody **jemand** (3)
someone **jemand** (3)
something **etwas** (2, 4, 5); something interesting / new **etwas Interessantes / Neues** (4)
sometimes **manchmal** (B)
son **der Sohn, ¨e** (B)
song **das Lied, -er** (3)
songbook **das Songbuch, ¨er** (2)
soon **bald** (8); soon thereafter **bald darauf** (8)
sore throat **die Halsschmerzen** (*pl.*) (11)
sorry! **tut mir leid!** (5)
sound **das Geräusch, -e** (8); to sound (like) **klingen (wie) (klingt), klang, geklungen** (11)
soup **die Suppe, -n** (3)
sour **sauer** (9)
south (of) **südlich (von)** (7)
South Africa **(das) Südafrika** (B)
South America **(das) Südamerika** (B)
southeast (of) **südöstlich (von)** (7)
southwest (of) **südwestlich (von)** (7)
souvenir **das Andenken, -** (10)
space: parking space **die Parklücke, -n** (7); space station **die Raumstation, -en** (6)
spaghetti **die Spaghetti** (*pl.*) (3)
Spain **(das) Spanien** (B)
Spanish (*language*) **(das) Spanisch** (B)
to speak **sprechen (spricht), sprach, gesprochen** (A)
speaker: stereo speaker **die Box, -en** (6)
specialized training **die Ausbildung** (5)
speeding ticket **der Strafzettel, -** (7)
to spell **schreiben (schreibt), schrieb, geschrieben** (A); how do you spell that? **wie schreibt man das?** (A, B); to cast a spell on **verwünschen, verwünscht** (8)
to spend **aus·geben (gibt . . . aus), gab . . . aus, ausgegeben** (3)
spice **das Gewürz, -e** (9)
spinach **der Spinat** (9)
spite: in spite of **trotz** (+ *gen.*) (12); in spite of that **trotzdem** (8)
spoon **der Löffel, -** (9)
sports jacket **das Sakko, -s** (A); to do sports **Sport treiben** (2)
spouse **der Ehepartner, -** / **die Ehepartnerin, -nen** (12)
spring **der Frühling, -e** (B); spring cleaning **der Frühjahrsputz** (6)
sprinkle **bestreuen, bestreut** (9)
sprouts: bamboo sprouts **die Bambussprossen** (*pl.*) (9); Brussels sprouts **der Rosenkohl** (9)
square: market square **der Marktplatz, ¨e** (6); square meter (m^2) **der Quadratmeter (qm)** (6)
squash **das Squash** (1)
stadium: soccer stadium **das Fußballstadion, Fußballstadien** (10)
stairway **die Treppe, -n** (6)

stairwell **das Treppenhaus, ¨-er** (10)
stamp **die Briefmarke, -n** (5)
to stand **stehen (steht), stand, gestanden** (2, 6, 9); to stand up **aufstehen (steht . . . auf), stand . . . auf, ist aufgestanden** (A); to stand (*s.th.*) up **stellen, gestellt** (9)
to starve **verhungern, verhungert** (12)
state **die Verfassung, -en** (3); **der Staat, -en** (10)
state-subsidized apartment building **das Wohnheim, -e** (12)
station: train station **der Bahnhof, ¨-e** (4, 6, 10)
stationery store **das Schreibwarengeschäft, -e** (6)
to stay **bleiben (bleibt), blieb, ist geblieben** (1); to stay overnight **übernachten, übernachtet** (6); to stay put **stecken·bleiben (bleibt . . . stecken), blieb . . . stecken, ist steckengeblieben** (11)
to steal **stehlen (stiehlt), stahl, gestohlen** (7)
to steer **lenken, gelenkt** (5)
steering wheel **das Lenkrad, ¨-er** (7)
stepfather **der Stiefvater, ¨** (8)
stepmother **die Stiefmutter, ¨** (8)
stereo speaker **die Box, -en** (6); stereo system **die Stereoanlage, -n** (6)
still **noch** (B)
to sting **stechen (sticht), stach, gestochen** (12)
stomach **der Bauch, ¨-e** (A); **der Magen, ¨** (11)
stomachache **die Magenschmerzen** (*pl.*) (11)
Stone Age **die Steinzeit** (12)
stop **die Haltestelle, -n** (10); bus stop **die Bushaltestelle, -n** (10); subway stop **die U-Bahnhaltestelle, -n** (10); to stop (*moving*) **halten (hält), hielt, gehalten** (4, 7); to stop (*a car*) **an·halten (hält . . . an), hielt . . . an, angehalten** (7); to stop (*doing something*) **auf·hören (mit), aufgehört** (1)
store **das Geschäft, -e** (2); department store **das Kaufhaus, ¨-er** (5); at the department store **im Kaufhaus** (5)
story **der Stock, Stockwerke** (6)
stove **der Herd, -e** (5, 6); tile stove **der Kachelofen, ¨** (6)
to stow **verstauen, verstaut** (7)
straight ahead **geradeaus** (10)
straighten **gerade·stellen, geradegestellt** (3); to straighten the books **die Bücher gerade·stellen** (3)
strange **komisch** (12)
strawberry **die Erdbeere, -n** (9)
street **die Straße, -n** (6, 7); one-way street **die Einbahnstraße, -n** (7); narrow street **die Gasse, -n** (10); streetcar **die Straßenbahn, -en** (7)
strict **streng** (8)
string **die Schnur, ¨-e** (9)
striped **gestreift** (10)
stuck: to get stuck **stecken·bleiben (bleibt . . . stecken), blieb . . . stecken, ist steckengeblieben** (11)
student **der Student, -en** (*wk.*) / **die Studentin, -nen** (A, B); fellow students **die Mitstudenten** (*pl.*) (A); student life **das Studentenleben** (4)
to study **studieren, studiert** (1)
subject: academic subjects **Schul- und Studienfächer** (1); favorite subject **das Lieblingsfach, ¨-er** (5)
subway **die U-Bahn, -en (Untergrundbahn)** (7); subway stop **die U-Bahnhaltestelle, -n** (10)
such **so** (3)
to suck **lutschen, gelutscht** (11)
suddenly **plötzlich** (8)
sugar **der Zucker** (9)
to suggest **vor·schlagen (schlägt . . . vor), schlug . . . vor, vorgeschlagen** (5)
suggestion **der Vorschlag, ¨-e** (5)
suit **der Anzug, ¨-e** (A); bathing suit **der Badeanzug, ¨-e** (5); to suit **stehen** (+ *dat.*) **(steht), stand, gestanden** (10)
suitcase **der Koffer, -** (2, 10)
summer **der Sommer, -** (B); last summer **letzten Sommer** (4); summer school **der Sommerkurs, -e** (3)
to sunbathe **sich sonnen, gesonnt** (11)
Sunday **der Sonntag** (1)
sunglasses **die Sonnenbrille, -n** (2)
sunny **sonnig** (B)
supermarket **der Supermarkt, ¨-e** (5, 6); at the supermarket **im Supermarkt** (5)
supper **das Abendessen, -** (1)
supposed: to be supposed to **sollen (soll), sollte, gesollt** (3)
sure **sicher** (3)
surface **die Fläche, -n** (7)
surfboard **das Surfbrett, -er** (2)
surname **der Familienname, -n** (*wk.*) (1)
surrounding area **die Umgebung, -en** (5)
survey **die Umfrage, -n** (4)
suspicion **die Ahnung, -en** (4)
to swear **fluchen, geflucht** (11)
sweater **der Pullover, -, der Pulli, -s** (2)
sweats **der Trainingsanzug, ¨-e** (2)
Sweden **(das) Schweden** (B)
Swedish (*language*) **(das) Schwedisch** (B)
to sweep **fegen, gefegt** (5)
sweet **die Süßigkeit, -en** (8); *adj.* **lieb** (10); **süß** (4)
to swim **schwimmen (schwimmt), schwamm, ist geschwommen** (7)
swimming pool **das Schwimmbad, ¨-er** (1, 5, 6); at the swimming pool **im Schwimmbad** (5); to go to the swimming pool **ins Schwimmbad fahren** (1); to swim in the sea **im Meer schwimmen** (1); swimming-pool attendant **der Bademeister, - / die Bademeisterin, -nen** (5); swimming trunks **die Badehose, -n** (5)
swimming: to go swimming **schwimmen gehen (geht schwimmen), ging schwimmen, ist schwimmen gegangen** (1)
Swiss (*person*) **der Schweizer, - / die Schweizerin, -nen** (B)
to switch on **an·machen, angemacht** (3)
Switzerland **(die) Schweiz** (B)
symptom **das Symptom, -e** (11)
syrup: cough syrup **der Hustensaft, ¨-e** (11)

T

T-shirt **das T-Shirt, -s** (2, 5)
table **der Tisch, -e** (B, 6); kitchen table **der Küchentisch, -e** (5, 6); living room table **der Wohnzimmertisch, -e** (6); night table **der Nachttisch, -e** (6); table lamp **die Tischlampe, -n** (9); table tennis **das Tischtennis** (3); to clear the table **den Tisch ab·räumen** (3); to set the table **den Tisch decken** (3)
tablet **die Tablette, -n** (11)
to take **nehmen (nimmt), nahm, genommen** (A, 3); to take along **mit·nehmen (nimmt . . . mit), nahm . . . mit, mitgenommen** (3); to take blood **Blut ab·nehmen** (11); to take care **Mach's gut** (*infor.*) (A); to take care of **sorgen für, gesorgt** (12); to take (a course) **belegen, belegt** (3); to take effect **wirken, gewirkt** (11); to take off (*clothes*) **aus·ziehen (zieht . . . aus), zog . . . aus, ausgezogen** (3); to take on (responsibility) **übernehmen (übernimmt), übernahm, übernommen** (12); to take out **weg·bringen**

(bringt . . . weg), brachte . . . weg, weggebracht (5); to take place **statt·finden (findet . . . statt), fand . . . statt, stattgefunden** (5)
tale: fairy tale **das Märchen, -** (4, 8)
talent **das Talent, -e** (3)
tall **groß** (A)
tame **zahm** (12)
tank **der Tank, -s** (7)
tanning salon **das Solarium, Solarien** (11)
to taste **probieren, probiert** (3); to taste good (to) **schmecken, geschmeckt** (+ *dat.*) (10)
tavern **die Kneipe, -n** (3)
tax **die Steuer, -n** (12)
taxi **das Taxi, -s** (3, 7); taxi driver **der Taxifahrer, - / die Taxifahrerin, -nen** (5)
tea **der Tee** (4, 9); tea kettle **der Teekessel, -** (9)
to teach **unterrichten, unterrichtet** (5)
teacher **der Lehrer, - / die Lehrerin, -nen** (A, 1)
team **die Mannschaft, -en** (8); baseball team **die Baseballmannschaft, -en** (8)
teapot **die Teekanne, -n** (9)
to tear **zerreißen (zerreißt), zerriß, zerrissen** (8)
to tease **ärgern, geärgert** (3)
technology **die Technik** (12)
teddy bear **der Teddy, -s** (8)
telegram **das Telegramm, -e** (2)
telephone **das Telefon, -e** (A, 2); telephone booth **die Telefonzelle, -n** (2); telephone card **die Telefonkarte, -n** (2); telephone number **die Telefonnummer, -n** (1); to telephone **telefonieren, telefoniert** (4)
to tell **sagen, gesagt** (5); to tell (a story, joke) **erzählen, erzählt** (3, 5); to tell jokes **Witze erzählen** (3)
ten **zehn** (A)
tender **zart** (9)
tennis **das Tennis** (1); tennis player **der Tennisspieler, - / die Tennisspielerin, -nen** (8); tennis racket **der Tennisschläger, -** (2); tennis shoe **der Tennisschuh, -e** (A)
tent **das Zelt, -e** (2, 5)
tenth **zehnt-** (4)
terrace **die Terrasse, -n** (6)
terrible **furchtbar** (4)
test **die Prüfung, -en**
tetanus **der Tetanus** (11)
text **der Text, -e** (12)
thanks **danke** (A); many thanks **vielen Dank** (10)
that **diese, dieser, dieses** (4); that (*subord. conj.*) **daß** (11); that is . . . **das ist . . .** (B); that way (*away from the speaker*) **hin** (10); to go that way **hin·gehen (geht . . . hin), ging . . . hin, ist hingegangen** (10); that's right **stimmt!** (4); that's why **deshalb** (7)
theater **das Theater, -** (4)
then **denn** (A)
there **da** (2); **dort** (7); **dorthin** (10); over there **da drüben** (B); there and back **hin und zurück** (10); there is **es gibt . . .** (6); is there . . . ? **gibt es . . . ?** (6)
thereafter: soon thereafter **bald darauf** (8)
therefore **deshalb** (7)
these **diese** (2, 4); these are . . . **das sind . . .** (B)
thesis (*for an advanced degree*) **die Diplomarbeit, -en** (12)
thing **das Ding, -e** (2); **die Sache, -n** (2); other things **Sonstiges** (8)
to think **denken (denkt), dachte, gedacht** (7); I think so **ich glaube schon** (3); to think about **nach·denken (über** + *acc.*) **(denkt . . . nach), dachte . . . nach, nachgedacht** (7); to think of **halten von (hält), hielt, gehalten** (12)
third **dritt-** (4)
thirst **der Durst** (3)
thirsty: to be thirsty **Durst haben** (3)
thirteen **dreizehn** (A)
thirteenth **dreizehnt-** (4)
thirty **dreißig** (A); at two thirty **um halb drei** (1)
this **diese, dieser, dieses** (2, 4); this evening **heute abend** (2); this is . . . **das ist . . .** (B); this way (*toward the speaker*) **her** (10); to come this way **her·kommen (kommt . . . her), kam . . . her, ist hergekommen** (10)
thorn **der Dorn, -en** (8)
those **diese** (4); those are . . . **das sind . . .** (B)
thought **der Gedanke, -n** (*wk.*) (7)
three **drei** (A); three times **dreimal** (3)
throat **der Hals, ¨e** (8); sore throat **die Halsschmerzen** (*pl.*) (11); throat lozenge **das Halsbonbon, -s** (11)
through **durch** (+ *acc.*) (7)
to throw **werfen (wirft), warf, geworfen** (3)
thunderstorm **das Gewitter, -** (9)
Thursday **der Donnerstag** (1)
thus **also** (2)
ticket **die Fahrkarte, -n** (4); ticket (*parking or speeding*) **der Strafzettel, -** (7); admissions ticket **die Eintrittskarte, -n** (5); movie theater ticket booth **die Kinokasse, -n** (5); plane ticket **der Flugschein, -e** (10); ticket booth **der Schalter, -** (5); at the ticket booth **am Schalter** (5); ticket counter **der Fahrkartenschalter, -** (10); ticket window **der Fahrkartenschalter, -** (7); train ticket **die Zugfahrkarte, -n** (6)
tie **die Krawatte, -n** (A); to tie to **binden (an** + *acc.*) **(bindet), band, gebunden** (12)
tied shut **zugebunden** (9)
tight **eng** (12)
tile stove **der Kachelofen, ¨** (6)
time **die Zeit, -en** (1, 4); **das Mal, -e** (4); at what time . . . ? **um wieviel Uhr . . . ?** (1); the last time **das letzte Mal** (4); for the first time **zum ersten Mal** (4); on time **rechtzeitig** (12); several times **mehrmals** (5); three times **dreimal** (3); what time is it? **wie spät ist es?** (1); **wieviel Uhr ist es?** (1)
timely **rechtzeitig** (12)
tip **das Trinkgeld, -er** (9)
tire **der Reifen, -** (7); **der Autoreifen, -** (9); flat tire **die Reifenpanne, -n** (7)
tired **müde** (3)
to **an** (+ *acc./dat.*); to the sea **ans Meer** (2); to (*a place*) **nach** (+ *dat.*) (10); **zu** (+ *dat.*); to the doctor **zum Arzt** (3); to the university **zur Uni** (2); to (a specific place already mentioned) **dorthin** (10)
toaster **der Toaster, -** (9)
today **heute** (B); what is today's date? **welches Datum ist heute?** (4)
together **zusammen** (2); **gemeinsam** (11); all together **alles zusammen** (5)
toilet **die Toilette, -n** (6); toilet paper **das Toilettenpapier** (4)
tolerant **tolerant** (B)
tomato **die Tomate, -n** (9); tomato sauce **die Tomatensoße, -n** (9)
tomorrow **morgen** (2); the day after tomorrow **übermorgen** (8)
tongue **die Zunge, -n** (11)
too **auch** (A)
too bad! **schade!** (3)
too **zu** (4); too heavy **zu schwer** (4)
tool **das Werkzeug, -e** (9)
tooth **der Zahn, ¨e** (11)
toothache **die Zahnschmerzen** (*pl.*) (11)

topic **das Thema, Themen** (4)
total **total** (4); to total (up) **aus·rechnen, ausgerechnet** (9)
tour of the city **die Stadtrundfahrt, -en** (7); bicycle tour **die Radtour, -en** (8); guided tour **die Führung, -en** (10)
tourism **der Tourismus** (10)
tourist bureau **das Fremdenverkehrsamt, ¨-er** (10); tourist class **die Touristenklasse** (5, 10)
towel: hand towel **das Handtuch, ¨-er** (5, 9); paper towel **das Papiertuch, ¨-er** (5)
town **der Ort, -e** (4); **die Stadt, ¨-e** (6); home town **die Heimatstadt, ¨-e** (6); old part of town **die Altstadt, ¨-e** (10); town hall **das Rathaus, ¨-er** (1, 6); at the town hall **auf dem Rathaus** (1)
tracks: set of train tracks **das Gleis, -e** (10); train track **die Schiene, -n** (10)
tradition **die Tradition, -en** (4)
traffic **der Verkehr** (7, 11); traffic jam **der Stau, -s** (7); traffic light **die Ampel, -n** (7); traffic roundabout **der Kreisverkehr** (10); traffic sign **das Verkehrsschild, -er** (7)
train **der Zug, ¨-e** (7, 10); passenger train **der Personenzug, ¨-e** (7); train agent **der Bahnbeamte, -n (ein Beamter) / die Bahnbeamtin, -nen** (10); train car **der Waggon, -s** (7); train station **der Bahnhof, ¨-e** (4, 5, 6, 10); at the train station **auf dem Bahnhof** (5); train ticket **die Zugfahrkarte, -n** (6); train track **die Schiene, -n** (10); train tracks (set of) **das Gleis, -e** (10)
training: specialized training **die Ausbildung, -en** (5); practical (career) training **praktische Ausbildung** (5)
trait **die Eigenschaft, -en** (12)
to translate **übersetzen, übersetzt** (8)
translator **der Übersetzer, - / die Übersetzerin, -nen** (12)
to transport **transportieren, transportiert** (7)
transportation: means of transportation **das Transportmittel, -** (7); public transportation **die öffentlichen Verkehrsmittel** (*pl.*) (7)
to travel **reisen, ist gereist** (1)
travel agency **das Reisebüro, -s** (6); travel bureau **das Reisebüro, -s** (10); travel experience **das Reiseerlebnis, -se** (7); to travel first class **erster Klasse fahren** (10); travel guidebook **der Reiseführer, -** (5)
traveler **der/die Reisende, -n (ein Reisender)** (10); traveler's check **der Reisescheck, -s** (7)
traveling **das Reisen** (10)
treasure **der Schatz, ¨-e** (8)
tree **der Baum, ¨-e** (8); tree house **das Baumhaus, ¨-er** (6)
trick **die List, -en** (8)
trip **die Reise, -n** (7); **die Fahrt, -en** (10); business trip **die Geschäftsreise, -n** (7); holiday trip **die Ferienreise, -n** (8); one-way trip **die einfache Fahrt** (10); round trip **hin und zurück** (10); **die Hin- und Rückfahrt** (10); to be on a trip **auf Reisen sein** (7); to go on a trip **verreisen, ist verreist** (3); to trip **stolpern, ist gestolpert** (8)
trout **die Forelle, -n** (9)
truck **der Lastwagen, -** (7)
true **wahr** (3); **treu** (8)
trunk **der Kofferraum, ¨-e** (7); trunk (*of an elephant*) **der Rüssel, -** (12); swimming trunks **die Badehose, -n** (5)
to try **probieren, probiert** (3); **versuchen, versucht** (8, 11); to try on **an·probieren, anprobiert** (10)
Tuesday **der Dienstag** (1)
Tunisia **(das) Tunesien** (B)
Turk **der Türke, -n** (*wk.*) / **die Türkin, -nen** (12)
Turkey **(die) Türkei** (B)
Turkish (*language*) **(das) Türkisch** (B)
to turn **ab·biegen (biegt . . . ab), bog . . . ab, ist abgebogen** (10); to turn off **aus·machen, ausgemacht** (3); to turn on **an·machen, angemacht** (3); **ein·schalten, eingeschaltet** (11)
turtle **die Schildkröte, -n** (12)
tusk **der Stoßzahn, ¨-e** (12)
to tutor **Nachhilfe geben** (3)
tutored: to be tutored **Nachhilfe nehmen** (3)
tutoring **die Nachhilfe** (3)
TV movie **der Fernsehfilm, -e** (12); TV reporter **der Fernsehreporter, - / die Fernsehreporterin, -nen** (5); TV room **das Fernsehzimmer, -** (10); TV set **der Fernseher, -** (2); to watch TV **fernsehen (sieht . . . fern), sah . . . fern, ferngesehen** (2)
twelfth **zwölft-** (4)
twelve **zwölf** (A)
twentieth **zwanzigst-** (4)
twenty **zwanzig** (A)
twice **zweimal** (5)
two **zwei** (A)
type **die Art, -en** (2); to type **tippen, getippt** (3, 6)
typewriter **die Schreibmaschine, -n** (2)

U

U.S.A. **die USA** (*pl.*) (B)
ugly **häßlich** (2)
Ukraine **(die) Urkraine** (B)
umbrella **der Regenschirm, -e** (5, 10)
unconsciousness **die Ohnmacht** (11)
underpants **die Unterhose, -n** (10)
undershirt **das Unterhemd, -en** (10)
to understand **verstehen (versteht), verstand, verstanden** (4)
underwear **die Unterwäsche** (10)
undressed: to get undressed **sich aus·ziehen (zieht . . . aus), zog . . . aus, ausgezogen** (11)
unemployed **arbeitslos** (5)
unfortunately **leider** (B)
union secretary **der Gewerkschaftssekretär, -e / die Gewerkschaftssekretärin, -nen** (12)
university **die Universität, -en** (1, 4, 5); **die Uni, -s** (*coll.*) (B, 1); at the university **auf der Universität** (5); university newspaper **die Unizeitung, -en** (4); university studies **das Studium** (1); to be at the university **auf der Uni sein** (1); to go to the university **zur Uni gehen** (1)
unmarried **ledig** (1)
untalented **unbegabt** (12)
until **bis** (2, 3, 4, 11); not until **erst** (4); not until four o'clock **erst um vier Uhr** (4); until four o'clock **bis um vier Uhr** (4); until four in the morning **bis um vier Uhr früh** (4); until eight o'clock **bis acht Uhr** (2)
up to **bis zu** (+ *dat.*) (10); up that way (*away from the speaker*) **hinauf** (10); to go up that way **hinauf·gehen (geht . . . hinauf), ging . . . hinauf, ist hinaufgegangen** (10)
upset: to get upset **sich auf·regen, aufgeregt** (11)
Uranus **der Uranus** (4)
urgently **dringend** (2)
to use **brauchen, gebraucht** (1, 7); to use violence **Gewalt an·wenden** (12)
used car **der Gebrauchtwagen, -** (7)
used: to get used to **sich gewöhnen (an + *acc.*), gewöhnt** (11)
useful **nützlich** (10)

usually **meistens** (9)
utilities **die Nebenkosten** (*pl.*) (6)

V

vacation **die Ferien** (*pl.*) (1); **der Urlaub, -e** (5); **die Ferienreise, -n** (8); vacation apartment/condo **die Ferienwohnung, -en** (10)
to vaccinate for **impfen (gegen** + *acc.*), **geimpft** (12)
vaccine **die Spritze, -n** (11)
to vacuum **staub·saugen, staubgesaugt** (6)
vacuum cleaner **der Staubsauger, -** (6)
Valentine's Day **der Valentinstag** (4)
valley **das Tal, ¨er** (7)
valuable **wertvoll** (2)
various **verschieden** (9)
vase **die Vase, -n** (3); **die Blumenvase, -n** (5)
veal cutlet **das Schnitzel, -** (9)
vegetable **das Gemüse, -** (9)
vehicle **das Fahrzeug, -e** (11)
verb **das Verb, -en** (A)
very **sehr** (B)
veterinarian **der Tierarzt, ¨e / die Tierärztin, -nen** (11)
vicinity **die Nähe** (6); in the vicinity **in der Nähe** (6, 7)
video **das Video, -s** (8)
videorecorder (VCR) **der Videorecorder, -** (A, 2)
view **der Ausblick, -e** (6)
vinegar **der Essig** (9)
violence **die Gewalt** (12); to use violence **Gewalt an·wenden** (12)
violin **die Geige, -n** (3)
visa **das Visum, Visa** (7)
visible **sichtbar** (11)
visit **der Besuch, -e** (3); to visit **zu Besuch kommen** (3); **besuchen, besucht** (1); **besichtigen, besichtigt** (7), **gekommen**
vocabulary **der Wortschatz, ¨e** (A)
volcano **der Vulkan, -e** (10)
volleyball **der Volleyball, ¨e** (1)

W

to wait **warten, gewartet** (7)
waiter **der Kellner, -** (5); **die Bedienung, -en** (9)
waiting room **die Wartehalle, -n** (10)
waitress **die Kellnerin, -nen** (5); **die Bedienung, -en** (9)
to wake up **auf·wachen, ist aufgewacht** (4); to wake (*s.o.*) up **wecken, geweckt** (8)
walk **der Spaziergang, ¨e** (10); to walk **gehen (geht), ging, ist gegangen** (A); to go for a walk **spazieren·gehen (geht . . . spazieren), ging . . . spazieren, ist spazierengegangen** (1); to take a walk in the park **im Park spazierengehen** (1)
walking: to keep on walking **weiter·gehen (geht . . . weiter), ging . . . weiter, ist weitergegangen** (10)
Walkman **der Walkman, -s** (2, 10)
wall **die Wand, ¨e** (B)
wallet **die Brieftasche, -n** (7)
waltz **der Walzer, -** (3)
to want **wollen (will), wollte, gewollt** (3)
warm **warm** (B)
to warn **warnen, gewarnt** (7)
to wash **spülen, gespült** (4); **(sich) waschen (wäscht), wusch, gewaschen** (2, 11); to wash the dishes **Geschirr spülen** (4)
washbasin **das Waschbecken, -** (6)
washing machine **die Waschmaschine, -n** (6)
wastebasket **der Papierkorb, ¨e** (3); to empty the wastebasket **den Papierkorb aus·leeren** (3)
watch (*n.*) **die Armbanduhr, -en** (A); to watch **an·sehen (sieht . . . an), sah . . . an, angesehen** (3); to watch out **auf·passen, aufgepaßt** (3); to watch out for **achten (auf** + *acc.*), **geachtet** (11); to watch TV **fern·sehen (sieht . . . fern), sah . . . fern, ferngesehen** (1, 2)
water: mineral water **das Mineralwasser** (9); water fowl **der Wasservogel, ¨** (12); to water **gießen (gießt), goß, gegossen** (3); to water the flowers/plants **die Blumen/Pflanzen gießen** (3)
watering can **die Gießkanne, -n** (6)
to wear **tragen (trägt), trug, getragen** (A, 2)
weather **das Wetter** (B)
Wednesday **der Mittwoch** (1)
week **die Woche, -n** (1); during the week **in der Woche** (1); every week **jede Woche** (3); last week **letzte Woche** (4)
weekend **das Wochenende, -n** (1); during the weekend **am Wochenende** (1); last weekend **letztes Wochenende** (4); over the weekend **übers Wochenende** (4)
weight: to lose weight **ab·nehmen (nimmt . . . ab), nahm . . . ab, abgenommen** (9, 11)
well **also** (2); **na** (3); to feel well **sich wohl·fühlen, wohlgefühlt** (11); well (*n.*) **der Brunnen, -** (8)
west (of) **westlich (von)** (7)
wet **naß** (3, 8)
whale: blue whale **der Blauwal, -e** (12)
what **was** (B); what for? **wofür?** (9)
wheel **das Rad, ¨er** (7); steering wheel **das Lenkrad, ¨er** (7)
when **wann** (B); **wenn** (*subord. conj.*) (2); **als** (*subord. conj.*) (5, 11); when I was eight years old **als ich acht Jahre alt war** (5)
when? **wann?** (1)
whenever **wenn** (*subord. conj.*) (3, 11)
where **wo** (B); where (from) **woher** (B); where to **wohin** (3); where are you going? **wo willst du denn hin?** (A)
whether **ob** (*subord. conj.*) (6, 10, 11)
which **welcher, welche, welches** (B)
white **weiß** (A)
who **wer** (A, B)
whole **ganz** (3); a whole lot **eine ganze Menge** (4)
whom (*acc.*) **wen** (4); (*dat.*) **wem** (4)
why **warum** (3); that's why **deshalb** (7)
wife **die Frau, -en** (B)
wig **die Perücke, -n** (11)
wild boar **das Wildschwein, -e** (12)
willingly **gern** (1)
to win **gewinnen (gewinnt), gewann, gewonnen** (4); to win the lottery **in der Lotterie gewinnen** (5)
wind **der Wind, -e** (8)
window **das Fenster, -** (B); ticket window **der Fahrkartenschalter, -** (7); window sill **die Fensterbank, ¨e** (5)
windowpane **die Scheibe, -n** (7); **die Fensterscheibe, -n** (8)
windshield wiper **der Scheibenwischer, -** (7)
(wind) surfboard **das Surfbrett, -er** (2)
windsurfing: to go windsurfing **windsurfen gehen (geht windsurfen), ging windsurfen, ist windsurfen gegangen** (1)
windy **windig** (B)
wine cellar **der Weinkeller, -** (6); wine glass **das Weinglas, ¨er** (5)
winter **der Winter, -** (B)
to wipe **wischen, gewischt** (7); to wipe clean **ab·wischen, abgewischt** (6)

wiper: windshield wiper **der Scheibenwischer, -** (7)
witch **die Hexe, -n** (7, 8)
with **bei** (+ *dat.*) (2, 3, 6, 10); **mit** (A, 3); with me **mit mir** (3); with your parents **bei deinen Eltern** (6); does it come with . . . ? **ist ein . . . dabei?** (6)
witness **der Zeuge, -n** (*wk.*) / **die Zeugin, -nen** (11)
wolf **der Wolf, ¨-e** (8)
woman **die Frau, -en** (A, B)
wonder **das Wunder** (4); no wonder **kein Wunder** (4)
woods **der Wald, ¨-er** (2, 7); to run in the woods **im Wald laufen** (2)
work **die Arbeit, -en** (1); **das Werk, -e** (8); to work **arbeiten, gearbeitet** (1); **funktionieren, funktioniert** (A); **wirken, gewirkt** (11); it's not working **es funktioniert nicht** (A)
workbook **das Arbeitsbuch, ¨-er** (3)
worker **der Arbeiter, - / die Arbeiterin, -nen** (5)
world **die Welt, -en** (7)
worried **besorgt** (3)
wound **die Wunde, -n** (11)
to write **schreiben (schreibt), schrieb, geschrieben** (A); to write down **auf·schreiben (schreibt . . . auf), schrieb . . . auf, aufgeschrieben** (11)
writer **der Schriftsteller, - / die Schriftstellerin, -nen** (5); detective novel writer **der Krimiautor, -en / die Krimiautorin, -nen** (12)
writing: in writing **schriftlich**
writing paper **das Briefpapier, -e** (5)
written **schriftlich** (10)
wrong **falsch** (2); to be wrong with (*a person*) **fehlen** (+ *dat.*), **gefehlt** (11); to get up on the wrong side of the bed **mit dem linken Fuß auf·stehen** (4)

X

X-ray **röntgen, geröntgt** (11)
xenophobia **der Ausländerhaß** (12)

Y

yacht **die Jacht, -en** (7)
year **das Jahr, -e** (2)
to yell **schreien (schreit), schrie, geschrien** (3)
yellow **gelb** (A)
yes (on the contrary!) **doch!** (4)
yesterday **gestern** (4); the day before yesterday **vorgestern** (4)
you (*acc.*) **dich** (2)
young **jung** (A)
your (*infor. sg.*) **deine, dein, deinen** (2); (*for.*) **Ihre, Ihr, Ihren** (2); (*infor. pl.*) **eure, euer, euren** (2)
your **dein(e)** (*infor.*) (B); **Ihr(e)** (*for.*) (B)
youth **die Jugend** (8)
youth hostel **die Jugendherberge, -n** (10); youth hostel ID card **der Jugendherbergsausweis, -e** (10); owner/manager of a youth hostel **die Herbergseltern** (*pl.*) (10)
Yugoslavia **(das) Jugoslawien** (B)

Z

zebra **das Zebra, -s** (12)
zeppelin **der Zeppelin, -e** (7)
zone: no-stopping zone **das Halteverbot, -e** (7)
zoo **der Zoo, -s** (10)
zoo director **der Zoodirektor, -en** (*wk.*) / **die Zoodirektorin, -nen** (12)

INDEX

This index is organized into three subsections: Culture, Grammar, and Vocabulary. The notation "n" following a page number indicates that the subject is treated in a footnote on that page.

CULTURE

GRAMMAR

VOCABULARY

Grateful acknowledgment is made for use of the following:

Photographs: *Pages 2, 9, 13, 24, 27, 28, 33, 48, 55, 62 (top)* © Stuart Cohen; *62 (center)* Thomas Lawrence, *Charles William, Baron von Humboldt.* The Royal Collection © Her Majesty Queen Elizabeth II; *62 (bottom), 69, 80, 85, 86* © Stuart Cohen; *93 (top and center)* Courtesy German Information Center; *93 (bottom), 110, 114, 120* © Stuart Cohen; *124 (top)* AKG London; *124 (bottom)* © Joke/Helga Lade Fotoagentur/Peter Arnold, Inc.; *140, 143, 148* © Stuart Cohen; *151* AKG London; *155* Charles F. Ulrich, *Immigrants in the waiting room of Castle Garden, New York*, 1884. Courtesy Balch Institute for Ethnic Studies Library, Henry Lucas Collection; *156 (top)* AKG London; *156 (bottom)* © Zefa-Hackenberg, Düsseldorf; *165* © Ulrike Welsch; *172, 180* © Stuart Cohen; *187* AKG London; *188, 204* © Stuart Cohen; *207* Carl Spitzweg, *Der Arme Poet*, 1839. Neue Pinakotheke, Munich/AKG London; *208, 209* © Stuart Cohen; *211 (clockwise from upper right)* © Stuart Cohen; © R. Waldkirch/H. Armstrong Roberts; © T. Krueger/Zefa-PH, Düsseldorf; AKG London; *212* © Stuart Cohen; *215* © W. Lowes/Helga Lade Fotoagentur/Peter Arnold, Inc.; *216* © Stuart Cohen; *220 (top)* The Bettmann Archive; *220 (bottom), 238, 244* © Stuart Cohen; *251 (top)* Carl Johann Baehr, *Caspar David Friedrich*, 1836. Gemäldegalerie, Dresden/AKG London; *251 (center)* Caspar David Friedrich, *The Chalk Cliffs of Rügen*, 1818. Oskar Reinhart Collection, Winterthur, Switzerland; *251 (bottom)* © John/Helga Lade Fotoagentur/Peter Arnold, Inc.; *257* © Ellis Herwig/Stock, Boston; *270* © Margo Granitsas/The Image Works; *274, 276* © Stuart Cohen; *285 (top)* The Bettmann Archive; *285 (bottom)* © Stuart Cohen; *304* © Comstock; *308, 313, 315* © Stuart Cohen; *319 (top)* Courtesy Bundesbildstelle, Bonn; *319 (bottom)* Egon Martzik/Helga Lade Fotoagentur/Peter Arnold, Inc.; *338* © D. and J. Heaton/Stock, Boston; *341* © Stuart Cohen; *351* © AP/Wide World Photos; *353 (top)* AKG London; *353 (bottom), 358, 368* © Stuart Cohen; *383 (top)* © UPI/Bettmann; *383 (bottom)* © Welsh/Helga Lade Fotoagentur/Peter Arnold, Inc.; *402* © David Simson/Stock, Boston; *410, 413, 417* © Stuart Cohen; *418 (top)* Franz von Lenbach, *Hedwig Dohm*, 1894. AKG London; *418 (bottom)* © Tom Haley/Sipa Press.

Videoecke stills courtesy of ZDF and PICS.

Realia: *Page 9* reprinted with permission from Suzy's Zoo®, San Diego, California. © Suzy Spafford; *29 Focus* / photo: Gamma Liaison; *58 Der Spiegel*; *92* Adapted from *Focus*; *130* from *Die Frustrierten III* by Claire Bretecher. Copyright © 1979 by Rowohlt Verlag GmbH, Reinbek; *144* Heinrich-Heine-Universität, Düsseldorf; *148 Focus*; *151 (left)* Coppenrath, Korsch, Sellmer. Published in *Focus*; *151 (right) Focus*; *159 Goslarsche Zeitung*; *177* Reprinted with permission of Dieter Hajek, illustrator; *183* © Globus-Kartendienst GmbH; 186 From *Das Haus*, June 1989. Reprinted with permission of Fa. Miele & Cie GmbH, Gütersloh; *192* Published in *Focus*; *248* © Globus-Kartendienst GmbH; *255* © *ADAC Motorwelt*; *276 Der Spiegel*; *279 Focus*; *292* Cartoon by Raymond reprinted with permission of *Bravo*; *314 Focus*; *317 Focus*; *349 Focus*; *371 Focus*; *375 (right) Focus*; *375 (left)* Philips; *406* From *Vielleicht sind wir eben zu verschieden* by Eva Heller (Oldenburg, Germany: Lappan Verlag, 1980). Reprinted by permission; *412 Focus.*

Readings: *Page 128* "mal eben" by Ralf Kaiser, from *Jugend vom Umtausch ausgeschlossen.* Copyright © 1984 by Rowohlt Verlag GmbH, Reinbek; *159 Goslarsche Zeitung*; *194* "Lebe wohl!" by Heiner Feldhoff, from *Literatur zum Anfassen* (Ismaning, Germany: Max Hueber Verlag); *255* © *ADAC Motorwelt*; *256* "Wo—vielleicht dort" by Jürgen Becker, from *Felder.* © Suhrkamp Verlag, Frankfurt am Main, 1964; *288* From *Der Tag, an dem Tante Marga verschwand* by Paul Marr. © Verlag Friedrich Oetinger, Hamburg, 1986; *291* "Ich habe zwei Heimatländer" by Sabri Çakir, from *In zwei Sprachen leben. Berichte, Erzählungen, Gedichte von Ausländern* (Munich: dtv, 1992); *323 Coupé*; *359* "Vornehme Leute, 1200 Meter hoch" by Kurt Tucholsky, from *Gesammelte Werke.* Copyright © 1960 by Rowohlt Verlag GmbH, Reinbek; *387* "Montagmorgengeschichte" by Susanne Kilian, from *Die Stadt ist Groß* (Weinheim und Basel: Beltz, 1976), p. 162; *390 Focus*; *391 Focus*; *421* From *Heimat in der Fremde* by Yüksel Pazarkaya (Stuttgart: Ararat Verlag, 1979). Reprinted with permission of the author; *425* "Frauen kommen langsam-aber gewaltig" by Ina Deter, from *Ich bereue nichts.* Phonogram GmbH, Hamburg.